D1571863

# LAW IN TRANSITION

Law has become the vehicle by which countries in the 'developing world', including post-conflict states or states undergoing constitutional transformation, must steer the course of social and economic, legal and political change. Legal mechanisms, in particular, the instruments as well as concepts of human rights, play an increasingly central role in the discourses and practices of both development and transitional justice. These developments can be seen as part of a tendency towards convergence within the wider set of discourses and practices in global governance. While this process of convergence of formerly distinct normative and conceptual fields of theory and practice has been both celebrated and critiqued at the level of theory, the present collection provides, through a series of studies drawn from a variety of contexts in which human rights advocacy and transitional justice initiatives are colliding with development projects, programmes and objectives, a more nuanced and critical account of contemporary developments. The book includes essays by many of the leading experts writing at the intersection of development, rights and transitional justice studies. Notwithstanding the theoretical and practical challenges presented by the complex interaction of these fields, the premise of the book is that it is only through engagement and dialogue among hitherto distinct fields of scholarship and practice that a better understanding of the institutional and normative issues arising in contemporary law and development and transitional justice contexts will be possible.

The book is designed for research and teaching at both undergraduate and graduate levels.

Series: Osgoode Readers
Volume 3

The Osgoode Readers offer interdisciplinary and cosmopolitan treatments of the essential elements of a variety of legal fields. Each chapter in an Osgoode Reader takes the form of a critical synthesis providing a succinct, engaging overview and analysis of contemporary issues and problems that are both shaping and being shaped by the law. The core of each Osgoode Reader consists of newly written chapters that build on each contributor's recent field-leading work, alongside chapters that are revised versions of recently published articles that have been thoroughly reworked to suit the focus and flow of the reader.

Osgoode Readers are distinguished by their attention to fresh perspectives dealing not only with traditional legal concerns but also with newer challenges posed by changes in social, ethical, economic and political environments. Osgoode Readers are organized and their analysis framed in ways that are alert to comparative-law insights and are intended to be relevant across legal jurisdictions.

Each Osgoode Reader is primarily aimed at upper-year LLB and JD, as well as graduate law, courses as either companion volumes or core prescribed readings. Most readers will also appeal to law scholars interested in keeping abreast of current developments in their own field, as well as researchers new to the field in question.

# Law in Transition

## Human Rights, Development and Transitional Justice

Edited by
Ruth Buchanan and Peer Zumbansen

·HART·
PUBLISHING

OXFORD AND PORTLAND, OREGON
2014

Published in the United Kingdom by Hart Publishing Ltd
16C Worcester Place, Oxford, OX1 2JW
Telephone: +44 (0)1865 517530
Fax: +44 (0)1865 510710
E-mail: mail@hartpub.co.uk
Website: http://www.hartpub.co.uk

Published in North America (US and Canada) by
Hart Publishing
c/o International Specialized Book Services
920 NE 58th Avenue, Suite 300
Portland, OR 97213-3786
USA
Tel: +1 503 287 3093 or toll-free: (1) 800 944 6190
Fax: +1 503 280 8832
E-mail: orders@isbs.com
Website: http://www.isbs.com

Hart Publishing is an imprint of Bloomsbury Publishing plc.

British Library Cataloguing in Publication Data

Data Available

ISBN: 978-1-84946-592-2

Typeset by Forewords, Oxon
Printed and bound in Great Britain by
CPI Group (UK) Ltd, Croydon CR0 4YY

# *Preface and Acknowledgements*

The volume presented here brings together seminal essays on the intersection between law & development, human rights and rights critique, and transitional justice. This constellation of discourses is of very recent origin, notwithstanding the long-standing substantive overlap between them. The idea to this collection first arose on the occasion of an international conference on law & development and transitional justice at Osgoode Hall Law School a few years ago, organised by the editors, in which it became obvious that a closer engagement between the participants in these discourses both held and holds significant promise in both theoretical and practical terms. While a number of law schools around the world have already been offering courses in law & development for some time, the field continues to remain considerably marginalised. All in all, only very few law schools have been including development-related courses in their curricula, but a slow trend to expand such offerings can be observed. The situation is still quite different in the area of transitional justice, which remains a boutique subject on offer at only a very small number of law schools. Meanwhile, transitional justice has become a highly prolific field of scholarly research and academic stature, with a growing number of dedicated research centres, a growing number of conferences in the field and an expanding field of journals explicitly devoted to the publication of work in this area.

This somewhat ambiguous status of both fields within the law school curriculum stands in considerable contrast to their enormous practical relevance. From the point of view of assessing the role of law in a context of increased global interaction, the engagement of international institutions, national governments, legal and economic experts and advisors in countries around the world, the centrality of both law & development and transitional justice is more than obvious. But it is precisely here that the openness and multidisciplinary nature of the continuing conceptual debate and imagination in both fields has a direct impact on the way in which theory can, and indeed does, inform practice. Despite an immensely rich theoretical repository in the respective areas of research, practice—in many cases—still just appears to happen without, apparently, being grounded in clearly discernible communication with this research.

The present volume aims at substantively contributing both to an approximation of theory and practice in this regard, and to the further development of conceptual refinement of the already-mentioned overlaps between law & development and transitional justice. The authors of this collection are, in different ways, all writing on these two aspects from a host of perspectives and use a variety of examples and case studies. On these grounds alone, the essays collected here should go a long way to introducing readers at the university student and law school level, as well as advanced researchers and practitioners, to some of the main dimensions of the extremely rich theoretical and conceptual debates in this area. The essays dealing specifically with the question of rights provide both a linkage between and a further sophistication of these fields, as they connect a long-standing engagement with the nature of rights, their origin and their application in diverse domestic and transnational contexts with the particular dynamics in law & development and transitional justice.

With the current epoch often referred to as one of global interactions, the specific contribution of law is worthy of being studied more closely. After the already contested enthusiasm over the 'end of history' following the collapse of the Soviet Union and the legal-economic emancipation of the Eastern European states had given way to a much more sober assessment of a post-1989 global legal-political consciousness in the view of the civil war in Kosovo, any attempt by lawyers to conceptualise legal answers to such global challenges would have to take account of this particular and poignant context. Yet it remains unclear how successfully lawyers have really fared in this regard. If the extremely polemic and ultimately inconclusive deliberations around the legality/legitimacy conflicts around 'humanitarian intervention' and, some years later, the so-called, 'War on Terror' were any indication, it appears that lawyers have been hard pressed to formulate both adequate terminology as well as reliable, functional instruments in response to these constellations. Surely, we can say that the famous Simma–Cassese debate over Kosovo[1] as well as the interventions by Martti Koskenniemi[2] and Anne Orford[3] have left a significant imprint on our current grasp of the limits of making law's voice heard in response to global-governance challenges, especially when considering the slippery slope between the arguments around Kosovo and those in favour of the invasion of Iraq in 2003. Yet it appears that even the currently proposed conceptual frameworks such as 'global administrative law' or 'global constitutionalism' are representative more of an attempt to capture the different dynamics and stakes in this complex relationship between law and globalisation than of an already arrived at set of conclusions and results.

We take the triad of law & development, transitional justice and rights as a platform from which it should be possible to inquire more concretely into the role of law in the context of state reformation, state change, post-conflict resolution and conciliation, on the one hand, and into the ways in which many of law's challenges in these contexts of change, renewal and reform mirror those of law in previous domestic contexts all along, on the other. In other words, we are taking the title of the collection presented here quite seriously in the way in which we posit that the triad merits a devoted study in its own right, in that this constellation can allow us to understand better how questions of legal-economic reform are inseparable from those touching upon retroactive, post-conflict and restorative justice, reconciliation, societal healing and state-building. Another way to reiterate this inseparability is to connect the question of the overlap between both fields—law & development and transitional justice—with that of rights and rights critique, not only because of the centrality of this concept in both areas, but also because a focus on rights allows us to see more clearly the continuities between

[1] B Simma, 'NATO, the UN and the Use of Force: Legal Aspects' (1999) 10 *European Journal of International Law* 1; A Cassese, '*Ex iniuria ius oritur*: Are We Moving towards International Legitimation of Forcible Humanitarian Countermeasures in the World Community? (1999) 10 *European Journal of International Law* 22.
[2] M Koskenniemi, '"The Lady Doth Protest Too Much" Kosovo and the Turn to International Law' (2002) 65 *Modern Law Review* 159.
[3] A Orford, 'Muscular Humanitarianism: Reading the Narratives of the New Interventionism' (1999) 10 *European Journal of International Law* 679.

legal conceptualisations in both the existing domestic and the emerging transnational contexts of law formation.

We are extremely grateful to the authors of the texts in this collection for making their work available to an audience of legal scholars, practitioners, sociologists, anthropologists and political scientists. In the tradition of the 'Osgoode Readers' series, inaugurated in 2006 in the area of environmental law, the present volume brings together some of the world's leading experts in the field. The volume is conceived to facilitate the teaching of both introductory and advanced courses, as well as to serve as a landmark repository of scholarship in the intersection of three of the most important legal research areas in the context of global governance today. We thank Richard Hart for his enthusiasm about this project, and Osgoode Hall Law School as well as the Social Sciences and Humanities Research Council of Canada for the financial support of this project. Finally, we are immensely grateful to Chris Engert in Florence, Italy, for his masterful editorial work on the contributions to this volume and to Tom Adams at Hart Publishing for his capable assistance in the book's final stages.

Peer Zumbansen

Tilburg & Toronto

Ruth Buchanan

Toronto

January 2014

The editors and publisher gratefully acknowledge the publishers of the following material, for permission to reprint from the sources indicated:

Chapter 5 of the book, by Makau Mutua, was originally published by Intersentia as 'A Critique of Rights in Transnational Justice: The African Experience' in G Ore Aguilar and F Gomez Isa (eds), *Rethinking Transitions: Equality and Social Justice in Societies Emerging from Conflict* (Antwerp, 2011) 31–45.

Chapter 6 of the book, 'Marks Indicating Conditions of Origin in Rights-Based Sustainable Development' by Nicole Aylwin and Rosemary J Coombe, is simultaneously printed in both this volume and in the *UC Davis Law Review*, Special Symposium Issue (2014) 47(3), 753–86. Both publishers have agreed to the simultaneous reprint of the article. The authors thank the editors and publishers for this privilege.

Chapter 8 of the book, by Sally Engle Merry, was originally published by Chicago University Press as 'Measuring the World: Indicators, Human Rights, and Global Governance' in D Partridge, M Welker and R Hardin (eds), *Corporate Lives: New Perspectives on the Social Life of the Corporate Form*, Wenner-Gren Symposium Series. *Current Anthropology*, Vol 52, Supplementary Issue 3, S83–S95.

Chapter 15 of the book, by Christian Joerges, was originally published by Routledge as 'Working through "Bitter Experiences" towards a Purified European Identity? A Critique of the Disregard for History in European Constitutional Theory and Practice' in EO Eriksen, C Joerges and F Rödl (eds), *Law, Democracy and Solidarity in a Post-national European Union: The Unsettled Political Order of Europe* (Oxford and New York, 2006) 175–192.

# Contents

## Part II: Transitional Justice and Development: Comparative and Transnational Perspectives

## Part III: Intersections and Prospects

# List of Contributors

**KIRSTEN ANKER**, BSc (Sydney, 1993), LLB (Sydney, 1995), PhD (Sydney, 2008), Assistant Professor of Law, McGill University.
kirsten.anker@mcgill.ca

**NICOLE AYLWIN**, BA (Windsor), MA (Ryerson) is currently the Executive Officer at the Canadian Forum on Civil Justice, a national not-for-profit organisation dedicated to the advancing of civil justice reform, and the Project Director at the Winkler Institute for Dispute Resolution at Osgoode Hall Law School.
naylwin@osgoode.yorku.ca

**RUTH BUCHANAN**, AB (Hons) Princeton, LLB (U Vic), LLM/SJD (U Wisconsin-Madison), Associate Professor of Law at Osgoode Hall Law School, Toronto.
rbuchanan@osgoode.yorku.ca

**ROSEMARY J COOMBE**, PhD/JSD Stanford University (Anthropology and Law), 1992. Full Professor and Tier One Canada Research Chair in Law, Communication and Culture, York University.
rcoombe@yorku.ca

**BRYANT G GARTH**, JD Stanford Law School (1975), PhD European University Institute (Florence 1979), Chancellor's Professor of Law, University of California, Irvine.
bgarth@law.uci.edu

**MORAG GOODWIN**, MA History (Hons; 1st) (Edinburgh, 1999); LLM International Law (dist; Nottingham, 2001); PhD (EUI, 2006). Associate Professor, International Law, Tilburg Law School.
m.e.a.goodwin@uvt.nl

**CHRISTIAN JOERGES**, First State Exam 1966; Dr jur 1970; Second State Exam 1972; Research Professor at the University of Bremen, Co-Director of the Centre of European Law and Politics and Senior Professor for Law and Society at the Hertie School of Governance in Berlin.
christian.joerges@sfb597.uni-bremen-de; joerges@hertie-school.org

**VIDYA KUMAR**, DPhil (Oxon); LLM (Osgoode Hall); BA (Hons) & LLB (Queen's University Canada); MA (University of Alberta), Lecturer in Law, University of Birmingham.
v.a.s.kumar@bham.ac.uk

**SALLY ENGLE MERRY**, BA Wellesley College (Boston, 1966), MA Yale University (New Haven 1968), PhD. Brandeis University (Boston, 1978). Professor of Anthropology, New York University.
sally.merry@nyu.edu

**MARTHA MINOW**, BA (Michigan); MA (Harvard); JD (Yale). Morgan and Helen Chu Dean and Professor of Law, Harvard Law School.
minow@law.harvard.edu

**ANANYA MUKHERJEE-REED**, PhD, Political Economy & Public Policy, University of Southern California, USA; Professor and Chair, Department of Political Science, York University, Toronto.
ananya@yorku.ca

**MAKAU W MUTUA**, SJD, LLM (Harvard Law School); LLB, LLM, University of Dar-es-Salaam, Tanzania. Dean and SUNY Distinguished Professor, SUNY Buffalo Law School, Buffalo, New York.
mutua@buffalo.edu

**ROSEMARY NAGY**, PhD, Associate Professor, Department of Gender Equality and Social Justice, Nipissing University, North Bay.
rnagy@nipissingu.ca

**VASUKI NESIAH**, BA Philosophy & Government, Cornell University, 1990, JD, Harvard Law School, 1993, SJD, Harvard Law School, 2000, Associate Professor of Practice, The Gallatin School, New York University.
vn10@nyu.edu

**OBIORA CHINEDU OKAFOR**, PhD, LLM (University of British Columbia); LLM, LLB (University of Nigeria), Professor of Law, Osgoode Hall Law School, York University, Toronto, Canada, Vice-Chairperson/Rapporteur, UN Human Rights Council Advisory Committee.
ookafor@osgoode.yorku.ca; ookafor@yorku.ca

**SUNDHYA PAHUJA**, BA/LLB (Hons), LLM, PhD (Lond), Professor of International Law, University of Melbourne, Research Professor in Law, SOAS, University of London.
s.pahuja@unimelb.edu.au

**KERRY RITTICH**, LLB (Alberta); SJD (Harvard). Professor of Law, University of Toronto Faculty of Law and at the Women's and Gender Studies Institute at the University of Toronto.
kerry.rittich@utronto.ca

**NAOMI ROHT-ARRIAZA**, JD, MPP (University of California, Berkeley, 1990). Professor of Law, University of California, Hastings College of Law, San Francisco.
rohtarri@uchastings.edu

**ISSA SHIVJI**, LLB (University of East Africa, 1970); LLM (London School of Economics, 1971); PhD (University of Dar es Salaam, 1982). Mwalimu Julius Nyerere Professor of Pan-African Studies, University of Dar es Salaam.
issashvji@gmail.com

**PEER ZUMBANSEN**, Licence en droit (Paris, 1991); Law State Exam (Frankfurt 1995), LLM (Harvard, 1998), PhD (Frankfurt, 1998); Habilitation (Frankfurt 2004). Professor of Law, Osgoode Hall Law School, Toronto. 2013 Inaugural Global Law Chair, Tilburg Law School.
PZumbansen@osgoode.yorku.ca

# List of Abbreviations

| | |
|---|---|
| ACLU | American Civil Liberties Union |
| ADPL | *Asociacion de Productores de Derirados Lacteos Cajamarca* |
| ALR | Australian Law Reports |
| A-N-P | Actors – Norms – Processes |
| AOC | *Appellation d'Origine Contrôlée* |
| CAVR | Commission for Reception, Truth and Reconciliation |
| CCR | Center for Constitutional Rights |
| CDC | Centers for Disease Control and Prevention |
| CEDAW | The United Nations Committee on the Elimination of Discrimination against Women |
| CEE | Central and Eastern Europe |
| CLR | Commonwealth Law Reports |
| COP | Communications on Progress |
| CSK | Czech Republic Koruna |
| CSO | Civil Society Organisation |
| CSR | Corporate Social Responsibility |
| Cth | Commonwealth |
| DCT | Draft Constitutional Treaty |
| DDR | Disarmament, Demobilisation and Re-integration of combatants |
| DLR | Dominion Law Reports |
| DPLF | Due Process of Law Foundation |
| ECAP | *Equipo de Estudios Comunitarios y Acción Psicosocial de* Guatemala |
| ECJ | European Court of Justice |
| ESCR | Economic, Social and Cultural Rights |
| EU | The European Union |
| FAO | The Food and Agriculture Organization of the United Nations |
| FFUNGO | Foreign-Funded Non-Governmental Organisation |
| FLR | Federal Law Reports |
| G20 | Group of Twenty Finance Ministers and Central Bank Governors |
| G77 | United Nations Group of 77 |
| GC | The United Nations Global Compact |
| GDP | Gross Domestic Product |
| GG | Global Governance |
| GI | Geographical Indication |
| GNP | Gross National Product |
| GRI | Global Reporting Initiative |
| HDI | Human Development Index |
| HDR | Human Development Reports |
| HIV/AIDS | Human Immunodeficiency Virus/Acquired Immune Deficiency Syndrome |
| ICC | International Criminal Court |
| ICCPR | International Covenant on Civil and Political Rights |
| ICDS | Integrated Child Development Services |
| ICSECR | International Covenant on Social, Economic and Cultural Rights |
| ICTJ | International Center for Transitional Justice |
| ICTR | International Criminal Tribunal for Rwanda |
| ICTSD | International Centre for Trade and Sustainable Development |
| ICTY | International Criminal Tribunal for the former Yugoslavia |
| IDA | International Development Association |
| IFI | International Financial Institution |

| | |
|---|---|
| IK | Indigenous Knowledge |
| ILM | International Legal Materials |
| ILO | International Labour Organization |
| IMF | International Monetary Fund |
| IP | Intellectual Property |
| IPR | Intellectual Property Right |
| IQ | Intelligence Quotient |
| L&D | Law and Development |
| LP | Legal Pluralism |
| LRA | The Lord's Resistance Army |
| MCC | Millennium Challenge Corporation |
| MDGs | Millennium Development Goals |
| MDM | Mid-day Meals |
| MICO | Marks Indicating Conditions of Origin |
| NATO | North Atlantic Treaty Organisation |
| NGO | Non-Governmental Organisation |
| NLC | Nigerian Labour Congress |
| NREGA | National Rural Employment Guarantee Act |
| ODI | Office for the Documentation and Investigation of the Crimes of Communism |
| OECD | Organisation for Economic Co-operation and Development |
| OHCHR | Office of the High Commissioner for Human Rights |
| OSCE | Organization for Security and Co-operation in Europe |
| PIR | Plan Integral de Reparaciones |
| PISA | Programme for International Student Assessment |
| PRSP | Poverty Reduction Strategy Paper |
| PUCL | People's Union for Civil Liberties |
| RBA | Rights-based Approach |
| RPF | Rwandan Patriotic Front |
| SAP | Structural Adjustment Programme |
| SCR | Supreme Court Reports (Canada) |
| TJ | Transnational Justice |
| TK | Traditional Knowledge |
| TL | Transnational Law |
| TRC | Truth and Reconciliation Commission |
| TREMF | Trade-related Market-friendly Human Rights |
| TWAIL | Third World Approaches to International Law |
| UDHR | Universal Declaration of Human Rights |
| UK | The United Kingdom |
| UN | The United Nations |
| UNCTAD | The United Nations Conference on Trade and Development |
| UNDP | United Nations Development Programme |
| UNESCO | The United Nations Educational, Scientific and Cultural Organization |
| UNFPA | The United Nation Populations Fund |
| UNHCR | The United Nations High Commissioner for Refugees |
| UNICEF | The United Nations Children's Fund |
| UNIFEM | The United Nations Development Fund for Women |
| UNTAET | The United Nations Transitional Administration |
| US | The United States of America |
| USAID | Unites States Agency for International Development |
| USD | United States Dollars |
| WB | The World Bank |
| WHO | The World Health Organization |
| WIPO | The World Intellectual Property Organization |
| WTO | The World Trade Organization |

# Introduction:
# Approximating Law and Development, Human Rights and Transitional Justice

PEER ZUMBANSEN AND RUTH BUCHANAN

## I. INTERSECTIONS

THE CONTRIBUTIONS TO this volume span the fast-growing areas of 'law and development', 'transitional justice' and 'human rights'. The participating authors are well aware of the challenges which arise out of the attempt both to cross and to relativise boundaries, as well as to bridge discourses. And perhaps the apparent ease with which the authors convened here navigate the complexity of the intersecting, and continuously evolving, scholarly discourses and academic–political practices will gloss over the intricacies of the exercise. But just how challenging the undertaking carried out by these authors really is becomes clearer when we realise that no area here is, in itself, easily categorised or comprehensively mapped out. Instead, the present volume intervenes at the cross-section of these three fields at a time in which considerable maturing, reflecting and revisiting has taken place in each of the respective areas, prompting us both to take stock now and to highlight the nature of the overlap, dialogue and cross-fertilisation of these discourses. The choice of our three areas of interest is by no means arbitrary: while human rights (HR) is arguably the oldest of the three legal fields in question here, it shares the inner complexity and dynamic content that characterise the other two. Law and development (L&D) is a somewhat younger field, but one with a tremendously rich, layered and contested history.[1] As scholars in the field have shown and as some of the contributors to this volume further illustrate, L&D brings into dialogue a wide range of legal and non-legal fields, and thus becomes part of scholarly and policy discourses ranging

---

[1] For a seminal statement, see D Trubek and M Galanter, 'Scholars in Self-Estrangement: Some Reflections on the Crisis in Law and Development Studies in the United States' [1974] *Wisconsin Law Review* 1062; see, some 30 years later, the reflections in D Trubek and A Santos, 'Introduction: The Third Moment in Law and Development Theory and the Emergence of a New Critical Practice' in D Trubek and A Santos (eds), *The New Law and Economic Development: A Critical Appraisal*, vol 1 (New York, Cambridge University Press, 2006). See also R Buchanan, 'A Crisis and its Afterlife: Some Reflections on "Scholars in Self-Estrangement"' in G de Búrca, C Fitzpatrick and J Scott (eds), *Critical Studies of Global Governance: Liber Amicorum for D Trubek* (Oxford, Hart Publishing, 2013).

from development studies,[2] economics and economic geography,[3] and trade law[4] to post-colonial studies.[5] A similar intersection of theoretical and deeply practice-driven approaches can be observed in the third area which this book is placing under scrutiny: transitional justice (TJ). While more will be said on this field later in this introduction, it deserves mentioning that, like HR and L&D, TJ continues to defy a straightforward categorisation, be that with regard to its basic assumptions or its aspirations,[6] its methodological foundations, or its theoretical versus practical aspirations.[7]

This introduction seeks to set the stage for the cross-examination of the three fields of scientific inquiry involved, which we understand to include legal as well as socio-economic, cultural and political practice. The latter cluster of connections is of particular importance in view of the acute awareness among TJ scholars of the need both to expand and to deepen their agenda's reach in order to address, with a view to long-term sustainability, the trajectories and the persistence of the social and economic grievances,[8] inequalities,[9] structural violence[10] or root causes[11] of societal conflict, exclusion and silencing. It will do so by first alluding to questions of context with regard to the emergence and continuing development of the three fields in a wider discursive universe of both 'law and society' and, more recently, 'law and globalisation' debates.[12] By not only situating the three identified areas against this background but also highlighting the interactions between them, we hope to show how any assessment of these fields is bound to be but a momentary snapshot, which only fleetingly highlights certain features, while obscuring others. In bringing together some of the most renowned experts in the three areas, we hope to shed at least some light on the intricacies as well as the stakes—methodological and, ultimately, political—in the areas under discussion here. Based upon the understanding that a primary objective of legal analysis ought to be the identification of the tension of 'winning' versus the

---

[2] JE Goldthorpe, *The Sociology of Post-Colonial Societies: Economic Disparity, Cultural Diversity, and Development* (Cambridge, Cambridge University Press, 1996); J Haynes, *Development Studies* (Cambridge, MA, Polity Press, 2008).

[3] PA David, 'Krugman's Economic Geography of Development: NEGs, POGs, and Naked Models in Space' (1999) 22 *International Regional Science Review* 162; R Peet, *Unholy Trinity: The IMF, World Bank and WTO*, 2nd edn (London, Zed Books, 2009).

[4] J Bhagwati, *The Economics of Underdeveloped Countries* (New York, McGraw Hill, 1966); JG Williamson, *Trade and Poverty: When the Third World Fell Behind* (Cambridge, MA, MIT Press, 2011).

[5] A Escobar, *Encountering Development: The Making and Unmaking of the Third World; with a new preface by the author* (Princeton, NJ, Princeton University Press, 2012); S Pahuja, *Decolonising International Law: Development, Economic Growth and the Politics of Universality* (Cambridge, Cambridge University Press, 2011); L Eslava and S Pahuja, 'Between Resistance and Reform: TWAIL and the Universality of International Law' (2012) 3 *Trade, Law and Development* 103.

[6] See, eg the excellent analysis provided by R Mani, 'Dilemmas of Expanding Transitional Justice, or Forging the Nexus between Transitional Justice and Development' (2008) 2 *International Journal of Transitional Justice* 253.

[7] C Bell, 'Transitional Justice, Interdisciplinarity and the State of the "Field" or "Non-Field"' (2009) 3 *International Journal of Transitional Justice* 5.

[8] I Muvingi, 'Sitting on Powder Kegs: Socioeconomic Rights in Transitional Justice' (2009) 3 *International Journal of Transitional Justice* 163.

[9] Z Miller, 'Effects of Invisibility: In Search of the "Economic" in Transitional Justice' (2008) 2 *International Journal of Transitional Justice* 266.

[10] Ibid; see Chapter 13 below.

[11] S Marks, 'Root Causes and Human Rights' (2011) 74 *Modern Law Review* 57.

[12] For an elaboration of this idea, see P Zumbansen, 'The Ins and Outs of Transnational Private Regulatory Governance: Legitimacy, Accountability, Effectiveness and a New Concept of "Context"' (2012) 13 *German Law Journal* 1269; see also Chapter 18 below.

'losing' interpretations and applications of legal instruments, our aim here is first to relativise the alleged uniqueness of the three fields with regard to long-existing core legal areas—such as contract or tort, administrative or constitutional law. By high-lighting how the interaction of such fields has repeatedly given rise to the formation of new legal arenas, we can point to the dynamic of mutual responsiveness between legal norms and societal developments. While restating this very basic premise of legal sociology might seem trite and unnecessary to some contemporary readers, we argue that this dynamic demands renewed attention in a legal education and professional context that is shaped by at least two powerful trajectories. In the next section, we review the development of the three identified fields against the background of a sig-nificant shift which has been occurring both within law schools and within the world of legal practice.

## II. BREAKING DOWN BOUNDARIES: LAW AND SOCIETY, LAW AND GLOBALISATION, LEGAL EDUCATION AND THE LEGAL PROFESSION

In the light of the seemingly unfaltering creativity on the part of legal scholars to extend the boundaries of existing legal fields in response to pressures, say, from tech-nological change,[13] social transformation,[14] and the fast-proliferating spheres of social and institutional practice,[15] the emergence and rapid consolidation of a new legal field has come to be seen as an ordinary event.[16] Yet, it appears as though the memory of truly innovative field-creations in law—such as in the exemplary cases of environ-mental[17] or cyberspace law[18]—are quite short lived, at least to the degree that scholars when they are confronted with the necessity (and the opportunity) to reflect upon the ways in which law reacts to change, for example under the rubric of internationalisa-tion or globalisation, continue to lament the absence of reliable analytical frameworks and definitions.[19] Meanwhile, the examples to be found in a field such as environ-

---

[13] R Brownsword and M Goodwin, *Law and the Technologies of the Twenty-first Century: Text and Materials* (Cambridge, Cambridge University Press, 2012); A Herwig, 'Transnational Governance Regimes for Foods Derived from Bio-technology and their Legitimacy' in C Joerges, I-J Sand and G Teubner (eds), *Transnational Governance and Constitutionalism* (Oxford, Hart Publishing, 2004) 199.

[14] L Peach, *Legislating Morality: Pluralism and Religious Identity in Lawmaking* (New York, Oxford University Press, 2002); K-H Ladeur and I Augsberg, 'The Myth of the Neutral State: The Relationship between State and Religion in the Face of New Challenges' (2007) 8 *German Law Journal* 143; AA An-Na'im, *Islam and the Secular State: Negotiating the Future of Shari'a* (Cambridge MA, Harvard University Press, 2008).

[15] DG Post, 'Anarchy, State, and the Internet: An Essay on Law-Making in Cyberspace' [1995] *Journal of Online Law*, available at http://www.temple.edu/Lawschool/dpost/Anarchy.html; J Hörnle, 'Disputes Solved in Cyberspace and the Rule of Law' (2001) 7 *The Journal of Information, Law and Technology* (now renamed the *European Journal of Law and Technology*), available at http://www2.warwick.ac.uk/fac/soc/law/elj/jilt/2001_2/hornle; V Mayer-Schönberger and M Ziewitz, 'Jefferson Rebuffed: The United States and the Future of Internet Governance' (2007) 8 *Columbia Science and Technology Law Review* 188.

[16] For the field of international law, see the remarkable essays in F Johns, RJ and S Pahuja (eds), *Events: The Force of International Law* (London, Routledge-Cavendish, 2011).

[17] G Teubner, L Farmer and D Murphy (eds), *Environmental Law and Ecological Responsibility: The Concept and Practice of Ecological Self-Organization* (Hoboken NJ, John Wiley & Sons, 1994).

[18] L Lessig, 'The Law of the Horse: What Cyberlaw might Teach' (1999) 113 *Harvard Law Review* 501.

[19] R Michaels, 'Globalization and Law: Law beyond the State' in R Banakar and M Travers, *Law and Social Theory*, 2nd edn (Oxford, Hart Publishing, forthcoming) 1, available at http://scholarship.law.duke.edu/faculty_scholarship/2862.

mental law, which emerged from and eventually grew beyond tort law responsibility,[20] or internet law, which both effectively and irreversibly[21] pushed beyond the confines of constitutional law and private law,[22] can be seen as important reminders of law's evolutionary nature,[23] causing it to resist ascriptions of simple causality or mere linear trajectory.[24] With these examples in mind, and although we can easily recognise the aspirations among our contemporaries to attribute an adequate label or even a specific status to emerging legal frameworks, we should nevertheless be mindful of the de facto normality of such struggles. In effect, such labelling anxieties multiply in the face of greater complexity, which serve to challenge the law in both form and substance with the alleged newness of a situation. In other words, law's relation to society in its ever-changing nature has always been a dynamic shaped by the competing forces of change and resistance, misunderstanding, overreaching, and trial and error.[25]

Compared to the immensely rich and, at the same time, precarious research and policy agenda of 'law and society',[26] the formula 'law and globalisation' describes a more recent, though no longer the newest, attempt at capturing the general meaning of law's operations in an increasingly interconnected global space.[27] Questioning existing methodologies, legal scholars, sociologists and anthropologists are examining the analytical and conceptual toolkits, the institutional orientation and normative

---

[20] G Gilmore, *The Death of Contract* (Columbus, OH, Ohio State University Press, 1974); D Kennedy, 'Distributive and Paternalist Motives in Contract and Tort Law, with Special Reference to Compulsory Terms and Unequal Bargaining Power (1982) 41 *Maryland Law Review* 563; PH Schuck, *Tort Law and the Public Interest: Competition, Innovation, and Consumer Welfare* (New York, WH Norton, 1991).

[21] L Lessig, *Code and other Laws of Cyberspace* (New York, Basic Books, 1999).

[22] HH Perritt Jr, 'The Internet is Changing the Public International Legal System' (2000) 88 *Kentucky Law Review* 885; J von Bernstorff, 'The Structural Limitations of Network Governance: ICANN as a Case in Point' in Joerges et al, n 14 above, 257; LM Ponte and TD Cavenagh, *Cyberjustice: Online Dispute Resolution (ODR) for E-Commerce* (Upper Saddle River, NJ, Prentice Hall, 2004).

[23] S Deakin, 'Evolution for our Time: A Theory of Legal Memetics', ESRC Centre for Business Research, University of Cambridge Working Paper No 242 (also published in (2002) 55 *Current Legal Problems*, 1–42), available at www.cbr.cam.ac.uk/pdf/WP242.pdf; P Zumbansen and G-P Calliess, 'Law, Economics and Evolutionary Theory: State of the Art and Interdisciplinary Perspectives' in P Zumbansen and G-P Calliess (eds), *Law, Economics and Evolutionary Theory* (Cheltenham-Northampton MA, Edward Elgar Publishing, 2011) 1.

[24] For the case of constitutional law see N Luhmann, 'Verfassung als evolutionäre Errungenschaft' (1989) 9 *Rechtshistorisches Journal* 176; see also RM Cover, 'Nomos and Narrative' (1983) 97 *Harvard Law Review* 4; EA Young, 'The Constitution outside the Constitution' (2007) 117 *Yale Law Journal* 408.

[25] See, eg LM Friedman, 'Coming of Age: Law and Society Enters an Exclusive Club' (2005) 1 *Annual Review of Law and Social Sciences* 1; R Buchanan, S Motha and S Pahuja, 'Introduction' in R Buchanan, S Motha and S Pahuja (eds), *Reading Modern Law: Critical Methdologies and Sovereign Formations* (Abingdon, Routledge, 2012) 1; P Zumbansen, 'Law's Effectiveness and Law's Knowledge: Reflections from Legal Sociology and Legal Theory' (2009) 10 *German Law Journal* 417.

[26] B de Sousa Santos, 'Law: A Map of Misreading. Toward a Postmodern Conception of Law' (1987) 14 *Journal of Law and Society* 279; G Teubner, 'How the Law Thinks: Toward a Constructivist Epistemology of Law' (1989) 23 *Law and Society Review* 727; R Cotterrell, 'Why Must Legal Ideas Be Interpreted Sociologically?' (1998) 25 *Journal of Law and Society* 171; B Garth and J Sterling, 'From Legal Realism to Law and Society: Reshaping Law for the Last Stages of the Social Activist State' (1998) 32 *Law and Society Review* 409; E Heger Boyle and JW Meyer, 'Modern Law as a Secularized and Global Model: Implications for the Sociology of Law' in Y Dezalay and B Garth (eds), *Global Prescriptions. The Production, Exportation, and Importation of a New Legal Orthodoxy* (Ann Arbor, University of Michigan Press, 2002).

[27] See the highly influential study by M Castells, *The Rise of the Network Society: Information Age: Economy, Society and Culture*, vol I, 2nd edn (Oxford, Blackwell Publishing, 2000), and two exemplary and very helpful depictions of the ways in which law has been reacting to globalization phenomena: G Teubner, 'The King's Many Bodies: The Self-Deconstruction of Law's Hierarchy' (1997) 31 *Law and Society Review* 763; P Schiff Berman, 'From International Law to Law and Globalization' (2005) 43 *Columbia Journal of Transnational Law* 485.

value judgements that are employed in the multi- and interdisciplinary context of globalisation studies.[28] Meanwhile, the challenge for lawyers and institutional educators to interpret and to translate the challenges of a globalising world into effective legal practice[29] as well as into the realities of a law-school classroom has only become greater.[30] It seems promising, then, that legal scholars have been showing a growing interest in better understanding the widely varied phenomena of globalisation and its impact on law, legal research and legal education.[31] Yet, despite ever-increasing efforts by lawyers and social scientists to study the complex relationship between domestic and global regulatory developments,[32] when can we actually be sure that the conceptual toolkits used in these undertakings are adequate? The same doubts appear to haunt (at least some areas of) legal education. While it is true that law schools around the world have been addressing the perceived need to adapt their curricula to the evolving prospects of a legal profession with an increasingly global reach,[33] most of such institutional undertakings remain marked by a concern which, first and foremost, regards the design of programmes that will provide graduates with the skills to offer optimal legal services in both domestic and global settings.[34] As a result, law school curriculum reformers, in trying to strike a balance between these two universes of legal practice, are prone to add introductory courses (such as 'Law and Globalisation' and 'Ethical Lawyering in a Global Context') to their curriculum, while, often enough, bowing to the pressures of the bar to maintain a distinct focus on core, blackletter, bread-and-butter courses. Meanwhile, and despite a long-standing and continuing tradition to

[28] See, eg DM Trubek, Y Dezalay, R Buchanan and JR Davis, 'Global Restructuring and the Law: Studies in the Internationalization of Legal Fields and the Creation of Transnational Arenas' (1994) 44 *Case Western Reserve Law Review* 407; J Comaroff and J L Comaroff, *Theory from the South: Or, How Euro-America is Evolving Toward Africa (The Radical Imagination)* (New York, Paradigm Publishers, 2011); D Chakrabarty, *Provincializing Europe: Postcolonial Thought and Historical Difference*, 2nd edn (Princeton, NJ, Princeton University Press, 2007).

[29] See, recently, Y Dezalay and BG Garth (eds), *Lawyers and the Construction of Transnational Justice* (Oxford, Routledge, 2012); HW Arthurs and Kreklewich, 'Law, Legal Institutions, and the Legal Profession in the New Economy' (2000) 34 *Osgoode Hall Law Journal* 1; MC Daly, 'The Ethical Implications of the Globalization of the Legal Profession: A Challenge to the Teaching of Professional Responsibility in the Twenty-First Century' (1998) 21 *Fordham International Law Journal* 1239.

[30] C Scott, 'A Core Curriculum for the Transnational Legal Education of JD and LLB Students: Surveying the Approach of the International, Comparative and Transnational Law Program at Osgoode Hall Law School' (2005) 23 *Pennsylvania State International Law Review* 757; G Torres, 'Integrating Transnational Legal Perspectives Into the First Year Curriculum' (2005) 23 *Pennsylvania State International Law Review* 801; H Dedek and A de Mestral, '"Born to be Wild": The "Trans-systemic" Programme at McGill and the De-Nationalization of Legal Education' (2009) 10 *German Law Journal* 889; P Zumbansen, 'Transnational Law, Evolving' in JM Smits (ed), *Elgar Encyclopedia of Comparative Law*, 2nd edn (Cheltenham, Edward Elgar Publishing, 2012) 898.

[31] See the symposia 'Navigating the Transsystemic—Tracer le Transsystemique' (2005) 50 *McGill Law Journal* 701 and N Chiesa, A de Luca and B Maheandiran (eds), 'Following the Call of the Wild: The Promises and Perils of Transnationalizing Legal Education' (2009) 10 *German Law Journal* 629, available at http://germanlawjournal.com/pdfs/FullIssues/Vol_10_No_07.pdf.

[32] S Sassen, 'The State and Globalization' in JS Nye and JD Donahue (eds), *Governance in a Globalizing World* (Washington DC, Brookings Institute, 2000) 91; A Stone Sweet, 'Constitutionalism, Legal Pluralism, and International Regimes' (2009) 16 *Indiana Journal of Global Legal Studies* 621.

[33] For one of the most recent examples, see the case of New York University School of Law's expansion through new law school campuses in Buenos Aires, Paris and Shanghai, available at http://www.law.nyu.edu/news/NYU_LAW_ANNOUNCES_STUDY-ABROAD_PROGRAM_CURRICULAR_ENHANCE-MENTS_THIRD_YEAR.

[34] See J Vescovi, 'Why Does Law School Cost So Much?', Columbia Law School, Communication Report (Summer 2006), available at https://www.law.columbia.edu/law_school/communications/reports/summer06/lawschoolcost.

push for a contextual study of business relations embedded in sociological analysis,[35] seminars in comparative or transnational law, legal culture or legal anthropology, and even international business transactions or international business law, are usually only taken by a self-selected group of specialised students in their last year of law school.

This fence-sitting is reflected, at least in part, in large parts of legal research; legal scholars, if the scope of research disseminated on the Social Science Research Network (www.ssrn.com) is any indication, likewise appear to focus their interests on matters of domestic significance, thus reflecting the primary orientation of legal practice for the majority of law school graduates. The world outside the nation state, even that of another nation state, remains one in which the majority of legal scholars is either not that interested, or sceptical about.[36] In contrast, then, while the apparently transnational scope of EU law appears to be a logical consequence of Europeanisation processes, there is also the risk of a distinct blind side. Pushing the boundaries of the European legal imagination towards a greater appreciation of the significance of studying law from both a comparative and, specifically, from a European and integrationist perspective, this energy-consuming effort sometimes has the tendency to push aside and, effectively, to render invisible important advances in the study of the historical and colonial pasts of the law of different countries (Member States).[37] This sometimes manifests itself in an apparent nonchalance towards the nation states' darker legacies,[38] as well as to their socio-economic specificities and their undeniable impact on European legal harmonisation projects.[39] This orientation towards the (once) bright lights of the European integration process today produces a strangely intriguing mixture of mundane love-of-self-as-consumer on the one hand[40] and a maturing interest in developing interdisciplinary research agendas to study the EU's deeper embeddedness in its colonial past on the other.[41]

In what could be seen as a parallel universe that persists in the blind spots of mainstream legal education today, increasingly sophisticated research approaches have been developing with regard to the prospects of and the forms in which legal analytical instruments and concepts—categories as well as basic understandings of nation state-

---

[35] S Macaulay, 'Elegant Models, Empirical Pictures, and the Complexities of Contract' (1977) 11 *Law and Society Review* 507; GC Shaffer, 'How Business Shapes Law: A Socio-Legal Framework' (2009) 42 *Connecticut Law Review* 147.

[36] M Minow, 'The Controversial Status of International and Comparative Law in the United States' (2010) 52 *Harvard International Law Journal Online*, available at http://www.harvardilj.org/wp.

[37] But, see C Joerges, 'Working through 'Bitter Experiences' towards a Purified European Identity: A Critique on the Disregard for History in European Constitutional Theory and Practice' in E Oddvar Eriksen, C Joerges and F Rödl (eds), *Law, Democracy and Solidarity in a Post-national Union: the Unsettled Political Order of Europe* (Oxford, Routledge, 2006) 335.

[38] See JHH Weiler, 'Epilogue' in C Joerges and N Singh Ghaleigh (eds), *Darker Legacies of Law in Europe: The Shadow of National Socialism and Facism over Europe and its Legal Tradition* (Oxford, Hart Publishing, 2003) 389; see the extensive commentaries on the project on the 'Darker Legacies of Law in Europe' in the symposium: D Augenstein (ed), 'European Integration in the Shadow of Europe's Darker Past: The "Darker Legacies of Law in Europe" Revisited' (2006) 7 *German Law Journal* 71.

[39] C Joerges, B Stråth and P Wagner (eds), *The Economy as a Polity: The Political Constitution of Contemporary Capitalism* (London, UCL Press, 2005); specifically on the area of corporate governance, see also the insightful essay by one of Europe's great comparatists: KJ Hopt, 'Common Principles of Corporate Governance in Europe?' in JA McCahery, P Moerland, T Raaijmakers and L Renneboog (eds), *Corporate Governance Regimes: Convergence and Diversity* (Oxford, Oxford University Press, 2002) 175.

[40] A Somek, 'Accidental Cosmopolitanism' (2012) 3 *Transnational Legal Theory* 371.

[41] P Dann and F Hanschmann, 'Post-colonial Theories and Law' (2012) 45 *Law and Politics in Africa, Asia, Latin America—Verfassung und Recht in Übersee (VRÜ)* 123.

originating legal institutions and processes—might or might not be adaptable to the regulatory challenges in a global space.[42] In this vein, scholarship on law and globalisation appears to have become an industry in its own right. Yet, the focal point of this burgeoning scholarship remains far from precise. In other words, it does not seem evident what precisely or specifically is the question that law and globalisation scholars are actually trying to answer. What does seem clear, however, is that the endeavours of legal scholars in this context have long become part of a multi-disciplinary study of global governance. As such, law and globalisation has become a field of scholarly inquiry that is belaboured by lawyers, political scientists, sociologists, anthropologists, geographers and political economists alike, which raises—yet again—important questions about how law should situate itself in relation to the approaches and methods of other disciplines.

## III. HUMAN RIGHTS, LAW AND DEVELOPMENT, AND TRANSITIONAL JUSTICE AS LEGAL FIELDS[43]

The contributions to the present volume can be read against the above-described background of an increasingly rich overlay of disciplinary engagements with globalisation phenomena. A distinctive trait of these engagements is the recognition that the success of any inquiry depends on the awareness of the methodological challenges arising from the unruly nature of the object or objects under scrutiny. Transitional justice, one of our core fields in this essay collection, is a case in point.[44] The same applies, arguably, to L&D, a field which has always been an area which can neither be neatly and clearly defined nor boxed into clear-cut categories. L&D has long been a battlefield for opposing concepts of law, political and economic order, and the role of institutional governance,[45] and, as such, has served as a laboratory for audacious experiments with explosive material. Categories such as 'progress',[46] 'development'[47] or 'order', and the often elusive promises of the rule of law,[48] are invariably contentious concepts, and, in the context of L&D, are frequently employed as bargaining chips in a high-stakes game over political and economic influence, autonomy and emanci-

---

[42] A rich account and analysis is offered by W Twining, *Globalisation and Legal Theory* (Evanston, IL, Northwestern University Press, 2000); see also the symposium on Twining's 2011 Montesquieu Lecture at Tilburg University on 'Globalization and Legal Research' in (2013) 4(3) *Transnational Legal Theory*.

[43] The following section draws on P Zumbansen, 'Knowledge in Development and Regulation, or How do we Distinguish between the Economic and the Non-Economic?' in Búrca et al, n 1 above.

[44] Bell, n 7 above, 5, 7: 'by 2009, we have a broad, multidisciplinary field that subjects its own origins, assumptions and political significance to radical critique. Unlike other fields of study, which have taken decades to reach this point, transitional justice can be argued to have experienced a dramatically compressed trajectory of fieldhood.'

[45] D Kennedy, 'Laws and Development' in J Hatchard and A Perry-Kessaris (eds), *Law and Development: Facing Complexity in the 21st Century—Essays in Honour of P Slinn* (London, Cavendish Publishing Limited, 2003) 17.

[46] T Skouteris, *The Notion of Progress in International Law Discourse* (The Hague, T.M.C. Asser Press, 2010); U Natarajan, 'TWAIL and the Environment: The State of Nature, the Nature of the State, and the Arab Spring' (2012) 14 *Oregon Review of International Law* 177.

[47] Escobar, n 5 above.

[48] J Rajah, *Authoritarian Rule of Law: Legislation, Discourse and Legitimacy in Singapore* (New York, Cambridge University Press, 2012).

pation.[49] While specific local contexts of L&D became the loci of such contestation, often enough under the magnifying glass of international and national development agendas, market integration and state reform,[50] one of the most striking discoveries to be made here relates to the fact that the contentious items in the L&D context are also those which have long informed a critical analysis of law and governance in the context of the nation state.[51] As such, the boundaries between the developing and the developed world, between those countries receiving and those exporting or providing legal (or economic) aid, become porous, and a legal theory of L&D can fruitfully build on its older domestic sister.

Among the important scholarly projects pursued by L&D scholars has been the discovery and analysis of the legal pluralist nature of the governance orders in the context of development.[52] With a growing awareness of the different ordering structures existing in the development context came the realisation that any legal order challenges the observer to acknowledge the parallels between, and the coexistence of, formal and informal law, hard and soft law, and legal and non-legal norms.[53] This realisation prompted L&D scholars not only to acknowledge but also to build upon the idea that many of the challenges pertaining to a law/non-law distinction that had been identified as specific to the development context were, in fact, detachable from any legal governance framework. Indeed, the inadequacy of the existing legal governance thinking pointed to the need for a different theoretical, but also doctrinal, attention.[54]

It is this realisation that allows for a better appreciation of the questionable foundations of a legal order, of the embeddedness of legal governance in a particular institutional setting (for example, the state) and at a particular moment in (geopolitical) time.[55] To the degree that the struggle over law reform in the context of development is seen as not entirely removed from contestations of the legal (political, economic) order in the domestic context,[56] L&D emerges as a field which is just as much concerned with the relationship of law to its (particular, local) social environment and context as has been the case for all other legal theoretical or legal sociological inquiries.[57] However, accepting this perspective also implies accepting the loss of an outside observer's standpoint. Precisely by acknowledging the inseparability of critical legal analysis in

---

[49] For a brilliant deconstruction of the post-war conceptual division between political and economic emancipation of former colonial states, see Pahuja, n 5 above.

[50] World Bank, *World Development Report 1996: From Plan to Market* (Oxford, Oxford University Press, 1996).

[51] The masterful analysis is still Trubek and Galanter, n 1 above.

[52] K Pistor and D Berkowitz, 'Of Legal Transplants, Legal Irritants, and Economic Development' in P Cornelius and B Kogut (eds), *Corporate Governance and Capital Flows in a Global Economy* (Oxford, Oxford University Press, 2003) 347; K Pistor, 'The Standardization of Law and its Effect on Developing Economies' (2002) 50 *American Journal of Comparative Law* 97.

[53] HW Arthurs, *Without the Law: Administrative Justice and Legal Pluralism in Nineteenth Century England* (Toronto, University of Toronto Press, 1988); RA Macdonald and J MacLean, 'No Toilets in Park' (2005) 50 *McGill Law Journal* 721; SF Moore, 'Law and Social Change: The Semi-Autonomous Field as an Appropriate Subject of Study' (1973) 7 *Law and Society Review* 719.

[54] Macdonald and MacLean, ibid. See also Scott, n 30 above, 757.

[55] B Aretxaga, 'Maddening States' (2003) 32 *Annual Review of Anthropology* 393.

[56] D Kennedy, 'Challenging Expert Rule: The Politics of Global Governance' (2005) 27 *Sydney Journal of International Law* 5.

[57] Cotterrell, n 26 above, 171; R Banakar, 'Law Through Sociology's Looking Glass: Conflict and Competition in Sociological Studies of Law' in A Denis and D Kalekin-Fishman (eds), *The ISA Handbook in Contemporary Sociology* (London, Sage Publications, 2009); P Zumbansen, 'Law's Effectiveness and Law's Knowledge: Reflections from Legal Sociology and Legal Theory' (2009) 10 *German Law Journal* 417.

the domestic and development contexts do we lose the comfort of being outside the very sphere which we are purporting both to study and to examine in a disinterested manner.[58] Instead, the demarcation of the L&D context from that of one's home legal system and jurisdiction becomes questionable in itself, because the assertions of law's precariousness in the development context apply to the domestic home context with equal force. Upon this basis, the distinction between governance challenges of 'there' and 'here' appears artificial. Indeed, the distinction seems designed to insulate the domestic context from critique while depicting the development context as deficient, and requiring aid and assistance. The identification of a series of legal governance questions as arising from within the context of a developing country inevitably leads to these questions having to be seen as being already pertinent much earlier, namely, already present and evident in the context of domestic legal critique.

A striking feature of this contextualisation of L&D as part of a larger exercise in investigating law's relationship to and its role in society, is the way in which the field opens itself up to an engagement and exchange with complementary discourses about regulatory places and spaces. Both legal scholars[59] and sociologists[60] have been scrutinising the conceptual and constituted nature of such regulatory spaces—spaces which escape a straightforward depiction from a single discipline's vantage point. Just as this critique has become pertinent with regard to the analysis of different, specialised regulatory arenas, ranging from labour[61] to corporate law,[62] from environmental[63] to criminal law,[64] altogether suggesting a methodological shift from comparative to

---

[58] Trubek and Galanter, n 1 above. See also DM Trubek, 'Toward a Social Theory of Law: An Essay on the Study of Law and Development' (1972) 82 *Yale Law Journal* 1.

[59] R Ford, 'Law's Territory (A History of Jurisdiction)' (1999) 97 *Michigan Law Review* 843; R. Buchanan, 'Border Crossings: NAFTA, Regulatory Restructuring and the Politics of Place' (1995) *Indiana Journal of Global Legal Studies* 371.

[60] Sassen, 'The State and Globalization', n 32 above, 91; idem, 'The Places and Spaces of the Global: An Expanded Analytic Terrain' in D Held and AG McGrew (eds), *Globalization Theory: Approaches and Controversies* (Cambridge, Polity Press, 2007) 79; D Harvey, 'The Sociological and Geographical Imaginations' (2005) *International Journal of Politics, Culture and Society* 211.

[61] DM Trubek, J Mosher and JS Rothstein, 'Transnationalism and the Regulation of Labor Relations: International Regimes and Transnational Advocacy Networks' (Labor and the Global Economy Research Circle, The International Institute, University of Wisconsin-Madison, January 1999) note 7; G Mundlak, 'De-Territorializing Labor Law' (2009) 3 *Law and Ethics of Human Rights* 188; HW Arthurs, 'Extraterritoriality by Other Means: How Labor Law Sneaks Across Borders, Conquers Minds, and Controls Workplaces Abroad' (2010) 21 *Stanford Law and Policy Review* 527.

[62] LC Backer, 'Private Actors and Public Governance Beyond the State: The Multinational Corporation, the Financial Stability Board, and the Global Governance Order' (2011) 18 *Indiana Journal of Global Legal Studies* 751; P Zumbansen, 'Neither "Public" nor "Private", "National" nor "International": Transnational Corporate Governance from a Legal Pluralist Perspective' (2011) 38 *Journal of Law and Society* 50.

[63] L Gulbrandsen, S Andresen and JB Skjærseth, 'Non-State Actors and Environmental Governance: Comparing Multinational, Supranational and Transnational Rule Making' in B Reinalda (ed), *The Ashgate Research Companion to Non-State Actors* (Farnham, Ashgate Publishing, 2011) 463; N Craik, 'Deliberation and Legitimacy in Transnational Environmental Governance', IILJ Working Paper 2006/10 (New York University, 2006); C Kamphuis, 'Canadian Mining Companies and Domestic Law Reform: A Critical-Legal Account' (2012) 13 *German Law Journal* 1456; S Seck, 'Home State Regulation of Environmental Human Rights Harms as Transnational Private Regulatory Governance' (2012) 13 *German Law Journal* 1360.

[64] N Boister, 'Transnational Criminal Law?' (2003) 14 *European Journal of International Law* 953; N Boister, *An Introduction to Transnational Criminal Law* (Oxford, Oxford University Press, 2012); RJ Currie, *International and Transnational Criminal Law* (Toronto, Irwin Law, 2010).

transnational law,[65] L&D has become a very active sphere for a renewed, critical and contextual analysis of law in a fast-changing and volatile environment.

This aspect has been underlined, perhaps most tellingly, by the recent approximation of L&D with the field of 'transitional justice', which testifies to an increasing awareness among interested experts of the close connections between investigations into the legacies of past injustices with programmes of future-directed legal and economic aid.[66] It is this disciplinary overlap and the growing intersections between L&D and TJ which allows for a critical investigation into their shared logics,[67] as several of the authors to the present collection illustrate. Due to concerns of space, the editors decided to omit the inclusion of a closely related field of scholarly analysis—literary critique—which prominently draws on novels and poetry to shed light on the relations between literature and academic trajectories of development, transitional justice and post-colonial studies.[68] Among such literature, we find works that treat themes closely connected to, and often overlapping with, the noted scholarly engagement: here, we find a vibrant literary[69] and cultural engagement with transition periods. After the seminal (inevitably colonial) portrayals by Joseph Conrad in *An Outpost of Progress* (1897) or *Heart of Darkness* (1899), post-colonial novels such as Chinua Achebe's *Things Fall Apart* (1958) and JM Coetzee's *Waiting for the Barbarians* (1980) poignantly scrutinise the slippery slope between 'us' and 'them' that inescapably pervades any intervention or development context. As Anne Orford has described in the context of public international law's attempts to address transnational military and civil conflict, we need to take a close look at the hidden, hegemonic aspirations of recent instances of humanitarian intervention.[70] Excavating the challenges of concepts such as 'change', 'reform' and 'progress', as they have been central to such seminal transitional justice debates as those concerning South Africa[71] and Sri Lanka,[72] Achmat Dangor's *Bitter Fruit* (2001)[73] or films such as Prasanna Vithanage's *Death on a Full Moon Day* have become inseparably intertwined with the scholarly discourse around these instances of transitional justice.[74]

[65] CM Scott, '"Transnational Law" as Proto-Concept: Three Conceptions' (2009) 10 *German Law Journal* 859; P Zumbansen, 'Transnational Legal Pluralism' (2010) 1 *Transnational Legal Theory* 141; Zumbansen, n 30 above.

[66] See, eg R Mani, 'Dilemmas of Expanding Transitional Justice, or Forging the Nexus between Transitional Justice and Development' (2008) 2 *International Journal of Transitional Justice* 253; P de Greiff and R Duthie (eds), *Transitional Justice and Development: Making Connections* (New York, Social Science Research Council, 2009).

[67] CJ Colvin, 'Purity and Planning: Shared Logics of Transitional Justice and Development' (2008) 2 *International Journal of Transitional Justice* 412.

[68] See EW Said, *Orientalism* (New York, Vintage Books, 1978); A Mbembe, *On the Postcolony* (Berkeley, CA, University of California Press, 2001).

[69] See the insightful discussion of the prose/poetry debate in India around the work of Rabindranath Tagore in D Chakrabarty, *Provincializing Europe: Postcolonial Thought and Historical Difference*, 2nd edn (Princeton, NJ, Princeton University Press, 2007).

[70] A Orford, 'Muscular Humanitarianism: Reading the Narratives of the New Interventionism' (2003) 10 *European Journal of International Law* 679.

[71] H Corder, 'Prisoner, Partisan and Patriarch: Transforming the Law in South Africa 1985–2000' (2002) 118 *The South African Law Journal* 772; A Gross, 'Reconciliation in South Africa' (2004) 40 *Stanford Journal of International Law* 40.

[72] J Derges, *Ritual and Recovery in Post-Conflict Sri Lanka* (London, Routledge, 2012).

[73] Corder, n 71 above; A Gross, n 71 above.

[74] See, eg G Weiss, *The Cage: The Fight for Sri Lanka and The Last Days of the Tamil Tigers* (London, Bodley Head, 2011).

The authors of the present collection of essays have a wide range of scholarly expertise as well as practical experience in L&D and TJ. These two areas have become pivotal signifiers of the ways in which lawyers interested in comparative and international law have, over time, developed very focused and nuanced approaches to the dynamics that characterise the emerging political and legal orders. Such transition states often result, for example, from military and/or political transformation due to either violent regime change or peaceful democratic transition, and raise pressing questions regarding the role of, say, criminal law and the persecution of the previous regime's human rights violations or that of international law in assisting or facilitating the new regime's legal–political consolidation.[75] With an almost overwhelming number of aspects to be addressed in a volatile development or transition context, scholars have fruitfully been debating how law, possibly aided by other disciplines, can adequately identify, address and eventually remedy the virulent questions arising in such contexts. In this vein, one of the field's leading scholars has observed that:

> The universe of transitional justice can be broadly or narrowly defined. At its broadest, it involves anything that a society devises to deal with a legacy of conflict and/or widespread human rights violations, from changes in criminal codes to those in high school textbooks, from creation of memorials, museums and days of mourning, to police and court reform, to tackling the distributional inequities that underlie conflict. A narrow view can be criticized for ignoring root causes and privileging civil and political rights over economic, social or cultural rights, and by so doing marginalizing the needs of women and the poor. On the other hand, broadening the scope of what we mean by transitional justice to encompass the building of a just as well as peaceful society may make the effort so broad as to become meaningless.[76]

Ruti Teitel, author of the widely acclaimed 2000 monograph on *Transitional Justice*, put the following questions at the outset of her investigation:

> How should societies deal with their evil pasts? . . . How is the social understanding behind a new regime committed to the rule of law created? Which legal acts have transformative significance? What, if any, is the relation between a state's response to its repressive past and its prospects for creating a liberal order? What is law's potential for ushering in liberalization?[77]

These questions have since been taken up within a wide range of scholarly and practical engagement, leading, inter alia, to the creation or further consolidation of specialised research institutions, including the International Center for Transitional Justice in New York City,[78] the Transitional Justice Centre at the University of Ulster,[79] and the Centre for Transitional Justice and Post Conflict Reconstruction in Ontario.[80] The

---

[75] RJ Goldstone, 'Foreword' in M Minow, *Between Vengeance and Forgiveness: Facing History after Genocide and Mass Violence* (Boston, MA, Beacon Press, 1999) ix–xiii; N Bhuta, 'New Modes and Orders: The Difficulties of a Jus Post Bellum of Constitutional Transformation' (2010) 60 *University of Toronto Law Journal* 799.

[76] N Roht-Arriaza, 'The New Landscape of Transitional Justice, in N Roht-Arriaza and J Mariecurrena (eds), *Transitional Justice in the Twenty-First Century: Beyond Truth Versus Justice* (Cambridge, Cambridge University Press, 2006) 1, 2.

[77] R Teitel, *Transitional Justice* (Oxford, Oxford University Press, 2000) 3.

[78] http://ictj.org/about.

[79] http://www.transitionaljustice.ulster.ac.uk/tji_about.html.

[80] http://tjcentre.uwo.ca.

increasing importance of TJ not only as an investigative pool but also as a platform for a border-crossing and interdisciplinary collaboration among human rights scholars, criminal lawyers, international lawyers, anthropologists and sociologists reflects on the complexity of issues addressed under the heading of TJ. It is this complexity that the present volume wishes to address in order to bring together the work of some of the leading scholars in the field. At the same time, however, the essays in this book encompass an even wider range of aspects than that already falling within the ambit of TJ. We approximate TJ with the equally complex field of L&D because we think that the issues just addressed in association with transitional justice have, in many ways, been central, explicitly or implicitly, to much of the work carried out by L&D scholars and practitioners. On the other hand, however, we believe that the dialogue between L&D and TJ about shared concerns and research targets is only in its early stages,[81] and is likely to produce a significant increase in our understanding of the intricate connections between development and aid policies, laws and economics on the one hand and the continuously proliferating field of transitional justice on the other.[82]

The collected essays in the area of L&D in this volume build on seminal scholarship since the 1970s, a time at which hopes even on the political left were particularly high with regard to the potential for law to play a significant role in the aid and assistance programmes that were being rolled out under the policy directives of the international organisations and the United States.[83] As terms such as 'development', 'aid' and 'reform' would suggest, one of the most treacherous aspects of the associated programmes was the implicit assumption of competence, authority and—arguably—righteousness in the design and delivery of such assistance programmes to countries around the world.[84] Critique against a predominantly Western- and, more precisely, United States-spirited wave of assistance and development programmes formed early and consistently, pointing to the pitfalls of policy programmes which all too often prioritised the relevance of private commercial enterprise over the pursuit of public policy[85] and, in dramatic ways, neglected to account for the causes of the current state of countries now receiving assistance.[86] Similarly, a poignant critique raised in the context of a number of humanitarian aid initiatives was the failure of those designing

---

[81] In that regard, see, eg de Greiff and Duthie, n 66 above; Y Selim and T Murithi, 'Transitional Justice and Development: Partners for Sustainable Peace in Africa?' (2011) 6 *Journal of Peacebuilding and Development* 58; see also S Buckley-Zistel, 'Connecting Transitional Justice and Development', presentation made at the Conference 'The Contribution of Civil Society and Victim Participation in Transitional Justice Processes' (2009), available at http://www.victim-participation.org/files/Buckley-Zistel.pdf; speech by UNDP Administrator H Clark, 'A Role for Development in Transitional Justice: the Arab Spring and Beyond', 14 November 2011, available at http://www.undp.org/content/undp/en/home/presscenter/speeches/2011/11/14/helen-clark-a-role-for-development-in-transitional-justice-the-arab-spring-and-beyond.html (last accessed 28 October 2012).

[82] See, eg the contributions to the *International Journal of Transitional Justice*, created in 2007, available at http://www.oxfordjournals.org/our_journals/ijtj/about.html.

[83] See the self-critical assessment by Trubek and Galanter, n 1 above, 1062.

[84] For a poignant deconstruction of the 'progress' v 'underdeveloped' assertions informing the World Bank's conceptualisation of developmental aid, see Pahuja, n 5 above.

[85] For an illustration of this approach, see the influential essay by RA Posner, 'Creating a Legal Framework for Economic Development' (1998) 13 *The World Bank Research Observer* 1.

[86] J Brohman, 'Economism and Critical Silences in Development Studies: A Theoretical Critique of Neoliberalism (1995) 16 *Third World Quarterly* 297; SN Ndegwa, 'A Case against Structural Adjustment' (1997) 2 *New Political Economy* 318 (1997); K Manzo, 'Africa in the Rise of Rights-based Development' (2003) 34 *Geoforum* 437.

the programme to consider more adequately the deeper root causes of the conflicts at the centre of the interventions.[87]

A pertinent aspect of the increasing overlap of L&D and TJ are the roles of law and, particularly, rights. Human rights have come to be seen as central to the assessments of states of underdevelopment and, as a consequence, the development of a rights regime, embedded in a system of 'rule of law', is seen as an essential prerequisite in the facilitation of societal, legal, economic and political progress.[88] However, as critics have long been arguing, human rights do not exist in a vacuum, but can only be explained within a comprehensive legal system, creating manifold rights and countervailing duties and obligations.[89] In the context of L&D, the critique of rights focused, even at an early stage, on the volatility of human rights assertions in precarious political conditions, characterised by socio-economic inequality and great disparities in the actually existing access to justice conditions. Even advanced stages of L&D reform, introducing concerns with the social, fell privy to a convincing critique of the programmes' failure to facilitate and consolidate a solid rights and entitlements regime, rather than complementing insufficient rule-of-law implements with arbitrary welfare or equity insertions.[90]

This focus on the centrality—but precariousness—of rights in the context of post-conflict, transitional states and emerging economies continues to be a central concern in the evolving regulatory and normative landscape of development and transitional justice. To the degree that human rights have come to represent institutionalised entitlements, which are both instruments of power as well as bargaining chips in struggles over autonomy and sovereignty, they play a central role in the continuing debates regarding the goals of development and transition.

These debates, to be sure, occur within an immensely complex context, rich with competing assertions of the conditions and trajectories of human rights developments and of the interests invested in granting rights to these or other concerns.[91] The scope of such contestations has, however, largely expanded, to the degree that policy concerns as expressed, for example, in the context of development or transitional justice programmes have become quasi-boundaryless. In other words, questions pertaining to the role of law in post-conflict Iraq or the World Bank's leadership in aid to Africa are, in many ways, no longer confined to these particular destinations. Instead, these concerns have become global in the way that they raise pressing questions which tie issues related to Iraq to those associated with global concerns with security and stability in the Middle East, with human rights protection, and with economic interests and geopolitical considerations. Likewise, any attempt even at helping or developing

---

[87] See, eg B Scholdan, 'Addressing the Root Causes: Relief and Development Assistance between Peacebuilding and Preventing Refugee Flow' (2000) *The Journal of Humanitarian Assistance*, available at http://sites.tufts.edu/jha/archives/category/bettina-scholdan.

[88] For a comprehensive discussion and critique, see A Santos, 'The World Bank's Uses of the "Rule of Law" Promise in Economic Development' in DM Trubek and A Santos (eds), *The New Law and Economic Development: A Critical Appraisal* (Cambridge, Cambridge University Press, 2006) 253.

[89] See, eg RL Hale, 'Coercion and Distribution in a Supposedly Non-coercive State' (1923) 38 *Political Science Quarterly* 470; MR Cohen, 'Property and Sovereignty' (1927) 13 *Cornell Law Quarterly* 8.

[90] K Rittich, 'The Future of Law and Development: Second Generation Reforms and the Incorporation of the Social' (2004) 26 *Michigan Journal of International Law* 199.

[91] See, eg J Kirkemann Boesen and T Martin, 'Applying a Rights-Based Approach. An Inspirational Guide for Civil Society' (Copenhagen, The Danish Institute for Human Rights, 2007), available at www.humanrights.dk/files/pdf/Publikationer/applying.

Africa (or India[92] or Latin America[93]) would have to start by taking into account the complex and intricate history of Africa's role in the world, a history that has been told too often from the colonisers' perspective and is now being told from within.[94] In other words, rights, development and transitional justice—the triad which provides the title elements to our book—have become the central grounds of contestation under the larger umbrella of 'global governance', the latter having attained the status of an adequately encompassing—as well as timely depiction of—regulatory and normative challenges which can no longer be confined to the level of the nation state or the sphere of international law.[95]

## IV. MAPPING GLOBAL GOVERNANCE DISCOURSES: CONVERGENCE, CONTESTATION AND CRITIQUE

The present volume can be read as a contribution to the body of scholarly responses to the changes in global governance since the end of the cold war, especially in the unfolding post-9/11 period, which have identified a reconfiguration, at the levels of both theory and practice, of formerly isolated fields and concerns, including human rights, law and development, as well as post-conflict or transitional justice.[96] The task of surveying each of these fields would be Sisyphean, not only because their boundaries appear, across a survey of various types of literature, as both fluid and porous, but also because the number of publications both within and among them continues to multiply. Furthermore, we have recognised that even the implied standpoint from which one might undertake such a survey cannot be presumptively assumed, either by ourselves as editors or by the individual contributors. There are no innocent starting points. This does not, however, imply an abdication of the responsibility to engage critically with these rapidly evolving discourses. Rather, the aim of the volume is precisely to draw attention to an extant body of critical scholarship that assumes this task. Not only do these essays individually offer nuanced accounts from a range of contexts in which human rights advocacy and transitional-justice initiatives are increasingly in collision with development projects, programmes and objectives,[97] but collectively they might be read as the beginning—partial and evocative, to be sure—of a methodological mapping of a reinvigorated and globalised field of critical legal scholarship.

[92] See, eg P Chatterjee, *The Nation and its Fragments: Colonial and Postcolonial Histories* (Princeton, NJ, Princeton University Press, 1993); idem, *The Politics of the Governed: Reflections on Popular Politics in Most of the World* (New York, Columbia University Press, 2004).

[93] See, eg A Anghie, *Imperialism, Sovereignty and the Making of International Law* (Cambridge, Cambridge University Press, 2005); D Bonilla Maldonado (ed), *Constitutionalism of the Global South: The Activist Tribunals of India, South Africa and Colombia* (New York, Cambridge University Press, 2013).

[94] See, eg the works by the late Chinua Achebe. In this regard, see also OC Okafor, *The African Human Rights System, Activist Forces and International Institutions* (Cambridge, Cambridge University Press, 2007).

[95] See, eg A Buchanan and RO Keohane, 'The Legitimacy of Global Governance' (2006) 20 *Ethics and International Affairs* 4 (2006); see also D Held and A McGrew (eds), *Governing Globalization: Power, Authority and Global Governance* (Cambridge, Polity Press/Blackwell Publishing, 2002); T Hale and D Held (eds), *Handbook of Transnational Governance. Institutions and Innovations* (Cambridge, Polity Press, 2011).

[96] See Rittich, n 90 above; S Pahuja, 'Rights as Regulation: The Integration of Development and Human Rights' in B Morgan (ed), *The Intersection of Rights and Regulation: New Directions in Sociolegal Scholarship* (Aldershot, Ashgate Publishing, 2007).

[97] On this, see also C Rodríguez-Garavito, 'Ethnicity.gov: Global Governance, Indigenous Peoples, and the Right to Prior Consultation in Social Minefields' ( 2011) 18 *Indiana Journal of Global Legal Studies* 263.

In the first part of the volume, the chapters explore the dimensions and dynamics of human rights discourse in the development context.[98] In recent years, the apparent convergence between the fields of human rights and development,[99] as expressed in various documents issued by the UN and by development institutions such as the World Bank, have attracted both praise and support from scholars and development practitioners.[100] Yet, until quite recently, human rights and development had, as a matter of professional expertise as well as practical application, moved along separate tracks.[101] Indeed, in many post-independence contexts, they were understood as emanating from distinct sources, requiring different sets of policies and programmes, and presenting potentially conflicting demands.[102] In light of this history, contemporary approaches that posit human rights and development as not only potentially congenial, but also axiomatically and self-evidently so, beg further inquiry.[103] As one of us writing with one of our contributions has observed elsewhere:

> despite the incorporation of human rights into the development agenda and efforts to represent the promotion of both human rights and development as fundamentally coterminous enterprises, it is clear that many questions concerning the links between social and economic rights and the trajectory of social transformation and economic development policy remain.[104]

These questions might also include '[h]ow economic development priorities are identified, which groups are consulted in the process of formulating them, how policies are implemented and risks and entitlements allocated, and how the associated costs and

---

[98] D Trubek, 'Toward a Social Theory of Law: An Essay on the Study of Law and Development' (1972) 82 *Yale Law Journal* 1; D Kennedy, 'Laws and Development' in J Hatchard and Amana Perry- Kessaris (eds), *Law and Development: Facing Complexity in the 21st Century* (London, Cavendish Publishing, 2003) 17; B Rajagopal, *International Law from Below: Development, Social Movements and Third World Resistance* (Cambridge, Cambridge University Press, 2003); R Buchanan, 'Reconceptualizing Law and Politics in the Transnational: Constitutional and Legal Approaches' (2009) 5 *Socio-legal Review* 21; Pahuja, n 96 above.

[99] S Engle Merry, 'Anthropology, Law, and Transnational Processes' (1992) 21 *Annual Review of Anthropology* 357; idem, 'New Legal Realism and the Ethnography of Transnational Law' (2006) 31 *Law and Society Inquiry* 975; C Antons and Volkmar Gessner (eds), *Globalisation and Resistance: Law Reform in Asia since the Crisis* (Portland OR, Hart Publishing, 2007); Y Dezalay and B Garth (eds), *Lawyers and the Rule of Law in an Era of Globalization* (Oxford, Routledge, 2012)

[100] P Alston and M Robinson, *Human Rights and Development: Towards Mutual Reinforcement* (Oxford, Oxford University Press, 2005), identify the effort to find 'ways in which the strengths, resources, and support of the international human rights and development communities can be mobilized in order to reinforce one another in their efforts to achieve shared goals' as a key objective of that landmark edited collection.

[101] I Shivji (1999) 'Constructing a New Rights Regime: Prospects, Problems, Prospects' (1999) 8 *Social and Legal Studies* 259: 'On the global terrain of social and political discourse, the developmental and the human rights discourses were locked in battle. They were polarized and became mutually exclusive. This meant that the developmental discourse and the human rights discourse ran parallel.'

[102] See, eg Shivji, ibid, 260, where he observes that: 'the liberal theory (of rights) ruled out of court any link between individual rights and economic justice, while developmental theory was prepared to sacrifice individual rights in the pursuit of socio-economic justice'.

[103] C Nyamu-Musembi and A Cornwall, 'What is the "Rights-Based Approach" All About? Perspectives from International Development Agencies', IDS Working Paper 234 (Institute of Development Studies, November 2004).

[104] R Buchanan, H Kijo-Bisimba and K Rittich, 'The Evictions at Nyamuma, Tanzania: Structural Constraints and Alternative Pathways in the Struggles over Land' in LE White and J Perelman (eds), *Stones of Hope: How African Activists Reclaim Human Rights to Challenge Global Poverty* (Stanford CA, Stanford University Press) 93.

benefits are distributed'.[105] Insofar as the proposed volume is offered as a response to these concerns, it seeks to address both the macrohistorical and legal-theoretical dimensions of these questions, as well as the dilemmas presented by their instantiation in particular (symbolic and institutional) locations.

The essays on transitional justice that are featured in the second part of the volume similarly engage with the complexity of increasingly intertwined discourses. It is here, in the amorphous and intensely belaboured field of international, local and mixed criminal courts and tribunals, global human rights discourse and human rights litigation,[106] truth commissions, village courts and assertions of retroactive justice,[107] that the internal dependency of these particularised discourses on the debates addressed in the areas of L&D, humanitarian intervention and occupation becomes visible. The intensive efforts of human rights activists, constitutional and criminal law experts over the past few years to bring human rights violators to justice,[108] while scrutinising the challenges arising from humanitarian interventions that were not authorised under public international law,[109] suggest a pressing need for a more encompassing and rigorous critical approach. It has become clear that a better understanding of the present situation of comparative constitutional politics, legal aid and law reform in post-conflict and transition societies crucially depends upon this rethinking.

While several of the chapters (eg Chapters 2 and 3) acknowledge the segmentation of these fields at the level of practice that, until quite recently, allowed experts in development, for example, to consider rights concerns as being somebody else's job,[110] and others (eg Chapter 6) document new actors and advocacy practices that have emerged in the era of rights-based development, all of the chapters in the present volume address the role of power inequalities, as well as the important place of social and political contestation in relation to recent developments. These approaches provide an important counterpoint to strands of scholarly and institutional discourse that have been much more sanguine, and even celebratory, regarding the potential for new, more

---

[105] Ibid.

[106] C Scott, 'Introduction to *Torture as Tort*: From Sudan to Canada to Somalia' in idem (ed), *Torture as Tort* (Oxford/Antwerp, Hart Publishing/Intersentia, 2001) 3; R Wai, 'Countering, Branding, Dealing: Using Economic and Social Rights in and around the International Trade Regime' (2003) 14 *European Journal of International Law* 35.

[107] M Usami, 'Retroactive Justice: Trials for Human Rights Violations under a Prior Regime' in BM Leiser and TD Campbell (eds), *Human Rights in Philosophy and Practice* (Aldershot, Ashgate Publishing, 2001) 423.

[108] See C Scott, 'Translating Torture into Transnational Tort: Conceptual Divides in the Debate on Corporate Accountability for Human Rights Harms' in idem, *Torture as Tort*, n 106 above, 45, and the other contributions in that volume; see also B Stephens, 'Translating Filártiga: A Comparative and International Law Analysis of Domestic Remedies for International Human Rights Violations' (2002) 27 *Yale Journal of International Law* 1; J Sarkin, 'Reparation for Past Wrongs: Using Domestic Courts Around the World, Especially the United States, to Pursue Human Rights Claims' (2004) 32 *International Journal of Legal Information* 426; AJ Carrillo, 'Bringing International Law Home: The Innovative Role of Human Rights Clinics in the Transnational Legal Process' (2004) 35 *Columbia Human Rights Law Review* 527.

[109] See A Orford, 'Muscular Humanitarianism: Reading the Narratives of the New Interventionism' (2003) 10 *European Journal of International Law* 679; M Koskenniemi, '"The Lady Doth Protest Too Much". Kosovo, and the Turn to Ethics in International Law' (2002) 65 *Modern Law Review* 159; AL Paulus, 'The War against Iraq and the Future of International Law: Hegemony or Pluralism?' (2004) 25 *Michigan Journal of International Law* 691.

[110] P Uvin, *Human Rights and Development* (West Hartford, CT, Kumarian Press, 2004).

encompassing, mechanisms of global governance, in order to avoid the errors and pitfalls of past practices.[111]

The discourse of convergence is illustrated, for example, by UN Secretary General Kofi Annan's 2005 report, entitled 'In Larger Freedom: Towards Development, Security and Human Rights for All'. The report cogently observed that 'we will not enjoy development without security, we will not enjoy security without development, and we will not enjoy either without respect for human rights. Unless all these causes are advanced, none will succeed.'[112]

Since the late 1990s, a growing number of international institutions and agencies have taken up this call to move towards a more integrated, or comprehensive, approach.[113] At the level of practice, one effect of these developments can be traced through the proliferation of projects under the increasingly capacious category of the rule of law.[114]

Our review of the convergence literature reveals a tendency to focus on the ways in which the fields can, or should, mutually enforce each other.[115] It is not uncommon to trace convergences between transitional justice and development upon the basis of their shared aspirations for a better future for the citizens of a particular nation, for example. The contributors to this volume, however, remind us to attend to the ways in which these types of discussion already assume the illusory narrative of progress that lies at the heart of the development project.[116] Along a different vector, even very robust and otherwise critical analyses of the relationship between development and human rights tend to focus on potential compatibilities, rather than on conflicts.[117] Yet the enthusiasm with which the discussion of potential synergies between the fields of development, human rights and transitional justice has been embraced by both scholars and practitioners has drawn scholarly and public attention away from the difficult choices and necessary trade-offs that are a routine part of the development enterprise.[118]

Rather than joining with the institutional or scholarly quest for an integrated approach, a number of the essays in this volume identify this move (towards a comprehensive approach) as a key aspect of contemporary developments which calls for a more differentiated analysis and critique.[119] One thing that is of particular interest

---

[111] H-O Sano, 'Development and Human Rights: The Necessary, but Partial Integration of Human Rights and Development' (2000) 22 *Human Rights Quarterly* 734; de Greiff and Duthie, n 66 above.

[112] 'In Larger Freedom: Towards Development, Security and Human Rights for All', report of UN Secretary General Kofi Annan, ch 1, http://www.un.org/largerfreedom/chap1.htm (last accessed 11 September 2012).

[113] See, eg the World Bank, *Development and Human Rights: the Role of the World Bank* (Washington, DC, IBRD, 1998).

[114] S Humphreys, *Theatre of the Rule of Law: Transnational Legal Intervention in Theory and Practice* (Cambridge, Cambridge University Press, 2010).

[115] Alston and Robinson, n 100 above.

[116] See Pahuja, n 5 above; Escobar, n 5 above.

[117] P Alston, 'Ships Passing in the Night: The Current State of the Human Rights and Development Debate Seen through the Lens of the Millennium Development Goals' (2005) 27 *Human Rights Quarterly* 755.

[118] R Buchanan, H Kijo-Bisimba and K Rittich, 'The Evictions at Nyamuma: Struggles over Land and the Limits of Human Rights Advocacy in Tanzania' in White and Perelman, n 104 above.

[119] S Pahuja, K Rittich, S Engle Merry, Chapters 1, 8 and 9, respectively, in this volume. See also L Eslava and S Pahuja, 'Beyond the (Post)Colonial: TWAIL and the Everyday Life of International Law' (2012) 45 *Journal of Law and Politics in Africa, Asia and Latin America—Verfassung und Recht in Übersee (VRÜ)* 195.

to us is the way in which law, in its technocratic guise, is increasingly understood as instrumental to each of these fields: human rights, development and transitional justice.[120] In a context in which enduring solutions to the world's problems—such as that embodied in the slogan inscribed on the entrance to the World Bank Building in New York, 'Our dream is a world free of poverty'—continue to elude the international community, institutions such as the World Bank have embraced the rule of law as a development strategy.[121] The rule of law is also understood as fundamental to the success of transitional justice initiatives, and is seen as essential to greater realisation of international human rights within given states. The turn to law plays an analogous role in each of these fields: in the context of deeply politicised policy decisions, a technocratic understanding of the rule of law both grounds and legitimates the interventions of international agencies in the domestic affairs of states. In this account, it is the understanding of law itself, and particularly the specific role which can be played by a particular conception of the rule of law in the international arena that is in transition, rather than human rights, development or transitional justice as such.

Our approach stands in contrast to previous exercises in bridge-building between these fields, which have sought to draw these separate strands together from within the functional logics or shared foundational assumptions of one, or occasionally two, fields.[122] Building upon shared foundations can serve to reinforce implicit assumptions, rather than subjecting them, as several of our authors do, to closer scrutiny. Within the fields in question, the shared founding assumptions arguably include the problematic dichotomies of old world/new world, civilised/barbaric, developed/underdeveloped, donor/recipient, as well as the hierarchies that are both supported and justified by these dichotomies. The unique contribution of the present volume is to pose the encounter between the fields without replicating or assuming the logics that underpin them. That is, this volume both offers a critical engagement with these developments and provides us with the opportunity to consider some of the risks presented by the convergence of the teleologies of human rights, development and transition. Consequently, it is not surprising that many of these chapters are cautious and cautionary, rather than celebratory, regarding recent developments.

In our contemporary engagement with critical scholarship on development, human rights and transitional justice we have found it useful to revisit the landmark critique of law and development formulated by David Trubek and Marc Galanter, who identified three categories, or grounds, of critique. These are the critique of universality, referring to the ethnocentrism of the liberal legalist paradigm; the critique of formal law's potency and the significance of informal ordering mechanisms; and the dark face of legal reform critique, which acknowledges that reform efforts may frequently have consequences such as empowering élites, or containing protest, not intended

---

[120] On this, see the analysis by S Engle Merry, Chapter 8 in this volume; see also GA Sarfaty, *Values in Translation: Human Rights and the Culture of the World Bank* (Stanford CA, Stanford University Press, 2012).

[121] See Pahuja, n 5 above, 185; Rittich, n 90 above; Trubek and Santos, *The New Law and Economic Development*, n 1 above.

[122] See, eg de Greiff and Duthie, n 66 above; Alston and Robinson, n 100 above; S McInerney-Lankford, 'Human Rights and Development: a Comment on Challenges and Opportunities from a Legal Perspective' (2009) 1 *Journal of Human Rights Practice* 51; R Peerenboom, 'Human Rights and Rule of Law: What's the Relationship?' (2004–05) 36 *Georgetown Journal of International Law* 809. See also the book review of *Transitional Justice and Development* by B Ugochukwu (2012) 13 *German Law Journal* 94.

by liberal reformers.[123] Although these insights have been taken up and expanded by critical scholars in a great many fields over the intervening decades, the persistence of ambitious, formalist and instrumental approaches to law reform in development- and transitional justice projects, most recently reframed in the language of rights, suggest that legal scholars and lawyers in development contexts continue to be loath to abandon their disciplinary commitments to legal efficacy, even in the face of con- siderable evidence to the contrary. For example, a number of scholars have recently both extended and illustrated the argument that, in the encounter with development agencies, human rights have largely become reformulated as a mode of regulation, in a manner that largely neutralises their potential to be used as a tool of the weak in contentious politics.[124] At the same time, critical scholarship also reminds us that the role of political mobilisation on the part of emergent activist groups within this development has never been more significant.[125] Kerry Rittich sums it up well when she notes that 'in second generation reforms, human rights are better understood not as the answer to the social deficit but as the terrain of struggle'.[126] In this contested and uncertain landscape, the work of critical legal scholars—including those whose essays are included in this collection and the many others cited herein—plays an increas- ingly vital role in questioning assumptions, containing expectations and challenging the power of entrenched institutions. The contributions to the present volume mark important milestones in the continuing engagement with law's role in development and transitional justice, and we trust that our readers will find in them a host of helpful and inspiring introductions to a field of discourse which is of growing impor- tance—both in interdisciplinary scholarship and in practice.

## OVERVIEW OF THE VOLUME

The first part of the book features work on the intersection of law & development and human rights. The first three chapters of the volume together provide a critical theoretical overview of the fields of development and human rights. The first chapter, by Pahuja, situates the project of development both historically, as a continuation of 'the benevolence of empire' and in relation to its capture by the field of international law, such that the problem of global poverty is understood and addressed within inter- national law and institutions. According to Pahuja, the result is 'a frame of refer- ence in which self interested and impoverishing behavior by the West is understood as altruism toward the rest'. Pahuja's chapter prompts a critical reconsideration of the development project, arguing that it constrains both how we can think about the causes of global poverty as well as the range of potential solutions we might marshal to address it. She argues that the development project represents an institutionalised

---

[123] Trubek and Galanter, n 1 above, 1083–84. See also Buchanan, n 1 above.

[124] Pahuja, n 96 above; idem, Chapter 1 in this volume; R Perry, 'Preserving Discursive Spaces to Promote Human Rights: Poverty Reduction Strategy, Human Rights and Development Discourse' (2011) 7 *McGill International Journal of Sustainable Development Law and Policy* 61.

[125] White and Perelman, n 104 above; Rajagopal, n 98 above; R. Buchanan, 'Writing Resistance into Inter- national Law' (2008) 10 *International Community Law Review* 445.

[126] K Rittich, 'The Future of Law and Development: Second-Generation Reforms and the Incorporation of the Social' in Trubek and Santos, n 1 above, 24.

set of knowledge practices, produced by an 'army of experts' primarily from the developed world that locate the causes of poverty within the poor state, and rule out of bounds the consideration of global or international causes. That international law or institutions might be complicit in exacerbating the difficulties of poor people and poor countries is 'simply not on the table'. Pahuja's chapter revisits a number of the core assumptions of development practice over the past 50 years, including free trade, conditionality and economic growth, provocatively suggesting that they have been adhered to as tenets of faith, rather than reason.

The contribution by Issa Shivji introduces the fields of both development and human rights as contentious, fragmented discourses. Shivji's analysis demonstrates the extent to which both discourses are the contingent products of historical struggle. He identified the UN debates over the right to self-determination in the 1960s and 1970s, during the efforts to promote a New International Economic Order, as pivotal. It was during this era that the developmental and human rights discourses became polarised. From the perspective of newly independent African states, to the extent that human rights discourses were posited as 'neutral' and 'universal', they were also anti-development, insofar as they could not acknowledge the particular histories, demands and aspirations of Third World peoples. Through the era of structural adjustment and since, the growing convergence of development and human rights discourses has led to the narrowing and technocratisation of the former, and the fragmentation and particularisation of the latter. Among the effects have been the marginalisation and containment of developmental concerns and proposals emanating from the Third World. According to Shivji, so long as the dominance of the North over the South in the world system is unacknowledged within human rights discourses, adding a 'developmental' dimension to human rights is unlikely to alter this trajectory.

Like Shivji, Ananya Mukerjee Reed argues that the meaning of both 'rights' and 'development' in the context of rights-based approaches to development is fundamentally contested. Her chapter focuses on problematising the meaning of development, rather than human rights. She offers a detailed critique of the capability approach, which she identifies as the dominant contemporary approach to human development. In this context, she discusses the work of Amartya Sen, which argues that rights are a key strategy by which we might formulate a response to the question 'how can we make the world less unjust?'.[127] Although Sen's recent work, in his own account, has moved beyond the transcendental institutionalism of Kant and Rawls, Mukerjee Reed illustrates the extent to which it still elides issues of structural inequality that, in her view, condition competing understandings of justice. In proposing an alternative, a 'social power' approach to development, she argues that 'it is imperative to introduce the issues of power and structural inequality into rights/development discourses if they are to be informed by transformative or "enabling" notions of justice'. Her chapter begins to move us toward a more nuanced understanding of both the potential and the limits of rights based approaches: while rights struggles can be a key part of broader social mobilisation, formalised rights can also function to normalise exclusionary practices and obscure structural inequalities.

A number of the authors in the first part of this book observe that the discourse of human rights undergoes a shift when it converges with development. They vary,

---

[127] A Sen, *The Idea of Justice* (Cambridge, MA, Harvard University Press, 2009).

however, in their assessment of the nature of that shift, and particularly in its impact on social justice. The chapter by Aylwin and Coombe argues that rights-based approaches to development, when implemented well, have some potential for improving social justice outcomes, while the chapters by Kumar and Okafor warn of the risks of present trends. While Aylwin and Coombe consider the potential of IP strategies such as the use of marks indicating conditions of origin (MICOs) as a way of securing greater benefits for local producers of a distinctive product such as Darjeeling tea or Mysore silk, they are not unaware of the potential downsides. Their chapter defines both 'rights' and 'development' in ways that account for power inequalities and collective, as well as individual, needs and aspirations. Rights-based development, in their account, has unleashed a new set of actors and a new brand of advocacy into the field. NGOs and social movements are increasingly using human rights standards (particularly social, cultural and economic rights) to confront the IP privileges granted to corporate actors by international financial institutions, trade regimes and governments. The focus is on the important role of non-state actors advocacy and activism, rather than legalistic avenues or technical expertise, in the securing of meaningful rights. Their discussion of development similarly moves well beyond traditional economistic approaches, to articulate an expanded conception that incorporates both environmental sustainability and cultural self-determination. While, in the view of the authors, 'MICOs are amongst the few IP vehicles likely to simultaneously satisfy needs for collective rights, local autonomy, economic improvement, and entrepreneurship in a global environment', their chapter also reveals a range of challenges for developing countries seeking to realise these benefits. There is no 'one size fits all' approach to IP-based development strategies—each programme must be evaluated and assessed on an ongoing basis in terms of the distribution of economic benefits and other impacts on local communities.

A well-known critical formulation of the argument about the implications of the convergence of rights and development is found in work of Upendra Baxi, who claims that the paradigm of universal human rights found in UNHDR is being supplanted by a new model, which he has described as 'trade related market friendly' rights.[128] The chapter by Obiora Okafor both tests this thesis and illustrates the potential effects of the convergence between development and human rights as conventionally understood and implemented by the World Bank and the IMF in the Nigerian context. It documents the effects of the implementation of a set of policy reforms between 1999 and 2005 that included the removal of 'subsidies' on petroleum products (and corresponding fuel price hikes), a dramatic reduction of the federal civil service and the privatisation of state-controlled enterprises. While the Nigerian state is lauded internationally for faithfully implementing the development policies imposed by the international financial institutions, Okafor's chapter powerfully documents the domestic costs of such policies in popular resistance, repression, human rights violations and the curtailment of labour rights.

Similarly, Kumar argues that the convergence of human rights discourse with labour rights leads to a depoliticisation of the latter. The chapter's brief genealogy reveals the extent to which the different historical trajectories of labour rights and human rights discourses underpin important practical and conceptual points of divergence.

---

[128] U Baxi, *The Future of Human Rights* (Delhi, Oxford University Press, 2002).

She argues that the focus of labour rights on the need to address unequal power relations between workers and employers sits uneasily within the 'universalist' aspirations of human rights discourse. As previous chapters have argued in different contexts, if care is not taken to ensure that issues of power and inequality are explicitly addressed at every level, the integration of human rights into development is likely to reinforce, rather than diminish, their impact.

The two final chapters in the first section examine the convergence of the fields of human rights and development through a consideration of the increasing significance of 'indicators' for each. The chapter by Sally Merry highlights two effects of the turn to indicators: as tools for knowledge and tools for governance. Indicators offer a technology for producing accessible and standardised forms of knowledge, but it is important to note the mechanisms by which this technology functions to consolidate power in the hands of experts and obscures the complex political and social choices that are embedded in those measures. According to Merry, indicators 'create a commensurability that is widely used to compare, to rank and to make decisions, even though the users recognise that these simplified numerical forms are superficial, often misleading and very possibly wrong'. She argues that the political struggles over what human rights mean and what constitutes compliance (highlighted by earlier chapters) are submerged in the turn to indicators by technical questions of measurement, criteria, and data accessibility. Merry's chapter draws on genealogies of statistics to compellingly illustrate the deep embeddedness of the 'modern fact' in contemporary practices of governance. Indicators are themselves also a technology of governance—'by establishing standards according to which individuals, organisations, or nations should behave, indicators should inspire those who are measured to perform better and improve their ranking'. But, by shifting the responsibility for governance/compliance from those in power to those who are governed, without giving the governed a role in the production of the indicators themselves, Merry points out that this technology can also produce alienation and resistance. The chapter by Kerry Rittich critically analyses a specific and almost universally lauded example of the turn to indicators in the Millenium Development Goals. Rittich's argument is that the MDG's themselves are a form of governance, a way of 'governing by measuring' that is increasingly entrenched in global regulation. Yet Rittich agrees with Merry that this mode of governance has some important potential shortcomings that beg for further consideration. Perhaps, she suggests,

> targeting a problem is not always as useful as situating a problem. Perhaps it encourages us to focus on symptoms rather than causes, perhaps it leaves unaddressed, and hence intact, the many direct and indirect sources of the problem we seek to solve or alleviate.

Part II of the book presents chapters with a particular focus on transitional justice (TJ). The chapters are written by authors with a long-standing and profound experience in the field and the increasingly vivid and globalised, scholarly academic discourse of TJ. It is against this background that their analysis seeks to strike a balance between serving a deep political commitment to TJ's aspirations on the one hand and critically engaging with the field's instrumentalist risks on the other. Highlighting the connection between TJ and law & development, which has also been emphasised by scholars such as Rama Mani and which is placed at the centre of this volume,

Naomi Roht-Arriaza forcefully highlights the blind spots of a TJ agenda that focuses on the violation of civil and political rights at the price of disregarding the economic conditions and inequalities: these, she argues, so often lie at the root of the circumstances that give rise to—as well as continue after—the transition processes have been launched. Drawing our attention to this conceptual omission in many TJ programmes, a point which is taken up also in the chapters by Nagy, Rittich and Goodwin, Roht-Arriaza argues for the need to place TJ agendas into the larger context of development politics. Without such contextualisation, any TJ effort is likely to miss the deeper economic roots of what would otherwise be perceived as political inequality. Focusing on a highly illuminating example in this regard, Roht-Arriaza describes the development of specially tailored reparations regimes in Guatemala and Rwanda, highlighting the importance of understanding reparations not merely as a 'deliverable', but as a 'process':

> The most important determinant of success is how things are done—that is, whether the discussion and delivery of reparations are set up in a way that makes the goals of acknowledgement, respect, the restoration of dignity, and civic interest in the betterment of lives a felt reality for the survivors.

Martha Minow, in her chapter, focuses on the availability of choices in directing TJ processes. In her helpful overview of efforts to institutionalise an international forum for criminal prosecution, Minow traces the emergence of ad hoc criminal tribunals in different transition contexts around the world (ICTY, ICTR) and places these in comparison with alternative approaches, including the creation of the Truth and Reconciliation Commission in post-apartheid South Africa. Her chapter paints an important picture of the role that truth commissions can play in deeply divided, conflictual societies to facilitate the devising of 'a new national narrative'. Meanwhile, Minow emphasises the significance of sometimes complementing truth inquiries with court-based trials as well as other state action, and doing so in a way that is sensitive to the conditions on the ground and to the need to establish a basis for truth seeking or conflict resolution: '[b]ut, simply knowing the truth is not sufficient; seeing public acknowledgement, receiving an apology, obtaining compensation, and benefiting from psychological and moral support are important elements at restoring many victims' sense of dignity, well-being, and respect'.

The chapter by Rosemary Nagy squarely engages with TJ from the perspective of a 'bigger picture', comprising global economic integration, 'democratisation' and standardisation. The chapter directs our attention to the leveling and standardising effect that TJ as a 'global project' can have when following upon military or political interventions, the original legality or legitimacy of which often will no longer be accessible for scrutiny once the problem-solving and state-building dynamic of TJ has begun to kick in. Echoing other scholars' concerns with TJ's saturatedness with often unquestioned human rights standards, Nagy highlights the asymmetric nature of 'globalised TJ', the roots of which she traces back to Nuremberg. Complementing Anne Orford's important analysis of the self-declared posture by the West as knight in shining armor who sets out to save the meek and promote human rights in Kosovo,[129] Nagy attracts

---

[129] A Orford, 'Muscular Humanitarianism: Reading the Narratives of the New Interventionism' (1999) 10(4) *European Journal of International Law* 679.

our attention to the discrepancy between the international community's disregard to the deeper causes for conflict or its resolution and its 'assistance' to install institutional and procedural aid in the period following economic and/or political collapse. Nagy's central contention is that TJ's 'legalistic focus' fails to look beyond egregious and much scandalised human rights violations at the structural and long-standing 'daily' violations, including those perpetrated against women, which frequently form an integral part of an institutionalised system of discrimination or exploitation, as in the case of legally sanctioned apartheid. By selecting preconceived types of rights abuses, the TJ framework falls short of recognising and addressing more deeply engrained 'patterns of violations' as part of structured violence and gender inequality.

Morag Goodwin's sobering account on the recent history of forced sterilisations of Romani women in the Czech transition context echoes Rosemary Nagy's concern with the bigger picture of discrimination, violence and exclusion routines and practices that predate political-legal transitions and continue after the alleged transition moment— precisely because of the frequent shortcomings in local TJ processes to adequately address and verbalise such forms of structural violence as they are entrenched in daily life. As Goodwin's chapter makes clear, it is the myopic focus of TJ processes to target 'political' forms of persecution with the 'state' or public officials in general as the main perpetrator. What remains outside that lens, however, are the myriad and extremely effective forms of daily live discrimination and exclusion, as in the case of the historically evolved treatment of Roma people. Especially where, as in many cases of Eastern European transition countries, the focus was on the change in system politics at alleged 'the end of history' (F Fukuyama), this led to a disregard of those forms of structural violence that were not directly related to the tension between communist, socialist or capitalist ideologies. As Goodwin observes, '[b]y focusing on those wronged for resisting Communism, the transition process excluded the Romani communities' experience of that political system precisely because it formed part of the everyday social pattern'. Beyond this poignant critique of the shortcomings of the politics of TJ, Goodwin's chapter illustrates the importance to place transition moments and periods within a larger context of time and space. By refusing to treat the transition in a particular place as circumscribed and, eventually, finite, it becomes possible to see how such transitions are often chances—more often than not, missed ones—of addressing long-standing tensions in a country's or a people's communal life. The task then becomes one of recognising and scrutinising the connections between such discrimination practices before, after and beyond a particular transition moment. In the case of the Roma, such a wider perspective brings into view the ties between the historical injustice towards the Roma and its continuation across Europe up to the present day. In conclusion, Goodwin's chapter makes a point that is one of the central contentions in the project that informs the present volume: as she notes that

> The process of transition, of which transitional justice is such a prominent part, is not just a coming to terms with the past, nor is it simply a statement of society's values in the present; rather it necessarily involves deeper constitutional questions of belonging and participation

she underlines the significance of treating TJ as part of a larger, critical project of scrutinising law's ability to identify, process and eventually address societal violence and inequality. Far from being a subject matter that concerns either those countries that emerge from century-long legacies of imperialism and colonialism or those that undergo fundamental political-economic 'system' change, TJ should be seen as a vehicle to study more comprehensively long-standing structural patterns of violence, discrimination and exclusion. Seen from this perspective, TJ echoes, takes up and reformulates many of the original concerns brought forward by legal pluralist scholars and rights activists in the 1960s and 1970s.

Kirsten Anker's chapter offers an illuminating comparative analysis on the role and effect of the apologies rendered by state leaders in both Australia and Canada to victims of historical injustice. Anker's chapter draws, inter alia, on legal pluralism to highlight the gap between the official agenda that informs and drives the 'apology' and the felt consequences in the complex socio-political relations marking the lives of the recipients of the apology on the ground. Through setting side-by-side the 'reconciliation' efforts in Australia with the target of addressing the 'stolen generations' and the Canadian attempt to bring justice to the victims of the Indian Residential Schools programme, it becomes possible to gain a deeper insight into the way in which highly publicised and attention-seeking efforts on the part of the state to address historical injustice lead to an unjustified confidence in law and state action to also remedy the deeper causes of this injustice. Here, Anker forcefully argues for a more comprehensive view on the relationship between state action in voicing apologies, convening inquiry commissions or creating education funds on the one hand and the continuing exclusion of the victims of this state-led and deeply entrenched violence on the other. Echoing Morag Goodwin's call for a constitutionalist perspective on the way in which TJ effectively addresses historical injustice—then and now—Kirsten Anker shows the importance of moving beyond a state-law perspective in order to more fully engage with the original targets of such reconciliation efforts on the same eye level.

> Reconciliation, in this context, can only ever be about learning to live with the imposition of the state's control over indigenous peoples, rather than working on a renewed relationship between peoples . . . An approach needs to be imagined in which indigenous law is not a curious social fact but a contributor to the ongoing conversation that makes a nation's law what it is.

Christian Joerges' chapter forms part of his comprehensive and rich engagement with Europe's legal and political past, which is driven by a keen interest in the historical trajectories of institutional, legal political structures of the EU's member states and their influence on the evolution of the EU. As the convenor and co-editor of one of the most important collective studies on the authoritarian past of several EU member states,[130] Joerges is well positioned to draw our attention to the stakes of European 'integration' as a complex and ongoing transition project. In his chapter in the present volume, Joerges critically engages with the failed Constitutional Treaty and with much of European constitutionalism in general. His analysis culminates in the poignant critique of the absence of historical awareness among those invested in EU constitutionalism.

---

[130] C Joerges and N Singh Ghaleigh (eds), *Darker Legacies of Law in Europe* (Oxford, Hart Publishing, 2003); see also the Review Symposium in *German Law Journal* 2006, available at http://www.germanlaw-journal.com/pdfs/FullIssues/pdf_Vol_07_No_02.pdf.

We cannot understand what is happening in the EU, nor what we are doing and what we are achieving or failing to achieve, unless we bring to mind the meaning of institutional changes, legal commitments, and political processes and aspirations, within historical perspectives.

Joerges' chapter is a comprehensive journey through the particular history of European integration, as well as a powerful testimony to the pursuit of a historically informed legal theory. By tracing the legal-political trajectories of administrative governance, parliamentary democracy and the pursuit of a—however varied—concept of a social welfare state through the individual histories of EU Member States, Joerges is able to shed significant light on the transition politics that are at work in the process of Europeanisation and globalisation. While focusing on the dramatic debates around the failure of the Constitutional Treaty in 2003 and their aftermath, the analysis of the tensions between market-driven and social justice aspiring, institutional politics within the EU provides a formidable basis on which to raise pertinent questions about the role of the state during and after the financial crisis, the prospects for 'social' democracy and transnational citizenship—which keeps the EU hostage till the present day. These questions, crucial to the European 'project', share numerous deeper concerns with those at the heart of the TJ instances described in other chapters.

The chapter by Vasuki Nesiah concludes part II of our collection and offers a poignant reflection on the apparent contradictions in TJ projects, aiming at both historical accountability and closure. Zeroing in on the example of post-Pinochet Chile, Nesiah makes a formidable presentation of how a TJ agenda that focuses on civil and political rights violations is prone to miss the actual socio-economic as well as legal context. Echoing the analysis by authors such as Nagy or Goodwin in the present volume, who underscored the tragic invisibility of everyday, structural violence, Nesiah extends this view to the economic sphere. Here she makes the fascinating observation that such a biased approach results in rendering an entire segment of perpetrators of human rights violations invisible. With Chile being one of the most infamous examples of economic development in the vein of Milton Friedman's Chicago School, a civil-political human rights-oriented TJ agenda misses those who helped install and consolidate the institutional infrastructure that supported the regime. Chile becomes a story primarily of Pinochet and his victims; his partners in economic leadership, be they internal actors (such as the Chilean bankers and the industrialists who supported Pinochet) or external actors (such as the Chicago School and the IMF economists), are pre-emptively acquitted. By drawing an analogy to Hannah Arendt's much discussed analysis of Adolf Eichmann's 'banality of evil', Nesiah highlights the parallels to the many instances where economic governance practices are excluded from the purview of an analysis which focuses on 'egregious' human rights violations such as torture, rape or murder, while at the same time dismissing economic organisation as 'merely technical and operational'. Complementing Rosemary Nagy's focus on the root causes of structural violence perpetrated against women, Nesiah shows how the disregard for the economic organisational context 'enables the continued power of both these selfsame actors and institutions that share responsibility for the socio-economic devastation of that period'.

Nesiah's contextualisation of such biased TJ agendas within the broader framework of an economically deterministic law & development project that is committed to 'progress', 'growth' and 'modernisation'—an idea which is taken up in Rittich's and Roth-Arriaza's chapters as well—gains even more traction as it is further embedded in a sharp analysis of the linkages between TJ, law & development and contemporary global governance reforms—effectively promoted by global financial institutions such as the World Bank, the IMF or, more recently, the 'troika' of the European Commission, the European Central Bank and the IMF.

It is this nexus between a predominantly human rights-driven TJ agenda, focusing on the redress of civil and political rights violations, on the one hand, and a undeterred, economistically oriented development ideology, on the other, that requires our attention in a context in which—especially after the 'humanitarian intervention' in Kosovo, the global spread of security (vs. freedom) politics following 9/11 and the legitimacy ambivalences of a 'duty to protect'—the boundaries between different fields and disciplines have long begun to become porous. As the chapter by Peer Zumbansen argues in the third part of the book, the demarcation between 'fields' such as 'TJ' or 'law & development' is but a matter of political choice. In the transnational context, however, such choices no longer reside within a more or less stably defined territory, constituency and governmental framework; instead, the direction, the means and the expected and pursued outcomes of both TJ and law & development projects are caught between the immediate pressure to 'act' in the face of identified 'problems', 'disasters' or 'catastrophes', system collapses or 'transitions' and a hopelessly fragmented, heterarchical landscape of competing actors and ideologies. TJ and law & development, then, become part of the much contested terrain of global governance and, as such, radicalise questions of participation, representation and redistribution that have for a long time marked the historical trajectory of nation states. This 'transnational replay' of right–left politics, however, occurs in the transnational arena in an altogether changed institutional and normative context. Without it being possible to depoliticise particular conflicts by delegating them to self-regulating markets while associating others with 'public purpose' for the protection of which we need to call upon the state, the transnational arena draws our attention to a constantly shifting architecture of actors, norms and processes, none of which can neatly or exclusively be associated with either the 'national' or the 'international', the 'public' or the 'private', the 'official' or unofficial. Zumbansen's chapter places the porosity of boundaries between TJ and law & development within the context of a fundamental extension of the sphere of the 'political', an extension which leads to a renewed interest in legal sociology, legal anthropology and legal theory in the attempt to map this multi-layered landscape.

The volume concludes with an epilogue by Bryant Garth that draws out and synthesises a number of themes from the preceding chapters and offers an agenda for future research. Garth notes that, while many chapters in the volume are unapologetic about their engagement with a quest for a more progressive transnational law, they are not naïve about the challenges and complexities of this struggle. A second theme, thrown into relief by the juxtaposition of the fields in the volume and in some tension with the first, is the politics of progress, that is, the inevitable debate over how to define 'progress'. Many chapters in the volume identify the progressivism that is embedded within each of these three discourses with a version of the 'contested and imperial politics of modernity'. As Garth observes, this tension 'between imposing notions of progress, on the one hand, and ideals of progressivism, on the other, is not going to vanish'. However, he does identify several matters that need to be considered by critical transnational legal theorists seeking to navigate this difficult terrain: first, the variable role of law in general in different national and local settings; secondly, the variable role of law in relation to progressive politics in particular contexts; and thirdly, 'how to relate the progressive ideal to imperial processes that skew what is considered to be legitimate progress and shape the impact of ideas and institutions that move across borders'. Each of these challenges calls on transnational legal scholars to attend closely to the specificity of law's role as it unfolds in the hands of particular actors, within a given territory and historical context. Garth both grounds and extends the volume through his concluding call for a complementary, sociologically oriented agenda for future research.

Part I

# Rights in Law & Development:
# Regulation, Possibility and Practice

# 1

# *Global Poverty and the Politics of Good Intentions*

SUNDHYA PAHUJA

## I. INTRODUCTION

I
N THE WEST, the terrain of a great deal of public debate around poverty is largely delimited by two figurations: activism and expertise. For the activist, fighting global poverty has become the moral cause of a new generation, inspiring rock songs and wristbands, and legions of celebrities for whom charity is the new accessory. For the expert, development is a technical project in which a body of knowledge, typically marshalled through the disciplinary lens of economics, is formulated for, and applied to, the problems of the developing world and then measured in a more or less scientific way.[1]

Despite their differences in sensibility, these figurations share two crucial things. First, development is the only problematic within which the question of material well-being and global wealth distribution can be addressed. Secondly, both experts and activists view international law as an instrumental means by which poverty may be addressed, but which is intrinsically secondary or epiphenomenal to the causes of poverty. This consensus takes form in, and finds application through, international institutional efforts directed toward global poverty reduction. It remains resilient despite what are, arguably, the manifest failures of the development project over the past 70 years.

In the face of this consensus, my thesis can be simply stated. In essence, I argue that international institutional attempts to address poverty (re)iterated in the idiom of development are likely to make the problem worse, rather than better. The international development project can be understood as a continuation of 'the benevolence of empire' in which interventions were conducted 'in the service of enabling the conditions of modernity to emerge, in the belief that these would serve better the interests and well-being of humanity'. The point of the characterisation is not to judge the sincerity of the 'good intentions', but to draw attention to the fact that 'what remains

---

[1] On the turn to indicators, see S Engle Merry, 'Measuring the World: Indicators, Human Rights and Global Governance' (24 August 2009), available at www.nyu.edu/ipk/files/docs/events/merry-measuring.doc; B Fine, 'Economics Imperialism and the New Development Economics as Kuhnian Paradigm Shift?' (2002) 30 *World Development* 2057.

indisputable is *the authority* with which such a gesture can be made, the vantage point from which it asserts itself' (emphasis added).[2]

Key to the production and maintenance of that authority are the intimacies between development and international law. The effect of international law in the world hinges largely on its capacity to authorise, including the practices which it authorises under the rubric of development. But development and international law also share a structural homology, so that, even as authority is vested upwards into the international community, responsibility is vested downwards into the nation state. The combination of the structural homology between international law and development with development's capture of the way in which poverty is understood and addressed within international law and institutions means that, even as the international community takes responsibility for global poverty (be it sincerely or not), it is not accountable for actions taken in the name of that duty. The unaccountability persists even as that sphere of action expands, in ways which often work against the interests of the world's poorest people. The result is a frame of reference in which self-interested and impoverishing behaviour by the West is understood as altruism towards the rest, or as being in the interests of poor states.[3]

Whether international law can be rehabilitated from this complicity or not remains an open question, but the argument calls us to rethink the development promise in a profound way. At the very least, it calls on us to be wary of the politics of good intentions, which continue both to shape contemporary international approaches to global poverty and to serve as their measure.

## II. INTERNATIONAL LAW, DEVELOPMENT AND POVERTY ALLEVIATION

Alongside securing peace, security and international order, the alleviation of poverty has been an explicit goal of contemporary international law since its institutional reinauguration in the 1940s. One of the four explicit aims in the Preamble to the UN Charter, for example, was the commitment to 'the [promotion] of social progress and better standards of life in larger freedom'.[4] We can also think of the motto of the World Bank, 'Our dream is a world free of poverty', as a paradigmatic example.[5] The same stated purpose applies to many international institutions, including the The Food and Agriculture Organisation of the United Nations (FAO), and the United Nations

---

[2] N Shaikh, 'Interrogating Charity and the Benevolence of Empire' (2007) 50 *Development* 83, 85.

[3] The effect of this combination is to allow the self-interest of rich countries in the form of market access and cheap primary commodities which conditionality effects, to be equated with altruism in the name of development. This recurring equation of altruism and self-interest is facilitated by the development story. See also G Rist, *The History of Development: From Western Origins to Global Faith* (London, Zed Books, 1997) 90–91.

[4] Charter of the United Nations, Preamble, available at www.un.org/en/documents/charter/preamble.shtml.

[5] See, eg the statement set in marble at the front entrance to the World Bank building: 'Our dream is a world free of poverty'; 'Working for a world free of poverty' as part of the World Bank logo, as on its homepage, available at www.worldbank.org; or the recent World Bank publication, *Our Dream: A World Free of Poverty* (New York, World Bank & Oxford University Press, 2010).

Development Programme (UNDP), as well as regional development banks, such as the Asian Development Bank.[6]

More people and institutions are reiterating this purpose, and more frequently, than ever before. One recent example is UN Secretary General Ban Ki-moon's address to the G20 summit in Toronto to 'stress . . . the concerns of the world's most vulnerable and the need for everyone to step up efforts to eradicate poverty'.[7] Since the wave of decolonisation in the 1950s and 1960s, however, the modern concept of development has been both central to the way in which the question of material need and distribution plays out internationally and deeply intertwined with the history of contemporary international law.

This dominance remains true to the present day, so that, when we talk about the persistence of global poverty, the solution is still always development. The efforts of the world to eradicate extreme poverty and hunger, for example, to empower women, to increase primary education, to reduce child and infant mortality, and to improve maternal health are declared to be the millennium development goals (MDGs).[8] Trade negotiation rounds which purport to focus on poor countries are labelled 'development rounds', and the way in which we turn to the problem of environmental degradation is sustainable development.[9] Even international military interventions have been statistically recast as development problems; money spent on security and post-war reconstruction in Iraq and Afghanistan, for example, is now being counted as development spending.[10] This shorthand is also indiscriminate, implicitly uniting diverse identities as swathes of nation states are grouped together as 'developing', not only in the face of the obvious differences between their societies, but equally whether the development project is moribund (as in Sudan) or seems to have been successful (as in Singapore).

This equivalence has been remarkably resilient, even in the face of its poor record. For, despite more than 60 years of development, the proliferation of a huge international bureaucracy and thousands of non-government organisations (NGOs) dedicated to bringing about the end of poverty, the gains have been modest, at best. Using the institutions' own terms, which hinge on monetary, income-based measures of poverty,

---

[6] The objective of poverty reduction ('reducing poverty' or 'reducing hunger') features in each of these institutions' self-descriptions: Asian Development Bank, 'About ADB' (2011), available at www.adb.org/About; Food and Agriculture Organization of the United Nations, 'About FAO' (2011), available at www.fao.org/about/en; and United Nations Development Programme, 'About UNDP' (2010), available at www.undp.org/about.

[7] UN News Centre, 'UN Brings Focus on Plight of World's Vulnerable to G20 Summit in Canada' (25 June 2010), available at www.un.org/apps/news/story.asp?NewsID=35158&Cr=MDG&Cr1.

[8] UN, 'Millennium Development Goals' (2010), available at www.un.org/millenniumgoals.

[9] Indeed, the first line of response to climate change has been a series of high level reports on the economics of climate change. See, eg N Stern, 'Stern Review: The Economics of Climate Change' (2006), available at www.hm-treasury.gov.uk/stern_review_report.htm; R Garnaut, 'The Garnaut Review 2011: Australia in the Global Response to Climate Change' (2011), available at http://www.garnautreview.org.au/update-2011/garnaut-review-2011/garnaut-review-2011.pdf. This is another performance of the 'economics imperialism' described in B Fine, 'Vicissitudes of Economics Imperialism' (2008) 66 *Review of Social Economy*, 235.

[10] A Muscara, 'Military Intervention Trumping Humanitarian Aid' (IPS, 10 February 2011), available at http://ipsnews.net/news.asp?idnews=54437; Department for International Development, 'Department for International Development Draft Structural Reform Plan' (27 July 2010), available at www.dfid.gov.uk/Documents/DFID_SRP.pdf.

recent World Bank statistics suggest that half the world's population live on less than the official poverty line of 2.50 USD per day, and many survive on far less than that.[11]

The World Bank's own statistics regarding improvements on various indicators show only marginal gains. If the clear decline in income poverty in China is excluded, then the percentage of people living below the poverty line in the rest of the world has barely declined over the past three decades.[12] This failure is especially marked given the world economy's 20-fold increase over the span of the twentieth century. During this time, not only has the world become much richer, but a colossal international bureaucracy has proliferated, specifically charged with the task of alleviating poverty. William Easterley estimates that over 2.3 trillion USD has been spent on foreign aid alone over the last five decades.[13]

Over the same period, inequality has also increased significantly. Just on an individualised level, the world's richest 450 individual people possess more wealth than the poorest 415 million people combined. In regional terms, the ratio of per capita income of Europe to Africa in 1960 was 30 to 1. By 2005, it had swollen to 40 to 1.[14] Along these lines, in his recent book entitled *Farewell to Alms*, economic historian Gregory Clark suggests that, at the present moment, both the poorest and the richest people who have ever lived, live on the earth today.[15] Even if Clark is only partly right, this is a dark fact. In combination with the statistics above, it is a telling indictment of our collective failure to address the poverty-related suffering of most of the people in the world. In addition to this failure, those states which have raised the standard of living of their general populations have almost invariably done so by specifically ignoring international developmental orthodoxies.[16]

Added to the mix of these puzzlingly small gains in poverty reduction, the ambiguous outcomes of the orthodox approaches to development and the growth of inequality, it is now unavoidably apparent that we are also using too many of the planet's resources, and too quickly. This is true not only in terms of carbon emissions, but also in relation to extreme biodiversity loss, the despoiling of the oceans and the introduction of an escalating array of chemical pollutants into the atmosphere, the soil and the waterways. I will return to this problem and what it might imply for the development project below, but let us turn first to the question of development as a proxy for the question of material well-being.

---

[11] The World Bank, 'Indicators' (2011), available at http://data.worldbank.org/indicator.

[12] Ibid.

[13] W Easterley, *The White Man's Burden: Why the West's Efforts to Aid the Rest have done so much Ill and so little Good* (Oxford, Oxford University Press, 2007) 4.

[14] See, generally, UN Development Policy and Analysis Division, 'World Economic and Social Survey 2010: Retooling Global Development, Chapter I Growth and Development Trends, 1960–2005' (2010), available at www.un.org/en/development/desa/policy/wess/wess_current/2010wess_chapter1.pdf.

[15] G Clark, *A Farewell to Alms: A Brief Economic History of the World* (Princeton NJ, Princeton University Press, 2007) 3.

[16] H-J Chang, *Bad Samaritans: The Myth of Free Trade and the Secret History of Capitalism* (New York, Bloomsbury Press, 2008).

### III. THE DIFFICULTY WITH DEVELOPMENT AS PROXY

One potential response to the observation that 'development' has become the universal frame of international approaches to poverty reduction is that development constitutes merely a word, or place-marker. What we intend when we use it, it might be said, is to indicate a general encapsulation of people improving their standard of living: what is important is the idea of getting better, or the progress which it implies. However, as Carl Schmitt reminded us in his 1929 essay, 'The Age of Neutralisations and Depoliticisations', concepts must be understood in terms of their concrete political existence.[17] Development is not just a neutral place-marker, and, as an idea, it does not simply mean a general improvement of any kind in the quality of life of people. Development has a very particular history, which is both a legacy of imperialism and intimately intertwined with the history of contemporary international law. It is not just a word; it is a specific way of knowing the world, which is both discourse and institutional machinery.

Decolonisation was crucial to the emergence of the concept of development as we now know it. The end of the Second World War, the success of independence struggles and the fatigue of empire meant that former colonies were increasingly decolonising. The universalisation of (European) public international law during the imperial period meant that the colonies could only decolonise through self-determination as nation states (and that, too, within former colonial boundaries, as expressed in the doctrine of *uti possedetis*). Yet, even as nation-statehood channelled the results of decolonisation through its monopoly over legal personality, successful struggles for independence still confronted the identity of the international community with difference.[18] During and after the period of decolonisation, what we might call the changing complexion of the international community potentially exposed international law's universal coverage as grounded in the geography of empire, and its claim to universality as founded in a hierarchy historically secured by racial difference.[19] It was modern development discourse that provided a way to maintain the universal claim and putative objectivity of international law in the face of these differences.

This maintenance was facilitated by securing the values being put forth as universal, in a new hierarchy anchored by the freshly minted, and ostensibly scientific, concept of gross national product (GNP). The concept of GNP, or gross domestic product (GDP), was born in the 1950s, around the same time as the concept of development.[20] Translated into numbers, it provided scientific ratification for the United States in its position as the world's most powerful nation. It also replaced race, which the Holocaust had made unpalatable even to the (then still) imperial powers, as the measure of superiority between peoples. Thus, even with the realisation of the promise of formal

---

[17] C Schmitt, 'The Age of Neutralizations and Depoliticizations (1929)', trans J McCormick (1993) 96 *Telos* 119.

[18] S Pahuja, 'Decolonisation and the Eventness of International Law' in F Johns, RJ Joyce and S Pahuja (eds), *Events: The Force of International Law* (Oxford, Routledge, 2011).

[19] S Pahuja, *Decolonising International Law: Development, Economic Growth and the Politics of Universality* (Cambridge, Cambridge University Press, 2011).

[20] T Mitchell, 'Economists and Economics in the Twentieth Century' in G Steinmetz (ed), *The Politics of Method in the Human Sciences: Positivism and Its Epistemological Others* (Durham NC, Duke University Press, 2005), 126; idem, 'The Work of Economics: How a Discipline Makes its World' (2005) 66 *Archive of European Sociology*, 297; D Greenwald (ed), *Encyclopedia of Economics* (New York, McGraw-Hill, 1982).

sovereign equality, nation states could still be ordered in a hierarchy, but with GDP, instead of race, as the securing value. What secured this ladder was not the idea of an immutable racial difference, but a promise—that the states at the bottom were included within the bosom of the international community and set on a path towards joining the ranks of the chosen few developed states at the top. This new hierarchy was one of desire,[21] structured around both a promise and a technical challenge. In this way, development immediately provided a means of ordering the world, in which everyone was included on formally equal terms, but in which a hierarchy—and essentially the old hierarchy—was maintained. Development became central to what Gilbert Rist has called the 'anti-colonial imperialism' of the cold war era,[22] quickly becoming the only idiom in which demands for greater material equality were issued both inside and outside the nation state.

The way in which development captured how poverty is understood and addressed within international law and institutions combines with the structural homologies between the two fields, so that global and historical causes of poverty cannot be recognised within international law and institutions, and a radical separation arises between those who are understood as the producers of knowledge and those to whom that knowledge is applied. The centrality of development to international institutions also provides meaning for justice as the symbolic horizon of international law, displacing the political contestation of meaning around that term and placing growth at the heart of institutional approaches to reducing global poverty. The combined effect is to allow the self-interested behaviour of the North to be understood as altruism toward the South.

## III.1. Localising the Causes of Poverty

Many volumes have been dedicated to the question of why some countries are poor. Several causes are proffered, both explicit and implicit, in the literature. One explanation locates the causes of poverty in the political and institutional culture of poor societies—they have corrupt elites, oppressive governments, or no formal laws and institutions.[23] In another explanation, the religious and philosophical traditions that underlie the institutions of poor countries are not adapted to a modern economy, and do not reward the industriousness or co-operative talents of their members; or blame is attributed to the absence of infrastructure, and the consequent limitations on investors and local entrepreneurs.[24] Another set of explanations suggests that physical endowments are to blame; some states have been unlucky in the geographic lottery (for example, by being landlocked).[25] Other analysts locate the causes of poverty in the

---

[21] JL Beard, *The Political Economy of Desire: Law, Development and the Nation* (Abingdon, Routledge-Cavendish, 2007).

[22] G Rist, *The History of Development: From Western Origins to Global Faith* (London-New York, Zed Books, 1997) 75.

[23] See, eg D North, 'Economic Performance through Time' (1994) 84 *American Economic Review* 359.

[24] See, eg T Homer-Dixon, 'The Ingenuity Gap: Can Poor Countries Adapt to Resource Scarcity?' (1995) 21 *Population and Development Review* 587.

[25] See, eg J Diamond, *Guns, Germs and Steel: The Fates of Human Societies* (New York, Norton, 1997); JL Gallup, J Sachs and A Mellinger, 'Geography and Economic Development', *Annual World Bank Conference on Development Economics 1998* (Washington DC, World Bank, 1999) 127.

history of slavery and colonial exploitation.[26] Yet others focus on unfair international trade rules, and the differential impact of the practices of some economies on others, or on the ways in which certain international lending practices have created an insurmountable debt burden for some states.[27]

These responses fall into four schematic categories: geographic causes; historical causes; international or global causes; and national or local factors particular to the poor country in question. For example, the idea that poor governance and corruption can explain a country's relative poverty represents local causes. That some people are culturally not adapted to capitalism similarly constitutes a local cause. Causes may also overlap, so the idea that colonialism created economic structures which have hindered a country's growth—such as a heavy reliance on producing one or two commodities—is both international and historical. The idea that global economic structures—including unfair trade rules and agricultural subsidies in rich countries—prevent poor countries from trading their way out of poverty also signifies international causes.

Undoubtedly, in relation to income poverty, many of these causes operate at the same time. Yet the institutionalised discourse of development repeatedly locates the causes of poverty only in local and present causes. It does not—perhaps cannot—take account of international (or global) and historical causes of poverty. In other words, the institutionalised development story offers a very specific explanation for global poverty. Understanding the causes of poverty in this way concentrates measures to address it in projects overwhelmingly directed at the transformation of the 'developing' society and its political, legal, economic and social structures. This transformative intervention effectively aims to produce what we think of as a 'modern nation state', able to compete effectively—and to trade freely—in an essentially benign international marketplace.

Many scholars, activists and international lawyers, particularly from the South, have critiqued this worldview. Important examples of such critique include the dependency theorists, the heterodox economistsand those agitating for the right to development.[28] However, because the international causes of poverty are simply not on the table in the development story, engagements which try to locate responsibility for global poverty at the global level do not have any bite in the context of international law and institutions. Myriad efforts over the last 60 years have not resulted in wholesale changes to the global terms of trade or in good-faith debt forgiveness. Instead, 60 years of development programmes have resulted in developing countries being compelled to open up more and more of themselves to the transformational interventions of a range of

---

[26] See, eg SL Engerman and KL Sokoloff, 'Colonialism, Inequality, and Long-Run Paths of Development' in A Vinayak Banerjee, R Bénabou and D Mookherjee (eds), *Understanding Poverty* (Oxford, Oxford University Press, 2006) 37.

[27] M Chossudovsky, *The Globalisation of Poverty: Impacts of IMF and World Bank Reforms* (Penang, Third World Network, 1997).

[28] See, eg R Prebisch, 'Five Stages in my Thinking on Development' in GM Meier and D Seers (eds), *Pioneers in Development* (Oxford, Oxford University Press, 1984) 175; H-J Chang, *Bad Samaritans: The Myth of Free Trade and the Secret History of Capitalism* (New York, Bloomsbury Press, 2008); E Reinert, *How Rich Countries Got Rich . . . and Why Poor Countries Stay Poor* (London, Constable, 2007); M Bedjaoui, 'The Right to Development' in *idem* (ed), *International Law: Achievement and Prospects* (Leiden, Brill, 1991) 1177.

international agencies, such as the World Bank, the International Monetary Fund and other UN bodies.[29]

Thus, over the same period as ballooning debt, the remit of the international financial institutions has expanded dramatically. The areas in which it is legal or legitimate to intervene in poor countries in the name of development has continued to widen. The conditions attached to loans have greatly proliferated, and where development institutions were once concerned with building bridges, they are now concerned with building democracy.[30]

International law is implicated in the way in which the development discourse explains poverty by international law's own structure. Through its focus on the nation state generally, in this context, it is a structure that localises responsibility to sites within poor countries, both at the national level and, increasingly, at the sub-national and local levels of government.[31] There is no jurisdiction within international law for calling actors (including the 'international community') to account for action taken on the international plane. The effects of this characteristic of international law are particularly acute in the context of development, which is understood as an international project which starts at the centre. Although international law authorises both the project and the interventions to actualise it, it does not create a concomitant responsibility; there is no global responsibility, only ever local responsibility.

## III.2. The Separation between the Location of Knowledge Production and its Application

International law and development are both implicated in a particular structure of knowledge, a structure we might call an 'export theory' of knowledge, in which knowledge is generated in one place—the developed world—for its consumption by others—the developing world. The structure is generated by the hierarchy produced by the narrative of development, in which some countries have attained the state of 'development' for which the others are striving. The characterisation of a state as 'developed' implies the possession of knowledge necessary to reach that state. Thus, this characterisation or naming involves the investiture of authority. The promise of inclusion, understood as involving a movement up the ladder through transformation or development, is to be made good through the application of technical knowledge, available in the places which have already attained the desired state.[32] In international law, this produces phenomena such as Brian Simpson's 'export theory of human

---

[29] See, generally, B Rajagopal, *International Law from Below: Development, Social Movements and Third World Resistance* (New York, Cambridge University Press, 2003).

[30] And increasingly with a gun. See P Collier, *The Bottom Billion: Why the Poorest Countries are Failing and What Can Be Done About It* (New York, Oxford University Press, 2008); see also W Easterly's review of the Collier book, entitled 'Foreign Aid Goes Military!' in *The New York Review of Books* (2008), available at www.nybooks.com/articles/archives/2008/dec/04/foreign-aid-goes-military.

[31] L Eslava, 'Decentralization of Development and Nation-Building Today: Reconstructing Colombia from the Margins of Bogotá' (2009) 2 *The Law and Development Review* 281.

[32] Beard, n 21 above.

rights', or, in development economics, what Erik Reinert describes as 'the export of economic rhetoric for others'.[33]

The explanatory content of the development story (and the localisation of the causes of poverty), combined with the location of knowledge and the investiture of authority in the developed world, provides a way to hold together the contradiction between the theories of development and the evidence of their results. Poor outcomes may then be blamed on the insufficiency of the transformation of the developing society, rather than on a flawed theory. This combination also enables the separation between the identity of the rich world as benefactor and the rich world as a self-interested actor in the global political economy.[34] The effect is to generate a frame of understanding in which the self-interest (of the rich) is equated with altruism, even when the two things are patently not commensurable. A good example of this is the way in which the conditionalities of the World Bank and International Monetary Fund interact with both the global trading order and international financial markets.

## IV. SELF-INTEREST AS ALTRUISM

### IV.1. Conditionalities and Global the Trading Order

Deeply embedded in the development project is the idea that free trade will bring development.[35] Resting on the theory of comparative advantage,[36] development orthodoxy asserts that countries will become richer by producing the things that they can produce most efficiently in their current condition and by selling those things in the global marketplace. In theoretical terms, this remains true even when some countries have nothing which they make more efficiently than others in absolute terms (in other words, when other countries produce everything more efficiently than they do). This is because the rational calculation of 'opportunity cost' ensures that the others will produce what they are absolutely best at in domestic terms, rather than just comparatively better at in global terms.[37]

Heterodox economists such as Ha-Joon Chang, Dani Rodrik and Eric Reinert question this orthodoxy. They expose the recipe of free trade as the path to wealth as both historically inaccurate and theoretically flawed. According to their analyses, the theory of comparative advantage on which free trade is founded is focused solely on short-term gains and can be justified only if one accepts the global status quo, a state of affairs which implies the continued underdevelopment of poor countries.[38] This is directly in conflict with the orthodoxy that free trade will bring development. Historically speaking, these thinkers argue, rich countries became rich by following

---

[33] AWB Simpson, *Human Rights and the End of Empire: Britain and the Genesis of the European Convention* (Oxford, Oxford University Press, 2001) 347; Reinert, n 28 above, 43.

[34] A Orford, 'Locating the International: Military and Monetary Interventions after the Cold War' (1997) 38 *Harvard International Law Journal* 443.

[35] See, eg the Preamble to the Marrakesh Agreement Establishing the World Trade Organization opened for signature 15 April 1994, 1867 UNTS 3 (entered into force 1 January 1995).

[36] See D Ricardo, *On the Principles of Political Economy and Taxation* (London, Black Horse Court, 1817).

[37] Reinert, n 28 above, 301.

[38] Ibid, 304.

precisely the opposite of the policies which the international development institutions such as the International Monetary Fund and the World Bank impose upon borrowing states. Famously, according to Chang, the rich countries have enriched themselves and, through international laws and institutions, including developmental conditionalities, have 'kicked away the ladder' so that poor countries are likely to remain in poverty if they play by the rules.[39]

But such explanations, which locate the causes of poverty, in part, in the international sphere, cannot be heard by the institutionalised discourse of development. Despite the historical, theoretical and economic critiques of the heterodox economists, the theory that free trade will bring development is resilient, and remains dominant within international instititutions.[40] The result of this dominance is that a great deal of developmental intervention is directed at restructuring the economies of poor countries as though they were participants in a global free market. This includes using the mechanism of conditionality to force poor countries to remove barriers to trade, including tariffs and subsidies, to allow money to move freely across borders, to orient production towards exports and to allow foreign direct investment. This coercive restructuring of state economies on the basis that free trade brings development, imposed as if there were actually an essentially benign global marketplace, takes place in the context of a global trading order which is anything but free. Given the real conditions of the global market, the policies prescribed are positively toxic for most poor countries.

Critiques are legion. Philosopher Thomas Pogge, for instance, points out that there is no such thing as free trade. Even as rich countries promise trade-led development, he argues, the current rules favour rich countries—by allowing them to protect their markets and subsidise exports through quotas, tariffs, anti-dumping duties, export credits and subsidies to domestic producers.[41] To sketch the financial magnitude of these subsidies, it is salutary to compare them to aid flows. Former Chief Economist of the World Bank, Nicholas Stern, estimated that, in 2002, rich countries spent about 300 billion USD on export subsidies for agricultural products alone—roughly six times their total development aid.[42] Cows in Europe famously receive annual subsidies of around 900 USD each, and in Japan of about 2,700 USD each—far above the annual income of most human beings, let alone the aid budget per capita.[43] Poor countries cannot match these subsidies, not only because they often cannot afford to, but also because they are prohibited from doing so by international law. This prohibition

[39] H-J Chang, *Kicking Away the Ladder: Development Strategy in Historical Perspective* (London, Anthem Press, 2003).
[40] World Bank, 'Global Challenges: Global Public Goods' (2010), available at http://go.worldbank.org/7XUN86PV10; WTO, 'Understanding the WTO: Basics' (2011), available at www.wto.org/english/thewto_e/whatis_e/tif_e/fact3_e.htm; International Monetary Fund, 'What We Do' (2011) http://www.imf.org/external/about/whatwedo.htm.
[41] T Pogge, 'Recognized and Violated by International Law: The Human Rights of the Global Poor' (2005) 18 *Leiden Journal of International Law* 771.
[42] N Stern, 'Dynamic Development: Innovation and Inclusion' (Munich Lectures in Economics, Munich, 19 November 2002), available at http://team.univ-paris1.fr/teamperso/page/files/BM%20Nicholas%20Stern.pdf.
[43] Development assistance in the same year was 8 USD to each Sub-Saharan African from Europe, or 1.47 USD to each African from Japan. M Wolf, *Why Globalization Works* (New Haven CT, Yale University Press, 2005) 215.

arises both from trade negotiations in the context of unequal bargaining power[44] and, perhaps more insidiously, from conditionalities contained in international agreements with the World Bank and the Inetnational Monetary Fund.[45]

As well as protecting their own markets and producers, on the other side of the equation rich countries manage their input costs through the use of 'escalating tariffs'. These are scales which apply low tariffs to raw materials—starting with no tariffs at all on those raw materials which cannot be grown or found in rich countries—and then raise the tariffs sharply with each step up the value chain. This ensures cheap raw materials for rich countries, whilst undermining manufacturing and employment in poor countries. Hence, Ghana and Côte D'Ivoire are confined to exporting unprocessed cocoa beans, Uganda and Kenya to raw coffee beans, and Mali and Burkina Faso to raw cotton.[46] There are many more examples which demonstrate how, despite the rhetoric, the current trade rules are not only not free, but in fact create capital flows and lost opportunities that hurt poor countries in ways which dwarf foreign aid flows.[47] Criticisms about the unfair trading practices of rich states also come from the other end of the political spectrum. The financial journalist and defender of (real) free trade Martin Wolf, for instance, denounces the treatment accorded to the poorest states in the trading regime as 'a disgrace'.[48] Wolf catalogues a litany of what he calls 'obscenities' arising from the EU's Common Agricultural Policy, US Cotton subsidies, Japanese farming subsidies and the licence payments demanded through the TRIPS Agreement, inter alia.[49]

Like other institutions, the World Bank understand the way that policies such as agricultural subsidies hurt poor countries, but because it has no jurisdiction over rich countries, it cannot do anything about them. What is more curious is that, even though institutions such as the World Bank are limited in this way, they continue both to espouse the ideology of free trade and to impose and support conditions which oblige poor countries to open their markets and liberalise their investment rules. Recommending these policies in a perfect world is already highly contested by the heterodox economists such as Chang, Rodrik and Reinert. Enforcing these policies in the global economic conditions of the real world could, at best, be the triumph of

[44] Pogge attributes the causes to the inequalities in bargaining power arising from the fact that countries 'with only 15.5% of the world's population . . . have 80.4% of the world's income and can therefore exact a high price for access to . . . markets'. Pogge, n 41 above, 724. Pogge is relying for these figures on The World Bank, *World Development Report 2005: A Better Investment Climate for Everyone* (New York, Oxford University Press, 2005), 257.

[45] Chossudovsky, n 27 above, 61; see also the feature-length documentary entitled *Life and Debt*, directed by Stephanie Black (Tuff Hong Pictures, 2001), which addresses the impact of the International Monetary Fund, the World Bank, the Inter-American Development Bank and current globalisation policies on a developing country such as Jamaica, available at http://www.amazon.co.uk/former-Jamaican-Minister-Michael-Manley/dp/B003Y4TS3E/ref=sr_1_1?s=dvd&ie=UTF8&qid=1341056462&sr=1-1.

[46] Stern, n 42 above, 25. In another speech, Stern estimates that full elimination of agricultural protection and production subsidies in rich countries would raise agricultural and food exports from low to middle income countries by 24% and total annual rural income in these areas by about $60 billion (about three quarters of the global poor live in such rural areas). Pogge, n 41 above, footnote 19.

[47] Pogge, n 41 above, 725.

[48] Wolf, n 43 above, 218.

[49] Ibid, 215. He also cites escalating or 'progressive' tariffs as grossly unfair, giving the example of Bangladeshi imports to the US, producing tariff payments of 331 million USD in 2001. Compare this to France, which exports to the US, producing tariff revenues of the same amount. But the total imports from France were 13 times larger. This shows how tariffs apply at the highest level on the very products which poor countries tend to export.

hope over experience and, in particular, over the more than 50 years of immiseration that these policies have caused.

The outcome, however, is to reinforce a trading system heavily skewed towards the interests of the rich world, in which the borders of poor countries are opened to sub-sidised products from the North, destroying local industries which cannot compete with artificially cheap imports, and in which poor countries are penalised for adding value to raw materials in ways which might potentially bring about industrialisation. These inequities are effected, in part, through international interventions in the name of development. The theoretical foundation that free trade brings to development is supported by a particular narrative of development in which the West is characterised as being essentially benign. The theory, untainted by critiques which would question this characterisation in the context of the global trading order, justifies the imposi-tion on the South of legally enforceable conditions which open borders and prevent defensive policy-making. The institutions which impose those conditions retain their putative legitimacy in the implicit reliance on the export theory of knowledge, and in the bifurcation of the identity of the West as benefactor and its identity as predator. The self-interested behaviour of rich countries can thus be presented as altruism because of the institutionalised development project.

## IV.2. Conditionality and finance

The relationship between conditionality and the global financial system is another example of the way in which the institutionalised development project enables self-interest to be understood as altruism. The debt-forgiveness campaign Jubilee 2000 estimates that over 100 countries need debt cancellation to enable them to meet their people's basic needs without taxing those below an ethical poverty line of three dollars a day. They point to the example of Kenya, which, in its 2005/2006 budget, spent more on debt repayments than on the combined total expenditure on water, health, agricul-ture, roads, transport and finance.[50]

While the debt question is complex and some debt is legitimate, there is a great deal of Third World debt which is illegitimate, having arisen through irresponsible lending during the oil boom of the 1960s and 1970s, often for strategic defence reasons connected to the cold war. Many of the projects funded were misconceived or failed. Many of the loans were to corrupt and/or racist governments known to be so by the lenders. Often everyone involved in the lending knew that repayment was never likely.[51] Combined with these problems of legitimacy, commodity prices declined dramatically over the same period. Most loans were denominated in hard currencies, such as the US dollar, exposing borrowers to risks from matters over which they have no control, such as US dollar interest-rate rises and currency volatility.[52]

In the aftermath of the repayment crises of the 1980s and beyond, the condition-ality mechanism of the international financial institutions has typically been used to

---

[50] Jubilee Debt Campaign, 'Why Should We Drop the Debt?', available at www.jubileedebtcampaign.org. uk/1%20Why%20should%20we%20drop%20the%20debt%3F+2675.twl.

[51] R Peet, *Unholy Trinity: The IMF, World Bank and WTO* (London, Zed Books, 2003), 78.

[52] Ibid, 76.

restructure poor economies, primarily to ensure loan repayment and the stability of the international banking system. As a result, debt servicing is made possible by cuts to public spending in health, education and food subsidies.[53] And, as shown above, continued funding from these institutions is conditioned on poor countries opening their markets to imports (often subsidised) from rich countries and to unrestricted foreign direct investment.

This pattern illustrates how the existence of Third World debt provides a very effective legal or juridified mechanism which transfers wealth and risk in opposite directions. In the commercial lending market, the lender bears the risk of the borrower not being able to repay the loan. In the situation of Third World debt, the lender is often acquitted of the full consequences of imprudent lending through the interventions of the international financial institutions. This institutional intervention occurs even as those same institutions extol the virtues of market disciplines for their (poor) clients. Risk is therefore transferred from those who can most afford it—rich countries and banks in rich countries—to the people of the Third World, who can least afford it. Wealth is transferred in the opposite direction, from the people who can least afford it—the citizens of Third World countries who need whatever public services that their state can afford—to rich countries, their banks and the shareholders of those banks.

## V. THE LIMITS TO GROWTH AND THE PLACE OF JUSTICE

The final problem with development's capture of how we understand questions of material well-being within international law and institutions is in the way in which it places growth at the heart of institutional approaches to reducing global poverty. This emplacement displaces contestation around the meaning of justice as the symbolic horizon of international law.[54] Because GDP was the lynchpin of the global order which was newly structured around a promise, the key to that promise—economic growth—had to lie at the heart of the project: economic growth was—and remains—the secret beating heart of the development story.

According to the theory of economic growth, the rising tide lifts all boats. In other words, by increasing overall wealth, even if the rich get richer, some of the wealth is bound to eventually trickle down to the poor. This idea took hold, and captured the Zeitgeist. It was quickly embraced by people of all political and geopolitical colours. Communism, which was equally, if not more, developmental than the First World, also embraced the need for growth as axiomatic. Hence, even if there was fierce contestation about how growth should be achieved, growth as the objective of development was immediately enthroned.

As time wore on and people began to realise the inadequacy of national income as the measure for development success, other definitions of development and, crucially, other measures of development were developed—perhaps most famously the Human Development Index devised by Mahbub Ul Haq and the UNDP in the 1990s. This measure adds life expectancy and literacy to GDP to come up with a single figure

---

[53] JK Walton and D Seddon, *Free Markets and Food Riots: The Politics of Global Adjustment* (Oxford, Blackwell Publishing, 1994).
[54] Pahuja, n 19 above.

index to indicate development. Amartya Sen, too, is famous for reconceptualising development as freedom, using what he calls the 'capabilities approach'.

But even the most famous reconceptualisations, such as Sen's, still have economic growth at their heart.[55] The shift has not been away from growth as the determinant, but towards growth 'plus'. International law and institutions have stayed very much within this paradigm; for example, the World Bank's most recent response to criticisms about the inadequacy of growth has been to shift to inclusive growth.[56] Many NGOs have tried to modify the formula by demanding what they call 'pro-poor growth'.[57]

The latest G20 summit declaration even reverses the emphasis, 'recognis[ing] that 2010 marks an important year for the MDGs, and reaffirm[ing] the commitment to assist the poorest countries', but situating that reaffirmation within, and dependent on, the main game of continued global growth: 'narrowing the development stern gap and reducing poverty are integral to our *broader objective of achieving strong, sustainable and balanced growth* and ensuring a more robust and resilient global economy for all'.[58]

Even within what are known as rights-based approaches to development, growth is still the engine of development, and therefore remains the main way to alleviate global poverty. Within liberalism, growth is understood as an alternative to redistribution as the way to address poverty.[59]

Leaving aside the well-known critiques about the social limits to growth and its ambiguous relation with the problem of inequality, a key problem with using gross national growth as the measure of the improvement of the quality of life is that it has the effect of setting the environment and development against each other. Within the vocabulary of international law, it seems impossible to be both for the environment and for economic justice. Indeed, historically, development and environment have often been antagonistic discourses. Common wisdom has typically suggested that we need to tackle poverty first and clean up later. People speak of an environmental Kuznets curve in which cities undergoing rapid development peak at a certain level of pollution and then quickly improve as the society becomes richer.[60] While this might be relevant for environmental degradation, such as air quality and the pollution of waterways, it is becoming clear that there are some things which cannot be reversed. Carbon emissions, for example, just keep increasing. Many of the world's species are facing imminent extinction, there is a huge loss in plant biodiversity and the oceans are being emptied of fish. None of these are reversible.

The environmental facts call into question a development promise based upon an infinitely expanding pie. An emphasis on growth is being maintained in the face of an

[55] Pahuja, n 19, 222; B Chimni, 'The Sen Conception of Development and Contemporary International Law Discourse: Some Parallels' (2008) 1 *Law and Development Review*, available at www.bepress.com/ldr/vol1/iss1/art2; U Baxi, *The Future of Human Rights* (Oxford, Oxford University Press, 2002).

[56] The World Bank, 'What Is Inclusive Growth?' (2009), available at http://siteresources.worldbank.org/INTDEBTDEPT/Resources/468980–1218567884549/WhatIsInclusiveGrowth20081230.pdf.

[57] M Ravallion, 'Pro-Poor Growth: A Primer' (World Bank Policy Research Working Paper No 3242, 2004), available at http://web.usal.es/~bustillo/RavallionPPGPrimer.pdf.

[58] The G-20 Toronto Summit Declaration, 26–27 June 2010, para 46, available at www.g20.org/Documents/g20_declaration_en.pdf.

[59] A Ellis and K Kumar, *Dilemmas of Liberal Democracies: Studies in Fred Hirsch's Social Limits to Growth* (London, Tavistock Publications, 1983) 3.

[60] D Stern, 'The Environmental Kuznets Curve' (International Society for Ecological Economics Internet Encyclopaedia of Ecological Economics, June 2003), available at http://www.ecoeco.org/pdf/stern.pdf.

overwhelming body of scientific evidence that suggests that we are already using the equivalent of 1.5 planets' sustainable resources.[61] If everyone on earth lived with the ecological footprint of an average (US) American, we would need approximately five planets to sustain the current population of the earth.[62] In the face of this, it is difficult to see how a good-faith promise of any kind of equivalence could be made. Given that the earth could sustain a population of around 1.8 billion people living at the current consumption levels of an average person in a high-income country, as opposed to the almost 7 billion that we currently have with vastly disparate consumption levels, what is it, exactly, that development is promising?

The implications of this fact have been recognised by states and international institutions in the promotion of 'sustainable development'. At its core, sustainable development means 'development that meets the needs of the present without compromising the ability of future generations to meet their own needs'.[63] In theory, sustainable development understands that the three intersecting spheres of society, the environment and the economy must all complement each other if development is to be sustainable. The goal, then, is to find the sweet spot, or point of overlap, between these three distinct spheres.[64]

However, in practice, without a fundamental redefinition of each distinct sphere, the sweet spot is a myth. Economic growth has been difficult to dislodge from the heart of the development project, and sustainable development is overtly directed towards sustaining growth-based development rather than sustaining the social, natural and political environment in which it takes place.[65] Yet even this more circumscribed horizon may not be achievable. Whether through the idea that technology will enable growing consumption through 'green growth',[66] or that we will 'clean up' after development has taken place, or that growth should be 'inclusive' or 'pro-poor',[67] even on its own terms, sustainable development is, at best, capable of producing less unsustainable development.

Within international approaches to global poverty alleviation, development is both process and horizon. It is both what we are trying to achieve and the way in which we achieve it. It is both the building of a bridge and the abstract promise of a better life. It is both the implementation of a law-reform project in the Pacific Islands and (as Jennifer Beard has put it) 'a numinous yearning for a better life'.[68] Because of this character as both process and horizon, development's relation to international law displaces the more open concept of justice which international law arguably promises as its horizon.[69] The idea that we can reduce poverty without affecting the distribution

[61] Global Footprint Network, 'World Footprint: Do We Fit on the Planet?' (2010), available at www.footprintnetwork.org/en/index.php/GFN/page/world_footprint.

[62] WWF International, 'Living Planet Report 2010: Biodiversity, Biocapacity and Development' (2010), available at http://assets.panda.org/downloads/lpr2010.pdf.

[63] World Commission on Environment and Development, 'Our Common Future' (Annex to UN General Assembly Document A/42/427, 1987), available at http://www.worldinbalance.net/pdf/1987-brundtland.pdf.

[64] B Hopwood, M Mellor and G O'Brien, 'Sustainable Development: Mapping Different Approaches' (2005) 13 *Sustainable Development* 38.

[65] Ibid.

[66] J Baskin, 'Is Sustainable Development Sustainable?', unpublished paper presented to Asian Development Bank (April 2011).

[67] Ravallion, n 57 above.

[68] Beard, n 21 above, 2.

[69] Pahuja, n 19 above.

or the accumulation of wealth is nonsense, but by centring the development story on growth, the promise to the poor is that they must invest their hopes of improving their material well-being in increases in the overall size of the pie. This is meant to increase the size of each crumb proportionately. The fact that this also increases the size of the rich countries' slice of the pie, or of the rich people in poor countries, is simply a collateral benefit of doing good for the poor. Here, self-interest and altruism are seen as made entirely commensurable by the concept of growth. Of course, according to this logic, there can be no question of the pie being shared differently, or really even countenancing the idea that the pie might be of a finite size.

This depoliticisation, by growth, of the meaning of justice interacts with the structural homology between development and international law to deradicalise current thinking on the best ways to address the question of global poverty. Because of development's centrality and the explanation of global poverty that it carries with it, international legal solutions to global poverty (including human rights based solutions) do not have any bite between nations, only within them. In other words, it is difficult, if not impossible, to use international law against action taken at the level of the international. The question of how we share the earth is removed from the table. Economic growth defers the question of distribution through an emphasis on a future horizon. International law's toothlessness means that calls for a more equitable global distribution of wealth have no bite.[70]

## VI. CONCLUSION

In his play about the martyrdom of the Bishop Thomas Beckett, TS Eliot writes:

> *The last temptation is the greatest treason:*
> *To do the right deed for the wrong reason.*

The line is meant to explain Beckett's realisation that his willingness to be sacrificed was wrongly motivated by the martyrdom which would come from it, rather than self-sacrifice without glory. Legal evaluation generally reverses this judgement and concentrates on the deed, not the reason. This reversal is necessary for balancing the interests of the well-intentioned actor with the protection of the person who is the subject of that action.

In the context of international law and development, though, this judgement is reversed once more. Interventions directed at bringing about 'development' are assessed primarily by reference to the intentions of the 'developer', rather than the effect of those actions on the 'developing'. This is exacerbated by the way in which accountability measures usually involve accountability to the donors, not to the subjects of

---

[70] A symptomatic case of this is when activists call for (legally binding) human rights: the way in which the structure of international law works means that those rights are directed at the nation state within which individuals are situated, and its municipal laws. They cannot be claimed, for example, against former imperial powers or against rich states and their subsidies, nor even against the international financial institutions. Similarly, calls to link labour standards to international trade would piggyback on the enforcement mechanisms of the trade regime to require poor states to respect human rights or labour standards—and incidentally privilege products from rich countries—surely, human rights in their most imperial guise?

developmental interventions. In other words, we, in the rich world, assess ourselves, and base that assessment on our intentions.

This effect is made possible by the explanatory narrative that development offers for the causes of poverty, and for the investiture of knowledge production in the rich world. The effect is ratified in law through its allocation of responsibility to the nation state. The cover of development shrouds with altruism, acts which work in the West's own self-interest. Often, the politics of good intentions can provide a cover for poor outcomes: even though we may have done the wrong things, we are assessed on the reason why we did them, not on their effects.

However, although good intentions might be morally relevant to the individual, when they are combined with the force of law, those intentions must be tempered by the responsibilities of power, even more so in the case of institutions. The responsibility of power is not answered by reference to intentions. Power brings us back to the question of authority, and the practices which law authorises. Nermeen Shaikh's 'benevolence of empire'[71] suggests that, although it is probably natural to think that one's own way of life is the best, it is quite another thing to have both the desire and the power to impose that way of life on others, be it out of self-interest or out of altruism, or a combination of the two. In intervening to bring about the conditions of modernity, even with the best intentions, the West is effectively arrogating to itself the right to develop the rest.

Even if we understand this arrogation to be a duty, rather than a right, it is difficult to see how the development promise can be made good, given the limits to growth. One way to proceed would simply be to recognise the impossibility of the promise and abandon it, fortifying the rich world with increasing violence and surveillance against the clamour to 'get in'. Some say that a version of this is already happening. But, arguably, we do not need such a dystopic vision of the future if we accept that what thinking about poverty and the environment together really means is that we need to rethink how we share the earth and how this sharing is to occur through international law.

The enormous political solidarity demonstrated at the recent protests in Toronto at the 2010 G20 summit—and, indeed, at every multilateral economic summit meeting since Seattle in 1999—shows that people do care about the suffering of strangers in far-away places, and about the state of the planet. The development project has captured a great deal of this energy for justice, but, to date, has only channelled it in ways which have shown themselves to be unlikely to alleviate global poverty. The visibly diminishing capacity of the earth to sustain us might provide the impelling political force that we need to make a shift away from development's certainties. However, even if Pogge is right in suggesting that it is easier to make good laws than good men,[72] we cannot simply argue for the reform of the laws and institutions which hurt the poor: we also need to think carefully about the institutional structures which support the production of those unfair laws in the first place.

Both development and international law are the children of imperialism, and carry

---

[71] Shaikh, n 2 above.

[72] '[M]orally successful rules are so much easier to sustain than morally successful conduct.' T Pogge, 'Severe Poverty as a Human Rights Violation' in idem (ed), *Freedom from Poverty as a Human Right: Who Owes What to the Very Poor?* (New York, UNESCO-Oxford University Press, 2007) 11, 26.

the legacy of that inheritance. They are also both institutionalised structures of knowl-edge, with ready armies of experts bearing solutions to the world's problems. The major differences between them are that law has a formal structure, and its promised horizon is the politically contestable notion of justice. Only by rejecting law's instru-mentalisation within the development project, and by refusing the replacement of the horizon of justice with the horizon of development, might there be a chance of har-nessing the widespread faith in international law and human rights in ways which save it for the poor, and which breathe life back into its powerful symbolic promise for . . . most of the world.[73]

---

[73] P Chatterjee, *The Politics of the Governed: Reflections on Popular Politics in Most of the World* (New York, Columbia University Press, 2004) 3.

# 2

# *Human Rights and Development: A Fragmented Discourse*[*]

### ISSA G SHIVJI

## I. HUMAN RIGHTS IDEOLOGIES AND DISCOURSES: CONTENTIOUS TERRAINS

IDEOLOGIES ARE NOT some neutral instruments to be picked up from shelves and wielded at will by altruistic actors; they are an articulation of material, social and power relations. They are determined by historically given circumstances, and constructed and reconstructed in the course of social struggles. Invariably, therefore, ideologies are intertwined terrains of contentions.

In a world divided and hierarchically structured between powerful countries, nations, peoples, states and classes, global discourses are no less ideological. And this applies fully and without qualification to the global human rights discourse, which I prefer to call by its orthodox name, rights-ideology.

In a situation in which rights, rule of law and democracy are presented as the ultimate good, a universal human value, a panacea to all our ills in Africa, it is important to remind ourselves that not only our sickness, but also the medicine on offer, are historically and socially determined. Nature did not posit the civilised, developed, rich and powerful North, on the one hand, and the backward, underdeveloped, poor and powerless South, on the other, as the original condition. This condition was created historically through the application of 'universal' violence. The violence, force and domination, in turn, were legitimised and rationalised through layers of historically and socially determined languages of religion, race, culture, ethnicity, etc, all of which, at one time or another, claimed superiority and universality just as human rights ideology does today.

Human rights are not absolutes which inhere in all human beings as an original condition only to be discovered with progress and civilisation—in this case, presumably, Western, Christian, European civilisation. They are a product of historical circumstances and social struggles. They are as contentious as any struggle can be.

In section II, I chart out in broad strokes the contention between developmentalist and human rights ideologies on the African continent over some four decades of the

---

[*] This is a revised version of the paper first presented at the International Colloquium on Challenges to Human Rights and Global Justice, held at Coimbra, 27–28 November 2008.

immediate post-independence period. My purpose is to locate these contentions in relation to larger social projects of national liberation and social emancipation generally, but, in particular, to show the fragmented nature of the human rights discourse. In section III, I paint in broad strokes the current globalisation or neo-liberal period in which, I argue, these discourses have metamorphosed—from development to poverty reduction and from human rights to humanitarian intervention. Embedded in my discussion is the question of whether the development/human rights discourses are part of the emancipatory or enslaving projects.

## II. A FRAGMENTED DISCOURSE

The Universal Declaration of Human Rights (UDHR) was born in the wake of the disastrous Second World War. Its human rights conceptions were heavily coloured by the need to provide an ideological counterpoint to the racist Nazi and fascist ideologies (see the preamble). The world hegemonies were being reconstituted upon the basis of a bipolar world, on the one hand, and the gathering storm of anti-colonial struggles, on the other. Particularistic ideologies of Nazism based upon racial purity and superiority were being countered by the universalistic language of the UDHR. Ironically, however, Nazi racism was a logical extension of the racist ideology which had hitherto rationalised and legitimised the imperial project (colonialism) throughout the Third World.[1] For instance, when the imperialist racist ideology was at its zenith, the West rejected Japan's attempt to 'include a clause on racial equality in the League of Nations Covenant'.[2] This was not so much the demonstration of the limits of equality (as Furedi contends), but much more the sign of the global ideological hegemony of the time, which was rooted in racial superiority and the civilising mission of the white race. An ideological construct based upon equal rights (human rights) was a world war away.

Indeed, as Furedi rightly observes, Woodrow Wilson's principle of the rights of nations to self-determination applied eminently only to Europe. Robert Lansing, Wilson's Secretary of State, could not be clearer when he stated, in the course of the Peace Conference:

> The more I think about the President's declaration as to the right of 'self-determination', the more convinced I am of the danger of putting such ideas into the minds of certain races. It is bound to be basis of impossible demands on the Peace Conference and create trouble in many lands.
>
> What effect will it have on the Irish, the Indians, the Egyptians, and the nationalists among the Boers? Will it not breed discontent, disorder and rebellion? Will not the Mohammedans of Syria and Palestine and possibly of Morocco and Tripoli rely on it?[3]

Thus, 'What was at stake was that sense of superiority which was so vital to imperial self-confidence'.[4] Between the wars, this self-confidence was undermined in various

---

[1] See T Hayter, *The Creation of World Poverty*, 2nd edn (London, Pluto, 1990) 19ff; E Said, *Culture and Imperialism* (London, Vintage, 1993) passim.
[2] See F Furedi, *The New Ideology of Imperialism* (London, Pluto, 1994) 5.
[3] Quoted in ibid, 13.
[4] Ibid.

ways by the reconstruction of, and the opposition to, the then hegemonic racial ideology.

First, as already argued, the imperial project could no longer be legitimised in particularistic racial terms. Hitler's Nazism made sure of that. Secondly, the participation of the coloured Japan in the war and its initial successes had weakened the underlying premise of racial superiority. For the colonised people, it was an eye-opener to see barbaric butchery between the civilised whites, which had hitherto been reserved for the non-whites, and to witness a non-white race (the Japanese) standing on its own and on an equal military footing against their masters. Subhas Chandra Bose's militant Indian Nationalist Army sought support from Japan and posed a greater and, probably, a more decisive threat to the British Raj than the passive and moderate Indian National Congress.[5]

The fact that the colonised peoples spontaneously felt the need to purge their consciousness of the racial inferiority drummed up by their colonial masters before they took up arms was true throughout much of the Afro-Asian world. This took varied ideological forms in different concrete situations, but was ultimately a reconstruction of the dominant racial ideology to produce, in the apt phrase of Wamba-dia-Wamba, 'ideologies of resistance'.[6] Powerful anti-colonial church movements in Africa, like the one in Kenya called Dini ya Musamba under Elijah Masinde, painted the statutes of Christ black. The intellectually profound, anti-imperialist treatise by Frantz Fanon, *The Wretched of the Earth*,[7] clearly and unambiguously postulated the stretching of the Marxist analysis in the colonial world because, here, race plays a central role in defining the 'native'. The so-called Western values are not only proclaimed to be universal, but also to be universalised through violence. So 'when the native hears a speech about Western culture, he pulls out his knife—or at least he makes sure it is within his reach'.[8]

> The violence with which the supremacy of white values is affirmed and the aggressiveness which has permeated the victory of these values over the ways of life and of thought of the native mean that, in revenge, the native laughs in mockery when Western values are mentioned in front of him. In the colonial context, the settler only ends his work of breaking in the native when the latter admits loudly and intelligibly the supremacy of the white man's values. In the period of decolonisation, the colonised masses mock at these very values, insult them and vomit them up.[9]

Thirdly, the shift of gravity from the Europe of colonies to the US (without colonies) as an imperialist superpower further facilitated the reconstruction of ideological hegemony from the language of 'racial superiority' to that of 'human equality' (human rights). The fundamental limits of the universalising language were, however, immediately apparent.

First, the war ended neither imperialism nor inter-imperialist rivalries at world level.

---

[5] See E Hobsbawn, *The Age of Extremes: The Short Twentieth Century, 1914–1991* (London, M Joseph, 1994) 216.
[6] Personal communication.
[7] F Fanon, *The Wretched of the Earth* (London, Penguin, 1967).
[8] Ibid, 33.
[9] Ibid, 33–34.

It placed both on a new level of the emerging cold war.[10] For the United States and its allies, the Soviet bloc was perceived and presented as a threat to the free world. It was the ideology of anti-communism and the free world which was the standard text during much of the 1950s and 1960s. The human rights debate arising in this context inevitably dovetailed into the politics and diplomacy of the cold war. The sub-text of the free world ideology was not so much to keep, maintain and propagate the freedom and rights of peoples, but to keep—strategically and economically—the states and peoples, particularly of the Third World, within the sphere of the free world. Thus, the right of nations to self-determination proclaimed by the US President as early as the First World War was given the status of a political principle in the United Nations Charter, but had no place in the human rights document, the UDHR. The four freedoms—freedom of expression and faith, and freedom from fear and want—proclaimed by Roosevelt in 1941 as the basis of the new international order and which inspired the UDHR did not include people's freedom from oppression and exploitation. Even the narrow Soviet Union's version of the right of peoples to self-determination to mean the process of formal independence continued to be opposed by the West, including the United States.[11]

Secondly, Hitler's violence, which had 'shocked the conscience of human beings world-wide, and laid the ground for a broad consensus that a new humanistic legal order would have to be established' (ie the UDHR),[12] did not mean that the new order would be without (universal) violence. There were two fundamental differences, though. The violence of the cold war era was far more ferocious and took place almost exclusively in the Third World. From the Korean War, through Vietnam, Palestine and Mozambique to the Gulf, systemic violence killed, maimed and devastated Third World peoples. But this violence was not supposed to shock the 'conscience of the human beings worldwide' because the Third World people were being killed in order to protect them against the evil incarnate—communism—during the cold war and in the interest of human rights post-cold war.

Thirdly, imperialism continued to support and nurture (through both overt and covert violence) dictatorial regimes in the Third World so long as they continued to keep their peoples and resources in the free world.[13] Under the spectre of anti-communism, even purely nationalist regimes (from Nasser to Nyerere) with policies to retain their resources within their countries evoked the wrath of imperialist (Western) states, which at the same time presented themselves as the champions of democracy and human rights. No wonder, then, that, for much of the sixties and seventies, Third World states paid little heed to human rights arguments. Intellectually the human rights discourse and debate was more the domain of Western liberals, Third World conservative academics and professions such as lawyers and political scientists rather than political cadres of liberation movements or activist intellectuals.

Over the first two decades of independence in Africa, the human rights discourse

[10] See, generally, M Walker, *The Cold War: And the Making of the Modern World* (London, Vintage, 1993).

[11] See A Cassese, *International Law in a Divided World* (Oxford, Clarendon Press, 1986) 416–17.

[12] P Alston (ed), *The United Nations and Human Rights: A Critical Appraisal* (Oxford, Clarendon Press, 1992) 10.

[13] See N Chomsky and ES Herman, *The Washington Connection and the Third World Fascism: The Political Economy of Human Rights* (New York, South End Press, 1979).

developed as a counterpoint to the developmentalist discourse. The dominant variants of the latter were grounded in some or other theories of social development. In Africa, the first two decades of post-independence period saw a raging debate between modernisation and underdevelopment/dependencia schools.[14] Regardless of the merits of these schools, the central point is that they placed the contentions on different paths of development at the centre of the agenda. Development as an ideological construct and a practical programme was seen and perceived as the central concern.

The dominant theme of the development discourse was, no doubt, economistic. Yet a significant, albeit minor, current attempted to transcend the economistic terrain. Such concepts as social development grounded in class struggles and a holistic approach rooted in classical political economy were often debated with great vigour, particularly in academia. These were the theoretical concerns which took concrete shape in the form of departments of development studies, and interdisciplinary and common courses in academic institutions. In these institutional frameworks, a holistic approach was consciously pursued, with varying degrees of success.

Knowledge (truth) was seen as 'the whole' and was not compartmentalised. Separation between politics and economics, between state and civil society, between the atomised individual and the social whole, between ideology and science, and between intellectual commitment and scientific neutrality was eschewed. The attack on what was called the bourgeois compartmentalisation of knowledge and segregation of life was both polemical and bitter, as epitomised in Josue de Castro's oft-quoted passage:

> [N]arrowness of outlook is characteristic of Western civilization. Since the middle of the nineteenth century a kind of university instruction has developed which is no longer interested in transmitting a unified image of the world, but rather in isolating, and mutilating, facets of reality, in the supposed interest of science. The tremendous impact of scientific progress produced a fragmentation of culture and pulverized it into little grains of learning. Each scientific specialist seized his granule and turned it over and over beneath the powerful lens of his microscope striving to penetrate its microcosm, with a marvellous indifference to and towering ignorance of everything around him. Recently in Europe and the United States an extreme development of this type of university education has created within the culture a sort of civilization *sui generis*—a specialists' civilization—directed by men whose scientific outlook is rigorous but who suffer from a deplorable cultural and political myopia.[15]

The global practical struggles of the time were articulated as those between the forces of national liberation and imperialism, on the one hand, and between the forces of socialism and capitalism, on the other. This was well summed up in the then popular Chinese slogan, 'Countries want independence, nations want liberation, people want revolution'.

The academic developmental discourse, contentious as it was, and the practical struggles underlying it filtered into the United Nations system as well. It thus found ideological legitimacy in the global political discourse. The result was a spate of resolutions, declarations and covenants on developmental concerns.

---

[14] See W Rodney, *How Europe Underdeveloped Africa* (Dar es Salaam, Tanzania Publishing House, 1972); B Hettne, *Development Theory and the Three Worlds* (London, Longman, 1990); M Mamdani, T Mkandawire and Wamba-dia-Wamba, *Social Movements, Social Transformation and the Struggle for Democracy* (Dakar, Codesria, 1988).

[15] J de Castro, *The Geography of Hunger* (London, Gollancz, 1954).

Within the UN system, the developmental discourse originating in the General Assembly and finding expression in declarations and resolutions was politically an extension of the domestic statist/developmentalist ideologies of many Third World, and particularly African, states. Intellectually, this discourse was grounded in the unequal international political economy, while organisationally it took off from such groupings of Third World countries as the United Nations Group of 77 (G77) and United Nations Conference on Trade and Development (UNCTAD). This movement originally began in a negative fashion as a non-aligned movement (not aligned either to NATO or Warsaw Pact countries), but eventually took on the form of a more positive economic bonding in opposition to what was perceived by the Third World leaders as unfair and inequitable practices of international trade and economic control. To some extent, therefore, it was essentially an anti-imperialist movement, albeit statist in orientation. It is the underlying anti-imperialist stance of the Third World development discourse which is what was centrally opposed by the dominant states of the North led by the US.

This is borne out by the fact that the right to self-determination often became the bone of contention between the West and the official Third World. Contrary to traditional belief reiterated in the dominant human rights discourse, it is not so much the issue of the divisibility of rights between political/civil and social/economic rights and the priority of the latter over the former, or the trade-offs, as it is often expressed,[16] which characterised the debate between the Third World and the West, but rather the sense of autonomy, however partially expressed in the right to self-determination, which was the real ground of contention. This can be seen in the debates on the two 1966 international Covenants on political and civil rights and on economic, social and cultural rights.

The UDHR itself did not dichotomise between political/civil and social/economic rights, nor did it contain the right to self-determination. Self-determination was seen as a political and organisational principle embodied in the UN Charter, rather than a rights issue. The US objection to social and economic rights was based much more upon the nature of the obligations of the state which this entailed, rather than the nature of rights as such.[17] The dichotomy between these two sets of rights became much more entangled in the ideological war between the Soviet Union and the US. The Soviet Union retaliated against accusations of breach of political and civil rights in the Soviet bloc by pointing out the breaches of social and economic rights in the US. This diplomatic cold war on the human rights terrain then—probably inaccurately—became extended to the West–South discourse largely because the socialist and Third World countries tended to vote together on many Third World initiatives, such as on the processes of decolonisation and the Palestinian struggle for self-determination.

The US objection to both Covenants (1966), resulting in non-ratification, was largely because of the inclusion of the identical Article 1(1) on self-determination. This reads: 'All peoples have the right to self-determination. By virtue of that right they freely determine their political status and freely pursue their economic, social and cultural development.'

---

[16] RJ Vincent, *Human Rights and International Relations* (Cambridge, Cambridge University Press, 1986) ch 5.
[17] Alston, n 12 above, 394–6.

The second paragraph was found to be offensive because of the perception (quite correct in the circumstances) of the West that it was directed against the interests of foreign, largely Western, capital involved in the exploitation of resources in the Third World and the transfer of profits from the South to the North. This, indeed, was the expansion of the meaning of the right of peoples to self-determination to include what many Third World publicists often called economic self-determination.[18] It is this aspect which was originally proposed by Chile to be included in the Covenants and which began to find expression in the documents and declarations proposed by Third World states and adopted by the General Assembly, where the Third World was in a majority. Thus, we had the Resolution on the Permanent Sovereignty of Natural Resources, 1962, the Charter of Economic Rights and Duties of States, 1974, and various resolutions and declarations to do with the New International Economic Order.

In spite of its original promise of strong anti-imperialism in both political and economic spheres, in the hands of Third World states the principle of self-determination was narrowed in three respects. Politically, the right to self-determination was limited to colonial and colonial-like situations, such as in apartheid South Africa. The right was considered to have exhausted itself once a country became independent. It was not applicable to peoples (nations) within an independent sovereign state. Secondly, as far as the right to economic self-determination was concerned, the term 'people' was conflated with the state. The right, therefore, was seen as belonging to the state. It became both statist and developmentalist in conception, and, in practice, the right to economic self-determination at international level became limited to trade-union-type demands of the Third World, ie demanding better and fairer terms of trade and laying claims to greater aid. The potential within the right of articulating and legitimising a stronger version of anti-imperialist struggles of the working people in the South was understandably not in the interest of the Third World states and therefore was not fully developed in the official discourse. Yet, to underscore once again, even in this limited form, the Third World version found only cursory mention in the dominant discourse of human rights largely originating and propagated by the West, which continued to focus on the universality of individual rights with monumental disregard for the social, economic and political disempowerment which the large masses of people in the Third World suffered under despotic regimes very often supported by the West.

And this is the point of my thesis so far. By and large, the dominant discourse in the Third World and that which the Third World pursued internationally was openly contentious, centrally developmental, probably economistic and often inevitably intertwined with the then superpower rivalry (the cold war). Nonetheless, it had achieved a measure of ascendancy and legitimacy for some of the major concerns of the peoples of the South. On the global terrain of social and political discourse, the developmental and the human rights discourses were actually locked in battle. They were polarised and became mutually exclusive. This meant that the developmental discourse and the human rights discourse ran parallel.

To be sure, there were always the middle-grounders from both sides of the discourse, who sought exactly that—a theoretical/conceptual middle ground. From the

---

[18] See A Cassese, *United Nations Law: Fundamental Rights—Two Topics in International Law* (The Hague, Kluwer Academic Publishers, 1979) 92–93.

human rights side, we had the development of such paradigms as the indivisibility of human rights, basic needs/rights schools, and human rights as integral. From the developmental side, we had such attempts as the Algiers Declaration.[19] Suffice it to say here that the middle ground became even more contentious because each side—inevitably—approached it from its own premises and outlook, thereby reflecting real-life social forces and interests. It is arguable whether the most valiant attempt at integrating the two discourses—the UN Declaration on the Right to Development—was a roaring success or just a gargantuan and meaningless diversion.[20]

Be that as it may, it was in this context and against this background that the human rights/democracy discourse made its forceful entry onto the African scene in the late 1970s. Whatever the pundits may say, the immediate genesis of this entry lay in the Carter doctrine. It was ideologically charged and came with the cold war package including its particular anti-developmental bias. This was so notwithstanding the fact that the African Charter of Human and People's Rights embodied a strongly statist version of the right to development. The essentially neo-classical paradigm of the newly emerging 'development' discourse (as opposed to that of the 1960s and 1970s, which were grounded in political economy)[21] became manifest in the various structural adjustment programmes (SAPs) imposed on African states by the international financial institutions (IFIs).[22]

Larger issues of even official Third Worldist political economy—unfair terms of trade, minimal aid, protectionism of Western markets, extraction of profits and resources by multinational corporations—which were the common currency of the developmentalist discourse of the 1960s and 1970s have not only disappeared, but been delegitimised. African states (among which, incidentally, Tanzania was leading), which were at the forefront of the demand for a New International Economic Order and UNCTAD's progressive deliberations, have been reduced to virtual supplicants with no say. In the Uruguay round, to cite one typical example, Africa was virtually marginalised from the negotiations, and continues to be marginalised in the various WTO rounds of negotiations.

The contemporary vocabulary itself is a dramatic reflection of the shift in the developmental discourse. It is not structural development, but adjustment which is at issue. And here it is the market, prices and fiscal mechanisms, rather than the social and political structures that underlie them, which are the centre of the focus.[23] The shifts are expressed even more dramatically in the academic discourse of radical political economy. We have come a long way (in a short time?) from the time when the state was either applauded as the agency of development or condemned as hijacking

---

[19] See IG Shivji, *The Concept of Human Rights in Africa* (Dakar, Codesria, 1989) *passim*; Cassese, ibid.

[20] See K M'Baye, 'Emergence of the Rights to Development as a Human Right in the Context of a New International Economic Order', Doc SS-78/CONF.630/8 (Paris, UNESCO, 1978). See also CE Welch and RI Meltzer (eds), *Human Rights and Development in Africa* (Albany, NY, State University of New York Press, 1985).

[21] See G Hyden, 'Changing Ideological and Theoretical Perpectives on Development' in U Himmelstrand, K Kinyanjui and E Mburugu (eds), *African Perspectives on Development: Controversies, Dilemmas & Openings* (Dar-es-Salaam, Mkuki na Nyota, 1994) 308–19.

[22] See P Gibbon, Y Banguri and A Ofstad (eds), *Adjustment, Authoritarianism and Democracy: The Politics of Economic Liberalisation in Africa* (Uppsala, Scandinavian Institute of African Studies, 1992).

[23] See M Mamdani, 'A Critical Analysis of the IMF Programme in Uganda' in Himmelstrand et al, n 21 above, 128–36.

a revolution.[24] The currency now is the non-government organisations (NGOs, many of them being foreign or foreign-funded—FFUNGOs), manned by development practitioners who draw up country policies (or 'policy inputs' as it is euphemistically called). 'Class' and 'working people' have been replaced (or displaced) by 'gender' and 'disadvantaged groups', and class struggles have been 'substituted' by rights literacy; nations and nationalities have been rechristened 'ethnicities and indigenous peoples', while culture and custom have been reconceptualised as religion and identities. Of course, Marxism has been harassed out by postmodernism, in which the concentrated expression of class consciousness—ideology—is fragmented into disparate discourses or narratives and meganarratives, while analysis is a story.

Interdisciplinary studies institutionalised in institutes and centres of development studies are now met with calls for respect for professional disciplines. The institutes themselves have been sidelined or converted into management schools.

The adjustment ideology both sidelined and villainised official developmentalist programmes and Third Worldist autonomy (self-determination?). The expected disastrous effect of adjustment on the large majority of the people, as field studies have documented, is supposedly adjusted by the so-called social dimensions programmes or adjustment with a human face.[25] It is here that human rights vocabulary is deployed as add-ons. Selective human rights (gender, children, etc) are grafted onto adjustment policy as part of programmes and projects of poverty alleviation, leaving the basic paradigms and premises of both of the human rights and adjustment discourses intact. In short, human rights are not in any sense an integral part of the adjustment paradigm.

From the human rights side, the radical fringes of the mainstream have, for some time now, tried to address the issues raised by the developmental discourse at the level of poverty alleviation and relief (minimalist) or empowerment (maximalist). Thus, we have debates over the integration of political/civil and social/economic rights; basic needs as basic rights; and the rights to aid,[26] to food[27] and to development, etc.

The intervention of the radical left/academia in the human rights discourse from the developmental perspective has been incoherent, inconsistent and more or less ignored. There is the work of the Permanent Peoples' Tribunal, which uses mock litigation to highlight larger issues of international inequality. It was the Lelio Basso Foundation behind this Tribunal which organised and proclaimed the Universal Declaration of the Rights of the People in 1966 (The Algiers Declaration, 1976).[28] Using the rights to self-determination, around 1988, it organised a mock trial of the International Monetary Fund (IMF) and the World Bank. They were charged with breaching, among other things, the right of peoples to self-determination because of the conditionalities and

---

[24] See IG Shivji, *Intellectuals at the Hill: Essays and Talks, 1968–1993* (Dar es Salaam, University Press, 1993) 200–19.

[25] P Gibbon, 'The World Bank and African Poverty 1973–91' (1992) 30 *Journal of Modern African Studies* 193.

[26] See K Tomasevski, *Development Aid and Human Rights Re-visited* (London, Pinter, 1993).

[27] See P Alston and K Tomasevski, *The Right to Food* (The Hague, Kluwer Academic Publishing, 1984); D Kowalewski, 'Transnational Corporations and the Third World's Right to Eat: The Caribbean' (1981) 3 *Human Rights Quarterly* 45; CD Brockett 'The Right to Food and International Obligations: The Impact of US Policy in Central America' in GW Shepherd and VP Nanda (eds), *Human Rights and Third World Development* (Westport CT, Greenwood Press, 1985) 125–47.

[28] See Cassese, n 18 above.

structural adjustment programmes that they imposed on Third World states and peoples.[29]

The Indian Supreme Court has been involved in developing public-interest litigation. This has largely involved expansion of the rules of *locus standi* and the flexible application of the rules of procedure to facilitate access to courts of the otherwise 'disadvantaged' groups. Indian courts have taken up some broader socio-economic issues (bonded labour, the plight of pavement dwellers, unhealthy conditions in quarries, the oppression of women, etc) and (*suo moto*) converted them into legal issues by expansive construction of human rights and directive principles of state-policy provisions in the Indian Constitution. This has now come to be called 'social-action litigation' by Indian academics and activist.[30] Generally, however, these developments remain largely untheorised and have made little dent in human rights discourse as such. In particular, it is doubtful if the varied ways of reformulating human rights (the right to life includes the right to livelihood, or, from human rights, the right to be human) has and can fully integrate larger developmental paradigms of domestic (class) and international political economy (imperialism) within the human rights ideology. All in all, the human rights discourse remains impervious to larger developmental paradigms.

To sum up this section, we have seen the globally divided nature of the discourse—divided between the human rights and the developmental discourse. Since the collapse of the Soviet Union, the cold war sting has probably been taken away from it. Nevertheless, the developmental concerns of the South remain, and have to be given expression within what has now become the dominant human rights/democracy discourse. I would submit that the way in which the human rights discourse has developed since has been in two apparently contradictory directions. On the one hand, the human rights discourse has continued to present itself as a universal and a neutral discourse. Thus, it is non-political and non-ideological. This premise and presentation form the heart of the dominant discourse in trying to win the hearts of the Third World people while simultaneously reproducing its dominant place in the world hegemonic system. This means that its original anti-developmental bias continues to be fundamentally reinforced, and done so, among other things, through further fragmentisation of the discourse (for instance, the incredible particularisation, reformulation and quantification of rights).

On the other hand, the building of consensus around the human rights discourse as an ideology requires 'making concessions', and thus taking on board the so-called developmental concerns of the people of the Third World. So developmental concerns expressed in the language of rights—the so-called social and economic rights—become add-ons in the human rights package. Consequently, the dominant-rights discourse de-legitimises the global developmental discourse while, at the same time, ostensibly taking on board the developmental concerns of the Third World people, which are fragmentised and particularised as needs, demands, entitlements and aspirations, in this order of acceptability. The radical reformulation of human rights in terms of the

---

[29] Permanent Peoples' Tribunal, 1988, On the Policies of the IMF and the World Bank.
[30] See M Gomez, *In the Public Interest: Essays on Public Interest Litigation and Participatory Justice* (Colombo, Legal Aid Centre, University of Colombo, 1993); J Cottrell, 'Third Generation Rights and Social Action Litigation' in A Paliwala and S Adelman (eds), *Law and Crisis in the Third World* (London, H Zell Publishers, 1993) 102–26.

rights to aid,[31] to food,[32] to be human,[33] to organise,[34] etc, at best highlights the deprivation of the large majority in the South and the double standards of the Northern states, but at worse contributes to further fragmentisation and quantification of the discourse, obfuscating the essential, valorising the inconsequential and disaggregating the social whole out of existence. What is more, and this is no doubt contentious and debatable, such interventions by radical intellectuals in the human rights discourse lends legitimacy to, and hegemonises, an ideology on a global level, which, as we have seen, has been anti-developmental (particularly pitted against national autonomous development in the Third World) and pro-imperialist in its origin as well as in its performance and practice.

What is important to emphasise here is that, as it presently stands, the human rights discourse is an expression not only of the contention at the level of the development discourse between the North and the South, but also of the hegemonic place and logic of the North over the South.[35] Adding on a 'developmental' dimension to human rights in the myriad conceptual ways which I discussed—the universality and indivisibility of human rights, basic needs as entitlements, the integrity of political/civil and social/economic rights, the rights to food, to aid, to relief, etc—does not challenge the world outlook or the social and political interests underlying the hegemonic place and the role of the North in the world capitalist system.

On the other hand, even minimalist developmental concerns of the Third World expressed in such forms as better terms of trade, debt relief, extraction of surplus, respect for state sovereignty, etc (ie concerns underlying the New International Economic Order) are sidelined and even de-legitimised. As for more radical versions of asserting autonomy in the form of national autonomous development,[36] it is even worse. These are positively demeaned or demonised as being labelled orthodox, visionary, fundamentalist anti-(human) rights.

In summary, my broad conclusion is that the human rights ideology/discourse in its hegemonic form forecloses basic issues of social and national inequality, inequity and social injustice inherent in the international imperialist order and domestic African (neo-colonial) formations. These were precisely the questions raised, even though partially and in a statist form, by the developmental discourse surrounding the New International Economic Order in which African countries such as Tanzania played a leading role. This developmental discourse ran parallel (and was, indeed, antithetic) to the human rights discourse.

The current hegemonisation of the human rights (rule of law, constitutionalism, multi-party democracy) discourse seems to have virtually annihilated the developmental discourse. Instead, the discourse is about and around adjustment, as opposed to development. But the basic problems and issues of the large majority of the African

---

[31] Tomasevski, n 26 above.

[32] Alston and Tomasevski, n 27 above.

[33] U Baxi, *Mambrino's Helmet: Human Rights for a Changing World* (New Delhi, Har-Anand Publications, 1994).

[34] Shivji, n 19 above.

[35] R Falk, 'Humanitarian Intervention: Imperatives and Problematics' in RP Claude and BH Weston (eds), *Human Rights in the World Community: Issues and Action*, 2nd edn (Philadelphia PA, University of Pennsylvania Press, 1992) 401.

[36] Third World Economics, 'An Alternative to the Crisis for Africa and the Middle East: Autonomous Economic and Social Development in Democracy', Bulletin No 10 (July 1992).

people and classes have not gone away. Adjustment pretends to address some of the phenomenal symptoms through projects and programmes of poverty alleviation.[37] The human rights community, on the other hand, attempts to find space for taking on board more progressive developmental concerns in the human rights discourse by reconceptualising existing rights and fabricating 'new' rights. This is the extent of integrating the 'developmental' and 'human rights' discourses in the current 'liberalisation' period. The early divergence and the current 'integration' of the two discourses are neatly represented in the following quotations from Julius K Nyerere, 23 years apart. In his *Stability and Change in Africa*,[38] written in 1969, Nyerere rhetorically asked:

> What freedom has our subsistence farmer? He scratches a bare living from the soil provided the rains do not fail; his children work at his side without schooling, medical care, or even good feeding. Certainly he has freedom to vote and to speak as he wishes. But these freedoms are much less real to him than his freedom to be exploited. Only as his poverty is reduced will his existing political freedom become properly meaningful and his right to human dignity become a fact of human dignity.[39]

This was in the heyday of developmentalist and Ujamaaist ideology and the one-party authoritarian state. The distance between developmental and human rights discourse could not be greater—it was a dialogue, if at all, of the deaf.

In 1993, addressing a Lutheran International Conference, Nyerere started off his speech in a serious effort to bring developmental (anti-adjustment) arguments on board through the rights discourse.

> Life is the most basic Human right. If justice means anything at all, it must protect life. That should be a constant underlying purpose of all social, economic, and political activities of government at all levels . . .
>
>    To have food, clothing, shelter, and other basic necessities of life; to live without fear; to have an opportunity to work for one's living; freedom of association, of speech, and of worship. All these things together are among the basic principles of living as a whole person in 'Freedom and Justice'. In other words, all are almost universally accepted as basic 'Human Rights'.[40]

Clearly, Nyerere is trying hard to marry the developmentalist discourse with the rights discourse. The concept of integrated rights—both the freedom of speech and the freedom to eat—is pretty acceptable. But this mellowed idealised introduction, probably necessary to be heard at all, is a far cry from the bold, confident, probably more realistic, assertion of 1969 that the freedom of expression means little to a starving person for whom the freedom to be exploited is more real. As a matter of fact, the interesting part of the 1993 speech is that the introduction trails off as the speech picks up Nyerere's more radical stance on the domination of African states and people by the states and IFIs controlled by the North. Although terms such as 'exploitation' are studiously avoided, the rights discourse, too, is abandoned. It seems to me that this is not only the limit of Nyerere's ideology, but that it also reflects the

---

[37] Gibbon, n 25 above.
[38] JK Nyerere, *Stability and Change in Africa* (Dar es Salaam, Government Publishers, 1969).
[39] Quoted in Shijva, n 19 above, 40.
[40] *Daily News*, 27 September 1993.

limit of the rights discourse to integrate fully the larger concerns of social development and emancipation.

This leads me to ask the question: Is it possible (and, if so, to what extent) to raise an anti-imperialist, nationally autonomous developmental agenda within the hegemonic human rights discourse without abandoning the perspective of the working people and obliterating class distance between the exploiter and the exploited?[41] This question has hardly been answered academically, even as life has begun to answer it in the dramatic events of this first decade of the new millennium.

## III. THE METAMORPHOSIS OF THE DEVELOPMENT AND HUMAN RIGHTS DISCOURSE IN THE ERA OF GLOBALISATION

The first generation of structural adjustment programmes had a very short life. They caused havoc in African societies and had to be repackaged and made more palliative with 'safety-valve' measures. The development discourse was thus transformed into a discourse on poverty reduction. The neo-liberal economic package with its economic conditionalities—de-regulation, liberalisation, marketisation, state withdrawal, etc—was now linked to a liberal political package with political conditionalities—multi-party, accountability, good governance, democracy and human rights. That there was an obvious internal inconsistency between economic and political conditionalities went virtually unheeded in the euphoria of democracy and pluralism. In my country, Tanzania, for example, the privatisation timetable was laid out by the IMF/World Bank. The state's National Bank of Commerce had to be privatised within a specified time-frame. The law enabling the privatisation of the bank was rushed through Parliament with little debate under a certificate of urgency. The same occurred with a number of other important pieces of legislation, such as the Mining Act of 1998. The very least that can be expected of a representative democracy is that the elected parliament has the 'sovereign' right to enact the laws of the country without external pressure: a law passed under duress is no different from a military decree!

As neo-liberalism gathered speed, the African states increasingly lost their basic sovereign power—the power to make policies, laws and determine the direction of the country——while citizens lost their basic right—the right to self-determination, that is, the right to participate in their own governance. Policy-making was taken over by a horde of donor-funded consultants who set priorities implicitly, but often expressly. In many cases and instances, the sovereign powers of the state were transferred to NGOs, which were funded by donors. Hegemonic powers and donor countries became development partners, and 30-year-old graduates from Harvard and Boston became development practitioners! Poverty-reduction discourse drained development of all its sovereign content, and the rights discourse—the monopoly of foreign-funded NGOs or FFUNGOs—became one huge stick to beat recalcitrant states with, rather than a terrain of struggle for the masses of the people. (I may be exaggerating—but exaggerating the essential truth.)

---

[41] P Corrigan and D Sayer, 'How the Law Rules: Variations on some Themes in Karl Marx' in B Fryer, A Hunt, D McBarnet and B Moorhouse (eds), *Law, State and Society* (London, Croom Helm, 1981).

Using Mamdani's[42] formulation in a slightly different context, we can say that the neo-liberal economic, political and human rights discourse undermined the very core of 'sovereignty' and 'citizenship'. The development and human rights discourses, which were parallel at best or fragmented at worse, merged into an orgy of a thought-less celebration of market fundamentalism and casino capitalism, on the one hand, and an unprecedented assault on humanity and human rights in the form of a war on terror, on the other. This was no longer a case of Western double standards in human rights, which had always characterised the dominant human rights discourse, but a forced regime with no standards at all! Just as financial speculators ruled the economy, so warmongers ruled the polity.

But the neo-liberal chickens are coming home to roost. The unfolding financial crisis should make us all rethink both the development and human rights discourses of the past half-century or so. Even more fundamentally, it should make us rethink the unequal and inhuman relationship between the North and the South, between the West and the rest, between unfettered power and enslaved people, all embedded in capitalist imperialism which has ruled the world for the last five centuries or more.

The central question in the realm of ideas is: What will be the new discourse which will allow us to raise and begin to grapple with the larger question of human emancipation?

The dominant human rights discourse, as we have known it, is too limited, if not actually depraved, to enable such a fundamental rethink. Nothing less than a full-blown emancipatory project is on the world-historical agenda. We need epochal rethinking and insurrectionist ideas beyond the mundane, the current and the obvious; thinking beyond the pragmatic, foreseeable future to an imagined humane future. We need to transcend the developmental and human rights discourses of the last millennium.

In the African intellectual community, such a rethinking is beginning. The liberatory ideas of Pan-Africanism and the unity of the continent are back on the African intel-lectual agenda. There is a re-evaluation, albeit hesitant and diffident, of the socialist emancipatory project. University campuses are beginning to wake up from the intense slumber imposed by neo-liberalism. To be sure, the pessimism of the intellect is still dominant, but the optimism of the will is on the horizon.

---

[42] M Mamdani, 'Darfur, ICC and the New Humanitarian Order: How the ICC's "Responsibility to Protect" Is Being Turned into an Assertion of Neo-colonial Domination', reprinted in *Pambazuka News*, available at http://www.pambazuka.org/en/category/features/50568/print.

# 3

# *Rights and Development: A Social Power Perspective*

ANANYA MUKHERJEE-REED

## I. WHY RIGHTS AND DEVELOPMENT? WHY NOW?

IN RECENT YEARS, we have seen a growing interest amongst scholars in exploring the connection between rights and development (see the introduction to this volume).[1] We can hypothesise two sets of reasons behind the emergence of the rights/development discourse. The first impetus comes from 'below'—from social movements and civil society actors. They see rights as a means of challenging the hierarchical and welfarist premise of conventional development, particularly with regard to the practices of states and development institutions. Alternatively, rights may provide a means of mobilising citizens and of demanding delivery on critical issues. The Right to Food movement in India is an example of this route.[2] The second impetus comes from 'above'—in part to manage the growing resistance to official development practices and in part to deal with the increasing failure of development institutions to deliver.[3] In this case, rights-based approaches are often used to formulate minimalist responses to structural issues. India's Food Security Act is such an example of a rights-based response to public pressure. There is a very legitimate fear amongst civil society actors that the Act may not only fail to address the issue of hunger, but may also have the effect of reinforcing the structural processes which engender hunger.[4]

Careful scrutiny of the perspectives from above and below reveal fundamental contestations about both the meaning and the content of rights, as well as the meaning and the content of development. It is this latter aspect upon which I wish to focus. Much of the rights/development discourses do not adequately problematise the notion of development; the notion of development that informs these discussions is most frequently a liberal understanding of development—such as that of human development,

---

[1] See the Introduction to this volume by Zumbansen and Buchanan.

[2] http://www.righttofoodindia.org/index.html.

[3] See 'Introduction', P Alston and M Robinson (eds), *Human Rights and Development* (New York, Oxford University Press, 2005).

[4] See Open Letter from the Right to Food Campaign on the Food Security Act, available at http://www.righttofoodindia.org/data/open_letter_from_right_to_food_campaignagainst_draft_national_food_security_act.pdf.

as developed by Amartya Sen, Mahbub ul Haq and Martha Nussbaum, amongst others.[5] The UNDP's Human Development Reports are centred around this concept. The Human Development Report 2000, entitled *Human Rights and Human Development*, is a key example of this approach.[6]

I begin by problematising the notion of human development, which I believe most intimately informs the emerging rights and development discourse. I first offer a critique of the notion with regard to three dimensions: (i) the understanding of social justice; (ii) the understanding of difference; and (iii) the understanding of agency. Following the work of Iris Marion Young, I argue that Sen's framework is rooted in a distributive paradigm of justice, and a notion of individual agency that does not necessarily enhance or deepen the potential for development. I then propose a distinct approach to development that uses alternative notions of justice, difference and agency, and suggest some questions about the potential relationship between rights and development that may be raised within this alternative framework.

To some extent, the alternatives which I discuss are based upon my analysis of the views articulated by the ongoing social movements. There is an issue of justification involved here: what justifies the choice of examining the notion of development from the perspective of movements and struggles? This is a question of epistemology which I cannot develop at length here. Arguably, however, there is much to be gained by contrasting official understandings of development with alternative ones, simply because they represent substantively different, if not conflicting, interests. The fact that one set of these interests attains officialdom whereas the others do not is a manifestation of the inequality of power that any meaningful discussion of development cannot justifiably eschew. The policy discourse around the current crisis of hunger is, to my mind, a prime illustration of this conflict over the very meaning of development. I will use this example throughout this chapter to develop my arguments.

The plan of the chapter is as follows. In Section II, I briefly discuss the dominant approaches to human development. In Section III, I critically examine these approaches. In Section IV, I offer an alternative approach. In the final section, I raise some questions about the role of rights in this alternative approach.

## II. CONCEPTUALISING HUMAN DEVELOPMENT

Much of the existing literature treats human development as an undifferentiated concept. While there are broad principles of agreement between different human-development scholars, it is important to recognise that multiple notions of human development may be possible, and, indeed, necessary. Let me begin by identifying two notions of human development:

- human development as the enhancement of opportunity, capability and freedom (hereinafter the capability approach); and

---

[5] M ul Haq, *Reflections on Human Development* (New York, Oxford University Press, 1997); MC Nussbaum, *Women and Human Development: The Capabilities Approach* (Cambridge-New York, Cambridge University Press, 2000); AK Sen, *Development as Freedom* (New York, Knopf, 1999).

[6] United Nations Development Program, Human Development Reports (HDRs), *Cultural Liberty in Today's Diverse World* (New York, United Nations, 2000).

- human development as a process of the reconfiguration of the matrices of social power (hereinafter the social power approach).

The first comprises the dominant institutionalised approach to human development. The second exists more as a critique than as a fully formulated approach within the human development paradigm. I have made a modest effort to give it such a formulation.[7]

As is well known, the primary philosophical formulation of the capability approach has been developed by Amartya Sen; Martha Nussbaum has enhanced the approach from a gender perspective. Mahbub ul Haq developed the primary policy tool based upon this approach, namely, the Human Development Index, which provides a measure of the development of people, rather than of economies. The core ideas of the approach are: universalism; a liberal and pluralist notion of the state; the priority of individual freedoms; formal equality; emphasis on individual agency; and a vision of liberal capitalism as a context in which opportunity and freedom are generated and individual human-agency thrives.[8]

The notion of capability is concerned with what people are actually able to do or be, as opposed to what they have or possess. In other words, it rejects the assumption that ensuring a certain amount of income or a basket of resources (such as basic needs) is equivalent to development. Unless these resources enable people to achieve what they value or to be who they wish to be, ie to enhance their capabilities, simply delivering them is not conducive to development. As Sen says, 'capability is thus a kind of freedom: the substantive freedom to . . . achieve various lifestyles'.[9] Drawing upon this notion of capability, Sen has argued that freedom should be considered as both the end and the means of development. The task of social change, in this view, consists primarily in eradicating the 'unfreedoms' that prevent the enhancement of capabilities.

Martha Nussbaum, in elaborating the capability framework from a gender perspective, has argued that Sen's 'perspective of freedom is too vague. Some freedoms limit others; some freedoms are important, some trivial, some good, and some positively bad.'[10] In her view, before the approach can offer a valuable normative perspective, 'we must make commitments about substance'.[11] She then goes on to specify 'a definite set of capabilities', which, she claims, are 'the most important ones to protect':

> Although this list is somewhat different from Rawls' list of primary goods, it is offered in a similar political-liberal spirit: as a list that can be endorsed for political purposes, as a moral basis for central constitutional guarantees, by people who have otherwise very different views on what a complete good life for a human being would be . . . A list of central capabilities is not a complete theory of justice. Such a list gives us the basis for a *decent social minimum* in a variety of areas.[12]

The idea of a decent social minimum is also found in Sen, and in successive Human

[7] A Mukherjee-Reed, *Human Development and Social Power: Perspectives from South Asia* (London, Routledge, 2008).
[8] Sen, n 5 above; Nussbaum, n 5 above.
[9] Sen, n 5 above, 75.
[10] Nussbaum, n 5 above, 74–5.
[11] Nussbaum, n 5 above; idem, 'Capabilities as Fundamental Entitlements: Sen and Social Justice' (2003) 9 *Feminist Economics* 33.
[12] Nussbaum, n 5 above, 74–75; emphasis added.

Development Reports (HDRs). In choosing which freedoms and capabilities need to be prioritised within a human development strategy, Sen has suggested using Adam Smith's evaluative criterion, 'the ability to appear in public without shame'.[13] In Sen's view, this criterion allows social needs and priorities to accommodate cultural differ- ence and human diversity. This ability, Sen has argued, is a distinct point of departure of the capability approach from other approaches, such as the basic needs approach, which seek to guarantee specific commodity bundles irrespective of cultural or material differences. The HDRs, in their actual task of human development policy formula- tion, originally gave priority to four specific types of capabilities: knowledge, health, a decent standard of living and human freedoms.[14] In 2004, cultural liberty was added (HDR 2004). In his recent work, however, Sen has emphasised that the capability approach should be valued more for the alternative 'informational focus' that it offers, rather than as a guide to specific policy choices or recommendations.[15]

In what follows, I wish to examine the capability approach critically along three principal themes:

1. the underlying conception of social justice;
2. the understanding of difference; and
3. the understanding of agency.

## II.1. Social Justice

Following Iris Young, I have recently argued that the paradigm of social justice, which informs the capability approach, is a distributive paradigm of justice.[16] The distributive paradigm sees social justice as the morally proper distribution of wealth, income and other material resources among the members of society. This distributive definition can also include non-material social goods such as rights, opportunity, power and self- respect.[17] I have argued that the capability approach, while departing somewhat from this focus on the distribution of things to the distribution of capabilities, still remains within the distributive paradigm. In Sen's most recent work on justice, the shift away from the distribution of things is even sharper: it now concerns the distribution of rights—particularly economic and social rights.[18]

What is the significance of this commitment to a distributive paradigm? This becomes clearer when it is seen in comparison with alternatives ways of thinking about justice. For example, Young speaks of an 'enabling conception of justice': while the distributive paradigm focuses on altering distribution within given structures, an enabling conception emphasises altering the structures/institutions which result in a certain distribution. While the first sees injustice as a problem of distribution, the latter sees injustice as oppression and domination. Injustice in the sense of domina- tion involves having to perform according to goals and norms that the people subject

---

[13] Sen, n 5 above, 74.

[14] United National Development Programme, Human Development Reports (New York, United Nations, 1990) 10.

[15] AK Sen, *The Idea of Justice* (London, Allen Lane, 2009).

[16] Mukherjee-Reed, n 7 above.

[17] IM Young, *Justice and the Politics of Difference* (Princeton, NJ, Princeton University Press, 1990) 16.

[18] Sen, n 15 above, 232–33.

to them have not participated in establishing. Justice in this understanding requires self-determination. Oppression involves processes such as exploitation, marginalisation, powerlessness, cultural imperialism and violence (both structural and direct), ie processes that impose constraints on self-development. For Young, justice requires the removal of these constraints.[19] While dominant development paradigms also speak to self-development or determination, their focus is usually on the individual dimension, rather than that of the collective. I have argued that this focus on the individual is not adequate for a notion of development. In the context of development, the issues of oppression, domination and injustice are better understood in relation to collectivities such as race, gender, religious/ethnic groups and so on. Individual stories of overcoming oppression/domination, however compelling, cannot be aggregated into a collective dynamic of transformation.

In the specific context of development, one can also speak of a notion of transformative justice, which focuses not only on changes in the underlying structures, but also on the agents—or subjects—who bring about this change and the process through which the change occurs. This aspect, that of agency, is particularly critical for any discussion of development, as I will argue below.

In his most recent work, Sen has proposed an approach to justice, which he calls a 'comparative realisation-focused' approach. This approach departs significantly from the classical approaches, which he calls 'transcendental institutionalism' (of which Kant and Rawls are two quintessential examples). Sen characterises transcendental institutionalism as one which seeks an ideal of justice and an ideal order of just institutions.[20] He argues that such a search is both unfeasible and unnecessary. It is unfeasible because there can be no consensus on any one ideal of justice; it is unnecessary because, even if there were such a consensus, it would be impossible to institutionalise it in a manner that would realise the ideal in practice. Sen's proposed alternative, the comparative realisation-focused approach, does not ask what justice is in any ideal sense, but rather poses the question: How can we make the world less unjust? My question is: How do we know what is less unjust? Sen argues that the key here is public discussion: reasoned debate can generate consensus for changes towards greater justice. Perhaps, but only if we abstract it from the inequality of power involved. In my view, Sen's account leaves out or deals inadequately with the problem of power inequalities.

As Jürgen Habermas has shown us, reasoned discussion is rendered difficult, if not impossible, when the various participants in the discussion are unequally situated. For a discussion to generate a legitimate consensus, it needs either to include only those who are equal or to take place within institutional arrangements that guarantee substantive equality between the participants involved. The first presents the problem of exclusion. The second reverts us back to a version of transcendental institutionalism, as Sen has described it. Unless we have an institutional arrangement that guarantees equality between participants, we cannot have a reasoned public debate. The broader question is one of power, and specifically the ability of certain actors to influence public discourse unfairly. Even if we find some procedural fixes to address the discursive inequities that result from unequal power relations, the problems remain (more

---

[19] Young, n 17 above.
[20] Sen, n 15 above.

on this below). To understand the salience of this argument, we only need to note the power relations institutionalised through what we call the 'free' media.

But even if we set this problem aside for a moment, can we answer the strategic question of how to reduce injustice if we abdicate from the more foundational question of what is justice? This inseparability of the normative and the strategic is a core issue of critical philosophy, and may not be so easily resolved. In the example of hunger, almost no one would disagree (at least openly) that our fellow citizens should be free from hunger. There is also some agreement that universal access to food should be enshrined as a right. But if we focus on the question of the realisation of this right—as Sen urges us to do—then we immediately confront a problem. There is no consensus on how the right to food should be guaranteed. Corporations argue for greater privatisation of food production, including increased corporate participation in food aid. Global justice movements, to the contrary, are arguing for the decommodification of food, corporate-free agriculture and complete community ownership and control of food production. These latter views are articulated within the framework of food sovereignty—a framework quite different from the notion of food security, which dominates the policy circles. Food sovereignty and food security embody substantively different notions of justice and different strategies of realising justice, most notably because they differ on the causality of injustice.

These differences do not arise from plurality, as Sen emphasises repeatedly. What is meant by the term plurality here is individual differences in ideas and understandings of justice or the divergence understandings of justice between different schools of thought. I wish to emphasise, instead, the different understandings of justice that arise from the unequal structural locations of the social actors in question—in this case, the farmers, on the one hand, and agribusiness, on the other. In other words, my concern is to delineate how structural inequality (rather than plurality) conditions understandings of justice.

What happens when such unequal participants enter into public discourse? Consider the 'failed' food summit in Rome in 2009.[21] It is believed to have failed in the specific sense that the Food and Agriculture Organization (FAO) failed to raise the 44 billion USD that it needs to eradicate chronic hunger (note that this amounts to 44 USD per person for the 1.07 billion chronically hungry in the world today). As startling as this is, there is much more at stake in this failure. In the lead up to the summit, the FAO undertook consultations with major stakeholders in order to arrive at a consensus strategy for chronic hunger. Several stakeholders were invited to forge such a consensus. For example, a civil society forum was held, the stated purpose of which was to 'ensure that the aspirations of the poor, the disadvantaged, the marginalized and the hungry are successfully voiced'. Farmers and agricultural workers—arguably the real producers of food—were invited to this forum; however, for the purposes of the summit, they were not recognised as producers, only as civil society. In contrast, a private sector forum, held at a separate meeting in Milan, brought together the largest agribusiness corporations. As the FAO said, 'the importance of securing a vital link with the private sector is seen as a key contribution to the Summit and to improving

---

[21] The Summit was held in Rome on 16–18 November 2009. See http://www.fao.org/wsfs/world-summit/en. See also A Mukherjee-Reed, 'The "Failed" Food Summit: An Analysis', *Oneworld South Asia*, 28 November 2009, accessible at: http://southasia.oneworld.net/weekend/the-failed-food-summit-an-analysis.

the food security of one billion people'. Note that food *security* is the agenda that the FAO and the entire policy community, as well as the corporate sector, share. Farmers and agricultural workers and the other participants in the civil society forum endorse the agenda of food *sovereignty*. This agenda of food sovereignty has found no place in the Summit Declaration (or in the policy discourse around hunger), even though it remains central to global justice movements.

In an immediate empirical sense, then, there does exist a consensus on food security, but none on food sovereignty. However, this consensus is obviously tainted by the inequality of power between the different stakeholders. Can we nonetheless argue that pursuing food security through increased corporatisation will make the world a little less unjust? There are two issues of concern here. First, less unjust according to who? Can claims arising from these fundamentally unequal locations be judged to be equally valid? This is a question of epistemology: a just epistemology. The second concerns the question of strategy: even if we accept food security as the consensus goal, how can it be realised? Rights are seen as a key strategy for realisation. For example, we can think of access to food—at least a certain amount—as enshrined into a justiciable right. But can such justiciability ensure an end to hunger? The empirical evidence on justiciable rights is not heartening.[22] However, as Sen correctly points out, the impossibility or unfeasibility of realising rights maximally should not deter us from asserting the ethical status of what those rights seek. In fact, as he further points out, the very process of claiming a certain right might stimulate much needed processes of social change. I will return to this below.

A further critical problem with regard to justiciability needs to be mentioned here. This concerns the corroboration between the right-holder and the obligation-bearer, without which a right does not really become a right. The rights discourse has seen an evolution of thinking with regard to the issue of corroboration—from an early history of perfect obligations towards what may be called imperfect obligations. This may have had the contradictory effect of making rights easier to formalise but more difficult to realise. Yet, this loosening of the corroboration is not necessarily accepted by social movements. In India, for example, the Right to Food movement clearly identifies the state as the obligation-bearer, with the requirement that the state intervenes in the production and distribution of food in very specific ways. Clearly locating the obligation to fulfil the right to food in the state, as the Right to Food movement seeks to do, can have far-reaching implications.

We can now summarise the above discussion. First, while the search for any consensus on a transcendental ideal of justice may indeed be unfeasible and unnecessary, it would be quite impossible to arrive democratically at a strategy for realising justice without focusing on the foundational question of what constitutes justice (and injustice). In the example that I have given here, the debate would focus on whether the goal to be realised is more food or greater control of the production of food. A simple consensus such as 'less injustice' means that less hunger does not advance us very far towards the realisation of that goal.

Secondly, given the problems of generating a democratic consensus, a major concern is to justify—politically and epistemologically—the particular path towards

---

[22] A Sengupta, 'On the Theory and Practice of the Right to Development' (2002) 24 *Human Rights Quarterly* 837.

justice that we choose to take. From whose perspective should we derive this justification: the philosopher, the corporation, the government, the large landowner, the small
farmer or the landless labourer (who is also, tragically, the hungry)? The problem
is more severe if the paths suggested by these actors appear contradictory. Indeed,
one argument, that business, governments and international institutions are increasingly making, is that the right to food requires more food and hence more corporate
involvement (including in food aid). A justiciable right to food, unaccompanied by
other kinds of structural change, can indeed justify such increased corporatisation.
This *problématique* emerges from the very nature of the distributive paradigm and
fundamentally affects the conceptualisation of rights. As Iris Young argues,

> rights are not fruitfully conceived as possessions. Rights are relationships, not things; they are
> institutionally defined rules specifying what people can do in relation to one another. Rights
> refer to doing more than having, to social relationships that enable or constrain action.[23]

In other words, the actual viability of rights is dependent on the underlying structures
and the social relations that are implied by them.

## II.2. The Understanding of Agency

As we know, much of the conventional literature on development sees institutions,
most importantly the state and international institutions, as the primary agent of
development. The critical difference between human-development approaches and conventional approaches is that the former see the institutions as the enablers of human
development; conventional approaches see the development of institutions itself as
development (the 'modern' state; the market; the corporate economy; etc). We can
identify two sets of problems in this view of agency.

First, many of the actions undertaken by states and institutions must rely primarily
on voluntarism: it requires actors such as large corporations and international institutions to act voluntarily, often in contradiction with their structural interests. The
limitations and contradictions of voluntarism are now well documented. A relevant
example can be found in the discourse on corporate social responsibility or self-regulation by corporations.[24]

In his conceptualisation of the connection between rights and development, Sen
emphasises the role of rights in overcoming precisely this problem of voluntarism.
Having a right to human development 'takes us beyond the *idea* of human development', by enabling individuals to make claims on other individuals and institutions to
ensure the fulfilment of their goals via the realisation of those rights.[25] In other words,
it makes it easier to 'locate accountability' in the system, and attempt to translate that
accountability into real social change. The UN Declaration on the Right to Develop-

[23] Young, n 17 above, 25.
[24] See, eg the UN Global Compact, available at www.unglobalcompact.org.
[25] United Nations Development Programme, HDR, *Human Rights and Human Development* (New York,
United Nations, 2000). See the Introduction by A Sen, 21; emphasis added.

ment sought to do exactly this, and its (very) limited success remains an indicator of the problems in this regard.[26]

Specifically, this illustrates the problem of corroboration between rights-bearers and obligation-bearers, ie of assigning obligations and responsibilities to the individuals and the institutions that are the designated agents of human development. Even if we accept some flexibility here, not much can be gained if rights are not attached to obligations. As I mentioned above, social movements seek to use rights not only to assert the ethical status of their claims, but also to realise them. There are several intractable complexities here. First, flexibility regarding the corroboration of rights-bearers and obligation-bearers might make it easier to institute rights, but would dramatically reduce their ability to address the underlying injustice. Secondly, such flexibility might allow the obligation-bearer to pass on the costs of bearing the obligation or to opt out of it somehow, as in the case of corporations which relocate to territories with weaker labour laws. Finally, there is the well-known problem of rights being violated where the aggrieved party is not in a position to challenge the violation. A prime example here are migrant workers who have (some) rights in countries such as Canada, but whose structural vulnerability prevents them from realising those rights. In fact, one may argue that the rights granted to them serve to exploit those structural vulnerabilities rather than to provide them with the tools with which to overcome them. Canada's formal schemes for migrant work lauded in the Human Development Report 2009 are examples of such an anomaly.[27]

This brings us to a key point about rights. Under certain circumstances, rights can be useful tools for realising justice and transcending the problems of welfarism and voluntarism that have historically plagued development. Central to these problems is a separation between the agents of development (such as the state) and the beneficiaries of development (such as the poor). A rights-based approach may help us to realise a more agent-centred vision of development, but only if we agree to engage fully with the *problématique* of power, in particular social power, as I argue below.

However, if we take rights simply as an instrument to realise a consensus, such as Smith's 'freedom from shame' threshold, Nussbaum's 'decent social minimum' or the Millennium Development Goals, then the pathway to justice remains tenuous. As I noted above, each of these seek distributional guarantees within highly unequal structures. They might be useful first steps, provided they keep open, rather than obfuscate, reasoned public debate on structural inequality. But the real arguments for systematically integrating a rights approach to development—as well as its limitations—are most apparent when we examine the question of (social) power.

---

[26] The Declaration on the Right to Development, adopted 4 December 1986, GA Res 41/128 UN GAOR, 41st Session, 3, Annex, UN Doc A/Res/41/128 Annex (1987).
[27] A Mukherjee-Reed, 'Migration and Unfreedom', *Oneworld South Asia*, 13 October 2010, available at http://southasia.oneworld.net/weekend/migration-and-unfreedom.

### III. AN ALTERNATIVE APPROACH: HUMAN DEVELOPMENT AND SOCIAL POWER

The critique above suggests several elements which are necessary for an alternative conceptualisation of development. These are:

- acknowledging the centrality of power and unequal power relations;
- a notion of social justice that goes beyond the distributive paradigm; and
- a notion of agency that overcomes this disjuncture between the agents and the beneficiaries of development.

Drawing upon the above, I propose an alternative notion which sees human development as the mobilisation of social power. The goal of such mobilisations is to address issues of structural inequality. Let me briefly discuss its main characteristics.

### III.1. Notion of structure

As opposed to the Rawlsian notion of basic structure, I take structure to be an essentially dualistic entity: on the one hand, it constitutes the conditions which actors confront and under which they act; on the other hand, structures are also produced by human action. Human action or agency both changes and reinforces structures. Structures also necessarily have multiple dimensions. These multiple dimensions exist in specific relationships with one another, and the specificity of these relationships and the interconnections between the dimensions is what constitutes structure. These interconnections are historically engendered. History ascribes a relative permanence, but not complete immutability, to structures. Most importantly, these interconnections between the multiple dimensions of structures are not neutral, but are embodiments of the underlying matrices of power.[28] The interconnectedness of the matrices of power is crucial to the understanding of human development. It suggests that human development cannot be addressed in a piecemeal manner, or as a *smorgasbord* of goals, however pragmatic they may be.[29]

---

[28] I draw this notion of structure from a number of seminal authors, including Marx. The most recent synthesis of the notion that I have drawn on appears in IM Young, *Inclusion and Democracy* (Oxford, Oxford University Press, 2000). The other authors upon whom I have drawn are: AK Bagchi, 'Freedom and Development as End of Alienation?' (2000) 35 *Economic & Political Weekly* 4408; RW Cox, *Production, Power and World Order* (New York, Columbia University Press, 1987).

[29] As Marilyn Frye said while alluding to her well-known metaphor of the bird cage: 'Consider a birdcage. If you look very closely at just one wire in the cage, you cannot see the other wires. If your conception of what is before you is determined by this myopic focus, you could look at one wire, up and down the length of it, and be unable to see why a bird would not just fly around the wire any time it wanted to go somewhere. Furthermore, even if, one day at a time, you myopically inspected each wire, you still could not see why a bird would have trouble going past the wires to get anywhere. There is no physical property of any one wire, nothing that the closest scrutiny could discover, that will reveal how a bird could be inhibited or harmed by it except in the most accidental way. It is only when you step back, stop looking at the wires one by one, microscopically, and take a macroscopic view of the whole cage, that you can see why the bird does not go anywhere; and then you will see it in a moment. It will require no great subtlety of mental powers. It is perfectly obvious that the bird is surrounded by a network of systematically related barriers, no one of which would be the least hindrance to its flight, but which, by their relations to each other, are as confining as the solid walls of a dungeon . . . It is now possible to grasp one of the reasons why oppression can be hard to see and recognize: one can study the elements of an oppressive structure

Structural inequality, as derived from this notion of structure, concerns the unequal relationships between collective entities or social groups, rather than between individuals. Social groups are defined from a structural social-relations perspective—as a 'collective of persons differentiated from others by cultural forms, practices, special needs or capacities, structures of power or privilege'.[30] In this view, social groups are expressions of social relations: 'a group exists only in relation to one other group . . . arising from social relations and processes'. They 'have similar structural locations that similarly condition their opportunities and life-chances, and similarly constrain or enable their ability to act as agents'.[31] This is substantially different from the notion of plurality, diversity or difference, which is typically the focus of identity politics. Relationships between these groups are structural; relations between groups are necessarily unequal. It is this structural inequality, I wish to argue, that should be the subject matter of human development.

## III.2. Power and Social Power

Power has been theorised in many different ways by a range of scholars, such as Michel Foucault, Nancy Fraser, Nancy Hartsock, Steven Lukes and Michael Mann.[32] Mann, most notably, writes about social power as the power exercised by the state over society through its various institutions. I take social power to do the exact opposite: the power of society to exercise power over the state or similar institutions. As such, my view of social power begins with a distinction between state power, economic power, political power and social power, a distinction that is stylistic but necessary for our purpose.[33]

John Friedmann, in his work *Empowerment*, gives us some important pointers drawing upon the rich tradition of Latin American thought on agency and power from below. In contrast to other forms of power, social power emanates at the local level, and from fundamentally different bases from which state power, economic power and political power arise. Friedmann identifies eight bases of social power: defensible life space; surplus time; knowledge and skills; appropriate information; social organisation; social networks; instruments of work and livelihood; and financial resources.

For Friedmann, levels of social power are determined by the levels of access and control over these bases. As social power is enhanced, so is political power, and it is eventually through the mobilisation of political power that transformations come about. Empowerment and development, in Friedmann's framework, constitute the increase in access to these bases of social power. But there is a clearly discernible

---

with great care and some good will without seeing the structure as a whole, and hence without seeing or being able to understand that one is looking at a cage and that there are people there who are caged, whose motion and mobility are restricted, whose lives are shaped and reduced'; see M Frye, *The Politics of Reality: Essays in Feminist Theory* (Trumansburg, NY, The Crossing, 1983) 18.

[30] Young, n 28 above, 90.

[31] Ibid, 90.

[32] N Folbre, *Who Pays for the Kids? Gender and the Structure of Constraint* (London, Routledge, 1994); M Foucault, 'Two Lectures' in M Foucault and C Gordon (eds), *Power/Knowledge: Selected Interviews and Other Writings, 1972–1977* (New York, Pantheon, 1980); N Fraser, *Unruly Practices: Power, Discourse, and Gender in Contemporary Social Theory* (Minneapolis, MN, University of Minnesota Press, 1989).

[33] J Friedmann, *Empowerment: The Politics of Alternative Development* (Oxford, Blackwell Publishers, 1992).

tension in Friedmann about the relationship between development as goal and development as process. If development is the increase in access to the bases identified above, then it begs the question as to how this increase in access is to materialise. One can think of two possible trajectories. The first is that development must first be effected through official policy (ie from above) in order to increase access to the bases of social power (this, in turn, leads to empowerment). The second is a trajectory from below: citizens/social groups attempt to increase their access to the bases of power through acts of struggle, ie the mobilisation of social power. While Friedmann seems to indicate the latter, he also sees an increase in the access to the bases as a prerequisite for empowerment and development.

The way out of this conundrum is to focus on the processes through which social and political power is mobilised. Thus, I wish to suggest a conceptualisation that sees human development as one of these processes of mobilising social power. But mobilisation for what goal? In order to delineate a notion of development, as it were, the focus should lie on the processes, not on any specific goal. The specific goals are to be determined by the struggles in question. But some discussion on what drives these mobilisations is necessary, in particular some reflections on the notion of justice which determines the goals which the various struggles adopt.

### III.3. Notion of Justice

As I pointed out above, the capability approach is located within a distributive paradigm of justice. Put very simply, the distributive paradigm is not concerned with structures or structural inequality. It is concerned with altering regimes of distribution within given structures. An alternative notion of justice would focus, on the other hand, on altering the structures which produce these distributions. This is what Young has called an 'enabling conception of justice'.[34] Its emphasis is on the creation of the institutional conditions necessary to enable social groups to challenge and alter structural inequality.[35] To go back to our example of the issue of hunger, this would entail two things: control over the production of food, land reforms, etc, as well as a policy process which is not systematically exclusionary.

### III.4. Agency

Agency, then, is the collective effort to address structural inequality by altering structural locations of social groups. Specifically, the goal of the agent, in this model, is not to change his or her individual relationship to structures (or components thereof), but the structure itself. Critical to this process will be the efforts to affect institutions, such

---

[34] Young, n 17 above, 39.

[35] The debate on approaches to social justice is obviously a substantive one and I adopt here a very specific formulation following Young. Of particular importance to the broader problematic of distributive/social justice are: BA Ackerman, *Social Justice in the Liberal State* (New Haven, CT, Yale University Press, 1980); GA Cohen, 'Where the Action Is: On the Site of Distributive Justice' (1997) 26 *Philosophy and Public Affairs* 3; R Dworkin, 'In Defense of Equality' (1983) 1 *Social Philosophy and Policy* 24; S-C Kolm, *Macrojustice: The Political Economy of Fairness* (New York, Cambridge University Press, 2005).

as the state, which have the power to alter incentive structures between social groups. This would involve forcing states to move beyond the provision of services, such as basic education or basic health care, into areas such as substantive fiscal redistribution; the redistribution of critical resources (for example, land); the decommodification of basic needs (for example, water, education); and devising policies that prevent private actors from contributing to structural inequality.[36] Needless to say, these types of action cannot emerge voluntarily from the state, but only through the mobilisation of social and political power by ordinary citizens. As such, the processes through which the forms of states and regimes are altered are themselves critical components of human development.

This kind of agency is mobilised irrespective of the degrees of access which agents have to the bases of social or political power. In this sense, this conception disagrees with the other approaches which see human development as a prerequisite for the mobilisation of agency. The social-power approach sees this relationship dialectically. Human development requires the mobilisation of agency from below; similarly, human development strengthens the mobilisation of such agency.

## IV. RIGHTS AND SOCIAL POWER: SOME QUESTIONS

The above discussion suggests several questions:

1. Is there any value added in taking social power and structural inequality as the focus of the rights/development discourse?
2. What role can rights have in the mobilisation of social power? Are rights to be treated as instruments for the mobilisation of social power? Is social power to be mobilised for the development of new rights? Which is more likely to address structural inequality?

I would argue that it is imperative to introduce the issues of power and structural inequality into rights/development discourses if they are to be informed by transformative or enabling notions of justice. As A Cornwall and C Nyambu-Musembi argue, rights-based approaches gained popularity in the 1990s precisely because they made possible the exclusion of global inequality from discourses on development. Associated with this popularity was also a severance between the rights-bearers and the duty-bearers.

In fact, even though rights-bearing approach language is being employed in the contexts of international cooperation and aid, it is quite clear that the funder countries, while insisting that they now see the people in the recipient countries as

---

[36] It might not appear pragmatic to suggest that states should be urged to take on responsibilities greater than delivering—or even guaranteeing—basic needs at a moment when they are resisting even that. But, as I have argued elsewhere, it is not possible to get states to deliver on basic needs, however minimal, unless citizens can challenge the state to address the structural causes behind the pervasive failure of basic needs guarantees. This is what one sees in the failure of the MDGs. The pitfalls of the 'pragmatism' inherent in such approaches to development can be understood best in terms of Habermas's classic distinction between *techne* and *praxis*. See J Habermas, *Theory and Practice* (Boston, MA, Beacon Press, 1973).

rights-bearers, do not see themselves as bearing any defined duties that contribute to the concrete realisation of these rights.[37]

Secondly, rights discourses may well endorse models of development that contradict the concerns of ordinary citizens. The World Bank, for instance, has embraced a right-based discourse simply to promote the privatisation of resources, most notably land, water and public utilities. As shown above, these trends are in direct contradiction to the directions in which global social movements are seeking change.

The current struggles in India over the enactment of the Food Security Act illustrates both the possibilities and the contradictions of rights-based approaches. On the one hand, it exemplifies *par excellence* how the power of social mobilisation can lead to the formalisation of a set of justiciable rights. The Right to Food Campaign, which grew out of public-interest litigations, has resulted in 44 'interim orders' issued by the Supreme Court. A number of key policy measures, such as the National Rural Employment Guarantee Act (NREGA), the Integrated Child Development Services (ICDS), the Mid-day Meals (MDM) scheme and, most notably, the Food Security Act mentioned above, are all consequences of this process.[38] Moreover, the Campaign led to the creation of judicial structures for monitoring and assessing the performance of the delivery of food as stipulated in the interim orders. The combination of social mobilisation and public-interest litigation has, indeed, been remarkable. On the other hand, and given the level of public action that it achieved, it is rather stunning that the Food Security Act, which is seen to be the ultimate formalisation of the demand mobilised by this process, encapsulates an absolutely minimalist idea of the right to food. As the Campaign has stated:

> This draft is not only a betrayal of the people of India but also is in contempt of the letter and spirit of the orders of the Supreme Court . . . This draft completely ignores the multiple entitlements which constitute the right to food of all ages of people and all sections of society including vulnerable groups . . . A legislation that promises a 'right' but in reality *reduces the existing entitlement* is completely unacceptable to the people of India and an affront on their dignity. (Right to Food Campaign, 2010)

Two points are critical here. The first is that the proposed act actually seeks to diminish the entitlements provided in the Supreme Court writ petitions. Why? Because, once the right is formalised, the government will have the legal obligation of ensuring sufficient resources for honouring the entitlement. Clearly, the Indian policy-making élite is wary of making such a commitment—even when hunger and malnutrition are at unprecedented levels. Ironically, as the Food Security Act envisions the right to food primarily as the commitment of the state to guarantee the poor a certain quantity of subsidised food grain, much effort is being made to limit the number of the poor.

---

[37] A Cornwall and C Nyamu-Musembi, 'Putting the "Rights-Based Approach" to Development into Perspective' (2004) 25 *Third World Quarterly* 1415.

[38] In April 2001, People's Union for Civil Liberties (PUCL) filed a 'writ petition' on the right to food in the Supreme Court (PUCL v Union of India and Others, Writ Petition (Civil) 196 of 2001). It was filed 'at a time when the country's food stocks reached unprecedented levels' while hunger in drought-affected areas intensified. The case was first brought against the Government of India, the Food Corporation of India and six state governments, with a backdrop of inadequate drought relief. Subsequently, the case was extended to the larger issues of chronic hunger and undernutrition, and all the state governments were added to the list of 'respondents'. This is popularly known as the Right-to-Food case. The legal basis of the case lies in Art 21 of the Indian Constitution, which guarantees the right to life and ascribes to the state the responsibility to protect it. Available at http://www.righttofoodindia.org/case/petition_sum.html.

While this is being framed as a contestation between various methodologies to ascertain the number of poor, one detects a concern to minimise, or at least contain, the absolute number of beneficiaries of this act. Secondly, the campaign also demanded protection from commercialisation and corporate involvement if they threatened to impinge on the right to food. These concerns are obviously excluded from the draft bill. None of this is, of course, surprising, but it nonetheless raises questions about the transformative role of rights, and, more fundamentally, about the relationship between rights and power.[39]

This is clearly manifested in the way the public debate about the right to food is evolving in India. While there is considerable public interest in institutionalising a universally guaranteed right to food, the government is insisting on a targeted approach. Under targeting, the state establishes criteria to determine which groups truly deserve the benefits which it chooses to offer. Universal regimes, on the other hand, give benefits to the entire population as a matter of right. In India's vast and growing landscape of hunger, targeting means choosing between the destitute, the poor and the barely surviving; or, if you like, the starving, the chronically hungry, the malnourished, the anaemic and the food insecure.

Naturally, where the need for support is so pervasive, targeting constitutes a rather difficult exercise: one that involves some serious questions of justice and democracy.[40]

First, we might ask if a right based upon targeting can be considered to be a right at all? It certainly cannot qualify as an inalienable right, as other human rights are, and would contradict the International Covenant on Economic, Social and Cultural Rights.[41] By vesting the authority to determine who is entitled to this right in the state, it reduces the right to a matter of discretion, or, at best, a highly tenuous and negotiable moral obligation. Legislation based upon such an unclear distinction between rights and discretion can be rather dangerous, particularly where so many lives (literally) hang in balance.

Secondly, targeting involves very serious questions of justice. How can the state justly choose the most deserving? How does it determine what is a just distribution of food? Can the question be settled justly if the poor and the hungry are systematically excluded from these discourses?

A targeted approach to food (or basic needs) denies self-determination. A universal approach avoids the injustice of violating self-determination. However, a universal approach may err in that it treats unequals as equals, by giving the hungry and the non-hungry the same right. But so does electoral democracy in deeply unequal societies. We nevertheless still guarantee some universal rights—the right to vote, for instance. And even if inequality prevents the substantive enjoyment of such universal rights by all, the way to reduce the conflict between democracy and inequality would be to reduce inequality rather than dilute democracy. The same goes for a right as

[39] After an extremely long, arduous and conflictual process; see http://www.righttofoodindia.org/data/right_to_food_act_data/RTF_campaign_response_to_Standing_Committee_recommendations%20on_NFSB_January_2013_English_summary.pdf.

[40] See A Mukherjee-Reed, 'Wrongs about the Right to Food', *Outlook India*, 8 September 2010, available at http://www.outlookindia.com/article.aspx?267030.

[41] International Covenant on Economic, Social and Cultural Rights. Adopted and opened for signature, ratification and accession by General Assembly resolution 2200A (XXI) of 16 December 1966; entry into force 3 January 1976, in accordance with Art 27, available at http://www2.ohchr.org/english/law/cescr.htm.

vital as the right to food—the solution is not to restrict the right but to remove the constraints that prevent it from being enjoyed equally by all. A targeted approach takes these constraints as given. It allows the state to invoke those constraints constantly, negotiate its targets and manoeuvre its obligations to the hungry. The state still retains the power to decide who it wants to feed and when. The citizens' right to food becomes a residual of state power.

Most critically, targeting removes from public scrutiny—and the purview of legislation—the fundamental reasons as to why the state's constraints come to exist in the first place. The government contends that there is neither enough money nor enough grain to guarantee universal access. Why is this the case? Could more money be available, for example, through greater pro-poor fiscal strategies? Could more grain be available by reversing policies which force farmers out of farming? It is precisely in this potential to raise such questions that the greatest strength of universalism lies. By giving every citizen a right to food, it creates an obligation for the state to reorder its priorities, rather than constantly pleading resource constraints. It reduces the state's room for manoeuvring its obligations towards reducing hunger. In sum, it gives citizens greater ammunition to scrutinise state power and how it is applied in defining constraints and priorities of public policy. Needless to say, by 'state power' I do not simply mean the power of particular governments, but the power of the state as an institution, which constitutes, and is constituted by, the unequal power relations that exist in society.

## V. CONCLUSIONS

The above discussion points to two main insights. The first is that it is important to see rights as one moment in a broader process of social mobilisation. When rights get formalised as a result of social struggles or mobilisation, then their transformative potential is greater, even if the actual content of the formalised rights does not fully accommodate the goals of the social struggles. What it unleashes, then, is an iterative process where social struggles can build on their initial successes and failures. If, on the other hand, rights are used as a tool to normalise or legitimise exclusionary practices and are applied within a development framework that consciously occludes relations of power, then the rights approach would run the risk of violating its fundamental ethical premise.

# 4

# Is a New 'TREMF' Human Rights Paradigm Emerging? Evidence from Nigeria*

OBIORA CHINEDU OKAFOR

## I. INTRODUCTION

IN *THE FUTURE of Human Rights*,[1] Upendra Baxi developed a germinal thesis on the steady supplanting, in our time, of the paradigm of the Universal Declaration of Human Rights (UDHR) by an emergent trade-related market-friendly human rights (TREMF) paradigm. In a subsequent contribution, Baxi ably applied this thesis to his analysis of the UN Norms on the Responsibilities of Transnational Corporations and Other Business Enterprises with Regard to Human Rights Norms formulated under the auspices of the (now defunct?) UN Sub-Commission on the Promotion and Protection of Human Rights.[2] As stated by Baxi himself, his overarching TREMF thesis is that:

> The paradigm of the Universal Declaration of Human Rights is being steadily, but surely, *supplanted* by that of trade related, market-friendly human rights. This new paradigm seeks to reverse the notion that universal human rights are designed for the attainment of the dignity and well-being of human beings and for enhancing the security and well being of socially, economically and civilisationally vulnerable peoples and communities.[3]

In my own view, a number of related sub-claims are embedded in Baxi's overarching thesis. These sub-claims will be isolated and discussed in the next section.

The objective of the present enquiry is to assess some of these sub-claims in the light of the available evidence regarding the intense contestations and confrontations that have occurred during the 1999–2005 period between the politically and economi-

---

* This chapter is a modified version of a previously published article entitled 'Assessing Baxi's Thesis on an Emergent Trade-Related Market-Friendly Human Rights Paradigm: Recent Evidence from Nigerian Labour-led Struggles' [2007] *Law, Social Justice and Development*, available at http://www.go.warwick.ac.uk/elj/lgd/2007_1/okafor.

[1] See U Baxi, *The Future of Human Rights* (Delhi, Oxford University Press, 2002) 131–66.

[2] U Baxi, 'Market Fundamentalisms: Business Ethics at the Altar of Human Rights' (2005) 5 *Human Rights Law Review* 1.

[3] Ibid, n 1 above, 132. Emphasis added.

cally transitional Obasanjo-led regime that governed Nigeria at that time and a local labour-led coalition.[4] To this end, the chapter has been organised into four main segments, including this introduction. In Section II, a more detailed explication of the particular sub-claims of Baxi's TREMF thesis, with which we are concerned in this chapter, is undertaken. This is followed, in Section III, by a description and an analysis of the character of the contestations and confrontations over socio-economic reforms that have characterised government/labour relations during Nigeria's immediate post-1999 economic and political transition. In Section IV, an assessment of the explanatory power of the Baxian thesis in relation to this Nigerian evidence is offered.

## II. ON THE NATURE OF THE BAXIAN TREMF THESIS

In the course of fleshing out his thought-provoking TREMF thesis, Baxi developed a number of distinguishable, but intimately related, sub-claims. Only some of these sub-claims concern us here. The first such sub-claim is that the emergent TREMF paradigm (unlike the UDHR paradigm) insists on promoting and protecting the collective human rights of various formations of global capital mostly at the direct expense of human beings and communities.[5] The distinctive quality here is Baxi's notion of the assignment of human (as opposed to ordinary legal) rights to various formations of global capital. To Baxi, the UDHR paradigm differs from the TREMF paradigm in this way because, although the UDH did make provision for a right to property that can be read to benefit any person (including presumably corporations and business associations), in the end, the notion of property in the UDHR is itself left substantially unsettled.[6] On the other hand, the TREMF paradigm makes the protection of the property interests of various formations of global capital central to its conception of the global social order. What is more, neither of the two main legally binding human rights covenants (the international covenant on civil and political rights and its sister covenant on economic, social and cultural rights) makes provision for property rights.[7] Thus, to Baxi, 'to say that the [TREMF paradigm] . . . is just an unfoldment of the potential of [the] UDHR is plainly incorrect'.[8]

The second sub-claim is that, much more than in the past, the progressive state (or, at a minimum, the progressive Third World state) is now conceived as one that is a good host to global capital; as one that protects global capital against political instability and market failure, usually at a significant cost to the most vulnerable among its own citizens; and as one that is, in reality, more accountable to the IMF and the World Bank than to its own citizens. According to this TREMF mindset, progressive states are those states that are much more soft than hard towards global capital.[9]

The third Baxian sub-claim is that the new global order also requires the reproduc-

---

[4] This is not, of course, the first time that Baxi's work on the interconnection among globalisation, development and human rights has been applied by other scholars. For instance, see A Anghie, 'Time Present and Time Past: Globalization, International Financial Institutions, and the Third World' (2000) 32 *New York University Journal of International Law and Politics* 243.

[5] Ibid.

[6] Ibid, 144.

[7] Ibid, 145.

[8] Ibid.

[9] Ibid, 141.

tion of a core of internal hardness within these same generally soft states. Thus, to paraphrase Baxi, a progressive state is also conceived, under the TREMF paradigm, as a state which is market efficient in suppressing and delegitimating the human rights-based practices of the resistance on the part of its own citizens, and which is also capable of unleashing (and, when necessary, does in fact unleash) a reign of terror on some of its citizens, especially those who actively oppose its excessive softness towards global capital.

The fourth such sub-claim is that, unlike the UDHR paradigm, the TREMF paradigm denies a significant redistributive role to the state.[10] In fleshing out this fourth sub-claim, Baxi argues that the UDHR paradigm which 'assigned human responsibilities to states . . . to construct, progressively and within the community of states, a just social order, national and global, that will at least meet the basic needs of human beings', is being pushed aside to a worrisome extent by a TREMF paradigm, which, in contrast, 'denies any significant redistributive role to the state; calls upon the state [and world order] to free as many spaces for capital as possible, initially by pursuing the three-Ds of contemporary globalization: deregulation, denationalization, and disinvestment'.[11]

These are the sub-claims the contextual and localised validity of which will, to some extent, be ascertained in this chapter. This will be done through a case study of government/labour confrontations over socio-economic reforms in Nigeria (1999–2005). To this end, the next section will focus on describing and analysing the nature of these government/labour confrontations. Emphasis will be placed on a discussion of the nature of the controversial reforms; the labour-led mass resistance to a key aspect of these reforms; the government's heightened repressive stance towards such resistance efforts; and the relative acquiescence—or, at least, studied ignorance—of key international actors in relation to the government's repressive behaviour.

Following the next section, the TREMF thesis will be situated within the specific Nigerian context and evaluated for its explanatory power in relation to that environment.

## III. THE GOVERNMENT/LABOUR CONFRONTATION IN NIGERIA (1999–2005)

### III.1. Neo-liberal Socio-economic Reform and Massive Fuel Price Hikes

Substantially in line with the earlier structural adjustment programmes (SAPs) that have been implemented in Nigeria and pursuant to the requirements of its latest IMF, World Bank (WB) and USA/EU inspired and backed socio-economic reform plan, the Obasanjo-led Nigerian government has, since 1999, embarked on a programme of state deregulation, denationalisation and disinvestment.[12] Sold as a homegrown

---

[10] Ibid, 139.

[11] Ibid, 139. Emphasis added.

[12] On the nature of earlier SAPs in Nigeria, see P Mosley, 'Policy-Making without Facts: A Note on the Assessment of Structural Adjustment Policies in Nigeria, 1985–1990' (1992) 91 *African Affairs* 227, 228–30; and JO Ihonvbere, 'Economic Crisis, Structural Adjustment and Social Crisis in Nigeria' (1993) 21 *World Development* 141, 143. For the IMF's and the WB's inspiration and support of the current reform

set of policies,[13] the main thrust of the current reform programme is the removal of subsidies on petroleum products (leading inexorably to massive fuel price increases), the retrenchment of about 40% of the staff of the federal civil service (euphemistically referred to as 'rightsizing') and the privatisation of state-controlled enterprises (leading, in most cases, to denationalisation and the creation of an economic bonanza for a tiny cabal).[14] This reform programme is most notably stated (or perhaps restated) in the so-called NEEDS Document.[15] In line with the dominant orthodoxy, this reform programme was often touted by the Obasanjo regime and its international backers as the solution to Nigeria's socio-economic woes.

While several contentious issues can be discerned from the above description of the Nigerian government's reform programme, the main focus of this government/labour confrontation during the 1999–2005 period was the rapid skyrocketing of motor-vehicle fuel prices in Nigeria.[16] As one of the three central and inextricable components of the government's reform programme, cumulatively massive and separately substantial increases in fuel prices were implemented by the Obasanjo regime. Between May 1999 and August 2005, fuel prices were hiked by a steep total margin approaching a huge 250% or so, bringing Nigerian fuel prices virtually in line with the prices that currently apply in many of the far richer developed countries. Yet, by the Obasanjo regime's own acknowledgement, the vast majority of the Nigerian population (over 70% by most accounts) were living below the poverty line.[17] What is more, as the then Lagos State Governor Ahmed Bola Tinubu noted, most Nigerians seemed to be worse off in 2005, after six years of formal democratic rule by the Obasanjo regime, than they were before 1999, when they were ruled by various military juntas. In the Governor's own words:

> the level of poverty in the country today is . . . unacceptable . . . There is nothing more heart-rending than hearing the teeming masses of our people cry daily that they are worse off economically and socially today than they were before the democratic restoration of 1999.[18]

Thus, the fact that the government/labour confrontation that concerns us here revolved mainly around fuel prices is not surprising, given the increasing poverty among a vastly impoverished Nigerian population and the centrality of the price of fuel to their survival within this harsh local economy.

---

programme see IMF, 'Semi-Annual Staff Report under Intensified Surveillance: Nigeria, 2004', IMF Country Report No 05/37 (February 2005) 1; S Amadi, 'Contextualizing NEEDS: Political and Economic Development' in S Amadi and F Ogwo (eds), *Contextualizing NEEDS: Economic/Political Reform in Nigeria* (Lagos, HURILAWS and CPPR, 2004) 12–19.

[13] See O Obasanjo, 'Briefing to the National Assembly on the Report of the National Political Reform Conference and Recent Debt Relief Granted to Nigeria', 26 July 2005, available at http://www.dawodu.com/obas42.htm (last accessed on 3 October 2005).

[14] See 'Trade Policy Report Review: Report by Nigeria', WT/TPR/G/147 (13 April 2005) 12; and *The Guardian*, 21 December 2003, available at http://www.dawodu.com/aluko75.htm (last accessed on 26 September 2005.

[15] See the National Economic Empowerment and Development Strategy (NEEDS) document, available at http://www.nigeria.gov.ng/eGovernment/Needs.PDF (accessed on 26 March 2006). For a critical assessment of the policy thrust of this document, see Amadi, n 12 above, 13.

[16] Hereinafter referred to as 'fuel prices'.

[17] See UNDP, Nigeria 2000/2001 Human Development Report (2001) 65; NEEDS, above n 15, 95.

[18] See *The Vanguard*, 15 September 2005, available at http://allafrica.com/stories/printable/200509150166.html (last accessed on 19 September 2005).

As might reasonably be expected, these massive fuel price hikes were as vastly unpopular among ordinary Nigerians as they were in the late 1980s and early 1990s, when the ruling military juntas implemented similar hikes at the behest of the IMF and the WB.[19] As in that earlier period, the Nigerian labour movement led a campaign of mass resistance to the implementation of these hikes. The next sub-section offers a brief analytical exposé of the story of this oppositional struggle.

### III.2. Labour-Led Mass Resistance

Charging—in Anghie-like terms—that the government's reform programme largely had the effect of 'augmenting inequality and impoverishment among the most vulnerable groups',[20] a coalition of activist forces that is led by the relatively powerful Nigerian Labour Congress (NLC) fought a sustained and gallant campaign of mass resistance against the massive fuel prices increases. This labour-led struggle against the harshness, in the specific Nigerian context, of the market logic of these fuel price hikes mainly took the form of general strikes that often paralysed the economy and always mobilised intense anti-government sentiment within the polity. Between 1999 and 2005, at least seven such strikes were called by the NLC and supported by a broad array of civil society groups. In a similar vein, a campaign of mass rallies and non-strike mass action was also called.

While nearly all of their acts of resistance were significant, the most significant of the seven general strikes that were mounted by this labour-led coalition in opposition to the fuel price hikes were the June 2000, June 2003 and June 2004 strikes. In response to the first increase of fuel prices announced in June 2000 by the Obasanjo government, the NLC led one of the most crippling and effective general strikes seen since the end of military rule in Nigeria. Oil workers were said to join public sector and transportation workers in ensuring the success of the strike.[21] Nigeria's main seaport in Lagos was blockaded, as were many highways.[22] International and domestic air flights were disrupted, and all fuel stations were closed.[23] Sporadic police and protester violence was reported across the country, and two police stations in the federal capital territory, Abuja, were burned down by irate mobs.[24] Similarly, after its call for dialogue with the government was basically ignored by the executive branch, despite being respected by the legislature and supported, to some degree, by some in the ruling party, the labour-led coalition launched another paralysing strike from 30 June 2003 that eventually lasted eight days. In the same vein, it took a failed NLC/government dialogue session and another three-day strike in June 2004 for the government to reverse that season's fuel price hike.[25] All of these strikes were relatively effective largely because they enjoyed the support of most Nigerians.

---

[19] See P Lewis, 'From Prebendalism to Predation: The Political Economy of Decline in Nigeria' (1996) 34 *The Journal of Modern African Studies* 79, 80–85.

[20] See Anghie, n 4 above, 252.

[21] See J Woodroffe and M Ellis-Jones, 'World Development Movement Report', available at http://www.wdm.org.uk/campaigns/cambriefs/debt/unrest.pdf (last accessed on 3 October 2005) 11.

[22] Ibid.

[23] Ibid.

[24] Ibid.

[25] Ibid.

The only non-strike mass campaign that this labour-led coalition conducted took place in September 2005. In what can be seen as a tentative and measured response to a court ruling that effectively held that the NLC could not organise anti-fuel price hike-strikes (since such strikes were, in the court's view, not related to the conditions of service of Nigerian workers),[26] the labour-led coalition decided to change its tactics somewhat and called for two weeks of rolling mass rallies to demonstrate the resistance of the vast majority of the Nigerian people to the government's sharp fuel price hikes. Peaceful demonstrations and rallies were held across Nigeria.[27] These events were massively attended.[28] For example, in Lagos, a mammoth crowd was mobilised which at one point stretched for nearly three kilometres.[29] NLC President Adams Oshiomole, the Catholic Archbishop of Lagos Olubunmi Okogie, Nobel prize-winner Wole Soyinka and Governor Bola Tinubu of Lagos state all supported and addressed this mass rally.

Thus, as shown above, the government's policy of massive fuel price increases (deregulation and disinvestment) in an atmosphere of mass grinding poverty met strong and sustained resistance from the vast majority of the Nigerian people, and it was the labour-led coalition that acted as the vanguard of this resistance campaign. Nevertheless, pressured as it was to wear a straitjacket that was largely tailored according to the familiar IMF/WB design, the Obasanjo government was predictably determined to push through this policy, even while massively alienating most of its citizens. Given the intensity of the local resistance to its objectives and the pressure it felt from the IMF/WB and other powerful global economic actors, this regime resorted all too often to tactics that were, at best, highly undemocratic and, at worst, brutally repressive. A brief version of the story of this repressive is told in the section that follows.

### III.3. The Obasanjo Regime's Assault on the Labour-Led Coalition and on Labour Rights

Although it made some modest concessions as a result of the mass resistance that was mobilised by the labour-led coalition against its series of massive fuel price hikes— including partially reversing some of the hikes[30] and declaring a time-limited moratorium in late 2005 on further hikes[31]—the Obasanjo regime's response to the labour-led

---

[26] See *Federal Government of Nigeria and another v Oshiomole and Nigeria Labour Congress*, Suit No FHC/ABJ/CS/52/2004, Abuja Division of the Federal high Court of Nigeria, 21 September 2004, per R Ukeje, CJ (on file with the author) 23–26. Hereinafter referred to as 'the Ukeje Ruling'.

[27] See http://news.bbc.co.uk/1/hi/world/africa/4244556.stm (last accessed on 3 October 2005).

[28] Ibid.

[29] Ibid.

[30] For instance, as a result of the June 2000 general strike, the government was forced to back down from almost all of its announced fuel price increases (that is from N20 to N30 and then back to N22 per litre). See http://news.bbc.co.uk/1/hi/world/africa/782242.stm (last accessed on 3 October 2005). In response to the June 2003 general strike, the government partially rescinded the fuel price increase. However, in line with its determination to implement its IMF/WB backed reforms, the government later raised these prices back to their pre-strike levels. See NLC, 'Report on the Fuel Price Strike 2003', available at http://www.nlcng.org/legislative/reportofthefuelstrike.htm (last accessed on 3 October 2005) 5.

[31] See O Obasanjo, '2005 Independence Day Speech', available at http://www.nigerianmuse.com/important_documents/?u=Obasanjo_independencespeech_October_1_2005.htm (last accessed on 5 October 2005). In this speech, Obasanjo announced that there would be no further fuel price hikes until the end of 2006 whatever the cost of crude oil or imported fuel in the international market. This was a very signifi-

resistance to the hikes was, for the most part, far from democratic. Indeed, it is better described as being mainly repressive of labour rights and freedoms.

Stung by the vast domestic popularity of the labour-led opposition, yet under great pressure to fit into the IMF/WB's straitjacket, the Obasanjo regime sought to defuse the negative effects on its already fragile popular legitimacy of the intense labour-led opposition to its fuel price hikes by attempting to limit, contain or stop entirely the general strikes that were called by the labour-led coalition. It made use of public appeals, obtained court rulings, and often ordered—or at least to a large extent tolerated—the harassment, assaults, detentions and killings perpetrated by the Nigerian police force on labour and allied activists, as well as on ordinary citizen protesters. While there are many examples of the kind of brutal repression to which this regime resorted, two specific examples will serve to illustrate this point. During the January 2002 general strike, Adams Oshiomole (the NLC president) and 10 other union activists were arrested and charged in court with 'organising an illegal strike'.[32] Approximately 20 and 16 NLC leaders were arrested and detained in Kaduna and Port Harcourt, respectively.[33] The police repeated and intensified this same pattern of brutality and repression during the June 2003 general strike.[34] Over sixteen lives were lost nationwide at the hands of police officers, and the police brutally assaulted dozens of others.[35] These two stories exemplify the Obasanjo regime's general reaction to the anti-fuel price hike resistance.

In a formally democratic, but still repressive, manner, the Obasanjo regime also pushed through legislation which sought to weaken significantly the labour-led coalition's capacity to paralyse economic and social activities in the country, and thus to reduce the coalition's ability to force the government to abandon or modify its highly unpopular fuel price increases.[36] This new legislation amended the Trade Unions Act of Nigeria and other allied legislation.[37] Under the new Act, labour unions could only declare a strike if their grievance with the government or their employer concerns a 'dispute of right' (defined as one arising directly and strictly from a collective agreement).[38] As such, strikes against fuel price hikes are presumably now outlawed under the new Act. Also health, education and other 'essential' workers (as defined under the Trade Disputes Act[39]) are now barred from ever declaring a strike.[40] Again, no labour union can declare a strike unless a simple majority of *all* union members

cant concession, given that, despite Nigeria's status as one of the world's largest oil producing countries, much of refined fuel consumed in Nigeria is now imported, and continues to be imported to date.

[32] See http://archives.cnn.com/2002/WORLD/africa/01/17/nigeria (last accessed on 3 October 2005).

[33] Ibid.

[34] See NLC, 'Report on the Fuel Price Strike 2003', available at http://www.nlcng.org/legislative/reportof-thefuelstrike.htm (last accessed on 3 October 2005) 6.

[35] Ibid.

[36] See the Trade Union (Amendment) Act, 2005, available at http://www.nigeria-law.org/TradeUnion(Amendment)Act2005.htm (last accessed on 23 September 2005). Hereinafter referred to as 'the new Act'.

[37] See the Trade Unions Act, Cap 437, Laws of the Federation of Nigeria, 1990; Decree No 4 of 1996; and Decree No 26 of 1996.

[38] See the new Act, n 36 above, s 6.

[39] See the First Schedule of the Trade Disputes Act, Cap 432, Laws of the Federation, 1990.

[40] See the new Act, n 36 above, s 6.

(not simply a majority of those who are present and vote) vote in favour of that course of action.[41]

As anti-Labour as the final legislation may seem, the original bill submitted to the National Assembly by the Obasanjo regime[42] was even more draconian. However, under pressure from the labour-led coalition and vocal sections of the Nigerian public, the National Assembly watered down that bill's much harsher proposals significantly. The three major, but highly consequential, amendments that the National Assembly made to the original bill was to expunge the government's proposal to ban strikes altogether, reduce the number of votes required for a union to declare a strike from a two-thirds majority to a simple majority, and expunge the mandate imposed on the Registrar of Trade Unions to deregister the NLC as the only central labour organisation in Nigeria.

Given the fact that the Obasanjo regime generally exhibited a broad semi-autocratic bent, it becomes apparent that the labour-led popular struggle against its reform project did not cause or create the autocratic instincts or behaviour of this regime.[43] However, the activities of this labour-led resistance to its IMF/WB inspired and supported fuel price hikes led to the intensification and accentuation of particular forms of government repression targeted at those who launched street protests and general strikes against the regime's highly unpopular policies and actions. It is therefore only logical that this regime singled out labour rights and freedoms for curtailment, and targeted the labour movement for weakening: it had to act in this repressive way in order to push the TREMF paradigm firmly through all the obstacles erected by a vastly resistant Nigerian population.

### III.4. The Western (Non-)Reaction: Studied Ignorance or Wilful Acceptance?

Although the Obasanjo regime is definitely not a 'bare knuckle' dictatorship of the Abacha kind,[44] given its visibly poor human rights record and in the light of Nigeria's very prominent stature both in Africa and in international relations, it is difficult to understand why the regime's behaviour was apparently acceptable to the international community. Why, one can ask, was the Obasanjo regime's suppression of labour rights and the labour movement in Nigeria any better or more benign than similar actions in Mugabe's Zimbabwe? Why did US President George W Bush claim in a manner that exemplified the favourable international view of the Obasanjo regime that 'because of your [Obasanjo's] forthrightness and your style and your commitment . . . I'm honoured to be here with you'?[45] Why did the then IMF resident representative in Nigeria laud President Obasanjo for his 'efforts to provide a brighter future for all

---

[41] Ibid.

[42] See A Bill for an Act to Amend the Trade Unions Act as Amended and for Matters Connected Therewith (on file with the author).

[43] See PC Aka, 'Nigeria Since May 1999: Understanding the Paradox of Civil Rule and Human Rights Violations under President Olusegun Obasanjo' (2003) 4 *San Diego International Law Journal* 209, 211, available at http://www.hrw.org/reports/2005/nigeria0705/1.htm (last accessed on 26 September 2005).

[44] On the nature of the Abacha regime, see A Olukotun, 'Authoritarian State, Crisis of Democratization and the Underground Media in Nigeria' (2002) 101 *African Affairs* 317.

[45] See http://nigeria.usembassy.gov/wwwhxaug03f.html (last accessed on 2 October 2005).

Nigerians'?[46] Does this international behaviour signify their studied ignorance or wilful acceptance of the crackdown on the labour-led coalition?

One of the most important of the many reasons that can be identified for this troubling Western/international attitude is that the Obasanjo regime was, on the whole, a strategic and key economic and political partner of the particular formations of global capital that have been most engaged with the Nigerian state, namely the key Western interests involved—be they the IMF/WB, the US/British governments or US/British investors. A dimension of this specific reason may be the fact that the regime faithfully implemented the key aspects of the reform agenda favoured by the IMF/WB and these key Western governments. Such reforms (especially the complete deregulation of the already largely denationalised petroleum sector) have enured or will probably enure in part to the benefit of many Western corporations, bankers, traders, investors and even citizens. These actors often benefit enormously from increased access to local markets, the sale of local refineries and increases in the prices of the fuel sold locally by the oil marketing multinationals.

The above evidence shows that substantive elements of the emerging shift towards the TREMF paradigm influenced the Nigerian government's thinking in their dogged implementation over time of a highly unpopular set of massive fuel price hikes. It also shaped the regime's desperately harsh reaction to the labour-led mass resistance to the hikes, and explains, in significant measure, the seeming international acceptance (or, at least, tolerance) of the supposedly democratic Obasanjo regime's repression of labour rights and movements.

## IV. ASSESSING THE BAXIAN TREMF THESIS

The focus of this section is to provide an analytical assessment of the possible explanatory power of the TREMF thesis in relation to the evidence that was discussed in the preceding section regarding the character of the government/labour confrontations over a key aspect of the Nigerian government's reform programme, and the seemingly studied ignorance or acceptance of the government's repressive behaviour by the international community. This evaluation will be conducted, in the first instance, through a consideration of each of the four sub-claims of the TREMF thesis that were isolated and briefly discussed in Section II. Following this discussion, further related insights will be offered.

Sub-claim one of the TREMF thesis, which posits that the emergent TREMF paradigm protects the collective human rights of global capital at the expense of the most vulnerable human beings, is, in my own view, proven to some extent by the discussion in Section III. To the extent that the praxis of the Obasanjo regime was that it went to great lengths and took serious political legitimacy risks in order to assign important property rights to elements of global capital (through the relative deregulation and denationalisation of the petroleum sector), its behaviour seems to support this particular sub-claim to a large extent. However, I reserve judgement, for now, as to the wisdom or otherwise of referring to the kind of entrenchment of property rights in favour of global capital that was witnessed in the Nigerian context as the

---

[46] See GG Moser, 'The IMF and Nigeria, an Enduring Relationship' (on file with the author) 1.

assignment of 'human' rights, as opposed to ordinary 'legal' rights. I agree with Baxi that, since many others have long appropriated the language of rights to the benefit of differing formations of global capital, the genie is already out of the discursive bottle. But to what extent must we reinscribe this discursive move? Is a refusal to name these TREMF rights 'human' in any sense an act of resistance? Of course, Baxi's thesis is, at one level, only descriptive as to the reality of the ongoing paradigmatic shift towards TREMF. In this descriptive sense, it is unassailable in my own view.

Sub-claim two insists that the emergent TREMF paradigm requires the (mostly Third World) states that want to earn the 'progressive' label to become good hosts (or—à la Baxi—good hostages) to the particular formations of global capital with which these states are engaged. This sub-claim is, in my view, largely proven by the discussion in Section III. To the extent that the Obasanjo regime went to great lengths, since 1999, to severely constrain labour rights in Nigeria and to weaken the Nigerian labour movement so as to make the country more hospitable to particular formations of global capital (such as the much sought after foreign investors) via the single-minded pursuit of its massive fuel price-hike policies in the face of massive disenchantment and resistance, there is strong evidence of the explanatory power of Baxi's TREMF thesis in this Nigerian context. Clearly, the Obasanjo regime sought to make Nigeria more hospitable to these elements of global capital by encouraging them to acquire very valuable property rights in the increasingly deregulated petroleum industry; undertook massive fuel price hikes to ensure that these property rights in the petroleum industry became even more valuable as a result of the increased profits that accrued from investing in them; and sought to ban, or at least tame, the general strikes and labour movement, which, in the government's view, created the kind of political instability that makes global capital averse to investing in the country. The regime has also sought to make the Nigerian state much more soft than hard towards the IMF/WB by faithfully adopting most of their demands for reform and being commended for so doing by these bodies, while all the while conveniently pretending that its key socio-economic reform policies are homegrown.[47]

As we have already seen, sub-claim three posits that the emergent TREMF paradigm in effect constructs the ideal (Third World) state as one that effectively implements the usually unpopular IMF/WB-style reform policies, and if necessary uses undemocratic, rough or even repressive tactics that overwhelm popular resistance to these policies. These are the kinds of states that often attract IMF/WB commendations.[48] This sub-claim is clearly supported by the evidence from Nigeria that is discussed in this chapter. As shown in Section III, the Obasanjo regime repeatedly and doggedly buried its fangs into the flesh of the labour coalition that led the mass resistance to its massive fuel price hikes. And, as we have also seen, this earned this regime the thinly veiled commendations (or, at the very least, the acquiescence) of various elements of global capital and their key promoters.

Sub-claim four, which argues that the emergent TREMF paradigm denies a significant redistributive role to the (Third World) state while favouring more and more

---

[47] See n 13 above.

[48] See IMF, n 12 above, 2, 9–10, 12 and 22; and IMF, 'Nigeria: 2005 Article IV Consultation', IMF Country Report No 05/302, 25 March 2005, paras 1, 6, 13 and 58 (describing Nigeria's actions in implementing its reform policies as 'commendable').

disinvestment and denationalisation on the part of states, is also demonstrated by the evidence discussed in Section III. In doggedly implementing its fuel price hike policy and justifying it as its attempt to remove and gradually end the policy of subsidising the cost of fuel to an already vastly impoverished Nigerian public, the Obasanjo regime accepted this aspect of the TREMF paradigm almost lock, stock and barrel.

Thus, in my own view, the 'living law' of human rights (rooted, as it must be, in the empirical evidence of social struggle/repression and social experience/propaganda, and thus of socio-legalities and counter-legalities) essentially grounds and supports Baxi's overall TREMF thesis. The Nigerian government's repressive behaviour under Obasanjo, the studied silence or acquiescence of many in the West who knew or ought to have known about the regime's excesses in defence of its TREMF-style organising ideology and the fact of that regime's very public and all-too-frequent endorsements by key elements and promoters of global capital all lend much credence to Baxi's germinal insight into the TREMF paradigm's rapid concretisation in our time as the dominant official frame of reference, even in the context of human rights questions.

It can, of course, be argued with much justification that the kind of solid paradigmatic shift toward TREMF that was and remains observable within Nigeria is more present at the official level than at the level of mass social movements or popular civil society actors (such as many elements within the Nigerian labour-led coalition). This case study itself shows a solid movement in a direction other than the official one; one that challenges and rejects the dominant shift towards TREMF, and offers a solid, if non-dominant, subaltern counter-normativity that can, under certain conditions, constrain the dominant TREMF norm to a modest extent (as witness Obasanjo's frequent modest retreats in the face of mass action by the labour-led coalition in Nigeria). Baxi is, of course, aware of the value of what he himself describes in another context as 'switching perspectives'[49] and anticipates this issue when he asks whether:

> there [are] any more possible ways of social and political struggle that may still ambush, both through the (Gramscian) wars of manoeuvre and position, the 'cunning' of late capital? How may the new [and old?] social movements (say the feminists and ecological) hunt and haunt the habitats of global capital?[50]

However, it must be understood that, as Baxi has suggested, the official (TREMF-loving and TREMF-dominated) discourse does not operate merely and only at the official level, but also breaches the boundaries of the unofficial and the popular in a manner that too often limits the terms of the unofficial anti-reform struggle itself. Baxi captured this point when he claimed, towards the end of *The Future of Human Rights*, that even the social movements that oppose and resist the turn towards TREMF orthodoxy are themselves doing so on terms set by the official discourse. And, what is more, as Baxi himself has suggested, it is the official TREMF discourse and practice that has largely constituted and constrained the lived experiences of the Third World subaltern (witness the Obasanjo regime's retreats without real surrender and its steady comebacks towards an effective 250% fuel price hike over five years or so).

It can also be argued that at no time has the UDHR paradigm been fully activated; and that the UDHR has always contained within it a counter-tendency that is

---

[49] Baxi, n 1 above, 137.
[50] Ibid, 134.

consistent with the TREMF paradigm. I agree with Baxi that the difference between this counter-tendency within the UDHR and the TREMF paradigm is a question of scale and intensity, and thus of character. In his words, 'while the appropriation of human rights logic and rhetoric [that is signified by the emergence of the TREMF paradigm] is not a distinctively novel phenomenon, it is the *scale* of the reversal now entailed that marks a radical discontinuity'.[51] It appears, then, that, in one sense, the TREMF human rights paradigm is an intense variant of earlier human rights para-digms. It shares continuities from the UDHR era—though not necessarily with the UDHR itself—but the discontinuities between them are so many, so enormous and so intense as to signal the emergence of a new paradigm. Since, at one time, the UDHR paradigm occupied a far more dominant place in the imagination of most govern-ments and social actors than it does today, it is to the gradual, but already substantial, loss of that dominant position and its many negative implications for human rights that Baxi's work in this area has thankfully alerted us.

In one sense, one of the things that the present chapter has attempted to do is to provide further empirical grounding for the somewhat distant possibility of a counter-narrative and counter-normativity, while at the same time recognising that, for now, little ground exists for optimism regarding the re-emergence to dominance (and not to mere competitive existence) of the UDHR paradigm; at least, not in the official dis-course of the more influential (Western) governments and of the relevant international economic institutions.

---

[51] Ibid, 155. Emphasis added.

# 5

# The Transformation of Africa: A Critique of Rights in Transitional Justice*

MAKAU W MUTUA

## I. INTRODUCTION

IN THE LAST two decades, the concept of transitional justice has come to represent the midwife for a democratic, rule-of-law state.[1] The script for the construction of such a phase is now regarded as an indispensable building block for sound constitutionalism, peace-building and national reconciliation in post-conflict societies or societies emerging out of abusive, authoritarian and fractured periods.[2] In fact, policy-makers and statesmen now increasingly realise that a human rights state that internalises human rights norms cannot be created unless the political society concretely addresses the grievances of the past. There is no future without a past, and the future is largely a result of the past. Unless we construct a future based upon the lessons of the past, we are bound to repeat our own mistakes and retard the development of our society.

The term 'transitional justice' captures two critical notions. First, it acknowledges the temporary measures that must be taken to build confidence in the construction of the post-despotic society. Secondly, by its own definition, transitional justice rejects a winner-takes-all approach as a beachhead to the future. In other words, transitional justice calls for deep concessions on either side of the divide. No one party or faction can be fully satisfied. Unyielding, non-concessionary demands can only foil the truce that is essential for national reconstruction. But equally important is the realisation that transitional justice rejects impunity for the most hideous offenders. To shield egregious perpetrators would only encourage a culture of unaccountability for past

---

* Originally published as: 'A Critique of Rights in Transitional Justice: The African Experience' in G Ore Aguilar and F Gomez Isa (eds), *Rethinking Transitions: Equality and Social Justice in Societies Emerging from Conflict* (Cambridge, Intersentia Ltd, 2011), 31–45. Republished with permission.
[1] See P Hayner, *Unspeakable Truths: Confronting State Terror and Atrocities* (Abingdon, Routledge, 2000).
[2] D Tutu, *No Future without Forgiveness: A Personal Overview of South Africa's Truth and Reconciliation Commission* (London, Random House, 1999).

abuses. Hence, a balance must be struck between justice for the victims and retribu-tion against offenders.[3]

However, the vast majority of states lack the requisite political will to effect trans-formative transitions. This is why most political transitions are either still born or aborted affairs. For Africa, this calls for soul-searching at all levels of society—within the political class, among the intelligentsia, in civil society and the general public. In other words, Africans must ask themselves: Is transitional justice a necessity for us if we are to create a democratic polity? If so, what vehicles should we construct to effect transitional justice, and what mandate shall we give such vehicles? But even as we ask these questions, we must remain mindful about the cost of abandoning transitional-justice measures. The reason for this is simple: we cannot exorcise the ghosts of the past without confronting them. The past will always be with us.

Even if we accept as a basic premise—which we do—that transitional justice pro-cesses and institutions are desirable and indispensable, we would be derelict not to interrogate the internal contradictions of the human rights project. I say so because the human rights project, which encompasses transitional justice, is an incomplete doctrine that is afflicted by gaping holes.[4] International human rights law, perhaps the most important transformational idea of our times, is fraught with conceptual and cultural problems. Human rights norms seek to impose an orthodoxy that would wipe out cultural milieus that are not consonant with liberalism and Eurocentrism. While it is useful to develop international standards for human rights, it is impera-tive that we understand the complexity of the diversity of our world, and work to create doctrinally inclusive and normatively multicultural formulae for dealing with human rights and social justice. Otherwise, we will lose the liberatory potential of human rights and fail to reconstruct societies that need recreation. While no society can truly emerge from a legacy of conflict and violence without the implementation of serious social-justice measures, such an exercise cannot be carried out in a cultural vacuum. For Africa, it is essential to recognise that communities and collectives are an integral part of social reality. As such, the individualist focus of the human rights corpus must be tempered with communalist or group-oriented approaches if human rights prescriptions are going to enjoy any legitimacy on the continent.

The last 50 years represents the entire period of the African post-colonial state, and gives us a fantastic window through which to interrogate the performance of the human rights project in Africa. But first, I will lay aside some misconceptions about the human rights corpus and the movement. At the outset, I need to address the subject of intellectual bias or normative location. Even though we aim to be objective, we are, nevertheless, products of our legacies and heritages, which have, in turn, forged our identity and philosophical outlooks. In this sense, true objectivity is an academic fiction, for no one can be truly objective. (In any case, if we were truly objective, we would be truly boring.) I thus plead my biases at the outset. I should also warn that, with regard to the subject in hand—that of the utility of human rights and liberalism in Africa—I adopt the view of an insider–outsider, an engaged sceptic who completely

---

[3] M Minow, *Between Vengeance and Forgiveness: Facing History after Genocide and Mass Violence* (Boston, MA, Beacon Press, 1998).

[4] M Mutua, *Human Rights: A Political and Cultural Critique* (Philadelphia, PA, University of Pennsyl-vania Press, 2002).

believes in human dignity but is not sure about the typology of political society that ought to be constructed to get us there.

I suggest that human rights are imprisoned in universality, one of the central proclivities of liberalism. This fact alone should give us pause about human rights because we ought to approach all claims of universality with caution and trepidation. I say this because visions of universality and predestination have often been intertwined throughout modern history, and not always happily: with an alarming frequency, liberalism's key tenets have been deployed to advance narrow, sectarian, hateful and exclusionary practices and ideas. So, at the purely theoretical level, we are chastised to look not once, but twice and again, at universalising creeds, ideas and phenomena. This is not to suggest that universality is always wrong-headed or even devious, although it has frequently been these things as well; rather, it is to assume that the universality of social phenomena is not a natural occurrence. Universality is always constructed by an interest for a specific purpose, with a specific intent and a projected substantive outcome in mind.

This critical view has special implications for Africa because it questions both the fit and utility of liberalism and human rights for the continent. If we agree that all social truths are initially local—even truths about the so-called natural attributes of human beings or the purposes of political society—what does this say about the assumptions of liberalism in Africa? If social truths are contextual, cultural, historical and time-bound, how can one find the relevance of the human rights project in Africa? This is not to say that local truths cannot be transformed into universal truths. They can, but the question for students of Africa is how one gets from here to there—in other words, what are the limitations of liberalism in general, and human rights in particular, as transnational projects? How do we turn local claims into universal human rights claims? If it is desirable to put liberalism in the service of Africa, how does one do so?

## II. HUMAN RIGHTS AND THE AFRICAN REALITY

Assuming these basic philosophical difficulties, how can human rights, as they are conceived, be of any help to the reconstruction and recovery of the African post-colonial state? Five decades after decolonisation, the African state is still haunted by crises of geographic, political and moral legitimacy. It is beset by the protracted reality of national incoherence and the ills of economic under-development. At its dawn, the African post-colonial state was handed a virtually impossible task—to assimilate the norms of the liberal tradition overnight within the structures of the colonial state while, at the same time, building a nation from disparate groups in a hostile international political economy. Instead, the newly minted African post-colonial elites chose first to consolidate their own political power. We can blame them now, as I have, but we must also understand that the first instinct of the political class is to consolidate itself and concentrate power in its own hands.

In the cold war context, this frequently meant stifling dissent, dismantling liberal constitutions, retreating to tribal loyalties or sycophantic cronies, and husbanding state resources for corruption or patronage purposes. In other words, any viable fabric of the post-colonial state started to crumble even before it was established. We know the rest—coups and counter-coups, military regimes and one-party dictatorships with the inevitable results of economic decay; the collapse of infrastructure; the fragmentation of political society; bilious retribalisation; religious, sectarian and communal conflicts and civil wars; and state collapse in a number of cases. The achievement of political independence from colonial rule turned into a false renaissance as one African state after another experienced transitional difficulties. While the African state retained some form of international legitimacy, its domestic writ was wafer thin. It is a miracle that many African states did not implode altogether, given the challenges to their internal legitimacy. Whatever the case, the liberal tradition failed to take hold as human rights were violated across the board.

However, the 1980s saw a resurgence of civil society and the reemergence of the political opposition. This started what has come to be loosely referred to as the Second Liberation. The entire continent was rocked by a wave of political liberalisation not witnessed since the 1950s and 1960s. Virtually all states succumbed to some form of political reform. In all cases, civil society and the political opposition sought a new social compact framed by the tenets of the liberal tradition. These were the rule of law, political democracy through multi-partyism, checks on executive power, limitations on the arbitrary use of state power, judicial independence, directly elected and unencumbered legislatures, the separation of powers, the freedoms of the press, speech, assembly and association—in other words, the whole gamut of civil and political rights or the full complement of so-called basic human rights.

It was as though Africans were asking to go back to the liberal constitutions imposed by the departing colonial powers. In some cases, new constitutional orders were established to respond to these demands. But a decade and a half after the frenzy to reintroduce the liberal tradition to the politics of Africa, we cannot count many blessings because the tumult of political liberalisation has yielded very mixed results. Optimists see a steady progression, even though the reversals have been many and discouraging. Pessimists, or what one might even want to call realists, see an African state that is a stubborn predator, unable and unwilling to accept reform. For every step forward, there seems to be several steps back. The near meltdown of Kenya in the aftermath of the December 2007 elections is only one case in point.

Is the African state unresponsive to human rights and the liberal tradition, or is the problem much more serious? The fault is variously placed on a bankrupt elite or political class; structural impediments within the state—ethnicity, religious zealotry, under-development, the failure to establish a legitimate political order, social cleavages; or an unyielding international economic order. Whatever the case, the jury for the current process of political liberalisation, which is taking place at the same time as economic globalisation, is still out. It is still too early to say for certain whether the African post-colonial state is ready for stabilisation and reclamation yet.

## III. CAN HUMAN RIGHTS RECOVER THE AFRICAN STATE?

The limitations that curtail the ability of the human rights corpus to respond to Africa's crises are conceptual and normative. The first limitation is simply one of the idiom in which the rights discourse is formulated. The language of rights, which is central to liberalism, is fraught with limitations which could be detrimental to the project of transforming deeply distorted societies. Inherent in the language of rights are indeterminacy, elasticity and the double-edged nature of the rights discourse. All of these characteristics open the rights language to malleability and misuse by malignant social elements, and make them a tool in the hands of those opposed to reform. South Africa is a case in point where a right-based revolution has been unable to transform fundamentally deeply embedded social dysfunction and the perverse legacy of apartheid. The choice of the rights idiom as the medium of choice to unravel the ravages of apartheid has been less than successful in spite of continued economic growth.

Another problem of the liberal tradition, which has been inherited by the human rights movement, is its unrelenting focus on individualism. This arises from liberalism's focus on formal equality and abstract autonomy. The human rights corpus views the individual as the centre of the moral universe, and therefore denigrates communities, collectives and group rights. This is one of the biggest assumptions of the human rights movement and is a particularly serious problem in Africa, where group and community rights are both deeply embedded in the cultures of the peoples and exacerbated by the multinational nature of the post-colonial state. The concept of self-determination in Africa cannot simply be understood as an external problem: it must, of necessity, be understood as encompassing the many nations within a given post-colonial state. In reality, this means that the individual rights of citizens within the state must be addressed in the context of group rights. Thus, group rights or the rights of peoples become important entitlements if the state is to gain the loyalties of its diverse citizens.

I do not deny that individualism is a necessity for any constitutional democracy, but I reject the idea that we can, or should, stop there in Africa. That would be a stunted understanding of rights from an African point of view. Indeed, for rights to make sense in the African context, one has to go beyond the individual, and address group identities in the political and economic framework of the state. Even in South Africa, for example, one of the states with an avowedly liberal interpretation of the rights language, there was an accommodation of group rights to language, culture and other forms of identity. One way political democracy deals with the question of multiple nations within one state is to grant autonomy to groups or to devolve powers through forms of federalism. But the paradox for Africa is that autonomous regimes or federalist arrangements have not worked well wherever they have been tried. These schemes have been unable to stem the combustible problem of ethnicity and reduce the legitimacy of the state. Ethnic groups retain a consciousness that stubbornly refuses to transfer loyalty from the group to the whole nation.

Secondly, the human rights movement's primary grounding and bias towards civil and political rights—and the impotence and vagueness of economic, social and cultural rights—is one of its major weaknesses in the African post-colonial context. Political democracy alone—without at least a strong welfare state or a social democracy—appears to be insufficient to recover the African state. The bias towards civil and political rights favours vested narrow class interests and kleptocracies which are entrenched in the bureaucratic, political and business sectors of society, and represent interests that are not inclined to challenge the economic powerlessness of the majority of post-colonial Africans. Yet the human rights movement assumes the naturalness of the market and the inevitability of employer/employee, capitalist/worker and subordinated labour relations. It seeks the regulation of these relationships, but not their fundamental reformulation.

By failing to interrogate and wrestle with economic and political philosophies and systems, the human rights movement indirectly sanctions capitalism and free markets. Importantly, the human rights corpus wrongly equates the containment of state despotism with the achievement of human dignity so that it seeks the construction of a political society in which political tyranny—not economic tyranny—is circumscribed. It thus seeks to create a society in which political tyranny is circumscribed or minimised. In so doing, it sidesteps economic powerlessness—the very condition that must be addressed if the African state is to be recovered. Political freedoms are clearly important, but, as South Africa has demonstrated, they are of limited utility in the struggle to empower populations and to reduce the illegitimacy of the state. It is an illusion to think of powerlessness and human indignity in the African context in purely political terms, as the human rights movement does, and to prescribe political democracy and the human rights doctrine as a panacea.

Real human powerlessness and indignity in Africa—the very causes of the illegitimacy of the African state—arise from social and economic conditions. This is why the human rights movement's recognition of secularism, capitalism and political democracy must be discussed openly to unveil its true identity so that we can recalculate its uses, and the limitations of these uses, to the reconstruction of the African state. To be useful to Africa's reconstruction, human rights cannot simply be advocated as an unreformed Eurocentric doctrine that must be donated as a gift to native peoples. Nor can it be imposed on Africa like an antibiotic, or be seen as a cure for the ills of a dark continent. My view is that this is how many in the West imagine what, for them, is a human rights crusade towards Africa. So far, this law and development model has not—and will not—work. Not only is it an imposition, but it also deals mostly with symptoms, while leaving the underlying fundamentals untouched.

To be of utility to Africa, and fundamentally transform the continent's dire fortunes, human rights must address economic powerlessness and the scandalous international order. Otherwise, it will promise much, while delivering little, as it did in the case of Rwanda, with the establishment of the International Criminal Tribunal for Rwanda and a false peace within the country; and as it also did in the wave of the so-called Second Liberation. The challenge for us is to work out how we can retool and rethink the human rights project as one of the vehicles for the reconstruction of the African post-colonial state. Unfortunately, to date, this is a task for which we have been found wanting.

## IV. RECONCEIVING TRANSITIONAL JUSTICE

Transitional justice concepts have to be freed from dogmatic universality in order to be useful to Africa. In this regard, notions of transitional justice ought to be reconstructed so that they are informed by a wider moral and social universe. The key to a successful transitional justice agenda is to imagine a more holistic approach to addressing human relationships in post-conflict, post-colonial situations. Reparative, retributive and adversarial notions of justice are limited, and may not be wholly legitimate in the eyes of victims. Sanctions against perpetrators—whether criminal, civil or political—are important in any transitional justice concept, but they are not enough. The problem is that such sanctions are not victim-centred at their core. Criminal sanctions, for example, are the revenge that society takes against the wrongdoer. Such sanctions thus mollify society at large, but may do nothing for the victim. Civil sanctions, such as compensatory damages, also respond to the material, but not the spiritual or metaphysical, damage. Thus, although the victim may be returned to the *status quo ante*, the restoration of material things may do nothing to heal the soul—the injured identity of gender, ethnicity, race, religion, political opinion or social status.

This is why I agree with Alex Boraine's 'holistic' approach to transitional justice and the five-pillar approach that combines elements of accountability, truth recovery, reconciliation, institutional reforms and reparations in one grand package of social reclamation.[5] A wider array of tools and approaches are necessary to address powerlessness in all its dimensions—social, economic, political, gender—to create a deeper democratic polity capable of repairing most hurts. It is these approaches that can ultimately tackle the hydra of impunity that corrupts the body politic and makes it virtually impossible for society to cohere into a nurturing instrumentality. That is why notions like *ubuntu*—the African philosophy of community wholesomeness—must be conceived as a new linchpin for the recovery of post-conflict societies.[6] This is not to say that traditional iterations of transitional justice contained in international humanitarian, human rights and international criminal law are vacuous or invalid. Rather, it is to recognise their limitations in addressing deeply embedded social dysfunctions that require more than criminal or civil sanction approaches.

In fact, the histories of several highly touted traditional transitional justice mechanisms point to these limitations. This is particularly true of international criminal tribunals, and much less so of truth commissions. Consider the International Criminal Tribunal for Rwanda (ICTR) and the International Criminal Tribunal for the former Yugoslavia (ICTY), for example. The ICTR followed the script of the Nuremberg tribunal. However, it is clear that, as constituted, the ICTR was intended to achieve neither the abolitionist impulses nor the just ends trumpeted by the United Nations. The tribunal is still disarticulated from political reconstruction and the normalisation processes necessary to bring humanity back to Rwanda. In the event, the Rwanda tribunal largely legitimises the Tutsi regime and allows the Tutsi a moral plane from which to exact their revenge on the Hutu. The ICTR would have made more sense in the context of a holistic and comprehensive settlement addressing the foundational problems that unleashed the genocide in the first place. As it is, the tribunal orbits in space, suspended from political reality and removed from both the individual and national psyches of the victims as well as the victors in the Rwanda conflict. The same analysis is applicable to the ICTY, where Serbs have seen themselves as its victims. The result is a failure of both institutions to inch society towards healing.

The Special Court for Sierra Leone has had more mixed, but arguably more promising, results because it was situated in the country itself, rather than outside, as was the case with the both the ICTR and the ICTY. The International Criminal Tribunal for Iraq, on the other hand, although situated in Iraq, has largely been a sham from

---

[5] A Boraine and S Valentine (eds), *Transitional Justice and Human Security* (Cape Town, International Center for Transitional Justice, 2006).
[6] Y Mokgoro, 'Ubuntu and the Law in South Africa' (1998) 4 *Buffalo Human Rights Law Review* 15.

both the domestic and international perspectives. It lacks credibility with Sunnis, who see it merely as a tool for revenge by the Shiites and the occupying American forces. Its unacceptably unfair, biased and compromised procedures and the absence of due process protections have made it a mockery of transitional justice. It remains to be seen whether the International Criminal Court can address any of these deficits, or whether it will simply remain the darling of lawyers, who see its utility as developing international criminal and humanitarian law, or of Western politicians, who see it as an instrument for assuaging their consciences for societal failures about which they did nothing—or very little—to stop.

The key, ultimately, is to understand that none of these processes—truth commissions, tribunals, sectoral reforms, prosecutions et al—will suffice by themselves, unless they are thought about and implemented in a holistic context that addresses the multiple, and often conflicting, vistas of powerlessness. Here, tackling impunity and building a democratic culture that is not premised solely on political rights will be key to the society of the future. I am not arguing that we should turn away from traditional systems of transitional justice; rather, I am arguing that these systems are incomplete and ineffective because they do not focus on people and victims, but are concerned with vindicating their own internal norms.

## V. THE LIMITATIONS OF TRANSITIONAL JUSTICE CONCEPTS

To be meaningful for Africa, transitional justice concepts should be comprehensive and all-inclusive if they are to break with past orthodoxies. I suggest a multicultural perspective in crafting effective solutions to legacies of conflict. In this view, I am alluding to the limits of normative Eurocentrism in the doctrine of international law.[7] While this critique of the exclusivity of international legal norms is not new, it has not been fully developed in human rights law and international humanitarian and criminal law. Yet these are critiques which are completely essential if transitional justice systems are to have any hope of success in the tormented societies in Africa. Without a doubt, what my analysis demands is a tall order. The question is whether there is both the intellectual rigour on the part of academics and the political will and vision on the part of states, civil societies and policy-makers to carry these ideas forward and develop them fully. These are questions which are complicated by the histories of conflict and the memories which they leave behind.

A survey of the anatomy of conflicts in the larger East African region—Kenya, Uganda, Rwanda, Sudan and Burundi—shows that democracy has not fared well. As such, many of these states are undergoing different iterations of 'transitions' from one thing or another. What is clear, however, is that these transitions have not accomplished much, and there have, indeed, been many reversals. Take, for example, the near collapse of Kenya after the 2007 elections just five years removed from the successful 2002 elections in which there was regime change for the first time. Clearly, the transition between 2002 and 2007 was not a successful one. In Rwanda, the Tutsi hegemony

---

[7] A Anghie, *Imperialism, Sovereignty, and the Making of International Law* (Cambridge, Cambridge University Press, 2005); JT Gathii, 'Imperialism, Colonialism, and International Law' (2007) 54 *Buffalo Law Review* 1013.

has once again been re-established under the guise of democracy and post-conflict transitional justice reconstruction. Burundi remains tense. In Sudan, an unstable peace barely holds in the south whereas, in the west region of Darfur, the government is committing genocide. How can you have a transition in one part of the country while committing genocide in the other? In Uganda, President Yoweri Museveni is creating the conditions for a perfect storm both in the north and everywhere else because of political despotism and a failed transition to democracy.

My panacea here is a call to go beyond tired notions of transitional justice and to introduce fuller concepts of 'restorative justice' that move away from criminal law formulations of sanctions and instead employ alternative dispute-resolution paradigms, such as indigenous courts, juvenile justice ideas and other novel vehicles that imagine the possibility of restoring a lost social balance. It is this lost social balance which is the chasm that caused the conflicts in the first place. Some may attack this approach based upon the localisation of the practices and norms, but I would argue instead that dominant Eurocentric cultures suffer from an over-emphasis of retribution, although they, too, have elements of restorative justice. Virtually all cultures have restorative justice impulses in them. But what is needed is the multiculturalisation of transitional justice to give it a truly universal imprint, much in the same way that the human rights corpus has been asked to become less Eurocentric and more inclusive.[8] There is some hope, as evidenced by the Claassen Principles and UN Draft Declaration of Principles of Restorative Justice in Criminal Matters, that transitional justice must move beyond the punitive to the more restorative, comprehensive and holistic transitional justice model. These principles are guided by their ability to heal; put victims at the centre; seek co-operation with perpetrators before confrontation; understand abominations as injuries to social relations; de-emphasise the punitive or criminality of offences and emphasise the causes of the abominations; and achieve community buy-in in crafting solutions and measures for accountability. In other words, this transitional justice approach requires the full participation of all the assets of the community—traditional, ethical, religious, civil society, political and moral. This is in marked contrast to traditional mechanisms, such as truth commissions or tribunals, which look primarily to formalised structures of criminal accountability and censure.

I believe that we have to reimagine the transitional justice agenda along these holistic perimeters, although I should caution that this is an arduous project. Secondly, it is important that the project does not do away with the progress made by traditional transitional justice systems. For example, it is clear that truth commissions have limitations. Even the most famous ones—such as South Africa's—have still left a lot to be desired. Most of them have lacked the political backing or framework to dig at the roots of the abominations, or to expose the rot that led to the pogroms in the first place. Most have been hampered by the cultures of impunity in which they were incubated. After all, how do the forces of reform—which are usually a minority in states emerging out of conflict—marshal sufficient political resources to overcome former regime elements?

In Kenya, for instance, the Report of the Task Force for the Establishment of a Truth, Justice, and Reconciliation Commission which I produced was buried by anti-reform elements in the Kibaki Government, even though it came to power on a clear

---

[8] Mutua, n 4 above.

mandate for fundamental change.[9] Six years later, the same people who shot down one truth commission are ostensibly interested in setting up another one after the genocidal violence of the 2007 elections. One has to wonder whether political interests have changed so much as to permit a genuine truth commission to be established in Kenya. Have Kenyans learnt any useful lessons between 2002 and 2008 that could be used to craft a more effective transitional justice project? Evidence suggests that the pogroms in the aftermath of the election indicate a deeper national psychosis that cannot be cured by a traditional truth commission or a retributive justice system alone. The nature of the abuses that took place, the proclivity of the political class to stoke ethnic hatred and the receptivity of the populace to misogyny and other forms of identity hatred suggests that a holistic approach to transitional justice is the only viable way forward.

We can employ dichotomy as a device to illustrate why traditional transitional justice notions have experienced large deficits. In this device, we can imagine a process of de-dichotomisation that is designed to free transitional justice from the tyrannies of Eurocentric legal paganism. The point of departure here is that dualism is a proclivity of Western liberal philosophy and the public imagination. Thus, good only makes sense in the face of evil, or right exists because of wrong. This Manichean white over black, superior/inferior, modern/traditional, savage/victim, progress/backward dualism has been an integral theme in European civilisation.[10] These dichotomies create illusions of moral certainty and policy inflexibility. Given this fixity, it is no wonder that there is reluctance within powerful countries and vested interests to entertain social, political and legal experimentation. This includes trials of emergent ideas in the area of transitional justice. However, I suggest that we break these dichotomies down because it is self-defeating to create water-tight categories that artificially stop social phenomena from naturally bleeding into each other. Whatever we do, it is not productive to bifurcate for the sake of it, either because jurists think it is heresy not to bifurcate or politicians are afraid that holistic approaches will reach to the bottom of the problem.

It is important to debunk one after the other of the many dichotomies of modern Western civilisation. For example, the modern/traditional schism imprisons us in a false jail and makes it difficult for us to cultivate non-Western notions to enrich transitional justice ideas. Another old-line distinction is between law and politics or the humanities. To traditional legal minds, law is supposed to be the neutral arbiter of social conflict and the dispassionate source of the allocation of power and its uses. Law is supposed to be impartial and objective, whereas politics is partisan and biased. The human rights movement was very good at insisting on this dichotomy at the height of the cold war for fear that it would be delegitimised as a tool for the capitalist, liberal and political democratic West.[11] These distinctions even found their way into the demonisation of economic and social rights as not rights at all in the way that political and civil rights are conceived in liberal market societies. This opposition

---

[9] Republic of Kenya, Report of the Task Force on the Establishment of Truth, Justice, and Reconciliation Commission (2003).

[10] M Mutua, 'Savages, Victims, and Saviors: the Metaphor of Human Rights' (2001) 42 *Harvard International Law Journal* 201.

[11] T Carothers, 'Democracy and Human Rights: Policy Allies or Rivals?' (1994) 17 *Washington Quarterly*, 106.

was voiced at a meeting to consider the ratification of the International Covenant on Economic, Social and Cultural Rights:

> One participant felt strongly that it would be detrimental for US human rights NGOs to espouse the idea of economic, social and cultural rights. Although they refer to important issues, they concern distributive justice rather than corrective justice, like civil and political rights. But distributive justice is a matter of policy, rather than principles; and human rights NGOs must deal with principles, not policies. Otherwise, their credibility will be damaged. Supporting economic demands will only undermine the ability of NGOs to promote civil and political rights.[12]

Attempts to locate political and civil rights on a different normative plane than economic and social rights—while attentive to political biases—have no scholarly defence or argument simply because it is impossible to imagine a right in one category that does not implicate a right in the other. As an analytical question, the distinction is purely fictional and has no basis in a normative argument. The same is true of the distinction between law and politics or the humanities. For the purposes of social transformation, such distinctions only serve to limit the potential of the transitional justice vehicles. Thus international criminal law needs to imagine itself as not in isolation from either geopolitics or the national political interests that animate and motivate political actors who will be subject to transitional justice projects. Nor would it make much sense for retributive justice processes to pay no attention to—or be separated from—the economic and social needs of victims or women, for instance. What kind of a lasting or effective solution would only focus on criminal sanctions for the perpetrators while leaving completely unattended the moral and material needs of vulnerable individuals and groups in society? Would that not simply leave intact the power structures of yesteryear and the fault lines that caused the pogroms in the first place? If such an approach does not address powerlessness in all its multiple dimensions, how would it hope to deal with impunity? The integration of various normative approaches that touch upon the human condition is the only viable method.

Other dualisms that vex transitional justice may include the use of criminal law without examining what civil law measures might be added. One looks at social wrongs as an affront to the individual while the other sees an offence as a wrong committed against the public. The search for a national peace that is substantive for individuals and communities cannot afford to put the two approaches at loggerheads. Instead, both should be integrated in a wholesome process. The same is obviously true of punitive, retributive processes common in adversarial systems. An imaginative approach needs to go beyond punishment and confrontation and craft hybrid systems that combine aspects of both, depending on the situation.

We can also identify the tension between national and international law as another drawback. International law, that 'gentle civiliser' of nations, is not meant to displace national or municipal law.[13] This is why international criminal tribunals, for instance, are less useful if they are unconnected to transitional processes taking place within

---

[12] M Rodriguez Bustelo and P Alston, Report of a Conference Held at Arden House (1986), quoted in 'US Ratification of the Covenant on Economic, Social and Cultural Rights: the Need for an Entirely New Strategy' (1990) 84 *American Journal of International Law* 365.

[13] M Koskenniemi, *The Gentle Civilizer of Nation: The Rise and Fall of International Law: 1870–1960* (Cambridge, Cambridge University Press, 2001).

states in the aftermath of conflicts. This critique is especially applicable to both the ICTR and the ICTY. But this dichotomy is extended to how conflicts are treated— whether they are national or international conflicts. So-called internal conflicts are less likely to draw international collective responses unless they are perceived to be extremely serious or to threaten the strategic interests of the major powers. This is in spite of the fact that the impact of the conflicts on individuals and groups is not diminished by the nature of it. The dichotomy evacuates people from the centre and replaces them with state interests. This is an additional hurdle that must be addressed by transitional justice advocates.

One can identify a cluster of schisms of justice/peace, justice/reconciliation and justice/democracy. The assumptions here indicate that the demands of justice would be incompatible with reconciliation, peace or democracy. This one-dimensional thinking—where justice is understood to be an end in itself—defeats the logic of transitional justice. By the nature of the objectives of transitional justice, it is not possible to have a winner-takes-all approach. Peace requires justice, but not full-throttled revenge. Reconciliation requires justice, but not in an extreme bias against either the victim or the perpetrator. To redeem the perpetrator without encouraging impunity requires a degree of conciliation on the part of the victim. Finally, there is a false belief that national security can be attained without human security. Recent conflicts within—and between—countries have shown that neither is possible without the other. The cases of Iraq, Afghanistan, Kenya and even the United States amply demonstrate the folly of treating one as separate from the other.

## VI. AS A WAY OF CONCLUSION

The subject of transitional justice is a difficult and complex one, particularly because it is a work in progress. Lessons from practice are still trickling in, and it will be some time before definitive data are accumulated. But one thing is clear—we know what does not work and what might work. What this chapter has attempted to do is to provide an opening to reconceptualise transitional justice projects and reformulate them from their traditionally narrow normative bases. Although it seems obvious, sufficient work has not been done on the indivisibility of the approaches to transitional justice. I am pleading for a more open mind to collapsing—or, at least, resisting the reification—of traditional totems of analysis and action. The human condition does not respond to abstracted categories. Rather, its complexity and density require a nuanced understanding of what will motivate individuals and groups to imagine a new and different life together. How we think about the choices that have to be made to create a viable bridge to this new society will depend on our ability to avoid intellectual rigidity and policy myopia. But none of these will bear fruit unless the political actors in Africa imagine a larger vision for the continent.

# 6

# Marks Indicating Conditions of Origin in Rights-Based Sustainable Development*

## NICOLE AYLWIN AND ROSEMARY J COOMBE

### I. INTRODUCTION

ON 3 SEPTEMBER 2010, the Registrar of Geographical Indications in India announced that the designation of Sandur Lambani had been granted the status of a geographical indication (GI), a form of intellectual property right (IPR) that recognises that a specific good has a quality, reputation or characteristic that is attributable to its geographical origin. The mark would be attached to goods containing a unique form of traditional embroidery, distinctive by virtue of the darning, cross-stitching, mirror work and natural dyeing and printing techniques developed over many years by Lambani craftswomen. Recognising the economic value that traditionally made products may have in global speciality markets, Sandur Kushala Kala Kendra, a non-governmental organisation (NGO), and the Karnataka State Handicrafts Development Corporation worked with, and on behalf of, all 300 craftswoman of the Lambani tribe in order to secure GI protection for their embroidery, ensuring that they alone could market and advertise this unique traditional product under the name Sandur Lambani.[1]

These craftswomen are not alone. Sandur Lambani embroidery joins a growing group of traditional Indian products, such as Darjeeling tea and Mysore and Kancheerpuram silk, which already enjoy GI protection. Writing in 2006 about a recent visit to India, legal scholar Madhavi Sunder noted that 'GI fever' had overtaken India's rural handicraft producers; in her words, 'Not even the makers of the famous laddus in Tirupati, who prepare these sweets for worshippers to offer to God in this popular Hindu pilgrimage site, have been immune to the frenzy'.[2]

The intellectual property (IP) frenzy in India is indicative of a larger trend in developing countries. As these countries attempt to meet the demands of the new global

---

* This chapter is simultaneously printed in both this volume and in the (2014) 47(3) *UC Davis Law Review*, Special Symposium Issue. Both publishers have agreed to simultaneous reprints of the article. The authors thank the editors and publishers for this privilege.
[1] See 'Sandur Lambani Embroidery Gets GI Tag', *The Hindu*, 30 September 2010, available at http://www.hindu.com/2010/09/30/stories/2010093051390500.htm (last accessed on 24 November 2010).
[2] M Sunder, 'IP3' (2006) 59 *Stanford Law Review* 44.

economy, they are also asked to find new ways of combating poverty while simultaneously protecting their unique traditional knowledge and culture. Increasingly, IP has been called upon to serve these global development needs.[3] IPRs have simultaneously become important sources of capital accumulation and the subjects of intense controversy in the last two decades as their range, scope and length have increased, as evidenced by the pressure put on the World Intellectual Property Organization (WIPO) to embark upon a development agenda.[4] Efforts to make IP better serve the needs of the world's more marginalised and vulnerable populations are often expressed in the vocabulary of international human rights norms. There is now a lively debate about the relationship between IP and human rights.[5] Moreover, academics and activists protesting the strength and reach of corporately held IPRs more generally now tend to frame their opposition in terms of countervailing rights, such as those of consumers, patients, communities, farmers, indigenous peoples and the users of cultural goods more generally.[6]

The intersection of IPRs with development and human rights suggests that IPRs are no longer regarded merely as tools to solve economic public goods problems and to advance capitalist accumulation. Indeed, they are implicated and deployed in agendas which are as seemingly unrelated as identity politics, rural development, ethical con-

[3] Commission on Intellectual Property Rights, 'Integrating Intellectual Property Rights and Development Policy', Report of the Commission on Intellectual Property Rights (London, September 2002), available at www.iprcommission.org.

[4] N Netanel (ed), *The Development Agenda: Global Intellectual Property and Developing Countries* (New York, Oxford University Press, 2008); D Gervais, *Intellectual Property, Trade and Development: Strategies to Optimize Economic Development in a TRIPS Plus Era* (New York, Oxford University Press, 2007); C May, *The World Intellectual Property Organization: Resurgence and the Development Agenda* (London, Routledge, 2007). For an overview and assessment of this and other development agendas pertaining to IP recently promoted in various international fora see P Yu, 'A Tale of Two Development Agendas' (2009) 35 *Ohio Northern University Law Review* 465.

[5] See, eg AEL Brown, 'Access to Essential Technologies: The Role of the Interface between Intellectual Property, Competition and Human Rights' (2010) 24 *International Review of Law, Computers and Technology* 51; AR Chapman, 'The Human Rights Implications of Intellectual Property Protection' (2002) 5 *Journal of International Economic Law* 861; RJ Coombe, 'Intellectual Property, Human Rights and Sovereignty: New Dilemmas in International Law Posed by the Recognition of Indigenous Knowledge and the Conservation of Biodiversity' (1998) 6 *Indiana Journal of Global Legal Studies* 59; W Grosheide (ed), *Intellectual Property and Human Rights: A Parodox* (Cheltenham, Edward Elgar Publishing, 2010); M Sinjela (ed), *Human Rights and Intellectual Property Right: Tensions and Convergences* (Leiden, Martinus Nijhoff, 2007).

[6] See, eg C Borowiak, 'Farmers' Rights: IP Regimes and the Struggle over Seeds' (2004) 32 *Politics & Society* 511; Y Chang, 'Who Should Own Access Rights? A Game-Theoretical Approach to Striking the Optimal Balance in the Debate over Digital Rights Management' (2007) 15 *Artificial Intelligence and Law* 323; P Cullet, 'Patents and Medicines: The Relationship between TRIPs and the Human Right to Health' (2003) 79 *International Affairs* 139; MG Hossain, 'The Protection of Community Rights and Plant Varieties: The Experience of Bangladesh', paper presented as part of an ICTSD Regional Dialogue on Asia, 18–21 April 2002, available at http://www.ictsd.org; P Jaszi, 'Rights in Basic Information' in R Melendez-Ortiz and P Roffe (eds), *Intellectual Property and Sustainable Development: Development Agendas in a Changing World* (Cheltenham, Edward Elgar Publishing, 2009) 5–20; P Kameri-Mbote, 'Community, Farmers' and Breeders' Rights in Africa: Towards a Legal Framework for *Sui Generis* Legislation' (2003) 1 *University of Nairobi Law Journal* 1; P Kameri-Mbote and J Otieno-Odek, 'Genetic Use Restriction Technologies and Sustainable Development' in Melendez-Ortiz and Roffe, ibid, 209–34, MJ Madison, 'Rights of Access and the Shape of the Internet' (2003) 44 *British Columbia Law Review* 433; C Lombard and RRB Leakey, 'Protecting the Rights of Farmers and Communities while Securing Long Term Market Access for Producers of Non-timber Forest Products: Experience in Southern Africa' (2010) 19 *Forests Trees and Livelihood* 235; N Ndlovu, 'Access to Rock Art Sites: A Right or a Qualification?' (2009) 64(189) *South African Archaeological Bulletin* 61.

sumption practices, the preservation of biological and cultural diversity, and indigenous self-determination. For example, as the tendency to treat all cultural forms as merely information emerges as a social ethos, IPRs are employed (and rhetorically deployed) by indigenous groups to prevent the exploitation of their traditional knowledge, to protect the cultural and economic value of their knowledge, and to affirm the rights of their community to control their own cultural resources.[7]

Under conditions of globalisation, the social justice norms of recognition, redistribution and respect for human dignity are now entailed in the discussion of IPRs' legitimacy in the extended social domains in which IPRs now figure. We take no position on the larger issue of whether IPRs should be considered as human rights, generally.[8] Nonetheless, it seems clear that IP is one means by which societies have historically attempted to protect and safeguard the cultural rights found in Article 15 of the International Covenant on Economic, Social and Cultural Rights. Culture, we will show, is increasingly regarded as a development resource, a marker of social cohesion, evidence of social capital, the basis for investing in rural development and a means of creating symbolic distinction in global markets.[9] As cultural rights and cultural resources assume new significance in international development arenas, we argue, IPRs will be shaped to meet these objectives.

In this chapter, we ask to what extent rights-based sustainable development objectives that capitalise upon cultural resources may be realised through the use of 'marks indicating conditions of origin' (MICO for short). We suggest that the expansion of this area of IP in developing countries cannot be appropriately dismissed merely as another instance of IP expansionism; instead, its legitimacy needs to be evaluated in terms of the qualities of empowerment, governance and the sustainability of local livelihood improvements that MICO initiatives enable. In short, we argue that rights-based sustainable development indicia provide promising ways to evaluate MICO initiatives, and that further promotion of MICOs for development demands a commitment to rights-based criteria if it is to avoid reproducing old forms of privilege or perpetuating new forms of injustice.

We will first explore the conditions under which IPRs and development have become inter-related, the reasons that this inter-relationship has put IPRs and their exercise into a rights-based normative framework, and the implications that this has for the future of IP policy and politics. We then explore the norm of sustainability that has become central to development theory and practice, and its implications for the way

---

[7] R Coombe and N Aylwin, 'Rethinking Cultural Heritage Ethics using Human Rights Norms' in R Coombe, D Wershler and M Zeilinger (eds), *Dynamic Fair Dealing: Creating Canadian Culture Online* (Toronto, University of Toronto Press, 2013).

[8] For analysis see P Cullet, 'Human Rights and Intellectual Property Protection in the TRIPS Era' (2007) 29 *Human Rights Quarterly* 403; P Yu, 'Reconceptualizing Intellectual Property Interests in a Human Rights Framework' (2007) 40 *UC Davis Law Review* 1039; LR Helfer, 'Toward a Human Rights Framework for Intellectual Property' (2007) 40 *UC Davis Law Review* 971. See also the sources cited in n 2 above.

[9] See, eg R Farhat, 'Neotribal Entrepreneurialism and the Commodification of Biodiversity: WIPO's Displacement of Development for Private Property Rights' (2008) 15 *Review of International Political Economy* 206; L Han, 'Cultural Products, Copyright Protection and Trade Rules' (2009) 4 *Frontiers of Law in China*, 196; GC Pigliasco, 'We Branded Ourselves Long Ago: Intangible Cultural Property and Commodification of Fijian Firewalking' (2010) 80 *Oceania* 161; AB Russell, 'Using Geographical Indication to Protect Artisanal Works in Developing Courntries: Lessons from a Banana Republic's Misnomered Hat' (2010) 19 *Transnational Law & Contemporary Problems* 705; AK Sanders, 'Incentives for the Protection of Cultural Expression: Art, Trade and Geographical Indications' (2010) 13 *The Journal of World Intellectual Property* 81.

in which we evaluate the successful use of IPRs in development practice. This leads us to an exploration of the increasing importance of cultural resources in sustainable development practices and the need to configure IP in order to value heritage resources and meet collective needs and aspirations. MICOs are then explored in terms of the qualities they have which make them appear as promising for sustainable development. We then examine a few MICO-based endeavours to illustrate how these might be evaluated using rights-based indicators. Finally, we conclude on an optimistic, but cautionary, note, by suggesting that great challenges lie ahead if MICOs are to secure the promise which they seem to offer for community-sustainable development based upon cultural resources while fulfilling human rights norms in the process of securing improvements in livelihood.

## II. INTELLECTUAL PROPERTY AND RIGHTS-BASED DEVELOPMENT

Concerns about the negative consequences that might flow from higher levels of international IP protection and stricter IP enforcement motivated a group of developing countries to put forward proposals in support of a WIPO Development Agenda in 2004.[10] The proposals sought to ensure that international IP policy took development objectives into account and was in compliance with state obligations, including those held under human rights treaties.[11] As a result of such proposals, WIPO now has a strong development agenda and has a number of initiatives that correspond with the UN Millennium Development Goals.[12] Ongoing efforts to incorporate development objectives at WIPO have also entailed more consideration of human rights, because development practice and theory have become human rights and have been used to develop measurable standards for assessing development projects. Development is no longer understood merely as an economic process, and human rights are no longer exclusively viewed as political objectives. The discourse surrounding development policy, funding, practice and accountability is increasingly rights-based:

> Rights-based development aspires to a more holistic integration of human rights as an
> ethical framework in the planning of projects designed for human improvement. Although
> the interdependence and indivisibility of human rights (civil/political and social/economic/

---

[10] This should be understood as a reminder rather than a new initiative. When WIPO became a UN agency in 1974, it bound itself to engage in measures to accelerate economic, social and cultural development. As a matter of public international law, it is also bound to act in a fashion that enables member states to meet their international obligations.

[11] '3D: Trade, Human Rights, Equitable Economy', Policy Brief on Intellectual Property, Development and Human Rights: How Human Rights can Support Proposals for a World Intellectual Property Organization (WIPO) Development Agenda (Geneva, Davinia Ovett, 2006), available at www.docs.google.com/gview?a=v&q=cache:X2sd9syjNTkJ:www.3dthree.org/pdf_3D/3DPolBrief-WIPO-eng.pdf+http://www.3dthree.org/pdf_3D/3DPolBrief-WIPO-eng.pdf&hl=en&sig=AFQjCNExgnPSO0ZTxLFDVBsWE4g2bOXsvg.

[12] For instance, in an attempt to address Goal 1, 'Eradicate Extreme Poverty and Hunger', WIPOs work on the protection of traditional knowledge aims to 'contribute to ensuring that local communities who conserve and maintain these resources and assets receive a fair share of economic benefits derived from their exploitation', while ensuring that, '[c]ommunities can also be empowered to trade in culturally distinct goods and services they derive from their knowledge systems and traditional creativity'. Clearly, there is now recognition within WIPO that IPRs have an important role to play in development and have functions that go beyond regulating the market of informational goods. For an overview of WIPOs work on the Millennium Development Goals see http://www.wipo.int/ip-development/en/agenda/millennium_goals.

cultural) has been much proclaimed, and internationally reaffirmed through the 1993 Vienna Declaration, this integration is perhaps most fully conceived in the emergence, content, and practice of rights-based development.[13]

As early as 1979, the Secretary General of the Commission on Human Rights affirmed, as a matter of general consensus, that:

> the central purpose of development is the realization of the potentialities of the human person in harmony with the community; the human person is the subject not the object of development; both material and nonmaterial needs must be satisfied; respect for human rights is fundamental; the opportunity for full participation must be accorded; the principles of equality and non-discrimination must be respected; and a degree of individual and collective self-reliance must be achieved.[14]

Accordingly, rights-based development takes seriously both social and economic rights as primary concerns.[15] It normatively shifts development assistance from a form of charity to a universal responsibility to provide peoples with an economic framework adequate to the pursuit of human dignity and social participation, an outlook now reflected in major NGO programmes, bilateral aid programmes and the Millennium Development Goals.[16] The principles of a rights-based approach include equitable participation, accountability, non-discrimination, empowerment and linkage to international rights instruments.[17] Unlike traditional development strategies, issues of justice in administration, political participation in decision-making and cultural propriety in project creation and implementation are to be taken into account. Principles of equality, equity and non-discrimination in the planning of projects and the distribution of benefits are emphasised.

Although the principles of rights-based development are generally agreed upon, the best means of implementing these principles in practice and of evaluating their success remain disputed.[18] Human rights practitioners Mac Darrow and Ampars Tomas suggest that rights-based approaches to development derive their legitimacy from their success or failure in redressing the asymmetries of power normally found in, and sometimes caused by, development projects.[19] In other words, redressing existing discriminatory patterns and avoiding new forms of deprivation are fundamental criteria for evaluating whether a project has fulfilled the human rights criteria. Political theorist Brigitte Hamm provides four criteria for implementation and evaluation: projects must reference the human rights obligations of states, practice non-discrimination with a focus on empowering

---

[13] J Ensor and P Gready (eds), *Reinventing Development?: Translating Rights-Based Approaches from Theory into Practice* (London, Zed Books, 2005) 14.

[14] Ibid, 14.

[15] BI Hamm, 'A Human Rights Approach to Development' (2001) 23(4) *Human Rights Quarterly* 1006.

[16] G Shafir and A Brysk, 'The Globalization of Rights: From Citizenship to Human Rights' (2006) 10 *Citizenship Studies* 275.

[17] CG Mokhiber, 'Toward a Measure of Dignity: Indicators for Rights-Based Development' (2001) 18 *Statistical Journal of the United Nations ECE* 158.

[18] Hamm, n 15 above, 1010; P Gready, 'Reasons to be Cautious about Evidence and Evaluation: Rights-Based Approaches to Development and the Emerging Culture of Evaluation' (2009) 1 *Journal of Human Rights Practice* 380; AJ Rosga and ML Satterthwaite, 'The Trust in Indicators: Measuring Human Rights' (2009) 27 *Berkeley Journal of International Law* 253.

[19] M Darrow and A Tomas, 'Power, Capture, and Conflict: A Call for Human Rights Accountability in Development Cooperation' (2005) 27 *Human Rights Quarterly* 489. See also A Mukherjee-Reed, Chapter 3 above.

disadvantaged groups, place an emphasis on inclusive participation in project planning and implementation, and comply with recognised principles of good governance.[20] As IP becomes implicated in development agendas, then, their bestowal, use and enforcement must be implemented in ways that meet these rights-based indicators. Human rights law, reporting and accounting mechanisms are measures that might ensure the integrity of projects that use IPRs to achieve development objectives by:

> identifying which obligations States and other actors have in relation to members of society, including the most vulnerable and marginalized groups . . . helping to identify which strategies and measures are needed by States and other actors in order to realize human rights and support development and . . . providing mechanisms capable of holding public and private actors accountable. A rights-based approach to development therefore supports more transparent policy-making and greater assessment of the impact of policies on the poorest members of society.[21]

If rights-based development brings two prominent areas of normative practice into a new relationship, it also reconfigures the political field in so doing. Rights-based development conceives of human rights in a fashion that speaks to the changes associated with economic globalisation, decentring the state and distributing its powers and responsibilities. The vertical pole of rights (state-individual) is not replaced, but is complemented with more horizontal relationships and networks of organisations acting to influence policy. In many cases, NGOs work with local producers, community-established collectivities and associations, local businesses and national regulators helping to create development initiatives that eschew purely legalistic interpretations of rights in favour of securing rights in political and social practices, and extending claim–duty relationships to subjects at the household, community, regional, national and international levels.[22]

---

[20] Hamm, n 15 above, 1011. Most good governance programmes have, as a core aim, the entrenchment of the rule of law with an emphasis upon improving the capacities of governments to uphold it, but the rights-based approach recognises a relationship between power, inequality and rights, and focuses on uncovering the power inequalities behind poverty to advocate for social change; the use of a rights vocabulary is believed to alter decision-makers' perceptions, creating new senses of obligation. A more radical rights-based approach sees development interventions as requiring that subjects of development become citizen-like actors in the process, measuring transformations in terms of justice, participation, empowerment and agency, which includes equity of access to processes of decision-making, participation that challenges established power and patronage structures, and building capacities for purposive choice into the institutional contexts in which choice is made. Opportunities for forging new alliances at different scales to construct transnational forms of citizenship may be a further objective. See TD Davis, 'The Politics of Human Rights and Development: The Challenge for Official Donors' (2009) 44 *Australian Journal of Political Science* 173. For a succinct overview of the ways in which development NGOS began to frame needs and claims as simultaneously development and rights issues and discussions of the potential and limits of rights as a basis for development see J Grugel and N Piper, 'Do Rights Promote Development?' (2009) 9 *Global Social Policy* 79; and the papers in S Hickey and D Mitlin, *Rights-Based Approaches to Development: Exploring the Potential and Pitfalls* (London, Earthscan, 2009).

[21] See n 11 above, 2.

[22] Using MICOs to help small producers to secure global markets for their locally made or traditionally produced goods is an excellent example of horizontal rights and development networking. In the case of Poronguito cheese, an example that is elaborated below, NGOs helped traditional cheese producers in Cajamarca to secure a collective mark for their cheese by co-ordinating with local producers and businesses as well as national institutions. By securing this collective mark, local producers were able to secure economic benefits for themselves and the community and were also able to ensure that they remained in control of their own working conditions and traditional modes of production.

Building the capacities of rights-holders to make claims and duty-holders to fulfil responsibilities involves multiple agencies on diverse scales.[23] The expanding role of non-state actors and the increasing importance of decisions made by transnational forums have been described by political theorists as the emergence of a 'global public domain'.[24] This is a domain in which 'the public' involves not just state governments, but corporations, international inter-governmental organisations, civil society organisations, citizen's movements and multilateral institutions in dialogue and deliberation. As they pertain to IP, these deliberations will include transnational dialogue, about both new entitlements and new exemptions (as we have seen with regard to traditional environmental knowledge). The term 'global public sphere' might better capture the deliberative, multi-sectoral nature of these new decision-making processes.[25]

In this field of politics, rules that favour global market expansion, such as the trade-based extension of IPRs, come up against a new advocacy that aims to promote, ensure and fulfil not only civil and political rights, but also economic, social and cultural rights.[26] IP agendas, such as those advanced by the WTO, may be quite detrimental to development and human rights, particularly given the perceived inflexibility of the obligations imposed by multilateral and bilateral trade agreements, and the harm inflicted on human rights by instrumentalist policies. Nonetheless, human rights-based development and IP are potentially complementary regimes.[27] Human rights, at their most basic level, are concerned with securing and promoting human dignity and ensuring human flourishing; there is no reason why intellectual property rights could not offer vehicles to support these pursuits.[28]

---

[23] Hamm, n 15 above, 1031.

[24] JS Ruggie, 'Reconstituting the Global Public Domain—Issues, Actors and Practices' (2004) 10 *European Journal of International Relations* 499. For a discussion of the growing role of NGOs in IP policy-making see D Matthews, 'The Role of International NGOs in the Intellectual Property Policy-Making and Norm-Setting Activities of Multilateral Institutions' (2007) 82 *Chicago-Kent Law Review* 1369.

[25] The term 'global public domain' is likely to confuse IP scholars, for whom the public domain has a status due to the lack of IP claimants and freedom of access to creative or innovative works as public goods. To some degree, these meanings overlap; political deliberations around the assertion that certain pharmaceuticals be freely available in the presence of catastrophic health needs, for example, is one that involves both an enhanced range of actors (civil society movements, NGOs and corporations) and a potential widening of public goods. However, the term 'global public sphere' seems to capture the deliberative, multi-sectoral nature of these new decision-making processes better. Although these may involve considerations of public goods, they also include deliberations around new entitlements and new exemptions in a transnational field of dialogue where the constitution of the public domain itself comes under scrutiny.

[26] As UN Secretary-General Ban Ki-Moon noted in the opening session of ECOSOC in April 2007, 'the rules of intellectual property rights need to be reformed, so as to strengthen technological progress and to ensure that the poor have better access to new technologies and products'. UNCTAD, *The Least Developed Countries Report 2007* (Geneva, United Nations, 2007), available at www.unctad.org/en/docs/ldc2007_en.pdf. The Commission on Economic, Social and Cultural Rights has also asserted the social function of IP and the necessity of states preventing IP from being used for purposes contrary to human rights and dignity.

[27] R Okediji, 'Securing Intellectual Property Objectives: New Approaches to Human Rights Considerations' in ME Salomon, A Tostensen and W Vandenhole (eds), *Casting the Net Wider: Human Rights, Development and New Duty-Bearers* (Mortsel, Intersentia, 2007) 242. For proposed action towards this end see J de Beer (ed), *Implementing the World Intellectual Property Organization's Development Agenda* (Waterloo, Wilfrid Laurier University Press, 2009).

[28] The Commission on Economic, Social and Cultural Rights has also asserted the social function of IP and the necessity of states preventing IP from being used for purposes contrary to human rights and dignity. General Comment No 17: The Right of Everyone to Benefit from the Protection of the Moral and Material Interests Resulting from any Scientific, Literary or Artistic Production of which he is the Author (Art 15, para 1(c) of the Covenant, 35 UN Doc E/C.12/GC/17, 12 January 2006).

Rights-based development aspirations, while most prominent in the work of bilateral development-aid donors, also influence the work of NGOs and social movements, and, in so doing, change the character of human rights struggles.

> Prevailing models for understanding NGOs as political actors are inspired largely by civil and political human rights and environmental advocacy, and characterize NGO advocacy as a process of building international support in order to force changes in individual states' behavior. But in a growing number of movements, especially involving economic and social rights, international actors play fundamentally different roles. Here, NGOs often work to weaken the roles of some international organizations, notably the International Monetary Fund (IMF) and the World Trade Organization (WTO) to alter the foreign and economic policies of powerful states, and to protect and broaden the options of national governments.[29]

At both the Convention on Biological Diversity and the WIPO meetings in recent years, for example, a more diverse range of IP options for developing-country governments have been championed by environmental, indigenous, development and health-oriented NGOs, many of which receive funding from aid organisations with social justice agendas.[30] These politics go beyond targeting single states as duty-bearers to their own citizens by focusing upon economic actors (including powerful governments) who are viewed as posing obstacles to the realisation of economic, social and cultural rights in other areas of the world. Traditional tensions between international NGOs and poor country governments are altered and sometimes reversed, 'as NGOs support and cooperate with governments and work against the constraining effects of trade rules, economic policy conditionality and corporate leverage'.[31]

This new brand of advocacy brings human rights standards to bear upon the practices of international financial institutions, trade regimes and corporations, as well as governments. Since the frontiers of commodification today involve cultural intangibles protected as informational goods, it is not surprising that much of this advocacy involves IP. By mobilising human rights principles as leverage against the norms of liberalisation and privatisation and by assigning accountability beyond the violating state, these struggles confront the IP privileges held by corporate rights-holders. The campaign for essential medicines and global HIV/AIDS treatment is,

---

[29] E Dorsey and P Nelson, 'New Rights Advocacy in a Global Public Domain' (2007) 13 *European Journal of International Relations* 190. See also E Dorsey and P Nelson, 'At the Nexus of Human Rights and Development: New Methods and Strategies of NGOs' (2003) 31 *World Development* 2013.

[30] C Deere, *The Implementation Game: The TRIPS Agreement and the Global Politics of Intellectual Property Reform in Developing Countries* (New York, Oxford University Press, 2009); AK Menescal, 'Changing WIPO's Ways? The 2004 Development Agenda in Historical Perspective' (2005) 8 *Journal of World Intellectual Property* 761.

[31] Deere, ibid, 190. See also K Raustiala and D Victor, 'The Regime Complex for Plant Genetic Resources' (2004) 58 *International Organization* 277.

perhaps, the best known,[32] but it is not singular.[33] The rights of governments to refuse to patent or to admit genetically modified foods, and the rights of citizens to refuse the commodification of life-forms, are championed by a new range of advocates.[34] Access to knowledge and open research networks are viewed as entitlements,[35] the rights of farmers to save seed over and above patents and plant breeders' rights are linked to food sovereignty[36] and asserted as aspects of self-determination, and states are provided with new legal resources to resist international trade pressures.[37] IP issues are thereby immersed in larger political conversations about livelihood sustainability.

## III. SUSTAINABILITY IN DEVELOPMENT

Just as rights-based norms have been deployed to counter trade-dominated understandings of IP, the concept of sustainability has provided policy-makers and community activists with alternative ways of thinking about economic development, resource use and social relations. Sustainability extends the time horizons in which actors conceive and evaluate projects, and promotes greater equity between social groups through new forms of governance which challenge the narrow principles of market efficiency. The foundations of the sustainability movement sit uneasily with neo-liberal, trickle-down economics in which development capacities are to be maximised with no necessary regard for participation, redistribution or social justice. Like neo-liberalism, sustain-

---

[32] Dorsey and Nelson, 'New Rights Advocacy', n 29 above, 187. See also SK Sell, *Private Power, Public Law: The Globalization of Intellectual Property Rights* (Cambridge, Cambridge University Press, 2003); E 't Hoen, 'TRIPS, Pharmaceutical Patents, and Access to Essential Medicines: A Long Way from Seattle to Doha' (2002) 3 *Chicago Journal of International Law* 27; P Roffe, G Tansey and D Vivas-Eugui (eds), *Negotiating Health: Intellectual Property and Access to Medicines* (London, Earthscan, 2005); L Helfer, 'Regime Shifting: The TRIPs Agreement and the New Dynamics of Intellectual Property Making' (2004) 29 *Yale Journal of International Law* 1; L Helfer, 'Regime Shifting in the International Intellectual Property System' (2009) 7 *Perspectives on Politics* 39; SK Sell, 'Cat and Mouse: Industries', States' and NGOs' Forum—Shifting in the Battle Over Intellectual Property Enforcement' (2009) available at SSRN: http://ssrn.com/abstract=1466156.

[33] See L Bernier, *Justice in Genetics: Intellectual Property and Human Rights from a Cosmopolitan Liberal Perspective* (Cheltenham, Edward Elgar Publishing, 2010); see also, more generally, D Halpert, *Resisting Intellectual Property* (New York, Routledge, 2005).

[34] S Safrin, 'Hyperownership in a Time of Biotechnological Promise: the International Conflict to Control the Building Blocks of Life' (2004) 98 *American Journal of International Law* 641; B Amani and RJ Coombe, 'The Human Genome Diversity Project: The Politics of Patents at the Intersection of Race, Religion, and Research Ethics' (2005) 27 *Law and Policy* 159; DB Resnik, *Owning the Genome: A Moral Analysis of DNA Patenting* (Albany, NY, State University of New York Press, 2003); D Harry, 'High-Tech Invasion: Biocolonialism' in J Mander and V Tauli-Corpuz (eds), *Paradigm Wars: Indigenous Peoples' Resistance to Globalization* (San Francisco, Sierra Club Books, 2006), 81.

[35] A Kapczynski, 'The Access to Knowledge Mobilization and the New Politics of Intellectual Property' (2008) 117 *Yale Journal of International Law* 804.

[36] AA Desmarais, *La Via Campesina: Globalization and the Power of Peasants* (London, Pluto Press, 2007); V Menotti, 'How the World Trade Organization Diminishes Native Sovereignty' in Mander and Tauli-Corpuz, n 34 above, 59; K Aoki, 'Weeds, Seeds & Deeds: Recent Skirmishes in the Seed Wars' (2003) 11 *Cardozo Journal of International and Comparative Law* 247; C Oguamanam, 'Agro-biodiversity and Food Security: Biotechnology and Traditional Agricultural Practices at the Periphery of International Intellectual Property Regime Complex' (2007) 215 *Michigan State University Law Review* 215; T Van Dooren, 'Inventing Seed: The Nature(s) of Intellectual Property in Plants' (2008) 26 *Environment and Planning D: Society and Space* 676.

[37] B Amani, *State Agency and the Patenting of Life in International Law: Merchants and Missionaries in a Global Society* (Aldershot, Ashgate Publishing, 2009); P Drahos, 'Four Lessons for Developing Countries from the Trade Negotiations over Access to Medicines' (2007) 28 *Liverpool Law Review* 11.

able development seeks to open up (state-dominated) economic systems, but it does so as a means to encourage the engagement of a wider variety of actors in the politics of development.[38] Sustainability has been suggested as a valuable conceptual framework for considering IP because it acknowledges the integrated importance of social, environmental and economic issues.[39] One initiative of this type involved Oxfam's efforts to increase consumption of Fairtrade-certified coffee for the benefit of small farmers and producer co-operatives by encouraging co-operation between NGOs and corporations, educating consumers and building new forms of social solidarity.[40]

The successful implementation of a certification scheme involves the deployment of IP (usually with a form of trademark) towards new ends. Marks certifying sustainability standards are only one part of a transnational commodity chain of assurance, governance and accountability which links actors and practices, but without this final indication the whole system would fail. The success of such projects depends upon a market for global social responsibility and the responsible exercise of the exclusive right to mark goods with indicia that confirm to the consumer that clear standards have been met. Marks that distinguish goods and services which have been certified to meet certain standards appear to be proliferating.[41] Although these certification programmes are privately operated, they often claim to promote the public interest and may be shaped by the motivation to restructure market incentives in order to achieve environmental and social aspirations.[42] Fairtrade and sustainable forestry certifications are but the best known of the MICOs which link environmental and equity concerns under the rubric of sustainability.

Indigenous peoples have made an ethos of environmental sustainability central to their global political platform and this ethos has been evoked in many international policy negotiations in order to find new means of protecting traditional knowledge (TK).[43] It

---

[38] M Raco, 'Sustainable Development, Rolled out Neoliberalism and Sustainable Communities' (2005) 37 *Antipode* 324, 330.

[39] D Marinova and M Raven, 'Indigenous Knowledge and Intellectual Property: A Sustainability Agenda' (2006) 20 *Journal of Economic Surveys* 587, 592. More generally see P Cullet, *Intellectual Property and Sustainable Development* (New Delhi, Butterworths, 2005); for an extensive discussion of the history of Fairtrade coffee, Fairtrade International and the benefits this moral economy of alternative globalization has provided to many communities in the Global South see G Fridell, *Fair Trade Coffee: The Prospects & Pitfalls of Market Driven Social Justice* (Toronto, University of Toronto Press, 2007). For a discussion of Oxfam's rationale see SH Holcombe and RC Offenheiser, 'Challenges and Opportunities in Implementing a Rights-Based Approach to Development: An Oxfam American Perspective' (2003) 32 *Nonprofit and Voluntary Sector Quarterly* 2, 268. The relevance of Fairtrade certification for food security and environmental sustainability is also addressed in D Jaffe, *Brewing Justice: Fair Trade Coffee, Sustainability, and Survival* (Berkeley CA, University of California Press, 2007).

[40] Shafir and Brysk, n 16 above, 275, 284.

[41] M Chon, 'Marks of Rectitude' (2008–09) 77 *Fordham Law Review* 2311; M Agdomar, 'Removing the Greek from Feta and Adding Korbel to Champagne: The Paradox of Geographical Indications in International Law' (2008) 18 *Fordham Intellectual Property Media, and Entertainment Law Journal* 541.

[42] E Mendieger, 'Law Making by Global Civil Society: The Forest Certification Prototype', working paper (2001), available at www.law.buffalo.edu/homepage/eemeid/scholarship/GCSEL.pdf, 16; *idem*, 'Multi-interest Self-governance through Global Product Certification Programs', Buffalo Legal Studies Research Paper No 2006-016 (July 2006), available at http://ssrn.com/abstract=917956; *idem*, 'Private Environmental Law Regulation, Human Rights and Community' (1999) 7 *Buffalo Environmental Law Journal* 123.

[43] The number of international instruments that refer to the protection of TK is now quite large. See RJ Coombe, 'First Nations' Intangible Cultural Heritage Concerns: Prospects for Protection of Traditional Knowledge and Traditional Cultural Expressions in International Law' in C Bell and R Patterson (eds), *Protection of First Nations' Cultural Heritage: Laws, Policy and Reform* (Vancouver, University of British Columbia Press, 2008), 313; *idem*, 'Protecting Traditional Environmental Knowledge and New Social Move-

is generally acknowledged that 'new intellectual property protection should allow for maintaining the social, political, cultural and physical environment where indigenous knowledge is created'.[44] A 'one size fits all' model for IP is arguably inappropriate in an ethos of sustainability that emphasises the maintenance of diversity in ecosystems, values and social systems. From a sustainability perspective, advocates argue, we need alternative approaches to allow for an ethic of environmental care, for the preservation of languages, for improved health and living standards, and for better political representation and participation to support a 'people–culture–country continuum'.[45]

Interestingly, what economists Dora Marinova and Margaret Raven offer as an example of one means of protecting indigenous knowledge outside of an IP system (and as an alternative means of sustainable indigenous development) is a protocol that contractually reproduces the mechanisms of a collective certification mark for local communities. They point to a partnership involving the multinational corporation Aveda, an Australian exporter (Mount Romance—The Sandalwood Factory) and a collective made up of indigenous elders (the Songman's Circle of Wisdom, a non-profit aboriginal organisation, certify that proper protocol is observed in collecting) that collectively ensure that an aboriginal community receives funds for the provision of sandalwood oil using their traditional knowledge of its properties.

> The World Perfumery Congress was alerted to the indigenous protocol in Cannes in 2004. The protocol establishes sourcing standards for sandalwood in Australia and provides a model for international Indigenous leaders to practice sustainable business across their own communities. It is the first protocol of its type in the world. Under the protocol, Aveda now sources its sandalwood in the Western Australian desert, led by Aboriginal wood harvesters from the camp at Kutkububba. Aveda pays a premium on top of the state-controlled price, which goes to the community. However, only a fifth of West Australian sandalwood harvesting is done by Indigenous communities. The money contributed by Aveda and Mount Romance will therefore form part of a working capital fund to assist Aboriginal communities to bid more effectively for the limited sandalwood licenses (the collection of sandalwood is conducted via a strict government licensing system). It is envisaged that the protocol will facilitate the development of other relationships between Indigenous people and multinational corporations like Aveda.[46]

To the extent that standards are maintained over local sourcing and the sandalwood oil has particular properties because of its area of origin, methods of location, collection or extraction, this 'accreditation' has all of the qualities of a MICO. Significantly, the protocol is based upon local cultural norms.

---

ments in the Americas: Intellectual Property, Human Right or Claims to an Alternative Form of Sustainable Development?' (2005) 17 *Florida Journal of International Law* 115.

[44] Marinova and Raven, n 39 above, 592.

[45] Ibid, 593.

[46] Agreements, Treaties and Negotiated Settlements Project (Melbourne, University of Melbourne, 2007), available at www.atns.net.au.

## IV. CULTURE AND HERITAGE IN DEVELOPMENT

[C]ulture has recently acquired a new visibility and salience in development thinking and practice.[47]

The incorporation of 'culture' into development agendas appears to have been prompted by UNESCO's expressed concern, in the World Culture Report of 1998, that a 'crippling lack of basic indicators of culture' amongst member states made the relationship between culture and development difficult to evaluate.[48] Cultural rights—that is, the rights to take part in cultural life, to enjoy the benefits of progress in the arts and sciences, to have minority and indigenous cultures protected, and to preserve and protect cultural heritage—are receiving renewed attention.[49] Evoking culture in development circles indexes the concerns about maintaining cultural diversity, respecting local value systems, ensuring social cohesion and ending discrimination against the socially marginalised.[50] It is widely recognised, however, that there is no simple way of preserving culture. As folklorist Kelly Feltault recalls:

> A fisherman asked me, 'How are you going to preserve my culture if you don't save my right and ability to fish?' His question brought together issues of public policy, culture, human rights, environmental management, and global capitalist economics—the precise location of his traditions . . . His question required another form of development, one based in political, economic and cultural rights and human security, rather than preservation and economic growth through the presentation of traditional culture.[51]

Cultural rights, particularly those that embrace identity claims, are an area of enhanced human rights concern.[52] They are exemplified by, but by no means limited to, indigenous rights, and may pertain both to individuals and to collectivities. These rights are increasingly recognised in national constitutions, as well as in regional and international legal instruments, shaping the practices of lending institutions as well as development agencies and NGOs, which increasingly view culture as a resource. Although culture as an asset is often framed in purely economic terms, culture conceived as a resource puts greater value on social cohesion, community autonomy, political recognition, local pride and cross-generational communications, and brings new issues, such as cultural misrepresentation, the loss of languages, and the preservation and valuation of local knowledge, to the fore. These concerns are integrally

---

[47] S Radcliffe, 'Culture in Development Thinking: Geographies, Actors and Paradigms' in *idem* (ed), *Culture and Development in a Globalizing World: Geographies, Actors, and Paradigms* (New York, Routledge, 2006) 1.

[48] CG Mohkiber, 'Toward a Measure of Dignity: Indicators for Rights-Based Development' (2001) 18 *Statistical Journal of the United Nations ECE* 155, 159.

[49] J Symonides, 'International Implementation of Cultural Rights by the International Community' (1998) 60 *International Communication Gazette* 7; R Albro and J Bauer, 'Introduction' to the special issue entitled, 'Cultural Rights: What they Are, Why they Matter, How they can be Realized' (2005) 2 *Human Rights Dialogue* 2.

[50] Radcliffe, n 47 above, 1.

[51] K Feltault, 'Development Folklife: Human Security and Cultural Conservation' (2006) 119 *Journal of American Folklore* 90.

[52] B Robbins and E Stamatopolou, 'Reflections on Culture and Cultural Rights' (2004) 103 *South Atlantic Quarterly* 419; Shafir and Brysk, n 16 above, 275; R Albro, 'Managing Culture at Diversity's Expense? Thoughts on UNESCO's Newest Cultural Policy Instrument' (2005) 29 *Journal of Arts Management, Law and Society* 1; Albro and Bauer, n 49 above, 12.

related to neo-liberalism, the growth of the 'knowledge economy' and the spread of new communications technologies that have enabled cultural forms to be reproduced and publicised at a speed and velocity never before experienced. Digitalisation, for example, has accelerated processes of social decontextualisation while simultaneously heightening our awareness of the exploitation of cultural heritage resources, and has thus enhanced political consciousness about the injuries that may thereby be effected.[53]

We have witnessed a growing possessiveness in relation to cultural forms at exactly the same time that culture is being revalued, not only by indigenous peoples,[54] but also by communities, regions and national governments, who see cultural expressions, cultural distinctions and cultural diversity as sources of both meaning and income.[55] IPRs figure centrally in these efforts to revalue traditions and revive heritage in a political terrain that involves many new stakeholders (individuals and governments certainly, but also businesses and archaeologists, curators and communities, development banks and universities). Cultural heritage protection, for example, links the preservation of natural and cultural environments to sustainability objectives that reconcile conservation and development goals. If IPRs have traditionally focused more on encouraging development in narrowly economic terms than on conservation functions, they are increasingly implicated in these new agendas in which 'culture and local specificity are integral',[56] communities are 'empowered'[57] and human rights are interpreted through vernacular structures of meaning.[58] Many of these projects make use of local knowledge and insist upon community participation while emphasising that cultural heritage is dynamic, flexible and adaptive. There appears to be a widespread belief that IPRs should be shaped to encourage this endorsement of cultural value through the use and development of TK innovations and practices (an agenda that the WIPO has, arguably, embraced), but great challenges lie before us.

The current methods of protecting IP are often too limited to recognise peoples' rights in relation to indigenous knowledge, for instance, and, to date, the so-called *sui generis* (unique) rights have been no more effective in terms of addressing social and livelihood needs without compromising the capacities of future generations to meet their obligations. Indigenous knowledge is more readily conceived of as capital when it is protected as IP, because most forms of IP serve as mechanisms for creating market-based values that may provide the equity necessary for some communities to

---

[53] RJ Coombe, 'The Expanding Purview of Cultural Properties and their Politics' (2009) 5 *Annual Review of Law and Social Sciences* 393.

[54] M Brown, *Who Owns Native Culture?* (Cambridge, MA, Harvard University Press, 2003); M Brown, 'Heritage Trouble: Recent Work on the Protection of Intangible Cultural Property' (2005) 12 *International Journal of Cultural Property*, 40; E Coleman and R Coombe, 'A Broken Record: Subjecting "Music" to Cultural Rights' in JC Young and C Brunck (eds), *Ethics of Cultural Appropriation* (Oxford, Blackwell Publishing, 2009) 179.

[55] M Ahmed, RJ Coombe and S Schnoor, 'Bearing Cultural Distinction: Informational Capitalism and New Expectations for Intellectual Property' (2007) 40 *University of California-Davis Law Review* 891; RJ Coombe, 'Legal Claims to Culture in and against the Market: Neoliberalism and the Global Proliferation of Meaningful Difference' (2005) 1 *Law, Culture and the Humanities* 32.

[56] Ensor and Gready, n 13 above, 11.

[57] For a critical understanding of this process see RJ Coombe, 'Owning Culture: Locating Community Subjects and their Properties' in M Busse and V Strang (eds), *Ownership and Appropriation* (Oxford, Berg Publishers, 2010) 105; idem, 'Cultural Agencies: 'Constructing' Community Subjects and their Rights' in M Biagioli, P Jaszi and M Woodmansee (eds), *Making and Unmaking Intellectual Property* (Chicago IL, University of Chicago Press, 2010) 79.

[58] Ensor and Gready, n 13 above, 17.

create wealth and perhaps break cycles of poverty.[59] A rights-based approach to the issue, moreover, would insist that opportunities be widely shared and efforts made to distribute benefits equitably. A sustainability perspective would suggest that the development of indigenous or traditional knowledge requires maintaining the social relations and practices through which a natural environment and its diversity are both maintained and reproduced. To the extent that biological and cultural diversity are regarded as being inter-related,[60] IP, as we know it, is far too limited. It promotes 'development' perhaps, but does nothing to ensure the sustainability of culture, not as a field of static works and practices of production, but as a way of living that shapes people's aspirations for improved livelihoods of their own design.[61]

As the fisherman's comment reminds us, the transformation of culture into an export commodity as part of a service industry that focuses on the past, as simply an asset of economic value, may depoliticise the processes that force people to rely upon their traditions when their traditional livelihoods have been destroyed and they have no alternative futures. Moreover, it discounts the capacity of tradition to serve as a dynamic resource for shaping peoples futures. Development divorced from self-determination fails to meet the rights-based indicators because it does not consider the ends as well as the means of development. In other words, within a human rights framework that values sustainability, community security must be addressed as a social good. Development projects and practices need to involve community members in decision-making about how reproductions of their heritage will be controlled, for what purposes and to achieve what kind of futures. Sustaining livelihoods, communities and traditions tied to resources requires a holistic, rights-based approach—whose legitimacy requires wide participation and democratic deliberation.

## V. MARKS INDICATIVE OF CONDITIONS OF ORIGIN (MICO)

Are IPRs capable of becoming more flexible in order to address these newly linked economic, social, cultural and environmental objectives? Geographical indications (GIs) are one means by which local conditions of production can be maintained, and traditional methods and practices recognised and valued through the exploitation of niche markets.[62] Used historically to protect the rural traditions of European elites, they are now favourably considered as vehicles to promote the development of others whose collective rights, traditions and cultural resources may thereby assume new value.[63] Indications of source, appellations of origin and geographical indications are

---

[59] Marinova and Raven, n 39 above, 587, 591.

[60] See discussion in SJ Zent and EL Zent, 'On Biocultural Diversity from a Venezuelan Perspective: Tracing the Interrelationships among Biodiversity, Culture Change and Legal Reforms' in CL MacManus (ed), *Biodiversity and the Law: Intellectual Property, Biotechnology and Traditional Knowledge* (London, Earthscan, 2007) 91.

[61] Coombe, 'Protecting Traditional Environmental Knowledge', n 43 above.

[62] See D Rangnekar, 'The Socioeconomics of Geographical Indications: A Review of Empirical Evidence from Europe' (May 2004) *Intellectual Property Rights and Sustainable Development* issue paper no 8.

[63] L Bentley and B Sherman, *Intellectual Property Law*, 2nd edn (Oxford, Oxford University Press, 2009) 976; D Gervais, 'Traditional Knowledge: Are We Closer to the Answer(s)? The Potential Role of Geographical Indications' (2009) 15 *ILSA Journal of International & Comparative Law* 551; AK Sanders, 'Incentives for and Protection of Cultural Expression: Art, Trade and Geographical Indications' (2010) 13 *The Journal of World Intellectual Property* 81; Sunder, n 2 above, 300; idem, 'The Invention of Traditional Knowledge'

unique in the field of IP protections; they are used to protect place-based distinctions in the market, and they are, in significant ways, inalienable, unlike the vast majority of IPRs which act primarily to promote alienability. Appellations of origin refer to geographical names that designate the origin of a good, in which 'the quality and characteristics exhibited by the product are essentially attributable to the geographical environment, including natural and human factors'.[64] Goods that have a quality, reputation or characteristic that is attributable to their geographical origin are covered by the TRIPs Agreement.[65]

If we take 'geographical origin' here to extend to natural and human factors (as it did historically and indeed, did in earlier drafts of the TRIPs Agreement[66]), then it is possible for marks of origin to designate a wide range of reputational characteristics. For example, certain agricultural goods from the Indian state of Kerala might bear an emblem of origin that indicates that they were produced in a 'GMO Free Zone', or by manufacturers committed to affirmative action for persons of castes traditionally discriminated against. In other words, although the goods might have no specific characteristics due to these conditions of origin, they may have a reputation essentially attributed to salient human factors that are linked to a geographical region. Nonetheless, it might be argued that the same objectives could be accomplished in a less complicated way through the use of more traditional categories of trademark, such as certification and collective marks.

As economists Cerkia Bramley and Johann Kirsten remind us, although most trademark laws prohibit the use of geographical terms or indicia that have not acquired secondary meaning because they are descriptive, this is not a bar to certification and collective marks.[67] Owners of certification marks cannot use them, however, because their holders must constitute an independent certifying authority required to ensure that all who use the mark are providing the good with the certified quality. Collective marks held by associations on behalf of their members are also usually bound to certain quality and cultivation controls within the area of production.

To avoid having to list all of these legal vehicles at each reiteration of this range, we have coined the term 'marks indicating conditions of origin' (MICOs) to indicate the larger field throughout this chapter. Different countries use different vehicles to

---

(2007) 70 *Law and Contemporary Problems* 97; B Sherman and L Wiseman, 'Toward an Indigenous Public Domain?' in L Guibault and PB Heugenholtz (eds), *The Future of the Public Domain* (Netherlands, Kluwer Law International, 2006), 259.

[64] M Gueze, 'Let's Have Another Look at the Lisbon Agreement: Its Terms in their Context and in Light of its Object and Purpose', paper prepared for the International Symposium on Geographical Indications jointly organized by the World Intellectual Property Organization and the State Administration for Industry and Commerce of the People's Republic of China, Beijing, WIPO/GEO/BEI/O7/10 (26–28 June 2007), available at www.wipo.int/edocs/mdocs/geoind/en/wipo_geo_bei_07/wipo_geo_bei_07_www_81756.doc. Many countries use the legal instrument 'denomination of origin' to add value to goods whose distinctive qualities are due to geographic conditions that include natural and human, or cultural factors.

[65] M Hopperger, 'Geographical Indications in the International Arena: The Current Situation', paper prepared for the International Symposium on Geographical Indications jointly organised by the World Intellectual Property Organization and the State Administration for Industry and Commerce of the People's Republic of China, Beijing, WIPO/GEO/BEI/O7/07 (26–28 June 2007).

[66] D Zografos, *Intellectual Property and Traditional Cultural Expressions* (Cheltenham, Edward Elgar Publishing, 2010) 176–77.

[67] C Bramley and JF Kirsten, 'Exploring the Economic Rationale for Protecting Geographical Indicators in Agriculture' (2007) 46 *Agrekon* 74.

accomplish similar things; a jurisdiction without a history of recognising geographical
indications may instead have a well-developed range of collective or certification marks
that may look more like a conventional group of trademarks found elsewhere. A more
encompassing term, such as MICOs, both enables us to refer to a more jurispruden-
tially diverse terrain and affirms legal pluralism. In international and transnational
arenas, more and more institutions have focused on the potential of MICOs as possible
tools for local and rural development.[68]

MICOs are seen as being especially promising in sustainable development and
rights-based development because the use of the legally protected name is not limited
to a single producer but to all producers within the designated area who adhere to the
code of practice; product reputation is the result of the activities of different agents
active in the same area of production, projected through traditions of practice over
time.[69] The distinguishing resources of a region, which will usually include terrain and
climate, may also be cultural and historical in nature. As one author summarises:

> GIs have features that respond to the needs of indigenous and local communities and
> farmers . . . [they] are based on collective traditions and a collective decision-making process;
> reward traditions while allowing for continued evolution; emphasize the relationship between
> human efforts, culture, land, resources, and environment; and—are not freely transferable
> from one owner to another.[70]

As another asserts: '[GIs] can present long term benefits as they create value, enhance
the marketability of goods and give an edge to developing countries to promote

[68] M Blakeney, 'Protection of Traditional Knowledge by Geographical Indications' (2009) 3 *International Journal of Intellectual Property Management Issues* 357; DR Downes and SA Laird, 'Innovative Mecha-nisms for sharing benefits of biodiversity and related knowledge. Case studies on geographical indications and trademarks', paper prepared for the UNCTAD Biotrade Initiative (1999), available at www.ciel.org; S Escudero, F Addor and A Grazioli, 'Geographical Indications beyond Wines and Spirits. A Roadmap for Better Protection for Geographical Indication in the WTO TRIPS Agreement' (2002) 5 *Journal of World Intellectual Property* 865; A Berenguer, 'Geographical Origins in the World', paper presented at the workshop 'Promoting Agricultural Competitiveness through Local Know-how'. Proceedings of the Mont-pellier Workshop (Washington DC World Bank Group, 2004); (MAAPAR, Paris; CIRAD, Montpellier); B Sylvander, 'Concerted Action: DOLPHINS Final Report, Synthesis and Recommendations' (January 2004), available at www.origin-food.org/pdf/wp7/dol_d8.pdf; GE Evans and M Blakeney, 'The Protection of Geo-graphical Indications after Doha: Quo Vadis?' (2006) 9 *Journal of International Economic Law* 3; P van de Kop, D Sautier and A Gertz (eds), *Origin-based Products: Lessons for Pro-poor Market Development* (Amsterdam, Royal Tropical Institute, 2006). For examples of regional studies see CM Correa, 'Protection of geographical indications in Caricom Countries', paper prepared for CARICOM (2002), available at www.crnm.org/documents/studies/geographical%20Indications%20%20Correa.pdf; E Mendes, 'An Investigation into the Potential for Products of Origin in the Western Cape, South Africa', Western Cape Department of Agriculture Report (2001) 154; D Sautier and C Sarfati, 'Indications géographique en Afrique francophone: rapport 2004 des actions d'appui INAO-CIRAD auprés de l'OAPI' (Montpellier, Cirad-Tera/Inao, 2005); D Rangnekar, 'Indications of Geographical Origin in Asia: Legal and Policy Issues to Resolve' in Melendez-Ortiz and Roffe, n 6 above, 273; S Wagle, 'Geographical Indications as Trade-Related Intellectual Property: Relevance and Implications for Human Development in Asia-Pacific', discussion paper (UNDP Asia-Pacific Trade and Investment Initiative, 2007).

[69] F Marty, 'Which Are the Ways of Innovation in PDO and PGI Products? Typical and Traditional Products: Rural Effect and Agro-industrial Problems' in F Arfini and C Mora (eds), *Proceedings of the 52nd European Association of Agricultural Economics Seminar, Parma, Italy, 19–21 June 2008*.

[70] F Addor and A Grazioli, 'Geographical Indications beyond Wines and Spirits: A Roadmap for a Better Protection for Geographical Indications in the WTO/TRIPS Agreement' (2002) 5 *Journal of World Intel-lectual Property* 865.

exports and rural development, thus generating sustainability and inter-generational equity'.[71]

The capacity to implement collective control over these marks is especially attractive both to development practitioners and to NGOs concerned with preventing new forms of inequality and hoping to encourage greater social cohesion. Moreover, MICOs are of interest to cultural heritage practitioners because they can be used with regard to products derived from the traditional practices of communities, and have a history of being used to protect traditional cultural expressions.[72]

Creating an exclusive right to a link between a product and its origin establishes a proprietary right for those who are entitled to use it.[73] However, unlike other IPs, such as privately held trademarks, MICOs are uniquely apt for supporting local collectivities because of the public nature of the rights that flow from their use.[74] Using a GI as a means of supporting local collectivities is, nonetheless, controversial; some critics argue that such a use is nothing more than a thinly veiled protectionist measure that can be used to undermine competition,[75] and that many countries, and the United States in particular, already offer adequate, TRIPs-level protection of domestic and foreign GIs through the trademark system.[76] Such an argument seems to presuppose that GIs constitute a wholly new regime of rights, rather than encompass the use of older forms of MICOs, such as certification and collective marks, which are well-known forms of trademark in most jurisdictions. The argument also overlooks the geopolitics of trade, which ensure that developing countries are often forced to compete in the global market without the protection and agricultural subsidies provided in developed countries. Finally, WTO member states have long made commitments to ensuring that developing countries could gain enhanced access to global markets, and it is only reasonable to expect that developing countries should seize upon one of the very few areas of TRIPs-protected IPRs that might provide them with some competitive advantage.[77] Consumer interests in securing knowledge about 'conditions of origin' for goods as well as the commitments on the part of states to human rights principles are also relevant considerations that militate against such purely economic arguments.[78]

As a tool in rights-based development practice, the introduction of GIs can aid the forging of collective rights that are indivisible from locality. Ecosystem specificities and local practices are maintained by turning these into symbolic differentiations that yield rents for those whose activities enrich and reproduce these distinctions. Communities

---

[71] D Zografos, 'Geographical Indicators and Socio-economic Development', paper presented at the 4th European Intellectual Property Institutes Network Conference, Zurich, April 2008, available at http://www.iqsensato.org/wp-content/uploads/2009/02/iqsensato-wp-3-zografos-dec-2008.pdf.

[72] Zografos, n 66 above, 103.

[73] Addor and Grazioloi, n 70 above, 183.

[74] I Calboli, 'Expanding the Protection of Geographical Indications of Origin under TRIPS: Old Debate or New Opportunity?' (2006) 10 *Marquette Intellectual Property Law Review* 181, 182.

[75] Ibid, 186.

[76] For examples of this argument see I Shalevick, 'Protection of Trademarks and Geographical Indications' (2008) 6 *Buffalo Intellectual Property Law Journal* 67; J Hughes, 'Champagne, Feta, and Bourbon: The Spirited Debate about Geographical Indications' (2008) 58 *Hastings Law Journal* 299.

[77] Agdomar, n 41 above.

[78] For studies advocating the extension and development of MICO protections that make cultural and human rights arguments for the projection of local identity-based products see DE Long, 'Is Fame All There Is? Beating Global Monopolists At Their Own Marketing Game' (2008) 40 *G Washington International Law Review* 123; RL Okedji, 'The International Intellectual Property Roots of Geographical Indications' (2007) 82 *Chicago-Kent Law Review* 1329.

and collectivities should thus benefit directly from the use of the GIs, but, as we shall see, these are often promoted by states, which may be more interested in increasing foreign exchange than in fostering community security. Creating sustainable livelihoods for more secure communities does, of course, contribute to the overall development of the nation state, but, from a sustainability and rights-based perspective, it should do so in a way that emphasises community participation, governance and capacity-building.

Evaluating the impact of the use of MICOs on rural development is complex. It might be argued that such a strategy risks fixing local practices, rather than enabling their ongoing generativity (although, in practice, they have proven to be capable of adjusting to shifting local circumstance). Few proponents of MICO strategies promote their general applicability; most urge careful consideration with regard to their govern-ance in assessing their capacities to serve as engines of rural development.[79] In any case, their success should not be measured only by standard development-assessment criteria, such as higher employment and income levels. From a sustainable and rights-based development perspective, careful attention to such indirect goals as biodiversity preservation, the protection of traditional knowledge, distributional equities and enhanced levels of social cohesion are also desirable.

The expansion of GIs to new forms of goods and services certainly has detrac-tors.[80] It is not our intention to enter into this debate or to argue for or against GIs on absolute grounds. We would, however, argue that it is inappropriate to evaluate the use of MICOs in abstract economic and philosophic terms that view them pri-marily as properties and/or exclusive rights to 'information' without consideration of their social function and consequence, their communicative objectives, their role in regional development policies for alleviating rural poverty and their capacity to build social capital.[81] As we will show, poorly implemented schemes to introduce MICOs are dangerous. They may give rise to new forms of local inequality, undesirable trans-formations of social relations and even further social disintegration if they are not adequately designed and regulated. However, they can also bear social dividends when they are well managed and adequately supported. Two studies of the consequences of using MICO will now be briefly summarised. A rights-based sustainable development framework assists us in evaluating these initiatives.

## VI. SUBJECTING MICOS TO SUSTAINABILITY AND RIGHTS-BASED DEVELOPMENT INDICATORS

GIs have attracted great new interest in the past decade as developing countries seek new ways of competing in a global economy.[82] Nonetheless, GIs may be 'sold' to

---

[79] E Barham, 'Translating *Terroir*: The Global Challenge of French AOC Labelling' (2003) 19 *Journal of Rural Studies* 127.

[80] Hughes, n 76 above.

[81] For one such study see S Munzer and K Raistala, 'The Global Struggle over Geographical Indications' (2007) 18 *European Journal of International Law* 337.

[82] For an excellent overview of the prospects for using indicators of geographical origin to improve the livelihoods of coffee growers, which links certifications guaranteeing socio-economic and environmental quality content with specific places and explores their use in promoting broader territorial strategies constructed around tourism, handicrafts and other agro-food products see B Daviron and S Ponte, *The Coffee Paradox; Global Markets, Commodity Trade and the Elusive Promise of Development* (London, Zed Books, 2005).

Third World countries (by NGOs, development aid agencies and lending institutions) without fair disclosure of the administrative costs involved, the technical expertise they require and the institutional investment they demand. Dwijen Rangnekar argues that the simple introduction of GIs will not generate positive social and economic trans-formation without collateral institutions, supporting policy measures and marketing strategies.[83] Empirical study of appellations in Europe suggests that producers with the most secure marketing networks tend to secure the lion's share of the values these yield.[84] Building supply chains is no easy feat for small producers; public investment will be necessary to prevent the most powerful private actors from monopolizing the opportunities that MICOs afford.

Daniel Gade's study of the use and management of the AOC (*Appellation d'Origine Contrôlée*) held in the commune of Cassis in Southern France[85] might be used to caution against any simple enthusiasm over the use of MICOs for promoting local goods. He argues that the AOC for local wine, developed to restrict industrial and residential development in the area, evolved historically so as to be controlled by an ever-smaller syndicate of producers who dictate the conditions of the appellation's deployment (routinely issuing dispensations to members when the weather does not easily enable these conditions to be met or profit margins to be sustained), limit the origins and the types of grapes/vines that can be used and thereby both restrict the variety of wines produced in the region and the number of producers. The syndicate also prevents the tenants—who grow most of the grapes—from using the appellations, and prohibits the establishment of co-operatives that would benefit smaller producers by introducing economies of scale and new technology. Grapes must be picked by hand, ensuring the continuation of a pool of subservient manual labour, and ceilings are put on the wages of harvest workers in order to keep production costs low.

Nonetheless, Gade believes that the vineyards would have been converted into residential developments early on, had they been denied appellation status. The syndi-cate's control of the appellation has enabled the commune to maintain a viticultural landscape that mitigates the impact of flooding and fire while sustaining a local tourist industry. Despite achieving some economic security for the region and some measure of regional ecoscape preservation, this is a use of a MICO that would fail most rights-based criteria because of its lack of inclusiveness, transparency and accountability, as well as its poor governance. It exacerbates, rather than mitigates, local inequalities while reducing both biological and cultural diversity. Government failures to ensure that management of the MICO meets the basic standards of good governance (or even the basic principles of administrative law), to insist upon an arm's-length relationship between those who govern the use of the mark and those who benefit from it, to insist upon a democratic decision-making process or to demand transparent standards of quality control are all obvious shortcomings. If we accept the veracity of Gade's

[83] Rangnekar, n 68 above, 291.
[84] D Rangnekar, 'The Socio-economics of Geographical Indications: A Review of Empirical Evidence from Europe', draft (October 2003), available at www.iprsonline.org/unctadictsd/docs/GIS_Economics_Oct03.pdf.
[85] D Gade, 'Tradition, Territory, and Terroir in French Viniculture: Cassis, France, and Appellation Con-trôlée' (2004) 94 *Annals of the Association of American Geographers* 848. Wayne Moran also criticises the French wine appellation strategy's propensity to entrench privilege and solidify structures of inequality, in W Moran, 'The Wine Appellation as Territory in France and California' (1999) 83 *Annals of the Association of American Geographers* 694.

observations and evaluations, this is an instance of a MICO being used primarily as a protectionist measure to entrench the privileges of local elites.

Anthropologist Anita Chan's fieldwork in northern Peru shows how 'denominations of origin' have been encouraged in a government initiative that cynically valorises 'tradition' while simultaneously promoting local industrialisation. Ceramic production has expanded dramatically since 'Chulucanas' became a protected mark, but so too has income inequality, labour exploitation and economic competition.[86] Traditional methods of production have actually been abandoned and collective inter-generational workshops replaced with individually owned factories due to the entrepreneurial efficiencies and unrealistic volume demands that national exporting strategies impose on those who seek to have their goods designated as 'National Folkloric Products'. These new standards were externally imposed, bore no relationship to existing social relations of production and decreased, rather than increased, social participation in the production of crafts and in the governance of their production. Moreover, nothing appears to have been done to educate consumers about the conditions of origin for these goods or to prevent their piracy abroad. Fewer people are now engaged in the industry (except as unskilled, low-paid labourers) and pieces of pottery bring in even less money to their producers, while envy, distrust and fear of misappropriation of design and know-how now characterise local social relations.

This Peruvian MICO initiative appears to meet none of the objectives of sustainability, social security or rights-based development which we have considered. Nonetheless, it is a project that was commended to the WIPO as indicative of 'best practices' of using IP to further rural development.[87] An examination of Peruvian national policy with regard to denominations of origin indicates that the government seeks to use place-based products as a means to reclaim 'national' products from foreign appropriation and to alleviate poverty.[88] To do so, however, the state has assumed legal entitlement to these denominations, privileging the protection of 'national' patrimony over considerations of local development, thereby promoting modern industrial criteria rather than local norms and practices, and restricting, rather than enhancing, social inclusion in the management of the MICOs and the allocation and extension of their benefits.

Peru is one of many developing countries that appears to have been 'sold' on a GI strategy as a new means of competing in a global economy without fair disclosure of the administrative costs, technical expertise and institutional investment that such a strategy requires.[89] Where these strategies succeed, extensive co-operation between the players in all the parts of the commodity chain and new sources of support for local producers appear to be necessary. For example, soft cheeses made in the Department of Cajamarca in the northern Andes have been targeted for development because these are considered 'typical products: they are simple, attached to a territory, and the quality of the *mantecosa* is closely linked to the local soils and climate which

---

[86] AS Chan, 'The Fortune of Networks: Neoliberal Seductions, Enterprising Artisans, and the Optimizing of Native Culture in Peru', paper presented at the American Anthropological Association Annual Conference, San Francisco CA, 21 November 2008. On file with the authors.

[87] Ibid.

[88] MA Sanchez del Solar, 'Denominaciones de origin en el Peru: desafios y opportunidades' (2008) 4 *Revista de la Competencia y Propiedad Industrial* 6.

[89] Evans and Blakeney, n 68 above.

determine the richness of the pastures and thus the quality of the milk'.[90] Mantecoso relies upon specific local knowledge and traditional know-how, is a symbol of local identity and involves the work of many small farmers producing milk in a particularly poor rural area. Although the product has evolved from a subsistence food to a commercial product only within the last 30 years, it has already achieved a national reputation for quality.[91] Nonetheless, the failure to protect the product from adulteration and to ensure that the use of the mark is linked exclusively to regional goods and tied to quality controls limits this MICO strategy. An association (the Associacion de Productores de Derirados Lacteos Cajamarca) of Cajamarca city cheesemakers was established in 1999 to improve the quality controls and enhance the marketing of these products, while promoting synergies between cheese, other regional foodstuffs and landscape amenities which have the potential to develop regional tourism further. The association has developed quality labels and has committed itself to the development of 'Poronguito', a collective mark awarded in the year 2000.[92] The extensive and expensive collective organisation necessary to this endeavour has been aided by non-governmental organisations (NGOs) that have facilitated dialogue between producers of *quesillo* (the curd used to make the cheese, which is generally provided by poor livestock producers in mountainous regions), small-scale cheese producers, speciality shops and the national institutions necessary to enable national marketing efforts. The latter are often distrusted in rural areas and amongst indigenous peoples. Still, even in this region, further work must be done to promote a greater sharing of benefits with small producers of *quesillo* (who are often women, often isolated, often exploited by middlemen, and physically and culturally distant from the end-product) as well as to reduce elite family control of direct marketing to consumers. Institutions for the governance of MICOs in this region must evolve in an inclusive and participatory fashion if they are to meet rights-based development indicators. Nonetheless, the growing links between local knowledge, social capital and collective action developing here make the project appear far superior to the exploitation of Chulucanas ceramics. In both instances, however, infrastructural support is necessary to enforce the MICOs and to prevent their infringement in wider markets.

Regionally based organisations that emphasise community building and democratic forms of governance have, in some cases, produced successful economies that turn on the identification and marketing of local product origins. A former staff member of the Inter-American Foundation, Kevin Healy, identifies the El Ceibo Cooperative of Bolivia as a prime example of success in such an endeavour. El Ceibo is an agricultural co-operative whose members farm cocoa beans and produce chocolate.[93] Since receiving its first funding from the Inter-American Foundation in 1978, it has grown from 12 members into a large and successful federation of over 36 co-operatives. Although the early objective was limited to improving the positions of farmers within

---

[90] F Boucher and A Gerz, 'Mantecoso Cheese in Peru: Organizing to Conquer the National Market' in van de Kop et al, n 68 above.

[91] Boucher and Gerz, n 90 above, 43.

[92] Ibid, 46, 48.

[93] K Healy, *Llamas, Weavings, and Organic Chocolate: Multicultural Grassroots Development in the Andes and Amazon of Bolivia* (Indiana IN, University of Notre Dame Press, 2001). For a more in-depth history see AJ Bebbington, *Technology and Rural Development Strategies in a Base Economic Organisation: 'El Ceibo' Ltd Federation of Cooperatives* (London, Overseas Development Institute, 1996).

the national market place, the federation has extended its reach globally. Its major international client is a small Swiss firm based in Geneva that distributes Third World products to customers who are willing to pay a higher price for goods that come from sustainable and equitable Third World farming communities—but it now exports chocolate to the US and Japan. As the market for sustainable, fair trade and organic products has grown, so has El Ceibo's success: a wrapper from an Organic Swiss Chocolate bar now reads:

> All Rapunzel products use ingredients purchased through the Eco-trade partners. For example, Rapunzel purchases cacao from a unique farmers co-operative in Bolivia. The El Ceibo co-op is a group of farmers that became world-class entrepreneurs to improve their quality of life.[94]

This Swiss chocolate company has clearly attempted to trade on the reputation of the El Ceibo farmers, who continue to benefit from the popularity of sustainable and organic niche markets. El Ceibo works as a collective mark and could be registered as a denomination of origin. Further delineation of the social, ecological and cultural dimensions of their cultivation methods could further serve to strengthen their market position as well as enhance their already strong reputation as an exemplar of fair-trade benefits and rights-based development.[95]

Maintaining a strong cultural identity has been an integral part of the El Ceibo strategy. Part of the success of the co-operative is credited to the use of indigenous models of community organisation and self-management, which has also facilitated new forms of social ritual. Enthusiasm for participation in the project has been maintained through social festivities in which the cultural history and mythology of the tree after which the co-operative is named and the traditional practice of its farming is celebrated though music, dance and all-night vigils. A short editorial promotion for one of these events asserts:

> Similar to the root of a tree is the culture of a people, a fact which is especially important in colonization zones. For when we leave behind our homelands and become involved in our new agricultural holdings as individual farmers, the risk of overlooking our rich traditions—the music, dance and our art forms—of our ancestors that mark us as distinct peoples become greater.[96]

The promotion of a strong cultural identity works in synchronicity with their MICO strategies, that is, the success of El Ceibo's cacao is dependent upon its ability to capitalise on the symbolic difference of the El Ceibo community. Moreover, while working to maintain its market share, El Ceibo has built a collective identity organised around markers of traditional culture and indigeneity.

---

[94] Healy, n 93 above, 147.
[95] For a recent description of their methods of cultivation, and the benefits of their obtaining both Fairtrade and organic certification status see http://www.globalexchange.org/campaigns/fairtrade/cocoa/Cocoa Bolivia.pdf.
[96] Healy, n 93 above, 147.

## VII. CONCLUSION

Recognising the contribution of poor peoples' knowledge to culture, technology and innovation is essential to development, as Madhavi Sunder argues. She notes that IP is a key vehicle for accomplishing this, provided that communities in developing countries are recognised not merely as the passive holders of an unchanging culture, but as actors capable of assuming agency in markets that value their efforts.[97] As we have shown, Sunder points to the creative use of GIs in India, where it is hoped that the introduction of these new IPRs will allow cultural diversity to thrive and rural artisans to remain in their villages, resisting the pull of city industry.[98] Indeed, it appears that many GIs have been registered for traditional weaving techniques and handicrafts.[99] Nonetheless, there are reasons to doubt the Indian government's capacity and commitment to fully implementing this strategy, as the Alternative Law Forum in Bangalore has found.[100] Although the Indian government has made impressive initiatives with regard to protecting and promoting new GIs for regional teas,[101] it appears to have done little to develop local governance structures for new GIs for handicrafts. Without support for governance and enforcement, the mere possession of a GI is a poor vehicle for community-livelihood security.[102] We have argued here that, even if we were to agree that developing markets for Third World cultural products is 'perhaps the most effective way to protect their traditions' by encouraging tradition-based innovation,[103] this will only be the case where an effective, rights-based governance infrastructure can be established and commitments to sustainability realised. A rights-based sustainability perspective, however, suggests that these responsibilities are not solely the burden of the state; transnational networks involving private parties, NGOs and the development agencies of governments of developed country may also be required to bear them.

The challenge in developing countries will be to ensure inclusive and representative governing bodies and industry organisations so as to avoid the dangers of larger entrepreneurs capturing the lion's share of the economic benefits and further disadvantaging the co-operatives of smaller producers and workers collectives. We also need further empirical studies in order to understand how MICO efforts have tended to affect relations between communities and the state historically, and to consider what impact these strategies have upon local power relations, the distribution of wealth and the availability of economic opportunity. More critical consideration of the role of

---

[97] Sunder, 'The Invention of Traditional Knowledge', n 63 above, 103. See, generally, JM Finger and P Schuler (eds), *Poor People's Knowledge: Promoting Intellectual Property in Developing Countries* (Washington, DC, World Bank and Oxford University Press, 2004).

[98] A fuller overview of GIs in India is found in S Singhal, 'Geographical Indications and Traditional Knowledge' (2008) 3 *Journal of Intellectual Property Law and Practice* 732.

[99] NS Gopalakrishnan, PS Nair and KB Aravind, 'Exploring the Relationship between Geographical Indications and Traditional Knowledge: An Analysis of the Legal Tools for the Protection of Geographical Indications in Asia', ICTSD Programme on Intellectual Property Rights and Sustainable Development (Geneva, ICTSD, 2007) 33–41, available at www.ictsd.org.

[100] P Iyengtar, Alternative Law Forum, Bangalore, India, presentation to the DFG-Forschergruppe Cultural Property Colloquium Series, Institute for European Ethnology, Georg-August-Universitat Gottingen, 18 June 2009.

[101] Rangnekar, n 68 above, 284–88.

[102] See note 100 above. For a longer discussion of the challenges in India see K Das, 'Prospects and Challenges of Geographical Indications in India' (2010) 13 *The Journal of World Intellectual Property* 148.

[103] Sunder, n 2 above.

NGOs in these processes is also desirable in order to ascertain the circumstances under which they foster community autonomy rather than promote community dependence. The resources offered by rights-based and sustainable development provide us with a significant matrix of principles to evaluate these strategies.

MICOs are amongst the few IP vehicles likely to satisfy simultaneously the needs for collective rights, local autonomy, economic improvement and entrepreneurship in a global environment, while promising enhanced social security through sustainable development and providing bases for cultural pride.[104] Their use, however, must be accompanied by new investments in infrastructure and the establishment of marketing channels that do not undermine local communities. Moreover, the use of MICOs must be accompanied by democratic governance structures that guarantee equity in the distribution of benefits, the equality of access to local participants, the transparency of criteria for using marks, and accountability in maintaining and enforcing locally developed standards in order to meet social, as well as economic, objectives.

The increasing use of MICOs in ethical marketing schemes, rural development projects and cultural heritage industries poses distinct challenges. Evaluating these projects cannot be accomplished by any simple blanket denunciation of IP expansion, by the vilification of new forms of property or by narrow emphases on the freedom of speech, which is, in any case, negligibly affected by these new forms of protection. Such new uses of IP should be subject to assessments based upon their social impact, their sustainability and the quality of their governance structures. If IP becomes the basis for new forms of commodity production, 'sustainable development' and 'fair trade' because of the growing tendency to link territory, resources, know-how and social capital, then it is imperative that we begin to subject IP management to new forms of scrutiny. We need to hold those who manage IP to enhanced standards of responsibility, in which the development of cultural, economic and social rights are truly integrated with respect for civil and political rights. Only then will we have a basis for evaluating these as strategies to achieve greater social justice.

---

[104] See, further, RJ Coombe and N Aylwin, 'Bordering Diversity and Desire: Using Intellectual Property to Mark Place-Based Products' (2011) 43 *Environment and Planning A: Society and Space* 2027.

# 7

# *Rethinking the Convergence of Human Rights and Labour Rights in International Law: Depoliticisation and Excess*

VIDYA KUMAR

## I. INTRODUCTION

T HE VERDICT IS still out on human rights in international law. On the one hand, human rights—like international law itself[1]—has offered, and to many offers still, a powerful legal and moral discourse promising justice, emancipation and progress.[2] On the other, its legacy has been under intense scrutiny for some time, and for good reason. That is to say, human rights, like international law,[3] has been exposed by powerful critiques to operate as a tool of domination, pursuing

* I would like to thank the editors of this collection for inviting me to deliver this paper at Osgoode Hall Law School's International Speaker Series in collaboration with the Comparative Research in Law and Political Economy Network (CLPE) and the Nathanson Centre for Transnational Human Rights, Crime, and Security. I would also like to thank R Buchanan, HW Arthurs and A Bogg for their advice and assistance in developing my thinking on the subject. All errors and omissions are, of course, my own.

[1] T Skouteris, *The Notion of Progress in International Law Discourse* (Cambridge, Cambridge University Press, 2010); MO Hudson, *Progress in International Organization* (Stanford CA, Stanford University Press, 1932); EW Searing, *Humanity and the Progress of International Law* (New York, New York Liberal Publishing Company, 1882); RA Miller and RM Bratspies, *Progress in International Law, Vol. 60. Development in International Law* (Leiden, Martinus Nijhoff Publishers, 2008).

[2] J Donnelly, *Universal Human Rights: In Theory & Practice*, 2nd edn (Ithaca, NY, Cornell University Press, 2003); M Ignatieff, *Human Rights as Politics and Idolatry* (Princeton, NJ, Princeton University Press, 2001); J Souter, 'Emancipation and Domination: Human Rights and Power Relations' (2008) 3 *In-Spire Journal of Law, Politics and Societies* 140.

[3] A Anghie, 'Francisco de Vitoria and the Colonial Origins of International Law' (1996) 5 *Social and Legal Studies* 321; BS Chimni, *International Law and World Order: A Critique of Contemporary Approaches* (Newbury Park, CA, SAGE Publications, 1993); M Sornarajah, 'Power and Justice in International Law' (1997) 1 *Singapore Journal of International & Comparative Law* 28; M Koskenniemi, *From Apology to Utopia* (Cambridge, Cambridge University Press, 2005), D Kennedy, *The Dark Sides of Virtue: Reassessing International Humanitarianism* (Princeton, NJ, Princeton University Press, 2004); S Marks, 'Empire's Law' (2003) 10 *Indiana Journal of Global Legal Studies* 449; S Pahuja, 'The Postcoloniality of International Law' (2005) 46 *Harvard International Law Journal* 459, C Chinkin, S Wright and H Charlesworth, 'Feminist Approaches to International Law: Reflections from another Century' in D Buss and A Manji (eds), *International Law: Modern Feminist Approaches* (Oxford, Hart Publishing, 2005).

imperialist aims and ends.[4] This chapter follows on the heels of these critiques and asks whether they are sustained in the context of international labour law: in particular, it asks what human rights discourse holds for workers in developed and developing countries? The chapter's starting point is the contention that any assessment of the relationship between human rights, international law and development—a relationship at the heart of this collection of essays—must incorporate an understanding of the effects of the post-war and 'post-wall'[5] convergence of the discourses of international labour law and human rights. Specifically, it argues that this convergence—best exemplified by the claim that 'labour rights are human rights'—results in the depoliticisation of international law in the following ways: first, at theoretical level, human rights discourse depoliticises international labour law by effacing the centrality of the conflict, and structural power disparity, between labour and capital (ie the conflict of class subordination); and secondly, human rights discourse depoliticises international law by externalising the impact and relevance of uneven economic development and colonial history from debates about whether 'core labour rights' ought to be adopted by, or applied to the trading practices of, developing countries and the international community.

## II. CONVERGENCE: MERGING INTERNATIONAL LABOUR RIGHTS AND INTERNATIONAL HUMAN RIGHTS

Human rights have become the *sine qua non* of rights discourse. Not only is rights discourse thought to be incomplete without them, but human rights have also eclipsed the *gravitas* and allure of labour rights in the twenty-first century:[6] of the two, the former indubitably possesses the more prevalent and forceful discourse in international law.[7] The reasons underlying the view that human rights discourse is, in some important way, stronger than that of international labour law are discussed elsewhere,[8] and are not as important as the widespread belief that this view is accurate and that

---

[4] DW Kennedy, 'The International Human Rights Movement: Part of the Problem?' (2001) 15 *Harvard Human Rights Journal* 99, 108–14; U Baxi, 'Voices of Suffering and the Future of Human Rights' (1998) 8 *Transnational Law & Contemporary Problems* 125; idem, *The Future of Human Rights*, 3rd edn (Oxford, Oxford University Press, 2007); C Douzinas, *The End of Human Rights: Critical Legal Thought at the Turn of the Century* (Oxford, Hart Publishing, 2000); idem, *Human Rights and Empire: The Political Philosophy of Cosmopolitanism* (London, Routledge-Cavendish, 2007); B Ibhawoh, *Imperialism and Human Rights: Colonial Discourses of Rights and Liberties* (Albany, NY, State University of New York Press, 2007); M Mutua, 'The Ideology of Human Rights' (1996) 36 *Virginia Journal of International Law* 589; idem, 'Savages, Victims and Saviours: the Metaphor of Human Rights' (2001) 42 *Harvard International Law Journal* 42; idem, *Human Rights: A Political and Cultural Critique* (Philadelphia, PA, University of Pennsylvania Press, 2002); K Kannabiran and R Singh, *Challenging the Rule(s) of Law: Colonialism, Criminology and Human Rights in India* (London, SAGE Publications, 2008).

[5] S Žižek, 'Post-Wall' (2009) 31(22) *London Review of Books* 10.

[6] J Atleson, 'The Voyage of the Neptune Jade: Transnational Labour Solidarity and the Obstacles of Domestic Law' in J Conaghan, K Klare and RM Fischl (eds), *Labour Law in an Era of Globalisation: Transformative Practices & Possibilities* (Oxford, Oxford University Press, 2004) 379; B Langille, 'Core Labour Rights—The True Story (Reply to Alston)' (2005) 16 *European Journal of International Law* 409, 437.

[7] P Alston, 'Labour Rights as Human Rights: The Not So Happy State of the Art' in idem (ed), *Labour Rights as Human Rights* (Oxford, Oxford University Press, 2005) 1.

[8] V Kumar, 'Labour Law Theory in the 21st Century: Recasting and Modernity', DPhil Thesis, University of Oxford (2008).

labour law discourse should therefore merge with or employ human rights discourse for strategic reasons.[9] The literature supporting this view that international labour rights are, or ought to be viewed as, human rights is too vast to be recounted here.[10] What is important to note is the increasing tendency of legal scholars to characterise labour law and rights as human rights.[11] Scholars do this most commonly by asserting that labour rights are human rights.[12] This declaration is frequently put forward as a self-evident fact,[13] as a claim requiring neither justification nor explanation.[14]

This convergence is surprising in the light of the fact that the genealogical histories of international labour law and human rights discourses are remarkably distinct—a detail that, as will be revealed, becomes important for workers in developed and developing countries alike. Although the term 'human rights' originates in the 1940s, it has a longer historical legacy. Beginning in the 1940s, the discourse of human rights replaced Thomas Paine's 'rights of man',[15] which was itself a replacement for the pre-legal,[16] religious concept of 'natural rights'.[17] These were not merely nominal substitutions, but reflected intangible and profound shifts within Western European societies and states from religious to putatively secular organising principles. International labour law discourse has a genealogy no less varied than that of human rights. It can be traced inter alia to powerful *fin de siècle* religious doctrines of the Catholic Church,[18] to the influence of nineteenth-century British, French, Swiss–Alsatian and Irish international labour law reformers (eg Robert Owen, Charles Hindley, Jerome Blanqui, Daniel Legrand and John Kells Ingram),[19] to the blend of idealism and practicality

---

[9] L Compa, 'Workers Freedom of Association in the United States under International Human Rights Standards' (2001) 17 *International Journal of Comparative Labour Law and Industrial Relations* 289, 308 (arguing that human rights give labour rights more respect in international law); J Bellace 'The ILO Declaration of Fundamental Principles and Rights at Work' (2001) 17 *International Journal of Comparative Labour Law and Industrial Relations* 269, 272–73 (arguing that convergence made the ILO's 1998 Declaration more acceptable).

[10] Kumar, n 8 above.

[11] JA Gross, 'A Long Overdue Beginning: The Promotion and Protection of Workers Rights as Human Rights' in idem (ed), *Workers' Rights as Human Rights* (London, ILR Press, 2003) 1; J Fudge, 'The New Discourse of Labour Rights: From Social to Fundamental Rights?' (2007) 29 *Comparative Labor Law and Policy Journal* 1, available at http://ssrn.com/abstract=974915 (last accessed on 20 March 2007).

[12] S Charnovitz, 'The Labour Dimension of the Emerging Free Trade Area of the Americas' in Alston, *Labour Rights as Human Rights*, n 7 above, 143, 168.

[13] VA Leary, 'The Paradox of Workers' Rights as Human Rights' in L Compa and SF Diamond (eds), *Human Rights, Labor Rights and International Trade* (Philadelphia, PA, University of Pennsylvania Press, 1996) 22; K Ewing, 'Human Rights and Industrial Relations: Possibilities and Pitfalls' (2002) 40 *British Journal of Industrial Relations* 138, 146; P Macklem, 'The Right to Bargain Collectively in International Law: Workers' Right, Human Right, International Right?' in Alston, *Labour Rights as Human Rights*, n 7 above, 61 and 63.

[14] B Hepple, 'Four Approaches to the Modernisation of Individual Employment Rights' in R Blanpain and M Weiss (eds), *Changing Industrial Relations & Modernisation of Labour Law* (The Hague, Kluwer Law International, 2003) 181, 188; CW Summers, 'Free Trade v Labor Rights/Human Rights: Doubts Definitions, Difficulties' in Blanpain and Weiss, ibid, 386, 387.

[15] T Paine, *The Rights of Man* (1791) (New York, Dover Publishing, 1999).

[16] M Freeden, *Human Rights: An Interdisciplinary Approach* (Cambridge, Polity Press, 2002) 62.

[17] M Cranston, 'Are There Any Human Rights?' (1983) 112 *Daedalus* 1; M Freeden, *Human Rights: An Interdisciplinary Approach* (Cambridge, Polity Press, 2002) 35.

[18] *Rerum Novarum*, 15 May 1891, available at http//www.vatican.va/holy_father/leo_xiii/encyclicals.

[19] JW Follows, *Antecedents of the International Labour Organization* (Oxford, Clarendon Press, 1951) 28, 31, 42, 201; P O'Higgins, '"Labour is not a Commodity"—an Irish Contribution to International Labour Law' (1997) 26 *Industrial Law Journal* 225, 233.

of the 1919 Paris Peace Conference,[20] to Marxism[21] and to the early twentieth-century need of nation states to regulate international competition for trade and investment.[22] International labour law discourse is a product of all of these things, and more. Accordingly, a single all-encompassing genealogy of either labour law or human rights discourse in international law would be both too messy and too long to canvass here if it were possible at all. These discourses are more Darwinian than creationist; rarely do they direct seekers to a single and incontrovertible ancestral source or moment of origin.

Leaving aside the question of the (im)possibility of proffering a single authoritative genealogical account of either discourse, this chapter draws attention to specific aspects distinguishing each discourse in order to gain important insights into the complex relationship between rights, international law and development. In essence, the differences between international labour rights and international human rights discourses—that they arise at different times, flow primarily from different watershed historical moments and institutions, and possess distinct rationales or purposes[23]—demonstrate not only that the foundational character of international human rights and labour rights is different in international law, but also that human rights discourse cannot accommodate important concerns addressed by international labour law discourse (namely, the centrality of class subordination or the labour–capital conflict, and the impact of colonialism on the needs, circumstances and development of national economies and labour markets). These two limitations of human rights discourse make the trend towards convergence, at best, theoretically and practically problematic, and, at worst, inherently capitalist and neocolonial.

## II.1. Historical Distinctions between Labour Rights and Human Rights

Labour rights were conceived as a form of international solidarity well before the modern human rights movement.[24] International labour rights addressed the fear of the spread of communism across Western Europe and the undesirable attendant consequences of this prospect: revolution and war.[25] The creation of the International Labour Organization (ILO) in 1919, the first institutional repository and legislator of international labour rights, was, in part, a response to the aftermath of Russia's Bolshevik Revolution in 1917: international labour law and rights were created to spoil the attractiveness of revolution for Western European workers by creating a

---

[20] J Van Daele, 'Engineering Social Peace: Networks, Ideas, and the Founding of the International Labour Organization' (2005) 50 *International Review of Social History*, 435.

[21] O'Higgins, n 19 above, 225–34 (noting the similarities between the ILO's and Marxist language).

[22] ILO created to address international competition and trade: N Valticos and G von Potobsky, *International Labour Law* (Deventer, Kluwer Law and Taxation Publishers, 1994) 163, para 10.

[23] VA Leary, 'The Paradox of Workers' Rights as Human Rights' in L Compa and S Diamond (eds), *Human Rights, Labor Rights and International Trade* (Philadelphia, PA, University of Pennsylvania Press, 1996) 22; R Adams, 'Voice for All: Why the Right to Refrain from Collective Bargaining is No Right at All' in Gross, n 11 above, 247.

[24] Charnovitz, n 12 above, 143, 168.

[25] Follows, n 19 above; P O'Higgins, 'The Interaction of The ILO, the Council of Europe, and European Labour Standards' in B Hepple (ed), *Social and Labour Rights in A Global Context: International and Comparative Perspectives* (Cambridge, Cambridge University Press, 2002) 56; Treaty of Versailles, 29 June 1919, 112 BFSP 1, Part XIII and Art 417.

'diametrically opposed' vision of social justice reform.[26] That vision advanced a just relationship between workers and employers by attenuating (though not eliminating) the exploitative effects of the former's subordination to the latter. Like national labour law regimes,[27] international labour law recognised the problem that uneven bargaining power between labour and capital posed for labour relations, industrial peace and lasting world peace:[28] its primary normative mission was to assuage this asymmetry that cultivated worker exploitation by private power.[29] The tripartite structure of the ILO meant that employers', national governments' and workers' interests were represented in the creation, negotiation and implementation of international labour rights.[30] By involving national governments in its legislative processes, the ILO wove each state's particular historical and economic circumstances, interests and concerns— including its past and present state of industrial and economic development—into a negotiated creation and implementation of international labour rights. In addition to accommodating national economic and labour market interests through tripartism, ILO resolutions were the first to recognise explicitly and address the impact of colonialism on the development of labour rights of indigenous peoples under colonial rule as well as after independence.[31]

Human rights discourse, in contrast, was rarely heard before the end of the Second World War, the creation of the United Nations and the promulgation of the Universal Declaration of Human Rights in 1948.[32] Modern human rights discourse emerged 30 years after the institutionalisation of international labour law,[33] and was primarily a response to the infamous legacy of Second World War: the Holocaust. Consequently, the predominant rationale underlying the institutionalised 'corpus'[34] of human rights of the twentieth century was the protection of the individual and individual dignity from the state's potential to abuse its power. The rationale underlying these rights was that human beings everywhere possess human rights by virtue of the fact that they

---

[26] F Maupain 'Is the ILO Effective in Upholding Labour Rights?: Reflections on the Myanmar Experience' in Alston, *Labour Rights as Human Rights*, n 7 above, 130, 89 ('The ILO had to face the implacable hostility of the Bolsheviks, who claimed to possess a "definite solution" of their own to the achievement of social justice'); ibid, 89, note 14: 'The ILO's reformist vision was diametrically opposed to the revolutionary option: the Marxist vision of social progress claims that the alienation of the proletariat can only be eliminated through the overthrow of the regime of private ownership of the means of production'.

[27] P Davies and M Freedland, *Kahn-Freud's Labour and the Law* (London, Steven and Sons, 1983); H Collins, 'Market Power, Bureaucratic Power and the Contract of Employment' (1986) 15 *Industrial Law Journal* 1; M D'Antona, 'Labour Law at the Century's End: An Identity Crisis?' in Conaghan et al, n 6 above, 33; J Howe, 'The Broad Idea of Labour Law' in G Davidov and B Langille (eds), *The Idea of Labour Law* (Oxford, Oxford University Press, 2011) 1, available at http://ssrn.com/abstract=1792187.

[28] Preamble of ILO's Constitution of 1919: available at http://www.ilo.org/ilolex/english/constq.htm (last accessed December 2010).

[29] Macklem, n 13 above, 61, 62.

[30] http://www.ilo.org/global/about-the-ilo/who-we-are/tripartite-constituents/lang–en/index.htm.

[31] L Rodríguez Piñero, *Indigenous Peoples, Postcolonialism and International Law: The ILO Regime (1919–1989)* (New York, Oxford University Press, 2005).

[32] AJ Langlois, 'The Narrative Metaphysics of Human Rights' (2005) 9 *International Journal of Human Rights* 369.

[33] K Drzewicki, 'The Right to Work and Rights in Work', in A Eide, C Krause and A Rosas, *Economic, Social and Cultural Rights: A Textbook*, 2nd edn (London, Martinus Nijhoff Publishers, 2001) 223, 224–25.

[34] Mutua, 'The Ideology of Human Rights', n 4 above 589. Mutua suggests that the Universal Declaration of Human Rights (1948), the International Covenant on Civil and Political Rights (1966) and the International Covenant on Social, Economic and Cultural Rights (1966) are widely presumed to constitute a definitive 'corpus' of human rights.

are human beings *without qualification*.[35] Consequently, international human rights—characterised as universal, identical and indivisible—aimed to prevent the violation of individual human dignity[36] by public authorities. They were, by design, the antidote to Nazi Germany and the nefarious excesses of fascism, totalitarianism and authoritarianism. The normative aspiration or mission of international human rights sought to protect universal elements of what it means to be a human being from the exercise of abusive sovereign power.[37]

## III. DEPOLITICISATION: TWO EFFECTS OF CONVERGENCE

If it were solely a descriptive or discursive exercise, perhaps little would be at stake in this merger of these distinct discourses. One could assert 'labour rights are human rights' without affecting the meaning and advancement of worker rights in either developed or developing countries. Yet this assertion is more than this. With convergence, not only do the salient institutional, historical and purposive differences between international labour law and international human rights virtually disappear, but, crucially, important conflicts in international law become depoliticised. That is to say, conflicts based upon particular power disparities—between workers and employers and between workers from developed countries and workers from developing countries—are effaced or externalised. And with them, the need that they be addressed disappears.

### III.1. Depoliticising Class: International Labour Rights as Human Rights

If human rights discourse rests upon a theory that views the conflict between the state (or sovereign) and the individual as central to—even definitive of—its normative mission, and views the idea that the violation of an individual's human dignity by the state as the most important or egregious problem necessitating legal intervention, it is then not a discourse that reflects international labour law's central concern of 'social justice'. Social justice in international labour law involves the creation of a just relationship between workers and employers, and requires states to adopt measures to redress the inequality of bargaining power between workers and employees in order to minimise the exploitative nature of private power on the wage–labour relation.[38] Social justice thus requires the state to address the conflict of class subordination in the public and private sphere in society and globally. Reframing labour law dis-

---

[35] J Shestack, 'The Jurisprudence of Human Rights' in T Meron (ed), *Human Rights in International Law: Legal and Policy Issues* (Oxford, Clarendon Press, 1984) 74; R Howse, 'The WTO and the Protection of Workers Rights' (1999) 3 *Journal of Small and Emerging Business Law* 131, 149.

[36] What constitutes a violation of human dignity? How can one know one's dignity is injured? Human rights scholars have been at best ambiguous at identifying which labour or employment issues or rights engage the question of human dignity and which do not. C McCrudden, 'Human Dignity', Oxford Legal Studies Research Paper No 10/2006, available at http://ssrn.com/abstract=899687 (last accessed on 27 April 2006) (absence of discussion of which labour issues or rights engage human dignity, which do not, and why); E Grant, 'Dignity and Equality' (2007) 7 *Human Rights Law Review* 299, 303.

[37] Macklem, n 13 above, 61–62.

[38] Valticos and von Potobsky, n 22 above, 25, para 19; Macklem, ibid; E Lee, 'Globalisation and Labour Standards: A Review of the Issues' (1997) 136 *International Labour Review* 173, 174.

course in human rights terms displaces international labour law's starting point, ie the inequality of bargaining power, replacing it with the declaration that 'human beings are equal'. As a consequence, convergence moves international labour law's conceptual foundation from the material *fact* of worker inequality and subordination to the *fiction* of the equality of all human beings.[39] This moves labour law discourse from a real or material starting point (ie redressing worker subordination and inequality) to an ideal one (ie declaring the equality of all human beings).

At first glance, this shift may not seem like much. Employees and workers are also human beings, so the convergence of labour law with human rights may, prima facie, make no difference.[40] But the shift puts much into question. For example, if labour rights are now to be understood as universal human rights, it is unclear whether international labour law must view the state as the primary antagonist of workers' interests. It unclear whether the ILO's Conventions, Resolutions and Declarations must now focus on protecting workers from state actions and view the state as the main antagonist to workers, rather than private power.

A second problem which this shift convergence necessitates is that employers are also human beings and will, therefore, possess universal human rights attaching to their dignity. If so, workers will—and must—have the same human rights as employers, such as freedom of speech or, if one assumes it is a human right (as some labour law scholars do),[41] the right to strike. But what human rights discourse does not and cannot tell us is what would be the meaning of granting an employer the human right to strike. Human rights discourse has not told us yet against whom employers would strike or when employers could or should exercise such a (universal) human right. Moreover, if a human rights discourse extends identical human rights to employers as employees, it may not be able to prevent employers from exercising free speech that may intimidate, threaten or coerce workers into not joining a union, not organising or voting 'No' in a strike ballot. It is not clear whether human rights discourse will—as labour law regimes have attempted to do[42]—prevent employers from engaging in such behaviour. It is also not clear whether human rights discourse will ask us to weigh differently the 'human dignity' of workers against that of employers in the protection and exercise of workers' 'human rights' in the light of the intractable problem of unequal bargaining power between employees and employers. Human rights discourse does not and, as it is presently framed, cannot tell us whether the human dignity of a 'worker-cum-human being' will be violated if he or she were laid off as a result of

---

[39] J-C Javillier, 'The Employer and the Worker: The Need for a Comparative International Perspective' in G Davidov and B Langille (eds), *Boundaries and Frontiers of Labour Law: Goals and Means in the Regulation of Work* (Oxford, Hart Publishing, 2006) 355, 370: 'Labour [law] . . . is born of realities, of the transation into legal terms the special constraints of the human condition at work'.

[40] JA Gross, 'Worker Rights as Human Rights: Wagner Act Values and Moral Choices' (2002) 4 *University of Pennsylvania Journal of Labor & Employment Law* 479, 489–90.

[41] Although there is debate about whether the right to strike is a human right, some have called for it to be recognised as such: KW Ewing, 'Laws Against Strikes Revisited' in C Barnard, S Deakin and G Morris (eds), *The Future of Labour Law: Liber Amicorum B Hepple QC* (Oxford, Hart Publishing, 2004) 60.

[42] For example, labour laws prohibiting such unfair labour practices by employers exist in Canada, the US and the UK: J Goddard, *Employment Relations Research Series No 29: Trade Union Recognition: Unfair Labour Practice Regimes in the USA and in Canada* (London, Department of Trade and Industry, 2004); A Bogg, 'The Mouse the Never Roared: Unfair Practices and Union Recognition' (2009) 28 *Industrial Law Journal* 390.

decisions made by employers owing to a downturn in the economy.[43] Even if workers' human rights are violated in such circumstances, redressing this infringement may violate employers' human rights, ie their freedom of contract or right to property.[44]

Consequently, with convergence, we do not know what happens when workers' and employers' human rights conflict: convergence holds labour rights and human rights to be one in the same. We do not know if, when or why some kinds of 'workplace' human rights trump others. Moreover, and critically, if human rights conflict, we do not know if their resolution will be made in favour of workers in principle, consonant with the purpose of international and national labour law regimes—ie to assuage the unequal bargaining power between workers and employers—or if there will be cases in which worker's rights must be or become subordinate to private power and capital in order to protect the human rights of employers.

When human rights discourse displaces the centrality of worker and class subordination in international labour law discourse, it depoliticises international labour law. Depoliticisation involves the erasure, displacement or de-emphasis of a political consideration, claim or aim of a discourse. Convergence robs international labour law discourse of its ability to respond to, and redress, the effect of a particular kind of power disparity both in society and globally: the asymmetrical power relationship between workers and employers in the workplace (and between labour and capital globally). This depoliticisation affects workers from developed and developing countries alike. That is, both have something to lose with convergence if human rights discourse does not view remedying the problem of labour's subordination to capital as being *central* to its rationale and normative mission, and both will be vulnerable in a human rights discourse that grants employers and workers identical human rights without viewing the protection of workers as overriding that of employers, or without viewing the abuse of private power as being acutely problematical for the majority of the world's workers who labour in the private sphere. If convergence is insisted upon, whether for strategic or principled reasons, human rights discourse will need to adopt new or different organising principles—ie principles that explicitly recognise and redress the causes and adverse effects of worker subordination to private power—if it is to avoid depoliticising labour rights in international law.

### III.2. Depoliticising Development: The Effect of Convergence on Core Labour Standards and Developing Countries and their Workers

In addition to effacing international labour law's mission of remedying worker subordination, the convergence of labour law and human rights discourses in international law depoliticises conflicts between workers from developed and developing countries, thereby making them difficult to perceive, raise and address. The ILO's adoption of 'core labour rights' in its 1998 'ILO Declaration on Fundamental Principles and

---

[43] Although labour and human rights scholars have tried to flesh out the meaning of 'human dignity', these questions are ultimately not addressed: McCrudden, n 36 above.

[44] S Anderman, 'Termination of Employment: Whose Property Rights?' in Barnard et al, n 41 above, 101.

Rights at Work'[45] is a useful example of the depoliticising effect of convergence in international law. It is discussed below in order to shed light on the problems that both developing countries and workers of developing countries face when convergence results in the universal application of 'core labour rights' upon developing countries and developed countries alike.

The first thing to note about the ILO's adoption of this Declaration in 1998 is that it is described as an unequivocal example of the convergence of labour rights and human rights in international law.[46] This is surprising in that nowhere in the Declaration is the phrase 'human rights' used. Nor did the ILO's governing body, in its description of the reasons for adopting the Declaration or in its description of which rights were fundamental rights or how they were chosen, mention 'human rights'.[47] Rather, the Declaration simply identifies four 'fundamental rights and principles' at work that all ILO members are required to respect and promote, whether or not they have ratified the relevant Conventions to which these rights and principles relate. The four fundamental rights and principles at work (which correlate to seven 'core' ILO conventions[48]) are: the freedom of association and the effective recognition of the right to collective bargaining; the elimination of forced or compulsory labour; the abolition of child labour; and the elimination of discrimination in respect of employment and occupation.[49]

Notwithstanding the absence of any mention of 'human rights', the 1998 Declaration has been widely described as an example of convergence par excellence.[50] By indicating a shift 'from the term "labour standards" to "labour rights and human rights"', the Declaration has apparently reflected that '[t]he basis of these rights is not wages or labour costs, but human rights'.[51] The Declaration has also 'elevated [core labour rights] to the status of human or fundamental rights . . . emphasis[ing] [their] universal nature'.[52] All seven conventions associated with the Declaration are said to be

[45] 'ILO Declaration on Fundamental Principles and Rights at Work', available at http://www.ilo.org/dyn/declaris/DECLARATIONWEB.static_jump?var_language=EN&var_pagename=DECLARATIONTEXT (last accessed on 1 March 2010; hereinafter the 1998 Declaration).

[46] B Langille, 'The ILO and the New Economy: Recent Developments' (1999) 15 *International Journal of Comparative Labour Labour and Industrial Relations* 229, 241, 253; P Alston, 'Core Labour Standards, and the Transformation of the International Labour Rights Regime' (2004) 15 *European Journal of International Law* 457, 484–92; P Alston and J Heenan, 'Shrinking the International Labor Code: An Unintended Consequence of the 1998 ILO Declaration on Fundamental Principles and Rights at Work?' (2004) 36 *New York University Journal of International Law & Policy* 221.

[47] ILO Governing Body Report: GB.270/3/1, 270th Session, Geneva, November 1999.

[48] Freedom of Association and Protection of the Right to Organise, 1948 (No 87); Right to Organise and Collective Bargaining Convention, 1949 (No 98); Forced Labour Convention, 1930 (No29); Abolition of Forced Labour Convention, 1957 (No 105); Equal Remuneration Convention, 1951 (No 100); Discrimination (Employment and Occupation) Convention, 1958 (No 111); and the Minimum Age Convention, 1973 (No138).

[49] http://www.ilo.org/declaration/lang--en/index.htm (accessed on 1 November 2013).

[50] R Adams, 'On the Convergence of Labour Rights and Human Rights' (2001) 56 *Relations Industrielles/Industrial Relations* 199; idem, 'Voice for All: Why the Right to Refrain from Collective Bargaining is No Right at All' in Gross (ed), *Workers' Rights as Human Rights*, n 11 above, 143, 145: '[i]n affirming these rights to be human rights, the Fundamental Declaration brings them under the umbrella of the broader international human rights consensus'.

[51] CW Summers, 'Free Trade v Labor Rights/Human Rights: Doubts Definitions, Difficulties' in R Blanpain and M Weiss (eds), *Changing Industrial Relations and the Modernisation of Labour Law* (Kluwer, The Hague 2003) 381; Alston and Heenan, n 46 above, 221; Bellace, n 9 above, 269, 272–73. Langille, n 46 above, 229.

[52] Fudge, n 11 above, 14.

'universally recognised as fundamental human rights',[53] which is not surprising, given that '[an] important aspect of the development of the human rights conception of the core labour rights agenda is to affirm their non-relativistic and universal character'.[54]

The main problem that this convergence poses for workers in developing countries stems from the fact that the universality it endows international labour rights above is fictitious; that is, convergence papers over pertinent conflicts between the interests of workers from developed and developing countries. The narrative that the 1998 Declaration transformed certain labour standards and rights into universally accepted human rights does not fit squarely with the events that brought the Declaration into being. The Declaration was often portrayed to have been widely, if not unanimously, adopted by ILO member states[55] when this was far from the case. The Declaration was highly contentious for developing countries,[56] and was only passed with 43 abstentions[57]—barely a quorum[58]—after many delegates from developing countries involved with the negotiations went home early having failed to reach an agreement in the first two weeks.[59] If the Declaration transformed core labour rights into universally recognised human rights, this contradicts the fact that many developing countries—from Latin America, the Middle East and Asia—did not vote in favour of it.[60] Putting aside for a moment the primary reason that many developing countries resisted the narrative of convergence advanced by the Declaration—namely, their fear that convergence will be used as a form of protectionism that will benefit the economies and workers of developed countries—it is important to note that the Declaration was not universally accepted, and the rights contained therein possess neither universal reach nor approval.

By reifying the universal acceptance of 'core universal rights', the narrative of convergence depoliticises the conflicts between workers in developing nations and developed nations,[61] conflicts rooted both in the present power disparities between these nations and in the logic and history of development stemming from colonial

[53] R Adams, 'Collective Bargaining: The Rodney Dangerfield of Human Rights' (2004) 50 *Labour Law Journal* 204, 207; B Hepple, 'New Approaches to International Labour Regulation' (1997) 26 *Industrial Law Journal* 353, 359, where he notes that the seven core conventions represent 'universal respect for fundamental human rights in the workplace'.

[54] Langille, n 46 above, 242.

[55] See below.

[56] http://www.ilo.org/global/about-the-ilo/press-and-media-centre/press-releases/WCMS_007990/lang–en/index.htm.

[57] For a list of those countries who abstained, see KA Elliot and RB Freeman, *Can Labour Standards Improve under Globalisation?* (Washington DC, Institute for International Economics, 2003) Box 5.2, 99.

[58] Langille, n 46 above, 249; Elliot and Freeman, ibid, 98. The vote was 273 for and 0 against, with 43 abstentions. A quorum of 264 was necessary for the motion to pass (700 delegates were eligible to vote). See http://www.ilo.org/global/about-the-ilo/press-and-media-centre/press-releases/WCMS_007990/lang-en/index.htm.

[59] Langille, n 46 above, 249.

[60] Elliot and Freeman, n 57 above, 99. The absence of universal support for the Declaration is less surprising if one also considers the historical events leading up to the Declaration's adoption. The divide between developed and developing countries over the adoption of core labour rights was foreshadowed two years earlier, when the World Trade Organization (WTO) rescinded an invitation to speak extended to the main campaigner of the 1998 Declaration (the ILO's Director General M Hansenne) following pressure from developing countries (ie India and Pakistan). VA Leary, 'The WTO and the Social Clause: Post Singapore' (1997) 1 *European Journal of International Law* 118, 119.

[61] R Munck, 'Globalisation Labour and Development: A View from the South' (2010) 72/73 *Transformation: Critical Perspectives on South Africa*, 205, 218.

relationships that have historically formed and characterised international law.[62] Convergence depoliticises these conflicts by defining them as conflicts lying outside the ambit of human rights discourse.

### III.2.a. The Present and Future Concerns of Developing Countries

In order to understand the connection between the convergence ushered in by the ILO's Declaration in 1998 and the objections to this convergence by developing countries, it is necessary to recognise that the debate about the Declaration—and about any future attempt to merge labour rights with universal human rights—cannot be separated from the fears expressed by developing countries and their workers that the adoption of these universal rights would be used as a protectionist tool to benefit the economies, markets and workers of developed countries. This fear is most likely to be realised if the Declaration, in addition to rebranding nominally labour rights as human rights, functions or is intended to function as a trade barrier to the economies of developing countries by reducing their comparative advantage in trade law.[63] Moreover, it is a fear situated within the context of a vast structural inequality in the economic wealth between developed and developing nations, or the Global North and South.[64]

Protectionism by developed countries against developing countries is one of the primary reasons that developing countries and their workers resist the narrative of convergence as it is one of the most important challenges that they face.[65] Consequently, protectionism can pit the interests of workers in the developed world against those in the developing world, as these interests are tied to their respective nations' economies and trade advantages.[66] Workers in developed countries, for instance, have an interest in developing countries' adopting 'universal' human rights if this counteracts the existing legitimate comparative advantage (such as lower labour costs) that many developing countries have in relation to developed countries in a way that

[62] Anghie, n 3 above, 321; Chimni, n 3 above; N Berman, 'In the Wake of Empire' (1999) 14 *American University International Law Review* 1515.

[63] M Busse, 'Do Labor Standards Affect Comparative Advantage in Developing Countries?' (2002) 30 *World Development* 1921.

[64] W Darity and LS Davis, 'Growth Trade and Uneven Development' (2005) 29 *Cambridge Journal of Economics* 141, 144–46; W Rodney, *How Europe Underdeveloped Africa*, rev'd edn (London, Howard University Press, 1981). For a useful discussion of the overlap between the categories of developed and developing nations, or West and non-West with the categories of Global North and Global South, see J Comaroff and JL Comaroff, *Theory from The South: How Euro-America is Evolving toward Africa* (Boulder, CO, Paradigm Publishers, 2012) 45. It is important for (occidental) labour scholars to recognise that the structural inequality in the international economic order between the Global North and South has been a preoccupation of (and ground for resistance) for Third Worldists for decades: M Berger, 'After the Third World, History, Destiny and the Fate of Third Worldism' (2004) 25 *Third World Quarterly* 9; U Baxi, 'What May the "Third World" Expect from International Law?' (2006) 27 *Third World Quarterly* 713; BS Chimni, 'Third World Approaches to International Law: A Manifesto' (2006) 8 *International Community Law Review* 3.

[65] JM Salazar-Xirinachs, 'The Trade–Labour Nexus: Developing Countries' Perspectives' (2000) 3 *Journal of International Economic Law* 376, 380; M Monshipouri, 'Promoting Universal Human Rights: Dilemmas of Integrating Developing Countries' (2001) 4 *Yale Human Rights & Development Journal* 25, 45; K Newland, 'Workers of the World, What Now?' (1999) 114 *Foreign Policy* 52, 57; K Dzehtsiarou, 'Civilising Globalisation' (2010) 12 *Journal of International Economic Law* 521, 252–53.

[66] Munck, n 61 above, 218.

enhances the job security of workers in Western developed nations.[67] This effect has not been lost on workers in developing countries, who have viewed the effect of convergence on trade as not necessarily 'an attempt by developed countries to better the lot of workers in developing countries, but rather to protect the domestic industry and jobs in the West'.[68]

The fear that the narrative of convergence is being employed to undermine the comparative trade advantage of developing countries is a fear not only about how it will harm these nations' economic development but also about the effect that this will have on the job market and on the job security of its workers. In the light of these fears, the problem with converting international labour rights into universal human rights for workers in developing countries is that human rights discourse (in contrast to labour law's discourse's tripartite nature) externalises the pertinent issues affecting workers in developing countries, such as:

- the differences in the labour markets and labour costs between developed and developing nations;
- the differing labour costs as a legitimate form of comparative advantage in international trade regimes; and
- the uneven economic development of, and disparities in, wealth between developed and developing nations.[69]

The universality of human rights discourse as presently framed is unable to identify, respond to or redress these conflicts rooted in the present power and wealth disparities between nations.

### III.2.b. The Concerns of Developing Countries Relating to the History of Development

In addition to the inability of universal human rights discourse to accommodate present concerns that developing countries and their workers have about how convergence advances protectionism by developed countries, convergence also rules out the need to understand and explore the historical reasons underlying the rejection of 'core labour rights' by workers in developing countries. This is because human rights discourse is necessarily ahistorical—it makes no allowances for the role or impact of the historical legacies of colonialism upon many developing countries, their economies, their workers and these workers' rights. By assuming that all human beings share identical universal human rights, human rights discourse cannot engage with the role that colonial history plays in the shaping of labour rights for workers in developing countries,[70] in the industrial and economic development of these countries vis-à-vis

---

[67] MJ Trebilcock and R Howse, *The Regulation of International Trade*, 2nd edn (London, Routledge, 1999) 21.

[68] K Kolben, 'The New Politics of Linkage: India's Opposition to the Workers Rights Clause' (2006) 13 *Indiana Journal of Global Legal Studies* 1, 20.

[69] Darity and Davis, n 64 above, 141, 153. See, generally, S Amin, *Global History: A View from the South* (Capetown, Pambazuka Press, 2011); see also BS Chimni, 'International Institutions Today: An Imperial Global State in the Making' (2004) 15 *European Journal of International Law* 1.

[70] Consumer Unity & Trust Society, 'Trade and Labour Standards: The State of the Debate' (2001) 6, available at http://www.cuts.org/linkages-interviews.htm.

developed countries,[71] or, vitally, in the arguments of unions and workers from developing countries rejecting the impact of convergence on trade advantages based on this very history.[72]

The link between uneven development and colonialism[73] and its impact upon the 'core labour rights' debate is more than merely outside the ambit of human rights discourse. It is an excess which can never be incorporated into human rights discourse, as its very absence from this discourse constitutes human rights as an ahistorical and apolitical narrative. Human rights are not contingent upon a nation's resources or the colonial history that lead ostensibly to its ('level' or 'stage' of) development; they cannot be rejected on political grounds.[74] Human rights discourse is—and, to retain its allure, must be—historically transcendent if it is to maintain its claim to universality. The (messy) legacy and impact of colonialism on whether workers from developing countries either desire or will benefit from core labour rights as human rights is externalised in a way that endows human rights with dazzling simplicity.[75] This is in stark contrast to the prosaic complexities which characterise international labour law discourse: negotiated tripartitism coupled with the recognition that labour rights redress pressing structural and historical material inequality that characterises the wage–labour relation.

## IV. CONCLUSION

The convergence of international labour law and human rights discourses comes at a risk, a risk borne by workers in developed and developing countries. Workers in both have much to lose if the discourse that advances their rights does not also, in the conceptualisation of these rights, explicitly recognise the acute need to redress the fundamental problem of labour's subordination to private power. And convergence, by assuming that the rights and interests of workers in both developed and developing countries are identical and universal, externalises in international law the relevance of the following concerns: the disparity of wealth between the Global North and the Global South, and the role that colonialism has played in structuring global economic development. By turning these otherwise intractable problems into an excess, convergence depoliticises labour law discourse in international law. This may secure the ascendancy of human rights discourse in international law, but the question remains: at what cost to workers?

---

[71] W Darity, Jr, 'A Model of "Original Sin": The Rise of the West and the Lag of The Rest' (1992) 82 *American Economic Review* 167.

[72] KL Mahendra, 'The All India Trade Union Congress Position' in J John and AM Chenoy (eds), *Labour, Environment and Globalisation: Social Clause in Multilateral Agreements, A View from The South* (New Delhi, New Age International Publishers Ltd, 1996) 44: '[Indian] trade unions are . . . conscious that the developing countries have not come out of the colonial past'.

[73] A Dutt, 'The Origins of Uneven Development—The Indian Subcontinent' (1992) 82 *American Economic Review* 146; S Amin, *Imperialism and Unequal Exchange* (Hassocks, Harvester Press, 1977); DK Fieldhouse, *The West and the Third World: Trade, Colonialism, Dependence and Development* (Oxford, Blackwell Publishers, 1999); G Prakash, 'Colonialism, Capitalism and the Discourse of Freedom' in S Amin and M van der Linden (eds), *'Peripheral' Labour? Studies in the History of Partial Proletarianization* (Cambridge, Cambridge University Press, 1997) 9–26.

[74] Bellace, n 9 above, 269, 272–73; Langille, n 47 above, 229.

[75] S Tharoor, 'The Messy Afterlife of Colonialism' (2005) 8 *Global Governance* 1.

# 8

# *Measuring the World: Indicators, Human Rights and Global Governance*\*

SALLY ENGLE MERRY

## I. INTRODUCTION

INDICATORS ARE RAPIDLY multiplying as tools for assessing and promoting a variety of social justice and reform strategies around the world. There are rule of law indicators, indicators of violence against women and indicators of economic development, among many others. Indicators are widely used at the national level and are increasingly important in global governance. Although the origins of indicators as modes of knowledge and governance stretch back to the creation of modern nation states in the early nineteenth century and the practices of business management a few centuries earlier, their current use in global governance comes largely from economics and business management. Development agencies such as the World Bank have created a wide range of indicators, including indicators of global governance and the rule of law, while gross domestic product is one of the most widely used and accepted indicators. Thus, the growing reliance on indicators is an instance of the dissemination of the corporate form of thinking and governance into broader social spheres. They are fundamental to modern forms of governmentality, be it in the service of corporate, state or reform modes of governance.

In the last few years, interest in using indicators to monitor human rights compliance has grown significantly. Technologies of audit developed in the sphere of business regulation have jumped domains to global governance. Indicators introduce into the field of global human rights law a form of knowledge production in which numerical measures make visible forms of violation and inequality that are otherwise obscured. Statistics on income, health, education and torture, for example, are useful in assessing compliance with human rights norms and progress in improving human rights conditions. The numbers convey an aura of objective truth and facilitate comparisons. However, indicators typically conceal their political and theoretical origins and the

\* This is an expanded version of S Engle Merry, 'Measuring the World: Indicators, Human Rights, and Global Governance' in D Partridge, M Welker and R Hardin (eds), *Corporate Lives: New Perspectives on the Social Life of the Corporate Form* (2011) Wenner-Gren Symposium Series. *Current Anthropology*, Vol 52, Supplementary Issue 3: S83–S95.

underlying theories of social change and activism. They rely on practices of measurement and counting which are themselves opaque.

The world of civil society organisations has also been transformed by the increasing use of statistical measures. There are demands for quantifying the accomplishments of civil society organisations and for 'evidence-based' funding. Donors to human rights organisations want indicators of success, such as reductions in trafficking in persons or diminished rates of poverty and disease. As donors move closer to business, they have adopted business-based means of accounting for productivity and accomplishments. The concept of 'venture philanthropy' underscores this new perspective. Recipient organisations are tasked with developing measures of what they have accomplished within the period of funding. Given the difficulties of measuring accomplishments such as 'increased awareness of human rights', NGOs tend to count proxies for these accomplishments, such as number of training sessions or number of people trained. Clearly, the use of quantitative measures of accomplishment and the introduction of ranking systems based upon these measures is transforming the way in which these organisations do their work.

This chapter considers two sociological aspects to the expansion of the use of indicators. The first is a knowledge effect. Numerical measures produce a world which is knowable without the detailed particulars of context and history. The constituent units can be compared and ranked according to a number of criteria. This knowledge is presented as objective and often as scientific. The interpretations lurk behind the numbers but are rarely presented explicitly. These numbers seem to be open to public scrutiny and are readily accessible in a way that private opinions are not. The second is a governance effect. Statistical measures of populations are clearly connected to eighteenth- and early nineteenth-century ideas that the people of a country represent its wealth, and that good governance requires measuring and counting these people.

As forms of knowledge, indicators rely on the magic of numbers and the appearance of certainty and objectivity that they convey. A key dimension of the power of indicators is their capacity to convert complicated, contextually variable phenomena into unambiguous, clear and impersonal measures. They represent a technology of producing readily accessible and standardised forms of knowledge. They submerge local particularities and idiosyncrasies into universal categories, generating knowledge that is standardised and comparable across nations and regions. They are a special use of statistics to develop quantifiable ways of assessing and comparing characteristics among groups, organisations, or nations. They depend on the construction of categories of measurement such as ethnicity, gender and income, and more elaborated concepts such as national income.

Indicators are a technology not only of knowledge production but also of governance. They are widely used for decisions such as where to send foreign aid, where to focus on human rights violators and which countries offer the best conditions for business development. Modern states use statistical information, some of which is bundled into indicators, to decide where to locate highways and railroads, where to build schools and hospitals, how to allocate taxes and how to deploy police forces to control crime, to give but a few examples. As the modern state came to see its wealth as its population, it put greater emphasis on counting and assessing the nature of the population. Standardised measures mean that the state can better administer its population, by knowing its birth and death rates and income levels, for example, and collect taxes.[1]

The use of statistical information in general, and indicators in particular, shifts the power dynamics of decision-making. Indicators replace judgements upon the basis of values or politics with apparently more rational decision-making upon the basis of statistical information. In theory, the process is more open, allowing the public access to the basis for decisions. As Theodore Porter argues, in the pre-modern world, aristocratic elites relied on non-numerical information circulated within small, private circles.[2] Statistical knowledge grew in importance with the birth of the modern state. The first great enthusiasm for statistics in Europe came in the 1820s and 1830s, and, by the mid-nineteenth century in France, statistics were thought to produce the broad public knowledge necessary for a democracy. Quantification provided an openness to public scrutiny. For French bridge and canal engineers in the mid-nineteenth century, for example, calculating public utility by numbers offered a defence against parochialism and local interests in the locations of railroads and canals.[3] The massive expansion of quantification in recent times comes from a political culture that demands more openness and seeks to drive out corruption, prejudice, and the arbitrary power of elites even at the cost of subtlety and depth.[4] This, Porter claims, is the power of numbers.

Yet statistical measures have embedded theories of value, which shape apparently objective decisions. Despite the increase in democratic openness produced by the use of statistics in decision-making, however, this is a technology that tends to consolidate power in the hands of those with expert knowledge. In many situations, the turn to indicators as modes of governance does not eliminate the role of private knowledge and elite power in decision-making but, rather, replaces it with technical, statistical expertise. Decisions that were carried out by political or judicial leaders are made by technical experts who constructed the measures and develop the processes of classification and counting which produced the numbers. In nineteenth-century France, for example, despite claims to rigorous definition and lack of ambiguity, statistical measures were often arcane and hard to understand, requiring careful interpretation by experts.[5] In the area of contemporary global governance, an increasing reliance on indicators tends to locate decision-making in the Global North, where indicators are typically designed and labelled.

Indicators provide a technology for reform as well as control. Indicators can effectively highlight deficits, areas of inequality, spheres of human rights violations and other problem areas. Reform movements depend on producing statistical measures of the wrongs which they hope to redress, such as human rights violations, refugee populations, disease rates, and the incidence of poverty and inequality. They are a valuable reform tool in their ability to reveal areas of state failure.

As indicators become increasingly central to global reform and global governance, it is critical to examine how they are produced and how the forms of knowledge

---

[1] See TM Porter, *Trust in Numbers: The Pursuit of Objectivity in Science and Public Life* (Princeton, NJ, Princeton University Press, 1995) 25.

[2] Ibid.

[3] Ibid, 121.

[4] Ibid, 85–86.

[5] Ibid, 74, 80–81.

which they create affect global power relationships. They influence the allocation of resources, the nature of political decisions and the assessment of which countries have bad human rights conditions. They facilitate governance by self-management, rather than command. Individuals and countries are made responsible for their own behaviour as they seek to comply with the measures of performance articulated in an indicator.

## II. DEFINING INDICATORS

Indicators are statistical measures that are used to summarise complex data into a simple number or rank that is meaningful to both policy-makers and the public. They tend to ignore individual specificity and context in favour of superficial, but standardised, knowledge. An indicator clearly presents the most important features relevant to informed decision-making about one issue or question.[6] Although indicators are quantitative, expressed in rates, ratios, or percentages, or numbers, some are based upon qualitative information converted into numbers. A recent effort to develop indicators for the United Nations' Committee on the Elimination of Discrimination against Women (CEDAW), for example, uses quantitative indicators such as literacy rates, maternal mortality rates and labour force participation rates that are sex disaggregated, along with qualitative indicators such as the existence of legislation for equal inheritance rights, policies such as quotas for girl children in educational institutions, and programmes such as legal aid services and shelters for female victims of violence. These qualitative measures are quantified by counting the number of laws, the number of shelters, etc, to produce a number.[7] Some indicators use a variety of qualitative measures to construct an ordinal numerical ranking, as is the case with rule of law measures which assess a country's rule of law on a scale of 1–5.[8] Many indicators are composites of other indicators, a blending and weighting of other indicators into a new bundle.[9]

The importance of understanding indicators emerged during my conversations about human rights reform with several senior UN staff members. They argued that it was impossible to engage in reform projects without indicators, and were working to develop indicators of early marriage. They confronted conceptual challenges in determining the age of marriage. Did marriage begin at the age of betrothal, the age at

---

[6] This document, reporting the discussion of an expert group meeting to develop an indicator for violence against women, convened by the United Nations Division for the Advancement of Women, the United Nations Economic Commission for Europe and the United Nations Statistical Division, describes indicators as follows: 'Indicators are part of the knowledge base needed to assist policy and decision-making. They help to raise awareness of an issue. Indicators, with their associated benchmarks, contribute to the monitoring of progress in achieving goals, and in policy evaluation. They enable an evidence-based comparison of trends over time, and within and between countries. Indicators on violence against women may also support the assessment of States' exercise of their due diligence obligation to prevent and address violence against women, and the effectiveness of related policies and other measures' (UN Expert Group Meeting Report, 8–10 October 2007, 4).

[7] See S Gooneskere, 'Introduction: Indicators for Monitoring Implementation of CEDAW' in *CEDAW Indicators for South Asia: An Initiative* (UNIFEM South Asia Regional Office, Centre for Women's Research (CENWOR), Columbia, Sri Lanka) 10–11.

[8] See K Davis, 'What Can the Rule of Law Variable Tell Us about Rule of Law Reforms?' (2004) 26 *Michigan Journal of International Law* 141, 152.

[9] See D Kaufmann and A Kraay, 'Governance Indicators: Where Are We, Where Should We Be Going?', Policy Research Working Paper 4370 (Washington DC, The World Bank).

the wedding ceremony, the age of first sex or the age of cohabitation? These events have different implications for human rights violations. The age of betrothal might flag forced marriage, since younger girls are less likely to exercise free choice. Not all societies have recognisable wedding ceremonies, nor do they necessarily lead to first sex or cohabitation. Age of first sex could indicate medical complications of early childbearing, such as fistula. Cohabitation might spell the end of a girl's schooling. One member of the UN staff sighed and noted that marriage is very complicated. Despite these complexities, they settled on cohabitation. I have since pondered this choice, thinking about the difference it would have made were another criterion chosen and wondering how the decision was made and by whom. What were the criteria? Was it the availability of data? To what extent was this decision based upon a theory of early marriage and particular health or social problems?

Indicators typically do not come with a discussion of such decisions or an analysis of the implications of the choice. Clearly, the selection of any criterion depends on how marriage is defined. Depending on which criterion is chosen, the indicator could measure how much early marriage and childbearing damage health, diminish women's schooling or prevent free choice of partners. The indicator submerges these issues and their surrounding theories. The essence of an indicator is that it is simple and easy to understand. Embedded theories, decisions about measures and interpretations of the data are replaced by the certainty and lack of ambiguity of a number. Like money, it appears to allow abstraction and easy comparison among groups and countries by converting values into numbers. But what information is lost? Does the number bury the messiness of difference and allow equivalence?[10]

A comparison with money is instructive, since it is the quintessential unit that flattens difference into commensurate values. The 'cash nexus' famously pointed to money's capacity to make comparison and exchange of items such as potatoes and sex possible.[11] But does money bury the messiness of difference and allow equivalence? As Bill Maurer notes, the apparent equivalence created by money is undermined by questions of morality and sociality. He examines alternative currencies such as Islamic banking or community currency in upstate New York, which are grounded in critiques of capitalism. Although the money in each system is technically fungible with the others, translation is not simple. The currencies coexist as convertible, but remain socially incommensurate in meaning and morality. Efforts to move between currencies or to do Islamic banking lead to awkward compromises. Maurer refers to the 'operation of the uncanny' as a way to think about the tension of things that are the same but always different.[12] Indicators rely on a similar alchemy: they create a commensurability that is widely used to compare, to rank and to make decisions, even though the

---

[10] Kaufman and Kraay emphasise the importance of sharing information on measurement error and the constituent elements of the indicator, but in their review of governance indicators note that many indicators do not make this information available; see ibid.

[11] As Mary Poovey argues, the origins of the idea of the modern scientific fact and its representation by numbers, themselves subject to manipulation according to fixed rules, occurred along with the invention of double-entry bookkeeping as a mode of business management; see M Poovey, *A History of the Modern Fact: Problems of Knowledge in the Sciences of Wealth and Society* (Chicago, IL, University of Chicago Press, 1998).

[12] See B Maurer, *Mutual Life, Limited: Islamic Banking, Alternative Currencies, Lateral Reason* (Princeton, NJ, Princeton University Press, 2005) 104–21.

users recognise that these simplified numerical forms are superficial, often misleading and very possibly wrong.

### III. HUMAN RIGHTS AND AUDIT CULTURE

The use of indicators to monitor compliance with human rights is a rapidly growing field. Until the late 1990s, many human rights activists resisted the use of indicators because of concerns about lack of data, oversimplification and bias.[13] For example, the Freedom House indicator, 'Freedom in the World', with its seven-point scale from 'free' to 'not free', based upon annual surveys starting in 1972, was widely seen as ideologically biased.[14] Efforts to develop indicators for social and economic human rights have faced difficulties in making the measures concrete.[15] Indicators measure aggregates while human rights are held by individuals.[16] Building a composite index of human rights performance promotes quick comparisons of countries along a scale, but ignores the specificity of various human rights and conceals particular violations. Measurement errors are also a major concern. There are significant differences in the quality of data on human rights violations among countries. The countries more concerned about human rights are likely to report a higher proportion of violations than those that resist human rights principles.[17]

Despite these concerns, the use of indicators is growing in the human rights field, migrating from economics through development to human rights compliance. UN agencies such as UNICEF, UNIFEM, the Commission on the Status of Women, the High Commissioner on Human Rights and the UN Statistical Commission are taking the lead. There are long-standing initiatives to develop statistical indicators among other UN agencies and programmes, such as the FAO, ILO, UNESCO, UNICEF, WHO and UNDP.[18] A set of indicators has been developed for the Millennium Development Goals.[19] Universities and non-governmental organisations (NGOs) are also active in collecting and systematising data. For example, the University of Maryland has a research project on minorities at risk, which examines the status and conflicts of politically active groups.[20] Many economic and social indicators, such as the World Bank Worldwide Governance Indicators and the UNDP Human Development Index, are used to assess compliance with social and economic human rights.[21]

---

[13] See M Green, 'What We Talk About When We Talk About Indicators: Current Approaches to Human Rights Measurement' (2001) 23 *Human Rights Quarterly* 1062, 1082–84; P Alston, 'R Lillich Memorial Lecture: Promoting the Accountability of Members of the New UN Human Rights Council' (2005) 15 *Journal of Transnational Law and Policy* 49, 71; AJ Rosga and ML Satterthwaite, 'The Trust in Indicators: Measuring Human Rights' (2009) 27 *Berkeley Journal of International Law* 253.

[14] See Alston, n 13 above, 72.

[15] See Rosga and Satterthwaite, n 13 above.

[16] See Green, n 13 above, 1085.

[17] See Alston, n 13 above, 71–74.

[18] R Malhotra and N Fasel, 'Quantitative Human Rights Indicators: A Survey of Major Initiatives', background paper for the UN Expert Meeting on Human Rights Indicators, Turku, Finland (2005), 15, available at   www.jus.uio/forskning/grupper/humrdev/Project-Indicators/Workshop06/Background/Malhotra&Fasel. pdf (last accessed on 17 December 2008).

[19] Available at http://mdgs.un.org/unsd/mdg/Default.aspx.

[20] Available at www.cidcm.umd.edu/inscr/mar; see also Malhotra and Fasel, n 18 above, 21.

[21] See E Filmer-Wilson, 'Summary Report of Material Collated regarding Practical Guidance to Implementing Rights-Based Approaches, Human Rights Analyses for Poverty Reduction and Human Rights

Development agencies have long used indicators. The recent shift to a rights-based approach to development[22] has brought human rights and development closer together and encouraged the use of economically based indicators for human rights compliance. The 2000 UNDP Human Development Report devoted a chapter to the value of indicators for human rights accountability.[23] The World Bank has collected and disseminated a wide range of socio-economic statistics derived largely from national statistical systems, as well as data on governance and the rule of law based upon expert and household surveys.[24] These are useful for monitoring compliance with social and economic rights in particular.[25] Economists at the World Bank have also played a critical role in developing indicators for international investment, such as its Doing Business project to assess business conditions around the world.[26] The 2009 Doing Business report ranked 181 countries on ten criteria for doing business, such as starting a business or dealing with construction permits, producing an overall 'Ease of Doing Business Index'.[27] Singapore ranked first, the US third and the Democratic Republic of the Congo last. The website offers a one-page explanation of the index and a caution about its limited scope. Despite these limitations, the index offers a readily understandable comparative exposition of business conditions around the world in one short table.

In his anthropological account of a European development project in Africa, Richard Rottenburg uses Latour's concept of centres of calculation to describe the production of such comparative, translocal knowledge. In order for a development bank to produce the knowledge necessary to monitor and control projects, it must know about projects around the world in comparable terms through their reports. Bank officials juxtapose these reports to create a common context that produces new knowledge. The process depends on producing representations of projects that travel (reports), that are immutable (certain in meaning, not shifting according to the teller) and that are combinable. Making reports combinable requires establishing in advance standardised procedures for measuring and aggregating the information in the report. By comparing the reports, the development bank produces translocal knowledge that allows it to monitor and control projects from a distance and to be accountable to the taxpayers.[28] This process, developed in the domain of economics and reliant on universalistic technical standards, provides a template for the production and use of indicators in other domains.

While there is considerable discussion of how to develop good indicators and cri-

---

Benchmarks from Development Actors and other Relevant Communities', for DFID (31 March 2005) 28, available at www.gsdrc.org/go/display/document/legacyid/1554 (last accessed on 19 December 2008). See also Green, n 13 above.

[22] See AK Sen, *Development as Freedom* (Oxford, Oxford University Press, 1999).

[23] See UNDP, 'Using Indicators for Human Rights Accountability', *Human Development Report 2000* (New York, United Nations, 2000) ch 5, 89–111.

[24] See Malhotra and Fasel, n 18 above, 15.

[25] See Green, n 13 above.

[26] See KE Davis and MB Kruse, 'Taking the Measure of Law: The Case of the *Doing Business* Project' (2007) 32 *Law and Social Inquiry* 1095, 1097.

[27] Available at www.doingbusiness.org/EconomyRankings.

[28] See B Latour, *Science in Action: How to Follow Scientists and Engineers through Society* (Cambridge MA, Harvard University Press, 1987); see also R Rottenburg, *Far-Fetched Facts: A Parable of Development Aid*, trans A Brown and T Lampert (Cambridge MA, The MIT Press, 2009) 181–82.

tiques of their errors of measurement, quality of data, embedded assumptions and simplification,[29] there is far less attention to the implications of the use of indicators for practices of global governance itself.[30] Within social science, however, there has been considerable attention to the impact on the practices of governance of these new political technologies based upon statistics and accountability—what has been called 'audit culture'.[31] Audit technologies are theorised as instruments for new forms of governance and power, 'agents for the creation of new forms of subjectivity: self-managing individuals who render themselves auditable'.[32] These technologies allow people to check their behaviour for themselves so that governments can withdraw from checking behaviour and simply check indicators of performance.[33] The self-checking practices become evidence of accountability from the perspective of the state. Marilyn Strathern's edited collection focuses on the new mechanisms for accountability established by the British government for evaluating and reimbursing university faculties.[34] The contributors argue that the new system places responsibility for compliance on the performer, not the checker. Thus, there is a shifting of responsibility that masks the underlying power dynamics: the indicator itself does the work of critique and the governed person seeks to conform to the terms of the government. Similar benefits devolve to treaty bodies that develop indicators: if the treaty body can persuade the country being governed to develop its own indicators, the committee can replace its practices of checking of country policies and actions with countries' self-checking.[35] The turn to indicator creation marks a shift in the way the administration of human rights law takes place. Instead of pressuring countries to conform to human rights laws upon the basis of ambiguous and contextualised accounts in country reports or case studies, reports in which each country is presented as shaped by its history, social structure, wealth and political agendas, indicators provide comparable information in numerical terms. The burden of assessment rests on the indicator itself, with its agreed-upon standards and means of measurement. Although the experts developing a set of indicators for monitoring compliance with human rights conventions argued that the numbers were not to be used to rank or shame countries, but only for assessing a country's progress over time, once an indicator has been created, such rankings are possible.[36] The reliance on numbers, with their apparently simple and straightforward meanings, produces an unambiguous and easily replicated field for judgement. Compliance becomes far more open to inspection and assessment.

Moreover, responsibility for compliance shifts to the monitored organisation or country itself, which must not only seek to comply but must also monitor and report the success of its efforts. The enforcement body moves away from the role of

[29] See Davis, n 8 above.
[30] But see Rosga and Satterthwaite, n 13 above.
[31] See M Power, *The Audit Society: Rituals of Verification* (Oxford, Oxford University Press, 1999); see also M Strathern (ed), *Audit Cultures: Anthropological studies in Accountability, Ethics, and the Academy* (Abingdon, Routledge, 2000).
[32] See C Shore and S Wright, 'Coercive Accountability: The Rise of Audit Culture in Higher Education' in Strathern, n 31 above, 57.
[33] See Strathern, n 31 above, 4.
[34] Ibid.
[35] See Rosga and Satterthwaite, n 13 above.
[36] See Turku Report, 'Report of Turku Expert Meeting on Human Rights Indicators, 10–13 March 2005 in Turku/Abo Finland' 7, available at http://web.abo.fi/institut/imr/research/seminars/indicators/Report.doc (last accessed on 17 December 2008).

an authority imposing criticisms to a body that registers performance in terms of already-established indicators. In other words, the process of assessing compliance shifts from the encounter between statements and rules in a quasi-judicial forum, such as a treaty body hearing, to the creation of the measure itself. Once the indicator has been established, compliance is simply a matter of recording performance according to the indicator. Treaty bodies are moving from asking countries to come up with their own indicators towards a universal set of indicators for all countries which can be assessed impartially by the treaty body.[37]

In sum, the expansion of the use of indicators in global governance means that political struggles over what human rights mean and what constitutes compliance are submerged by technical questions of measurement, criteria and data accessibility. Political debates about compliance shift to arguments about how to form an indicator, what should be measured and what each measurement should represent. These debates typically rely on experts in the field of measurement and statistics, usually in consultation with experts in the substantive topic and in the national and international terrain. They build on previous research studies and knowledge generated by scholars. The outcomes appear as forms of knowledge, rather than as particular representations of a methodology and particular political decision about what to measure and what to call it. An indicator provides a transition from ambiguity to certainty, from theory to fact, and from complex variation and context to truthful, comparable numbers. In other words, the political process of judging and evaluating is transformed into a technical issue of measurement and counting by the diligent work of experts. The practices of measuring phenomena that are relatively easily counted, such as money or inventories of goods, are transplanted into domains far less amenable to quantification, such as the frequency of torture or the prevalence of ill health. The technologies of knowledge developed in the economic domain move uneasily into these newer fields.

Despite the political significance of indicators and the numbers that they generate, much of the discussion about indicators takes a highly technical approach, debating issues such as the quality of measures, the data available, the difficulties in comparing across countries, the sample size, the data-collection techniques, and the costs of stand-alone and detailed surveys in comparison to shorter modules attached to existing surveys.[38] For indicators to be credible, they must appear to be neutral, scientific and objective. This set of expectations explains the pervasive role of researchers and scholars in the process, who bring their technical expertise and knowledge of other forms of data collection to the process. It explains the intimate, but often uneasy, relationship between researchers and policy advocates in the indicator production process.

Indicators serve disparate and sometimes contradictory goals: producing scientific knowledge, monitoring and controlling behaviour, and identifying and reforming social problems. Indicators are simultaneously a form of objective knowledge, a means of governance of people and organisations, such as NGOs, and an advocacy tool. Contestation over these three goals has deep historic roots, stretching back at least until the beginnings of government statistics in the nineteenth century. They recur in

---

[37] See Rosga and Satterthwaite, n 13 above, 4.

[38] See S Walby, 'Indicators to Measure Violence Against Women: Invited Paper', Expert Group Meeting on Indicators to Measure Violence Against Women Working Paper 1 (2007 UN Statistical Commission and Economic Commission for Europe, UN Division for the Advancement of Women, UN Statistics Division); see also Kaufmann and Kraay, n 9 above.

contemporary debates about indicator production. In one meeting of a UN group developing an indicator, for example, some of those attending were knowledgeable about research and statistics while others worked in countries around the world in UN offices or for NGOs. The group confronted the difficulty of deciding whether the goal of an indicator is to develop a scientific descriptive tool for theory development, a policy tool to assess government policies or NGO programmes, or an advocacy tool to shame governments for poor performance. These goals are all quite different. The first is to produce scientific knowledge, the second is to facilitate organisational management and the third is to promote reform. Each suggests a somewhat different approach to formulating questions and selecting items.

However, these approaches are also interdependent. The value of an indicator for both policy and advocacy objectives depends on its scientific credibility, while the policy and advocacy goals are important in promoting indicator development and encouraging countries to co-operate in data collection. The documentation on several expert-group meetings to develop indicators indicates that participants have very different forms of knowledge and expertise. Some have scientific research expertise while others are more familiar with the local conditions in the sites that are being surveyed. The documents produced by these meetings suggest that local, vernacular knowledge is less influential than technical knowledge. For example, UNIFEM and the UN Division for the Advancement of Women, along with the UN Economic Commission for Europe and the UN Statistics Commission, held a series of meetings and discussions, and produced expert reports to establish an indicator of violence against women. The reports from the 2007 expert group meeting indicate that it combined academic experts housed in universities with substantial research experience with people from NGOs, governments and the UN who have carried out surveys in various countries.[39] Papers by participants included reports from Mexico, Ghana, Korea and Italy, as well as overviews from Africa, Europe, Latin America and the Caribbean, the Asia/Pacific region and Western Asia. The final report surveyed studies from the UNHCR, the US, the UK, the EU, Palestine and the UN Millennium Project (UN Division for the Advancement of Women 2007). Despite this broad international participation, however, the theoretical framework was based upon the work of experts, much as development banks rely on standardised forms of knowledge. There is no other way to develop compatible data. As in other indicator processes, it is the expert who is charged with defining the terms, reporting the research already done on the topic and proposing the measures of an indicator. The process requires universal categories. It founders on cultural difference.

The creation of indicators for human rights compliance by UN treaty bodies monitoring the six major human rights conventions[40] follows a similar process. The first step is the expert report that looks at the existing survey research, distils a set of questions and measurement strategies, and proposes a set of standards. The second step is a set of meetings over two or three years that brings together academic experts with representatives from UN agencies, governments and NGOs to discuss the report and individual country studies and to settle on a set of items. The overarching framework

---

[39] See Walby, n 38 above.
[40] See Goonesekere, n 7 above. See also 'Report on Indicators for Monitoring Compliance with International Human Rights Instruments' UN Doc HRI/MC/2006/7 (2006); Turku Expert Group Meeting on Human Rights Indicators, 10–13 March 2005, available at ww.abo.fi/instut/imr/indicators/index.htm.

is already set, but the indicator is now being groomed to travel. The third step is determining the source of the data, be they already existing or newly acquired through financing self-standing surveys or attaching questions to existing studies. Questions of reliability, ease of administration and costs of data collection are very important. The fourth step involves assessing whether the data conforms to similar indicators.[41] If it seems quite divergent, there may be an effort to weight or adjust the findings. Questions of reliability, ease of administration and costs of data collection are very important. The goal is to produce a set of universal categories that are simple, easy and inexpensive to administer and quantify.

Indicators are sometimes challenged by those subject to them. Individuals and groups may object to the definition of the criteria as well as the process of measurement. For example, the UN Permanent Forum on Indigenous Issues led an effort to include consideration of the condition of indigenous peoples in global indicators such as those developed to assess the Millennium Development Goals (MDGs) and the Human Development Index.[42] A series of workshops and regional meetings beginning in 2004 produced a report from a workshop in Ottawa in 2006, which complained that indigenous peoples were not included in the development and implementation of the MDG indicators, that the indicators were inaccurate from the perspective of indigenous peoples because they did not incorporate indigenous conceptions of well-being or assess these communities accurately, and that the practices of aggregation used by global indicators erased the particular experience of indigenous minorities. For example, the report said that the measures focused on materialistic assessment of goods more than reciprocity in social and economic relations. The report recommended disaggregating indigenous peoples and developing indicators that address the specific situation of indigenous peoples, such as their relationship to the land or the transmission of indigenous languages. They proposed measures such as the percentage of indigenous peoples who recognise their indigenous language as their mother tongue and the percentage of fluent indigenous language speakers in indigenous communities (Ottawa Report 2006). This report was presented to the Permanent Forum in May 2007 at its Sixth Session.

Insofar as the Permanent Forum represents indigenous people, this effort is a political contestation of the content of indicators by those who are subject to their governance. Of the 12 participants in the 2006 Ottawa meeting, at least eight were heads of indigenous organisations and two were members of the secretariat of the Permanent Forum. The other two appear to be experts in research on indigenous issues. In this report and in the Permanent Forum discussions, indigenous people did not contest the use of indicators per se, but only how they failed to account for their experiences. They wanted a better indicator, not its elimination. An indicator responsive to indigenous concerns seemed to offer a way to increase public attention to the difficulties faced by indigenous peoples. Yet, in order to produce this translocal knowledge, it is necessary to eliminate some of the particularities of indigenous experience and its diversities to produce a standardised representation of truth.

Individuals, populations and nations that are being measured by global indicators

---

[41] See Kaufmann and Kraay, n 9 above.
[42] See J Taylor, 'Indigenous Peoples and Indicators of Well-Being: Australian Perspectives on United Nations Global Frameworks' [2008] *Social Indicators Research* 87, 111, 112.

differ greatly in their power to challenge or change the indicators. Relatively weak countries have far less ability to change the indicators than powerful ones. Those who are drawing up and using the indicators clearly have more ability to adjust or refine them. Participatory processes in indicator construction clearly help to produce a more accurate measure, but participants differ greatly in their power to make changes. According to the MDG list of indicators from January 2008, indigenous people have not yet been included as a separate category, nor have their concerns been incorporated within this set of 48 indicators.[43]

Thus, the creation of indicators reveals a slippage between the political and the technical. The slippage occurs in the way in which issues and problems are defined, in the identity and role of experts, in the relative power of the people engaged in producing and using indicators, and in the power and clout of the sponsoring organisation. Through the apparatus of science and measurement, the indicator displaces judgement from governing bodies onto the indicator itself, which establishes the standards for judgement. Nevertheless, indicators are inevitably political, rooted in particular conceptions of problems and theories of responsibility. They represent the perspectives and frameworks of those who produce them, as well as their political and financial power. What gets counted depends on which groups and organisations can afford to count. However, indicators differ significantly between those produced by a powerful organisation, such as the World Bank, which scores and ranks countries, and more participatory processes, such as the OHCHR human rights indicators, in which the experts provide a framework but the choice of indicators, methods and data collection lies, to a somewhat greater extent, with the countries being measured.

## IV. THE GENEALOGY OF INDICATORS

Where did indicators come from? What is their genealogy? Since their creation in practices of financial management and governance in Europe perhaps four centuries ago, they have migrated across sectors and nations. The use of numerical information to understand the world reflects the creation of what Mary Poovey calls the 'modern fact' as a form of knowledge.[44] The modern fact is basic to the ways in which Westerners have come to know the world. It has organised most of the knowledge projects of the last four centuries.[45] Numbers are the epitome of the modern fact because they seem to be simple descriptors of phenomena and resist the biases of conjecture and theory since they are subject to the invariable rules of mathematics. Numbers have become the bedrock of systematic knowledge because they seem free of interpretation, as neutral and descriptive. They are presented as objective, with an interpretive narrative attached to them by which they are given meaning. Numbers can be assigned to observed particulars in a way that makes them amenable to such manipulations and makes them amenable to a knowledge system that privileges quantity over quality and equivalence over difference.[46]

---

[43] Available at http://mdgs.un.org/unsd/mdg/Host.aspx?Content=Indicators/OfficialList.htm.
[44] See Poovey, n 11 above, xii.
[45] Ibid, xiii.
[46] Ibid, 4.

However, Poovey shows that numbers are not non-interpretive but embody theoretical assumptions about what should be counted, how to understand material reality and how quantification contributes to systematic knowledge about the world.[47] Establishing the understanding of numbers as an objective description of reality outside interpretation was a project of modernity. Although some see facts as interpreted, the idea that numbers guarantee value-free description is still pervasive.[48] Poovey argues that the early nineteenth-century combination of numbers and analysis enabled professionals to develop systematic knowledge through non-interpretive descriptions. The nineteenth-century separation of numbers from interpretation made numbers different in kind from analytical accounts, locating them in a different stage in knowledge-producing projects. Since the numbers were different in kind from other knowledge, they could be developed by a special class of professionals who worked with them. Experts—professional knowledge producers—took responsibility for managing this different kind of knowledge, knowledge that existed prior to policy and could be used in neutral ways to inform it.[49]

Statistics became increasingly important as a technology of governance in nineteenth-century Europe. As scholars of the intellectual history of statistics indicate, numbers as an instrument of knowledge production were developed first for business transactions, exemplified, in particular, by the invention of double-entry bookkeeping, and subsequently as instruments of state governance.[50] The use of numerical measures by states for administration and tax collection stretches back millennia, but it is only with the development of the modern state that statistics have been used to describe the characteristics of populations themselves. Quantification, with its aura of objectivity, became increasingly important to a variety of government and business functions in the nineteenth century, from developing cost–benefit measures for locating railroad lines to the need to measure life-spans by life insurance companies in the mid-nineteenth century.[51]

In her history of the rise of statistics as a discipline in England and France in the nineteenth century, Libby Schweber[52] notes that statistics were fundamental to the new project of administering a population and attending to issues such as public health, poverty, and the rates of birth and death in a population. Foucault analysed the nineteenth-century interest in population statistics as a shift to governance designed to enhance the capacities of the nation.[53] The use of numerical measures of population by age, birth and death rates, health, poverty and other criteria constituted the population as a measurable entity that could be known in new ways.[54] Increasingly, statistics became the basis upon which governments assessed their resources, human and natural, and developed policies for promoting public health, diminishing population decline and 'degeneracy', and alleviating poverty. Similar technologies were vital

[47] Ibid, xii.
[48] Ibid, xxv.
[49] Ibid, xv.
[50] Ibid.
[51] See Porter, n 1 above, 106–21.
[52] See L Schweber, *Disciplining Statistics: Demography and Vital Statistics in France and England, 1830–1885* (Durham NC, Duke University Press, 2006).
[53] M Foucault, 'Governmentality' in G Burchell, C Gordon and P Miller (eds), *The Foucault Effect: Studies in Governmentality* (Chicago, IL, University of Chicago Press, 1991) 87–105.
[54] See Poovey, n 11 above; Porter, n 1 above; Schweber, n 52 above.

to the governance of the newly formed colonies of the nineteenth century. Bernard Cohn argues that the British imperial government in India developed strategies of classification and counting that made possible the acquisition of control over the complexity of Indian society.[55]

These studies of the rise of statistical knowledge indicate that there were three simultaneous uses of statistics in the nineteenth century, which were often in tension with one another. The differences are quite similar to those of the contemporary indicator movement in the field of human rights. First, statistics were a means of providing a scientific description of a population, delineating its character in a way that was neutral in terms of policy but which still provided knowledge of its shape and composition. Secondly, statistics were used as a mode of understanding the population of a nation as a resource, in order to govern it more effectively. Thus, statistics were linked to strategies of management and control over populations. Thirdly, statistics were deployed as a mode of reform, a way to identify problems such as poverty and public health deficits. For example, in the 1860s in France, a panic about the declining population led to a focus on the possible consequences of wet nurses for infant mortality. Statistics confirmed that there was at least a relationship between wet nurses and infant deaths.[56] Each of these uses of statistics suggests a different strategy for gathering information, a different mode of interpretation, and a different choice of subjects of counting and measurement.

## V. DATA COLLECTION: THE PROBLEM OF COUNTING

Indicators depend on the collection of comparable data, which means defining phenomena that can be counted. As donors demand evidence-based programming, NGOs must come up with statistical measures for what they have accomplished. Activists jockeying for funding are pressed to engage in activities that can produce measurable outcomes in relatively short time periods. For those with broad social change agendas, bigger accomplishments must be replaced with small, countable activities. For example, a feminist women's centre in which I studied in the 1990s initially sought to transform gender relations and diminish violence through requiring batterers in domestic violence cases to attend eight months of two-hours-a-week training sessions. When its funding shifted from community development money to the judiciary, there was suddenly a new set of expectations of carrying forward a substantial caseload. The staff had to shorten the training programme, develop a more therapeutic and less critical way of dealing with violent men in domestic battery cases, and count the number of clients which it handled on a monthly basis. Thus, their agenda shifted from transforming the community and gender relations to providing services to battered people and to those who hit them.[57]

Not only do systems of accounting affect the internal work of an organisation, they also shape the competitive advantage of alternative programmes. As a group of justice

---

[55] BS Cohn, *Colonialism and its Forms of Knowledge: The British in India* (Princeton, NJ, Princeton University Press, 1996).

[56] See Schweber, n 52 above.

[57] S Engle Merry, *Gender Violence: A Cultural Perspective* (Malden, MA, Wiley Blackwell, 2009) 54–75.

advocates at the World Bank told me, objective measures tend to benefit activities with clear contributions to economic well-being, such as road building, in comparison to those that offer far more ambiguous and long-term measurable benefits, such as local justice initiatives. Indicators are an apparently neutral technology of knowledge production with important implications for power relations. They are the political tools of the present.

Indicators require converting dimensions of social life into something that can be measured. Some things are more easily measured than others, however, and require less interpretation. Infant mortality is easier to count than the rule of law, for example. However, even phenomena that seem quite countable, such as infant mortality, depend on practices of birth and death registration and reporting mechanisms. Many indicators assess phenomenon that are very difficult to quantify, such as justice or the protection of human rights. One solution is to create quantifiable proxies for the phenomenon. For example, if the goal is increasing the consciousness of human rights, this could be assessed by an attitude survey or by a count of the number of training sessions that an organisation has carried out. The latter is clearly less expensive.

Expertise is fundamental to data collection. Who does the counting and what kinds of training they have both have a critical impact on the data produced. Data collection can be handled by highly trained data collectors who can flexibly adapt their methods to the situation, or by untrained and unsophisticated data collectors who must follow rigid rules.[58] The skill of the data collector determines how rigidly the data must be defined; more flexible approaches demand more skilled collectors. As Theodore Porter notes, those who are charged with counting confront the ambiguities of classification, but, once routine practices are established and compromises reached with regard to how the classification is done, those who use them, such as newspapers or public officials, have little opportunity to rework the numbers.[59]

Those who design an indicator must decide which data collection methods they can use, depending, in part, on how much they can spend on collecting information. Data collection is expensive, especially for a global cross-country comparison. Cost is often a trade-off against accuracy. For example, in their survey of recent efforts to develop human rights indicators, Rajeev Malhotra and Nicolas Fasel describe four kinds of data: (i) events-based data upon human rights violations, primarily of civil and political rights, and generally collected by civil society organisations; (ii) socio-economic statistics, usually collected by governments, and their administrative records, which can be used to assess compliance with social and economic rights; (iii) household perception and opinion surveys that offer perspectives of public opinion on governments and their policies, such as governance, human rights and democracy; and (iv) data based upon expert judgements, which focuses primarily on civil and political rights.[60] The first and second are more reliable, but they are also more expensive than the third and fourth.

A common approach in cross-national comparisons is to survey in-country 'experts' about their perceptions of their country. Sending questionnaires is clearly cost effective. This approach is often used by World Bank surveys on governance indicators to assess

---

[58] See Porter, n 1 above, 35.
[59] Ibid, 42.
[60] Malhotra and Fasel, n 18 above, 5–22.

whether laws are enforced or whether there is extensive corruption in a government.[61] However, there are limitations to the knowledge which this approach provides. A questionnaire sent to a Latin American expert by the World Justice Project, an indicator initiative to measure the rule of law founded by the American Bar Association along with a large number of other US, Canadian and international bar associations and other organisations, illustrates the problem.[62] The World Justice Project has already spent two years and 1.1 million USD developing the index. Justice experts from Yale and Stanford Universities as well as judges and lawyers in The Hague, where the ICC, the World Court and the ICTY are located, worked on the index.[63] It has partnered with the Vera Institute of Justice in New York. Thus, this is a Global North initiative.

The index is based upon four universal principles, one of which is 'whether the process by which the laws are enacted, administered and enforced is accessible, fair and efficient'.[64] One source of information for this indicator is a 'Qualified Respondent's Questionnaire'. The labour law segment of the questionnaire, sent to 'highly qualified persons with knowledge of the rule of law in their country', including academics, practicing professionals, and current or former government officials and judges, poses a number of questions requiring extensive knowledge of national practices. The respondent is asked to answer according to 'your perception of how the laws are applied *in practice* to the following situations in your country'. One question asks, 'How likely is a person's application for employment to be rejected because this person is: of another race? Of a different religion? Female? Homosexual or transgender? A foreign national? Physically disabled?'. The respondent is given four choices for each category, ranging from very likely to very unlikely (as well as 'don't know'). Since the answers might vary with the employer, the questionnaire suggests that the respondent should assume a medium-sized clothing manufacturing company located in the country's largest city, wholly owned by national citizens. In order to fill in the other characteristics of the putative applicant, the form says that he should be considered a male of the dominant race and ethnicity, a citizen, 36 years old, without a criminal history, who has worked for the company for 16 years (presumably to cover the next question, which asks about the likelihood of being fired). Clearly, a full answer to these questions requires extensive research into a wide range of employment situations in various parts of a country—yet the invitation to participate says it should take less than an hour to complete the questionnaire. The designers clearly do not anticipate that the respondent will engage in research, or even search out existing research. Instead, the questionnaire seeks the opinion of someone who is 'knowledgeable'. Thus, expertise based upon experience is converted into expertise based upon numbers.

Indicators at the global level inevitably rely on local data collection processes, although they may be created and managed at international level. Local centres may understand the process differently, carry out the measurement tasks in different ways, or resist co-operating with national and international expectations. It is striking that all of the global governance indicator projects I have looked at are created in the

---

[61] Kaufmann and Kraay, n 9 above, 7 and 15.

[62] See www.worldjusticeproject.org.

[63] *International Herald Tribune*, 3 July 2008, available at www.iht.com/articles/ap/2008/07/03/europe/EU-Rule-of-Law.php.

[64] Available at www.worldjusticeproject.org.

Global North, which sets the agenda, names the indicator and assembles the criteria, while data collection typically takes place mostly in the Global South. As the use of indicators enhances the exposure of nations to international scrutiny and potentially control, there may be forms of local resistance to the process.

## VI. NAMING INDICATORS

One of the critical ways that an indicator produces knowledge is by announcing what it measures, such as 'rule of law' or 'poverty'. Neither of these categories is self-evident. When sponsoring organisations name their indicators, they interpret what the numbers mean. Labelling is essential to producing a measure that is readily understood by the public and simple in its conception. Labels do not necessarily accurately reflect the data that produce the indicators, however. How indicators are named and who decides what they represent are fundamental to the way in which an indicator produces knowledge.

Indeed, statistical measures create new categories. An indicator may even create the phenomenon that it is measuring, instead of the other way around. IQ is whatever it is that the IQ test measures, for example. Here, the process of measurement produces the phenomenon which it claims to measure. As Porter points out, although the categories of enumeration may be highly contingent at first, once they are in place they become extremely resilient and come to take on permanent existence as a form of knowledge. He uses the category of Hispanic in the US census as an example of this phenomenon.[65] One of the most well known examples of this process is the introduction of the census in India by the British colonial authorities in the nineteenth and twentieth centuries.[66] To increase legibility, the population census classified individuals by caste, religion, gender and other criteria. The British arranged the castes in an orderly hierarchy and sought to collect 'objective' information about caste identities. However, the caste categories in existence at the time were relatively fluid, situational, segmented and local. In place of a wide range of forms of ritual and social exclusion in practice, the British selected pollution by touch as the key marker of low caste status. Thus, the category 'Untouchability' emerged as a distinct, all-India category. By redefining castes in terms of categories that applied across the subcontinent, the British rendered caste into a far more fixed and intractable social entity, but one that could be more readily counted and compared.[67]

### VI.1. Using Indicators for Governance

As tools of governance, indicators are commonly developed by powerful bodies seeking to manage and control populations or allocate resources. They may also be used to

---

[65] See Porter, n 1 above, 42.
[66] See Cohn, n 55 above; S Randeria, 'Entangled Histories of Uneven Modernities: Civil Society, Caste Solidarities and Legal Pluralism in Post-colonial India' in J Keane (ed), *Civil Society—Berlin Perspectives* (Cambridge, Cambridge University Press, 2006); NB Dirks, *Castes of Mind: Colonialism and the Making of Modern India* (Princeton, NJ, Princeton University Press).
[67] See Randeria, n 66 above, 19.

rank countries or organisations or to determine eligibility for a benefit. Indicators are not only directed at helping decision-makers decide where to build a railroad or in what country to invest, but also at promoting self-governance among the governed. By establishing standards according to which individuals, organisations or nations should behave, indicators should inspire those who are measured to perform better and improve their ranking. Students in the US are very familiar with the role that grades play in their educational lives. One of the reasons for creating indicators for treaty compliance is to promote nations taking steps to improve their performance according to the numerical standards of human rights treaties. Countries some-times respond by emphasising their status on indicators where they rank highly. For example, when Lithuania reported to the committee that monitors compliance with the Women's Convention, CEDAW, on 2 July 2008, which I observed, the government representative, the Secretary of the Ministry of Social Security and Labour, pointed out that, according to the World Economic Forum's Report Global Gender Gap Index 2007, Lithuania was among the countries that had made the most significant progress among the top 20 countries and now occupies fourteenth place. The minister also noted that Lithuania was in second place in the employment rate of women raising children below 12 years of age according to the EU Report on Gender Equality in 2008. Clearly, the minister was using these rankings to point out how well her country was succeeding in diminishing gender discrimination (CEDAW/C/LTU/Q/4).

The governed often shift their behaviour in ways designed to improve their score, although they may do so in ways not desired by the producer of the indicator. As AnnJanette Rosga and Margaret Satterthwaite note, indicators have a relatively short life before those who are governed by them begin to change their behaviour in order to enhance their score.[68] While this may be the desired outcome, it may also produce strategies to 'game' the indicator. For example, some colleges downgraded by the US News and World Report for low rates of alumna-giving divide their alumnae gifts made in one year into three annual payments. Although some highly ranked colleges have recently refused to participate at all, those ranked lower have relatively little power to challenge or change the system of ranking.

As indicators shift responsibility for governance from those in power to those who are governed, they may undermine autonomy, a sense of trust and willingness to co-operate among certain kinds of populations. Marilyn Strathern and her colleagues criticise the Research Assessment Exercise programme of the British government which has introduced indicators of faculty productivity and activity as the basis for allocating revenues to academic departments.[69] As Strathern argues, this mechanism creates the standards to which universities then seek to govern themselves, but, for professionals who work long hours with low pay under conditions of autonomy, this regime suggests a lack of trust and leads to alienation and resistance, producing exhaustion and withdrawal.

The turn to indicators is part of a new form of governance, one that engages the person in governing himself or herself in terms of standards set by others. This new form of governance emphasises 'responsibilisation', in which individuals are induced to

[68] See Rosga and Satterthwaite, n 13 above.
[69] See Stathern, n 31 above.

take responsibility for their actions.[70] In some of the most successful examples, such as grades in school, the indicator comes to shape subjectivity, defining for the individual his or her degree of merit. These indicators promote self-management, what Nikolas Rose calls 'government at a distance'. He argues that new systems of governance have emerged in the post-war period that seek to control individual behaviour through governance of the soul.[71] In the liberal democracies of the post-war period, citizens are to regulate themselves, to become active participants in the process rather than objects of domination. Rose dates the formation of this self-managing system of governance to the 1950s, but sees a major expansion during the era of neo-liberalism and the critique of the welfare state.[72] However, Andrew Kipnis criticises Rose's emphasis on the connection of audit culture and neo-liberalism, since similar practices of monitoring occur in China under a very different political regime.[73]

## VI.2. Indicator Governance and the Corporate Form

Indicators are a basic technology of corporate management and control, but as they move into the previously distinct domain of human rights and humanitarianism, the boundaries between business, the state and what is commonly referred to as 'civil society' blur. In practice, the corporation is increasingly intertwined with these other domains of society both in discourse and in management strategy. The spread of its techniques of auditing and counting to the state and civil society is an instance of this seepage of the corporate form. Here, I will identify three forms of interchange.

The first is the donors' demand for performance evaluations of civil society organisations by foundations and governments. Social justice and humanitarian organisations face an increasingly onerous burden of quantifying their accomplishments, even when they are difficult to measure and the data are expensive to produce, as discussed above. A further step in this direction is the US government's move to create indicator-based development funding. The Millennium Challenge Corporation (MCC), started in 2004, relies on competition among countries to allocate funding. Countries that perform better on the indicators established by the MCC are more likely to receive funding. This system replaces the earlier use of conditions that have to be met by countries receiving development aid. This approach emphasises a country's responsibility for its governance and embodies the argument that effective government is fundamental to development.

The key concern of the MCC programme is controlling corruption through promoting 'good governance'. Countries are measured by 17 indicators, grouped into three broad categories: ruling justly, investing in people and encouraging economic freedom. The indicators are all developed by other organisations. Five of the six governance indicators were developed by the World Bank, while two are from Freedom House.

---

[70] See P O'Malley, 'Governmentality and the Risk Society' (1999) 28 *Economy and Society* 138.

[71] See N Rose, *Governing the Soul: The Shaping of the Private Self* (London, Routledge, 1989); idem, 'The Death of the Social? Re-figuring the Territory of Government' (1996) 25 *Economy and Society* 327; idem, *Predicaments of Freedom* (Cambridge, Cambridge University Press, 1999).

[72] See Rose, *Governing the Soul*, ibid, 226–27.

[73] See AB Kipnis, 'Audit Cultures: Neoliberal Governmentality, Socialist Legacy, or Technologies of Governing?' (2008) 35 *American Ethnologist* 275.

Health and education indicators come from UNESCO and WHO, whereas economic freedom ones are from the World Bank and the Heritage Foundation's trade-policy indicator. The MCC also uses the Corruption Perceptions Index of Transparency International and the US State Department Human Rights Report.[74] The process of selection involves four steps. The MCC board identifies eligible countries from the low- and middle-income range, publishes the selection criteria, develops scorecards for each country and, upon the basis of these scorecards, selects some for assistance. Countries selected by the board as eligible are invited to submit proposals for an MCC compact. A few countries with a low score on one of the policy indicators are selected each year to participate in the Millennium Corporation Threshold Programme/0 to help raise their score and become eligible for an MCC grant. The Threshold Programme is run by USAID.[75]

In a discussion of this programme in January 2008 at the American Enterprise Institute entitled, 'Can Indicator-based Competition Make Foreign Aid Work?', speakers emphasised that the turn to indicators is result of the emphasis on accountability. The overarching idea is to replace conditionalities with competition. Under this indicator approach, countries know what is expected of them and can compete for funds according to these standards. However, at this event, the representative from the UNDP said that he thought the mechanism was too complex, and conditions should be loosened.[76] These examples suggest that work associated with the promotion of development, human rights and good governance is increasingly being channelled by reliance on indicators.

The corporate form is also moving into domains of state and civil society governance with its engagement in process of indicator development and data collection. Corporations are increasingly involved in the expensive and highly technical process of collecting and analyzing data and writing reports for NGOs, governments and UN agencies. For example, a recent initiative of US AID East Africa and the US AID Inter-agency Gender Working Group to develop a compendium of monitoring and evaluation indicators of violence against women and girls was developed by MEASURE Evaluation in collaboration with a technical advisory group of experts. The advisory group consisted of experts from UNHCR, USAID, CDC, UNFPA, WHO, academics, independent consultants and several people from MEASURE Evaluation, one of whom authored the report.[77] MEASURE Evaluation describes itself as providing technical leadership:

> through collaboration at local, national, and global levels to build the sustainable capacity of individuals and organizations to identify data needs, collect and analyze technically sound data, and use that data for health decision-making. We develop, implement and facilitate state of the art methods for and approaches to improving health information systems, monitoring and evaluation, and data use; and we collect, share, and disseminate information, knowledge, and best practices in order to increase the use of data and advance the field of health monitoring and evaluation in many countries.

[74] Available at www.mcc.gov/mcc/bm/doc (last accessed on 22 August 2009).
[75] Available at www.mcc.gov/mcc/panda/programs/threshold/shtml.index (last accessed on 20 July 2009).
[76] Available at www.aei.org/event/1627 (last accessed on 20 July 2009).
[77] SS Bloom, 'Violence against Women and Girls: A Compendium of Monitoring and Evaluation Indicators' (2008), available at http://www.prb.org/igwg_media/violenceagainstwomen.pdf.

The organisation is funded by USAID and works in partnership with the University of North Carolina, Tulane University and ICF Macro, among others, revealing the collaboration of academic, government and corporate actors.

ICF Macro is a large corporation that includes a programme, MEASURE DHS, which, since 1984, has provided technical assistance for 240 Demographic and Health Surveys in 75 countries around the world. ICF Macro is based in the Washington DC area and maintains offices across the US. It conducts projects for private and public sector clients in more than 125 countries. It has annual revenues of approximately 150 million USD and more than 1,100 employees, and, in 2009, joined with ICF International.[78] Similarly, an OECD educational testing programme, the Programme for International Student Assessment (PISA), hired an international contractor—an Australian company—to work with each participating state to carry out the assessment. Student questionnaires and tests were developed by the international contractors, the PISA governing board and functional expert groups.[79] The development of data and analysis, and sometimes even the indicators themselves, is clearly a blend of public and private activity that brings together corporations, academics, NGOs, governments and UN bodies, as well as local, national and international organisations. Data collection and analysis companies typically come from developed countries and often work in developing countries.

Not only are corporations increasingly involved in producing the data and measures that make up indicators used in the public domain, but efforts to persuade corporations to be more socially responsible have also adopted this technology. As social movement activists, the UN and other NGOs seek to control the human rights, environmental, labour and corruption practices of corporations, they have turned to the same strategies of governance that corporations exported to the social reformers. The emerging field of corporate social responsibility (CSR) relies on indicators of corporate performance to assess companies. The UN's Global Compact (GC) and the Global Reporting Initiative (GRI), two of the most widely used global CSR systems, both rely on indicators to assess compliance with their general principles and both are voluntary. The GC website claims that it is the largest corporate citizenship initiative in the world. It says it launched the programme in the year 2000 and, as of May 2007, had more than 3,000 companies from 100 countries, as well as over 700 hundred civil society and international labour organisations, participating in the initiative. The Global Reporting Initiative is an international network of business, civil society, labour and professional institutions. This group has created a Reporting Framework through a consensus-seeking process. By 2006, more than 1,000 organisations from nearly 60 countries had formally declared their use of the GRI Guidelines according to a Global Compact Report.[80] The GRI developed a set of detailed indicators which the GC adopted to implement its general principles.

The Global Compact Annual Review 2007 describes its monitoring process as a system of periodic reports by every signatory company every two years detailing its

[78] Ibid.

[79] See A von Bogandy and M Goldman, 'The Exercise of Public Authority through National Policy Assessment', IILJ Working Paper 2009/2 Global Administrative Law Series (24 March 2009) 13.

[80] 'Making the Connection: The GRI Guidelines and the UNGC Communication on Progress', UN Global Compact and Global Reporting Initiative (drafted 2006) 3, available at www.unglobalcompact.org (last accessed on 21 August 2009).

compliance with the 10 GC principles, articulated as indicators, plus its support for the MDGs. The 10 principles cover human rights, labour, environmental issues and corruption. The reports are called communications on progress. They should include: a statement of continued support for the GC by the chief executive officer or other senior executive; a description of the practical actions of the company's efforts to implement the GC principles and to undertake partnerships projects in support of broad UN goals such as MDGs; and measurements of expected outcomes, using, as much as possible, indicators or metrics such as the Global Reporting Initiative Guidelines. If a company fails to file a report within three years of signing on or two years from its previous communication on progress, it will be defined as inactive and dropped from the GC group.[81]

The 2008 Guidelines for Communications on Progress advocate presenting information about commitment, the systems in place to ensure compliance, such as policies, programmes and management systems, activities and measures of outcomes. It recommends that reports should 'Use performance indicators appropriate for your company's size, sector and unique operating environment, and also allow for benchmarking and comparability'. In other words, companies are invited to develop their own metrics.

> Companies should develop systems and evaluation programmes to assure that the information they are recording, collecting, analysing and disclosing is accurate and reliable. Importantly, this need not be a highly complex and expensive process, but could be as simple as a local Global Compact network peer review programme.[82]

The guidelines to reporting stress that it is important to produce reliable and specific measures in order to assess progress, rather than to focus only on policies or activities. 'Specific measurements that track actual performance are essential for ensuring continuous improvement.'[83]

Some of the internal benefits claimed for the process are discussion and awareness of these issues in the company while external benefits are enhancing the corporation's reputation.[84] Thus, the CG represents another example of the mobilization of the argument that social responsibility is good for business, not just morality.

The guidelines use over 30 indicators developed by the GRI. Some focus on behaviour, while others ask for numbers of training sessions or policies and management programmes. The following list of illustrative indicators is characteristic of the GC approach of enumerating trainings or policies more than actual behaviour.

- **HR 1** Percentage and total number of significant investment agreements that include human rights clauses or that underwent human rights screening. (HR = human rights.)
- **HR 3** Total hours of employee training on policies and procedures concerning aspects of human rights that are relevant to operations, including the percentage of employees trained.
- **HR 4** Total number of incidents of discrimination and actions taken.

---

[81] See Annual Review 2007, available at www.globalcompact.org (last accessed on 21 August 2009).

[82] United Nations Global Compact, 'The Practical Guide to the United Nations Global Compact Communications on Progress (COPs)', revised version of 2004 report (2008) 15, available at www.unglobalcompact.org (last accessed on 21 August 2009).

[83] Ibid, 17.

[84] Ibid, 18.

- **HR 5** Operations identified where the right to exercise freedom of association and collective bargaining may be at significant risk, and actions to support these rights.
- **HR 6** Operations identified as having significant risk for incidents of child labour and measures to contribute to eliminate child labour.
- **SO 5** Public policy positions and participation in public policy development and lobbying. (SO = society.)
- **SO 2** Percentage and total number of business units analyzed for risks related to corruption.
- **SO 3** Percentage of employees trained in organization's anti-corruption policies and procedures.[85]

The guidelines suggest that companies check with their human resources, employee relations, supply management, legal, media and public relations, public affairs or corporate relations offices for this information.

The GRI focuses on sustainability reporting guidelines. In 2006, the organisation published its third generation of guidelines, performance indicators and indicator protocols, called GRI G3.[86] The indicators developed for the GRI can be used to address the 10 principles of the GC. Although there are some differences, overall, the two voluntary reporting mechanisms cover roughly the same issues.

Thus, the monitoring system for GC and GRI is quite similar to that of UN treaty bodies, in which a governing organisation confronts the dilemma of judging compliance based upon information provided by the organisation being judged. Like treaty body reports, the information requested focuses more on the existence of polices and training programmes than on actual changes in behaviour. Treaty bodies typically cope with this situation by politely asking for more information and focusing more on information about laws and policies than on performance data. Nevertheless, treaty bodies constantly request more statistical data on outcomes and performance, and are currently seeking to develop indicators for human rights. In both of these monitoring systems, indicators seem to offer a solution to the lack of independent information available to those who seek to govern.

## VII. CONCLUSIONS

In sum, indicators are a political technology that can be used for many different purposes, including advocacy, reform, control and management. In some ways, indicators are like witchcraft. Witchcraft is the power to guide the flow of supernatural forces for good or harm. It is pervasive in societies that see supernatural forces as powerful actors in the world. Misfortunes and disease are the result of hostile supernatural forces, but healing and recovery from psychic and physical illness also rely on the mobilisation of supernatural powers. Sometimes, the same person is both a witch and a healer, since both depend on the ability to control these forces. Like witchcraft, indicators are a technology that exercises power, but in a variety of ways, depending on who is using it for what purpose. And, like witchcraft, indicators presume a system

---

[85] Ibid, 21, 33 and 39.
[86] See n 80 above, 5.

of knowledge and a theory of how things happen that is hegemonic and rarely subjected to scrutiny, despite its critical role in the allocation of power.

As the world becomes ever more measured and tracked through indicators, it becomes increasingly important to sort out the technical and political dimensions of this new technology. Indicators produce readily understandable and convenient forms of knowledge about the world, which shape the way in which policy-makers as well as the general public understand the world. Those with long use have become naturalised as well as hegemonic, as in the case of grades for school performance. This is a form of knowledge production and governance that has expanded from its economic, corporate origins to a wide array of uses in national and global governance. Indicators contribute to the calcification of categories, such as caste, race or gender, which are subjected to categorical definition and measurement. The use of these statistical techniques, with their aura of certainty, is producing new knowledge of the social world and new opportunities for governance through self-governance. The expansion of indicator technology into new domains and spaces of governance is another way in which the corporate form is reshaping contemporary social life.

# 9

# *Governing by Measuring: The Millennium Development Goals in Global Governance*

KERRY RITTICH

## I. INTRODUCTION

'ERADICATE EXTREME POVERTY and hunger.' 'Achieve universal primary education.' 'Promote gender equality and empower women.' 'Reduce child mortality.' 'Improve maternal health.' 'Combat HIV/AIDS, malaria and other diseases.' 'Ensure environmental sustainability.' 'Develop a global partnership for development.' Here, in all their sweeping ambition and apparent simplicity, are the Millennium Development Goals (MDGs). Further elaborated by the identification of an expanding list of related targets and indicators,[1] agreed upon at a UN Summit in 2000 and referred to in countless policy documents and public relations exercises both inside and outside the UN since that time, the MDGs have become the most visible effort on the international plane to both identify and address the social deficit in the global order.

Commitment to the MDGs is routinely said to be 'universal', and virtually all states have coalesced around the MDGs, accepting them as the template for global progress on an inter-related set of social objectives. What is perhaps more noteworthy than the high-level support that they have garnered among states and international institutions is the extent to which the MDGs have permeated the global public sphere and entered global public consciousness. An astonishingly wide range of actors and organisations now routinely invoke the MDGs, and it has become commonplace to hear someone recite the fact that a billion people live on less than $1 a day. That countless policy and advocacy documents emanating from politicians, global technocrats and civil society groups alike now either cite this 'fact' or simply take the MDGs as the starting point of discussion about issues ranging from poverty itself to the effects of globalisation writ large reflects the extent to which the MDGs have been internalised both as an account of the global social deficit and as a programme of action for remedying it.

Moreover, states have tied themselves to a timeline, pledging to achieve the MDGs

---

[1] At this point, there are 21 targets and 60 indicators associated with the MDGs. See UN, Millenium Development Goals Indicators, Official List of MDG Indicators, available at http://mdgs.un.org/unsd/mdg/Host.aspx?Content=Indicators/OfficialList.htm (last accessed on 24 August 2012).

by the year 2015. Yet despite ongoing commitment to the MDGs[2] and claims that they have 'galvanized unprecedented efforts to meet the needs of the worlds poorest',[3] the MDGs are far from on track to realisation. By some measures—absolute numbers of poor, for example—poverty rates are now worse than before the MDGs were adopted.[4] A similarly grim picture emerges in respect of maternal health: more women are dying now in childbirth than in the year 2000. As the head of the WHO observed, '[d]espite two decades of effort . . . the world has failed to make a dent'.[5] Despite claims that the MDGs can still be met by the year 2015 as long as we do not continue with 'business as usual',[6] it would take an extraordinary, and probably unwarranted, degree of optimism to conclude that their achievement will come to pass, if only because there is little reason to conclude that 'business as usual' is about to be disturbed, at least in ways that are likely to advance the position of the poor. As a report by the Secretary-General of the United Nations puts it, there are critical gaps in the follow-through on aid and trade commitments.[7] Aid flows have remained well below their target levels since the MDGs were adopted, and have tailed off still further in recent years. Trade negotiations, too, remain mired in disagreements between the North and the South,[8] and the failure of the Doha round of trade negotiations at the WTO indicates that it is unlikely that developing countries will see the enhanced access to rich country markets that they seek anytime in the near future.[9]

While high-profile proponents of the MDGs point to progress on individual goals such as the treatment of malaria[10] and official support for the MDGs remains intact, it is unclear how much such successes can be attributed to the MDGs and it is increasingly hard to sustain the thesis that the MDGs, as a project, are succeeding. Even if it is too soon to pronounce the death of the MDGs *tout court*, we do not have to wait until 2015 to know that, at some level, the MDGs have already 'failed'.[11] One possible response is, of course, to lament the lack of political will that has produced this state of affairs and to call for redoubled efforts to achieve the MDGs. But the fact that donor nations face economic crises and increasing pressure on their budgets makes this seem like both a hollow response and an unlikely solution. At the same time, whatever the fate of the MDGs, myriad pressures virtually ensure that the concerns

[2] UN, 'High-Level Event', news update, 25 September 2008, available at http://www.un.org/millenniumgoals/2008highlevel (last accessed on 12 July 2009).

[3] See UN, 'A Gateway to the UN System's Work on the MDGs', available at http://www.un.org/millenniumgoals (last accessed on 12 July 2009).

[4] B Milanovic, *Worlds Apart: Measuring International and Global Inequality* (Princeton, NJ, Princeton University Press, 2005).

[5] R Seal and K Manson, 'Why Are Mothers Still Dying in Childbirth?', *The Guardian*, 28 September 2008, available at http://www.guardian.co.uk/world/2008/sep/28/sierraleone.internationalaidanddevelopment (last accessed on 12 July 2009).

[6] Ibid.

[7] UN, 'Launching Report by MDG Gap Task Force, Secretary-General Underscores Need for Quantitative, Qualitative Shift in Efforts to Halve Extreme Poverty', news update, 4 September 2008, available at http://www.un.org/News/Press/docs/2008/sgsm11777.doc.htm (last accessed on 12 July 2009).

[8] Ibid.

[9] BBC, 'World Trade Talks End in Collapse', *BBC News*, 29 July 2008, available at http://news.bbc.co.uk/2/hi/business/7531099.stm (last accessed on 12 July 2009).

[10] See, eg the discussion between Bono and Jeffrey Sachs, *MDG Blog*, available at http://blogs.ft.com/mdg/author/bono (last accessed on 12 July 2009).

[11] Any such assertion must remain contestable, if only because the counterfactual is unavailable: it is impossible to know, for example, if things might have been even worse without the MDGs.

and issues they embody will continue to surface on the international agenda. There are reasons, moreover, to think that future efforts to address such concerns and issues, as well as to promote other social justice agendas, will partake of some of the salient features of the MDGs. If there is any truth to this intuition, then it would be wise to start the process of appraisal sooner rather than later.

Before we attempt to find solutions, if indeed there are 'solutions', to the concerns and issues embodied by the MDGs, we need to better understand what we are doing now. Not only do we need to consider our actions in response to the social deficit; we need to consider how we conceive of and locate the social deficit in the first place. Indeed, we need to consider whether, and how, we might produce some of the problems that we then seek to solve through the MDGs. Paradoxically, this is particularly important with the MDGs precisely because the project commands such widespread assent and because the initial, even 'natural', reaction to it is, '*of course it is a good idea. Who could be against it?*' Thus, another possible response is to take this prospect of failure to raise some basic questions about the MDGs. Whatever the role of political will or its lack, the stasis on the MDGs may reflect unresolved tensions or conflicts among the goals or ambiguities about their nature and content. It may also be linked to structural features of the project itself. Finally, it may be, in part, a consequence of the broader institutional and policy environment in which the MDGs are situated. If so, it may be useful to analyse the terms of reference that are embedded in the MDGs and to probe the mechanism by which the project operates. For example, we may need to consider what is not, as well as what is, contained within the MDGs, and we may gain insight from attending to the frame or context in which they operate, including other global governance projects.

With this in mind, what follows is a discussion of two issues: the first is the relationship between the MDGs and development initiatives in the international economic order; the second is the phenomenon that I will call 'governing by measuring'.

The MDGs are described as a 'respon[se] to the world's main development challenges'[12] and are widely accepted as the principal international initiative on the global social deficit. Thus, the relationship of the social deficit to the current path of development seems to be a central question: is economic development part of the problem, part of the solution, or might it be both in different ways? One possibility, of course, is to think of the MDGs as addressing discrete and distinct pathologies and problems that are susceptible to special initiatives. However, the issues that the MDGs seek to address may also be symptomatic of a wider malaise and connected to general trends in social and economic development. To put it another way, the poverty, inequality, deprivation and disempowerment of the types targeted by the MDGs may be exceptional on the global landscape because, for example, they are confined to particular areas and populations or arise in specific cultural contexts. But what if such concerns belong in the zone of the normal? And what if, rather than merely natural, social or cultural phenomena, they are actually produced or reinforced by the ordinary rules and institutions, both national and international, through which we now promote economic development and other objectives? This discussion does not attempt to comprehensively analyse, let alone resolve, these issues. However, it does aim to indicate how and why any assessment of the MDGs might require an examination of the

---

[12] UN, n 1 above.

broader context in which development occurs, as well as an evaluation of other initiatives adopted by the key international institutions that work on issues of development, poverty alleviation and social justice.

In addition, the MDGs might be illuminated by reflection on the process of 'governing by measuring'. The MDGs partake of the increasingly pervasive strategy of identifying goals and benchmarking progress through indicators in order to provoke social and economic transformation. In common with other such initiatives in the international order,[13] the MDGs are premised on the idea that a focus on specific targets and the identification of measures that can be compared across different jurisdictions gives us both a clear picture of the real state of the world's social deficit and a means to identify the 'best practices' in state policy and regulation that might remedy it. The implicit, if not explicit, claim, moreover, is that initiatives based upon these targets and measures will galvanise action and generate positive change in ways that reliance conventional state-driven, 'top-down' processes of policy and norm generation, including those of international law, either have not or will not.

Yet problems do not simply identify themselves. Although the official claim is that the MDGs 'synthesize in a single package, many of the most important commitments made separately at the international conferences and summits of the 1990s',[14] this is a somewhat sanitised, if diplomatic, account of their history.[15] The MDGs embody a necessarily selective, even idiosyncratic, reading of the international commitments of the previous decades. And rather than simply reflect the global consensus on social development, the MDG goals, targets and indicators bear the imprint of other international governance projects too, some of which are, at this point, controversial for either normative or institutional reasons.

What is most of interest here are the MDGs as a particular mode of conceptualising and tackling public concerns and issues. A key part of the appeal of the MDGs, I want to propose, lies in their overall structure, in particular their reliance on benchmarks and indicators. The attraction of benchmarks and indicators is that they present as non-ideological: they are just 'facts', beyond political dispute and contestation; for this reason, they can be used as the basis for disinterested assessment of progress and common action. Yet, as much as the MDGs simply appear to marshal facts and indicators as the basis for problem solving, the MDGs should also be understood as an exercise in knowledge production. The MDGs work by placing particular facts and issues in the global spotlight. In so doing, the MDGs operate to standardise the reception of the global social-justice deficit and to diffuse a particular view of the nature of global problems across states and communities. Important, consequential decisions are also made in the identification of targets and the choice of indicators by which the goals are then pursued and their attainment measured. The corollary is that

---

[13] See, eg OECD, 'Paris Declaration on Aid Effectiveness: Ownership, Harmonisation, Alignment, Results and Mutual Accountability' (2005), available at http://www.oecd.org/development/effectiveness/34428351.pdf (last accessed on 12 July 2009).

[14] See UN, n 1 above.

[15] For a discussion of the background to their adoption and the competing agendas of the UN and the other multilateral agencies, see D Hulme, 'The Making of the Millennium Development Goals: Human Development Meets Results-Based Management in an Imperfect World', Working Paper (Washington DC, Brooks World Poverty Institute, 16 December 2007).

other conceptions of that deficit, as well as other issues and other dimensions of the identified issues and problems, remain in the shadows.

If the claims or forms of knowledge that the MDGs rely upon are themselves linked to particular economic and political projects—economic development projects or legal reform projects, for example—and if they work in tandem with some regulatory and policy initiatives and at odds with others, then as the term 'governing by measuring' is intended to suggest, the MDGs might themselves be understood as a mode of governance or, at minimum, an element of other governance projects. These possibilities raise normative and political questions, including questions about how the MDGs are likely to intersect with other modes of rule-making at international and domestic law. They also raise deeply practical questions, including questions about how facts and indicators are identified as relevant, and who the actors and institutions involved in the selection process are. In short, if the goals, benchmarks and indicators both reflect and influence policy and regulation, if they have potential implications for the manner in which we govern, then the processes by which they are selected and promoted, and the effects of the entire enterprise of measuring may be worth considering in more detail. This is particularly true if the MDGs reflect a commitment not only to particular goals, but also to particular modes of pursuing those goals.

## II. SITUATING THE MILLENNIUM DEVELOPMENT GOALS: IDENTIFYING THE 'PROBLEM' OF DEVELOPMENT

Assuming that development can even be thought of as a single project or process, what does global development look like at the present moment? How is it best accounted for? Is it a story of general progress marred by persistent, but tractable, problems? Is it a more nuanced and uneven process, something that varies considerably among states? Or is it a fundamentally dark and troubling narrative? As it turns out, the 'truth' and the 'facts' surrounding these basic issues are deeply contested; depending on how the data are read and the events are characterised, very different pictures of the problem that development aims to solve may be generated.

To begin to probe this terrain, let me contrast two recent accounts of global development. Both are by pedigreed, distinguished and well-situated development economists with long histories of engagement with the central international institution concerned with development research, namely, the World Bank. The first is Paul Collier's *The Bottom Billion*;[16] the second is Branko Milanovic's *Worlds Apart*.[17] Despite the fact that they both tackle basic questions about development, and both do so as 'insiders' to the contemporary development project, they tell fundamentally different stories about the trajectory of global economic development.

In one sense, the titles themselves give away the general arguments. For Collier, the story of development, and of the persistence of poverty, is one of general economic progress, darkened only by the plight of those at the bottom who have the misfortune to live within states that are persistent laggards. These he identifies as the coterie of

---

[16] P Collier, *The Bottom Billion: Why the Poorest Countries are Failing and What Can Be Done About It* (Oxford, Oxford University Press, 2008).

[17] Milanovic, n 4 above.

nations, largely in sub-Saharan Africa and Central Asia, who have failed to integrate successfully into the global economy because they are beset by identifiable, discrete and recurring problems. For Milanovic, however, the current story is best captured by the steadily growing distance among states in the global order: what he describes is the divergence in the growth trajectories between the states of the first world and virtually everyone else, certainly if China and India are excluded. As his account reveals in riveting detail, this distance has been widening, not narrowing, since 1980, so much so that we are hard pressed to reach any other conclusion than that this gap will simply continue to grow.

As is evident, these two accounts diverge over the basic issue: the identification of the problem of development. In its simplest form, for Collier, the problem is poverty caused by lack of economic growth; for Milanovic, it is the unequal fates and fortunes of states within the global order. However, Collier and Milanovic also diverge over the magnitude of the development deficit, how they identify the root of the deficiency and where they place the emphasis in the remedy. For Collier, the focus is the specific characteristics of the states that are 'failing'. Collier's distinctive contribution to contemporary development policy debates is the identification of four 'traps' which, he claims, are in operation in those states at the bottom and that, implicitly if not explicitly, account for their failure to succeed: the conflict trap; the natural resource trap; the 'landlocked with bad neighbours' trap; and the 'bad governance in a small country' trap.[18]

For Milanovic, by contrast, the story is fundamentally a relational one: what matters is not simply, or even primarily, the absolute status of the countries themselves, but rather how they are situated in the international order and whether their prospects in relation to other states are improving or declining. It is the stunning distance between the fortunes of different states to which he draws our attention, and the extent to which the current global order fails to generate the economic progress for so many of them that, ultimately, he takes to be politically, morally and statistically relevant. Milanovic is less overtly diagnostic about the causes of this growing global inequality than Collier is about the persistence of the 'bottom billion'. However, the stark contrast that Milanovic draws between the post World War II era until 1980, a period in which global inequality was diminishing, and the period from 1980 and 2000, during which inequality spiked sharply higher, invites us to consider possibilities that we are drawn away from considering in Collier's account. To wit, Milanovic suggests that broader practices and institutions in the international order, rather than merely the unfortunate characteristics of developing states, may be centrally implicated in the problem of growing inequality. Perhaps the introduction of particular trade, investment and development policies during the period in which inequality grew, rather than merely bad governance explained as internal corruption, could have something to do with the problem.

What is worth emphasising is that the differences reflected in these two accounts of development are not differences that can be resolved simply by reference to facts and evidence. Instead, they reflect disagreement on prior, more basic issues: the nature of the problem to be solved and where we should look for its likely sources. Indeed, Milanovic's explicitly relational account raises the question of whether we can appre-

---

[18] Collier, n 16 above.

ciate or even recognize a problem outside of the wider (global) context in which it is situated.

As it turns out, such questions are also central to the MDGs. Despite the widespread normative commitment to the MDGs, there is an unresolved debate in the international order about the relationship between economic growth on the one hand and poverty reduction, inequality and other social objectives on the other. Since about 1980, the international financial and economic institutions (IFIs) have taken the position that welfare gains are largely coterminous with economic growth, while maintaining that the fundamental condition of poverty alleviation (and the achievement of other social objectives too) is the adoption of policies and rules to facilitate greater private-sector economic activity. In recent years, 'pro-poor' policies have been grafted onto the standard formulation of market reforms, and nods have been made in the direction of greater environmental and labour protection too. However, such additions have not disturbed the fundamental commitment to market-centred, export-focused and privately led economic growth.[19] Within the IFIs, if not necessarily elsewhere, development is still fundamentally imagined as a process of integrating local and national into global markets through strategies of trade and capital market liberalisation and the promotion of stable, rule-based, investor-friendly regulatory regimes.[20] The claim is that these strategies will provide the basis of economic growth without which social issues, including those targeted in the MDGs, can never hope to be successfully tackled.

Yet, even among economists, this is a controversial position.[21] There are many indications that orthodox reforms have failed to generate a secure foundation for sustained growth; in the short to medium term, they have often been responsible for pronounced economic downturns as well as increased poverty rates and widening income inequality. By contrast, states that pursued heterodox development strategies have often fared better.[22] Thus, 'facts' have undercut the argument automatically connecting market-centred development policies to economic growth and welfare gains at a quite basic level.

As a number of economists now point out, there are good theoretical foundations, including some within the neoclassical and institutional economic theory, to these observed facts of increased poverty and inequality. While openness may lead to greater economic growth, arguments about the benefits of economic openness are often overstated and sometimes simply wrong, both in respect of particular states and in respect of specific groups within them.[23] For example, financial liberalisation may leave

---

[19] K Rittich, 'The Future of Law and Development: Second Generation Reforms and the Incorporation of the Social' in D Trubek and A Santos (eds), *The New Law and Economic Development* (Cambridge, Cambridge University Press, 2006).

[20] This should be understood as the governing regulative ideal, not a description of the global regulatory order itself, which, for political and historical reasons, is infinitely more complex and varied in its institutional structure.

[21] JE Stiglitz, 'Is There a Post-Washington Consensus Consensus?' in N Serra and JE Stiglitz (eds), *The Washington Consensus Reconsidered: Towards a New Global Governance* (Oxford, Oxford University Press, 2008).

[22] See JKM Ohnesorge, 'Developing Development Theory: Law and Development Orthodoxies and the Northeast Asian Experience' (2007) 28 *University of Pennsylvania Journal of International Economic Law* 219.

[23] Stiglitz, n 21 above; D Rodrik, 'Death of Globalisation Consensus', *Emirates Business 24/7*, 13 July 2008, available at http://news.bbc.co.uk/2/hi/business/7531099.stm (last accessed on 12 July 2009).

states at risk of sudden investment outflows, while deregulation may simply shift risks and burdens among market participants rather than eliminate costly impediments to economic activity as the dominant regulatory narrative holds.[24] Indeed, experience with financial crises seems to confirm that, far from imposing burdens, it is the absence of adequate regulation which may prove to be truly costly. Even states that are now classified as 'winners' in the development game may periodically suffer widespread economic upheaval. But they may also experience widening poverty and disadvantage even in the midst of economic growth, in part because global economic integration increases vulnerability to volatile external forces.[25] This (now quite common) disjuncture between growth and improved welfare often arises from the concentration of the gains from economic growth within particular groups, sectors or regions. It may also reflect the (related) fact that the very legal and economic reforms that promote enhanced growth rates can be violently disruptive to existing economic activities and modes of subsistence and/or traditional forms of life. Yet reforms typically leave those who directly experience any associated losses in the process of change to manage them on their own as best they can.

For all of these reasons and more, a broad range of critics and interlocutors, including some within other international institutions, maintain that orthodox strategies to promote growth through economic openness and integration have, at best, an ambiguous relation to the achievement of social objectives; at worst, they are part of the problem. For example, they may lead, directly or indirectly, to human rights violations, exacerbate social inequality of various types or intensify environmental problems. In addition, they typically reduce the scope for democratic decision-making on critical issues of social and economic policy, thus undermining basic norms about economic and political self-determination in the international order.[26] Because interventions to implement such policies are disproportionately visited on states in the South but are designed and promoted by technocrats and states in the North, they have become a persistent irritant in global diplomatic and political relations and a source of complaint about the legitimacy of international institutions as well. As a result, standard legal and institutional reforms associated with development remain a source of deep contention among development economists themselves, between development economists and human rights scholars and advocates, between the North and the South, and between those that benefit from liberalising economic reforms and those who perceive themselves to be harmed by them.

The relationships between economic growth and both poverty and inequality are complex; any claims about thm are, in any event, almost certainly dependent on the specific histories and institutional contexts of different states. What seems important for our purposes is less the resolution of these debates than the fact that the standard view of 'good' global governance for economic growth is incorporated into the MDGs

---

[24] H de Soto, *The Other Path: The Invisible Revolution in the Third World* (London, IB Taurus, 1989); idem, *The Mystery of Capital: Why Capitalism Triumphs in the West and Fails Everywhere Else* (New York, Basic Books, 2000).

[25] See, eg the labour crisis in China occasioned by the global economic slowdown. R Ke, 'Global Financial Crisis spills over China's Labour Market', *China Features*, 11 November 2008, available at http://sify.com/finance/fullstory.php?id=14795188&VSV=chieco (last accessed on 28 July 2009).

[26] P Alston and M Robinson (eds), *Human Rights and Development: Towards Mutual Reinforcement* (Oxford, Oxford University Press, 2005).

themselves. The result of this incorporation, I want to suggest, is twofold. First, it introduces the possibility of internal conflict within the MDG project itself, as the pursuit of one goal may undercut another. Secondly, it rules out of consideration a diverse range of heterodox rules, institutions and strategies, no matter how much they might be indicated, either in general or in particular contexts.

The incorporation of governance strategies into the MDGs is clearly evident in the manner in which Goal 8—'Develop a global partnership for development'—is elaborated. The first target that is identified is this: 'Develop further an open trading and financial system that is rule-based, predictable and non-discriminatory'.[27] A series of further targets then follows, including: 'Address the special needs of the least developed states' (Target 8b) and 'Deal comprehensively with the debt problems of developing countries through national and international measures to make debt sustainable in the long term' (Target 8d).[28] These subsidiary targets appear to be designed to create space for the most greatly disadvantaged to benefit from the global economic order. However, they also stabilise a particular approach to rule-based development. As the goal of a global development partnership is translated into the objective of a further liberalised and juridified global economic order, we get no inkling of the fact that, far from a plausible basis of a global partnership, parts of this rule-based order have been associated with adverse effects for particular regions and groups, and, accordingly, have provoked resistance on the part of important developing states.[29]

The significance of the global governance agenda is not limited to the issue of forging a development partnership. It is possible to imagine some of the MDGs as problems that can be tackled separately and apart from any changes to the basic rules and institutions of the current global regulatory order. It is also possible that progress on economic and social development go together, and that all of the objectives embedded in the MDGs are harmonious, both with each other and with larger governance and development strategies. Weighing against this, however, is the fact that social indicators such as mortality and morbidity have worsened in the face of fiscal austerity drives, a standard part of the development reform package in the last generation.[30] Similarly, while universal primary education is a goal that clearly serves social objectives, as well as development strategies premised upon participation in high-skill, high-velocity labour markets,[31] like access to healthcare, access to education has often been impeded rather than advanced in the drive towards cost recovery and the implementation of user fees, both of which have been common features of contemporary development strategies.

Objectives like poverty reduction, gender equality and environmental sustainability, too, all have connections to processes of economic growth that are uncertain at best. India, for example, charts both impressive economic growth rates and increasing economic insecurity for significant parts its population; for this reason, the govern-

---

[27] UN, n 1 above.

[28] Ibid.

[29] A Beattie and F Williams, 'WTO Chief Drops Plans to Press Ministers for Outline Doha Deal', *Financial Times*, 13 December 2008, 10.

[30] Russia still stands as the most dramatic example; life expectancy, particularly among men, fell dramatically in a few short years as a consequence of the harsh economic conditions that surrounded the transition to market economy.

[31] OECD, *The OECD Jobs Study: Evidence and Explanations* (Paris, OECD, 1994).

ment of India has resisted the reduction of agricultural subsidies, a cornerstone of current trade negotiations, fearing the consequences for the many people whose lives and livelihoods depend on agricultural production.[32] The goal of environmental sustainability seems as far away on the horizon now as it was in 1992 when, following the Earth Summit in Rio de Janeiro, the UN Framework Convention on Climate Change was opened for signature and the objectives of the Kyoto Protocol were first formulated.[33] While there are many ways to account for the lack of progress on a better relationship between development and environmental objectives,[34] the task has not been assisted either by the presumption against regulation in the global regulatory order,[35] or by the priority given to the exploitation of natural resources as a strategy to promote economic growth. Similar tensions beset efforts to tackle medical and health objectives. For example, combating HIV/AIDS has been rendered more difficult and expensive by the standardisation of trade-related intellectual property rules at the behest of the pharmaceutical industry in 1994 and instituted as part of the shift towards a rules-based trade regime.[36]

In short, rather than objectives that are inevitably advanced by 'an open trading and financial system that is rule-based, predictable and non-discriminatory', it is not difficult to find indications that some of the MDGs have been badly served, and some even impeded, by aspects of the very rules-based system that is in place. The possibility that trade and financial liberalisation, for example, may have an adverse effect on social objectives is not news now, nor was it when the MDGs were formulated in the year 2000. It has now been more than 20 years since the first systemic analysis of the shortcomings of orthodox economic reforms promoted by the international financial institutions was released.[37] The East Asian financial crisis of 1997–98 clearly demonstrated the volatility and risks of contagion inherent in liberalised financial markets. The economic pain that ensued in the region is well documented, and myriad studies and proposals to reform the architecture of the global economic order have been in circulation since that time, mostly to no avail.[38] It has often been observed that trade negotiations, as well as the regimes that have emerged from them, operate to the disadvantage of developing states;[39] even within the WTO, it is conceded that the current round of trade talks should be more clearly focused on development goals.[40] Nonetheless, there is little evidence that such a shift in focus is, in fact, underway;

[32] PG Thakurta, 'Trade-India: Rare Unity against West's Agricultural Subsidies', *Inter Press Service*, 27 July 2008, available at http://ipsnews.net/news.asp?idnews=34116 (last accessed on 12 July 2009).

[33] See Kyoto Protocol to the United Nations Framework Convention on Climate Change (adopted 10 December 1997, entered into force 16 February 2005) (1998) 37 *International Law Materials* 32.

[34] K Mickelson, 'South, North, International Environmental Law, and International Environmental Lawyers' (2000) 11 *Yearbook of International Environmental Law* 52; JT Roberts and BC Parks, *A Climate of Injustice: Global Inequality, North–South Politics, and Climate Policy* (Cambridge, MA, The MIT Press, 2007).

[35] IFI Shihata, *Complementary Reform: Essays on Legal, Judicial, and Other Institutional Reforms Supported by the World Bank* (The Hague, Kluwer Law International, 1997).

[36] SK Sell, *Private Power, Public Law: The Globalization of Intellectual Property Rights* (Cambridge, Cambridge University Press, 2003).

[37] G Cornia, R Jolly and F Stewart (eds), *Adjustment with a Human Face* (Oxford, Clarendon Press, 1987).

[38] JE Stiglitz, *Globalization and its Discontents* (New York, WW Norton, 2002).

[39] BL Das, *WTO: The Doha Agenda: The New Negotiations on World Trade* (London, Zed, 2003).

[40] WTO Ministerial Declaration, adopted 20 November 2001, WT/MIN(01)/DEC/1, available at http://www.wto.org/english/thewto_e/minist_e/min01_e/mindecl_e.htm (last accessed on 29 July 2009).

instead, emerging Third World economic powers such as Brazil and India are exerting their collective muscle to prevent the continued liberalisation of trade.[41] Overtly or quietly, states and even entire regions such as Latin America have begun to disengage from relationships with the international development banks; while some are simply no longer in need of funds, others are unwilling to continue the process of subjection to policy and regulatory oversight that accessing funds from the international financial institutions has come to entail.

Despite widespread discussion of such issues in development circles, it is difficult to find any imprint of these concerns, whether on the MDGs themselves or in the debate that surrounds them. For example, at the World Summit held in 2005, where the MDGs remained a linchpin of the global agenda, the denunciation of terrorism, support for peace building, disaster relief, humanitarian assistance, management reform at the UN, strengthening human rights machinery, a new 'democracy' fund and support for the rule of law all appeared on the agenda for action.[42] But whether such commitments reflect the agenda of developing countries or advance the MDGs in any meaningful way is doubtful. Commitments on trade are centred on further trade liberalisation, while those concerning debt relief remain weak: there is an 'agreement to consider additional measures to ensure long-term debt sustainability' and 'where appropriate to consider' additional debt relief.[43] Apart from a commitment to more aid to fight poverty—a commitment that is already ringing hollow—few demands beyond the open-ended commitment to achieve the goals themselves are placed on the international community.

### III. GOVERNING BY MEASURING

The MDGs are the exemplary effort to advance social objectives at global level. But they are also representative of the turn toward new governance in the international order, a turn marked by the embrace of empiricism and 'problem-solving' through benchmarking. New governance here refers to a broad array of governance practices and regulatory strategies that eschew reliance on top-down processes of regulation and norm generation that are legislated through formal political channels and enforced by legal institutions. Yet while such initiatives consciously avoid conventional law-making processes, they aim to serve many of law's purposes. In general, new governance is premised on the idea that identifying goals and quantifiable targets and pursuing those targets with measurable indicators, monitoring progress or regress through peer and external surveillance, diffusing 'best practices' from better performers to laggards, and revising those practices on the basis of feedback and cumulative gains in knowledge is often the most promising way to generate desired change.

New governance initiatives emerged in the EU in part to address problems of regulatory co-ordination among the Member States, and in part to respond to specific regulatory concerns that were not addressed in the 'hard' regulatory project of

---

[41] See n 9 above.

[42] UNGA, '2005 World Summit Outcome', UN Doc A/Res/60/1 (24 October 2005), available at http://daccessdds.un.org/doc/UNDOC/GEN/N05/487/60/PDF/N0548760.pdf?OpenElement (last accessed on 12 July 2009).

[43] Ibid.

building the common market.[44] At about the same time, a convergence of factors—from political deadlocks to the regulatory vacuum associated with the atrophy and dysfunctionality of the administrative state—generated an impetus for regulatory experimentation outside of conventional rule-making processes in the US.[45] In recent years, new governance has migrated beyond these contexts and entered the lexicon of international development policy[46] and, in at least a limited way, become integrated into the governance projects of the international financial and economic institutions. Indeed, in the world of development policy, governance is not only the product of measurement; it has also become the subject of measuring itself. For example, various divisions within the World Bank have embarked on ambitious projects to measure the 'quality' of governance within states,[47] the best known of which is the Doing Business Project, which purports to measure the ease of transacting, investing and engaging in business in different states, and hence the prospects for development, by evaluating and ranking the regulatory constraints upon investors in 10 different areas.[48] As these initiatives disclose, there is burgeoning interest in the possibilities of new governance across quite different theatres of regulation.

New governance initiatives exhibit both continuities and differences with other global governance strategies, old and new, and many regimes are appropriately thought of as hybrid.[49] Rather than comprehensively describe or analyse the issues that they raise,[50] the objectives here are merely, first, to identify some of the processes and properties that are both characteristic of new governance and relevant to the operation of the MDGs, and, secondly, to explore how, rather than solve difficult governance problems, such processes and properties may also serve to mask or avoid them. The MDGs share with many other new governance ventures a preoccupation with measuring at the methodological or operational level. While these methodological features or characteristics do not determine the fate of the MDGs, some appreciation of the deeply conjoined processes of governing and measuring may illuminate the extent to which decisions about process can, in turn, drive choices about goals, targets and indicators. It may also serve to problematise the facial equivalence among the different goals and explain why lofty initiatives like the MDGs often fall short of their objectives, and sometimes go

---

[44] J Scott and DM Trubek, 'Mind the Gap: Law and New Approaches to Governance in the European Union' (2002) 8 *European Law Journal* 1.

[45] W Simon, 'Toyota Jurisprudence: Legal Theory and Rolling Rule Regimes' in G de Búrca and J Scott (eds), *Law and New Governance in the EU and the US* (Oxford, Hart Publishing, 2006).

[46] See C Sabel, 'Bootstrapping Development: Rethinking the Role of Public Intervention in Promoting Growth' in V Nee and R Swedberg (eds), *On Capitalism* (Stanford, CA, Stanford University Press, 2007); R Hausmann, D Rodrik and C Sabel, 'Reconfiguring Industrial Policy: A Framework with an Application to South Africa', HKS Working Paper No RWP08-031 (2008), available at http://papers.ssrn.com/sol3/papers.cfm?abstract_id=1245702 (last accessed on 12 July 2009).

[47] D Kaufmann, A Kraay and M Mastruzzi, 'Governance Matters VI: Aggregate and Individual Governance Indicators', World Bank Policy Research Working Paper 4280 (2007), available at http://www-wds.worldbank.org/servlet/WDSContentServer/WDSP/IB/2007/07/10/000016406_20070710125923/Rendered/PDF/wps4280.pdf (last accessed on 12 July 2009); see also Ohnesorge, n 22 above, 219.

[48] The World Bank Group, *Doing Business* (various years), available at http://www.doingbusiness.org/Downloads (last accessed on 12 July 2009).

[49] DM Trubek and L Trubek, 'Hard and Soft Law in the Construction of Social Europe: The Open Method of Coordination' (2005) 11 *European Law Journal* 343.

[50] K Rittich, 'Good Governance and New Governance: Taxonomizing the Relationships', international law seminar (International Law Association British Branch and University College London Faculty of Laws, 2008).

awry entirely. The overall aim is to provoke a more sophisticated and discerning attitude towards the factual and normative claims that are made, both in respect of individual targets and indicators and in support of projects like the MDGs as a whole. Although governing by measuring purports to inject greater clarity, focus and objectivity into the otherwise messy and contestable processes of policy formation, it may in fact produce unwarranted certainty about the degree of stasis and change as well as the trajectory of progress. When governance itself is subject to measurement, these risks are particularly acute and potentially far-reaching.

In brief, governing by measuring suffers from a number of risks. First, problems are not self-evident, and goals may be arbitrarily or contestably identified. As described earlier, they may be contestable at the highest level; however, the potential for disagreement is replicated at lower levels as well. For example, a bureaucrat or technocrat may have one idea of what the appropriate objective is in respect of environmental regulation; a business owner, worker, consumer or community member may have a very different one.

Secondly, specific targets and indicators may be reductively defined in relation to the overall goal or objective to which they are linked. For obvious reasons, targets may be chosen because of their susceptibility to measurement, rather than because they best instantiate or embody the goal or because they are the most illuminating indicator of progress toward or regress from it. To put it another way, we may measure what we can measure most easily, rather than what most needs measuring. If goals are at all broad, targets and indicators are likely to reflect partial visions of the goal or heighten some dimensions of a problem or phenomenon at the expense of others. Targets and indicators may also be political or ideological, insofar as they reflect prior assumptions about what is needed or desirable in the way of policy or regulatory reform. As a result, targets and indicators may be poor, or simply contestable, proxies for the underlying goals that they purport to advance.

Thirdly, indicators may be misleading, particularly when they are compared across jurisdictions. This risk increases where indicators are composite measures and either reflect or require complex judgements, as is typically the case when regulatory regimes themselves are subject to benchmarks. Apparently similar data sets may not be commensurable on closer scrutiny, and sometimes indicators are also simply wrong in the most basic of ways about the facts that they purport to measure.

Fourthly, it is now clear that the heavy reliance on the monitoring and certification required for benchmarking and ranking itself entails risks. Monitors may have no particular expertise in the issue that they are assessing, and either miss, or misevaluate, critical pieces of information as a result; think of the ubiquitous presence of accounting firms such as PricewaterhouseCoopers in the monitoring of corporate codes of conduct, including compliance with labour standards and human rights.[51] For related reasons, monitors may well overreach, 'certifying' facts or conditions that they are in no real position to report upon reliably. Monitors may also be subject to bad incentives, particularly when they are private rather than public, where they have a stake in the outcome of the monitoring, whether because they are the source of

---

[51] M Barenberg, 'Toward a Democratic Model of Transnational Labour Monitoring' in B Bercusson and C Estlund (eds), *Regulating Labour in the Wake of Globalisation: New Challenges, New Institutions* (Oxford, Hart Publishing, 2008) 37.

the norms that they are measuring and their compensation is implicitly linked to the outcomes that they report and/or because they perform other services for the firm or entity that has retained them. In addition, monitoring and certification may induce others to forego analyses and assessments that they otherwise would, and perhaps should, undertake. It is almost certain that certifications will be taken at face value by some, whether or not there is any good reason for them to be relied upon; providing information that people can rely upon in lieu of making their own assessments is, after all, the purpose of certification.

Finally, rankings may be of dubious value or actually counterproductive. Rankings may induce competition according to criteria set by outsiders, whether or not they are the best criteria or conducive to the best use of time and resources; consider, for example, the effects of test score rankings on school curricula. To the extent that significant material or symbolic benefits are at stake, those who are ranked may be induced, or even feel compelled, to manipulate their numbers by fair means and foul, paradoxically undermining the factual reliability of rankings at the same time as they enhance their status. Ranking may also detract from relational or structural analysis of issues and, in so doing, induce confusion about the sources or causes of the variables measured at the end.

Far from merely theoretical concerns, the MDGs project appears to exhibit some, if not all, of these problems.[52] First, the issue of goal identification. Take poverty reduction, the most well-known and widely cited of the MDGs and, arguably, the linchpin of the project as a whole. It is hard to be against poverty reduction, and virtually no one, in fact, speaks against it. But as the foregoing comparison of *The Bottom Billion*[53] and *Worlds Apart*[54] discloses, the story of development at the global level can be told in different ways and the principal problem of development is not self-evident: instead, it emerges from different readings of the global order and different perceptions and judgements of what is significant about the direction of change.

With this in mind, what if we were to question the goal of poverty reduction and ask, what if growing inequality and the balance of power and resources—between South and North, or between élites and working people both within and across states—were identified as the problem instead? What difference would it make in how we see the issue of development? Might paths of transformation open up that are now closed? Are there specific regulatory strategies that are now off the table that might be back under consideration? What would it mean for the rest of the MDGs, indeed, for the formulation of the project as a whole? It seems entirely possible, for example, that a focus on inequality rather than poverty reduction might end up having an impact on Goal 8, the global development partnership. We can imagine, at minimum, that it would alter the chosen targets and indicators. Merely asking these questions, however, raises the possibility that the process might also work in reverse. That is, goals such as poverty alleviation may be chosen not simply 'in the air'. but because they are compatible, or more compatible, with other stated goals and other regulatory and policy initiatives. Development, for example, as well as specific initiatives like land titling

---

[52] See also A Heuty and SG Reddy, 'Achieving the Millennium Development Goals: What's Wrong with Existing Analytical Models?' (Harvard Center for Population and Development Studies, 2006), available at http://ssrn.com/abstract=802804 (last accessed on 12 July 2009).

[53] Collier, n 16 above.

[54] Milanovic, n 4 above.

reform, is now routinely proclaimed to be in the service of both growth and poverty alleviation. At this point, we can begin to observe how, due to the links between the information in circulation and the perception of the problem 'to be solved', the MDGs might operate as part of a project of knowledge production. Specifically, the repeated and widespread dissemination of claims concerning the degree and nature of poverty reinforce the perception that poverty itself, rather than something else, is self-evidently the problem that should be addressed.

Putting the self-reinforcing nature of the project aside and assuming that, quite independent of the MDGs, there was general agreement that poverty reduction is, in fact, the right global objective, what if it ultimately turns out that poverty is itself (partly) a function of inequality? To put it another way, what if tackling inequality— in its various forms and through a variety of means—were itself the best way to reduce poverty? More to the point, what if bracketing inequality—and the factors and processes that appear to contribute to it—actually prevents the successful reduction of poverty? As the first part of the chapter described, these questions are not marginal to the MDGs; rather, they lie at the heart of contemporary development debates.[55] Without trying to answer them, it is useful to reiterate that defining the problem is not as straightforward as it seems. Different actors, institutions and interest groups can be expected to have different views on what matters, and these views may very well be linked to other objectives and projects in the international order to which they are committed. If the goals themselves were open to continuous revision, such differences might matter little. But it may be the case that the initial identification or definition of the problem matters a great deal—for example, it may send us down one road as opposed to another; it may involve or implicate some institutions rather than others; it may empower, or disempower, some constituencies rather than others.

A related problem concerns omissions from the MDGs and the reduction of goals to specific targets or objectives. As described earlier, the MDGs incorporate a regulatory model that is, at best, ambiguous in its social and distributive effects and, at worst, may pose problems to the achievement of some of the goals. But if the particular focus of the governance agenda in the MDGs raises concerns, so do the governance issues that it excludes. An international lawyer might, for example, be struck by the absence of any reference to international law in the MDGs. He or she might wonder if 'good governance' is foundational to the MDGs, then why not 'achieving universal respect for human rights'? After all, the official position is that human rights are linked to the success of development goals such as poverty alleviation.[56] Similar observations might be made about the role of domestic regulation and even private law in achieving the MDGs. Third World scholars and activists, feminists, indigenous peoples' advo-cates and workers' representatives are all groups with a deep interest in the problems targeted by the MDGs, and all have identified legal reforms as part of their agenda. Labour and employment laws, environmental protections, tax policy and property laws, for example, have all been identified as areas of interest and sites of conflict and, for this reason, often figure centrally in their aspirations for change. Rather than mere

---

[55] Stiglitz, n 21 above; P Krugman, 'Inequality and Redistribution' in Serra and Stiglitz, n 21 above.
[56] UNDP, *Human Development Report 1999* (Oxford, Oxford University Press, 1999); The World Bank, *World Development Report 2000/2001: Attacking Poverty* (Oxford, Oxford University Press, 2001); A Sen, *Development as Freedom* (New York, Knopf, 1999).

expressions or elaborations of good governance as understood within the policy mainstream, however, their projects almost invariably involve different legal entitlements,
different conceptions of human rights, different sources of normativity and different
institutional arrangements, both domestic and international.

References to international law, human rights and other legal norms are also an
obvious omission in Goal 3, 'Promote gender equality and empower women', for
example. Gender equality and empowerment is a broad, encompassing agenda and
it, like poverty alleviation, now receives almost universal assent at the normative level.
However, the main focus in the MDGs—the target variable for gender equality—is
school enrolment rates: 'Eliminate gender disparity in primary and secondary education, preferably by 2005, and at all levels by 2015'. Apart from the uncertainty of the
target—is the timeline a deadline or a mere preference? Do primary and secondary
education have equal status as objectives?—the first thing to observe is that this is
a very narrow reading of what the promotion of gender equality might be thought
to require. The second is that there is no shortage of alternative visions of gender
equality in the international order, many of which focus on human rights, legal
reform and governance issues writ large. Gender equality norms are well entrenched
in international law, located in documents ranging from the UN Human Rights Covenants and the Convention on the Elimination of All Forms of Discrimination against
Women,[57] to the more recent 'soft law' declarations and Platforms for Action such as
those emanating from the UN Fourth World Conference for Women in 1995.[58] While
equal access to education is an element of all of them, none of these initiatives gives
education pride of place in the achievement of gender equality. None, that is, except
the gender equality programme now advanced by the World Bank.

After years of being on the receiving end of human rights and gender discrimination complaints, in 2001 the World Bank explicitly embraced gender equality as
a development strategy.[59] However, rather than rely upon existing gender equality
norms in international law, the Bank generated its own definition of, and strategy for,
gender equality. It also provided a new narrative of the relationship between gender
equality and development. Far from harming women and impeding gender equality as
critics contended, the Bank asserted that the new opportunities that markets open up
will benefit women more than men by inducing families to make new investments in
women and girls. They can, it is claimed, even be expected to help redress the well-
known disparity in unpaid work between men and women.[60]

It is not necessary to adjudicate the promise of this market-based strategy for gender
equality and empowerment to observe that it is the equal opportunity approach, and
from this framework primarily, that makes raising girls' school enrolment rates look
like the obvious or natural starting point. A focus on equality in education closely
tracks the gender equality agenda promoted by the Bank, as does the second target

[57] Convention on the Elimination of All Forms of Discrimination against Women (adopted 18 December
1979, entered into force 3 September 1981), 1249 UNTS 13.
[58] 'Beijing Declaration and Platform for Action' in 'Report', Fourth World Conference on Women (17
October 1995) UN Doc A/CONF.177/20, 4.
[59] For a discussion of the rationale, see the World Bank, *Engendering Development: Through Gender
Equality in Rights, Resources, and Voice* (Oxford, Oxford University Press, 2001).
[60] Ibid; see also K Rittich, 'Engendering Development/Marketing Equality' (2003) 67 *Albany Law Review*
575.

identified with the goal of gender equality, raising the share of women in non-agricultural wage employment. Situated within a broader context, however, including the frame of international gender equality norms, what most comes to the fore are questions such as how such targets are identified, for what reasons and by whom. Many parties with a stake in the issue would contest the conception of gender equality and empowerment reflected in the MDGs, and it is almost certain that there would be broad disagreement about whether a focus on school enrolment and the promotion of wage labour represent the best line of attack on gender inequality. Despite the claim that the MDGs are drawn from the commitments of the international summits and conferences of the 1990s, elements of the international gender equality agenda with equal, or better, claim to attention are left out of the equation entirely. This, in turn, raises questions about the relative power of different institutions and actors to set the agenda for institutional and regulatory change in the international order. Who exactly was consulted here when the issue of gender equality was on the agenda?

The choice of indicators by which targets are measured may be as complex and controversial as the targets themselves, particularly when these indicators are subject to measurement and used as standards of the adequacy of governance. The exemplary case here is the Doing Business report series of the World Bank.[61] One of the criteria for the quality of governance according to the parameters defined in the project concerns the ease of hiring and firing workers, and one of the targets of measurement is job-security provisions. Under the 'Employing Workers' indicator, states that provide security against arbitrary termination of employment, or those that require termination or severance pay for workers when contracts of indefinite term come to an end, are deemed to be less business-friendly than those that allow employers complete latitude in such decisions. Accordingly, states with such rules receive a lower score on the governance assessment than those without them.

Two brief observations will suffice to suggest why such a governance measure might be both controversial and problematic. The first is that the establishment of a norm against protection or compensation upon job termination and the treatment of the worker as mere commodity conflicts outright with existing rules and norms in international law, namely, those contained in the conventions or treaties of the International Labour Organisation (ILO). These are long-standing norms that are widely subscribed to by states, they are enshrined in various human rights treaties and they are the subject of promotion by the ILO. They are also commonly found in both industrialised and developing states and, despite fears and claims to the contrary,[62] in general appear to generate no adverse consequences for either employment or economic growth and may, in fact, contribute to better economic outcomes.[63] Job security is also a matter that directly engages the conflicting interests of workers and employers, as well as broader concerns about social welfare and economic security. It is not surprising, then, either that labour advocates and the ILO strongly objected to the use of such an indicator to measure the adequacy of labour market governance or that the indicator itself has been modified in response to the passage of a bill in the US Congress objecting to both

---

[61] See n 48 above.
[62] OECD, *The OECD Jobs Study: Evidence and Explanations* (Paris, OECD, 1994); IMF, *World Economic Outlook: International Financial Contagion* (Washington DC, IMF, 1999); World Bank, *World Development Report 1995: Workers in an Integrating World* (Oxford, Oxford University Press, 1995).
[63] OECD, *OECD Employment Outlook 2006: Boosting Jobs and Incomes* (Paris, OECD, 2006).

its content and its use.[64] As this controversy indicates, the choice and construction of the indicator may be a normatively charged enterprise. We can also begin to appreciate how decisions about goals, targets and indicators in the MDGs might engage, in negative as well as positive ways, the concerns and initiatives of other international institutions. This again raises fundamental questions: who determines the indicators? What opportunities are there to contest and alter them?

There is a deeper problem, however. Because of a failure to distinguish between the form of the law and the substantive entitlements of the parties, the report may draw unsafe conclusions or make faulty assertions about the extent of job security and the cost of termination in particular jurisdictions. Thus, even assuming that the objective were itself uncontroversial, the Employing Workers indicator appears to generate fundamentally unreliable information about the state of labour market governance. For example, on the assumption that employment contracts in common law jurisdictions reflect the US norm of 'employment at will'—that is, an employer is free to fire an employee for good or bad reasons, or for no reason at all—Canada is ranked as having a highly business-friendly employment law regime. However, important job termination entitlements in many common law jurisdictions, including Canada and the UK, exist apart from statutory entitlements and are secured via contract law, through vehicles such as the implied contractual term of reasonable notice.[65] While such entitlements do not prevent the termination of employment, they can, and often do, make it more expensive to take such action; that is, they impose costs on employers of precisely the sort that Doing Business identifies as an impediment to economic activity. If the private law rules that structure these decisions do not figure in the analysis of labour market governance except as proxies for desirable labour market flexibility, indicators may be distorted or misleading even on their own terms. Here, we can see the significance of disciplinary frameworks and assumptions, not only in the choice of indicators but also in how they are interpreted. As most students of law would observe, determining what the law 'is' can be a complex exercise, raising questions not susceptible to easy resolution or singular answers. Even apart from questions of enforcement, the gap between the law in the books and the law in action, or simply the facts in any given case, the state of the law will depend on how legal doctrines and statutory provisions have been interpreted and the relative weight given to competing, and perhaps conflicting, lines of authority in the case law. The risk of failing to consider such complexities in the selection and construction of indicators is clear: the result may be inherently unreliable conclusions about the very thing that is, in theory, being measured.

In addition, indicators may alternatively dampen or inflate perceptions of the problem for which they stand as a proxy; a small, but significant, example will illustrate the possibilities here. In 2008, the World Bank reported that poverty rates were considerably higher than previously announced, and that progress towards eliminating

---

[64] United States House of Representatives Report No 111-151, 44–45 (2009). Subsequent to its passage, the World Bank announced that the Employing Workers indicator did not reflect Bank policy and should not be used for policy advice. See Bank Information Center, 'F Praises Changes to World Bank "Doing Business" Report', available at http://www.bicusa.org/en/Article.11123.aspx (last accessed on 29 July 2009). References to labour rights and changes to the indicator are reflected in subsequent reports, such as World Bank, *Doing Business 2010: Reforming through Difficult Times* (Basingstoke, Palgrave Macmillan, 2009).

[65] See, eg *Machtinger v HOJ Industries Ltd* [1992] 1 SCR 831.

poverty was therefore slower than expected and less than previously reported. This is because the figure chosen to measure the number of people living in poverty was adjusted upward to US$1.25 a day from US$1.00 a day, the measure of poverty adopted in the MDGs.[66] It is not, of course, the case that there were many more poor people on the day that this was announced than there had been the day or week before, and it may well be that the new benchmark is a more accurate measure of the extent of 'real' poverty than the earlier one. But it may also be that both benchmarks are faulty or misleading in important ways.[67] Whatever the answers, the change in the poverty measure both destabilises a central pillar of the MDGs and puts the spotlight on the malleability, manipulability and contestability of any standard that is adopted. This, too, returns us to basic questions. Who decides on the benchmarks? By what processes are they determined? Who has input into their determination? How are discretion and judgement exercised when they are decided? How revisable are they, and what provokes a reconsideration of the standards that are adopted?

Even with agreement on targets and benchmarks, indicators may be misleading when they are compared across different jurisdictions; they may even be misleading concerning the state of affairs within states. For example, developing economies are, almost definitionally under current measures, less commodified than industrialised economies. But neither poverty nor its reduction correlates in any simple way with the extent of commodification.[68] Someone may be much more deprived living on US$1 a day as a slum dweller in a city than he or she would have been living a more tra-ditional existence and engaging in subsistence activities in a rural area. Hence, if we are interested in poverty reduction understood in terms of real welfare gains, or if we want to determine what types of poverty are increasing and what types of interven-tion might be useful in response, it may be less helpful to focus on simply the dollar figure alone than to consider other factors and variables, some of which require non-quantitative research and are inherently less susceptible to measuring.[69]

The difficulty may also be approached from the other direction. It is unlikely, for example, that many people in industrialised countries would be identified as poor according to the criteria adopted under the MDGs. But the actual cost of living, the rise of more precarious employment, and the fact that alternatives to the purchase of goods and services on the market are increasingly foreclosed for many people in the industrialised world means that there are growing numbers of people suffering from real material deprivation there too. If we are interested in remedying global poverty, such developments should be of deep interest, particularly if there are systemic con-nections between the poor in different locations, something that can no longer be ruled out. A singular fixation on the extent of 'absolute poverty', whether defined at US$1

---

[66] S Chen and M Ravallion, 'The Developing World is Poorer than We Thought, but No Less Successful in the Fight against Poverty', World Bank Policy Research Working Paper No 4703 (2008), available at http://ssrn.com/abstract=1259575 (last accessed on 12 July 2009).

[67] Reddy and Heuty, n 52 above, argue that such measures do not reliably correlate with extreme poverty in any useful way.

[68] Ibid.

[69] For a recent discussion of the pitfalls of assuming that either growth or welfare gains are reliably captured through increases in market-based economic activity and reflected in increased GDP alone, see J Stiglitz, A Sen and J-P Fitoussi, 'Report by the Commission on the Measurement of Economic Performance and Social Progress' (2009), available at www.stiglitz-sen-fitoussi.fr.

or US$1.25 and even if adjusted for purchasing power parity, may actually be a barrier rather than an aid to perceiving the changing face and varied nature of global poverty.

Finally, governing by measuring may say both too much and too little about the most important thing, the best way to actually achieve beneficial change in any given context. This critical issue may ultimately rest on things that remain almost entirely outside the MDGs: questions of institutional context, links with broader economic and political issues, the extent of political accountability, both domestic and international, and processes of mobilisation and democratic empowerment.

## IV. GOVERNING BY MEASURING: OBSERVATIONS, QUESTIONS, AND UNCOMFORTABLE POSSIBILITIES

In the last few decades, the international landscape has become populated with 'platforms for change' and 'programmes of action' on the environment, gender equality, racism—fill in the blank here—to which all states, and increasingly non-state actors, too, have dutifully committed themselves. The MDGs simply take this process to the next stage: we might think of the MDGs as the 'meta-platform' for change. Sometimes these initiatives are the catalysts to legal and institutional reform and/or broader structural transformation, but we have enough experience to know that, just as often, they are not. The MDGs have attracted unprecedented amounts of scholarly and institutional attention and energy. In a short period of time, they have virtually come to 'stand in' for the very problems that they seek to address. If, however, we are now actually farther away on some of these goals than we were at the start, perhaps it is time to ask some more probing questions, not simply about why we have not achieved specific MDGs, but whether the MDGs, as a project, exemplify the most promising way either to think about the social deficit or to attempt transformative change on a global scale.

The MDGs are symptomatic of increasingly entrenched trends in the management and regulation of global issues. Not only is the project invested in measurement practices and the pursuit of quantifiable targets and goals at a constitutional level; it proceeds on the basis that there are 'proper' goals that can, and should, be pursued, all within a policy and institutional environment that is largely given. For the MDGs as other projects, the norms, rules, practices and institutions currently identified with good governance come to form the context, matrix or background in which all other international initiatives and normative projects must operate. It is clear that holding these governance norms stable while focusing, laser-like, on specific problems holds a deep attraction; perhaps, the very capacity to stabilise these norms is itself part of the attraction. Whether it advances other projects, however, is another question. Perhaps targeting a problem is not always as useful as situating a problem. Perhaps it encourages us to focus on symptoms rather than causes; perhaps it leaves unaddressed, and hence intact, the many direct and indirect sources of the problem that we seek to solve or alleviate.

The structure of the MDGs suggests that the individual goals are, in some sense, commensurable or, at minimum, that they can be thought of and approached in a roughly similar way. But perhaps this mode of ordering and classifying problems is more confusing or distracting than illuminating. How helpful is it to aggregate such a Borgesian list of objectives?[70] In what sense is it plausible to think of tackling child mortality, for example, in the same manner as forging a new development partnership?

How much does the focus on measurable goals achieve? What if other less measurable, but no less important, goals are displaced? What if some things are just not fundamentally measurable? Can complex endeavours like ensuring environmental sustainability, for example, be reliably reduced to simple indicators?

Can the MDGs be disconnected from the wider context—economic, sociological, political, regulatory, ideological and cultural—from which they emerge and in which they are situated? Divorced and disembedded from context and history, how much can be said about how to tackle them? Once translated from general goals to particular problems and issues, is it safe to say that the MDGs even always refer to the same things?

Should we re-evaluate our (growing) preoccupation with measuring itself? It has long been observed that information about developing countries is typically gathered for a purpose, and that the relevant measures are not simply chosen through some normatively neutral process.[71] Even the designation of large parts of the world as poor is an event that is both recent and controversial.[72] Perhaps these insights should be revived in the assessment of the MDGs; perhaps if they were, we would see illuminating continuities with older endeavours. Even if we retain our interest in the goals, we may then be better equipped to face the following conundrum: whether, as conceived, the MDGs assist us in grappling with these complexities or whether instead they serve to obscure them.

These are difficult issues. But they suggest that below the apparently certain, measurable surface of the MDGs are more questions than answers. If we were to reflect systematically on the structure of the project and the other endeavours to which it is linked, it might change the questions that we ask; this, in turn, might affect our perceptions both of the problems and of the modes of conceiving of more just global futures.

---

[70] Foucault's famous discussion of classification in *The Order of Things* begins with a reference to a fictional taxonomy of animals drawn from an essay by JL Borges. This taxonomy includes animals 'belonging to the Emperor' and 'that from a long way off look like flies'. See M Foucault, *The Order of Things: An Archaeology of Human Sciences* (New York, Vintage Books, 1973), Preface.

[71] A Anghie, 'Time Present and Time Past: Globalization, International Financial Institutions, and the Third World' (2000) 32 *New York University Journal of International Law and Politics* 243.

[72] B Rajagopal, *International Law from Below: Development, Social Movements, and Third World Resistance* (Cambridge, Cambridge University Press, 2003).

Part II

Transitional Justice and Development:
Comparative and Transnational Perspectives

# 10

# Reparations and Development*

## NAOMI ROHT-ARRIAZA

### I. INTRODUCTION

IN THE WAKE of a civil conflict in the 1980s that took some 69,000 lives, the government of Peru established an Integrated Reparations Policy aimed at providing reparations to survivors who had suffered human rights violations or violations of international humanitarian law. As part of this programme, the regional government in affected areas held public meetings for local people to express their views on the priorities for 'collective reparations'. Although the process, according to observers, did not adequately reach out to women, youth or other community members, it did result in a list of priority projects, including schools, markets, roads and rural electrification. As a result of this process, a new school was built.

Halfway around the world, the World Bank, in conjunction with the local government, developed a Poverty Reduction Strategy Paper (PRSP) stressing the importance of health and education for development. As part of the PRSP-based loan-approval process, the regional government held public meetings for local people to express their views on priorities for 'development projects'. Although the process, according to observers, did not adequately reach out to women, youth or other community members, it did result in a list of priority projects, including schools, markets, roads and rural electrification. As a result of this process, a new school was built.

What is the difference between these two scenarios, from the perspective of international law, of the domestic government, or of the parents of the schoolchildren? The question has become an urgent one, as reparations programmes try to reach large numbers of people in the wake of civil strife or dictatorships. As the number of the potential beneficiaries of such programmes and an awareness of the collective dimensions of harm have grown, attention has moved from solely individual reparations to those involving services for entire communities. This creates an overlap with other government efforts, generally given the heading of 'development', which has proven problematical, but, at the same time, reflects the increasing overlap between

---

* This chapter is based in part upon a longer paper by N Roht-Arriaza and K Orlovsky, entitled 'A Complementary Relationship: Reparations and Development' in P de Greiff and R Duthie (eds), *Transitional Justice and Development: Making Connections* (New York, Social Science Research Council, 2009).

the 'transitional' or 'post-armed conflict' justice[1] agenda and that of development and its corollary, 'development assistance'. This chapter briefly considers this convergence, and a few of the issues that it raises. It first traces the theories of reparations and of development that create possibilities for convergence, then focuses specifically on the provision of forms of both collective and individual reparations that raise problems, as well as illustrate the potential for these converging practices.

## II. THE CONVERGENCE BETWEEN TRANSITIONAL JUSTICE AND DEVELOPMENT: REPARATIONS

Reparation to individuals and communities (rather than states) emerges from human rights law's right to a remedy, as well as from some provisions of international humanitarian law. It is increasingly discussed as an element of the larger spectrum of transitional justice measures, including truth-seeking or investigation, criminal prosecutions and/or civil suits against rights violators, removal of such violators from security forces or other public employment, memorialisation, local reconciliation efforts, and the disarmament, demobilisation and reintegration of combatants (DDR). One useful insight of the transitional justice field has been the inter-relationship of these different efforts. As Pablo de Greiff, Brandon Hamber and others have pointed out, truth—whether uncovered through trials or truth commissions, or both—not followed up with concrete action to make amends will leave many victims frustrated, while reparations alone, without truth-telling or justice, will be seen as payment for silence or 'blood money'.[2] Likewise, DDR programmes that serve ex-combatants while ignoring the misery and lack of economic prospects of the victims will create resentment and division, rather than reconciliation or reintegration.

The victims' legal right to reparation for serious harms that they have suffered is a core concept of human rights instruments, where it is generally articulated as a right to a remedy. It is articulated in the 2005 United Nations 'Basic Principles on the Right to a Remedy and Reparation for Victims of Gross Violations of International Human Rights Law and Serious Violations of International Humanitarian Law' (UN Basic Principles).[3] According to the UN Basic Principles, a victim of the said violations has the right, under international law, to (i) equal and effective access to justice; (ii) adequate, effective and prompt reparation for harm suffered; and (iii) access to the relevant information concerning the violations and reparation mechanisms. Such repa-

---

[1] I acknowledge at the outset the shortcomings of 'transitional' and 'post-armed conflict' as labels. I use them, according to conventions in the literature, to refer to situations in which massive violations of humanitarian law or serious human rights violations constituting crimes under national and international law have occurred in the recent past, followed by a change in regime and/or a negotiated or imposed end to the fighting. I acknowledge that there are significant differences between a 'post-dictatorship' and a 'post-armed conflict' situation.

[2] P de Greiff, 'Justice and Reparations' in idem (ed), *The Handbook of Reparations* (Oxford, Oxford University Press, 2006) 451; B Hamber, 'Narrowing the Micro and Macro: A Psychological Perspective on Reparations in Societies in Transition' in ibid, 580.

[3] UN Basic Principles, VII, 11, available at *www2.ohchr.org/english/issues/remedy/principles.htm*. For a thorough examination of the UN basic principles, and other sources of the right to reparation in international law, see D Shelton, 'The United Nations Principles and Guidelines on Reparations: Context and Contents' in K de Feyter, S Parmentier, M Bossuyt and P Lemmens (eds), *Out of the Ashes: Reparations for Victims of Gross and Systematic Human Rights Violations* (Antwerp, Intersentia, 2005) 11.

ration 'should be proportional to the gravity of the violations and the harm suffered',[4] and may take the form of restitution, compensation, rehabilitation, satisfaction and guarantees of non-repetition.[5] The right to a remedy or to reparations is also articulated in specialised conventions, non-binding instruments and the Rome Statute of the International Criminal Court.[6]

Reparations are distinguished from reconstruction and from victim assistance (i) by their roots as a legal entitlement based upon an obligation to repair harm and (ii) by an element of recognition of wrongdoing, atonement or making good. Reparations are, therefore, a limited category of response to harm, and generally address violations of basic civil and political rights such as massacres or disappearances, rather than larger issues of social exclusion or denial of economic, social or cultural rights.[7]

The transitional justice movement, in its origins, focused almost exclusively on violations of civil and political rights. Indeed, the politics of transition in Latin America in the 1980s and South Africa or Eastern Europe in the early 1990s, where the movement emerged, required a focus on rule of law and democratisation, and a soft-pedalling of more contentious distributive justice issues.[8] Although some early writers, such as Rama Mani, insisted that distributive justice was an integral part of post-armed conflict reconstruction,[9] for the most part academics and practitioners alike largely ignored both the economic roots of conflict and the inter-relationship between redistributive and other forms of justice.

This began to change somewhat in the early 2000s. Several factors intervened. The performance of the international and mixed criminal tribunals, while useful in many ways, did not seem to affect the daily realities of much of the population in the territorial states. They focused on the stories of the perpetrators, and the victims and witnesses only played passive roles. As one result, practitioners and parties began placing more emphasis on non-prosecutorial strategies focused on victims, including reparations. Truth commissions, which focused on disappearances, massacres and summary executions, began incorporating long-standing structural inequalities, corruption and the violations of economic, social and cultural rights into their narratives of the causes and consequences of conflict.[10] A new generation of academics and activists began insisting that avoiding a recurrence of conflict requires sustained attention to the economic and social as well as the ideological or political causes of civil wars and dictatorships. There were other points of convergence: an insistence that the beneficiaries of post-armed conflict programmes or policies have a voice in their design, and that 'transition' may be too narrow a time-frame for processes of social and legal reconstruction that may take decades or generations.

---

[4] Basic Principles, ibid, IX, 15.

[5] Ibid, IX, 19–23.

[6] See N Roht-Arriaza, 'Reparations Decisions and Dilemmas' (2004) 27 *Hastings International & Comparative Law Review* 157, 160–65.

[7] This is not to argue that reparations for violations of economic, social and cultural rights are not possible, simply that no programme to date labelled as reparations has attempted to redress such violations in the absence of concurrent violations of basic civil and political rights.

[8] See P Arthur, 'How "Transitions" Reshaped Human Rights: A Conceptual History of Transitional Justice' (2009) 31 *Human Rights Quarterly* 321.

[9] R Mani, *Beyond Retribution: Seeking Justice in the Shadows of War* (Cambridge, Polity Press, 2002).

[10] See, eg the difference in narratives of the early Chilean Truth and Reconciliation Commission (1991) with the later Sierra Leone one (2004).

## III. THE CONVERGENCE BETWEEN DEVELOPMENT AND
## REPARATIONS: DEVELOPMENT

Like transitional justice, development has multiple definitions and embodies multiple discourses. The dominant economic model focuses on export-led growth and integration into global markets as the surest paths to economic advancement. During the 1980s and early 1990s, the 'Washington consensus' held that growth, and thus development, was a function of opening up economies, selling state assets and shrinking the public sector. The result, in many countries, was a contraction of economic activity and cutbacks in services, such as public health and education, which might overlap with the efforts of many reparations programmes. In the post-'consensus' era, even the international financial institutions (IFIs) and donor agencies now pay lip service to the need for increased government services in these areas, and for a direct focus on poverty alleviation (rather than regarding it as a trickle-down consequence of growth). The Millennium Development Goals (MDGs), approved by governments in the year 2000, are the most well-known expression of the mainstream policy objectives for reducing poverty and improving well-being.[11]

Starting in the 1980s and increasingly today, development economists, academic experts and even international financial institutions,[12] as well as national and international aid agencies and governments, recognise that growth and other macro-indicators alone do not capture many of the essential aspects of a development process. There is broad agreement that the social exclusion of large sectors of a population, combined with other factors, including geography, level of conflict and 'governance', are crucial variables in determining development levels.[13]

Amartya Sen[14] and other theorists postulated that development entails creating the conditions for all people to develop their fullest possible range of capabilities. This view, widely espoused by the United Nations Development Programme (UNDP) and other aid agencies, results in attention being directed to a much wider set of development indicators. The UNDP's Human Development Index has, since the 1990s, ranked countries in terms of measures such as infant morbidity and mortality, educational level and women's rights, as well as by GDP growth. Along the same lines, devel-

---

[11] The MDGs were developed out of the eight chapters of the United Nations Millennium Declaration, signed in September 2000. The eight goals are: eradicate extreme poverty and hunger; achieve universal primary education; promote gender equality and empower women; reduce child mortality; improve maternal health; combat HIV/AIDS, malaria and other diseases; ensure environmental sustainability; and develop a global partnership for development. For the most part, the goals are to be achieved by 2015.

[12] The most important IFI for purposes of this discussion is the World Bank Group, itself divided into a commercial arm (the International Finance Corporation), which makes market-rate loans, and the International Development Association, which loans at below-market rates to very poor countries for both projects and support of government budgets. Regional banks, like the Inter-American and Asian Development Banks, also provide project finance. The International Monetary Fund, in contrast, does not provide project finance but serves as a lender of last resort in cases of currency or commercial imbalance. The IMF sets conditions on its loans that are often echoed by the World Bank as well as by commercial and state lenders, in effect making it very difficult for states which defy its prescriptions to borrow money. This is slowly beginning to change with the advent of states such as Venezuela and China willing to lend under different conditions, but it is still the norm. See JM Cypher and JL Dietz, *The Process of Economic Development*, 2nd edn (Abingdon, Routledge, 2004) ch 17, 555.

[13] See, eg J Sachs, *The End of Poverty: How We Can Make it Happen in Our Lifetime* (Harmondsworth, Penguin Books, 2006).

[14] A Sen, *Development as Freedom* (Oxford, Oxford University Press, 1999).

opment practitioners have begun focusing on the micro- as well as the macro-level, looking at village-level interventions and community-driven processes as important components of development success.[15]

Reparations may have an impact on development by facilitating social integration. Recent research explores the link between social integration and economic development. Kaushik Basu, for example, finds that

> once a group of people is left outside the system or treated as marginal over a period of time, forces develop that reinforce its marginalization. The group learns not to participate in society and others learn to exclude members of this group, and participator inequity becomes a part of the economic and societal 'equilibrium'.

Therefore, because people evaluate how trustworthy or likely to succeed others may be in an economic endeavour based, in part, upon the identity characteristics of the individual, marginalised groups (whether by race, class or victim status) tend to stay marginalised and unable to break out of poverty. The solution, according to Basu, lies in fostering a sense of 'participatory equity', so that the marginalised belong to their society and also have rights like others.[16] It is this vision of development, especially as it concerns the life conditions and chances of excluded or marginalised sectors, where the clearest overlap with reparations occurs.

In the 1990s, alongside the concern with opening up economies, came a new focus on 'governance', which has, over time, brought the concerns and techniques of transitional justice and development experts closer together. After years of focusing on markets as the sole drivers of growth, IFIs and donor governments finally realised that markets could not operate properly without an overarching set of rules provided by the state. They thus turned their attention to strengthening certain aspects of state performance, including judicial and legal-system reform and anti-corruption efforts, and tying external support to 'good governance'.[17] In particular, lending and aid agencies have focused a large amount of their resources on 'rule of law' programming, aimed simultaneously at modernisation of codes and courts to facilitate open markets and at improving access to justice for the population, especially those who have never seen courts as useful defenders of their rights. While the overall effect of this surge in interest in 'rule of law' is unclear, the focus on the justice sector has at least led to greater sensitivity among some development specialists to the particular needs and characteristics of post-conflict societies, and to a renewed focus on the state's capacity to carry out any of the goals assigned to it, whether these involve development processes or justice, or both.[18]

---

[15] See, eg Sachs, n 13 above.

[16] K Basu, 'Participatory Equity, Identity, and Productivity: Policy Implications for Promoting Development', CAE Working Paper #06-06 (May 2006).

[17] See, eg the Millennium Challenge Account.

[18] Thus, the World Bank, USAID and the major European aid organisations as well as UNDP have created specialised units focusing on transitional and/or post-armed conflict states. See, for instance, the Millennium Challenge Account (2004), available at http://www.cfr.org/pakistan/foreign-aid-millennium-challenge-account/p7748.

## IV. TENSIONS AND SYNERGIES

There are obviously tensions between reparations programmes and the larger development agenda. If nothing else, budgets are finite, and competition for resources is particularly fierce in a post-armed conflict or post-dictatorship context, where the economy and infrastructure may be damaged or destroyed and common crime is likely to surge. Fiscal stability and a need to create a favourable investment climate may conflict with the additional social spending and need for additional government revenues that a reparations program will demand.

At the same time, there are potential synergies. Reparations, from an individual victim's perspective, may be a necessary step towards creating a sense of recognition as a citizen with equal rights and of civic trust of citizens towards their government.[19] These, in turn, are preconditions for the (re-)emergence of the victims and survivors as actors with the initiative, drive and belief in the future that drives sustainable economic activity. While all transitional justice measures share this aim, reparations constitute its most concrete, tangible and, to some degree, personalised expression. Reparations payments, at least if past and current administrative programmes are a guide, will never be large enough to make a difference on a macro-economic scale. Nonetheless, reparations payments may have positive effects on rebalancing power relations within families and at the local community level. Even small amounts, under certain conditions, may unleash the energy and creativity of previously marginalised sectors (especially women and indigenous peoples). Reparations in the form of services can improve health, education and other measures of well-being that are essential to development in ways that 'normal' programmes for the provision of these services will miss because they are not attuned to the specific potential and needs of survivors, including the need to have their individual harms acknowledged.

Moreover, individual and collective reparations may have important spillover effects on other aspects of development. These include linkages to other issues, such as civil registry and titling, potential strengthening of the state's ability to be an effective service provider, and the ability of civil society and business groups to interface with the state (through procurement and otherwise) in a 'normal' fashion. Interaction with the state around reparations, if positive, can increase awareness of the population as rights-bearing citizens, which can, in turn, spill over into a demand for access to justice and for effective (and transparent) government.

Just as reparations may affect development, however, development can also contribute to an improved ability to provide effective reparations. At the simplest level, a desperately poor country with little in the way of government infrastructure will face greater difficulties in financing and distributing reparations than a richer, more organised one. The lack of a government presence in the interior of a country which is emerging from conflict will make it difficult to organise the provision of reparations, or even to know what the potential beneficiaries of a reparations programme need or want. In particular, many reparations, especially in-kind services, require a delivery system. To the extent that these services can be channelled through already functioning pension, education or health systems, they are more likely to be competently provided. Moreover, development efforts focused on fighting corruption, public

---

[19] See de Greiff, 'Justice and Reparations', n 2 above.

administrative reform and even security sector reform might make the state more effective in delivering reparations. This has implications for the timing of reparations: it may take some time to build up the required physical, financial and human infrastructure to ensure an adequate reparations programme. While this is by no means an argument for delaying the provision of reparations, it may lead to the recognition that the benefits of reparations may accrue, only in part, to the initial victims and survivors of the violations, and may, in part, be inter-generational.

## V. THE COMPONENTS OF A REPARATIONS PROGRAMME

Both individual and collective reparations are important components of a sufficiently complex and integrated reparations effort. Individual reparations recognise specific harm to an individual, and an individual's worth as a rights-bearing citizen. Such recognition may not be otherwise satisfied, and this is integral to (re-)gaining civic trust. Such individual recognition becomes especially important where government has previously treated the affected population as an undifferentiated mass or as second-class citizens.

Individual reparations need not be limited to monetary compensation: they can also take the form of restitution—of land, other property, jobs, pensions, civil rights or good name—and of physical, mental and legal rehabilitation. Individual reparations may be symbolic as well as material: for example, the Chilean government's delivery of a personalised copy of the Truth and Reconciliation Commission's report with a letter indicating where the name of each individual victim could be found had a profound reparative value to the individuals involved.[20] Other individual reparations may include the exhumation and dignified reburial of those killed, apologies to individual survivors or next-of-kin, or the publication of the facts of an individual case. Individual reparations can also take the form of government service packages, for example, enrolment in government health plans, preferential access to medical services, or scholarships.

Collective reparations may serve other, albeit overlapping, functions: to respond to collective harms and to harms to social cohesion (especially in places with a strong sense of collective identity), to re-establish social solidarity and to maximise the effectiveness of the existing resources. The objective is not to choose one form of reparation over another, but to understand the strengths and limitations of each, and to combine them in a culturally appropriate and creative manner.

Collective reparations consider the individual in the context of societal ties. Use of the term may refer to reparations to a particular social, ethnic or geographical group, or simply to a community that has suffered harm to its cohesion and social fabric as such, and thus is being repaired *qua* community. This approach clearly raises the difficulty of assigning victims to groups or communities for reparation purposes, a problem magnified by demographic and social shifts during the course of an armed conflict, especially widespread displacement and migration. In practice, collective reparations have most often been conceptualised as either non-individualised modalities of distribution, or public goods tied to specific communities or particularly hard-hit regions. Thus, while access to scholarships or hospital privileges would constitute indi-

---

[20] E Lira, 'The Reparations Policy for Human Rights Violations in Chile' in de Greiff, ibid, 55.

vidual reparations, the building of schools or health clinics in affected communities, open to all residents, would be collective reparations. Some modalities of reparations are collective in form, but still remain largely limited to the victims, and may be targeted at group-based harm.[21] Examples include psychosocial accompaniment for groups of victims, exhumations of mass grave sites in specific communities, the titling of collective lands, the restitution of sites of communal worship, or micro-credit or other producer-targeted projects that target groups of widows or the like. As with individual reparations, these forms of collective reparations may include material, as well as symbolic, measures, restitution and satisfaction as well as compensation.

Most existing proposals and programmes, at least in theory, combine both an individual and a collective component. The law creating the Peruvian Integral Reparations Policy specifies multiple modalities, including the restitution of civil rights, reparations in health, education and housing, symbolic and collective reparations, and others. Reparations may be paid to individual victims or their next-of-kin, or to collectivities, defined as:

> The peasant and native communities and other population centers affected by the violence, that present certain characteristics such as: a concentration of individual violations, destruction, forced displacement, breaks or cracks in local authority structures, loss of family or communal infrastructure; and organized groups of non-returning displaced, who come from the affected communities but have resettled elsewhere.[22]

Peru granted hard-hit communities around 100,000 soles (33,500 USD) each for development projects of their choosing. The first 440 community projects ranged from irrigation, electrification, water and school and road improvements, to projects to raise small livestock (*cuyes* or guinea pigs), improve tourist infrastructure or create a computer centre for a small town. It is too early to evaluate the effectiveness of these projects or of the process by which they were allocated, although an initial monitoring project found shortcomings in the way in which the projects were chosen. Conceptually, the projects were unrelated to the nature or type of harms that they were ostensibly redressing, which obscured their purposes among the beneficiaries. The process of community participation in choosing projects was skewed towards local government officials, with few women participants.[23] Of course, problems in local participatory processes are ubiquitous in development work, and reparations practitioners might look to development specialists to craft better ways of encouraging and reflecting participation. Individual reparations, on the other hand, had not, as of 2010, been forthcoming, in part due to difficulties with creating a victim registry as well as to lack of financing.

The Guatemalan National Reparations Programme, in theory, includes both an individual compensation component and a large component of collective reparations, including psychosocial and cultural reparations, productive projects for women, and

[21] R Rubio-Marin, 'Gender and Collective Reparations in the Aftermath of Conflict and Political Repression', unpublished draft.

[22] Ley que Crea el Plan Integral de Reparaciones, Ley 28592 (2005) Art 7, available at http://www.internal-displacement.org/idmc/website/countries.nsf/%28httpEnvelopes%29/FE5565C4326AF8AEC12575160 0582F51?OpenDocument.

[23] APRODEH-ICTJ, 'Sistema de Vigilancia a Reparaciones', Reporte Nacional de Vigilancia del Programa de Reparaciones Colectivas, 2008, available at www.aprodeh.org.pe/reparaciones/sistema/reparaciones/reportenacional.pdf.

education, health and housing benefits for the affected communities. In practice, the major component of actual disbursements has been in individual reparations and in support for the exhumations of mass graves, although, beginning in 2008, the programme is being revamped to focus more on community-generated projects. In Morocco, the reparations paid by the Equity and Reconciliation Commission include collective reparations focused on the building of infrastructure, including schools, clinics and women's centres in the hardest-hit areas of the country. Individual reparations in Morocco took the form of compensation granted to individuals and were distributed through their local post office, along with a personalised letter of apology and acknowledgement, an explanation of the ruling in their individual case, and an application form for health coverage.[24]

Generally speaking, human rights practitioners and theorists writing about reparations have discouraged the use of non-exclusive goods and services as the principal, or even a principal, form of reparation. This would be, they argue, the provision of development funds as reparations, confusing the nature and purposes of both. At an individual level, social reconstruction conflated with reparations will have a limited psychological impact, especially for those seeking individual reparations. Brandon Hamber notes that genuine reparation and the process of healing does not occur only or primarily through the delivery of an object or acts of reparations, but also through the process that takes place around the object or act.[25] In addition, victims may consider the upgrading of their communities to be a right. Advocates have pointed out that using reparations funds to provide non-exclusive goods or services to underserved populations (including—but not limited to—the victims) allows the government to escape too easily: it need only do what it should be doing anyway and slap a reparations label on it.[26] Moreover, the beneficiaries are likely to confuse the results as a product of official largesse, rather than a legally defined obligation.

Governments tend to prefer the use of collective reparations, and often for precisely these pragmatic reasons. It may allow them to funnel programmes into existing ministries, seem more efficient and less likely to be politically sensitive, require less new bureaucracy, and seem more acceptable to budget-conscious managers and creditors. Non-exclusive reparations also avoid problems with either singling out the victims or creating new resentments. They allows the government to take credit for the programmes, rather than foregrounding the past harms and the existence of a legal obligation. Aid agencies also prefer to speak of 'victim assistance' and not of reparations, a more politically loaded term.

Despite the limitations of non-exclusivity and the danger of confusion, there may be some substantial advantages to these kinds of collective reparations in the context of larger-term development if they are used to complement some kind of individual reparations. In conditions where there is a scarcity of resources and a large number of victims, the choice may be between collective reparations, on the one hand, and no material reparations, or individual compensation so meagre as to be insulting, on the other. Non-exclusive access for larger segments of an affected population, including

---

[24] ICTJ, 'Truth-Seeking and Reparations in Morocco', April 2008.
[25] Hamber, n 2 above, 580.
[26] See Roht-Arriaza, n 6 above; see also de Greiff, 'Justice and Reparations' and *The Handbook of Reparations*, n 2 above; Rubio-Marin, n 21 above.

the victims and the perpetrators, avoids creating new resentments, or conversely may avoid the stigmatisation and continuing marginalisation that victim-only programmes may engender. In addition, collective reparations can be designed to maximise their symbolic impact through naming ceremonies, in combination with symbolic reparations of different kinds, or the like.

These kinds of processes may help to rebalance power at local level by altering the dynamic between the victims and the local power structure. After many armed conflicts, the victors constitute the local (official or de facto) leadership: they have the most resources (often as a result of appropriating the resources of victims), they are protected by impunity from any kind of accountability, and they have sometimes morphed into local mafia or crime bosses. Victims, on the other hand, tend to be among the worst-off members of the community, whether because of the lack of one or more breadwinners, a lack of land or health problems. Despite the return of peace, they tend to continue to be largely powerless and marginalised. As described earlier, this creates difficulties in fully engaging a substantial sector of the population in development efforts.

Under these circumstances, a well-designed reparations programme can help rebalance local power. Most obviously, it can put much-needed resources into the hands of the worst-off, which, in turn, may underscore and makes public the state's evaluation of who was wronged. But even services such as schools, roads or health centres that will benefit everyone living in the area, including perpetrators, bystanders and rescuers as well as the victims,[27] may help to rebalance power in favour of the victims. If services needed by all come to the community because of the needs—and, even better, the efforts—of the victims and the survivors, this provenance provides them with a source of status and pride in the eyes of their neighbours. One source of status in many cultures and communities is the ability to bring resources to bear for the common good, to be a benefactor.[28] By making it clear that the victims are the reason why the services arrive, even if these services benefit everyone, collective reparations can begin to address an existing power imbalance. This may, in turn, allow for broader participation by the victims in local governance.

The dangers of governments downplaying the rights-based, obligatory nature of reparations, allowing them to be perceived as merely largesse, may be just as applicable to individual compensation payments. In Guatemala, for example, victims' groups have complained that cheques to the victims of human rights violations are perceived as being equivalent to the cheques issued at the same time to civil patrollers (who were often human rights violators) to compensate them for forced labour. In this situation, there are also (with rare exceptions) few symbolic or apologetic aspects to the handover of funds, and groups report that people are confused and upset by the

---

[27] These categories are obviously fluid: the same individual may fall into more than one category, eg rescuing some people while attacking others; within families, there are often representatives of all of them. It may be impossible to benefit only the 'right' victims; Peru's PIR, for example, excludes members of subversive groups, but this provision has raised a host of criticisms that the exclusion is discriminatory and sweeps much too broadly.

[28] This phenomenon takes different forms in different cultures. It is (derogatorily) talked about as the ability to act as a godfather, big man or mover and shaker, but the same impulse motivates, at least in part, large wedding feasts and hefty donations to the ballet or new hospital wing.

different amounts being handed out to different families, notwithstanding the fact that there was a clear logic behind the differing amounts.[29]

Individual reparations in the form of lump-sum cash payments can create other types of difficulty. Some evidence about reparations negotiated in, or ordered by, the Inter-American system suggests that large payments (admittedly, an order of magnitude larger than those offered by most administrative reparations programmes) provoked community dislocations: historic leaders were abandoned in favour of a host of newcomers promising that they could obtain more and better reparations, towns were flooded with hucksters promising fast cheques, long-lost and unknown family members suddenly appeared, and some recipients were assaulted or threatened into turning over the proceeds of their cheque.[30] Intra-family dynamics were also impacted: while, in some cases, women were empowered by receiving disposable cash in their name, in others, male relatives quickly laid claim to the compensation paid to their wives and mothers.[31]

The development impact of reparations may be different in some cultural contexts, depending on whether reparations are made in kind or through cash payments, and whether they attempt to compensate material loss, rather than wrongful death. Restitution in kind includes housing materials, farm or grazing animals, seeds, work and domestic implements, such as hoes and pots. While economists will argue that providing goods, rather than cash, is inefficient,[32] there are a few reasons why preferring in-kind replacement of goods over cash might vary the impact on both the reparatory effect and the long-term development.

First, the symbolic values are different: replacement goods are a tangible connection to what was lost, whereas money is generic. This is why international law traditionally favours restitution if at all possible, and considers compensation only for goods (and people) that cannot be replaced. Secondly, the relative values of money and goods are different in certain societies. Of all the potential types of reparation, money is the most controversial: in some places, it is considered 'blood money', a perception which is exacerbated when the money is given for the loss of a loved one, rather than for material losses and displacement. In others, money is associated with colonial impositions and the necessity of wage labour; in some places, it measures wealth and worth, while in others wealth is measured in cattle, pigs or other goods, and personal worth is a function of giving away assets, rather than saving them. In many traditional cultures, different kinds of money have had different uses, with cash often associated with more crass, commercial dealings and other products (*pom incense*, shells, offer-

---

[29] Amounts depended on the nature of the violation (ie was the victim killed) and also on how many family members suffered the violation, to deal with situations in which entire extended families were nearly wiped out. Amounts ranged from Q20,000 to Q44,000 (2,608 USD to 5,737 USD).

[30] M Mersky and N Roht-Arriaza, 'Guatemala' in Due Process of Law Foundation, *Victims Unsilenced: The Inter-American Human Rights System and Transitional Justice in Latin America* (Washington DC, DPLF, 2007). Elizabeth Lira notes a similar result in the Mapuche areas of Chile, where 'in very poor communities the economic reparations distorted family relations of solidarity and negatively affected family and community networks'; see Lira, n 20 above, 63.

[31] This information is based upon discussions in Guatemala regarding reparations paid as a result of Inter-American cases, especially interviews with Olga Alicia Paz of ECAP and with massacre survivors in Plan de Sanchez. See also Mersky and Roht-Arriaza, ibid.

[32] Welfare economists stress the ability of cash recipients to satisfy a wider range of preferences, and the smaller administrative costs of cash disbursements. DM Hausman and MS McPherson, 'Beware of Economists Bearing Advice' (1997) 18 *Policy Options* 16.

ings, etc) being seen as valuable in solemn contractual or important inter-personal dealings.[33] While, in many cases, these differences may be nothing more than residual at this point, when highly symbolic, emotion-fraught goods are at stake, they may resonate. Thus, in Rwanda, reparations paid from one community to another shortly after the genocide under traditional notions of *Gacaca* (community justice)[34] took the form of cattle—the traditional marker of wealth in east Africa—not cash. In East Timor, reparations for property and personal damage under the Community Reparations Procedures included young pigs or chickens and ceremonial beads.[35]

At the same time, the line between personal losses and property losses may not be the same in all societies. In some places, domestic animals may be seen as sentient beings more akin to the extended family, while in others even crops and domestic goods may have spirits. This is especially true in the world view of indigenous cultures. Thus, when these things are lost, the loss may be felt as more than the loss of 'mere' property. It is quite striking, in the testimonies of victims, how often people enumerate losses of crops, domestic animals and tools with great specificity, even decades after the losses took place.

Thirdly, restitution in goods, rather than cash, may change the intra-family and gender-based effects of the payment. The domestic economy tends to be the sphere of women, while the cash economy is that of men. Control of the resources will thus tend to depend on whose sphere they belong in, so that provision of goods will more likely retain them in the hands of women. Domestic animals, in particular, are more likely than cash to be used for improving the family's nutrition or to augment an income stream that is under the control of women. In turn, studies show that income controlled by women is more likely to be spent on nutrition and the education of children.

Admittedly, restitution in kind may not be practicable in urban areas, nor have the same resonance in all cultures, even rural ones. But even there, care should be taken to think about culturally appropriate and economically beneficial forms of non-cash individual payments, whether these be housing materials, for example, or tools that would give the victims the means to live with dignity. Thought should also be given to the nature and size of the available markets: if the things people most need cannot be bought locally, cash payments may end up benefiting urban or foreign élites and not creating any kind of multiplier effect at local level. They may even serve to drain the local economy of human resources, as when people use their reparations payments to send their young people abroad to work as migrant labour.

---

[33] There is a vast literature on commodities, gifts, and currencies and their meaning. See, eg A Strathern and PJ Stewart, 'Objects, Relationships and Meanings' in D Akin and J Robbins (eds), *Money and Modernity: State and Local Currencies in Melanesia* (Pittsburgh, PA, University of Pittsburgh Press, 1999) 164–91 (speaking of the Nuer of East Africa: 'Limits on the interconvertibility of money and cattle are based on the idea that money "has no blood" and does not carry the procreative power that cattle do. The fact that humans and cattle do have blood is given by Nuer as the reason why cattle can stand for people in reproductive exchanges (bridewealth, blood payments) as pigs do in New Guinea'). See also CA Gregory, *Gifts and Commodities* (London, Academic Press, 1982).

[34] I do not refer here to the 'legal gacaca' created to hold low-level perpetrators accountable but the spontaneous version that sprung up in the years immediately following 1994.

[35] See P Burgess, 'A New Approach to Restorative Justice—East Timor's Community Reconciliation Processes' in N Roht-Arriaza and J Mariezcurrena (eds), *Transitional Justice in the Twenty-first Century: Beyond Truth versus Justice* (Cambridge, Cambridge University Press, 2006) 176.

## VI. CONCLUSIONS

It is under a capabilities-centred, bottom-up approach to development that the strongest links can be made to transitional justice generally, and reparations programmes in particular. Like development more broadly, reparations is a process, not a deliverable. The most important determinant of success is how things are done—that is, whether the discussion and delivery of reparations are set up in a way that makes the goals of acknowledgement, respect, the restoration of dignity and civic interest in the betterment of lives a felt reality for the survivors.

A well-designed and -implemented reparations programme can have follow-on and spill-over effects that affect longer-term development. Such a programme can help to create sustainable, culturally relevant change while addressing both root causes and the immediate needs of the survivors. While the two processes are different and should not be conflated or merged, there are a number of ways in which they can strengthen and complement each other. Indeed, care should be taken to ensure that reparations programmes complement development efforts (and related state functions), rather than duplicate them.

Post-armed conflict reconstruction and initial economic development planning will overlap with the time-frame in which reparations are being negotiated for the victims of the conflict—after the initial emergency and humanitarian aid has ended, but before a business-as-usual phase sets in. The lack of adequate provision and sequencing has meant that many reparations programmes only come about 20 or more years after the end of the violations that they are meant to redress, when both their material and symbolic effects are attenuated. It may be, however, that a time lag is inevitable, and that reparations should be conceived of as a multi-generational effort that takes into account the multi-generational effects of trauma.[36] Thus, reparations for the first generation could focus on livelihood reconstruction, psychosocial and medical assistance and dignification, while, for the second and third generations, a focus on education and social empowerment would be appropriate.

Both collective and individual reparations can contribute to dignification—or not. Collective reparations should not be automatically rejected by human rights groups or non-government organisations. Instead, they should be designed to maximise both the perception that victims are contributing to their community and the ability of victims' and survivors' groups to establish priorities for social spending. While individual reparations are important, they need not be entirely, or even mostly, made up of a one-time cash award. In particular, periodic pensions, in-kind restitution of domestic animals, housing materials, seed and tools may have more positive effects in rural communities. Conversely, reparations must have at least some individualised component to fulfil its goals—the provision of basic services, no matter how needed or how well executed, will not serve the same functions.

Reparations cannot, and should not, replace long-term development strategies. But they can be designed to be the initial 'victim-friendly' face of the state, creating habits of trust and rights possession among their target population that will set the stage for a more positive long-term interaction between the state and a sizeable group of its citizens.

---

[36] For a discussion of the multigenerational effects of genocide, repression and other trauma see, generally, Y Danieli (ed), *International Handbook of Multigenerational Legacies of Trauma* (New York, Springer, 1998).

# 11

# *Making History or Making Peace: When Prosecutions Should Give Way to Truth Commissions and Peace Negotiations**

## MARTHA MINOW

NOTIONS OF FUNDAMENTAL human rights help people to name and to respond to mass atrocities. The rhetoric of 'rights' implies an institutional structure of adjudication for enforcement, but sometimes neither criminal prosecution nor civil litigation suits the scope of the harms or the needs of the community. Severe human suffering is incommensurate with the instruments of rights enforcement. Asked about justice after serving as a witness at an international criminal tribunal following the killing of her husband and two sons, one woman said, 'How can you measure justice against all that I have suffered?'[1]

Commissions of inquiry, exemplified by the South African Truth and Reconciliation Commission (TRC), offer an alternative to criminal and civil litigation for expressing community condemnation of human rights violations.[2] Commissions of inquiry afford opportunities for naming perpetrators, hearing from survivors and reporting on larger societal patterns which have contributed to the degradation and terrorisation of large numbers of people. Truth commissions can prompt monetary and symbolic reparations, educational programmes, memorials and projects to strengthen democratic institutions; such commissions put the victims and survivors at the centre of attention and seek to restore their dignity and produce enduring acknowledgement of their

* Thanks to Taki Flevaris and Matt Perault for research assistance. This draws in part on M Minow, 'Instituting Universal Human Rights Law: The Invention of Tradition in the Twentieth Century' in A Sarat, B Garth and RA Kagan (eds), *Looking Back at Law's Century* (Ithaca NY, Cornell University Press, 2002).

[1] Quoted in E Stover, 'Witnesses and the Promise of Justice in The Hague' in E Stover and HM Weinstein (eds), *My Neighbor, My Enemy: Justice and Community in the Aftermath of Mass Atrocity* (Cambridge, Cambridge University Press, 2004) 104, 115.

[2] See RA Wilson, *The Politics of Truth and Reconciliation in South Africa* (Cambridge, Cambridge University Press, 2001); M Minow, *Between Vengeance and Forgiveness: Facing History after Genocide and Mass Violence* (Boston MA, Beacon Press, 1998); C Villa-Vicencio and W Verwoerd, *Looking Back, Reaching Forward: Reflections on the Truth and Reconciliation Commission of South Africa* (London, Zed Books, 2000). The burgeoning literature on truth commissions includes these useful overviews: M Freeman, *Truth Commissions and Procedural Fairness* (Cambridge, Cambridge University Press, 2006); N Roht-Arriaza and J Mariezcurrena (eds), *Transitional Justice in the Twenty-first Century: Beyond Truth versus Justice* (Cambridge-New York, Cambridge University Press, 2006).

suffering. To achieve the goals of shaping collective memory and building a cultural commitment to condemning torture, politically motivated rape and murder, and other crimes against humanity, a commission of inquiry offers genuine strengths. Moreover, the emphasis on hearing victims' stories and placing them in larger collective narratives of remembrance makes truth commissions potentially able to provide immediate and personal gestures of respect for human dignity.[3]

Yet, if pursued as a substitute for criminal prosecution or civil litigation, truth commissions may seem inadequate, for they fail to exact punishment, they do not pin down individual responsibility and they do not formally enforce human rights norms. Especially, given the trade of amnesty for testimony modelled by the TRC, truth commissions may seem to be a pale and disappointing compromise that water down, rather than strengthen, human rights. Moreover, truth commissions seem better at assembling facts than producing common understanding, reconciliation or social change.[4]

Commentators, in recent years, have repeatedly listed the strengths and limitations of both commissions of inquiry and human rights trials, without developing analytic steps for matching the institutional response with the needs of the community. Even when a nation proceeds with both trials and truth commissions, the decision-makers often lack clarity concerning what goals each mechanism is to accomplish, and hence, the scope of each.[5] Clarity requires weighing what might be contrasting priorities for the local, most directly affected society and the 'international community'.

When weighing priorities, decision-makers encounter potential conflict between peace and accountability. Framed in these terms, it may seem that human rights require accountability, rather than peace.[6] Indeed, the choice between trials and truth commissions seems to echo the potential choice presented to an international prosecutor by a target of investigation. Luis Moreno-Ocampo, the first prosecutor of the International Criminal Court, asked an audience of 400 lawyers and teachers what they would do if a target of investigation for crimes against humanity requested to postpone prosecution—not even to forgo it—so that the targeted political leader could negotiate peace in a region of conflict.[7] Human rights advocates are likely to view this as an unaccep-

---

[3] See, generally, Roht-Arriaza and Mariezcurrena, ibid.

[4] N Roht-Arriaza, 'The New Landscape of Transitional Justice' in ibid; Mariezcurrena, n 2 above, 1.

[5] See CW Ling, 'Forgiveness and Punishment in Post-conflict Timor' (2005) 10 *UCLA Journal of International Law & Foreign Affairs* 297; WA Schabas, 'The Sierra Leone Truth and Reconciliation Commission' in Roht-Arriaza and Mariezcurrena, n 2 above, 21, 35.

[6] The grant of blanket amnesty to alleged perpetrators is an extreme measure, sometimes pursued in the name of peace, but at times reflecting the political power of the perpetrators and their supporters. If granted with conditions, such as participation in a truth commission, amnesties may play a role in social reconstruction.

[7] Remarks of L Moreno-Ocampo, 'Pursuing Human Dignity, Facing History and Ourselves', Harvard Law School Facing History Conference, 4 November 2005. The audience was evenly and vigorously divided over the question. The Office of the Prosecutor released a statement on 12 July 2006 noting that the 'Ugandan Minister for Security, Mr Amana Mbabazi, was here as part of a regular exchange between the Office of the Prosecutor and the Government of Uganda. The Office of the Prosecutor was updated on the peace talks currently underway in Southern Sudan. The Government of Uganda did not ask for any withdrawal of the warrants of arrest.' ICC-OTP-20061712–149-En. The Global Policy Forum explains: 'In 1987, J Kony formed the Lord's Resistance Army (LRA), claiming to seek the establishment of a Ugandan national government based on Christian principles and the Ten Commandments. Over the course of its existence, the LRA has killed thousands of civilians, and abducted an estimated 20,000 children, forcing them to be sex slaves and child soldiers. In January 2004, Ugandan President Yoweri Museveni became the first head of state to refer a case in his country to the ICC. While this was a historic moment for the Court,

table option, inviting a sacrifice of principle for practical improvement of conditions. Yet peace, if secured, may provide more immediate and personal benefits for human dignity than the pursuit of litigation would in the midst of conflict. Freedom from the risk of violence simply offers more safety and liberty than continued violent conflict does.[8] Many people think that it would wrongly sacrifice justice to limit prosecutions and turn to a truth commission even in a setting such as early twenty-first century Northern Ireland, following the long-sought-after negotiated end of the violent 'troubles'.[9] Perhaps forgoing prosecutions seems to be an undue sacrifice of justice because it may involve admitting that there are more cases than the system can handle, or acknowledging that the negotiated peace depends, in part, on the continuing participation of key individuals who would otherwise be targets of prosecution.

Yet the embrace of peace and negotiated power-sharing are genuine accomplishments not to be underestimated in the face of decades of deadly violence, terrorist attacks, mass imprisonment, hunger strikes and failed peace negotiations. Should the international community condemn Northern Ireland if it does not pursue prosecutions against domestic human rights abuses? Even raising the question risks neglecting the courage and the difficult steps, and the fragility of the peace negotiations, and could jeopardise the practical transformation of daily life that those negotiations produced, ending the long-standing conflict and ensuring safety and decency for individuals and families previously living in fear of escalating violence and abuse. Even though institutional innovations like truth commissions expose the continuing weakness in human rights enforcement, they signal real regard for the dignity and interests of people. In this light, seeming trade-offs between peace and justice may be better understood as contrasts between unsentimental respect for human life and safety, and their abstract idealisation. Basic acknowledgement of human safety and coexistence can, consistent with human rights, trump even the justifiable outrage over the murder and bombing of civilians. While many nations pursue both trials and truth commissions—simultaneously or in a series—or truth commissions instead of trials, the distinctive relationship between human rights and each institutional response warrants close consideration.[10]

## I. THE EMERGENCE OF LEGAL RESPONSES TO MASS ATROCITY

After World War II, the Allies followed their wartime identities as the upholders of democracy and the rule of law with the International Military Tribunal trials in Nuremberg and Tokyo. In so doing, the Allies used the model of domestic criminal

---

the continuation of LRA violence has complicated the case in Uganda. ICC investigators have been slowed by ongoing debates over the merits of seeking justice in a society where peace still does not exist, and whether or not Ugandans should rely on methods of traditional justice, rather than international criminal trials. In October 2005, the ICC reignited these debates when it issued indictments for five of the top LRA officers. The articles and documents below track these and other issues facing the ICC investigations in Uganda.' Available at: http://www.globalpolicy.org/intljustice/icc/ugandaindex.htm.

[8] For specific discussion of these issues, see MJ Guembe and H Olea, 'No Justice, No Peace: Discussion of a Legal Framework Regarding the Demobilization of Non-state Armed Groups in Colombia' in Roht-Arriaza and Mariezcurrena, n 2 above, 120, 126–35, 138–39.

[9] Remarks of Rory Brady, former Attorney General of Ireland, Harvard Law School, 11 July 2007.

[10] See Roht-Arriaza, n 4 above, 9 (discussing the simultaneous use of truth commissions and trials in Sierra Leone and East Timor, and their sequential use in the former Yugoslavia).

prosecution to articulate and enforce human rights norms, at the same time enlarging the content of these norms with crimes against humanity and genocide as new articulations.

By the 1950s, the UN undertook efforts to codify the principles of the Nuremberg and Tokyo trials. Even though contemporaneous critics characterised the trials as the victors' travesties of justice, over time, the trials received credit for helping to launch an international movement in support of human rights. This movement pushed forward the notion that individual defendants can, and should, be held responsible and punished for violating human rights norms, including crimes against humanity and genocide. The trial process stood out as a recognised vehicle for collecting factual accounts, building a historical record and supplying a basis for punishment. With its dramatic live testimony, the criminal trial could also host public accounts of what happened, who was responsible and why it should be condemned.

But cold war politics chilled proposals for a permanent international criminal court. A leader in the Nuremberg and Tokyo efforts, the US pressed on the brakes during the 1950s, 1960s and 1970s, especially as it became a potential target for charges of war crimes in Vietnam. Individual countries pursued the criminal justice approach to human rights violations; Germany, France Canada, and Israel pursued trials of Nazi figures. Nevertheless, the absence of a permanent international criminal court meant silence in response to mass murders in Cambodia, South Africa, Kurdistan, and elsewhere.

International law continued to formalise many human rights norms during this post-war period; the Hague and Geneva Conventions and the two Protocols of 1977 both reflected and energised an emerging international human rights consciousness. Yet the model of criminal justice languished until the US and other Western nations found themselves unable and unwilling to intervene militarily in the cascading violence in the former Yugoslavia. National leaders and advocates from non-governmental organisations pressed for action, and the UN established an International Criminal Tribunal for the former Yugoslavia (ICTY) in 1992, after invoking a generous interpretation of its authority to respond to threats to international peace and security (the conflict was generally viewed as internal to one collapsing nation). The UN authorised a similar ad hoc tribunal (ICTR) after the embarrassment of global inaction leading up to the genocide in Rwanda. The prosecutions pursued by the ICTY developed and applied human rights norms, but also revealed the real difficulties posed by international criminal prosecutions: (i) having the ability to find and arrest the key perpetrators; (ii) managing the time and money needed to mount the legal and evidentiary prosecutions with responsible and competent prosecutors, investigators and defence counsel; (iii) dealing with the vulnerability of the adversarial process to being hijacked by a prominent defendant's delays, drama and insistence on proceeding without counsel; and (iv) translating collective international conflicts into the framework of individual criminal responsibility. The ICTR, located in Arusha, Tanzania, produced notable convictions—including the first one to name rape as a war crime—but also confronted sharp criticisms for its sluggishness, its physical remoteness from Rwanda, its confusing relationship with domestic prosecutions proceeding in Rwanda and its cost.

Given these origins, recent efforts to pursue international criminal prosecutions for human rights violations appear, to many, as a distant second-best response when the US and other countries have failed to halt mass atrocity. Unable or unwilling to intervene to stop mass killings and rapes, the international community will sponsor trials after the fact. Supporters hope that international criminal tribunals will create official records of human rights violations, produce public acknowledgement of violations, and locate individuals to blame and punish. The structure of individualised prosecutions can also clarify that others of the same ethnicity, religion or background did not commit violations and thus should not be swept up in a wave of guilt by association. Fundamentally, the tribunals are meant to give palpability to the ideals of human rights, while locating violations in the past, rather than in a never-ending present.

However, in practice, the tribunals are marked by slow progress, cumbersome procedures and widespread uncertainty about their effectiveness. Convictions, a long time coming, enforce both traditional and newly named human rights, but may do little to alter the day-to-day experience of the victims and the survivors. The capacity to deter mass human rights violations is unclear at best, and even the capacity to pursue and punish large numbers of perpetrators is limited.

Nonetheless, the ad hoc international criminal tribunals produced enough support to revive plans for a permanent International Criminal Court (ICC). In 1998, 120 of the world's nations—but not the US—voted to create such a court. Designed to have jurisdiction over genocide, crimes against humanity, war crimes, and the crime of aggression, the ICC is also meant to co-operate with, and not displace, domestic justice systems. The Court actually took effect in the summer of 2002, after 60 nations signed the authorising treaty, and even in its initial years, pursued notable investigations and received referrals from nations and from the UN Security Counsel.[11]

The ICC could become a vehicle for generating reputable and regularised prosecutions for human rights violations. It could produce public records that cut through the myths and distortions spawned by repressive regimes. It could, of course, become the subject of politicised bickering or it could become bogged down in procedural wrangling, and it could become a place of technical expertise and debate such that it has little effect on public memory or deeper articulations of human rights. Given that its jurisdiction is limited to instances in which the domestic regime fails to pursue action, it may, over time, generate greater capacity within member states to pursue human rights violations. But such results will take years, if not decades, to be realised.[12] In the

---

[11] As of summer 2007, the Prosecutor was pursuing an investigation of alleged mass killings and rapes in the Central African Republic between 2002 and 2003, arising during the armed conflict between the government and rebel forces. The Court's Pre-Trial Chamber issued arrest warrants upon finding reasonable grounds to believe Ahmad Harun, State Minister of the Interior for the Government of the Sudan and head of the 'Darfur Security desk', and militia/Janjaweed lea Ali Kushayb were responsible for murder, rape, torture, the forced displacement of entire villages, other war crimes and crimes against humanity in Darfur between 2003 and 2004. It also issued arrest warrants for Joseph Kony, the leader of Lord's Resistance Army in Uganda, and four LRA lieutenants based upon charges that they orchestrated the killing of thousands of civilians and the enslavement of thousands more children over two decades of conflict with Ugandan President Yoweri Museveni's government. Further, it confirmed charges against Lubanga Dyilo for individual criminal responsibility, under Art 25(3)(a) of the Rome Statute, for war crimes in the Democratic Republic of the Congo with the war crime of enlisting children under the age of 15; the war crime of conscription of children under the age of 15; and the war crime of using children under the age of 15 to participate actively in hostilities. See the International Criminal Court's website, at http://www.icc-cpi.int/cases.html.
[12] The use of hybrid tribunals, combining international presence with domestic participants, is one variant pursued as an alternative to ICC action—but is also spurred by the ICC's presence as an impending alternative should the domestic legal system fail to act. See S Katzenstein, 'Hybrid Tribunals: Searching for Justice in East Timor' (2003) 16 *Harvard Human Rights Journal* 245.

meantime, the ICC, like the ad hoc tribunals, invites characterisation as a symbolic, but ineffective, tool for international human rights. The *New York Times Magazine*, for example, devoted a cover story to the ICC titled, 'If Not Peace, Then Justice'.[13] The story begins:

> The UN is not going to stop the genocide in Darfur. The African Union is not going to stop the genocide in Darfur. The US is not going to stop the genocide in Darfur. NATO is not going to stop the genocide in Darfur. The European Union is not going to stop the genocide in Darfur. But someday, Luis Moreno-Ocampo is going to bring those who committed the genocide to justice.[14]

Litigation beyond criminal trials may also enforce human rights. Civil actions filed in the US under the Alien Tort Claim Act and the Torture Victim Protection Act can prompt media inquiry as well as adversarial fact-finding into charges of human rights violations by officials, groups, and corporations.[15] These actions face legal and practical obstacles, but can produce judicial and media investigations highlighting human rights abuses around the world.

## II. TRUTH COMMISSIONS

Prior to the development of the ad hoc tribunals and the permanent ICC, nations such as Chile, Cambodia and Uganda suffered terrifying incidents of terror and violence without the subsequent domestic political will or confidence to prosecute human rights violators. Domestic barriers proved especially pronounced in nations where the violence was chronic and pervasive. Advocates seeking to articulate and enforce human rights pursued reporting by non-governmental organisations and journalists, and also developed commissions of inquiry exposing and documenting torture, murders and other human rights violations that would otherwise have been denied and covered up by repressive regimes.[16]

The leading example resulted from a secret investigation led by courageous journalists and religious leaders. The Brazilian report, *Brasil: Nunca Mais* [*Brazil: Never Again*],[17] in many ways inspired truth commission inquiries that took more public forms elsewhere. This report documented 144 political murders, 125 disappearances and over 1,800 incidents of torture. Its summary volume became a best-seller and

---

[13] E Rubin, 'If Not Peace, Then Justice', *New York Times Magazine*, 2 April 2006, cover, 42. See K Anderson, 'Review Essay: Goodbye to All That? A Requiem for Neoconservatism' (2007) 22 *American University International Law Review* 277, 331 (describing this *New York Times* story as 'perhaps its saddest cover story in years').

[14] Rubin, ibid, cover.

[15] The first such effort was *Filartiga v Pena-Irala*, 630 F2d 876 (2d cir 1980). In 2007, the American Civil Liberties Union and the British human rights charity Reprieve filed suit in California on 31 May against logistics consulting company Jeppesen Dataplan Inc with claims that the company aided the Central Intelligence Agency in transporting terrorism suspects to settings outside the US where they faced torture or degrading and inhumane interrogation in violation of international human rights. See B Mongoven, 'The Alien Tort Claims Act: An Activist Tool for Change, Stratfor, 7 June 2007', available at http://www.stratfor.com/products/premium/read_article.php?id=289914.

[16] Some definitions require an inquiry to be official—and sanctioned by the state—to count as a truth commission. See Freeman, n 2 above, 18.

[17] The unofficial report by the Commission of Inquiry investigating the systematic use of torture based on military trial transcripts between 1964 and 1979.

produced enormous public reaction, contributing largely to Brazil's early adoption of the United Nations Convention against Torture in 1985. The UN then itself sponsored the creation of a truth commission for El Salvador. This more public effort gathered evidence that otherwise might have been destroyed or suppressed, but it did not generate a widespread national acknowledgement of the human rights violations.

Other inquiries have collected testimony from survivors and issued public reports tracing the causes of periods of mass atrocity. The most dramatic example is South Africa's TRC, created by the first democratically elected parliament after the nation negotiated a peaceful transition from apartheid. Because this negotiated peace included a promise to launch a process for granting amnesty to participants in past conflicts, the TRC established a committee to receive applications from individuals seeking amnesty. It gave amnesty to only a few hundred of the over 9,000 applicants, stringently applying the statutory requirements that applicants tell the whole truth of their violations, which must have been committed solely for political purposes and only using means commensurate with those purposes. The TRC also used a separate human rights committee to collect statements from the survivors of violence on all sides of the preceding conflicts. Some 22,000 offered statements. Many people testified in public hearings that were broadcast around the nation.

Spawning controversy—especially among the opponents of the amnesty process—the TRC nonetheless provided vivid and unforgettable proof of human rights violations that had long been denied by members of the apartheid government. It also gave voice to survivors of violence at the hands of secret police, other government officials and opposition groups. Ultimately producing a five-volume report as well as memorable national broadcasts of live testimony, the TRC most remarkably indicated the possibility of making public the names and conduct of human rights violators without unleashing vigilante revenge against them. Individual survivors received some solace in gaining acknowledgement from the government and the watching nation and world, and also gained facts from exhumed mass graves, government files and amnesty applications concerning who ordered what, who killed whom, what exactly was the instrument of torture and where the loved one's bones now lie.

The TRC included sector-wide inquiries into the roles of the business community, the judiciary, the medical profession and the mass media. The final report offered analyses of the contributions of these larger factors to the perpetuation of human rights abuses and to the maintenance of a system that dehumanised and demoralised the majority of the population. Investigations of the uses of violence by the African National Congress and other resistance groups produced condemnations of their use of force in the final report, but the report clearly treated the abuses committed by the government, in the name of the people, as the more severe wrong.

The TRC received accolades but also critiques from both domestic and international audiences. The absence of criminal punishment—and the granting of amnesty—offended many who found this an unacceptable trade of justice for truth-telling.[18]

---

[18] A constitutional challenge to that effect failed before the South African Constitutional Court. See *Azapo v President of the Republic of South Africa*, CCT 17/96, Constitutional Court, 25 July 1996. See also A Neier, *War Crimes: Brutality, Genocide, Terror, and the Struggle for Justice* (New York, Times Books, 1998); RI Rotberg and D Thompson (eds), *Truth v Justice: The Morality of Truth Commissions* (Princeton, NJ, Princeton University Press, 2000); CL Sriram, *Confronting Past Human Rights Violations: Justice vs. Peace in Times of Transition* (New York, Frank Cass, 2004).

Other critics charged that the TRC was itself a kind of oppressive witch-hunt, lacking the protection of adversarial hearings and the presumption of innocence. Supporters emphasised the possibility of a path to reconciliation, rather than hostility, and evoked both religious views and a cultural tradition of humane inclusion. One empirical study reported that those who accepted the work of the TRC were more likely than those who did not also to report relative reconciliation with the past.[19]

Domestic and international advocates pressed for truth commissions in Bosnia, Cambodia, Rwanda, Sierra Leone, East Timor, Northern Ireland and the Middle East, and in sub-national settings, including Greensboro, North Carolina. In some cases—where there are too many people to prosecute, or too much time has passed for reliable and admissible evidence to be found—a truth commission may appear more feasible than criminal prosecutions, but still seem like a second-best solution.[20] In other circumstances—when complex and multiparty conflicts persisted over many years, where oppression produced silence and denial about mass atrocity or where the courts themselves were associated with the oppression—a truth commission may seem more promising than criminal or civil litigation as a means for digging out the broad historical causes of human rights violations or for advancing respect and restoration of the human rights of victims.

The Cambodian Documentation Center's work in gathering testimony and other evidence helped to build pressure for a tribunal and preserved evidence for it, and at the same time explored broad historical inquiry into the context of the atrocity.[21] Even as a tribunal finally gets underway to address the decades-old mass killings in Cambodia, a truth commission might offer public acknowledgement and a broader inquiry into the causes of the genocidal Khmer Rouge regime.[22] The Iranian Human Rights Documentation Center collects evidence and issues reports both to promote acknowledgement of decades-long human rights violations and to prepare materials should a tribunal ever become possible.[23] In Greensboro, North Carolina, in the US, a commission of inquiry issued a report into targeted killings by the Ku Klux Klan after criminal trials proved unavailing.[24] After the report emerged, a successful civil lawsuit generated more public education and accountability.[25]

A truth commission may be deployed during the same time that litigation addressing the mass atrocity proceeds.[26] In this case, co-ordination between the two tracks requires careful consideration of timing, shared information and fair process[27]—and

---

[19] JL Gibson, 'Moves toward Democracy: Overcoming Apartheid: Can Truth Reconcile a Divided Nation?' (2006) 603 *Annals* 82. See also Stover and Weinstein, n 1 above.

[20] See Ling, n 5 above, 297.

[21] See Cambodian Documentation Center, www.*dccam.org*.

[22] K Sok, 'Documenting the Truth Khmer Institute', available at *www.khmerinstitute.org/articles/art10.html*.

[23] The author has been on the board of the Iranian Human Rights Documentation Center since its founding. For its activities and reports see *www.iranhrdc.org*.

[24] For a description of the commission and access to its report see www.greensborotrc.org.

[25] SA Bermanzohn, *Through Survivors' Eyes: From the Sixties to the Greensboro Massacre* (Nashville, TN, Vanderbilt University Press, 2003).

[26] For an examination of this pattern in Sierra Leone see Schabas, n 5 above, 21, 35.

[27] For a discussion of problems if the relationship between a tribunal and a truth commission is not clarified in advance see A Tejan-Cole, 'The Complementary and Conflicting Relationship between the Special Court for Sierra Leone and the Truth and Reconciliation Commission' (2003) 6 *Yale Human Rights & Development Law Journal* 139.

concerted efforts to clarify to the watching public the distinctive tasks and practices of the truth commission and the trials.[28] In Sierra Leone, early accounts indicate that the truth commission effectively focused on the 'small fry' perpetrators—including child soldiers—while the Special Court directed its attention to the 'big fish'.[29] Simultaneous proceedings accomplished different goals and, with the help of co-operative personalities, avoided undermining each other.[30] In other contexts, a truth commission may start first and help identify the information relevant to proceeding later with criminal trials[31]—making the choice not one between truth and justice, but about which one to pursue first.[32]

## III. A TRUTH COMMISSION ALONE OR IN CONJUNCTION WITH TRIALS CAN ADVANCE HUMAN RIGHTS

Even if the sole criterion were advancing human rights, assessing when to use a truth commission raises difficult choices and, in practice, criteria of political feasibility and costs also play important roles.[33] A truth commission may be a more effective mechanism than litigation for devising a new national narrative. A commission can produce an actual document, useful for public education, or could prompt work by historians, curriculum developers, artists and others to devise cultural resources that acknowledge the sources and details of mass violations of human rights. Such an effort would have the capacity to examine the roles of multiple sectors and actors in perpetrating human rights violations.[34] If the justice sought is broad enough to entail reconstructing memory and community, these avenues could be more effective than court actions, removed from public sight and framed in adversarial terms.[35] A truth commission can give more time and space for the testimony of victims, while courts must be centred on the particular claims against defendants and, at the same time, must protect their rights. A truth commission may also equip the members of a divided society better to build a sense of national unity; to this end, South Africa's TRC addressed violations committed by all sides, promoting informal meetings of reconciliation and articulating a narrative devoted to building a shared future.

Even if it falls short of these aspirations, a truth commission can accomplish the

---

[28] See Schabas, n 5 above, 38–40. A commission may explicitly pursue restorative justice while the criminal trials stress retributive justice—and a post-conflict society may need both. See P Burgess, 'A New Approach to Restorative Justice—East Timor's Community Reconciliation Process' in Roht-Arriaza and Mariezcurrena, n 2 above, 176, 200–01.

[29] S Horovitz, 'Transitional Criminal Justice in Sierra Leone' in Roht-Arriaza and Mariezcurrena, n 2 above, 43, 54–55.

[30] Ibid, 56.

[31] See EG Cueva, 'The Peruvian Truth and Reconciliation Commission and the Challenge of Impunity' in Roht-Arriaza and Mariezcurrena, n 2 above, 70, 85–89.

[32] See E Lutz, 'Transitional Justice: Lessons Learned and the Road Ahead' in Roht-Arriaza and Mariezcurrena, n 2 above, 325, 327.

[33] See Sriram, n 18 above, identifying external influence, balance of forces among former opponents and scope of abuses as key factors in the selection of mechanisms to respond to human rights abuses, based on a study of El Salvador, Honduras, Argentina, South Africa and Sri Lanka.

[34] See J Ramji, 'Reclaiming Cambodian History: The Case for a Truth Commission' (2000) 24 *Fletcher Forum of World Affairs* 137.

[35] See HM Weinstein and E Stover, 'Introduction: Conflict, Justice, and Reclamation' in Stover and Weinstein, n 1 above, 1, 14–20.

critical task of public acknowledgement and condemnation of a violent past, and mark a national commitment to turn the corner and respect human rights. Trials can work in this same direction by articulating human rights norms and producing sanctions against a limited number of individuals for their violation. But trials are no better than truth commissions at building a culture of respect for human rights and preventing future violations. Criminal trials have not moved multi-national Bosnia towards national unity. Even though the ICTY has tried to pursue prosecutions of both Serbs and Croats, members of each group tend to view the ICTY as biased in favour of their enemies.[36] Scholars have found little evidence that human rights trials themselves promote reconciliation.[37] Nor is there evidence that criminal prosecutions console the victims of violence or help them to overcome a damaged sense of self, frozen grief and other psychological harms.[38] Testifying in a trial can be empowering to victims, but, by itself, does not produce healing.[39] The delays and financial expenses associated with criminal trials—which can often last for years and cost hundreds of thousands of dollars—may make a time-limited truth commission a more practical mechanism for highlighting human rights norms and acknowledging their violation. Neither history nor its observers have yet shown that international criminal courts deter human rights violations.[40]

The political context will affect the perceived legitimacy of criminal trials. Hence, ongoing instability and insufficient resources may make international control of a tribunal located outside the affected nation seem necessary, yet remote international trials may do more for global human rights activists than for the most directly affected victims and their neighbours. A criminal trial administered pursuant to the occupation or domination by foreign powers may fail to secure much legitimacy in any audience.[41] Yet the political context will also determine whether a truth commission can obtain the mandate, membership, and resources necessary to conduct an effective inquiry and produce a meaningful report. Indeed, unless a truth commission is guaranteed independence, public participation in the design of the commission and adequate time and resources, it should not proceed.[42] Moreover, even in the most promising context, a truth commission risks losing its legitimacy if it 'names names' without providing due process, the cross-examination of witnesses and full opportunities for defence—yet it may also seem unimpressive if it produces no assignment of responsibility for the violations. The Indonesia–Timor Leste Commission of Truth and Friendship assigned responsibility to the Indonesian military, police and civilian government for widespread and systematic gross violations of human rights, but its limited mandated excluded the first 23 years of Indonesia's invasion and occupation of Timor Leste

---

[36] Stover and Weinstein, ibid.

[37] Ibid.

[38] J O'Connell, 'Gambling with the Psyche: Does Prosecuting Human Rights Violators Console their Victims?' (2005) 46 *Harvard International Law Journal* 295.

[39] LE Fletcher and HM Weinstein, 'Violence and Social Repair: Rethinking the Contribution of Justice to Reconciliation' (2002) 24 *Human Rights Quarterly* 573.

[40] See MA Drumbl, *Atrocity, Punishment, and International Law* (Cambridge, Cambridge University Press, 2007).

[41] See J Peterson, 'Unpacking Show Trials: Situating the Trial of Saddam Hussein' (2007) 48 *Harvard International Law Journal* 257.

[42] See PB Hayner, 'Accountability for International Crime and Serious Violations of Fundamental Human Rights: International Guidelines for the Creation and Operation of Truth Commissions: A Preliminary Proposal' (1996) 59 *Law & Contemporary Problems* 173.

(during which more than 100,000 Timorese were killed). The Commission named no names of individual wrongdoers and made no recommendation for prosecution, and attracted criticism from the UN, the Catholic Church and many non-governmental organisations for its limited approach.[43]

Assistance to victims can be supplied in the context of both trials and truth commissions, but there are more opportunities in a truth commission for the victims to tell their stories without interruption and, perhaps, to have the experience of being heard and acknowledged. For some individuals and some communities, this direct experience more effectively enacts the recognition of human rights than does the focus on the defendant that criminal and civil trials create.[44] The Trust Fund for Victims of the ICC has provided concrete medical and psychological assistance even while the trial process pursuing human rights violations in the Congo lumbers slowly towards actual hearings.[45] But simply knowing the truth is not sufficient; seeing public acknowledgement, receiving an apology, obtaining compensation, and benefiting from psychological and moral support are important elements to restoring many victims' sense of dignity, well-being and respect.[46]

## IV. CONCLUSION

Responses to mass atrocity test the meaning of human rights, for anything short of full protest and denunciation may seem to condone the violence, expressing a diminution of human worth. The locution of human rights as developed largely in the West, with liberal assumptions, summons up the institutions of courts and laws; 'full protest and denunciation' seem to require criminal prosecution with punishment, or civil litigation with court-ordered remedies. Measured in terms of precedent-setting doctrine, individual punishment or court-ordered damages of trials, the processes and products of truth commissions look modest and fragile. Criminal trials and even civil litigation are more likely to enforce and extend human rights doctrine and build international institutions devoted to human rights. When a truth commission has inadequate resources or authority, it will be too compromised to accord respect and alter public memory.

Yet the realisation of human rights may take instead, or simultaneously, the path of inquiry, attention, recognition and commemoration.[47] This can be the path afforded by truth commissions; it can also be an approach that deepens the significance of trials

---

[43] See, eg Joint NGO Statement on the Handover of the Commission of Truth and Friendship Report, available at http://www.humanrightsfirst.info/pdf/080715-HRD-joint-NGO-stat-handover-comm-truth-friendship-ret.pdf.

[44] See MJ Aukerman, 'Extraordinary Evil, Ordinary Crime: A Framework for Understanding Transitional Justice' (2002) 15 *Harvard Human Rights Journal* 39; R Aldana-Pindell, 'In Vindication of Justiciable Victims' Rights to Truth and Justice for State-Sponsored Crimes' (2002) 35 *Vanderbilt Journal of Transnational Law* 1399.

[45] ICC Trust Fund for Victims Assists Kivu Rape Victims, available at www.*rnw.nl/int-justice/.../icc/DRC/090127-icc-Kivu*.

[46] See B Hamber, 'Dealing with the Past: Rights and Reasons: Challenges for Truth Recovery in South Africa and Northern Ireland' (2003) 26 *Fordham International Law Journal* 1074.

[47] See F Haldemann, 'A Different Kind of Justice: Transitional Justice as Recognition, Global Fellows Forum', 7 February 2006, available at www.nyulawglobal.org/fellowsscholars/documents/haldemannpaper.pdf.

for both the participants and the observers.[48] Indeed, societies can use both trials and truth commissions, but need then to co-ordinate them—whether to proceed simultane-ously or in a series—in order to enhance human rights enforcement, recognition and commemoration.[49]

It is in this light that it may be worth entertaining the postponement of prosecu-tion, if not its suspension altogether, in order to facilitate peace negotiations, to provide healing for victims, to explore whether a truth commission or alternative commemoration would be more effective and meaningful in the particular context, or set the society on a firmer grounding to prevent future recurrence of violence.[50] As Helena Cobban notes, 'war and conflict themselves inflict major violations on all the human rights of people living in the areas directly affected'.[51] At the same time, peace negotiated without accountability can undermine present and future peace by leaving abusers to believe that they can avoid consequences for their human rights violations.[52] The meanings of human rights initiatives to the specific community most directly affected should matter as much, if not more, than the interests of a global human rights community or the advocates that claim to speak for it. This is because human rights are meant to recognise specific and real humans, not simply an abstract ideal.

---

[48] Drafters of the Rome Statute, authorising the International Criminal Court, provided that the inter-ests of victims may justify presentation of facts even where the defendant pleads guilty. Rome Statute of the International Criminal Court, Article 65, Section 4, UN Doc A/CONF.183/9*, available at http://www.un.org/law/icc/statute/romefra.htm.

[49] Tejan-Cole, n 27 above, 139.

[50] H Cobban, *Amnesty after Atrocity?: Healing Nations after Genocide and War Crimes* (Boulder, CO, Paradigm Publishers, 2006).

[51] *Just World News*, 30 May 2005, available at http://justworldnews.org/archives/001274.html.

[52] See 'Sudan: Peace Deal Must Tackle Past Abuses', *Human Rights News*, 18 November 2004, available at http://hrw.org/english/docs/2004/11/18/sudan9684.htm.

# 12

# Transitional Justice as Global Project: Critical Reflections*

## ROSEMARY NAGY

### I. INTRODUCTION

T RANSITIONAL JUSTICE AS a field and practice has grown greatly over the last 15 years or so, including: the institution of international criminal tribunals, hybrid courts and the International Criminal Court (ICC); the development of a 'right to truth' and a 'right to reparation' under international law; the transnational proliferation of truth and reconciliation commissions; the expansion of transitional justice scholarship so that there are now a dedicated journal, research centres and academic programmes; and the birth of international and regional transitional justice non-governmental organisations. In other words, transitional justice has become a well-established fixture on the global terrain of human rights. It entails an insistence against unwilling governments that it is necessary to respond to egregious violence and atrocity. The international community provides fragile new governments with important financial, institutional and normative support for reckoning with the past, attending to the needs of victims and setting the foundations for democracy, human rights and the rule of law.

Yet there also appear worrisome tendencies of the international community to impose 'one-size-fits-all', technocratic and decontextualised solutions. To what extent does transitional justice appear from on high as the 'saviour' to the 'savagery'[1] of ethnic, especially African, 'tribal' conflict? Steeped in Western liberalism, and often located outside the area where conflict occurred, transitional justice may be alien and distant to those who actually have to live together after atrocity. It is accused of producing subjects and truths that are blind to gender and social injustice. And, in a post-9/11 world, transitional justice may increasingly be shaped by 'the appropriation of the language of "transition" and "democratization" in furtherance of an apparently global project [that has] few effective international legal constraints'.[2]

---

* An earlier version of this article was published in (2008) 29 *Third World Quarterly* 275.
[1] M Mutua, 'Savages, Victims and Saviors: The Metaphor of Human Rights' (2001) 42 *Harvard International Law Journal* 201.
[2] C Bell, C Campbell and F Ní Aoláin, 'Justice Discourses in Transition' (2004) 13 *Social & Legal Studies* 307.

All this suggests a timely need to reflect critically upon transitional justice as a global project. By 'global project', I refer to the fact that transitional justice has emerged as a body of customary international law and normative standards. I call it a 'global' project, rather than an 'international' one, in order to capture the three-dimensional landscape of transitional justice (local, national, global) and its location within broader processes of globalisation. It is a 'project' by virtue of the fairly settled consensus—a consensus that has largely moved past the initial debates of 'peace versus justice' and 'truth versus justice'—that there can be no lasting peace without some kind of accounting, and that truth and justice are complementary approaches to dealing with the past. The question today is not whether something should be done after atrocity, but how it should be done. And a professional body of international donors, practitioners and researchers assists or directs in figuring this out and implementing it.

In the first section of this chapter, I critically introduce how the scope of transitional justice is typically defined and implemented. In the remaining sections, I employ the categories of when, to whom and for what transitional justice applies in order to challenge troubling features of its standardisation. I do not wish to deny that national governments and local actors are active agents in their own transitional processes. Rather, my concern is to call attention to the ways in which their horizon of options may be channelled or streamlined. In engaging themes of gender, power and structural violence, this chapter offers a cautionary investigation of the worrying ways in which the scope of transitional justice can be depoliticised and narrowed. The reflections undertaken here are intended to be suggestive in nature and to raise questions for further research. For the sake of convenience, I presume a fairly singular (Westernised) international community, acknowledging here its rather nebulous and frequently divided nature.

## II. DEFINING THE SCOPE OF TRANSITIONAL JUSTICE

It is not often remarked that figuring out how to implement transitional justice is necessarily a task of first determining the problem. Transitional justice seeks to redress wrongdoing but, inevitably, in the face of resource, time and political constraints, this is a selective process. Transitional justice thus involves a delimiting narration of violence and remedy. This raises, as Christine Bell and Catherine O'Rourke put it, 'fundamental questions about what exactly transitional justice is transiting "from" and "to"'.[3] Although there is no single definition of transitional justice, I suggest that predominant views construct human rights violations fairly narrowly.[4] Structural and gender-based violence are excluded or marginalised. There is a privileging of legal responses which are, at times, detrimentally abstracted from the lived realities. Little

---

[3] C Bell and C O'Rourke, 'Does Feminism Need a Theory of Transitional Justice? An Introductory Essay' (2007) 1 *International Journal of Transitional Justice* 35.

[4] R Mani, *Beyond Retribution: Seeking Justice in the Shadows of War* (Malden, MA, Polity Press, 2002), provides the one of the broadest holistic approaches that incorporates distributive justice, including at the global level. But Mani also explicitly understands her approach as encompassing transitional justice rather than replacing or overthrowing it. Idem, 'Rebuilding an Inclusive Community after War' (2005) 36 *Security Dialogue*, 524.

attention, if any, is paid to the role that established Western democracies have in violence. Together, these tendencies profoundly affect the perceptions of the nature of violence, victimhood and perpetration, and they skew the direction of truth, justice and reconciliation.

According to the UN Secretary General's 2004 Report on the Rule of Law and Transitional Justice, transitional justice refers to:

> the full range of processes and mechanisms associated with a society's attempts to come to terms with a legacy of large-scale past abuses, in order to ensure accountability, serve justice and achieve reconciliation. These may include . . . individual prosecutions, reparations, truth-seeking, institutional reform, vetting and dismissals, or a combination thereof.[5]

For reasons of space, my analysis will focus on the predominant institutions—trials and truth commissions. My main concern is how the implementation of trials and truth commissions tends to structure their conceptions of violence and justice. Their implementation ought to be assessed within the context of an overarching assumption 'that a focus on legal processes is adequate to resolve individual and social harm', as Laurel Fletcher and Harvey Weinstein put it.[6] Furthermore, the privileging of legal approaches has occurred within an international climate where 'the prevalent liberal-democratic ideal . . . tends to favour freedom and liberty over equality'.[7]

The predominance of the legalist paradigm, which focuses on generating elite and mass compliance with international humanitarian norms,[8] can partly be explained by the profound need to restore the rule of law in conflict and post-conflict societies. But another reason is that law is perceived as a safe, neutral, universal way to engage with other countries.[9] Kieran McEvoy notes that law speaks to qualities such as rationality, certainty, objectivity and uniformity that are highly prized in times of social rupture. However, law's 'seductive' lure is grounded on a presumption of law as a closed system of knowledge that articulates how the world ought to be.[10] This does not see law—or its application—as infused with politics, social structures, cultural meanings and so forth. Consequently, for example, a narrow fixation on judicial mechanisms in Iraq shields analysts from asking normative questions about the illegitimacy or justifiability of the occupation or about whether 'justice' is even possible in such a context.[11] International law is 'brought' to war-torn countries, though this may be resisted, as we have recently seen with Rwanda's neo-traditional *gacaca* (community justice) courts and Uganda's call to use *mato oput* (a local reintegration ritual) and

---

[5] United Nations Secretary-General, 'Report on the Rule of Law and Transitional Justice in Conflict and Post-Conflict Societies', S/2004/616 (2004) para 8.

[6] LE Fletcher and HM Weinstein, 'Violence and Social Repair: Rethinking the Contribution of Justice to Reconciliation' (2002) 24 *Human Rights Quarterly* 584.

[7] Mani, *Beyond Retribution*, n 4 above, 151.

[8] See L Vinjamuri and J Snyder, 'Advocacy and Scholarship in the Study of International War Crimes Tribunals and Transitional Justice' (2004) 7 *Annual Review of Political Science* 347.

[9] B Oomen, 'Donor-Driven Justice and its Discontents: The Case of Rwanda' (2005) 36 *Development and Change* 893.

[10] K McEvoy, 'Letting go of Legalism: Developing a 'Thicker' Version of Transitional Justice' in K McEvoy and L McGregor (eds), *Transitional Justice from Below: Grassroots Activism and the Struggle for Change* (Oxford, Hart Publishing, 2008) 15–45.

[11] For example, E Stover, H Megally and H Mufti, 'Bremer's "Gordian Knot": Transitional Justice and the US Occupation of Iraq' in N Roht-Arriaza and J Mariezcurrena (eds), *Transitional Justice in the Twenty-First Century* (Cambridge, Cambridge University Press, 2006) 229–54, is completely agnostic on these points.

other healing mechanisms, rather than the ICC. Internationalised legal 'justice' risks being abstracted from lived realities. For instance, gendered advances in international criminal law still mean that 'any woman' could serve as a witness in landmark cases because individuals are subsumed under 'larger principles which their testimony helps establish'.[12]

In the following analysis, I point to general trends and draw on several prominent country examples to illustrate the ways in which the scope of transitional justice is channelled. These cases include the South African Truth and Reconciliation Commission (TRC) (1996–2003), which looms large on the transitional justice landscape as a model or lesson. Sierra Leone and East Timor each represent significant developments in global practice because they pair trials with truth commissions. Moreover, the Special Court for Sierra Leone (established in 2002 and still in operation) and the Special Panel for Serious Crimes in East Timor (1999–2005) are hybrid courts. Sierra Leone's Truth and Reconciliation Commission (2000–05) and East Timor's Commission for Reception, Truth and Reconciliation (2001–05) both demonstrate tentative advances in the ability of truth commissions to provide extensive accounts of gender-based violence, social injustice and external influence. Finally, Iraq and Afghanistan present troubling situations of seeking truth, justice and reconciliation in the midst of occupation and conflict.

I turn now to the categories of when, to whom and for what transitional justice applies. I argue that these categories function to hone transitional justice into a particular kind of solution to address particular kinds of problems. The focus on specific sets of actors for specific sets of crimes channels transitional justice towards a fairly narrow interpretation of violence within a somewhat artificial time-frame and to the exclusion of external actors.

## III. WHEN TRANSITIONAL JUSTICE APPLIES

The when of transitional justice is tied to the very conception of transition. Whether transiting from authoritarianism to democracy or from war to peace (to democracy), transitional justice has typically appeared salient only after massive direct violence has been brought to a halt. In part, this appearance has to do with the emphasis within the literature on prosecution, truth-telling, reparation, reconciliation and reform, and less so on peace accords, transitional administration or disarmament, demobilisation and reintegration. Transitional justice also implies a fixed interregnum period with a distinct end; it bridges between a violent or repressive past and a peaceful, democratic future. Notions of 'breaking with the past' and 'never again', which align with the dominant transitional mechanisms, mould a definitive sense of 'now' and 'then'.

This can problematically obscure continuities of violence and exclusion. For example, the efforts of the South African TRC to promote the 'new' South Africa met with considerable challenge and resistance in the face of ongoing police violations of human rights, political violence, racialised socio-economic inequalities, de facto geo-

---

[12] KM Franke, 'Gendered Subjects of Transitional Justice' (2006) 15 *Columbia Journal of Gender and Law* 813, 820.

graphic apartheid, and general racism and xenophobia.[13] More generally, to construct transition as a break with past violence also neglects the domestic violence that many women face in a militarised society and after male combatants have returned home. There is some evidence to suggest that violence against women actually increases in the 'post-conflict' period.[14] This can occur due to post-traumatic stress, due to the need of men to reassert control in their homes, which had been headed by women during the war, or due to the sense of dislocation, powerlessness and unemployment that combatants may face upon their return.[15]

In Iraq and Afghanistan, the transition has been constructed as being 'from' a repressive police state under Saddam Hussein or 'from' cycles of war and repression culminating in the Taliban regime.[16] This neatly avoids the current matter of foreign military intervention, and implies that the transitional problem has to do with 'then', and not the 'now' of occupation, insurgency and the war on terror. (And, as I discuss below, it implies that the problem has to with 'them', not 'us'.) Although prosecution, vetting, reparation and truth-telling are taking, or will take, place in the midst of violence and insecurity, the concern of these transitional mechanisms is the history prior to 2001 in Afghanistan and prior to 2003 in Iraq. The 'to' of transitional justice is thus insulated from the current reasons for and causes of instability.

Of course, with the ICC's indictments in Uganda, the DRC and Darfur, we do see prosecution being used to effect a transition in the midst of conflict. Yet the ICC is facing situations in which actual prosecution cannot take place due to the difficulties of arrest. Even if trials begin, they may have little or even a detrimental political effect. For instance, some Acholi leaders opposed the ICC's involvement in northern Uganda because they feared it would jeopardise peace talks with the Lord's Resistance Army (LRA).[17] While the ICC indictments may, perhaps, be credited with bringing the rebels to the negotiating table, international criminal justice is nonetheless seen by many Acholi as contravening traditional values. And, given the ICC's failure to seek accountability for violations committed by the Ugandan government, including massive forced removals, the 'to' of transition is only partial.

One concern with the consistent emphasis on applying transitional justice only when

---

[13] R Nagy, 'The Ambiguities of Reconciliation and Responsibility in South Africa' (2004) 52 *Political Studies* 709; K Lalloo, 'Citizenship and Place: Spatial Definitions of Oppression and Agency in South Africa' (1998) 45 *Africa Today* 439; N Valji, 'Creating the Nation: The Rise of Violent Xenophobia in the New South Africa', unpublished Masters thesis (York University, 2003), available at http://www.csvr.org.za/papers/papnv1.htm (last accessed on April 2004).

[14] C Duggan and AM Abusharaf, 'Reparation of Sexual Violence in Democratic Transitions: The Search for Gender Justice' in P de Greiff (ed), *The Handbook of Reparations* (Oxford, Oxford University Press, 2006) 627. F Ní Aoláin, 'Political Violence and Gender During Times of Transition' (2006) 15 *Columbia Journal of Gender and Law* 829, 848, notes that there may be an increase in reporting rather than in incidents.

[15] C Chinkin and H Charlesworth, 'Building Women into Peace: the International Legal Framework' (2006) 27 *Third World Quarterly* 946. See also Ní Aoláin, n 14 above.

[16] For example, see Democratic Principles Working Group, 'Iraqi Opposition Report on the Transition to Democracy' (2003) 14 *Journal of Democracy* 14; USIPeace Briefing, 'Establishing Justice and the Rule of Law in Iraq: A Blueprint for Action' (Washington, USIP, 2003), available at http://www.usip.org/pubs/usipeace_briefings/2003/0801_ESIraq_law.html; Afghanistan Independent Human Rights Commission, 'A Call for Justice' (2005), available at http://www.aihrc.org.af/Rep_29_Eng/rep29_1_05call4justice.pdf.

[17] See T Allen, *Trial Justice: The International Criminal Court and the Lord's Resistance Army* (London, Zed Books, 2006). A similar fear was voiced in 1995 when the ICTY indicted Milosevic prior to the conclusion of a diplomatic solution.

there is massive repression, conflict or war is, as Anne Orford argues, that 'the literature gives the sense that large-scale human rights violations are exceptional' and 'the
focus is not on genocide or human rights violations in liberal democratic states'.[18] She
'unsettles' this assumption by examining the 'the everydayness and bureaucratization
of genocide and of massive human rights violations' through a reading of Australia's
(1997) 'Bringing Them Home' report on the separation of Aboriginal and Torres Strait
Islander children from their families.[19] Similar examples can be found in other settler
states: in Canada, the Truth and Reconciliation Commission regarding Indian Residential Schools and the Qikiqtani Truth Commission investigating dog slaughter and
Inuit relocation, and in the US, the Maine Wabanaki Child Welfare Truth and Reconciliation Commission.[20] The use of transitional justice in these settings of consolidated
democracy, which are 'non-transitional' in a paradigmatic sense, serves to challenge
our notions of transition so as to include incremental transitions from colonial to
postcolonial states.[21]

## IV. TO WHOM TRANSITIONAL JUSTICE APPLIES

The more pressing concern, to follow on the above, has less to do with when justice
is transitional than with to whom transitional justice applies. Because transitional
justice almost always applies to non-Western developing countries, it is vulnerable to
the general challenge that critics raise against the supposed universalism of human
rights. The general thrust of this challenge is that the West arrogates the universal to
itself and then brings all others into its fold of humanity.[22] The case of Iraq is most
obviously liable to this charge. As noted above, the artificial time-frame of transitional justice applies only to Saddam's Iraq. This glosses over the illegality of the
US-led invasion, the damages caused by the corrupt UN oil-for-food programme, the
ongoing insurgency, and the human rights abuses committed by American soldiers at
Abu Ghraib and elsewhere. Furthermore, as David Chandler writes, when Paul Bremer
created the Iraqi Special Tribunal:

> Commentators everywhere insisted on the importance of a fair trial, on 'justice being seen
> to be done,' not so much for Saddam's benefit as for the political and educational benefit
> of the Iraqi people. Implicit in this discussion was the idea that the Iraqi people could not
> move on without a thorough accounting of the past; that without this process there were
> not ready for the freedom their Western liberators offered them. Here responsibility for
> chronic violence and instability of the Iraqi people was shifted away from the actions of the
> intervening powers and placed with the psychological immaturity of the Iraqi people.[23]

[18] A Orford, 'Commissioning the Truth' (2006) 15 *Columbia Journal of Gender and Law* 863.
[19] Ibid, 854.
[20] There is also the Greensboro (North Carolina) Truth Commission on civil rights violence in that town in 1979.
[21] See R Nagy, 'The Scope and Bounds of Transitional Justice and the Canadian Truth and Reconciliation Commission' (2013) 7(1) *International Journal of Transitional Justice* 52.
[22] See E Darian-Smith and P Fitzpatrick, 'Laws of the Postcolonial: An Insistent Introduction' in idem (eds), *Laws of the Postcolonial* (Ann Arbor, MI, University of Michigan Press, 2002) 1–15.
[23] D Chandler, *Empire in Denial: The Politics of State-Building* (London, Pluto, 2006) 172.

Prosecution and other transitional mechanisms were put in place to teach Iraqis, and not America or its allies, about the rule of law and human rights.

Neither paternalism nor asymmetry is confined to the Iraqi case. Charges of paternalism have been voiced, for example, regarding the transitional administrations run by the international Peace Implementation Council in Bosnia-Herzegovina, and by the UN in East Timor. The different High Representatives to Bosnia have used their sweeping authority to impose legislation that was rejected by democratically elected parliamentarians, to ban political parties, and dismiss elected officials.[24] In East Timor, Anne Orford documents how post-colonial reconstruction treats the country as a 'blank slate in terms of existing knowledge and experience, marked by cronyism, incompetence and corruption. The people of East Timor are portrayed as lacking a state, ethics, skills and respect for human rights'.[25] Suzanne Katzenstein notes that, in the building of the Special Panels for Serious Crimes, 'many East Timorese in the judiciary felt sidelined by the UN staff', due to lack of consultation on institutional design. Mentoring programmes quickly disintegrated when UN personnel entirely took over the tasks at hand, and East Timorese became 'sick of internationals coming in and conducting "workshops"'.[26]

As for the asymmetrical features of globalised transitional justice, these go right back to the Nuremburg precedent of victor's justice. Alongside the Ugandan case noted above, victor's justice has prevailed in the ICTY's refusal to investigate alleged violations of international humanitarian law committed by NATO during its bombing campaign in Kosovo, and in the ICTR's halted investigation of the governing Rwandan Patriotic Front for war crimes. Furthermore, geographic 'zones of impunity'[27] are being created due to the state-centric nature of international law. For instance, the ICC does not apply to non-state parties except in the instance of Security Council referral, which will inevitably be limited by veto politics. There is also the US's active campaign against the ICC. Over 100 countries, some of which have poor human rights records and have shown little ability or interest in domestic criminal procedures, have been induced by the US to sign bilateral agreements refusing extradition to the ICC.

Third country prosecution can overcome the jurisdictional limits of other institutions or domestic amnesties. But, as Christiane Wilke points out, the universality of 'justice without borders' is fairly particularistic: 'either some of the victims have the citizenship of the prosecuting state, or the perpetrators (and some of the victims) are physically present in the country'.[28] The result is highly uneven, globally speaking: the likelihood of pursuing justice is largely confined to liberal democracies that have the resources and political interest to mount a case. And even when a case is mounted, the challenges of extradition and the lining up of different legal systems can result in a watering down of charges, as seen when the British House of Lords reduced Spain's

---

[24] A Orford, *Reading Humanitarian Intervention: Human Rights and the Use of Force in International Law* (Cambridge, Cambridge University Press, 2003); Chandler, ibid.

[25] Ibid, 139.

[26] S Katzenstein, 'Hybrid Tribunals: Searching for Justice in East Timor' (2003) 16 *Harvard Human Rights Journal* 245, 256.

[27] CL Sriram and A Ross, 'Geographies of Crimes and Justice: Contemporary Transitional Justice and the Creation of "Zones of Impunity"' (2007) 1 *International Journal of Transitional Justice* 45.

[28] C Wilke, 'A Particular Universality: Universal Jurisdiction for Crimes against Humanity in Domestic Courts' (2005) 12 *Constellations* 84.

draft charges against General Pinochet from thirty to three.[29] (And, of course, Jack Straw let Pinochet go home.)

International criminal justice also appears frequently unable to respond to violent conflict that spills across borders. Currently, as Chandra Lekha Sriram and Amy Ross explain, the ICC is mandated to investigate human rights violations in northern Uganda but not LRA activities in southern Sudan or support by the Sudanese government of the LRA during Sudan's North–South civil war. The ICC has no jurisdiction in Sudan except for in Darfur, and only over Sudanese nationals there.[30] As another example, Charles Taylor did not face trial for crimes he committed in Liberia, his own country, or neighbouring Côte d'Ivoire because the Special Court for Sierra Leone does not have extraterritorial jurisdiction.[31]

The pursuit of transitional justice in East Timor is especially illustrative of zones of impunity. From 1974 to 1999, the people of East Timor suffered death and destruction under the illegal Indonesian occupation, with violence culminating during the 1999 plebiscite on autonomy. Under the subsequent United Nations Transitional Administration (UNTAET), the Serious Crimes Investigative Unit was created to investigate and prosecute crimes at the Special Panel for Serious Crimes (comprised of two international and one East Timorese judge). Although Indonesia and UNTAET signed a memorandum of understanding regarding the exchange of evidence, the Serious Crimes Unit was unable to gain access to Indonesian suspects, and thus those with the 'greatest responsibility' remained beyond the reach of the Dili-based court.[32] The UN did not set up a process to address those responsible in Indonesia, indicating that Indonesia is obligated to do so. Under severe pressure, the Indonesian government established an ad hoc court to deal with violations in East Timor, but it convicted only one (Timorese) perpetrator, acquitted all of the Indonesians, and some military officers implicated in atrocities have actually been promoted.[33]

The Indonesian president's treatment of East Timor independence as a national humiliation,[34] combined with the limited mandate of East Timor's hybrid court, have resulted in a 'near universal perception within Indonesia that the 1999 violence was the result of conflict between two opposing East Timorese factions, rather than a military-orchestrated terror campaign'.[35] But the problem is not simply Indonesia's intransigence. The problem also lies with the international community. Hybrid courts are touted as a means of doing 'justice on the cheap', and there was a widespread perception among the East Timorese that the international community did not care about their plight.[36] Indeed, the Special Panel was shut down in 2005 due to lack of

[29] F Webber, 'The Pinochet Case: The Struggle for the Realization of Human Rights' (1999) 26 *Journal of Law and Society* 523.

[30] Sriram and Ross, n 27 above, 57.

[31] Ibid, 59.

[32] See CL Sriram, *Globalizing Justice for Mass Atrocities: A Revolution in Accountability* (London, Routledge, 2005); Human Rights Watch, 'East Timor: UN Security Council Must Ensure Justice', *Human Rights News*, 29 June 2005, available at http://hrw.org/english/docs/2005/06/28/eastti11231.htm (last accessed on 30 July 2007).

[33] Human Rights Watch, 'Justice Denied for East Timor' (2004), available at http://www.hrw.org/backgrounder/asia/timor/etimor1202bg.htm.

[34] Ibid.

[35] J Nevins, 'Restitution over Coffee: Truth, Reconciliation and Environmental Justice in East Timor' (2003) 22 *Political Geography* 684.

[36] Sriram, n 32 above, 88.

international political and donor support. (The UN Secretary-General has since recommended the resumption of the tribunal's investigative functions, but not judicial functions.) The UN Commission of Experts recommended in its 2005 report that an international tribunal be established under Chapter VII of the UN Charter if Indonesia's 'manifestly inadequate' ad hoc courts do not improve.[37] Yet, even if an international tribunal were created, which appears unlikely, it would not address the broader injustices of occupation and exploitation. It would say little about Australian, American, British and Japanese support of Indonesia's occupation, or how Indonesian control and impoverishment of the East Timor coffee sector (a major reason for the occupation) fit into cold war politics and volatile price shifts after 1989.[38]

Thus, the East Timor situation points to a further concern that transitional justice operates in such a way that 'the international community is absent from the scene of violence and suffering until it intervenes as the heroic saviour'.[39] Foreign involvement in violence—through indifference, funding, training, cross-border raids or conflict economies in arms, diamonds or oil—is largely absent from, or negligible in, the official transitional justice records. This occurs most starkly with prosecution because trials create rather individualised accounts of human rights crimes. Truth commissions are better equipped to paint the larger picture of violence. For the most part, however, truth commissions do not investigate the role of outside actors in internal human rights violations.[40] In recent exceptions, the Sierra Leone truth commission has addressed the role of foreign actors in the conflict quite extensively, including Liberia's Charles Taylor, Libya, the diamond industry and the international community, which abandoned Sierra Leone in its hours of need. And, to return to the East Timor case discussed above, the Commission for Reception, Truth and Reconciliation (CAVR) holds the international community accountable for providing military backing to the Indonesian government and holds Indonesia and other states liable for reparation.

## V. TO WHAT TRANSITIONAL JUSTICE APPLIES

Even when truth commissions do investigate the role of outside actors—and the majority do not—their primary focus is the direct perpetrators and direct victims of crimes against humanity and violations of international humanitarian law. The issue, therefore, is not only to whom transitional justice applies, but also to what it applies. By and large, transitional justice pertains to genocide, torture, disappearance, massacre, sexual violence and other war crimes. In the privileging of legalistic approaches, transitional justice tends to focus on gross violations of civil and political rights (arbitrary or indefinite detention, severe assault, ill-treatment, etc) or criminal acts (the destruction of property, the abuse of children, etc). Consequently, structural violence and social injustice are peripheral in the 'from' and 'to' of transitional justice.

---

[37] UN Commission of Experts, Summary of the Report to the Secretary-General of the Commission of Experts to Review the Prosecution of Serious Violations of Human Rights in Timor-Leste (Then East Timor) in 1999, S/2005/458, para 17, 29.

[38] See Nevins, n 35 above, 682, 690–93.

[39] Orford, n 18 above, 862.

[40] PB Hayner, *Unspeakable Truths: Confronting State Terror and Atrocity* (New York, Routledge, 2001) 75–76. Some earlier exceptions include the truth commissions in Chad, Chile, El Salvador and Guatemala.

This trend parallels the general neglect of economic, social and cultural rights (ESCR) that continues to dog human rights theory and practice.

The social and political costs of this narrow framing are vividly apparent in the South African experience. Although the TRC clearly recognised apartheid as a crime against humanity, its mandate narrowly defined both the victims and the perpetrators as those who had suffered acute bodily harm. Apartheid thus featured as the context to crime, rather than the crime itself.[41] The everyday violence of poverty and racism—and, consequently, the ordinary victims and beneficiaries of apartheid—were placed in the background of truth and reconciliation. Because the TRC report largely appeared as a depoliticised chronicle of wrongful acts, it did not sufficiently depict the ways that illegal acts of torture, killing and terror were intrinsic to legally sanctioned apartheid.[42] Admittedly, there were understandable logistical reasons for limiting the scope of inquiry, and the TRC did hold a series of hearings on the role of civil society. But, as I have argued elsewhere,[43] the overall effect was to relieve the beneficiaries of obligations pursuant to national reconciliation and to gloss over the suffering of millions in the 'new' South Africa. This has had lasting effects on the perceptions of justice and racial reconciliation in South Africa, including the debate and lawsuit over corporate reparations.[44]

In thinking of the costs elsewhere of a similarly narrow framing of what transitional justice addresses, I point to the powerful call for a shift in praxis made by Louise Arbour when she was the UN High Commissioner for Human Rights:

> [Transitional justice], without losing its *raison d'être*, is poised to make the significant leap that would allow justice, in its full sense, to contribute as it should to societies in transition . . . It must reach to—but also beyond—the crimes and abuses committed during the conflict that led to the transition, and it must address the human rights violations that pre-dated the conflict and caused or contributed to it. With these aims so broadly defined, transitional justice practitioners will very likely expose a great number of discriminatory practices and violations of economic, social, and cultural rights.[45]

Louise Arbour points to East Timor's CAVR to show how a truth commission might widen the scope of what transitional justice addresses. CAVR's statistical accounting of fatal human rights violations looks beyond the direct result of military operations to include death due to hunger and illness.[46] There is a separate chapter on forced displacement and famine, which affected nearly every person living in that time period. (In contrast, the South African TRC could only include findings of specific violations of ESCR by treating arson as 'severe ill-treatment'. There was considerable criticism of its refusal to treat forced displacement in a similar manner.) CAVR, in its chapter

---

[41] See M Mamdani, 'Reconciliation without Justice' [November/December 1996] *South African Review of Books* 46.

[42] See R Nagy, 'Violence, Amnesty and Transitional Law: "Private" Acts and "Public" Truth in South Africa' (2004) 1 *African Journal of Legal Studies* 1.

[43] R Nagy, 'The Ambiguities of Reconciliation and Responsibility in South Africa' (2004) 52 *Political Studies* 709.

[44] See R Nagy, 'Postapartheid Justice: Can Cosmopolitanism and Nation-Building be Reconciled?' (2006) 40 *Law and Society Review* 623.

[45] L Arbour, 'Economic and Social Justice for Societies in Transition' (2007) 40 *New York University Journal of Law and Politics* 2.

[46] East Timor CAVR, 'Chega! Final Report of the Commission for Reception, Truth and Reconciliation in East Timor' (2005), available at http://www.cavr-timorleste.org/en/chegaReport.html, ch 6.12, 5.

on violations of social, cultural and economic rights, addresses the use of the education system as a propaganda tool, the manipulation of the coffee market, de-development and environmental degradation.[47] It also provides recommendations regarding the rights to freedom from hunger, an adequate standard of living, education, culture, basic health and a sustainable environment. Unfortunately, as too often seems the case with truth commissions, the East Timorese government and the international community have largely ignored the truth commission's report.[48]

Engendering transitional justice will be an important corollary to taking up Louise Arbour's call. Until very recently, women and gender have been glaringly absent from transitional justice programmes. Masculinist determinations of the transitional problem have centred on political violence with, as noted above, an emphasis on 'extraordinary' violations of civil and political rights. This construction disregards and treats as 'ordinary' the private or intimate violence that women experience in a militarised, unequal society. It also fails to reflect the myriad of social and economic harms that are disproportionately placed upon women, and widows in particular, both during and after repression or armed conflict.[49]

When 'truth' is structured around extraordinary violence, women predominantly bear witness on behalf of deceased partners, children and grandchildren, in other words, as indirect or secondary victims. Consequently, women's stories of violence and suffering do not fully emerge. Rosemary Jolly remarks, in the South African case, that 'the TRC lacked the social and structural context to be able to conceive of these women as victim-survivors, authors and subjects of their own narratives'.[50] When women do appear as victim-survivors[51] in their own right, it is overwhelmingly as the victims of sexual violence, something to which it is incredibly difficult to give public testimony. Women-only workshops and hearings can alleviate this difficulty, but, as Corey Levine argues in the East Timorese context, women-centred hearings should not neglect other forms of gender-based suffering, such as losing a limb due to a landmine when searching for food or facing discriminatory inheritance laws.[52] Certainly, it is an important advance for women's rights to recognise that sexual violence constitutes a crime against humanity, war crime or genocide, rather than simply being a spoil of war or violation of honour. But international criminal jurisprudence, Katherine Franke points out, has problematically created 'mis-recognition' or 'over-recognition' of women. It pins the female victims of sexual violence to an essentialised identity that makes it difficult to 'script new social possibilities', particularly where rape is highly stigmatised. Furthermore, 'it fails to capture the array of manners in which women suffer gross injustice'.[53] As Augustine Park puts it, 'international law is not a

---

[47] Ibid, ch 7.9, 3ff.

[48] Human Rights Watch, *2007 World Report: East Timor*, available at http://www.hrw.org/legacy/wr2k7/.

[49] See E Rehn and EJ Sirleaf, *Women, War and Peace: The Independent Experts' Assessment on the Impact of Armed Conflict on Women and Women's Role in Peace-building* (New York, UNDP, 2002).

[50] RJ Jolly, 'Desiring Good(s) in the Face of Marginalized Subjects: South Africa's Truth and Reconciliation Commission in a Global Context' (2001) 100 *South Atlantic Quarterly* 623.

[51] Discussion of women as combatants, perpetrators or collaborators is beyond my scope.

[52] C Levine, 'Gender and Transitional Justice: A Case Study of East Timor' (Canadian Consortium for Human Security, 2004), on file with author.

[53] Franke, n 12 above, 822.

silver bullet to alleviate the structural barriers, constraints and challenges that entrench girls' vulnerability in peacetime and wartime'.[54]

Truth commissions are better positioned to address the marginalisation of women and girls because they look at patterns of violations. For example, the Sierra Leone TRC's extensive and far-reaching recommendations include the repeal of discriminatory inheritance, marriageable age and other customary laws, amendments to laws pertaining to domestic and sexual violence, the promotion of skills training, education and the economic empowerment of women, and the setting up a Gender Commission.[55] These recommendations follow extensive gendered analysis in other sections of the report and go well beyond a sexualised accounting of gender-based violence to challenge structural inequality. Unfortunately, the Sierra Leone government has done 'next to nothing' to implement the recommendations, despite being legally bound to do so, and despite the recent provision of external debt relief.[56]

## VI. CONCLUSION

In the determination of who is accountable for what and when, transitional justice is a discourse and practice imbued with power. Yet, it can be strikingly depoliticised in its application. Artificial time-frames and zones of impunity produce restricted accounts of violence and remedy. A narrow, legalistic focus on gross violations of civil and political rights overlooks the ways in which structural violence and gender inequality inform subjective experiences of political conflict, injustice and their consequences. Where structural violence enters the picture, it is largely in the background. Where gender enters the picture, it is fixated on sexual violence against women, neglecting sexual violence against men and non-sexual violence against women.

Efforts within the global project of transitional justice to retract from one-size-fits-all solutions must guard against the kinds of channelling highlighted in this chapter. To do so requires a broader approach that encompasses structural violence, gender inequality and foreign involvement. This challenge speaks to the very legitimacy of a globalised transitional justice, as well as to the efficacy and legitimacy of mechanisms designed to help those who must live together after atrocity. International law and transnational norms must have a heightened role in transitional circumstances precisely because national legal and political systems are weak or corrupt. At the same time, remote institutions and narrowly conceived mechanisms and analyses will not change ordinary people's lives for the better.

---

[54] ASJ Park, '"Other Inhumane Acts": Forced Marriage, Girl Soldiers and the Special Court for Sierra Leone' (2006) 15 *Social & Legal Studies* 316.

[55] Sierra Leone TRC, *Witness to Truth: Report of the Sierra Leone Truth and Reconciliation Commission* (Accra, Graphic Packaging, 2004), available at http://www.trcsierraleone.org/drwebsite/publish/index.shtml, vol 2, ch 3, paras 107–11, 316–76.

[56] L Graybill, 'Debt Relief: a Panacea for Sierra Leone?', *CSIS Africa Policy Forum*, 9 February 2007.

# 13

# Holding Up a Mirror to the Process of Transition? The Coercive Sterilisation of Romani Women in the Czech Republic Post-1991*

MORAG GOODWIN

## I. INTRODUCTION

T
OWARDS THE END of 2004, the Czech Ombudsman (known as the Public Defender of Rights) received complaints from ten Romani women who alleged that they had been sterilised without their full and informed consent in the period 1991–2003. In the course of the investigations that took place throughout 2005 into the complaints by both the Ombudsman and the Ministry of Health, which established an advisory board to review the allegations at the Ombudsman's request, a further 77 women came forward with similar complaints. The vast majority identified themselves as Romani.

Although these cases all took place, without exception, in the post-Communist period, and ostensibly involved the actions of private actors, this chapter will suggest that they are intimately entwined with late Communist policy towards Roma in the Czech Republic. This link to the past suggests the need for critical consideration of the nature of the transition process as it took place in the Czech Republic post-1991, and, in particular, calls for reflection upon a transition process that had as its *telos* human rights-based liberal democracy. Debates about transitional justice are slowly shifting from the question of how best to achieve transition to a liberal democracy—more forgiveness, less criminal sanctions or vice versa, and all the institutional options in between[1]—to a more thorough-going critique of the problems inherent to the concept

* This project was begun in the context of a 2008 CLPE Visiting Fellowship at Osgoode Hall Law School, and the author is grateful to Osgoode for their hospitality and financing. A version of this paper was presented at the 3rd Osgoode Constitutional Law Roundtable, 21–22 February 2008, and at the EUI European Outcasts Workshop, Florence, 5–6 May 2008, and benefited from the feedback of participants at both. Special thanks to Euan MacDonald (Edinburgh) and Thomas Mertens (Nijmegen/Leiden) for their comments. The usual disclaimer applies. The research for this chapter was completed in January 2009.

[1] See, among the wealth of literature on transitional justice, R Teitel, *Transitional Justice* (Oxford, Oxford University Press, 2000); J Elster, *Closing the Books: Transitional Justice in Historical Perspective*

and processes of transitional justice itself.[2] This process is occurring as the field of global transitional justice studies, now well established, begins to interact with more established sub-disciplines such as 'law and development', and is increasingly influenced by the subtleties of constitutional thinking.[3] This chapter hopes to contribute to this debate by reflecting simply upon the way in which the Czech process of transition entrenched patterns of societal domination, thereby effectively excluding one group in particular from membership in the body politic. The suggestion is that it is not surprising that it is this particular ethnic group that is overwhelmingly the victim of coercive sterilisation in the present.

The first part of this chapter (Section II) will consider the cases and the legal context of the post-1991 sterilisation cases. The second part (Section III) will consider in brief the Romani experience under Communism, dealing, in particular, with the policy of sterilisation that formed a central element of the later Communist regime's attempt to deal with the 'Romani problem'. The nature of the Czech process of transition will be briefly described and considered from the perspective of the Romani experience in the third and fourth parts (Sections IV and V). The final part of the chapter (Section VI) will suggest some insights which this particular example may have for the global transitional justice project.

## II. COERCIVE STERILISATION IN THE CZECH REPUBLIC POST-1991

### II.1. The Cases

The complaints of non-consensual sterilisation made in the period 1991–2003 relate to a number of different hospitals in different regions of the country, and concern different medical teams. However, there are a number of commonalities between the cases that have affected the way in which the authorities—both the government and the courts—have dealt with them. Without exception, the complaints investigated by the Ombudsman concerned procedures carried out in the context of Caesarean section deliveries. Almost without exception, the procedures were carried out upon the basis of a perceived medical need by the doctors in question—typically, that the complications of the delivery which made an emergency Caesarean section necessary deter-

---

(Cambridge, Cambridge University Press, 2004); R Teitel, 'Transitional Justice Genealogy' (2003) 16 *Harvard Human Rights Journal* 69; S Chesterman, *You, The People, The United Nations, Transitional Administration and State-Building* (Oxford, Oxford University Press, 2004); P Van Zyl, 'Dilemmas of Transitional Justice: The Case of South Africa's Truth and Reconciliation Commission' (1999) 52 *Journal of International Affairs*, 647; M Minow, 'Making History or Making Peace: When Prosecutions Should Give Way to Truth Commissions and Peace Negotiations', Chapter 12 in this volume. See also J Waldron, 'Redressing Historical Injustice' (2002) 52 *The University of Toronto Law Journal* 135.

[2] For recent attempts to get this debate going see R Nagy, 'Transitional Justice as Global Project: Critical Reflections', Chapter 13 above. See also R Teitel, 'Transitional Justice in a New Era' (2002–03) 26 *Fordham International Law Journal* 893.

[3] For a good introduction to these critiques see P Zumbansen and SA Ahmed, 'The Transnational Law of Transitional Justice: A Bridging Exercise', CLPE Research Paper 12/2008, Vol 04 No 03 (2008), available at http://www.comparativeresearch.net/papers.jsp; for consideration of these critiques (and their possible tensions) in light of South Africa's transitional process see R Nagy, 'Postapartheid Justice: Can Cosmopolitanism and Nation-Building be Reconciled?' (2006) 40 *Law and Society Review* 623. See also P Zumbansen, 'Sociological Jurisprudence 2.0: Updating Law's Inter-disciplinarity in a Global Context', Chapter 18 below.

mined that the mother's life would be placed at risk in any subsequent pregnancy, and thus that the removal of the possibility of such a pregnancy was in her best interest.

Despite the fact that Czech law sets out strict conditions for the performance of sterilisation procedures, all of which are designed to ensure that the individual under-going the procedure has given her free and informed consent and is fully aware of the consequences of her decision,[4] the Ministry of Health advisory board concluded that the overwhelming majority of the complaints were without foundation. In its opinion, the health of the women had not been impaired and the treatment had been in their own best interest. The ministry's dismissal of all but a handful of the most egre-gious complaints was determined, first, by the board's finding that there was no racial pattern to the complaints, and, secondly, by its interpretation of Czech law concerning sterilisation, which views medical interventions performed without consent as not con-stituting a criminal offence where the action is taken *lege artis*.[5]

Three of the cases were taken up by the Supreme State Prosecutor's Office, to which the Ombudsman added a further 54 cases. However, the defence of *lege artis*, in combi-nation with the statute of limitations, prevented any criminal prosecutions from being brought.[6] The ministry concluded its investigation in September 2005 and, following the issuing of updated guidelines for medical staff on the procedure for obtaining full and informed consent for sterilisations, considers the matter closed.[7] The Ombudsman published his report into the complaints in December 2005.[8]

While the investigation by the authorities into the complaints was still ongoing, a number of victims turned to the civil courts, seeking compensation for the harm done to them. In the first such case, the Regional Court in Ostrava found that, although an illegal act had violated the victim's right to physical integrity, it dismissed the claim for financial compensation on the grounds that the statute of limitations had expired.[9] However, on 12 October 2007, damages of just over US$25,000 were awarded against a hospital, again in Ostrava, as compensation for a non-consensual sterilisation pro-cedure carried out as the victim was giving birth to her second child. This ruling was overturned on appeal, with the Olomouc High Court finding that, although the complainant, Ms Červeňáková, had been sterilised without her consent, her complaint exceeded the three-year statute of limitation period allowed for compensation claims of this sort; in so finding, the High Court applied a 2008 amendment introducing the

---

[4] The specific requirements are laid down in the Health Care Act and Sterilization Directive, Ministry of Health Directive No LP-252-3-19.19.11.71. See, further, O Motejl, 'Final Statement of the Public Defender of Rights in the Matter of Sterilizations Performed in Contravention of the Law and Proposed Remedial Measures' (hereinafter the Ombudsman's Report) (Brno, 23 December 2005), available in the official English version at: http://www.ochrance.cz/en/dokumenty/dokument.php?doc=400; see also M Kopalová, 'Coercive Sterilisation in Czech Republic: Civil and Criminal Law Aspects' (2006) 2 *Roma Rights Quarterly* 27. Ms Kopalová is a lawyer acting for a number of the victims in the civil trials.

[5] For further details on the guidelines issued in relation to medical malpractice see Kopalová, n 4 above, 29.

[6] ERRC, 'Czech State Attorneys Will Not Punish Doctors for Forced Sterilisations of Romani Women', *Snapshots from Around Europe*, 20 November 2007, available at http://errc.org (last accessed on 23 January 2008).

[7] See Ombudsman's Report, n 4 above, s 2.

[8] Ibid.

[9] Judgment of 11 November 2005; the case has been appealed by both the victim, Ms Ferenčiková, and the plaintiff, Vitkovice hospital.

new limitation period retroactively.[10] A number of other civil cases were still ongoing at the time of writing, but are likely to fall foul of this limitation ruling.

## II.2. Interpreting the Cases

These cases have been interpreted in two different ways. Both interpretations limit themselves to a contemporary accounting of the connections between the cases—a limitation which I wish to challenge. The first interpretation concerns the medical aspect of consent; the second, the ethnicity of the victims.

The approach of the Czech government has been to see the issue of post-1991 sterilisations as hinging on the definition of full and informed consent. The government's approach defines and determines the main actors as female patients, on the one hand, and the hospital medical staff, on the other. From this framing, ie by defining the issue as one of consent, the Ministry of Health's advisory board found that no real harm had been done to the majority of the women, as the procedures had been performed as a consequence of medical diagnosis and thus fell within an understanding of the women's own best interest, regardless of whether they had fully understood the consequences of the procedure. Any wrongdoing, therefore, was, according to the ministry, limited to failing to ensure that the women were fully informed and of failing to keep adequate records.[11] As a consequence of this analysis, the matter was closed by issuing new guidelines on obtaining consent for sterilisation procedures.

The other approach, which was that taken by the victims, focuses on the shared ethnicity of the victims. This approach sees the individual doctors as part of a collective medical culture that discriminates against Roma and is prejudicial to Romani family norms, in particular, the desire for a large family. For the victims, therefore, the issue of consent is secondary, with the failure to follow the statutory procedure for establishing free and informed consent seen as exposing wider contemptuous attitudes towards Roma. The complaint of the victims thus goes much deeper than the reading of the government and concerns their equal worth as human beings.

However, while the victims are right to stress that the majority of the victims of these sterilisations belong to a specific racial group, this, I suggest, is only a part of the story. What both the victims and the authorities appear to miss—the authorities by ignoring the racial aspect, the victims by viewing the actions of the medical staff as deliberately targeting them—is the counter-intuitive fact that, while the medical staff in various hospitals across the country did not appear to target the Romani women specifically, their individual actions nonetheless formed a clear pattern of indirect effect. Without intention, these cases appear to mirror the historical experience of the Roma communities under Communism.

---

[10] For reporting of the case in English see CM Wong, 'Court Reverses Sterilization Case', *The Prague Post*, 12 November 2008; available at www.praguepost.com (last accessed on 15 January 2009).

[11] See Ombudsman's Report, n 4 above, ss 3.2–3.3.

## III. ROMANI EXPERIENCES UNDER COMMUNISM IN CZECHOSLOVAKIA

The story of Roma in Europe is a complicated and contested one.[12] The currently predominating understanding of the term 'Roma' (Rroma) is as a collective of transnational ethnic groups, mainly concentrated in Europe, and Central and Eastern Europe in particular, although scattered throughout the world.[13] It is a word used in the singular, yet it is an overarching term to describe a variety of groups that allegedly all share some common essence, or *řomanipé* ('Romaniness').[14] Their origins,[15] culture[16] and population numbers continue to be shrouded in mystery and speculation.[17] What

---

[12] The best introduction remains A Fraser, *The Gypsies* (Oxford, Blackstone Press, 1992). For a particular focus on Central and Eastern Europe see W Guy (ed), *Between Past and Future: the Roma of Central and Eastern Europe* (Hatfield, University of Hertfordshire Press, 2001), especially the chapter by Nicolae Gheorghe and Thomas Acton. For a good introduction to contemporary attitudes to the Roma within Europe see I Pogány, *The Roma Café* (London, Pluto Press, 2004). For information on Romani socio-economic exclusion in today's Europe see D Reingold, MA Orenstein and E Wilkens, *Roma in an Expanding Europe: Breaking the Poverty Cycle* (Washington DC, World Bank Publications, 2005), available at http://web.worldbank.org.

[13] See E Marushiakova and V Popov, 'Historical and Ethnographic Background: Gypsies, Roma and Sinti' in Guy, n 12 above. Marushiakova and Popov are ethnographers who have published extensively on the Roma of Central and Eastern Europe; they provide a breakdown of current Romani sub-groups in Central and Eastern Europe, and provide a glimpse of the fascinating array of diversity between them.

[14] This common bond is perhaps best summed up by Hancock's observation that 'Members of one group might deride members of another group as not being real "Gypsies", and when pressed will say it is because "they are not like us" . . . when asked whether they are Gypsies or *gadžé* they will say they are Gypsies'. Hancock's claim is not that Roma share a sense of being a single people but that the fundamental nature of Romani identity is the division of the world into Roma and *gadžé* (non-Roma) and that from this flows the related notion of *řomanipé* ('Romaniness'). Hancock has suggested in the same article that '*řomanipé* may be seen as the Gypsies' transportable homeland'. I Hancock, 'The East European Roots of Romani Nationalism' (1991) XIX *Nationalities Papers* 5.

[15] The most commonly accepted version of Romani origins understands the Roma as originating in India, migrating westwards and arriving in Europe at the beginning of the second millennium; this is supported by linguistic evidence, with the Romani language being most closely related to Hindi. The reasons for the migration and the time-frame are both disputed. See Fraser, n 12 above; for the linguistic evidence see Y Matras, *Romani. A Linguistic Introduction* (Cambridge, Cambridge University Press, 2002). The Indian-origins thesis has taken on an official aura; see, eg OSCE High Commissioner on National Minorities, 'Report on the Situation of Roma and Sinti in the OSCE Area' (The Hague, 2000) 17. This is, however, contested by some sociologists and anthropologists who suggest that Romani origins are better located in Europe's need for scapegoats and the repressive measures against vagabonds across much of seventeenth-, eighteenth- and nineteenth-century Europe. See W Willems, *In Search of the True Gypsy. From Enlightenment to Final Solution* (London, Frank Cass, 1997); see also J Okely, 'Some Political Consequences of Theories of Gypsy Ethnicity' in A James, J Hockey and A Dawson (eds), *After Writing Culture: Epistemology and Praxis in Contemporary Anthropology* (London, Routledge, 1997); L Lucassen, W Willems and A Cottaar (eds), *Gypsies and Other Itinerant Groups* (Great Britain, Macmillan, 1998).

[16] One of the most mysterious aspects of Romani culture concerns their alleged nomadism. The belief that Roma are nomadic stems from the peripatetic nature of the occupations that Romani groups undertook in early modern Europe. However, very few Romani families remain nomadic, with Roma being forcefully settled in Western Europe in the nineteenth century and in the east during the Communist era. For details see Fraser, n 12 above.

[17] Population numbers on Roma vary wildly from between 5 and 15 million. The difficulty in collecting accurate census data is a combination, inter alia, of legal prohibitions in many European countries on collecting racial data, of grave distrust on the part of the Romani of the good faith of authorities in requesting the information, and of efforts by Roma to deny their own identity. For the latter in a specific instance see G Duijzings, 'The Making of Egyptians in Kosovo and Macedonia' in C Govers and H Vermuelen (eds), *The Politics of Ethnic Consciousness* (London, Macmillian, 1997); see, more generally, C Cahn, 'The Unseen Powers: Perception, Stigma and Roma Rights' (2007) 3 *Roma Rights Quarterly* 3. For a report on

is beyond dispute is that, however one chooses to date their arrival or appearance within Europe, the Romani experience has been marked both by a centuries-long separation from wider society,[18] and of a growing hostility and brutality directed towards Romani communities by Europe's emerging states. This hostility and exclusion is a continuous feature of European history and persists today across the old East–West divide.[19]

It was this hostility and the desire to control closely those on the margins of society that led to Roma becoming a genuinely global people. In medieval times, expulsion had been more or less a local matter, seeing travellers moved on to other towns, and later expelled from whole domains or realms. Certain countries also used concentration as a means of dealing with the 'Gypsy problem'; in the course of 1749, for example, the Spanish authorities executed a carefully orchestrated round-up of all the Gypsies in Spain—men, women and children—and sent them to forced labour in places of the government's choosing, all their possessions being confiscated and sold.[20] During the course of the sixteenth century, Portugal developed a policy of deportation, and was the first country to adopt transportation overseas as a solution to the problem of those Roma who had been born in the country and could not simply be expelled to a neighbouring state. In 1574, a Romani man and his family were forcibly transported to Brazil, and from that date a Portuguese practice of sending Romani women to Africa and men to service in the galleys established itself; large-scale group expulsions switched from Africa to Brazil a century later.[21] By the beginning of the eighteenth century, groups of Roma were being forcefully rounded up by the Portuguese authorities and transported to both India and Africa. This practice was picked up and copied by other countries. The Spanish sent Roma and others into the army, for example, or to its holdings in North Africa, but not, interestingly, to the American colonies; in 1570, Phillip II forbade Gypsies from entering these areas and ordered his officials to arrange for them to be shipped back to Spain should they appear there. England, however, had no such qualms about the use of the Americas as a dumping ground for undesirables, and the 1597 Vagrancy Act saw considerable numbers of Roma and other itinerants shipped to do hard labour in the American colonies. There are neither figures on the numbers of those transported overseas nor any details as to their reception by the locals.

This European story and the particular manifestations which it assumed in the area of today's Czech Republic necessarily form the backdrop to the Communist attitude

---

the difficulty of collecting Romani statistics see PER Report, 'Roma and Statistics' (2000), available at http://www.per-usa.org/Reports/PERStrasbourg.pdf.

[18] See the insightful comments on the mutual miscomprehension of Romani and *gadžé* norms in SG Drummond, *Mapping Marriage Law in Spanish Gitano Communities* (Toronto, UBC Press, 2006) 110–18; for a vigorous response to the prejudices of the majority see I Hancock, *We Are the Romani People* (Hatfield, University of Hertfordshire Press, 2002) Chapter 5 in particular.

[19] For up-to-date country-by-country details of discrimination and abuse against Roma see the European Roma Rights Centre website: http://errc.org. For an attempt to understand the multidimensional aspect of anti-Romani prejudice and exclusion in contemporary Europe see M Goodwin, 'Multidimensional Exclusion: Viewing Romani Marginalisation through the Nexus of Race and Poverty' in D Schiek and V Chege (eds), *European Union Non-discrimination Law: Comparative Perspectives on Multidimensional Equality Law* (Oxford, Routledge-Cavendish, 2009) 137–58.

[20] A Fraser, 'The Present and Future of the Gypsy PAST' (2000) 13 *Cambridge Review of International Affairs* 17, 29.

[21] Details in this paragraph are taken from Fraser, n 12 above, 168–71.

towards Roma in Czechoslovakia. The Europe-wide marginalisation and history of cruelty—the persecution, enslavement, expulsion and killings—found its zenith in the inclusion of Roma as a racial category marked for extermination in the Holocaust.[22] The attempted annihilation of the Roma was particularly successful in the Czech lands of Bohemia and Moravia, and a mere 600 Roma are thought to have survived the Second World War from a pre-war population of *circa* 8,000.[23] The destruction of the pre-war Czech Romani population and the imbalance it created between the two constituent republics had an important influence upon early Czechoslovakian Communist policies towards the Roma.

Communist ideology took a particular approach to the Roma. Roma failed to meet the standards laid down in Marxist–Leninist doctrine for qualification as a nationality, with the consequence that Romani culture or difference was perceived as a social problem.[24] Yet the approach was not straightforwardly hostile, at least in intent. The regime's antipathy towards the 'deviant' lifestyles of the Roma was a consequence of the ideological commitment to modernise society[25]—a process that required the common effort of the whole population—and, as such, was different to the doctrines of racial inferiority under Nazi control.

Following the failure of earlier policy initiatives,[26] which saw the forced removal of the Romani communities from Slovakia and their dispersal and resettlement in the Czech lands, a new policy was introduced in 1972 that was undoubtedly more benevolent in intention than resettlement. It sought the 'all-embracing cultural and social integration of the Roma' by means of a gradual levelling up of the average living standard of the Roma to the rest of society. As part of the launch of this policy, a body was established to deal with Romani issues exclusively in the Czech lands: the Commission of the Government of the Czech Socialist Republic for Gypsy Population Issues. The reports of this body show clearly that the high birthrate in Romani communities—the population had doubled between 1950 and 1970—was held to be an excessive 'risk factor' that impeded the assimilation of the Roma.[27] Moreover, in the reports the low socio-economic status of Romani families and their related inability to care adequately for their children and bring them up properly, which led to poorer health and development derangements not found in the rest of the Czech population,

---

[22] Although Roma have either been excluded or marginalised within the mainstream historical consideration of the Holocaust, there are now a number of histories of Roma in the Second World War available. See, in particular, D Kenrick and G Puxon, *The Destiny of Europe's Gypsies* (London, Heinemann, 1972); D Crowe and J Kolsti (eds), *The Gypsies of Eastern Europe* (London, ME Sharpe, 1991; as well as the comprehensive D Kenrick (ed), *The Gypsies During the Second World War. Volume 2. In the Shadow of the Swastika* (Hatfield, University of Hertfordshire Press, 1999).

[23] See Fraser, n 12 above, 267.

[24] A Central Committee of the Communist Party of Czechoslovakia Politburo Resolution of 8 April 1958, entitled 'On Work with the Gypsy Population in the Czechoslovak Republic', noted that the Roma could not be considered an ethnic group and were solely a 'socially and culturally backward population featuring characteristic lifestyles'. Cited in the Ombudsman's Report, n 4 above, 44.

[25] W Connor, *The National Question in Marxist–Leninist Theory and Strategy* (Princeton, NJ, Princeton University Press, 1984); see also Z Barany, 'Politics and the Roma in State-Socialist Eastern Europe' (2000) 33 *Communist and Post-Communist Studies* 421.

[26] The details that follow are taken from the Ombudsman's Report, n 4 above, 44–52, from Fraser, n 12 above, 274–82, and from W Guy, 'The Czech Lands and Slovakia: Another False Dawn?' in idem, n 12 above.

[27] DJ Kostelancik, 'The Gypsies of Czechoslovakia: Political and Ideological Considerations in the Development of Policy' (1989) XXII *Studies in Comparative Communism* 307, 316.

combined to see the Romani population labelled as being of 'low quality'. One of the recommendations for overcoming this in the reports was birth control, one strongly recommended method of which was sterilisation.

This recommendation took practical form in the design of social security benefits. One particular rule of an act dating from 1988 provided for a one-off monetary or material allowance of up to 5,000 Czech koruny (CSK)[28] (in exceptional cases, CSK 10,000) to citizens 'undergoing medical intervention under special regulations in the interest of a healthy population and over-coming unfavourable living conditions of the family within one year of intervention (sterilisation)'.[29] Access to this particular social benefit was thus tied to being willing to undergo sterilisation. While this benefit was open to all citizens and not explicitly targeted at the Roma in the text of the legislation, the vast majority (over 90%) of those affected by it—including those who volunteered for sterilisation not fully understanding the implications of their decision, or who were sterilised without their consent in the process of giving birth and applied *ex post facto* for the benefit—were Romani.[30]

Although the prevalence of desperate poverty among Romani communities meant that they were always more likely to be seduced by the benefit, the implementation of the provision was also systemically focused on the Roma. The Ombudsman's report suggests 'large-scale interference by social workers based upon persuading women into, preparation and administrative/organisational procurement of sterilisation'. Furthermore, the report noted, '[i]t is entirely typical . . . that applications for sterilisation from a single town were written into entirely identical forms, often clearly on a single typewriter, using identical justifications'. Those justifications often contained a single word, 'Romo'. As such, the Czech Ombudsman found that the state had, in full awareness, used sterilisation as a social tool to curb Romani-population growth, and that its reasons for doing so had strongly eugenic overtones.[31]

## IV. THE GENERAL PROCESS OF TRANSITION IN THE CZECH REPUBLIC

There is not sufficient space here to do justice to the obvious complexities of any process of transition;[32] consequently, this section will simply highlight the main features of the Czech process. The 1993 Velvet Revolution divided what was Czechoslovakia into two new republics. Despite sharing a communist regime for 50 years, the response of the two new republics was markedly different in the implementation and thoroughness of the process of 'de-Communisation'.[33]

The process in the Czech Republic was designed to purge the new republic of the

[28] At today's exchange rate, approx US$ 300.

[29] See Ombudsman's Report, n 4 above, 25.

[30] R Pellar and Z Andrš, 'Report on the Examination in the Problematics of Sexual Sterilization of Romanies in Czechoslovakia' (1989); summarised in Ombudsman's Report, n 4 above, 25–27.

[31] Ombudsman's Report, n 4 above, 72.

[32] For a detailed overview see 'Czechoslovakia' in NJ Kritz (ed), *Transitional Justice: How Emerging Democracies Reckon with Former Regimes. Volume 2. Country Studies* (Washington DC, United States Institute of Peace Press, 1997).

[33] For a detailed comparison, N Nedelsky, 'Divergent Responses to a Common Past: Transitional Justice in the Czech Republic and Slovakia' (2004) 33 *Theory and Society* 65–115.

people and institutions that had dominated the Communist regime. Quickly after the fall of the regime, political prisoners were released and repressive laws were abrogated. Attempts were made under the 1990 Act on Extra-Judicial Rehabilitation to rectify wrongs done, such as the cancellation of decisions expelling students from university or the firing of employees from positions for political reasons. Efforts were made to return confiscated or nationalised property and compensation was paid to the families of those who had been executed or who had died in prison. Reparation efforts were limited, however, focusing solely on the most serious injustices committed by the Communist regime—a limitation imposed, according to David and Choi, by the sheer scale of the repression.[34]

The process of societal acknowledgement of Communist oppression was delivered largely through symbolic acts of Parliament, such as the celebrated 1993 Act on the Illegitimacy of the Communist Regime, which declared the old regime illegitimate and honoured acts of resistance to it. There was no truth commission in the Czech Republic, and attempts at prosecution for political crimes resulted in a dismal number of convictions: eight guilty verdicts, five of which received suspended sentences.[35] However, the 1993 Lustration Act was punitive in comparison with similar enactments in other countries, and was rigorously enforced in comparison with a comparable act in Slovakia;[36] all those named in the secret-police files were presumed guilty and members of the old regime were prevented from holding senior posts in the new administration, with the Act twice being extended.

While acknowledging the impact of the scale of repression and of a devastated economy on the unique mixture of retribution, restitution and forgiveness of the Czech transitional process, what is clear from numerous accounts, although not explicitly noted by their authors, is that the efforts to rectify the wrongs of the past focused almost entirely on active political resistance to Communism. Suffering which was not overtly related to resistance to Communism itself was not included in the accounting under transition.

## V. TRANSITIONAL TUNNEL VISION: THE REFUSAL TO 'SEE' ROMANI EXPERIENCES

Efforts were made both in the immediate post-1991 period and subsequently to include Romani experiences in the wider process of transition, to have them viewed as part of the crimes of Communism. As early as 1978, the civil society organisation Charter 77 issued a document in which they alleged that the practice of sterilisation was being used as a means of preventing births among the Romani minority and, as such, constituted

---

[34] Between 1948 and 1989, approximately 234 people were judicially executed and more than 4,000 died in unclear circumstances; 262,500 people were jailed for political reasons; in the 1950s and 1960s, about 100,000 class enemies were held in 18 concentration camps and subjected to an extremely harsh regime; thousands were evicted from their homes, hundreds of thousands lost their jobs in purges that followed 1948 and 1968 and private property was entirely nationalised. For further details and literature see R David and SYP Choi, 'Forgiveness and Transitional Justice in the Czech Republic' (2006) 50 *Journal of Conflict Resolution* 339, 397–98.

[35] Ibid, 346–49; R David and SYP Choi, 'Victims on Transitional Justice: Lessons from the Reparations of Human Rights Abuse in the Czech Republic' (2005) 27 *Human Rights Quarterly* 392, 401.

[36] Nedelsky, n 33 above.

a genocidal policy.[37] Following the opening up of the state files, a study was conducted based upon an evaluation of the statistical data and upon interviews with the women affected into the possibility of racial bias in the policy of tying financial benefit to consent to sterilisation. The study found that there had been a steady increase in the number of sterilisations following the introduction of this clause, and that the implementation of the measure was strongly suggestive of eugenic impulses.[38] Charter 77 took the same opportunity to examine state documents and released another report on the sterilisation of Romani women in 1990. This highlighted the pressure that social workers exerted on women to undergo the procedure and made the motives behind the policy as expressed in official documents of the time widely known; the report included, for example, an official document from Eastern Slovakia which justified the application of the policy to the Roma as concerning 'citizens showing an extensively negative attitude to work and learning, a high crime-rate, an inclination to alcoholism, female promiscuity, and last but not least, lagging behind the cultural and social development of other population groups'.[39]

These studies formed the basis of complaints to the General Prosecutor's Office in the period 1990–91, which requested a statement from the new Ministry of Health and Social Affairs. The ministry's statement was restricted to commenting on the 1988 policy, and categorically denied any link between the policy and a particular ethnic group, noting that it applied to all population groups equally—an explanation accepted in full by the General Prosecutor's Office. In 1997, the authors of the 1990 study addressed a complaint to the Office for the Documentation and Investigation of the Crimes of Communism (ODI). The ODI came to an almost identical conclusion: that the legal provisions on sterilisation applied to all citizens, regardless of gender or ethnicity.[40] This marked the end of the official responses to the efforts to include the Romani experiences within the general reckoning with the past.[41]

Inga Markovits has noted, in connection with the East German experience, that, in order to remember, it is necessary to know.[42] Despite the information being available and being brought to the attention of the relevant officials, there was an official refusal to take cognisance of it—a point which is all the more noteworthy given that many of the founding members of Charter 77 went on to play a prominent role in the transition process as the Republic's new political elite. But how was it that the past was filtered to eliminate Romani experiences?[43]

---

[37] Charter 77 Document No 23/1978; quoted in Ombudsman's Report, n 4 above, 24–25.

[38] For example, although the measure was meant to apply only to women over the age of 35 with four children, it was routinely applied to women who did not meet those criteria and the amount paid out was highest for those who were childless. See the summary of the main findings of the study in the Ombudsman's Report, n 4 above, 25–27.

[39] Charter 77 Document No 3/1990; quoted in Ombudsman's Report, n 4 above, 27–28.

[40] See Ombudsman's Report, ibid, 35–37.

[41] The issue, however, has not gone away—a government advisory group recommended in 2007 that a state fund be established to compensate the victims of the Communist-era involuntary sterilizations, a claim rejected by the then-government. R Johnston, 'Will the State Compensate Women Sterilized against Their Will?', Free Radio Europe, 24 July 2007, available at http://romove.radio.cz/en/article/21568.

[42] I Markovits, 'Selective Memory: How the Law Affects What We Remember and Forget about the Past: The Case of East Germany' (2001) 35 *Law and Society Review* 513, 520; see also the contributions in E Christodoulidis and S Veitch (eds), *Lethe's Law: Law and Ethics in Reconciliation* (Oxford, Hart Publishing, 2001).

[43] For an article reflecting upon the general socio-economic neglect of Roma in the processes of transition see Z Barany, 'Orphans of Transition: Gypsies in Eastern Europe' (1998) 9 *Journal of Democracy*

## V.1. Drawing the Boundaries of Transitional Reckoning

The failure to include Romani experiences under Communism in the process of transition can be seen as stemming, in part, from the seemingly neutral way in which the lines were drawn to frame the activities subject to investigation. Drawing definitional lines is, of course, necessary in any process of justice, be it transitional or not;[44] however, boundary-drawing in transitional processes is rarely morally arbitrary (as Posner and Vermeule suggest[45]), but is guided by a moral compass that decides both who is deserving of justice for past wrongs as well as the more basic question of whether those wrongs actually count as wrongs at all. The answer to these questions arguably reveals not only the underlying societal pathologies of the past society, but also determines, in part, whether those pathologies—those patterns of domination—flow silently into the future. As Teitel notes in her seminal study, 'What is deemed just [in the context of transitional justice] is contingent and informed by prior injustice'.[46]

The focus on the crimes of the recent past of Communist regimes makes taking the year 1948 as the historical starting point for any accounting seem logical.[47] Yet, while the drawing of a temporal line appears to determine the events to be included, and thereby the victims that are included, the decision to take 1948 as the starting point arguably only makes sense where the experiences of a certain group are already determined as the focus of the enquiry, ie not the ethnic Germans and Hungarians who were forced to flee; not the Jews and the Roma, the central victims of the Holocaust. In the case of the Czech transition, the period of 1948–89 makes most sense where the predetermined focus is the political crimes of Communism, under which the majority reserves the category of general victim for itself. All other histories are then subsumed within this particular version of history.

The Czech focus—the category of the victims and the temporal boundaries selected—is explicable in that transitional justice tends to highlight acts that are above and beyond acts of the ordinary everyday. In the context of South Africa, for example, a number of commentators have noted the way in which the process of transitional justice there highlighted particularly grievous acts of violence such as torture and murder, but generally overlooked the violence of apartheid itself.[48] In the South

---

142. However, there appears to be no literature on the exclusion of Roma from processes of transitional reckoning, despite many detailed country accounts.

[44] For a detailed assertion that transitional justice differs little from ordinary processes of justice see EA Posner and A Vermeule, 'Transitional Justice as Ordinary Justice' (2003–04) 117 *Harvard Law Review* 762.

[45] Ibid, 808. The example which they give of the exclusion of property-restitution claims in the Czech Republic between 1945 and 1948 in order to prevent claims by ethnic German and Hungarian citizens forced from the country in the immediate post-war period may appear morally arbitrary to the uncommitted outsider, but is clearly not so to the average Czech citizen. The fact that Jews, too, were initially excluded and subsequently included suggests that their exclusion was considered wrong and was therefore rectified.

[46] Teitel, n 1 above, 6. See also JJ Linz, *The Breakdown of Democratic Regimes: Crisis, Breakdown & Reequilibration* (Baltimore, MD, The J Hopkins University Press, 1978).

[47] For an account of how the present rules over the past and the law's complicity in this see Markovits, n 42 above, 513–15.

[48] For example, Nagy, n 3 above, 623. Also, RA Wilson, *The Politics of Truth and Reconciliation in South Africa: Legitimizing the Post-Apartheid State* (Cambridge, Cambridge University Press, 2001); R Nagy, 'Violence, Amnesty and Transitional Law: "Private" Acts and "Public" Truth in South Africa' (2004) 52 *Political Studies* 709. See, in the context of gender bias, E Rooney, 'Engendering Transitional Justice: Questions of Absence and Silence' (2007) *International Journal of Law in Context* 173.

African process, apartheid acted largely as the context to crimes rather than being prioritised as the crime itself, despite the official recognition of apartheid as a crime against humanity in international law, and acknowledged as such by the Truth and Reconciliation Commission.[49] In the Czech context, acts of political resistance marked the extraordinary, and the harms of Communism itself—its ideology of racial inferiority and its attempted social engineering—were viewed simply as a backdrop. Instead of a general accounting of the victims of Communism, the Czech process therefore saw victimhood reserved for the ordinary Czech citizen who had either chosen resistance and had been punished or who had suffered as a consequence of the choice of another to resist, such as a relative or friend. This limiting of victimhood to a certain category of victim becomes explicit in a comment by the government-appointed Commissioner for Human Rights. In justifying his refusal to support the establishment of a state fund to compensate the victims of involuntary sterilisation under Communism, he is reported as saying: 'Endless amounts of wrongs were committed under communist rule. My wife, for example, wasn't allowed to go to secondary school, let alone university—she's not getting any compensation.'[50]

By focusing on those wronged for resisting Communism, the transition process excluded the Romani communities' experience of that political system precisely because it formed part of the everyday social pattern. There was nothing extraordinary about societal interference with, and persecution of, the Roma. It is the refusal to consider the experiences of the Other, in this case the Roma, that makes the framing of the period for which reckoning is necessary—the starting point of transition or what is being transited from—seem logical (or arbitrary), where it does, in fact, represent a revealing choice.

## V.2. Entrenchment and Continuation of Unacknowledged Wrongs

This conscious drawing of historical boundaries of reckoning and of memory, it is suggested, risks entrenching, and thereby perpetuating, other equally heinous wrongs that were not the focus of enquiry, precisely because they were not included within the scope of the collective writing of the national past. In failing to include the policies and practices of sterilisation in the accounting of Communist crimes, past society has been effectively absolved of those crimes. Moreover, by not being included in the catalogue of Communist wrongs, the policy of sterilisation is discounted as an actual wrong, for which society cannot, therefore, be held accountable. In being defined as a non-crime, there is a strong sense in which a policy that was strongly eugenic in nature has been rendered acceptable—a justifiable response to the socio-economic circumstances that the Romani communities allegedly brought upon themselves. In not being included, the views of the civil servants and social workers with regard to the 'low

---

[49] See The Truth and Reconciliation Commission, 'Findings and Recommendations: Legal Framework within which the Commission Made Findings in the Context of International Law', vol 6, s 5, ch 1, para 19, available at http://www.info.gov.za/otherdocs/2003/trc/5_1.pdf. I am grateful to Euan MacDonald for this point.

[50] Johnston, n 41 above. In May 2007, the Czech Council for Human Rights put forward a plan that would compensate the women sterilized between the period 1966 and 1991, but the plan was rejected by the government upon the basis that it might set a precedent for largely unverifiable malpractice suits.

quality' and other negative attributes of the Romani population are given credence—a suggestion supported by the intense marginalisation and prejudice against the Roma in today's Czech Republic.[51]

In addition, by setting the temporal boundary of inclusion as 1948, earlier wrongs—in the present case, the Romani genocide that decimated the Czech Romani population and the centuries of European efforts to persecute, exclude and marginalise Romani communities—are obviously excluded from the transitional reckoning. While a boundary clearly needs to be drawn, the exclusion of certain actions or events can have an anaesthetising effect, as the nature of transition easily risks creating a wall between the past and the future. But if the defining of the period being transited from is restrictive, both in terms of time periods and in terms of those affected, there is a danger of the perception becoming embedded in society that 'history' has been put to rest. In the present case, the restrictive historical reckoning of the transition process failed to include important elements of collective history, including the difficult relationship between the Czech majority and the Romani minority, which continued its established pattern during Communism. In effect, the Roma have been written out of society's collective history by being excluded from the Communist snapshot, giving credence to the widespread Czech belief that, following their near annihilation in World War II, there is no such thing as a Czech *Rom*/Roma.

This exclusion from the past has obvious consequences in the present. One of the earliest actions of the newly constituted Czech Parliament in 1993 was to pass a new nationality law containing provisions designed to exclude the Roma from the new Czech citizenship and to define them, instead, as Slovak. Following years of international pressure, the law was eventually amended.[52] However, the continuing legacy of this episode can, arguably, be seen in the census data for the year 2000. Whereas a 1997 government report put the number of Czech Roma unofficially at 200,000, the 2000 census found only 11,000 people willing to identify themselves as Romani, in comparison with the 33,000 self-identifying Roma in 1990.[53]

Moreover, in constituting a bridge between what has gone before and the possible futures of a given society, transitional justice is written into the foundations of those available futures. In the words of Peer Zumbansen: 'the law of new beginnings is, in fact, tainted and burdened by the past experiences of law that question the acceptable meaning and substance of the term itself'.[54]

The history of abuse under Communism, itself part of the long and shared history of separation and misunderstanding between the Roma and non-Roma, finds expression today in the position of the Roma as the most cripplingly poor and

---

[51] For evidence of contemptuous attitudes towards the Roma see nn 53 and 56 below.

[52] For details of the law and of the campaign to repeal these clauses see J Siklova and M Miklusakova, 'Law as an Instrument of Discrimination: Denying Citizenship to the Czech Roma' (1998) 7 *East European Constitutional Review*, available at http://www.law.nyu.edu/eecr/vol7num2/special/denyingcitizenship.html. It should be noted that Slovakia retaliated in kind, thus leaving the Roma of the former Czechoslovakia without citizenship and without access to any of the benefits that citizenship entails for the greater part of the 1990s.

[53] Figures taken from C Cahn, 'The Unseen Powers: Perception, Stigma and Roma Rights' (2007) 3 *Roma Rights Quarterly* 3.

[54] P Zumbansen, 'Transitional Justice in a Transnational World', CLPE Research Paper No 40/2008, available at http://papers.ssrn.com/sol3/papers.cfm?abstract_id=1313725, 6.

marginalised group in society.[55] The failure to speak of Romani experiences under Communism within the transitional process has arguably allowed the prejudices that motivated the sterilisation policy and its targeted application to the Romani communities to go unchecked; instead, it vindicated them.[56] Being targeted for eugenical practices is symptomatic of a wider phenomenon. Intricately intertwined with the desperate multifaceted poverty in which many Roma are today caught up is the widespread, deeply entrenched and bitter prejudice against Romani individuals and communities.[57] The wave of violence against the Roma that found particular expression in the Czech Republic throughout the 1990s in cases of police brutality and of individual acts of skinhead/extreme right violence, coupled with a near complete impunity for their actions within the justice system,[58] finds contemporary expression in everyday systematic discrimination. The continuing refusal to see the Roma as citizens of equal worth is reflected, for example, in the overwhelming segregation of Romani children in schools for the mentally handicapped (as recently recognised by the European Court of Human Rights in *DH and others*[59]). As such, society at large remains a hostile place for Czech Roma.[60] The transition that was meant to mark a break with the past has, instead, allowed a major societal pathology to continue as a social normality.

## V.3. The Teleology of Transition

The pattern of Czech history and the contemporaneous attitudes of the majority of Czechs were not the only drivers of the transition process. While the countries of Central and Eastern Europe took individual transition paths, they did so within a broader context of a set ideology of what the end of that transition should be. The fall of Communism marked the 'end of history'; transition was a path to liberal multi-party democracy, to a free media, to the rule of law and to a free market economy.[61] Thus, although the distinct experiences of law are embedded in particular histories, a transnational law of transitional justice has—as Zumbansen suggests—emerged from

---

[55] In 2003, the UNDP reported of the Roma in Bulgaria, the Czech Republic, Hungary, Romania and Slovakia that, 'by such measures as literacy, infant mortality and basic nutrition, most of these country's four to five million Roma endure conditions closer to sub-Saharan Africa than Europe'. UNDP, 'Avoiding the Dependency Trap: The Roma Human Development Report, 2003', available at http://roma.undp.sk (last accessed on 23 September 2007).

[56] For one explanation of the way in which anti-Romani prejudices both drive and are driven by socio-economic exclusion, with the former causing and justifying the latter and the latter, in turn, justifying the prejudice, see Goodwin, n 19 above.

[57] For empirical details see R Fawn, 'Czech Attitudes towards the Roma: "Expecting more of Havel's Country"?' (2001) 53 *Europe-Asia Studies* 1193.

[58] See P Hockenos, *Free to Hate: The Rise of the Right in Post-Communist Eastern Europe* (New York, Routledge, 1993), charting the rise of the far right across Central and Eastern Europe in the wake of newly discovered freedoms; see ch 6 on the Czech Republic.

[59] *DH and Others v the Czech Republic*, European Court of Human Rights, Grand Chamber Judgment of 13 November 2007, Application No 57325/00.

[60] For a detailed picture of the contemporary situation of the Roma in the Czech Republic go to http://errc.org and select country 'Czech Republic'. For an example, on 17 November 2008, anti-Romani demonstrators from the far right Workers' Party in the Czech city of Litvinov clashed with riot police in their attempt to reach a Romani settlement, presumably with the aim of carrying out a pogrom.

[61] See, eg Posner and Vermeule, n 44 above, 768.

the Nuremberg Trials onwards, in which transitional justice institutions rely heavily on formal law.[62] Yet the ability of law—constitutional law, human rights law or criminal law—to address past injustices adequately is increasingly open to question.[63] Where the boundaries of historical reckoning define which past injustices matter, the transition process also determines the avenues open to the victims for redress: how one, as a nation, makes sense of the crimes of the past informs the understanding of who is to be protected in the future, as well as the means chosen to protect them.

The teleological process of transition in the Czech Republic arguably depoliticised what was an inherently political process; and it did so, it is suggested, on two levels. The first is that, as recognised by Nagy and others, the construction of liberal democracy works to privilege certain responses, and, in doing so, ignores structural and gendered aspects of violence, as well as questions of social injustice; for example, the decision to focus on political resistance over structural poverty or other economic issues was, in part, determined by the privileging of civil and political rights in the liberal model.[64] The necessity of an individual justice response to the post-1991 sterilisation cases, ie criminal prosecution or a civil claim for damages and the refusal on the part of the authorities to confront the structural elements of the cases, were, arguably, also shaped here. However, there is, perhaps, another level at which the rapid shift to a human rights-based, rule of law-focused, democratic system has worked to depoliticise the process of transition.

The process of transition, of which transitional justice is such a prominent part, is not just a coming to terms with the past, nor is it simply a statement of society's values in the present; rather, it necessarily involves the deeper constitutional questions of belonging and participation. The teleological nature of transition and the reliance on formal law to answer questions of past injustice also worked to allow Czech society to avoid, and to excuse itself from, consideration of the self-definitional question of who that society is. Pre-political questions of inclusion and exclusion, of defining a constitutional vernacular, were, instead, replaced by a characterisation of the state's relationship with its citizens as the entrenchment of civil and political human rights in a document marked 'constitution'.[65] This dynamic is, arguably, contained in the very essence and in the language of transition itself. By characterising a society as being in transition, the suggestion is that an already constituted society is moving either through conflict or from one regime to another, but that the society itself, albeit marked by whatever tragedy makes such a break with the past necessary, remains already constituted. As a result, transitional constitutional discussions have a strong tendency to focus on the rights and institutions to be contained in a 'new' democratic order, in which those rights are human rights as law, not as sites of political contestation. This dominance of rule-of-law talk in situations of transition is, to borrow the

---

[62] Zumbansen, n 54 above.

[63] See, eg L McGregor, 'Reconciliation: Where is the Law?' in S Veitch (ed), *Law and the Politics of Reconciliation* (Aldershot, Ashgate Publishing, 2007).

[64] Nagy, n 2 above, 3–4. Nagy quotes Mani as stating that 'the prevalent liberal-democratic ideal . . . tends to favour freedom and liberty over equality': R Mani, *Beyond Retribution: Seeking Justice in the Shadow of War* (Oxford, Polity Press, 2002) 17.

[65] See Teitel, n 1 above. See also A Schaap, 'The Time of Reconciliation and the Space of Politics' in Veitch, n 63 above, especially 25–29.

language of Anne-Marie Slaughter, an example of the colonisation of the political by the legal.[66]

The skipping over of the metaconstitutional questions of belonging is, of course, in part a practical response to divided societies; however, this fixture of the transitional project is arguably also normative, taking sustenance from the liberal multicultural project,[67] as well as the international law principle of *uti possidetis*, which views allowing groups to go their own way as independent entities as unacceptable. The failure to instigate a process of mutual engagement in a dialogue about the practice of constitutionalism in Czech society has been noted in other processes, notably South Africa,[68] and may suggest a strong propensity within the global transitional justice project to smooth over metaconstitutional questions. This, of course, has fundamental implications for the perpetuation of power structures within society, and suggests that the strong liberal teleology of the current project of transitional justice is ill-suited to address questions of structural domination, with all the attendant consequences to which this myopia leads.[69]

## VI. WHAT IMPLICATIONS, IF ANY, FOR THE TRANSITIONAL JUSTICE PROJECT?

This chapter has attempted to engage critically with the global project of transitional justice on a bottom-up basis, by taking ostensibly unconnected cases of wrong-doing and attempting to understand them within a transitional justice process informed both by critiques from the law and development field, and those of critical constitutionalism. By viewing these cases through a historical lens, we gain a picture of a present-day fractured society and of a group that is consistently, and across all areas of life, denied their equal worth both as human beings and as citizens. The everyday 'violence' against Roma may not be formally political in that the state is not explicitly implicated, at least not at the national authority level,[70] but it is nonetheless political in that these contemporary cases should not be seen in isolation from the historical experience of targeted sterilisation practices or from wider contemporary attitudes to the Roma. Moreover, these cases are political in that they cannot be separated from the transition process itself. As is clear from the field of law and development, and

[66] A-M Slaughter, 'Pushing the Limits of Liberal Peace: Ethnic Conflict and the "Ideal Polity"' in D Wippman (ed), *International Law and Ethnic Conflict* (Ithaca, NY, Cornell University Press, 1998) 128–44, 134. For a predominantly legal focus see Teitel, n 1 above; see also the Report of the Secretary General to the Security Council, The Rule of Law and Transitional Justice in Conflict and Post-conflict Societies, 23 August 2004, S/2004/616. For a useful mapping of the role of law in transitional justice theory see C Bell, C Campbell and F Ní Aoláin, 'Justice Discourses in Transition' (2004) 13 *Social & Legal Studies* 305, especially 308–10. See also Zumbansen, Chapter 18 below.

[67] See, eg W Kymlicka, *Multicultural Citizenship: A Liberal Theory of Minority Rights* (Oxford, Oxford University Press, 1995).

[68] See Nagy, n 3 above.

[69] For an analysis of the unfairness inherent in the practice of constitutionalism between dominant and minority cultures see J Tully, *Strange Multiplicity: Constitutionalism in an Age of Diversity* (Cambridge, Cambridge University Press, 1995); see also P Pettit, *Republicanism: A Theory of Freedom and Government* (Oxford, Oxford University Press, 1997).

[70] There are numerous examples of local authorities explicitly implementing racially discriminatory policies against the Roma; for example, a two-metre-high wall was built in Ústí nad Labem to separate the Romani community from its non-Romani neighbours. See reports of the incident at http://errc.org.

as Nagy has so explicitly drawn out in the transitional context, the practice and discourse of transitional justice is imbued with power.

The cases under consideration here act not only as a window onto the exclusionary biases of the transition process but must themselves be viewed within the context of that exclusion—it is in this sense that the cases act as a mirror, directing light onto the story of the past and reflecting its dark shadows back to the present. If this is the case, civil actions against the hospitals that carried out the procedures are unlikely to redress the harms done.[71]

One should, of course, be extremely cautious about attempting to draw inferences from a single example. However, as a minor contribution to the ongoing debate about the practices and processes of transitional justice, from which scholars more knowledgeable in this field than I may be able to draw lines of connection to other examples, it is to be hoped that the following generalisations, while obvious, may nonetheless be of interest. First, the defining of the boundaries of transitional justice—the choice of victims, the temporal focus—is neither neutral nor arbitrary, but reflects societal power relations. Secondly, the act of defining those boundaries not only reflects the structures of power, but, in excluding the everyday relations of domination, may also serve to entrench them. Finally, transitional justice projects should not ignore the metaconstitutional questions of belonging and membership, however difficult such questions might be for divided societies, and even where, as in the case of transition in Central and Eastern Europe, a (majority) society may not present itself as divided. While the initial post-conflict phase may not be an appropriate juncture at which to raise fundamental and far-reaching questions of a constitutional nature, what the cases at hand arguably suggest is that the process of transition cannot be deemed to be completed until those discussions have taken place, if it can, indeed, ever be properly characterised as concluded (the agonistic model of constitutionalism explicitly eschewing an end point[72]). More importantly, there is little chance of justice being done to all the victims without the initiation of a constitutional conversation.

The extent to which the avoidance of metaconstitutional questions behind an overtly legal approach is written into the global project of transition is a question for others to answer. What I have hoped to do in this chapter is to provide an illustration of the consequences of failing to address exclusive constitutional forms and patterns of power in society; and to raise the question of whether the nature of transition itself is complicit in perpetuating the victimhood of a marginalised and vulnerable group.

---

[71] This is the subject of a longer paper and draws heavily upon the work of J Llewellyn and her claims regarding restorative justice. See J Llewellyn, 'Dealing with the Legacy of Native Residential School Abuse in Canada: Litigation, ADR, and Restorative Justice' (2002) 52 *University of Toronto Law Journal* 253.

[72] For a model of agonistic constitutionalism see Tully, n 69 above. See also C Mouffe (ed), *The Democratic Paradox* (London, Verso, 2000).

# 14

# Symptoms of Sovereignty? Apologies, Indigenous Rights and Reconciliation in Australia and Canada

KIRSTEN ANKER

## I. INTRODUCTION

EARLY ON THE morning of 13 February 2008, hundreds of thousands of Australians packed into public squares and venues all around the country in order to witness freshly elected Prime Minister Kevin Rudd deliver on one of his election promises: a long-awaited apology to the 'stolen generations' of indigenous[1] children forcibly removed from their families and placed into foster homes, mission schools and labour-training institutions between the 1880s and 1970s. The Prime Minister's audience heard him say 'sorry' for past wrongs and the suffering caused, express hope for the healing of the nation and for a 'new chapter' in Australian history, and offer the apology in the spirit of reconciliation.[2]

These sentiments were repeated, in very similar terms, in June 2008, when Canadian Prime Minister Stephen Harper offered a formal apology to those affected by *his* country's removal and assimilation policies: the survivors of Canada's Indian residential schools, their families and their communities. He announced the establishment of an Indian Residential Schools 'Truth and Reconciliation Commission' as a 'positive step in forging a new relationship between aboriginal peoples and other Canadians . . . based on the knowledge of our shared history, a respect for each other and a desire to move forward together'.[3]

While it may be tempting to speculate about the coincidence of the apologies, locally distinct factors, such as the Australian election in 2007 and the 2006 settlement of a class action over Residential School injuries in Canada, also do much to explain the timing. Likewise, the similarity in the language of the apologies detracts attention

---

[1] Whereas 'indigenous' is more common in international contexts, the Canadian constitution uses 'aboriginal peoples' as the collective name; in the Australian Native Title Act (Cth) 1993, the reference is to 'Aboriginal Peoples and Torres Strait Islanders'. I use indigenous and aboriginal more or less interchangeably.

[2] Text of Prime Minister Rudd's apology, 13 February 2008, available at http://www.aph.gov.au/house/rudd_speech.pdf.

[3] Text of Prime Minister Harper's Apology, 11 June 2008, available at http://www.pm.gc.ca/eng/media.asp?id=2149.

from the concrete differences in government strategies: the class action settlement in Canada included compensation for all former students, with the apology coming only after Harper relented to pressure from Aboriginal groups and other political parties, while in Australia, the apology was explicitly framed as a symbolic action alone, with compensation to be left to the standard avenues of litigation.

Nevertheless, there is a 'parallel of imaginative dispositions'[4] in these apologies that invites comparison, one fed by common histories as British colonies with indigenous populations, but also by their contemporary realities as economically successful, multi-ethnic states subscribing to human rights and democratic standards. My grounding argument in this chapter is that, in engaging in the discourse of reconciliation to address past injustices against indigenous peoples, the two apologies present a common set of 'symptoms' which are characteristic of sovereignty in the modern state. Plying a version of sovereignty as unlimited, unchallengeable and monologic, I argue, the apologies re-enact an original injustice that ignored the limits, challenges and multiplicities posed by the presence of indigenous peoples. In this way, they undermine their reconciliatory intentions.

Or do they? This grounding argument can be complicated in two ways: first, by considering the broader political and legal context of reconciliation in both nations, so that reconciliation can be seen as consistent with, and even necessary to, the assertion of state sovereignty, and secondly, by attending to the claim that the power of sovereignty is maintained by symbolic, as well as material, means, so that these symptoms are not conclusive.

To dig first a little deeper into the discourses of reconciliation, we can start by looking back, 12 years prior to the apologies, to when William and Donald Gladstone, Heiltsuk First Nation members from southern British Columbia, who had been arrested for selling herring spawn on kelp contrary to fisheries regulations, heard from the Supreme Court of Canada that their constitutionally protected traditional right to collect and trade spawn could be limited by general legislative objectives in the interests of 'reconciling' distinct aboriginal societies with the broader political community. According to the Court, the 'recognition and affirmation' of aboriginal rights in section 35 of the constitution has, as its purpose, not only the recognition of the fact that the land in North America was already occupied by distinctive aboriginal societies, but also the reconciliation of that fact with the assertion of Crown sovereignty over Canada.[5]

Apart from the shared factor of indigenous people and colonisation, what do aboriginal rights[6] and the two apologies have in common? They seem to be different responses to different problems, the first, a legal and rights-based response to the fact of prior occupation by indigenous peoples, the second, a moral and therapeutic response

---

[4] T Clark and R de Costa, 'A Tale of Two Apologies' (Fall 2009) *Canada Watch* 36–37, 36, 40, available at http://robarts.info.yorku.ca/files/2012/03/CW_2009_Multiculturalism.pdf.
[5] *R v Gladstone*, [1996] 2 SCR 723.
[6] It is difficult to find a common term that captures a similar area of law in both countries. In Australia, 'native title' is the inclusive term for a compendium of rights over land held by aboriginal peoples and Torres Straight Islanders, which may include exclusive possession, the right to control resources or just the right of access for specific purposes such as hunting. In Canada, aboriginal title is a species of the generic category aboriginal rights, although, in a specific sense, aboriginal rights are those based upon cultural practices—hunting, fishing, forestry—thereby constituting less than occupation of a territory. I have mainly used 'rights' as the common term, shifting to native title or aboriginal title when more precision is required.

to the attempted destruction of them as peoples. So, are the Canadian Supreme Court and Prime Ministers Rudd and Harper speaking about the same reconciliation? In Section II, I will show that both indigenous rights recognition and the apologies in Canada and Australia aspire to post-colonial justice through 'reconciliation', but will stress—and this is the first complication—that this term is marked by a profound ambiguity relating to sovereignty and the nature of law. My analysis of the content and staging of the two apologies in Section III of this chapter will show that the symptoms of sovereignty, and the related understanding of law as exclusively posited and determined by the state, prevent governments from recognising—and addressing—the foundational injustice entailed in assuming physical control and legal jurisdiction over indigenous peoples. Nevertheless, turning to rights, jurisprudence suggests that the notion of reconciliation itself is used to require indigenous peoples to live with this assumption as a historical and unavoidable fact.

The second complication arises if the power of sovereignty is understood to act not only through direct acts of force, but also through symbolic means. Sovereignty has, for a long time, been understood as the concentration of final and absolute political authority within a territory in one entity, such as a monarch or the state.[7] This had been justified by political philosophers such as Thomas Hobbes and Jean Bodin as necessary to prevent endless conflict and thus to secure individual security and freedom.[8] Since their time, various limitations—such as natural or divine law, the consent of the governed, a constitution, the rule of law or fundamental individual rights—on sovereign power have been widely accepted.[9] Nevertheless, the idea that there is only 'one law' posited by the state (or, in the case of common law, declared by judges) in any given territory remains the dominant model of sovereignty.[10] For example, even though native title in Australia is described as the result of the 'intersection' of aboriginal law with common law, this intersection is historically located at the date that Britain claimed sovereignty, after which only common law could create new rights.[11]

However, the claim that in fact there is only one source of law is problematical if one can point to any law that is irreducible to the rules of the state, or to the indeterminate and thus prolific meanings of those rules themselves.[12] Claims to absolute sovereignty are then best understood, as John Griffiths suggests, as normative arguments or expressions of an ideology—that the state should have a monopoly on law—that attempt to out-shout all other possibilities.[13] Just as European monarchs used public

---

[7] The territorial integrity of sovereign states in Europe was recognised in the Treaty of Westphalia of 1648, although Francis Hinsley traces the concept of sovereignty to the Roman Empire when the will of the Emperor became conflated with the laws of a territorial community: FH Hinsley, *Sovereignty*, 2nd edn (Cambridge, Cambridge University Press, 1986) 41–42.

[8] J Bodin, *Les six livres de la république* (1576); T Hobbes, *Leviathan* (1651).

[9] See B Tamanaha, *On the Rule of Law: History, Politics, Theory* (Cambridge, Cambridge University Press, 2004) 52–55; T Fleiner and L Basta Fleiner, *Constitutional Democracy in a Multicultural and Globalized World* (Heidelberg, Springer, 2009) 229–30.

[10] See, eg Justice Kirby's declaration that 'there is but one law applicable to, and binding upon, all the people of Australia' in *Commonwealth v Yarmirr* (2001) 208 CLR 1, 115.

[11] Ibid, 37 (Gleeson CJ, Gaudron, Gummow and Hayne JJ); *Yorta Yorta Aboriginal Community v V* (2002) 194 ALR 538, 552 (Gleeson CJ, Gummow and Hayne JJ).

[12] See M Davies, 'The Ethos of Pluralism' (2005) 27 *Sydney Law Review* 87 for a characterisation of legal theory in terms of 'one' and 'many'.

[13] J Griffiths, 'What is Legal Pluralism?' (1986) 24 *Journal of Legal Pluralism and Unofficial Law* 1, 3.

spectacle—the magnificence of jewels[14] or the terror of public executions[15]—to imprint the power of sovereignty on the minds and bodies of their subjects, state sovereignty is a story told in symbols because it is about purveying an idea as much as forcefully enacting law. The ideology of monopoly, together with racist assumptions about the lack of law or government in indigenous societies, of course, enabled colonial governments in the nineteenth and twentieth centuries in Canada and Australia to assume the right to take over indigenous lands and communities.[16] Yet, in practice, the 'intersection of normative orders' was, and continues to be, both messier and more interesting than a one-time transfer of law-making power. Indigenous law and state law interact in practical, discursive and symbolic ways.[17] Furthermore, it is in the radically open-ended symbolic dimension that the state's performance of finality fails.

First, though, if reconciliation is part of a larger 'transitional justice' story, we need to begin by understanding how justice for the indigenous peoples in Canada and Australia has become reconciliation or even 'truth and reconciliation'. What kind of transitions are contemplated or made possible by the recognition of indigenous rights or the performance of parliamentary apology rituals? Section II of this chapter provides an overview of the connections between reconciliation, justice and transition in Australia and Canada. It concludes by drawing out the ambiguities of reconciliation in indigenous rights cases, which see the discourse of justice sacrificed to that of certainty and compromise.

In the remarkably standardised vocabulary of reconciliation, the desire for transition in the form of collective or institutional change in order to address past injustice is frequently expressed in the revolutionary terms of drawing a line between an old 'then' and a new 'now',[18] as the image of 'chapters' used in both apologies evokes so well. In Section III, I argue that the articulation of this change in the apologies is deficient in that it does not accurately identify the past wrong as lying in the power of the state to carry out removal policies. Furthermore, whereas apologies purport to work towards reconciliation by building trust and restoring agency to the victims through the power to forgive, the staging of these apologies undermines the agency of the people receiving them. However, I conclude that the symbolic nature of displays of sovereignty may work to undo these deficiencies. As symbols can both powerfully enforce the status quo and remain radically open to reinterpretation, an apology has the potential to transform the colonial relationship not by breaking with past, but by providing a living resource for its continual reconstruction. In particular, where the symbols are those of an unsurrendered indigenous sovereignty, these cannot be contained as benign rituals.

---

[14] B Lenman, 'The Exiled Stuarts and the Symbols of Sovereignty' (2001) 25 *Eighteenth Century Life* 185, 185.

[15] As Foucault's account of the 1757 execution of Damiens so vividly illustrates: M Foucault, *Surveillir et Punir* (Paris, Gallimard, 1975) 9–11.

[16] See S Banner, 'Why *Terra Nullius*? Anthropology and Property in Early Australia' (2005) 23 *Law & History Review* 95; M Borch, 'Rethinking the Origins of *Terra Nullius*' (2001) 32 *Australian History Review* 222. The early periods of colonisation in Canada were more equivocal with respect to First Nation's law: see J Webber, 'Relations of Force and Relations of Justice: The Emergence of Normative Community between Colonists and Aboriginal Peoples' (1995) 33 *Osgoode Hall Law Journal* 623.

[17] For example, the question of proof has entangled different legal orders at many levels: see K Anker, 'The Truth in Painting: Cultural Artefacts as Proof of Native Title' (2005) 9 *Law Text Culture* 91.

[18] A Schaap, *Political Reconciliation* (New York, Routledge, 2005) 90–91.

## II. IMAGINATIVE DISPOSITIONS

Canada and Australia are among many countries around the world in which reconciliation has become part of the everyday political vocabulary as shorthand for healing, restorative justice and community, principally in coming to terms with, and transitioning from, past conflict and widespread human rights abuses.[19] There are a number of specific differences, though, in the resonances of the term reconciliation in these two countries. In Australia, reconciliation is an era-defining term in contemporary politics and popular discourse which readily comprehends both the apology to the stolen generations and the legal recognition of traditional rights as participating in the nation's coming to terms with its colonial past. In Canada, the language of reconciliation has become most associated publically with political responses to the residential schools issue rather than with aboriginal rights. The courts' use of 'reconciliation' in aboriginal rights jurisprudence as an interpretive principle for section 35 thus appears as distinct from residential schools reconciliation. The following sub-section will elaborate how reconciliation has articulated past and future, conflict and community, and justice and injustice in these different contexts.

### II.1. Australia: The Reconciliation Movement and the Recognition of Native Title

The Rudd apology came as a spectacular highlight in a longer history of an Australian 'reconciliation movement' formally launched with the creation of the Council for Aboriginal Reconciliation in 1991 by Prime Minister Paul Keating's government.[20] To its supporters, reconciliation represents the chance for Australians to form a unified community whose former rifts have been healed by owning up to the injustices of the past, and by committing to 'justice and equity for all'.[21] Accounts of crimes and abuses visited on indigenous peoples, such as those made public in the 1996 Royal Commission Report on the stolen generations, *Bringing Them Home*,[22] are part of the process of coming to terms with the past, and form an all-important collective narrative in which to ground the new 'we'.

While the Report recommended a formal apology as necessary to reparations to the stolen generations, John Howard, who was Prime Minister between 1996 and

---

[19] For an overview of this global movement, see E Daly and J Sarkin, *Reconciliation in Divided Societies: Finding Common Ground* (Philadelphia, PA, University of Pennsylvania Press, 2007); see further C Knox and P Quirk, *Peace Building in Northern Ireland, Israel and South Africa: Transition, Transformation and Reconciliation* (New York, St Martin's Press, 2000); JP Lederach, *Building Peace: Sustainable Reconciliation in Divided Societies* (Washington, DC, United States Institute of Peace Press, 1997); E Yamamoto, *Interracial Justice: Conflict and Reconciliation in Post-civil Rights America* (New York, New York University Press, 1999); C Prager and T Govier (eds), *Dilemmas of Reconciliation: Cases and Concepts* (Waterloo, Wilfred Laurier Press, 2003); M Brant Castellano, L Archibald and M DeGagne (eds), *From Truth to Reconciliation: Transforming the Legacy of Indian Residential Schools* (Ottawa, Aboriginal Healing Foundation, 2008).

[20] See D Short, *Reconciliation and Colonial Power: Indigenous Rights in Australia* (Aldershot, Ashgate Publishing, 2008) 1–2, 110, 161 and passim.

[21] See, eg Council for Aboriginal Reconciliation, 'Australian Declaration Towards Reconciliation' (2000), available at http://www.austlii.edu.au/au/other/IndigLRes/car/2000/9/pg1.htm, and ReconciliAction Network, 'What is Reconciliation?', available at http://reconciliaction.org.au/nsw/education-kit/what-is-reconciliation.

[22] Human Rights and Equal Opportunity Commission, 'Bringing Them Home: Report of the National Inquiry into the Separation of Aboriginal and Torres Strait Islander Children from their Families' (Sydney, HREOC, 1997).

2007, consistently refused to issue an official apology, maintaining that to do so would require 'Australians of this generation . . . to accept the guilt and blame for past actions and policies over which they had no control', and that everybody's interests were best served by what he termed 'practical reconciliation' (addressing issues such as health, life expectancy and education) rather than 'empty symbolism'.[23] In contrast, Keating's iconic Redfern speech in 1992 had strongly invoked a 'we'—non-indigenous Australians—who are responsible: *we* did the dispossessing, *we* took lands and smashed the traditional way of life, *we* took children from their mothers, *we* practiced discrimination and exclusion.[24] Because of Howard's stand against it, an apology to the stolen generations became the most high profile reconciliation 'issue', leading to massive public participation in events such as 'Sorry Day', the Sydney Harbour Bridge Walk in 2000, the Sea of Hands[25] and the signing of 'Sorry Books'.

But in Australia, reconciliation has also engaged with the acknowledgement of a more fundamental truth: that aboriginal and Torres Straight Islander peoples are the original owners and custodians of the land, with their own continuing laws and traditions. This acknowledgement was formalised in the *Mabo* decision of 1992, in which the common law recognised 'native title' for the first time in Australian history,[26] and overruled the only previous case on the matter, *Milirrpum v Nabalco* (1971).[27] Indeed, as Keating put it in the Redfern speech, in finally doing away with 'the bizarre conceit that this continent had no owners prior to the settlement of Europeans' and enshrining this fundamental truth in law, *Mabo* provided a crucial turning point in the reconciliation process.[28] For Keating and his government, 'recognition'—both of past wrongs and of distinct aboriginal traditions—became necessary to the creation of a reconciled political community.

Two of the three majority judgments in *Mabo* certainly manifest a 'jurisprudence of regret', as Jeremy Webber has coined it, which reflects the objectives of the reconciliation movement.[29] Acknowledging and turning from the injustices and human rights violations of the past are key to the decision of Justices Deane and Gaudron, for instance, who describe a 'conflagration of oppression and conflict which was . . . to spread across the continent to dispossess, degrade and devastate the aboriginal peoples and leave a national legacy of unutterable shame'.[30] Together with Justice Brennan, the justices lay responsibility for these wrongs on a principle which they identify, in

---

[23] 'Opening Ceremony Speech', Australian Reconciliation Convention, 26 May 1997, available at http://www.austlii.edu.au/au/other/IndigLRes/car/1997/3/speeches/opening/howard.htm.

[24] P Keating, Redfern Park Speech, 10 December 1992, available at http://www.nswalp.com/redfern-speech. See also F Brennan, 'Reconciliation in the Post-Mabo Era' (1993) 61 *Aboriginal Law Bulletin* 18.

[25] A public art installation in every major Australian city consisting in thousands of plastic hands planted in the ground bearing the name of a signatory to a petition in support of reconciliation. See http://www.antar.org.au/sea_of_hands.

[26] *Mabo v Commonwealth (No 2)* (1992) 175 CLR 1. See N Sharp, *No Ordinary Judgment: Mabo, the Murray Islanders' Land Case* (Canberra, Aboriginal Studies Press, 1996); MA Stephenson and S Ratnapala (eds), *Mabo: A Judicial Revolution* (St Lucia, University of Queensland Press, 1993); P Russel, *Recognizing Aboriginal Title: The Mabo Case and Indigenous Resistance to English-Settler Colonialism* (Toronto, University of Toronto Press, 2005).

[27] *Milirrpum v Nabalco* (1971) 17 FLR 141.

[28] Keating, n 24 above. See also Brennan, n 24 above.

[29] J Webber, 'The Jurisprudence of Regret: The Search for Standards of Justice in Mabo' (1995) 17 *Sydney Law Review* 5.

[30] *Mabo*, n 26 above, 104.

a handful of Australian property cases, as the 'doctrine of *terra nullius*',[31] by which inhabited colonies could be treated as uninhabited for the purposes of European settlement if the occupants were considered 'uncivilised' and lacking in government or laws. The rejection of *terra nullius* as the basis of beneficial Crown ownership of land and the recognition of a form of traditional title which survived the acquisition of sovereignty in *Mabo* led to its reputation as a 'revolution' that represented a new beginning for Australian law brought into conformity with 'contemporary notions of justice and human rights'.[32]

'National shame', as Desmond Manderson has argued, may be a more appropriate response to the past than the intergenerational guilt eschewed by Howard, as it entails a deep realisation about not only how 'we' non-indigenous Australians—our culture and our law—have been implicated in the treatment of the indigenous peoples upon the basis of their difference from us, but also an empathy for their suffering that lays the foundations for community with them. The contradictory identification on which shame rests—and its troubled vision of community—is destabilising, but it is this instability that is a force for deep change in a reconciliation project.[33] Something of this tension between difference and commonality is central to Andrew Schaap's idea that reconciliation sustains post-colonial politics teleologically as the never-to-be-reached community of political adversaries, and is thus premised on acting with others in diversity rather than as the unified 'we' that is the focus of mainstream reconciliation discourse.[34]

Similarly, the recognition of a *sui generis* title—one that takes its characteristics from indigenous law—as a question of equality is based upon a tension between what we have in common and what makes us unique and different. As Charles Taylor famously describes it, recognition is so compelling in the justice claims of minority groups such as aboriginal peoples because it unites two opposite tendencies inherited from Enlightenment thinking: the idea of universal dignity that demands respect for what is innately human in all of us and the idea of the authentic, unique self.[35] *Sui generis* aboriginal rights respond to the claim that it is just that equal respect be accorded to the unique and specific ways which indigenous peoples have of relating to the land.

*Mabo*, the reconciliation movement and the academic and popular discourse in which they are embedded in many ways prompted a profound rethinking of Australian history and the place of indigenous peoples in the nation's politics. The shame of past wrongs, the 'rejection of *terra nullius*' and the urge towards recognising aspects of

[31] Although a principle of international law whose relevance to Australia is debated, and consequently irrelevant as a precedent as such, *terra nullius* may, nonetheless, be understood as a contemporary shorthand for a discourse of power that informed the government's approach to indigenous rights to land, and thus relevant to the court's attempt to initiate a new legal 'truth'. See D Ritter, 'The Rejection of *Terra Nullius* in *Mabo*: A Critical Analysis' (1996) 18 *Sydney Law Review* 5.

[32] *Mabo*, n 26 above, 30 (Brennan J). See, eg Stephenson and Ratnapala, n 26 above. Its revolutionary aspects were downplayed by others responding to concerns that the rejection of settled law amounted to flagrant 'judicial legislation': see G Nettheim, 'Judicial Revolution or Cautious Correction? *Mabo v Queensland*' (1993) 16 *UNSW Law Review* 1.

[33] D Manderson, 'Unutterable Shame, Unuttered Guilt: Semantics, Aporia and the Possibility of Mabo' (1998) 4 *Law Text Culture* 234.

[34] Schaap, n 18 above, 77–84.

[35] C Taylor, 'The Politics of Recognition' in A Gutman (ed), *Multiculturalism: Examining the Politics of Recognition* (Princeton, NJ, Princeton University Press, 1994) 26–32.

traditional indigenous life through *sui generis* rights infiltrated the public imagination and destabilised received understandings of history, law and even geography, as I can personally attest. Reconciliation has arguably become a 'people's movement', giving many white Australians a vehicle to get involved in change at the community level.[36] In practical terms, native title put indigenous interests in land on the official-property map and, through compulsory negotiation requirements in the Native Title Act passed the year following *Mabo*, built consultation and agreement-making with indigenous peoples into the day-to-day corporate practices of primary industry proponents. Indigenous law in various forms, such as painting and dancing, has been accepted in court as evidence of title, and trial judges find themselves confronting the reality of indigenous protocols—gender-specific knowledge about 'country', grandmother avoidance, mourning bans—in conducting native-title hearings.[37]

The limits on transformation, however, are clearly stated in the *Mabo* decision. The original acquisition of sovereignty by Britain—also undermined by the rejection of *terra nullius*—is declared non-justiciable as an act of state. The possibility of using *Mabo* to argue for the non-extinguishment of an original Aboriginal sovereignty was later held 'untenable' in *Coe v Commonwealth*.[38] Furthermore, the obligation to conform to contemporary notions of justice is limited to those changes which will not fracture the 'skeleton of principle' which structures the Australian legal system, and which guarantees the 'peace and order of Australian society'.[39] The skeleton at stake here is the feudal doctrine of land tenure, in which the Crown holds a 'radical title' to Australia enabling it to grant valid land titles, so that native title was permanently extinguished over those lands, and the native title-holders were legally and finally dispossessed.

In this light, the instauration of a new post-colonial community in Australia thus comes at the expense of addressing two of the most foundational injustices for indigenous peoples: loss of sovereignty and loss of land.[40] With community autonomy and dispossession frequently cited as being at the root of indigenous poverty and disadvantage,[41] these two elements are also crucial to 'practical reconciliation' that would focus on improving health indicators and standards of living. Furthermore, with the passage of the Native Title Act 1993 and its 1998 amendments, subsequent High Court decisions have replaced the language of justice, equality and human rights—and a concern for the big picture of colonisation and the responsibilities of those who are its benefactors—with a technical focus on statutory interpretation and the language of certainty for governments and third parties.[42] The Court has emphasised the 'fragility'

---

[36] H Reynolds, 'A Crossroads of Conscience' in M Grattan (ed), *Essays on Australian Reconciliation* (Melbourne, Black Inc, 2000) 55.

[37] See L Anderson, 'The Law in the Desert: Alternative Methods of Delivering Justice' (2003) 30 *Journal of Law & Society* 120.

[38] (1993) 118 ALR 193.

[39] *Mabo*, n 26 above, 30.

[40] See S Motha, 'Reconciliation as Domination' in S Veitch (ed), *Law and the Politics of Reconciliation* (Aldershot, Ashgate Publishing, 2007) 72–76.

[41] However, see the argument by P Sutton that this orthodoxy largely ignores the reality that many endemic problems, such as poor health, alcoholism and domestic violence, result from a deeply embedded 'clash of cultures': 'The Politics of Suffering: Indigenous Policy in Australia since the 1970s' (2001) 11 *Anthropological Forum* 125, 133–35.

[42] G Nettheim, 'The Search for Certainty and the Native Title Amendment Act 1998 (Cth)' (1999) 22 *University of NSW Law Journal* 564, 565.

of native title so that it is more readily found to be permanently extinguished by other interests in land.[43] These are the limits in the extent to which the truth of Australia's 'bizarre conceit' will be taken on board.

## II.2. Canada: Healing, Truth and a Just Settlement

In Canada, it was the report of the Royal Commission on Aboriginal Peoples in 1996 that provided a focal point for public awareness about colonial history, with particular emphasis on residential schools and the assimilative and discriminatory premises of the schools policy.[44] Although not a prominent term in the report, reconciliation is used to refer the 'renewal of relationships' between the aboriginal peoples and the state, which can be traced back to the 1970s and the negotiation of the first modern treaties, and the involvement of aboriginal leaders in discussions prior to the repatriation of the constitution in 1982 and in subsequent constitutional reform.[45] Arguably, reconciliation as political practice in North America also has a much older history located in indigenous traditions such as the Haudenosaunee 'condolence' ceremonies, which would seek to re-establish harmony and balance after the passing of a *roiiane* or 'chief', after the commission of an offence and prior to the signing of a treaty.[46]

The Commission argued that the mistakes of colonisation, which had left many aboriginal communities with debilitating social problems, could only be redressed by 'a national policy of reconciliation and regeneration' which entailed a complex notion of multinational citizenship and coexisting, self-governing peoples.[47] However, in the context of a ballooning number of litigated cases detailing rampant physical and sexual abuse of residential schoolchildren at the hands of officials, as well as awareness of the ongoing impact of the residential school experience on aboriginal families and communities, public reconciliation discourse in Canada has attached itself more specifically to the residential school issue.

In response to the report's recommendation of a public apology, the Minister of Indian and Northern Affairs presented a 'Statement of Reconciliation' to survivors in 1998, offering regret on behalf of all Canadians for the legacy of colonial policies, and apologising specifically for the physical and sexual abuse suffered at the schools. However, the alternative dispute resolution programme established shortly afterwards to deal with the tort-based harms of residential schools was widely criticised as being inadequate: it did not compensate for loss of culture or other social harms such as alienation from family and community, the process itself was legalistic and dehumanising,

---

[43] A Reilly, 'From a Jurisprudence of Regret to a Regrettable Jurisprudence: Shaping Native Title from *Mabo* to *Ward*' (2002) 9 *Murdoch University Electronic Journal of Law* [38].

[44] Royal Commission on Aboriginal Peoples, 'Final Report. Volume 1. Looking Forward, Looking Back' (Ottawa, Minister of Supply and Services, 1996).

[45] Ibid, ch 7.

[46] See W Fenton, *The Great Law and the Longhouse* (Norman, OK, University of Oklahoma Press, 1998) 135–202; M Pomedli, 'Eighteenth Century Treaties: Amended Iroquois Condolence Rituals' (1995) 19 *American Indian Quarterly* 319.

[47] N 44 above, ch 7. See also M Walters, 'The Jurisprudence of Reconciliation: Aboriginal Rights in Canada' in W Kymlicka and B Bashir (eds), *The Politics of Reconciliation in Multicultural Societies* (Oxford, Oxford University Press, 2008) 173.

and consultation with First Nations communities had been inadequate.[48] A House of Commons Standing Committee report on the programme, responding to the criticisms of survivors, the Assembly of First Nations and other organisations, recommended a process that would allow Canadians to hear survivor's stories because of the need for empathy in the healing process.[49] When a class action over residential school abuse was settled in 2006, the agreement included the establishment of a public enquiry in the form of a Truth and Reconciliation Commission, a common payment for attendance at schools and funding for community healing projects. The government resisted including a prime ministerial apology as part of the package, but reversed its decision in June 2008, recognising that the absence of an apology was 'an impediment to healing and reconciliation'.[50]

A larger ambit for reconciliation in the Canadian political arena along the lines of the Commission's 'renewal of relationships' can be traced, although it has flowered less prominently than in Australia, or at least has been branded less consistently. After Prime Minister Trudeau's 1969 White Paper proposal to replace special Indian status and rights with universal and individual rights failed, the report of the Indian Claims Commission on the nature of grievances surrounding Indian claims noted that a 'satisfactory settlement' would require nothing less than 'redetermining the place of Indian people within Canadian society . . . with them as the major partner in the enterprise'.[51] The impetus for the federal government to reconsider this place was fuelled by the Supreme Court's decisions in *Calder*[52] and *Baker Lake*[53]—the first in the modern era to acknowledge the inherent rights of indigenous peoples to land and resources—and by the growing confidence of groups such as the James Bay Cree, whose roadblocks threatened the development of hydroelectricity projects in Quebec in the early 1970s, in asserting their rights through direct-action protests.[54]

In 1973, the federal government introduced its 'Comprehensive Land Claims' policy, which proposed to resolve outstanding claims to traditional territories via negotiated agreements. In 1982, the repatriation of the constitution included a new section, section 35, which 'recognized and affirmed' existing aboriginal and treaty rights in sub-section (1). Aboriginal self-government, although rejected as a constitutional amendment by public vote following the 1992 Charlottetown Accord, was recognised as an inherent section 35 right by the federal government 1995.[55]

The courts, too, have often taken the position that matters between Aboriginal

---

[48] N Funk-Unrau and A Snyder, 'Indian Residential School Survivors and State-Designed ADR: A Strategy for Co-optation?' (2007) 24 *Conflict Resolution Quarterly* 285, 295–97.

[49] See, eg the statements of members of the Committee cited in P Regan, 'An Apology Feast in Hazleton: Indian Residential Schools, Reconciliation and Making Space for Indigenous Legal Traditions' in Law Commission Canada (ed), *Indigenous Legal Traditions* (Vancouver, UBC Press, 2007) 57.

[50] N 2 above.

[51] N 44 above, ch 7.

[52] *Calder v British Columbia (Attorney General)* [1973] SCR 313.

[53] *Hamlet of Baker Lake v Minister of Indian Affairs and Northern Development* [1979] 87 DLR (3d) 342.

[54] For a history of this, see S McCutcheon, *Electric Rivers: The Story of the J Bay Project* (Montreal, Black Rose, 1991); H Feit, 'Hunting and the Quest for Power: The J Bay Cree and Whiteman Development' in RB Morrison and CR Wilson, *Native Peoples: The Canadian Experience*, 3rd edn (Toronto, Oxford University Press, 2004) 171–207.

[55] See Minister of Indian Affairs and Northern Development, *The Government of Canada's Approach to Implementation of the Inherent Right and the Negotiation of Aboriginal Self-Government* (1995), available at http://www.ainc-inac.gc.ca/al/ldc/ccl/pubs/sg/sg-eng.asp.

nations and the Crown are best resolved by negotiation rather than litigation, supported by the finding in *R v Sparrow*[56] that section 35(1), in representing the culmination of a long struggle by aboriginal associations and others for the constitutional recognition of aboriginal rights, 'provides a solid constitutional base upon which subsequent negotiations can take place'.[57] Indeed, it is in the development of the jurisprudence around section 35 that cases following *Sparrow* begin to identify reconciliation as one of the objectives of the section, and to argue for negotiation as a path to reconciliation.[58] It is in these cases that we begin to understand the role that reconciliation plays in restructuring the relationships between aboriginal peoples and the state.

## II.3. The Ambiguity of Reconciliation

What is striking about the landmark Canadian cases, from an Australian perspective, is the absence of anything resembling *Mabo*'s 'jurisprudence of regret'. In *Sparrow*, *Van Der Peet*,[59] *Gladstone* and *Delgamuukw*,[60] reconciliation may point the way to a renewed relationship between the Crown and Aboriginal Peoples, but there is little rhetoric of facing up to historic truths and turning from past injustice. One obvious distinguishing factor is the history of treaty-making between colonists and aboriginal peoples in North America, initially as part of the fur trade, but later to secure both military alliances and the surrender of aboriginal lands, which was absent in Australia.[61] The practice became official policy in the Royal Proclamation of 1763, which reserved unsurrendered land to the 'several Nations or Tribes of Indians' and provided that such land could only be ceded to, or purchased by, the Crown. Nineteenth-century cases in Canada and the US confirmed that the Indians possessed a form of land title, which the Chief Justice Marshall of the US Supreme Court held to be derived from their prior occupation,[62] and the Privy Council in *St Catharine's Milling* held to be derived from the Royal Proclamation itself.[63] Officially, the law had done the right thing.

Yet, as the court admits in *R v Sparrow*, 'the rights of the Indians were often honoured in the breach'.[64] Furthermore, the treaty policy had never been systematically pursued in British Columbia.[65] However, territorial claims by First Nations in this province launched the modern era of aboriginal rights, and, in *Calder v BC*, a

---

[56] *R v Sparrow* [1990] 1 SCR 1075.

[57] Ibid, 1105 (Dickson CJ and La Forest J).

[58] *Delgamuukw v British Columbia* [1997] 3 SCR 1026, 1123 (Lamer CJ); *R v Van Der Peet* [1996] 2 SCR 507, 668 (McLachlin J).

[59] *Van Der Peet*, ibid.

[60] *Delgamuukw*, n 58 above.

[61] For a Canadian history, see JR Miller, *Compact, Contract, Covenant: Aboriginal Treaty Making in Canada* (Toronto, University of Toronto Press, 2009).

[62] See *Worcester v Georgia* (1832) 6 Peters 515, 542–44.

[63] *St Catherines Milling & Lumber Co v The Queen* (1888) 14 App Cas 46, 54–55.

[64] N 56 above. US President Jackson's apocryphal response to the *Worcester v Georgia* was 'J Marshall has made his decision, now let him enforce it!' Jackson was responsible for the forced re-location of over 13,000 Cherokee in what is known as the 'trail of tears': T Perdue and M Green (eds), *The Cherokee Removal: A Brief History with Documents* (Boston, MA, Bedford/Saint Martin's, 1995) 176–79.

[65] Treaty No 8 extends into the north-east corner of British Columbia, and the province also entered into treaties covering small areas on Vancouver Island, but lack of funds apparently halted this process: see the dispatch from Governor D in 1861 quoted in *Calder v British Columbia*, n 52 above, 330 (Judson J).

majority in the Supreme Court of Canada recognised that Indian title existed because 'when the settlers came, the Indians were there, organized in societies and occupying the land as their fore-fathers had done for centuries'.[66] This finding is presented as consistent with *St Catharine's* and supported by a line of US decisions dating back to the Marshall decisions. *Calder* seems to be in continuity with the past, correcting a mistake in British Columbia, rather than manifesting a revolution in the law.

It may also be that courts, largely bound by precedent and existing constitutional structures, are not readily the instruments of reconciliation and the reconstruction of relationships, as the Canadian Royal Commission on Aboriginal Peoples suggests.[67] In that case, it remains to be understood why the Australian High Court was drawn to speak in such clearly revolutionary terms. Indeed, the reasoning of Justice Toohey in *Mabo*, who also found for the existence of native title in Australia, resembled much more that of his Canadian counterparts in accepting the continuity of this doctrine that was widely applied elsewhere in the British Empire, merely adopting it into Australian law. One explanation is that Justices Brennan, Gaudron and Deane were acutely aware of a 'crisis of truth' provoked by the earlier *Milirrpum* decision, in which the anthropological fact that the Yolngu claimants had a complex system of law was made to surrender to the legal fact that Australia had been treated as a settled—unoccupied—colony in the common law.[68] Australian law had both to explain this lacuna and to rescue itself from it, and the dramatic rejection of *terra nullius* performed this rhetorically. Native title restored the tainted legitimacy of the common law.

In continuity with this argument, reconciliation itself in Australia has been seen as a foil that offers 'post-colonial' legitimacy by including indigenous peoples in a nation-building agenda, but permits stronger claims for land, political autonomy and reparations to be sidelined. Indigenous Australians must 'forgive and forget'. Indeed, the Council for Aboriginal Reconciliation had been created to head off a campaign for a national treaty, ostensibly to educate non-indigenous Australians about indigenous issues so that they would be prepared for a treaty process and better understand the claims for justice made by indigenous peoples. However, as Damien Short notes, '"education" for the non-indigenous rather than "justice" for the indigenous emerged as the dominant theme of the [reconciliation] process'.[69] Treaty activist Kevin Gilbert makes it clear that the 'feel good' reconciliation discourse has bitter overtones: 'What are we to reconcile ourselves to? To a holocaust, to massacre, to the removal of us from our land, from the taking of our land?'[70] Without reparations, a treaty or a return of a political and economic base, he argues, 'the reconciliation process can achieve nothing'.[71]

Mark Antaki and Coel Kirkby have likewise observed that reconciliation emerges as an ambiguous objective in Canadian Aboriginal rights cases.[72] In *Sparrow*, it is used

---

[66] Ibid, 328 (Judson J). Hall J also identifies possession since time immemorial as the basis for Indian title, 352.

[67] N 44 above, 'Opening the Door'.

[68] See Ritter, n 31 above, 15–17.

[69] Short, n 20 above, 127.

[70] K Gilbert, *Aboriginal Sovereignty: Justice, the Law and the Land* (Canberra, Burrambinga Books, 1993) 2.

[71] Ibid.

[72] M Antaki and C Kirkby, 'The Lethality of the Canadian States (Re)cognition of Aboriginal Peoples' in A Sarat and J Culbert (eds), *States of Violence: War, Capital Punishment and Letting Die* (Cambridge, Cambridge University Press, 2009) 215.

to explain the limits that section 35 puts on the power to extinguish title assumed by the federal government under its section 91 legislative power over 'Indians and land reserved for Indians'. As the culmination of a history of the Crown's fiduciary duty towards aboriginal peoples, section 35 means that 'federal power must be reconciled with federal duty' and calls for a 'just settlement' for aboriginal peoples, explains the court, quoting Professor Lyons.[73] 'It renounces the old rules of the game under which the Crown established courts of law and denied those courts the authority to question sovereign claims made by the Crown.'[74]

In specific cases of proposed government regulation, *Sparrow* held that the reconciliation of power with duty required a compelling objective—such as resource conservation—for the infringement of any aboriginal rights or title. This was a break from the relatively blanket-power to extinguish rights assumed by the Crown in the past.

However, in *R v Van Der Peet*,[75] the purpose of section 35 is said to be to reconcile the prior occupation of distinctive aboriginal societies with the sovereignty of the Crown. Picking up on this, the *Gladstone* case added that limits to aboriginal rights are inherent in section 35 because of the need to reconcile distinctive aboriginal societies with the broader political community and with Crown sovereignty. In *Gladstone*, the *Sparrow* test for infringement shifts to one of balancing aboriginal rights with a broader range of legislative objectives (including the recognition of the historical reliance of non-aboriginal groups on resources). Furthermore, as Justice Lamer suggests in *Delgamuukw*, aboriginal territorial rights might be justifiably infringed not just by conservation measures, but by 'the development of agriculture, forestry, mining, and hydroelectric power . . . the building of infrastructure and the settlement of foreign populations to support those aims'.[76] In effect, reconciliation is used to 'justify unilateral governmental infringement of Aboriginal rights for the benefit of other Canadians'[77] in order to maintain 'societal peace'.[78]

A first sense for reconciliation, that of restoring relationships, may be made out in the characterisation of section 35 as enshrining respect for the historical fiduciary duties of the Crown towards aboriginal peoples and effecting a just settlement in the wake of colonisation through the negotiation of land-claim agreements. However, to reconcile is also to acquiesce or resign oneself to some inevitable, but undesirable, situation. The second sense is palpable in the fact that although, as Justice Lamer concludes in *Delgamuukw*, 'we are all here to stay', it is the aboriginal peoples who must acquiesce to the Crown's ultimate sovereignty over them and its capacity to infringe their rights. It is facts or juridical claims that are to be reconciled, rather than peoples, and the limits of constitutional sovereignty act as a pre-set limit to any renewal of

---

[73] N 56 above, 1106 (Dickson CJ and LaForest J).
[74] Ibid.
[75] *Van Der Peet*, n 58 above.
[76] *Delgamuukw*, n 58 above, 1111.
[77] K McNeil, 'Reconciliation and the Supreme Court: The Opposing Views of Chief Justices Lamer and McLachlin' (2003) 2 *Indigenous Law Journal* 1, 17.
[78] *Van Der Peet*, n 58 above, 668 (McLachlin J).

relationships.[79] As the court bluntly states in *Sparrow* as a premise to the history of Crown recognition of title, 'the sovereignty of the Crown has never been in doubt'.[80]

To these first two versions of reconciliation, Mark Walters would add reconciliation as a kind of accounting, rendering inconsistent things consistent.[81] This sense is perceptible in the limits placed on aboriginal rights by ordinary legislative objectives, according to which aboriginal rights become simply one more interest for the state to balance—an inconsistent element to reconcile—rather than the representation of a partnership or a just settlement with distinct constitutional protection.[82]

As Brenna Bhandar argues, the transition to a post-colonial democracy requires a historical narrative to support it, and in Canada, this has been a seamless, progressive narrative of nation formation.[83] Elements that would rupture contemporary political and economic structures—such as indigenous sovereignty or rights to the commercial exploitation of resources—are subsumed into the assertion of crown sovereignty or excluded by a construction of the proper aboriginal subject in terms of cultural authenticity and the traditional past.[84] In recent developments in the *Haida Nation* case, the Crown's assertion of sovereignty and de facto control over indigenous lands and resources is held to give rise to a duty to act honourably and to engage in negotiations. The court seems to suggest that Crown sovereignty is still an open wound that requires an ongoing process of reconciliation and negotiation in order to establish legitimacy. Yet, as Bhandar observes, defining reconciliation as a process that began with the assertion of sovereignty ignores racist policies from the nineteenth and twentieth centuries that brought so much violence and injustice to indigenous peoples. Instead of dealing with these injustices face on, the court projects a kinder, more 'honourable' vision of sovereignty back into the past. Reconciliation is not failed by these problematical turns; it is, in fact, a necessary element in closing off the meaning of the past occupation of aboriginal peoples for the present generation.

## III. SYMPTOMS OF SOVEREIGNTY

The limits on recognition through indigenous rights, in which the discourse of reconciliation may be seen as complicit, have a clear material and economic component, but they also speak to deeply embedded understandings of state sovereignty and law. The following section will elaborate these understandings by taking up two instances of contradiction in the apologies and linking them to symptoms of sovereignty in rights jurisprudence.

As exemplified in the Australian reconciliation movement and the recommendations of the Canadian Royal Commission on Aboriginal Peoples, apologies are frequently

---

[79] Walters, n 47 above, 178.

[80] N 56 above, 1103 (Dickson CJ and La Forest J).

[81] Walters, n 47 above, 167.

[82] Ibid, 182.

[83] B Bhandar, '"Spacialising History" and Opening Time: Resisting the Reproduction of the Proper Subject' in S Veitch (ed), *Law and the Politics of Reconciliation* (Aldershot, Ashgate Publishing, 2007) 94.

[84] This refers to Chief Justice Lamer's definition of aboriginal rights in *Van Der Peet* as those practices, traditions and customs that were central to aboriginal societies prior to contact with Europeans. In many cases, this test has resulted in courts restricting rights to non-commercial practices such as subsistence fishing or logging for personal use: see *Van Der Peet*, n 58 above; *R v Sappier*; *R v Gray* [2006] 2 SCR 686.

seen as necessary to repairing past injustices and as contributing to reconciliation as the regeneration of a national polity. While *apologia* in ancient Greek was a speech in defence, modern usage has it that an apology is made to the wronged party precisely in the absence of a defence, excuse or justification for the injurious act. It is the exposure of defencelessness that makes an apology a remedial speech act, for it reverses the original imbalance of power in which one party harmed the other.[85] Political apologies by powerful institutions may work for different reasons, however. In a careful analysis of the links between apology and reconciliation, Pablo de Greiff concludes that official apologies help to restore in citizens an all important attitude of trust in institutions.[86] And while institutions need to become trustworthy—with concrete actions such as legal accountability, reparations, truth-telling and institutional reform—he argues that apologies can cement an attitudinal change towards trust by interpolating citizens in a commitment to shared norms and values considered as binding.[87] In confirming a normative community, apologies are then about more than just the charisma of the speaker or an empty ritual.

Our two apologies ground their gestures towards the restoration of relationships in norms of equality and respect for human rights and dignity. They also ask for acceptance and thus semantically recognise the agency of indigenous peoples, redressing the denial of agency in the removal policies. However, as the analysis below will show, these norms are undercut by structural contradictions and limitations that are symptomatic of the dominance of state law and its assumption of a unilateral, declaratory power. Nevertheless, in the end, this is a story that tells itself too neatly and assumes too much. As a public symbol that will be memorialised and referred to by future generations, a political apology has an uncontrollable life that goes beyond the person of the prime ministers and the moment of delivery. Taking the apology rituals as a whole reveals other symptoms, symptoms of the symbolic life of apology that cannot be reduced to singular sovereignty and posited law.

### III.1. Identifying the Wrong

Many writers on the topic consider apology to require, at a minimum, that the wrongdoer admit responsibility and express regret: 'My actions caused you harm. Your suffering was my fault.'[88] Prime Minister Rudd's apology names both the actions taken by the state and their consequences:

> We apologise for the laws and policies of successive Parliaments and governments that have inflicted profound grief, suffering and loss . . . We apologise especially for the removal of

---

[85] See N Tavuchis, *Mea Culpa: A Sociology of Apology and Reconciliation* (Stanford CA, Stanford University Press, 1991) 15–22.

[86] P de Greiff, 'Apologies in National Reconciliation Processes' in M Gibney, R Howard-Hassmann, J-M Coicaud and N Steiner (eds), *The Age of Apology: Facing Up to the Past* (Philadelphia, PA, University of Pennsylvania Press, 2008) 131.

[87] See also A Lazare, *On Apology* (Oxford, Oxford University Press, 2004) 43–58.

[88] See Tavuchis, n 85 above, 19; de Greiff, n 86 above, 129; J Lind, *Sorry States: Apologies in International Politics* (Ithaca, NY, Cornell University Press, 2008) 16. Tracing this ethic of responsibility back to a Weberian account of modernity, see J Olick and B Coughlin, 'The Politics of Regret: Analytical Frames' in J Torpey (ed), *Politics and the Past: On Repairing Historical Injustices* (Lanham, MD, Rowman & Littlefield Publishers, 2003) 46–50.

Aboriginal and Torres Strait Islander children from their families, their communities and their country.

For the pain, suffering and hurt of these Stolen Generations, their descendants and for their families left behind, we say sorry. To the mothers and the fathers, the brothers and the sisters, for the breaking up of families and communities, we say sorry. And for the indignity and degradation thus inflicted on a proud people and a proud culture, we say sorry.

Prime Minister Harper's apology follows a similar pattern:

I stand before you . . . to apologize to aboriginal peoples for Canada's role in the Indian residential schools system. The government of Canada now recognizes that it was wrong to forcibly remove children from their homes and we apologize for having done this. We now recognize that it was wrong to separate children from rich and vibrant cultures and traditions, that it created a void in many lives and communities, and we apologize for having done this. We now recognize that, in separating children from their families, we undermined the ability of many to adequately parent their own children and sowed the seeds for generations to follow, and we apologize for having done this.

If an apology is to communicate recognition of the wrongfulness of the behaviour and to express genuine regret, then it ought to include a promise of non-repetition.[89] Harper makes no explicit promise or undertaking of non-repetition, but the apology imagines a future in which repetition would not be possible: '[t]here is no place in Canada for the attitudes that inspired the Indian residential schools system to ever again prevail'.

Rudd's apology moves that the 'Parliament resolve . . . that the injustices of the past . . . never, never happen again'. Those who object to the continuation under Rudd of the Northern Territory National Emergency Response introduced by the Howard administration in 2007 as being a heavy handed and aggressive takeover of indigenous communities that some liken to an earlier era of protectionism[90] would be cynical of this promise. Furthermore, present governments cannot literally bind those of the future. On the other hand, as Janna Thompson points out, states both make and keep long-term commitments—treaties, for example—which are desirable because they promote political stability and individual security.[91] The more embedded a promise becomes in the legal and political structures of a state—in treaties, legislation or a constitution—the more reliable that promise appears. Thus, the movement in Australia to amend the constitution so as to prohibit the use of the 'races power' for discriminatory purposes, or to sign a *makarrata* or treaty with indigenous peoples,[92] can be seen as a way of attempting to institutionalise the government's trustworthiness, to use de Greiff's terms.

But rather than pin the evaluation of the apologies to some deferred action that puts 'words' into 'practice', I am interested here in taking what Prime Minister Howard

[89] M Minow, *Between Vengeance and Forgiveness: Facing History after Genocide and Mass Violence* (Boston MA, Beacon Press, 1998) 112.

[90] See http://stoptheintervention.org/facts. See also generally J Altman and M Hinkson, *Coercive Reconciliation: Stabilise, Normalise, Exit Aboriginal Australia* (Melbourne, Arena Publications, 2007).

[91] J Thompson, 'Apology, Justice, and Respect: A Critical Defense of Political Apology' in Gibney et al, n 86 above, 31–44, 38.

[92] See S Brennan, G Williams and B Gunn, '"Sovereignty" and Treaty-Making between Indigenous Peoples and Australian Governments' (2004) 26 *Sydney Law Review* 307.

eschewed as mere symbols seriously: that is, what the apologies themselves perform in the limit of their promise. Both texts apologise for the role of the state in carrying out laws and policies that were unjust. In popular, as well as academic, discussions of removal practices, this injustice is often put down to the values, ignorance and prejudice of the times, such as being in the best interests of the child, the best interests of aboriginal peoples, or the best interests of society or progress.[93] 'We now recognize that it was wrong', says Harper, but removal policies were hitherto justified by the assumption that 'aboriginal cultures and spiritual beliefs were inferior and unequal'.[94] The apology implies that it is these attitudes that must not be repeated.

But crucially, in the historical context of neither nation was it illegal, unconstitutional or otherwise beyond the power of the state to act in the way in which it did. In Canada, to suggest as much would be to question the validity of the governing legislation, the Indian Act, which is still in force, and the limits of the federal power under section 91(24) of the constitution over Indians and lands reserved for Indians which made them wards of the state. In Australia, it was precisely the issue of the constitutional validity of acts of removal that was tested in the 'stolen generation' case, *Kruger v Commonwealth* (1997).[95] The Chief Protector of Aborigines in the Northern Territory was authorised by a legislative ordinance 'to undertake the care, custody, or control of any aboriginal . . . if, in his opinion it is necessary or desirable in the interests of the aboriginal'.[96] The High Court held that there were no express or implied limitations in the constitution that would have imposed equality or human rights standards in order to render the actions of the Chief Protector taken under the ordinance unconstitutional.

As Alexander Reilly points out with regard to the Australian apology, by declining to resile from the power of the state to enact or enforce removal laws, the apology effectively confirms the power to pass such laws.[97] Removal laws are thus explained as resulting from the (legitimate) use of state power for (illegitimate) racist ends based upon misjudgements of indigenous cultural difference or the misguided assumption that assimilation was possible and necessary. The apology consequently only challenges the attitudes of people who make and carry out the law rather than accounting for state power, and thus, Reilly argues, 'perpetuates an assumption of sovereignty that made possible the forced removal of Aboriginal children in the first place'.[98] These arguments point us to the elephant in the room: unconstrained and unchallenged, sovereign power is the mute ground upon which unjust laws—even those that egregiously destroy the most basic rights and freedoms supported in a liberal democratic framework—may still be law.

---

[93] See, eg the discussion page at http://www.turning-point.ca/?q=node/19491; R Chrisjohn and S Young, *The Circle Game: Shadow and Substance in the Residential School Experience in Canada* (Penticton, BC, Theytus Books, 1995) ch 1; R Van Krieken, 'The "Stolen Generations" and Cultural Genocide: The Forced Removal of Australian Indigenous Children from their Families and its Implications for the Sociology of Childhood' (1999) 6 *Childhood* 297, 298; T Barta, 'Sorry and Not Sorry: How the Apology to the Stolen Generations Buried a History of Genocide' (2008) 10 *Journal of Genocide Research* 201, 202.

[94] N 3 above.

[95] 190 CLR 1.

[96] Aboriginals Ordinance 1918 (NT), s 6.

[97] A Reilly, 'Sovereign Apologises' in J Evans, A Genovese, A Reilly and P Wolfe (eds), *Sovereignty: Frontiers of Possibility* (Honolulu, Hawaii University Press, 2012).

[98] Ibid, 197–98.

In the apologies, then, sovereignty is a no-go zone. In the same way that an assumption of a monopoly on sovereignty in the apologies limits the identification of the wrong, it also limits what can be recognised within aboriginal rights doctrine. In Australia, the land title recognised by the common law has its source in the 'traditional laws and customs' of the claimant group: this is the meaning of 'intersection'. But this intersection has a use-by date, because, after Britain's assertion of sovereignty, the common law is the only law, and no new law or new legal rights from another source can be recognised. For the Yorta Yorta Aboriginal Community, who experienced a heavy impact of colonisation from the early days of settlement, this meant that their claim to native title based upon traditional laws and customs recently 'revived' from what was taught to them by their parents and grandparents was refused. Based upon a lack of evidence from an interim period of practices that matched earliest accounts of local traditional culture, as well as the claimants' description of their culture as 'sleeping' and being 'woken up', the Australian High Court determined that the Yorta Yorta Community had stopped being the normative society relevant to native title law at the time that they stopped following their traditional laws. And because a society and its law were said to be 'inextricably entwined', the contemporary community was thus a new society following new law that could not be recognised due to the principle of exclusive sovereignty.[99]

In Canada, the *sui generis* character of aboriginal rights—and the goal of reconciliation—is said to be grounded both in the common law and in the aboriginal perspective on the rights. Nevertheless, the aboriginal perspective 'must be framed in terms cognizable to the Canadian legal and constitutional structure'.[100] Furthermore, Aboriginal practices will not be recognised as rights where they are considered to be incompatible with Crown sovereignty, as Justice Binnie held was the case with the Mohawk cross-border trade and mobility right claimed in *Mitchell v MNR*.[101] The common register suggested by the reconciliation of perspectives is qualified by the state's unchallenged sovereignty.

For John Borrows, one sticking point is the double standard in the question of proof in Canada: aboriginal peoples have to marshal witnesses, experts and volumes of historical, anthropological and other evidence to support their claims, while Crown sovereignty and title to land is a fact that 'has never been in doubt' and thus requires no proof, regardless of abundant evidence of political and physical contestation of this claim 'from the outset'.[102] Furthermore, he argues, no cogent theoretical justification is proposed for Crown sovereignty. The unwillingness to revisit the legitimacy or the monopoly of Crown sovereignty in either Canada or Australia, and the brick walls that this erects in the recognition of title and in the capacity to acknowledge adequately the wrong done to indigenous peoples, is perhaps one of the greatest stumbling blocks on the path to transforming the colonial relationship.

---

[99] *Yorta Yorta*, n 11 above, 552–54 (Gleeson CJ, Gummow and Hayne JJ). See K Anker, 'Law in the Present Tense: Continuity and Tradition in *The Yorta Yorta Aboriginal Community v Victoria*' (2004) 28 *Melbourne University Law Review* 1.

[100] *Van Der Peet*, n 58 above, 551 (Lamer CJ).

[101] *Mitchell v MNR* [2001] 1 SCR 911.

[102] J Borrows, 'Sovereignty's Alchemy: An Analysis of *Delgamuukw v British Columbia*' (1999) 37 *Osgoode Hall Law Journal* 537. See also P Macklem, *Indigenous Difference and the Constitution of Canada* (Toronto, University of Toronto Press, 2001) 107–31; M Walters, 'The Morality of Aboriginal Law' (2006) 31 *Queen's Law Journal* 470, 502–17.

## III.2. The Possibility of Refusal

Some accounts provide that the way in which an apology restores agency to victims and works towards reconciliation is by according them the power to forgive.[103] In these accounts, genuine apology must incorporate the possibility that it may be refused, as this is one way of earning the trust of the addressee. If it is possible to extrapolate from interpersonal power dynamics to state apologies, a political apology that makes the state vulnerable in this way would thus be enacting a certain loss of control, a limitation to the unilateral power of the state to declare how things are. Although there is understandable scepticism of vulnerability and the exchange of power in accurately explaining official apologies,[104] Harper and Rudd both invoke this element of apology.

Harper's apology directly 'asks the forgiveness of the aboriginal peoples of this country for failing them so profoundly'. As was fitting for the official status of the apology, it was delivered in Parliament. However, this also meant that it was also orchestrated and controlled by the government. For example, aboriginal leaders were initially told that they would not be given the opportunity to respond. Eventually, one hour before the event, the representatives of five different aboriginal organisations were given permission to speak and formally accepted the apology before the Commons.

The conferral of agency that is crucial to the structure of a successful apology was thus significantly impeded by the respondents' lack of control over the circumstances in which these responses were given. Furthermore, the staging of the whole ceremony would have made a rejection appear in bad faith: indeed, formal responses by aboriginal organisations that were more cautious and equivocal, which criticised the present government and highlighted the continuing oppressive policies only appeared outside of the event.[105] Turning to Rudd's speech, he requested 'that this apology be received in the spirit in which it is offered as part of the healing of the nation'. Unlike the Canadian apology, indigenous witnesses sitting in the public gallery of the Australian House of Commons were given no formal role, signifying more directly that the apology was complete without any action on their part.

In offering these apologies, the Canadian and Australian states have engaged in an act characterised semantically by interpersonal and reciprocal relations rather than unilateral action, but then transformed that act into one that effectively purports to determine, single-handedly, that an apology has been completed. This is, once more, symptomatic of the singular, monologic and positive quality of law associated with state sovereignty in which the state alone lays down definitive rules and determines the outcomes of their application.

A similar pattern—invoking a two-way process but treating it as a unilateral act—can be observed in relation to 'recognition' as a core concept in rights jurisprudence. Recognition only makes sense as an ethical principle because it is interactive: we cannot do it for ourselves. For GWF Hegel, on whom Charles Taylor drew heavily in his work, recognition is the basis of ethical community because an individual's self-consciousness—a subject's humanity—only emerges through recognition by another

---

[103] J-M Coicaud and J Jonsonn, 'Elements of a Road Map for a Politics of Apology' in Gibney et al, n 86 above, 77–91, 79; Lazare, n 87 above, 52.
[104] De Grieff, n 86 above, 130.
[105] See Quebec Native Women's Association statement, 11 June 2008, available at http://www.faq-qnw.org/pressrel-en.html.

subject. This interaction might result in domination, the recognition of another as an object, but ultimately an imbalance is undesirable because the dominant party likewise needs the recognition of a full human subject, so, in Hegel's ideal ethical state, there is an equilibrium of mutual recognition.[106]

As mentioned in Section II, recognition compellingly combines the elements of universal dignity and authentic difference. If the self is considered to pre-exist its relation with others as a monologic subject, these elements produce a tension that will always manifest as a difficulty in finding the appropriate grounds for recognition. For example, if aspects of one way of life are to be recognised as proprietary, what will constitute the standard of 'property'? How are such aspects to be selected? The 'other' will always be recognised 'in terms of' (and in terms which subjugate it to) the 'self'. In contrast, with the self understood, as Hegel's theory proposes, as dialogically and iteratively created through the recognition of others, the terms of recognition are themselves constituted in the process. Taylor develops this into a contemporary theory for strong political recognition in culturally plural democracies: that is, recognition as a cultural dialogue in which the values that ground the terms of recognition (recognising which differences upon the basis of which commonalities) are constantly shifting as a result of an ongoing 'fusion of horizons'.[107]

In legal discourse, however, the version of recognition remains a monologic one, tied to the positivist notion of law as something laid down in a unidirectional manner by a central authority and applied to individuals and groups. Recognition is a technical term that merely connects a 'this' (a fact scenario, such as a pattern of land use) to a 'that' (the ability to claim legal consequences, such as an injunction to prevent others from using the land) via the medium of legal rights. Thus, although Australian native title and Canadian aboriginal title and rights are both *sui generis* and defined in part by indigenous law, monologic recognition depends on constructing that law as a social fact, and therefore as a question of evidence and 'cognition' which hypostatises indigenous peoples and their ways.[108]

Having to demonstrate the existence of their traditional laws or establish the necessary historical use of land clearly does not sit well with the view that many indigenous peoples have of the legitimacy of their own law. For instance, in discussions with their barrister in preparation of their claim to 'sea country' off Australia's northern coast, Yolngu people put to him the rhetorical question that, if they know it is the Yolngu who own 'sea country' under their law, 'why is it not sufficient . . . simply to state this to the court?'[109] As if to insist on the illegitimacy of the assertion of sovereignty over their lands, during the hearing (held in their community), the Yolngu chose to insert their law, *rom*, into the proceedings through the performance of key ceremonies relating to the power of *rom*. As Frances Morphy puts it, these responses to the court's assertion of jurisdiction effectively declare that 'we know we are encapsulated, but we are not colonised'.[110]

---

[106] GFW Hegel, *Phenomenology of Mind (1807)*, trans JB Baillie (New York, Harper Torchbook, 1967) 229.
[107] The term is borrowed from Hans Georg Gadamer: Taylor, n 35 above, 67.
[108] Antaki and Kirkby, n 72 above, 218.
[109] F Morphy, 'Performing Law: The Yolngu of Blue Mud Bay Meet the Native Title Process' in B Smith and F Morphy, *Effects of Native Title: Recognition, Translation, Co-existence* (Canberra, CAEPR, 2007) 32.
[110] Ibid, 31.

In a recent judgment by Canadian Chief Justice McLachlin, the language of *sui generis* seems to have been replaced by that of translation, and the 'framing' role of the common law is that the pre-sovereignty practice of aboriginal peoples should be translated into the modern legal right that 'fits' it.[111] Consequently, in *Marshall and Bernard*, in which the defendants were using a claim to aboriginal title as a defence to charges of taking timber without a provincial licence, McLachlin held that Mi'kmaq use of land should be evaluated according to standards of 'possession similar to title at common law'. The result was that, with no direct evidence of use of the timber-cutting sites in question (although evidence of proximate settlements), and a statement by a Mi'kmaq chief that exclusive control of land was not desired in Mi'kmaq traditions, the court found an absence of aboriginal title. The question of the Mi'kmaq perspective is reduced to understanding the significance of timber cutting to Mi'kmaq culture, or to confirming the fit with common-law property, rather than contributing (as Justice Le Bel in dissent notes) to the development of property standards and the understandings of the rights themselves; in other words, contributing as a source of law. Justice Le Bel's approach moves closer to taking indigenous law as 'real law' that is able to contribute principles, arguments and a normative imagination to legal decisions, and that would constitute a transformed colonial law rather than reconciling aboriginal peoples to their fate as subjects of the Crown.

## III.3. The Openness of Symbols

We have seen that the state's assertion of absolute power works to undermine both the apologies and the recognition of rights as a way towards a post-colonial nation in Australia and Canada because it maintains the selfsame problematical assumptions that grounded colonial policy—namely, that indigenous law was either invisible or inferior, and that there were no limits to what the state could do in pursuing its vision of bringing indigenous peoples under the control of the dominant legal system. In coming to terms with the limits of the apologies, however, it is worth noting a few small details easily undetected in concentrating on official written texts. These details—questions of staging, ritual and symbolism—make us realise that it is problematical to take the dominant version of sovereignty as the only message.

At the Canadian apology, attendees were greeted by the sound of drumbeat and the smell of sweetgrass, the herb burnt in some North American indigenous cleansing ceremonies.[112] Harper himself participated in the cleansing by 'washing' himself with smoke. Tokenistic? Perhaps, and we would do well to heed the warning of Val Napoleon that participating in indigenous ceremonies may feel good for non-indigenous people but will not achieve reconciliation without addressing fundamental power imbalances in concrete ways. In particular, she argues that indigenous rituals remain

---

[111] *R v Marshall*; *R v Bernard* [2005] 2 SCR 220, [48]. The characterisation of native title as a problem of transation (from the 'spiritual' to the 'legal') is also prominent in Australia: see, *Western Australia v Ward* (2002) 213 CLR 1, 15 (Gleeson CJ, Gaudron, Gummow and Hayne JJ).

[112] L Dueck, 'When is an Apology Too Much? Or Not Enough?', *The Globe and Mail*, 12 June 2008, available at http://www.theglobeandmail.com/archives/when-is-an-apology-not-enough-or-too-much/article691095.

mere window-dressing without robust recognition of the political and legal systems from which they derive.[113]

But it is difficult to account for the powerful way that law affects us through our senses; and different laws engage different senses. The drumbeat, a sound symbolic of both the heartbeat and the footsteps of a people on mother earth, was described by one observer as '[a]n interesting technique which First Nations used to fully alert our spirits to the occasion'.[114] When heard up close, this sound practically forces itself into one's chest cavity, demanding that the symbolism of the beating heart of the people be lived out physically and, at least in that moment, not rationalised away.

In Australia, indigenous peoples may not have been given the floor during the apology, but the day before, at the official opening of the 42nd Parliament, local Ngunnawal elder Matilda House performed a 'welcome to country' ceremony in the Members' Hall of Parliament House: a contemporary version of a traditional welcome in which acknowledging the custodians or 'traditional owners' of lands is crucial for visitors. Again, these ceremonies—increasingly commonplace in the opening of public events in Australia—may simply be a safe gesture of recognition in which non-indigenous people participate knowing that the symbolic rights claims which they represent are unenforceable. However, as Kristina Everett describes it, the awkwardness that is often felt by non-indigenous people witnessing these symbolic manifestations of unsurrendered sovereignty in the buildings and public spaces that are most unproblematically the domain of 'whites' is unsettling: 'indigenous agency', she writes, 'once acknowledged in performance, cannot be fully directed by the nation state to serve its own ends'.[115] Because of the symbolic and discursive nature of rituals such as apologies and even land claims, their meaning cannot be determined in advance. The openness of symbols to future generations of interpretation does not threaten the mechanical strength of the state, but it does undermine its claim to be the sole source of legal meaning.

## IV. CONCLUSION

The links that I have sketched in this short comparison have allowed us to see that, despite local particularities in the way the forces of colonisation engaged with indigenous peoples, and differences in contemporary responses to historical injustices such as dispossession and child-removal policies, certain discursive and structural commonalities emerge between Canada and Australia. These are that, notwithstanding the recognition of continuing indigenous polities with autonomous and functioning legal orders, state sovereignty remains assumed, unchallenged and largely unconstrained. Reconciliation, in this context, can only ever be about learning to live with the imposition of the state's control over indigenous peoples, rather than working on a renewed relationship between peoples. Calls for reconciliation processes to include the robust recognition of indigenous sovereignty via an overhaul of political structures must also

---

[113] V Napoleon, 'Who Gets to Say What Happens? Reconciliation Issues for the Gitksan' in C Bell and D Kahane (eds), *Intercultural Dispute Resolution in Aboriginal Contexts* (Vancouver, UBC Press, 2004) 184.

[114] Dueck, n 112 above.

[115] K Everett, 'Welcome to Country . . . Not' (2009) 79 *Oceania* 53, 64.

pay attention to the way state sovereignty is understood and put into effect through the daily routine matters of the law, both practical and symbolic. An approach needs to be imagined in which indigenous law is not a curious social fact but a contributor to the ongoing conversation that makes a nation's law what it is.

The monopoly of sovereignty is something that holds sway over us through symbolic means. While the gestures of recognition and the deference to manifestations of indigenous sovereignty cannot be taken at face value, neither can it be assumed that they are meaningless unless they are backed up by concrete measures. In the same way that a constitution is said to be a 'living document' available to speak to the concerns of different eras, so too is an apology a resource for continuing to make sense of the past, and for continuing to argue about what 'is' in the present. The effect of these political apologies is thus not determined by whether the prime ministers really 'meant' what they said, judged either by their personal charisma or by the actions that they subsequently take. Once performed, the apologies cannot be undone, and they will evolve in ways that the state cannot control.

# 15

# *Working through 'Bitter Experiences' towards a Purified European Identity? A Critique of the Disregard for History in European Constitutional Theory and Practice*

CHRISTIAN JOERGES

## I. INTRODUCTION: TWO INTER-DEPENDENT THESES

THIS CHAPTER OSCILLATES between two poles or aspirations. The first is to present reflections on the constitutionalisation process, which comprises both Europe's accomplishments and its performance in the light of a specific theoretical perspective, namely, the deliberative strand of theories of democracy. However, my objective in this respect is not to enrich this theoretical debate; instead, I will focus on the transformation of theoretical deliberation into legal concepts, and suggest that conflict of laws would provide the proper legal form for the constitutionalisation of Europe. The second pole is complementary. Its main message is stated in the title: European constitutionalism and the European Convention both failed to pay proper regard to the weight of history when embarking on the adventure of writing a European Constitution. Neither the weight nor the differences in European historical experiences and memories have been taken into account. These experiences, especially in the twentieth century, were 'bitter', if not traumatic—albeit in different ways and to different degrees. In the case of Germany, the most appropriate term to capture its specific situation may be found in Bernhard Schlink's term *Vergangenheitsschuld*.[1] This notion is a construction with two components, which, through their conflation, exhibit a specific tension. The importance of the first element of the term—*Vergangenheit*, or the past—is obvious. Ideas about European unity are old. But the integration process that we are experiencing and studying was initiated after, and under the

---

[1] B Schlink, *Vergangenheitsschuld und gegenwärtiges Recht* (Frankfurt aM, Suhrkamp Verlag, 2002); the essays in B Schlink's collection deal mainly, but not exclusively, with the assessment of wrongdoing in criminal law proceedings in the past. But see, for the present context in particular, 'Die Gegenwart der Vergangenheit', 145–56.

impression of, the Second World War. The remnants of this past have been engraved in the design of Europe, and thus remain somehow present in the EU, even after, or especially because of, its enlargement. To put it even more strongly, we cannot understand what is happening in the EU, nor what we are doing and what we are achieving or failing to achieve, unless we bring to mind the meaning of institutional changes, legal commitments, and political processes and aspirations, within historical perspectives. It seems equally obvious, for a German at least, to qualify this past with the second component of Schlink's term, ie first and foremost with German guilt and the 'bitter experiences' related to it.[2] The conflation of the two components in Schlink's term produces a tension which the term *Gedächtnispolitik*—the politics of memory—captures quite well.

My thesis that important links exist between the two poles of this essay—European constitutionalism and European historical experiences—is not just a reflection upon Europe's bellicose past and the Holocaust. Historical conflicts both between European nation states and within European societies are present in all important areas affected by the integration process. This essay will briefly address two of them, namely, the debate on Europe's 'social model' and European citizenship. Again, the message will be a critical one: European constitutionalism has not taken into account the weight of historical experiences in Europe's presence and the weight of memory politics in contested political issues.

All of these references to history and the insistence that European constitutionalism should regain a historical consciousness should not be read as a purely negative critique. This critique also has a positive side. It may be best submitted as a bold and daring thesis: Europe should, by working through its past(s), renew and deepen its *acquis historique*; it may, in such processes, not only obtain or acquire a better understanding of topical and contested issues of 'the integration project', but also renew the legitimacy and even the dignity of the integration project as such.

## II. THEORETICAL FRAMEWORK: HOW DO HISTORY AND LAW INTERACT?

How history and law interact seems so obvious that the argument should not, and, indeed, does not, need any authoritative support. Nonetheless, I start with a well-known passage from Jürgen Habermas's contribution to the *Historikerstreit*:

> Our form of life is connected with that of our parents and grandparents through a web of familial, local, political, and intellectual traditions that is difficult to disentangle—that is,

---

[2] I am neither referring to personal guilt nor to the moral 'duty to remember', but to something factual which social psychology and trauma research will be able to decipher. Suffice it to cite from one of Jürgen Habermas' pertinent essays: 'Aber liegt nicht seit jener moralischen Katastrophe, in abgeschwächter Weise, auf unserer aller Überleben der Fluch des bloßen Davongekommensein? Und begründet nicht die Zufälligkeit des unverdienten Entrinnens eine intersubjektive Haftung—eine Haftung für entstellte Lebenszusammenhänge, die das Glück oder auch die bloße Existenz der einer einzig um den Preis des vernichteten Glücks, des vorenthaltenen Lebens und des Leidens der anderen einmäumen?', J Habermas, 'Geschichtsbewußtsein und nationale Identität: Die Westorientierung der Bundesrepublik' in idem, *Eine Art Schadensabwicklung* (Frankfurt aM, Suhrkamp Verlag, 1987) 164. Habermas, at times, and especially when it comes to the German past, writes very personally. Suffice it, therefore, to indicate that he is reflecting upon how the trauma of the Holocaust affects the self-consciousness of the later generations.

through a historical milieu that made us what and who we are today. None of us can escape this milieu, because our identities, both as individuals and as Germans, are indissolubly interwoven with it. This holds true from mimicry and physical gestures to language and into the capillary ramifications of one's intellectual stance . . . we have to stand by our traditions, then, if we do not want to disavow ourselves . . .[3]

This is the personal dimension. Its political complement was written out in the Habermas/Derrida manifesto published in the *Frankfurter Allgemeine Zeitung* of 31 May 2003:

Contemporary Europe has been shaped by the experiences of the totalitarian regimes of the twentieth century and through the Holocaust—the persecution and annihilation of European Jews, in which the Nazi regime made the societies of the conquered countries complicit as well . . . A bellicose past once entangled all European nations in bloody conflicts. They drew a conclusion from that military and spiritual mobilisation against one another: the imperative of developing new, supranational forms of co-operation after the Second World War.[4]

These statements will not provoke much opposition; however, the constellations to which they refer have not had much impact on my profession. This may seem surprising, it may be uncomfortable and difficult to explain, but it is a fact.[5] There is little explicit reflection by lawyers and legal historians on the shadows of the past in institutionalised Europe in legal history, not even in contemporary legal history.[6] This is not to say that legal historians are not ready to confront the law's 'darker legacy'. They may be accused of having avoided this topic for too long, but this avoidance has been over for some decades now, especially in Germany. It would, of course, be absurd to

---

[3] J Habermas, 'On the Public Use of History' in idem, *The New Conservatism* (Cambridge, MA, The MIT Press, 1990) 233.

[4] Cited from the transation in J Habermas and J Derrida, 'February 15, or What binds Europeans Together: A Plea for a Common Foreign Policy, Beginning in the Core of Europe' (2003) 10 *Constellations* 291, 296.

[5] For an instructive recent overview see T Keiser, 'Europeanization as a Challenge to Legal History' (2005) 6 *German Law Journal* 473, available at http://www.germanlawjournal.com.

[6] Such a statement requires qualifications. There is a new sensitivity to the differences in the perception and evaluation of the integration project in the European 'demoi-cracy'; see, in particular, J Lacrois and K Nicolaïdes (eds), *European Stories: Intellectual debates on Europe in National Contexts* (Oxford, Oxford University Press, 2010). Furthermore, there are, of course, important contributions to a historical interpretation of Europe in the legal literature on European integration. Suffice it to mention here JHH Weiler, 'The Community System: The Dual Character of Supranationalism' (1981) 1 *Yearbook of European Law* 267; idem, *The Constitution of Europe: 'Do the New Clothes Have an Emperor' and Other Essays on European Integration* (Cambridge, Cambridge University Press, 1999); M Kaufmann, *Europäische Integration und Demokratieprinzip* (Baden-Baden, Nomos Verlag, 1997); A von Bogdandy, 'A Bird's Eye View on the Science of European Law' (2000) 6 *European Law Journal* 208; A Somek, 'Constitutional Erinnerungsarbeit: Ambivalence and Translation' (2005) 6 *German Law Journal* 357, with references to his much more comprehensive work; U Haltern, *Europarecht und das Politische* (Tübingen, Mohr Siebeck, 2005); see also idem, 'Europäische Verfassung und europäische Identiät' in R Elm (ed), *Europäische Identität: Paradigmen und Methodenfragen* (Baden-Baden, Nomos Verlag, 2002) 252–61. Haltern's contribution is the most systematic and comprehensive. It also reflects most explicitly on the linkages between theorising Europe, reconstructing it historiographically and determining the potential role of law as *Sinnsprecher* (instantiation). My reservations against his effort to understand law and integration in the light of the essence of the political will, reason and interest, which Haltern employs (see also his 'Pathos and Patina—The Failure and Promise of Constitutionalism in the European Imagination' (2003) 9 *European Law Journal* 14) would not enable me to address the law's darker legacy. In a nutshell, I am not troubled at all by a lack of the element of political will in institutionalised Europe, but I am concerned with the complacency of constitutionalists. No rule is without exceptions, however; a notable one is C Closa, 'Dealing with the Past: Memory and European Integration', J Monnet Working Paper 01/11 (2011), available at www.JeanMonnetProgram.org.

accuse them of ignoring European history altogether. Quite to the contrary, Thorsten Keiser recently observed that Europe has attracted much attention since the Treaty of Maastricht, and has, with the Convention process, become 'one of the most important reference points of legal historical research'.[7] The primary effort of pertinent studies in the fields of private law is, however, to reveal a common cultural heritage which, in the past, is said to have formed the basis of an *ius commune europaeum*, which can now be revitalised in the search for legal unity. The equivalent in public law has been revealed by Felix Hanschmann.[8] Leading exponents of German constitutional thought such as Josef Isensee[9] and Paul Kirchhof[10] invoke a cultural communality of historical experience that is now to become the bearer of a common polity upon the basis of which a united Europe can be, and indeed should be, constituted.

These latter positions contrast drastically with the theoretical assumptions that prevail in general historical research.[11] Not surprisingly, it is also much richer and differentiated. Historians began early[12] and continue to explore the integration process, including its institutionalisation, in all its details. The intensity of the historical research into World War II, the Third Reich and the Holocaust is simply breathtaking. In addition, historical investigations which interpret the history of the integration process in the light or the shadow of European crises and failures are both available, and meet with considerable interest.[13] Yet concerns that are, indeed, very similar to my own personal uneasiness with contemporary legal history are being articulated.[14] Historians have not taken sufficient note of the diversity in Europe's historical memories, complains Konrad H Jarausch.[15] Not being a historian, I cite once more:

> Europe did possess a vague sense of cultural commonality before 1914, but that did almost disappear during the two world wars. The dominant languages such as Latin, French, and later English, and, in a regional sense also German, provided a communication medium for the educated élites. The social origin and intermarriage of the aristocracy or commercial bourgeoisie was another bond. The intensity of economic exchanges created a sense of togetherness. During imperialism, the issue of race also played a role by defining European simply as white . . . The rise of nationalism, the fierce hostility of World War I, the

---

[7] Keiser, n 5 above.

[8] F Hanschmann, '"A Community of History": A Problematic Concept and its Usage in Constitutional Law and Community Law' (2005) 6 *German Law Journal* 1129; idem, '"Geschichtsgemeinschaft": Ein problematischer Begriff und seine Verwendung im staats- und Europarecht' (2004) *Rechtsgeschichte* 150.

[9] J Isensee, 'Abschied der Demokratie vom Demos' in D Schwab et al (eds), *Staat, Kirche, Wissenschaft in einer pluralistischen Gesellschaft (Festschrift für P Mikat)* (Berlin, Duncker & Humbolt, 1989) 705–40.

[10] P Kirchhof, 'Europäische Einigung und der Verfassungsstaat der Bundesrepublik Deutschland' in J Isensee (ed), *Europa als politische Idee und als rechtliche Form* (Berlin, Duncker & Humblot, 1993) 63–101.

[11] See the references in Hanschmann, n 8 above, especially notes 47ff; see also B Stråth, 'Methodological and Substantive Remarks on Myth, Memory and History in the Construction of a European Community' (2005) 6 *German Law Journal* 255.

[12] See, in particular, W Lipgens, *A History of European Integration* (Oxford, Clarendon Press, 1982).

[13] See, eg M Mazower, *Dark Continent: Europe's Twentieth Century* (London, Penguin, 1998).

[14] KH Jarausch, 'Zeitgeschichte zwischen Nation und Europa. Eine transnationale Herausforderung', typescript, on file with the author.

[15] 'Die Überwölbung eines Ensembles von disparaten Nationalgeschichten bleibt ebenso unbefriedigeng wie die teleologischen Anstrengung, das aufklärerische und liberal-demokratische Erbe Europas herauszustellen, oder das Bemühen, die gegenwärtigen Integrationsversuche in die Vergangenheit vor 1945 zurückzuprojizieren. Gerade weil Erkenntnisinteressen, Wertbezüge und europäischen Geschichte gänzlich unvermeidlich.' See also Stråth, n 11 above.

destruction of the Central and East European Empires in the suburban Paris treaties of 1919, the breakdown of trade, the repetition of the War in 1939, etc, practically destroyed this sense of cohesion . . .

After World War II, some residual feeling of cultural affinity grew from below and was promoted by specific sectors of the European population. The common suffering of war and oppression by the Nazis animated members of the resistance movements; the shared project of restoring cultural monuments and reviving high culture called for a degree of co-operation; moreover, the eclipse of European power led to a joint defensiveness against popularising cultural influences from America or ideological subversion from the Soviet Union. But, in spite of similar social patterns . . . the nation-states were not so damaged that they did not make a come-back and culture remained organised on a national level . . .

Powerful factors have continued to limit the emergence of a European cultural identity.[16]

How to cope with cultural diversity and divergent historical memories: this seems to be the challenge that Europe is facing. Is it necessary to underline the importance of this point after enlargement? Not only did the accession countries from Central and Eastern Europe have their own national pasts, they also had other reasons for wishing to join the founding nations; last, but not least, they were not involved in the writing of institutionalised Europe's *acquis historique*.[17]

Historians will respond to these challenges. We can even assume that, sooner or later, legal historians will listen and talk to both historians and jurists. At present, however, it is impossible to anticipate such developments. Nevertheless, it is all the more important to reflect, at the very least, on the methodological difficulties of an integration of Europe's pasts into our understanding of institutionalised Europe and European law. Reinhart Koselleck dealt with this relationship between 'History, Law and Justice' some 20 years ago when addressing German legal historians, albeit at a very general level.[18] Historians, Koselleck argues, have traditionally quite openly acted like judges in their accounts of history. Although they have become conscious of this role and sought to define their accounts more cautiously and subtly, they cannot avoid talking, explicitly or implicitly, about the justice or injustice of situations, changes or catastrophes.[19] There is a link between history, legal history and law. However, there is also a fundamental difference in the approaches of historians and legal historians. Inherent in the category of law is the *telos* of repeated application, which requires respect for formalism (Koselleck: 'the maximum of formalism') because the law has to ensure that its principles, procedures and rules all transcend the individual case. In their analyses of the preparation and adoption of legislative acts, the approaches of lawyers and historians are remarkably similar. However, when it comes to the study of the development of the enactment, the legal historian has to respect the law's *proprium*.[20]

---

[16] KH Jarausch, 'A European Cultural Identity: Reality or Hope?', typescript, on file with the author.

[17] On this latter point see F Larat, 'Present-ing the Past: Political Narratives on European History and the Justification of EU Integration' (2005) 6 *German Law Journal* 273.

[18] R Koselleck, 'Geschichte, Recht und Gerechtigkeit' in D Simon (ed), *Akten des 26. Deutschen Rechtshistorikertages* (Frankfurt aM, Klostermann, 1987) 139–49, cited from the reprint in idem, *Zeitschichten. Studien zur Historik* (Frankfurt aM, Suhrkamp Verlag, 2000) 336–58.

[19] Ibid, 349.

[20] Ibid, 352.

This is all quite abstract, but it is nevertheless helpful because it makes us aware of what is bound to happen once political processes end with a juridical act. It is not just that lawyers, as they did with the Draft Constitutional Treaty (DCT) in so many books, start to apply their methods of interpretation to the text that they received. They will also project their understanding of the meaning of the political sphere into their interpretations, and will bring their visions of the social functions of law and its normative aspirations to bear. The case of the European Economic Community is particularly illustrative here. What, legally speaking, was new and promising in this Treaty? What kinds of commitments had the signatories accepted? What kind of post-national legitimacy could the new entity claim? How could the rule of law in the European Community be strengthened? In his account of the European Community's *raison d'être*, Joseph Weiler has famously and convincingly underlined three rationales: Europe was about ensuring peace, promoting prosperity and overcoming discrimination on grounds of nationality.[21] These are all lessons that Europeans had learned from their pasts. The importance of both their juridification in the Treaty and their subsequent implementation cannot be overestimated. Yet they are by no means sufficiently substantiated to document some comprehensive unity or to exclude fundamental disagreements about the ends of the Community, about its legitimacy and its *finalité*. A comprehensive legal history informing us about the different national ways to write European law is still to be written. In Germany alone we can identify at least three schools of thought, each of which promotes its own distinct vision of democratic positivism, functionalism and ordo-liberalism.[22] This diversity would certainly become much richer through the inclusion of more legal traditions. And such an exercise could inform us about both the law's and the European Union's capacity to live with pluralism and diversity.

### III. *UNITAS IN PLURALITATE*

If legal scholarship has invested so little, what can we expect from intergovernmental conferences or even from the Convention? I am not aware of any analysis of the use of history and of memory politics in the Convention process.[23] Just one text element refers explicitly to the past, namely, the Preamble.[24] In the original version of the

---

[21] JHH Weiler, 'Fin-de-siècle Europe: Do the New Clothes Have an Emperor' in idem, *The Constitution of Europe*, n 6 above, subtly commented on by Z Bankowski, 'The Journey of the European Ideal' in A Nortan and J Francis (eds), *A Europe of Neighbours? Religious Social Thought and the Reshaping of a Pluralist Europe* (Edinburgh, Centre for Theology and Public Issues, 1999) 149–72.

[22] See C Joerges, 'What is Left of the European Economic Constitution? A Melancholic Eulogy' (2005) 30 *European Law Review* 461. Even with national communities, the perceptions of what is noteworthy differ considerably. Ordo-liberalism, in my view, the intellectually most interesting and practically most influential German contribution to European law, is not part of the mindset of the general German European law scholarship.

[23] So much has been done—the review essay by M Große Hüttman, 'Das Experiment einer europäischen Verfassung' (2005) 28 *Integration* 262, presents six German language volumes—that I may easily have overlooked pertinent efforts.

[24] For the text see OJ C310/2004, 1 of 16 December 2004, also available at http://european-convention. eu.int. For an instructive analysis see A von Bogdandy, 'Europäische Verfassung und europäische Identität' (2004) 59 *Juristen Zeitung* 53, especially 55ff; for a brief synopsis of the preambles to the different versions of the European Treaties see Larat, n 17 above.

Convention, this was quite a euphemistic document. At the very end of the whole process, however, in June 2004, the intergovernmental conference, following a Polish initiative, changed the Preamble quite considerably. The first two, somewhat ostentatious, passages were dropped, and the reference to 're-united Europe' was replaced by a 'Europe, re-united after bitter experiences'.

## III.1. Constitutionalisation

One could have imagined a more substantiated reference. The 'bitter experiences' are simply copied from the Preamble of the Polish constitution.[25] Poland, indeed, had particularly bitter experiences, and this notion will have very clear connotations. But what is their meaning in the ensemble of 27 Member States? More important, perhaps, and certainly painful, the formula can be read as comprising the suffering of European nations. Might it comprise German suffering? But why is there no mention of 'the persecution and extermination of the European Jews, in which the Nazi regime also involved the societies of the countries they had conquered'?[26] There is neither an official interpretation available nor can one detect traces of discussions, let alone controversies, of Europe's 'bitter experiences'. This seems to be shaming enough. The intergovernmental silence may even be telling in a specifically political way. The revised Preamble seems to present what Germans call a *Verschlimmbesserung*: an improvement, in that it no longer just documents European pride, and a worsening, in that it documents self-pity, instead of shame and guilt. It continues to do what Tony Judt analyses so intriguingly and movingly in the epilogue of his recent *Postwar* as a pan-European style of *Vergangenheitsbewältigung*.[27] It does what the Germans have done for decades after the war, namely, to forget about their former citizens. It does what the Western Europeans have done, namely, to remember their liberation from the occupier but to forget about their own involvement; and it does not liberate Eastern Europeans from the perverse interpretation of exterminative racism as a machination of capitalism. What a self-deception! We must not infer from the absence of the darkest side of our past in the official constitutional agenda that we have escaped from its shadows.

The real challenge, we concluded in our introductory observations, is the challenge of European diversity. How to accomplish 'unity in diversity' (*unitas in pluralitate*), the motto of the European Union according to Article IV-1 of the DCT? Nicolaus Cusanus operated with his *coincidentia oppositorum* in a framework that too few Europeans understand. And, in the context of the Convention process, we must certainly ask how the Union's motto might be transformed into law. The answer submitted in the next section is this: through an understanding of European law as a new species of conflict of laws. This suggestion, it is submitted, is not only an appropriate response to the diversity of European pasts, but is also, as the following section will argue, the one that is most compatible with the state of the EU. It is a specifically legal conceptualisa-

---

[25] Which reads: 'Mindful of the bitter experiences of the times when fundamental freedoms and human rights were violated in our Homeland'.

[26] Thus, Habermas and Derrida, n 4 above.

[27] T Judt, *Postwar: A History of Europe since 1945* (New York, Penguin, 2005) 803–31.

tion, which is not, of course, meant to replace theoretical and philosophical efforts to define the vocation of European integration.

In the presentation of my version of European constitutionalism, I have to refrain from any systematic appraisal of the plethora of suggestions that have been submitted during the last two decades (or previously). To prepare my own argument, it is sufficient to focus on just one learned sceptic, namely, Dieter Grimm, who has continuously and consistently defended the notion of constitutionalism against its transposition into Europe's post-national constellation. Pertinent suggestions, Grimm warns, are all at odds with the important functions which we are expecting the constitutions of democratic polities to serve. To cite from Grimm's lucid recent summary of his argument:[28] '[The constitution] constitutes the public power of a society[29] . . . People expect the constitution to unify their society as a polity . . . The constitution is regarded as a guarantee of the fundamental consensus that is necessary for social cohesion.'[30] But here the law ends: 'Integration as a collective mental process cannot even be ordered by law.'[31]

What cannot be guaranteed through constitutions within the nation state is unlikely to occur within the Union.[32] Here, an empirical observation can be made. The legitimacy of the EU, in the traditional Weberian sense, is eroding. What the proponents of the European constitution assume is that it will help to compensate for these failures and will foster social integration. This, however, is unlikely to happen, or, as we can say by now, this assumption has already proved to be erroneous.

Grimm's argument insists both fairly and coherently on the specifics of constitutional law in democratic societies. He could have, following Giandomenico Majone's example,[33] pointed to Occam's razor, which prescribes 'not to introduce new terms unless they actually improve our understanding of the processes and phenomena under investigation', and vice versa: the Constitutional Treaty is, legally speaking, a treaty. It could not mutate through some fiat of the Convention. It did not transform into anything other than an intergovernmental act. There is no good reason, Grimm concludes, for any conceptual camouflage.

The argument is correct—yet it remains somehow unconvincing. It is certainly important to remember that the juridification of democracy was achieved in nation states, and that we must not equate transnational entities, including the EU, with states or fully fledged federations. But this caveat does not tell us how to respond to post-national constellations. The quest for the constitutionalisation of the EU and for a cure to its 'democracy deficit' reflects the erosion of nation-state governance, the emergence of transnational governance—and the quest for its legitimation. To rephrase this concern, Grimm asks us to adhere to our inherited dichotomy of national constitutional law and international treaty law, assuming that the entrance into the post-national constellation is legally insignificant. Grimm, of course, does much to

---

[28] D Grimm, 'Integration by Constitution' (2005) 3 *International Journal of Constitutional Law* 193; for an update see D Grimm, 'The Achievement of Constitutionalism and its Prospects in a Changed World' in P Dobner and M Loughlin (eds), *The Twilight of Constitutionalism?* (Oxford, Oxford University Press, 2010) 3–22.

[29] Ibid, 194.

[30] Ibid, 194.

[31] Ibid, 196.

[32] Ibid, 197.

[33] In his *Dilemmas of European Integration* (Oxford, Oxford University Press, 2005) 14.

turn this assumption into a normatively and sociologically substantiated argument. What he fails to do, however, is to explore alternatives to the type of legitimacy that statal constitutional law provides, and to address the transnational deficiencies of that law. Europeanisation and globalisation may require precisely this.

## III.2. 'Deliberative' Supranationalism

How do we find out? Since we seek to find out how constitutional law interacts with its societal environment, and, in particular, with Europeanisation and globalisation, it seems appropriate to consider how the closest neighbouring disciplines, especially integration research and international relations theory, conceptualise these developments. Clearly, this is still too general a question, which does nothing but expose us to a rhapsody of approaches which pursue questions that the law does not pose, and which it is ultimately unable to answer. However, it is easy to see that we have a methodological problem in common, namely, the tensions between our categories and the changes in the context to which these categories refer explicitly or implicitly. Our core categories, in national constitutional law and in international law, just as in international relations theory, all refer to the nation state as their basic unit. This dependence has been called the 'misery of methodological nationalism' by Michael Zürn.[34] His diagnoses deal with the contextual conditions of political action:[35] the nation state, he argues, is no longer in a position to define its political priorities autonomously (as sovereign), but is, instead, forced to co-ordinate them transnationally. It is not only the members of nation states (national citizens) who must recognise their political actions; states, too, have also become accountable to the transnational bodies in which their politics are subjected to evaluation. To be sure, national governments vehemently continue to defend their fiscal powers. 'Whilst resources remain at national level, the formulation of politics has been internationalised and recognition transnationalised.'[36] Parallels with what we observe in the legal system are readily apparent. Like Zürn, we can argue that the entry of law into the post-national constellation is not at our—or the law's—disposition. We can observe how the law responds to this multidimensional disaggregation of statehood and, in addition, become aware of the demands articulated at the transnational (European) level of politics, on the one hand, and at national and regional levels, on the other. We will then understand the pressure and requests for an adaptation of national law, and the honest and not so honest references to an institutionalised integration *telos*, etc.

This, as Immanuel Kant famously and sarcastically observed,[37] is the point at which

---

[34] 'Politik in der postnationalen Konstellation. Über das Elend des methodologischen Nationalismus' in C Landfried (ed), *Politik in einer entgrenzten Welt. 21. wissenschaftlicher Kongreß der Deutschen Vereinigung für Politischen Wissenschaft* (Cologne, Verlag Wissenschaft und Politik, 2001) 181–203; idem, 'The State in the Post-National Constellation—Societal Denationalisation and Multi-Level Governance', ARENA Working Paper 35/1999 (Oslo, 1999). Similarly, U Beck, 'Beyond Methodological Nationalism. Towards a New Critical Theory with Cosmopolitan Intent' (2003) 10 *Constellations* 453 (their differences in the use of the term need not concern us here).

[35] Ibid, 188–91.

[36] My transation; ibid, 188.

[37] I Kant, 'The Contest of Faculties' in idem, *Political Writings*, 2nd edn, H Reiss edn (Cambridge, Cambridge University Press, 1991).

lawyers tend to cease to rely on reason but instead content themselves with authoritatively deciphering certified texts such as the Treaty and/or its interpretation by an institutionalised authority such as the ECJ. To turn one of Kant's famous sayings[38] upside-down, this may be the way it operates in practice, but it does not suffice in theory. We cannot content ourselves with such self-perceptions or officious self-descriptions of the claims of validity raised by institutionalised Europe. In addition, or even instead, we must ask ourselves whether these claims might 'deserve recognition'.[39] This type of critical reflection is inevitable simply because we know about the 'indeterminacy' of law and its inability to determine its own application.

What is true for legal decision-making holds equally true for the conceptual exercises that lawyers, especially German lawyers, call 'theories'. It is essential to understand that these exercises cannot rely exclusively on the authority of our given texts or on the authority of social science. The insights, debates and approaches of political science cannot be translated literally into the language of the law and of legal discourses. Systems theory can provide us with the most elegant framework to substantiate this insight.[40] However, we do not need to subscribe to this framework. The law must discover for itself, with categories of its own, whether and, if so, how it can overcome 'the misery of methodological nationalism'.

Jürgen Neyer and I submitted a response which we coined 'deliberative' (as opposed to traditional or doctrinal) supranationalism—and continue to defend and elaborate this concept.[41] Briefly, we did not suggest that deliberation in transparent or opaque transnational bodies would constitute democratic transnational or European governance. Instead, we started from below, with the simple observation that no Member State of the EU can take decisions without causing extra-territorial effects on its neighbours.[42] Provocatively put, perhaps, but brought to its logical conclusion, this effectively means that nationally organised constitutional states are becoming increasingly incapable of acting democratically. They cannot include all those who will be affected by their decisions in the electoral processes, and, vice versa, citizens cannot influence the behaviour of the political actors who are taking decisions on their behalf.

---

[38] 'That may be all right in theory, but does not do in practice'; I Kant, 'Über den Gemeinspruch: Das mag in der Theorie richtig sein, taugt aber nicht für die Praxis', vol 9 of *Werkausgabe* edited by W Weischedel (Darmstadt, Wissenschaftliche Buchgesellschaft, 1971) 125ff.

[39] See J Habermas, 'Constitutional Democracy: A Paradoxical Union of Contradictory Principles?' (2001) 29 *Political Theory* 766.

[40] See G Teubner, *Networks as Connected Contracts* (Oxford, Hart Publishing, 2011) 17ff.

[41] For a restatement on which the following remarks draw see C Joerges, "Deliberative Political Processes' Revisited: What Have We Learnt about the Legitimacy of Supranational Decision-Making' (2006) 44 *Journal of Common Market Studies* 779; idem, 'Rethinking European Law's Supremacy: A Plea for a Supranational Conflict of Laws' in B Kohler-Koch and B Rittberger (eds), *Debating the Democratic Legitimacy of the European Union* (Lanham, MD, Rowman & Littlefield, 2007) 311–27; thereafter, for example, 'Unity in Diversity as Europe's Vocation and Conflicts Law as Europe's Constitutional Form' in A Greppi and R Nickel (eds), *The Changing Role of Law in the Age of Supra and Transnational Governance* (Baden-Baden, Nomos Verlag, forthcoming 2014); Jürgen Neyer's latest restatement is *The Justification of Europe: A Political Theory of Supranational Integration* (Oxford, Oxford University Press, 2012). See also C Joerges and F Rödl, 'Reconceptualising the Constitution of Europe's Post-national Constellation—By Dint of Conflict of Laws' in I Lianos and O Odudu (eds), *Regulating Trade in Services in the EU and the WTO: Trust, Distrust and Economic Integration* (Cambridge, Cambridge University Press, 2012) 762–80.

[42] This argument was first submitted in C Joerges, 'Taking the Law Seriously: On Political Science and the Role of Law in the Process of European Integration' (1996) 2 *European Law Journal* 105 and restated in idem, 'The Impact of European Integration on Private Law: Reductionist Perceptions, True Conflicts and a New Constitutionalist Perspective' (1997) 3 *European Law Journal* 378.

Hence, it is only through a supranationally valid law that democratic governance can be accomplished. Deliberative supranationalism seeks to identify principles and rules that serve precisely this end. It is a concept that is well anchored in real existing European law, in doctrines such as the following: the Member States of the Union may not enforce their interests and/or their laws unboundedly; they are bound to respect European freedoms; they may not discriminate; they may only pursue legitimate regulatory policies approved by the Community; they must co-ordinate in relation to the regulatory concerns that they may follow; and they must design their national regulatory provisions in the most Community-friendly way.

## III.3. Europeanisation via Conflict of Laws Methodology

The primary function of these types of norms is co-ordinative. It represents a 'proceduralisation' of the category of law in the sense that Jürgen Habermas and others have defined this legal paradigm.[43] Deliberative supranationalism pleads for a proceduralised understanding of European law, for a 'law of law production'.[44] In order to illuminate its specific status, I have qualified European law as a new species of conflict of laws.[45] Conflict of laws seeks to identify the appropriate legal responses in multi-jurisdictional constellations. It is an old discipline which, in its modern (post-1848) development, shares all the weaknesses of methodological nationalism. Its methodology, however, is rich and adaptable to vertical conflicts between different levels of governance, as well as to the diagonal conflicts which result from the assignment of different competences to different levels of governments in constellations which require the co-ordination or subordination of such partial competences.[46] It is, furthermore, an approach to the resolution of complex conflict constellations, which is by no means appropriate only within international settings, but is likewise appropriate within national legal systems. It is an approach which reflects the continuous need for law production, and seeks to ensure the law's legitimacy through proceduralisation. It is precisely this need which is constitutive for the EU. To rephrase our initial thesis, the constitutionalisation of Europe should not seek to replace national constitutional law. Instead, it should be prepared to work continuously on Europe's *unitas in pluralitate*. This process can be characterised as a constitutional conflict of laws paradigm.

It cannot be the objective of this essay to elaborate this version of supranationalism much further. Suffice it to restate that deliberative supranationalism continues to do what conflict of laws has done during its long history, namely, to identify the rules and

---

[43] See, as a brief summary, J Habermas, 'Paradigms of Law' in M Rosenfeld and A Arato (eds), *On Law and Democracy: Critical Exchanges* (Berkeley, CA, University of California Press, 1998) 13–25.

[44] FI Michelman, *Brennan and Democracy* (Princeton, NJ, Princeton University Press, 1999) 34.

[45] N 41 above; see, previously, C Joerges, 'Transnationale 'deliberative Demokratie' oder 'deliberativer Supranationalismus'? Anmerkungen zur Konzeptualisierung legitimen Regierens jenseits des Nationalstaats bei R Schmaltz-Bruns' (2000) 7 *Zeitschrift für Internationale Beziehungen* 145; idem, 'The Europeanization of Private Law as a Rationalisation Process and as a Contest of Disciplines—an Analysis of the Directive on Unfair Terms in Consumer Contracts' (1995) 3 *European Review of Private Law* 175.

[46] See, similarly, C Schmid, 'Selective Harmonisation: Vertical, Horizontal and Diagonal Conflicts: Diagonal Competence Conflicts between European Competition Law and National Regulation: A Conflict of Laws Reconstruction of the Dispute on Book Price Fixing' (2000) 8 *European Review of Private Law* 155.

principles which frame multi-jurisdictional constellations. In the EU, it does this with much more strength and with orientations which form the fundamental achievements of the *acquis communautaire*: the Member States have, in principle, to recognise their laws mutually; however, they remain autonomous where domains and orientations which they regard as essential are concerned. The guarantee of this type of autonomy can be understood as an institutionalisation of tolerance in the trans-legal sense of this notion.[47] All this is not to say that the arguments, critiques and scepticism towards this vision of supranationalism do not deserve to be considered. What I understand to be the strength of the argument—namely, its perception of the democracy failure of constitutional states—also points to a practical weakness of the EU which the theory of deliberative supranationalism cannot cure.

## IV. EXEMPLARY ILLUSTRATIONS

Does all this have anything to do with Europe's praxis? Are all these matters merely for the Preamble and not for the actual contents of a Constitutional Treaty? How compatible or dysfunctional are they when brought to bear on the mundane world of European affairs? My thesis is that Europe's pasts are present in our daily business and not just in debates about memorials for the European Jewry and/or the Roma and the Sinti, about surrender and/or liberation days, about resistance and/or collaboration, about genocide trials and the remuneration of forced labour, or about the true nationality of Albert Einstein. In order to substantiate my assertion, I could now go into a huge spectrum of topics—only to get lost there. It would be both pointless and, at the same time, too abstract simply to insist that there are varieties of capitalism in Europe, that Scandinavian welfarism has always been distinct, that the history of antitrust in post-war Germany differs from that of Italy, that the French *planification* and *services publiques* are not identical with Germany's *Ordoliberalismus* and its *Daseinsvorsorge*. My argument is much stronger and more specific: it concerns the 'bitter experiences' to which European societies have responded individually, in concert or collectively, and my assertion is that it would be beneficial for Europe to reflect upon its working through its pasts. Two of the topics addressed explicitly and implicitly in our agenda seem particularly appropriate for exemplary discussions, namely, 'social Europe' and 'European identity and European citizenship'. The advantage of this focus is that I can be very brief, though other topics are equally important. One is the rule of law and of experiences with the deformalisation of public governance, though this may be too subtle. Another such topic is enlargement, but this is too large to be dealt with *en passant*.[48]

---

[47] See R Forst, 'Toleration, Justice and Reason' in C McKinnon and D Castiglione (eds), *The Culture of Toleration in Diverse Socities: Reasonable Tolerance* (Manchester, Manchester University Press, 2003); J Habermas, 'Religion in der Öffentlichkeit. Kognitive Voraussetzungen für den 'öffentlichen Vernunftgebrauch' religiöser und säkularer Bürger' in idem, *Zwischen Naturalismus und Religion* (Frankfurt aM, Suhrkamp Verlag, 2005) 119–54.

[48] For a particularly thought-provoking starting point see T Judt, 'The Past is Another Country: Myth and Memory in Post-war Europe' in J-W Müller (ed), *Memory and Power in Post-war Europe: Studies on the Presence of the Past* (Cambridge, Cambridge University Press, 2002) 157–83; in legal literature see J Přibáň, 'European Union Constitution-Making, Political Identity and Central European Reflections' (2005) 11 *European Law Journal* 135; A Sajó, 'Legal Consequences of Past Collective Wrongdoing after Communism' (2005) 6 *German Law Journal* 425, all of them with rich references.

## IV.1. Social Europe and the Disregard for History in the Convention Process

I will not try to summarise the vast topical debates on social Europe here. Instead, I will address a neglected dimension of this debate, namely, the ambivalent legacy of 'the social' (the efforts to find a stable response to the social conflicts in capitalist societies) as a constitutional issue.

### IV.1.a. Rechtsstaat v Sozialstaat

The patterns of debate on social justice, democracy and the rule of law are enormously stable. It all starts, in German memory, with Max Weber's warning that the intrusion of values of social justice into the legal system (the turn to substantive rationality) will threaten the law's formal rationality and the rule of law as such.[49] Or should we understand 'social justice' as an inherent promise of true democracy? Hermann Heller was probably the first to deliver a systematic constitutional theory in which a social model and the rule of law were synthesised, and the *soziale Rechtsstaat* presented as the best, or the only, conceivable democratic response to the tensions between the classes in capitalist societies.[50] Heller's defence of social democracy resonates famously in the commitments of Germany's Basic Law,[51] but it was never uncontroversial. Two types of arguments are particularly important: in the neo-liberal and monetarist view, the quest for a 'social' democracy is economically irrational and risks destroying our freedoms. This second aspect was drastically articulated by von Hayek's characterisation of welfarism as a 'road to serfdom'.[52] The authoritarian and populist right never cared about the law's rationality. Deformalisation was inevitable, but should—and this was the fascist and national socialist conclusion in the 1920s and 1930s—be compensated by strong political leadership representing *il movimento* or *das Volk* directly. This is no longer the vocabulary of modern populism. What remains a common credo of populist movements is their anti-modernism, their instrumentalisation of anxieties, their appeal to collective cultural or national—but always exclusionary—identities. How far away is our darker past? The issue that has just resurfaced in the, at present, most intensively discussed book on the Third Reich in Germany, Götz Aly's *Hitler's Volksstaat*.[53] Aly not only underlines how the Nazis cared about the welfare of their *Volksgenossen*, but also points to very uncomfortable continuities in social policies.

---

[49] M Weber, *Economy and Society* (Berkeley, CA, University of California Press, 1978) 873–874; on socialism see his 'Socialism' in idem, *Political Writings* (Cambridge, Cambridge University Press, 1994) 272–303.

[50] See W Schluchter, *Entscheidung für den sozialen Rechtsstaat: Hermann Heller und die staatstheoretische Diskussion in der Weimarer Republik*, 2nd edn (Baden-Baden, Nomos Verlag, 1983); D Dyzenhaus, *Legality and Legitimacy: C Schmitt, H Kelsen and Hermann Heller in Weimar* (Oxford, Oxford University Press, 1997). Important texts by Heller have been made accessible by AJ Jacobsen and B Schlink (eds), *Weimar: A Jurisprudence of Crisis* (Berkeley, CA, University of California Press, 2000).

[51] Art 20 para. 1: 'Die Bundesrepublik Deutschland ist ein demokratischer und sozialer Bundesstaat.' (The Federal Republic of Germany is a democratic and social federal state).

[52] FA von Hayek, *The Road to Serfdom* (London, George Routledge & Sons, 1944).

[53] G Aly, *Hitler's Volksstaat. Raub, Rassenkrieg und nationaler Sozialismus* (Frankfurt aM, Simon Fischer, 2005). For a critical review with many references see, eg M Spörer, available at http://hsozkult.geschichtee. hu-berlin.de/rezensionen/2005-2-143. To mention Aly is not to acknowledge that statements like 'the defence of the *Sozialstaat* is a defence also of expropriation and robbery' reflect the ambivalences of the social state particularly well.

This has become a subtext of the renewed debates on the compatibility of freedom and social justice, between the *Rechtsstaat* and the *Sozialstaat*.[54]

### IV.1.b. Social Europe in the Draft Constitutional Treaty

Hermann Heller's legacy was strong in post-war Germany. And Germany, in its search for a synthesis of a social model and the rule of law, did not choose a *Sonderweg*. The responsibility for ensuring welfare, balancing social inequalities and creating infrastructure for economic development has become a common feature of the European nation state. It is in this abstract sense that we can identify 'a European social model' as one of the four dimensions of 'a multi-function state that combines the Territorial State, the state that assures the Rule of Law, the Democratic State, and the Intervention State'.[55]

Given the strength of this tradition, it was predictable that the Convention, even though this was not originally foreseen, would have addressed this precarious dimension of the integration project. The ambition of the Convention to design a document of constitutional dignity left no choice. A refusal to enlarge the agenda would have damaged the political credibility of the whole endeavour. Working Group XI on Social Europe had a belated start, but worked all the more intensively.

This had an impact. Social Europe became a visible dimension of the Draft Constitutional Treaty.[56] It rests mainly on three pillars: the commitment to a 'competitive social market economy';[57] the recognition of 'social rights'[58] to be implemented by the European Court of Justice; and the introduction of 'soft law' techniques for the co-ordination of social policies.[59] It is, however, once again both remarkable and deplorable that all of these elements were introduced by political fiat and without much reflection on historical experience. Joschka Fischer and Jacques Villepin, to whom we owe the assignment of constitutional dignity to the concept of the 'social market economy', knew they were giving a political signal—though, apparently, not much more. Nobody seems to have explained that the '*soziale Marktwirtschaft*' was Germany's post-war historical compromise, supported by the Christian Democrats, the trade unions and both Christian churches.[60] No one seems to have recalled the ambivalent past of this project. No one seemed to know or care about the reasons

---

[54] Aly receives attention for his continuity theses. On 11 August 2005, www.haaretz.com reproduced the report of the Deutsche Nachrichtenagentur on an infamous contribution of Oskar Lafontaine to the electoral campaign of Germany's new Left Party ('The state is obligated to prevent family fathers and women from becoming unemployed because of Fremdarbeiter (foreign workers) taking away their jobs by working for low wages').

[55] S Leibfried and M Zürn, 'Reconfiguring the National Constellation' in idem (eds), *Transformations of the State* (Cambridge, Cambridge University Press, 2005) 1–36, 8; for prominent historical confirmation see T Judt, *Postwar: A History of Europe since 1945* (New York, Penguin Press, 2005) 791ff; idem, *Ill Fares the Land* (New York, Penguin Press, 2010) 127ff.

[56] N 24 above.

[57] Art 3(3).

[58] See Title IV of the Draft Constitutional Treaty (n 24 above).

[59] See, especially, Art I-14(4) of the DCT; the assignment of a competence 'to promote and co-ordinate the economic and employment policies of the Member States' has been repealed. Art I-11(3) as amended on 22 June 2004.

[60] See M Glasman, *Unnecessary Suffering: Managing Market Utopia* (London, Verso, 1996) 96ff; C Joerges and F Rödl, 'The "Social Market Economy" as Europe's Social Model?', EUI Working Paper Law No 2004/8 (2004), slightly revised version in L Magnusson and B Stråth (eds), *A European Social Citizenship? Preconditions for Future Policies in Historical Light* (Brussels, Lang, 2005) 125–58.

which the German Constitutional Court had given for its rejection of the idea of a constitutionalisation of the market economy in its seminal *Investitionshilfe* judgment, handed down in 1954.[61] The standard response in the debates on the social dimension of the Convention to the openness and indeterminacy of the formula in the Constitutional Treaty was that all modern constitutions need to resort to programmatic commitments. Germany is then cited again as an exemplary case. The future *Gestalt* of the *soziale Rechtsstaat* was, indeed, by no means clear at the time of the adoption of the Basic Law. However, as indicated, it was quite clear how the *soziale Markt-twirtschaft* would try to give a specific content to the social commitments of the Basic Law, and it was apparent that this 'third way' met with broad political and societal support. The Bundesverfassungsgericht also found broad support for the view that the concrete design of Germany's social model should be left to the legislature and was not prescribed by the Basic Law.

Would such awareness have made a difference? It might, at least, have led some of the actors to proceed with more caution and to be more careful with their promises. The same holds true for two other pillars of 'social Europe'. What should make us trust in the capability of the ECJ to accomplish social progress through the powers that it has in the interpretation of the new social rights? It is difficult to understand upon what kind of evidence the Convention's Working Group XI may have based its conclusion 'that the open method of co-ordination has proved to be a useful instrument in policy areas where no stronger co-ordination instrument exists' without taking note of the experience which we have had with the deformalisation of social commitments.

*IV.1.c. Social Europe and the French Referendum*

It was no longer possible to be more cautious in the presentations of 'social Europe' after the campaigns in France had got off the ground. It seemed that Pandora's box had been opened.[62]

There is little doubt that the perceived dismantling of the French welfare state through the integration process, the portrayal of Europe as neo-liberal deregulation machinery, and the anxieties that such portrayals of Europeanisation and globalisation provoked amongst the French had a substantial impact on their '*non*'. Political commentators and academic observers hold this view; solid opinion polls confirm their point.[63] The French referendum is certainly not one-dimensional. Among the mixed motivations which seem to have guided the French, the disappointing insight that Europe could no longer be understood as just a *grande France* may have been as important as Joachim Schild assumes.[64] The attention this event attracted in the com-

---

[61] *Bundedverfassungsgericht* in 5 BVerfGE 7 (1954). On the contemporary discussion in Germany see G Brüggemeier, *Entwicklung des Rechts im organisierten Kapitalismus*, vol 2 (Frankfurt aM, Syndikat, 1979) 269ff.

[62] See D della Porta and M Caiani, 'Quale Europa? Europeizzazione, Identità e Conflitti', typescript, on file with the author; J Schild, 'Ein Sieg der Angst—das gescheiterte französische Verfassungsreferendum' (2006) 28 *Integration* 187; especially enlightening for non-French observers is J-L Andreani, 'France solidaire et France libérale', *Le Monde*, 15 June 2006.

[63] For a detailed discussion see della Porta and Caiani, n 62 above.

[64] Schild, n 62 above, 199.

munity of European constitutionalists is nevertheless disappointing.[65] What I seek to underline—and what the comments cited confirm, at least implicitly—is the presence of France's past, which manifests itself in the patterns of the debate. It seems to me unsurprising that the kind of European future which the Draft Constitutional Treaty had so vaguely outlined, and which its proponents had so confidently proclaimed, could not cope with this past.

## IV.2. Identity and Citizenship

What does it mean to be a citizen of the EU? No other issue brings law and history in general, and law and 'bitter memories' specifically, together so intimately. Precisely for this reason, the idea of a constitutional conflict of laws deserves to be considered as a means to avoid the pitfalls which the concept of European citizenship entails.

It is difficult, even impossible, to avoid Habermas and the notion of constitutional patriotism when one enters this arena. As, in particular, Jan-Werner Müller has explained,[66] it was not Jürgen Habermas but Dolf Sternberger[67] who constructed this constitutional patriotism. Habermas adopted *Verfassungspatriotismus*, transforming it into a cornerstone of his political theory in such a way that he could introduce the idea of constitutional patriotism into the European constitutional discourse.[68] Does Habermas's constitutional patriotism abstract too rigidly from the social, political and cultural embeddedness of 'really existing' human beings, as has been argued so often? This critique is not valid. It is the great achievement of Sternberger and Habermas's constitutional patriotism that this is not a substantive concept of identity.[69] But it is, nevertheless, a concept which is embedded in a specific culture and *Lebenswelt*, designed to mirror Germany's transformation into a constitutional democracy.[70] Is it too 'thick' to become a European concept, or, if deprived of its German connotation, too 'thin' to represent Europe's *unitas*?[71]

Habermas later substantiated and modified his position. Constitutional patriotism, he explained, does not assume that citizens will identify with abstract constitutional

---

[65] See C Joerges, 'On the Disregard for History in the Convention Process' (2006) 12 *European Law Journal* 2.

[66] J-W Müller, *Constitutional Patriotism* (Princeton, NJ, Princeton University Press, 2007) 15ff.

[67] '"Verfassungspatriotismus." Rede bei der 25-Jahr-Feier der "Akademie für Politische Bildung" in Tutzing am 29.6.1982' in M-L Recker (ed), *Politische Reden 1945–1990* (Frankfurt aM, Deutscher Klassiker Verlag, 1999) 702ff.

[68] J Habermas, *Staatsbürgerschaft und nationale Identität* (St Gallen, Erkner, 1991). The short monograph was reprinted in idem, *Faktizität und Geltung* (Frankfurt aM, Suhrkamp Verlag, 1992) 632–60, translated as *Between Facts and Norms* (Cambridge, MA, The MIT Press, 1998) 491–515.

[69] Ibid. See also J Habermas, *Die Zukunft der menschlichen Natur. Auf dem Weg zu einer liberalen Eugenik?* (Frankfurt aM, Suhrkamp Verlag, 2004) 124.

[70] On the 'militancy' and its credentials in this process see G Frankenberg, 'Der lernende Souverän' in idem, *Autorität und Integration. Zur Grammatik von Recht und Verfassung* (Frankfurt aM, Suhrkamp Verlag, 2003) 46–72; this example illustrates perfectly how problematical it would be to try to transmit social learning into another society—and how useful inter-societal observation and critique can be.

[71] See M Kumm, 'Thick Constitutional Patriotism and Political Liberalism: On the Role and Structure of European Legal History' (2005) 6 *German Law Journal* 319; M Mahlmann, 'Constitutional Identity and the Politics of Homogeneity' (2005) 6 *German Law Journal* 307. See also FC Mayer and J Palmowski, 'European Identities and the EU—The Ties that Bind the Peoples of Europe' (2004) 42 *Journal of Common Market Studies* 573, with historical dimensions and a more cautious view than their title suggests.

principles. *Verfassungspatriotismus* is a conscious affirmation of political principles as citizens experience them in the context of their national histories.[72] He deepened this point in his discussion on the meaning of culture and of the, in his view misconceived, idea of guaranteeing cultures through collective rights: culture is of an intrinsic importance for our lifestyle; the human mind (*Geist*) is culturally constituted[73]—and culture is perpetuated only through the acceptance of its addresses and the conviction that it is worthwhile maintaining this tradition.[74]

A European concept of citizenship which seeks to achieve a deepened integration through some form of intentional 'identity politics' would then be fundamentally misconceived. European citizens are not expected—by Habermas—to forget their histories and cultural traditions. They cannot escape from them anyway, they should develop them further and they should learn to live with this variety. In 1988, Habermas opined:

> By and large, national public spheres are still culturally isolated from one another . . . In the future, however, a common *political* culture could differentiate itself from the various *national* cultures.[75]

This differentiation between a 'European-wide political culture' and many other cultural spheres which remain national resembles an exercise in conflict-of-laws methodology, inspired by systems theory and its notion of functional differentiation. It is a conceptually all-too-artificial and, sociologically speaking, unrealistic suggestion.[76] A conflict-of-laws approach would be much simpler: let the differences persist, but subject these national communities to rules and principles which ensure mutual respect and coexistence. Do not create some elitist public space, but ensure that the national political cultures can observe and criticise each other.[77]

Notwithstanding its inclusion in the Treaty of Maastricht, the concept of European citizenship has remained a playing field mainly of political scientists and legal theorists. Lawyers trying to come to terms with Europeanisation processes in the fields which they examine have difficulties in transforming it into legal concepts with a potential of structuring their inquiries. But it is at this level of concreteness that 'European

---

[72] J Habermas, 'Vorpolitische Grundlagen des demokratischen Rechtsstaates?' in idem, *Zwischen Naturalismus und Religion*, n 47 above, 106–18, 111.

[73] 'Kulturelle Gleichbehandlung—und die Grenzen des postmodernen Liberalismus', ibid, 279–323, 306.

[74] Ibid, 313. In his recent essay, 'Die Krise der Europäischen Union im Lichte der Konstitutionalisierung des Völkerrechts—Ein Essay zur Verfassung Europas', in J Habermas, *Zur Verfassung Europas: Ein Essay* (Frankfurt aM, Suhrkamp Verlag, 2011) 39–96, Habermas has moved to another construct, arguing that Europeans have a twofold citizenship as nationals and Europeans. It seems to me that he undervalues the intensity of the traditional ties of Europeans to their home-polities. In this respect, K Nicolaïdes's notion of 'demoi-cracy' seems more realistic and normatively attractive; see her essay, 'The Idea of European Demoicracy' in J Dickson and P Eleftheriadis (eds), *Philosophical Foundations of EU Law* (Oxford, Oxford University Press, 2012).

[75] J Habermas, 'Citizenship and National Identity', Appendix II to *Between Facts and Norms*, n 68 above, 507. Original emphasis.

[76] See B Peters, 'Public Discourse, Identity, and the Problem of Democratic Legitimacy' in EO Eriksen (ed), *Making the European Polity: Reflexive Integration in the EU* (Abingdon, Routledge, 2005) 84–124.

[77] See K Eder's intensive work on the Europeanisation of public spheres, in particular 'Zur Transformation nationalstaatlicher Öffentlichkeit in Europa, Von der Sprachgemeinschaft zur issuespezifischen Kommunikationsgemeinschaft' (2000) *Berliner Journal für Soziologie* 167; K Eder and C Kantner, 'Transnationale Resonanzstrukturen in Europa. Eine Kritik der Rede vom Öffentlichkeitsdefizit in Europa' in M Bach (ed), *Die Europäisierung nationaler Gesellschaften* (Wiesbaden, Westdeutscher Verlag, 2000) 306–31. See also H-J Trenz, 'Einführung: Auf der Suche nach einer europäischen Öffentlichkeit' in A Klein et al (eds), *Bürgerschaft, Öffentlichkeit und Demokratie in Europa* (Opladen, Leske & Budrich, 2003) 161–68.

citizenship' can deploy a great potential. It is a concept through which the inherited schism between the European 'market citizen' (Hans Peter Ipsen) who enjoys private autonomy in the great European economic space and the un-Europeanised political citizen who exercises his or her political autonomy under the umbrella of a constitutional state can be gradually overcome. This potential has materialised in many fields. The most interesting example that I know of is from the not so mundane world of European company law, which I will not explore here.[78]

There are many more examples. They all could serve to illustrate in great detail how legal systems are reconstituting themselves in Europeanisation processes. This is by no means a linear or necessarily beneficial process. However, what is so important to underline, in my opinion, is that it is false to conceptualise European law as a ready-made or steadily growing *corpus juridicus* which will gradually replace national legal systems. What we have to develop is an analytical understanding of these processes. What we have to learn is how to organise and stabilise the balance of private and public autonomy in such a way that the European law of law production (*Recht-Fertigungs-Recht*) deserves recognition. But I must refrain from substantiating these visions any further here. What should have become plausible, however, is their potential to link law to history.

## V. CONCLUDING REMARKS

The past—good or bad—is with us. Does it matter whether we make ourselves aware of it? We should try to learn from the past, especially in the cases where it has been unpleasant. We may then even have a 'duty to remember'.[79] These answers may seem self-evident, even emotionally appealing, but appearances can deceive. Until now (and, indeed, for the foreseeable future) Europeans have had to live with different, and in many respects conflicting, historical memories—and there is no authority entrusted with deciding about such conflicts. It is all the more important to be aware that 'the glance in the mirror'[80] tends to have unsettling effects both in one's own lifeworld and in the political sphere.

There is no choice conceivable to come to terms with this *problématique*. It may well be, as Armin von Bogdandy observes in his evaluation of the Preamble,[81] that negative connotations are unlikely to further identity-building. We can therefore argue against 'identity politics' altogether. We should not assume, however, that we can

---

[78] But see C Joerges, 'The Challenges of Europeanization in the Realm of Private Law: A Plea for a New Legal Discipline' (2004) 14 *Duke Journal of Comparative and International Law* 149, 173ff; also available at http://www.iue.it/PUB/law04-12.pdf. Fields such as anti-discrimination and labour law may appear more exciting. Mechanisms of Europeanisation from below are instructively documented in the latter field by S Sciarra (ed), *Labour Law in the Courts: National Judges and the European Court of Justice* (Oxford, Hart Publishing, 2001).

[79] P de Greiff, 'The Duty to Remember: The Dead Weight of the Past, or the Weight of the Dead of the Past?', typescript, on file with the author.

[80] M Stolleis, 'Reluctance to Glance in the Mirror: The Changing Face of German Jurisprudence after 1933 and Post-1945' in C Joerges and NS Ghaleigh (eds), *Darker Legacies of Law in Europe: The Shadow of National Socialism and Fascism over Europe and its Legal Traditions* (Oxford, Hart Publishing, 2003) 1–18.

[81] 'Europäische Verfassung und europäische Identität', n 24 above, 57.

control the biases that insert themselves into narrative structures.[82] We can observe that this infiltration becomes consciously politicised, that it is simply impossible not to instrumentalise the past in general, and 'bitter experiences' in particular.

As Jan-Werner Müller observes, it is all under way:[83] the 'politics of regret', the exchanges regarding the recognition of guilt, the apologies by political leaders, the debates about memorials in schoolbooks, the painful self-interrogations in so many quarters about collaboration and involvement in the Holocaust. Is there a chance that these often painful processes and contestations will create a new sensitivity, that Europeans will learn something about themselves, from and for their neighbours, which will be beneficial for their Union? Could one even hope that the European project will derive a new legitimacy out of these confrontations with the bitter experiences in European nations' pasts? Jan-Werner Müller is sceptical and cautious. Mutual observation tends to provoke cross-border blame and to promote shame as governmental politics.[84]

Back to the Constitutional Treaty: can Europeans really hope to 'forge a common destiny' while remaining 'proud of their own national identities and history'—as the Preamble suggests—if they fail to confront their pasts? 'Working through the past' is a European burden and 'from the very beginning, the integration of Europe represents the remedy to centuries of imperialism, war and other kinds of inter-state conflict, and is shown as the only possible alternative to Europe's self-destruction and decay'.[85] This insight we may share. However, it will not suffice as an orientation when trying to come to terms with our past. Somewhat paradoxically, it is the Holocaust that Europeans seem to recognise as a point of negative communality. To cite *Postwar* again:

> The new Europe, bound together by the signs and symbols of its terrible past, is a remarkable accomplishment; but it remains forever mortgaged to that past. If Europeans are to maintain this vital link—if Europe's past is to continue to furnish Europe's present with admonitory meaning and moral purpose—then it will have to be *taught* afresh with each passing generation. The 'European Union' may be a response to history, but it can never be a substitute.[86]

---

[82] H White, *Metahistory: The Historical Imagination in Nineteenth-Century Europe* (Baltimore, MD, J Hopkins University Press, 1973).
[83] Müller, n 66 above, 93ff.
[84] Ibid. See also JQ Whitmann, 'What is Wrong with Inflicting Shame Sanctions?' (1998) 107 *Yale Law Journal* 1055, 1088–91.
[85] Larat, n 17 above.
[86] Judt, n 27 above, 831. Original emphasis.

# 16

# The Trials of History: Losing Justice in the Monstrous and the Banal

## VASUKI NESIAH

## I. INTRODUCTION: ATTENDING TO THE PAST

TRANSITIONAL JUSTICE HAS brought a transformation in international human rights law over the last two decades.[1] Born in the post-World War II Nuremberg trials, the field gained global momentum[2] only in the early 1990s. Within a five-year period, four major truth commissions were established—in Chile (1990), El Salvador (1992), Guatemala (1994) and South Africa (1995)[3]—and international tribunals were launched to address both the war crimes in the former Yugoslavia (1993) and the genocide in Rwanda.[4] These initiatives were symptomatic of an invigorated demand for post-conflict justice that came to mark the end of wars,

---

[1] Transitional justice is a sub-field of human rights focused on redress of past mass atrocities in contexts of political transition through a family of mechanisms that include trials, truth commissions, reparation programmes, memorials and institutional reform initiatives. The rationale for such special mechanisms emerges from the sense that the scale and intensity of abuses that accompany war and authoritarianism exceeds the goals and institutional capacity of the ordinary criminal justice system. These contexts may range from short, intense periods of violence, such as the one-hundred-day Rwandan genocide, to periods of entrenched abuse, such as more than four decades of apartheid.

[2] In this intervening period, there were key transitional justice initiatives following the military dictatorships in countries such as Argentina and Greece; however, these did not catalyse the global 'justice cascade' that we see post-1989. E Lutz and K Sikkink, 'The Justice Cascade: The Evolution and Impact of Foreign Human Rights Trials in Latin America' (2001) 2 *Chicago Journal of International Law* 1.

[3] While the Argentina Truth Commission in 1983 introduced this new institutional mechanism to the international human rights community, it was in the 1990s that they became more widespread after similar institutions were established in Chile (1990), El Salvador (1992), Guatemala (1994) and South Africa (1995). For an overview of truth commissions around the world see P Hayner, *Unspeakable Truths: Facing the Challenges of Truth Commissioners* (London, Routledge, 2002). In some ways, the earliest truth commission was the Nunca Mas (Never Again) project in Brazil—an unofficial initiative that was inaugurated in 1979 and took more than half a decade to finish. However, this project was undertaken in secret and only became public upon the publication of the report in 1985 (available at http://www.utexas.edu/utpress/excerpts/excattop.html (last accessed on 14 July 2011).

[4] In 1999, the International Criminal Tribunal for the former Yugoslavia (ICTY) became the first international court to bring charges against a sitting head of state when it indicted Slobodan Milošević for war crimes and crimes against humanity. Established just two years after the ICTY, the International Criminal Tribunal for Rwanda (ICTR) was tasked with investigating and prosecuting those responsible for the genocide and all the serious violations of international law that took place in Rwanda in 1994 (see http://www.ictr.org).

dictatorships and periods of mass atrocity in many parts of the world.[5] Commissions and tribunals were often accompanied by reparations policies for the victims. Memorials were built to honour the dead, and reform proposals were enacted under the global mantra of *nunca mas*, or never again.[6] Today, when the guns cease, the international human rights community urges that victims should not be asked to forgive, forget and turn their focus forward to peace.[7] Even if these are wars that have gone on for many years, the passage of history cannot be a licence to forget.[8] The field of transitional justice is born out of the promise of redress and recompense through courts and commissions that turn their gaze back to the crimes that have been committed, and assert the importance of historical accountability.[9]

It is worth underscoring that historical reckoning is presented here as endogenous to the very concept of justice. In fact, it is argued that, in the aftermath of war, conflict and periods of authoritarian rule, it is particularly important that we not only address human rights violations and their immediate impact, but also that we adopt the long view and incorporate a historically focused engagement with a nation's human rights record. Drawing on international laws and norms, transitional justice mechanisms are designed to address this ambitious (historical) task,[10] which involves

---

[5] Other transitional justice efforts during this period are many and varied—they extend from post-Cold War policies of lustration and restitution in some East European countries, to the calls for accountability and mock tribunals by the so-called 'comfort women' from a range of South East Asian countries for sexual crimes by the Japanese military in World War II, to a range of commissions of inquiry (and concomitant reparation programmes) that were set up to address violations related to the ongoing conflicts in Northern Ireland, Sri Lanka and elsewhere.

[6] It is not insignificant that four of the six commissions and tribunals mentioned above were led by international actors; all are marked by international influence, including the normative and doctrinal influence of international human rights and humanitarian law. These transnational involvements are echoed in the development of international laws and norms in the decade that followed in ways that reverberate back to deepen and legitimate the terrain for international engagement. For instance, the principle of universal jurisdiction represents the idea that some acts are such an affront to our conscience that any court anywhere has jurisdiction irrespective of where and when those acts took place—concomitantly, it underscores the notion that such justice processes are legitimately matters of international concern and engagement rather than matters that are solely internal to the nation concerned. In some cases jurisdiction is exercised transnationally: Liberia's Charles Taylor was indicted by the Sierra Leone Special Court in 2003, apprehended in Nigeria in 2006, tried and then found guilty and sentenced in the Special Court in The Hague in 2012. See N Roht-Arrriaza, *The Pinochet Effect: Transnational Justice in the Age of Human Rights* (Philadelphia, PA, University of Pennsylvania Press, 2005).

[7] E Barkan, *The Guilt of Nations: Restitution and Negotiating Historical Injustices* (New York, Norton, 2000).

[8] The argument is made that accountability is not only a moral and legal obligation, but also of instrumental value in affirming the rule of law and in rebuilding a nation. DF Orentlicher, 'Settling Accounts: The Duty to Prosecute Human Rights Violations of a Prior Regime' (1991) 100 *Yale Law Journal* 2537.

[9] Within the field, terms such as justice and accountability are defined broadly to include a range of goals—from prosecution of perpetrators to truth about the human rights record, reparations for victims and national reconciliation. Not all transitional justice institutions may pursue all these goals, but they may see the goals as interconnected and situate their mandate in relation to a multiplicity of goals. For instance, a commission's primary focus may be investigation and research, but many commissions also make recommendations regarding prosecutions, advance policy proposals regarding reparations, encourage legal and political reform measures, and see their work as promoting reconciliation.

[10] This normative call to examine the past is complemented by doctrinal developments in human rights law contesting statutes of limitations and other constraints on prosecuting historic gross human rights violations. The Convention on the Non-applicability of Statutory Limitations to War Crimes and Crimes against Humanity declares that no statutory limitations apply to war crimes and crimes against humanity. See Arts 1 and 4 of The Convention on the Non-applicability of Statutory Limitations to War Crimes and Crimes Against Humanity, GA Res 2391 (XXIII), annex, 23 UN GAOR Supp (No 18), 40, UN Doc A/7218 (1968), entered into force 11 November 1970. Similarly, the Rome Statute stipulates that genocide, crimes

not only accountability for past crimes, but also a call to situate these crimes historically so that we can address their enabling conditions; reparation for past wrongs, but
also reform that is grounded in a study of past mistakes in order to deter their repetition more solidly. Within the transitional justice field, these multiple objectives were
sometimes seen to be embodied in courts, commissions, reparation programmes and
institutional reform policies, which were seen as the four parallel, but complementary,
pillars of the field.[11]

This call to attend to the past is not new to our political imagination. For instance,
Sophocles' *Antigone* remains an iconic figure in discussions of what constitutes justice
in the aftermath of war precisely because of this concern. After the war that killed her
brothers, Antigone argues with Creon that you cannot move on until you honour the
dead and deal with the past. The dissenting voice of Antigone represents the importance not only of giving the past its due, however agonised and troubled it may be, but
also the critical importance that this holds for the present and future.[12] We have heard
a more legalistic echo of this closer to home—during the course of his first year in
office, there were insistent calls for the Obama administration to pursue accountability
for the abusive treatment of prisoners in Guantánamo, Abu Ghraib and elsewhere.[13]
Moreover, these calls insist that these abuses need to be situated in the history of US
foreign policy and overseas military action.[14] The argument made by the American

against humanity, and war crimes 'shall not be subject to any statute of limitations'. Part 3 of the Rome
Statute of the International Criminal Court, 2187 UNTS 90, lays out the general principles that are to
govern its applicability. It clarifies that, while the ICC will not have retrospective reach for crimes committed
before it came into force (see Art 24), this provision ensures that perpetrators who fall within ICC jurisdiction will be vulnerable to future prosecution irrespective of the passage of time (see Art 29). See www.
untreaty.un.org/cod/ICC/STATUTE/99_corr/3.htm. See also RA Kok, *Statutory Limitations in International
Law* (The Hague, Asser Press, 2007) 119–20. See the discussion of doctrinal developments on gross human
rights violations as imprescriptible in V Nesiah, 'Missionary Zeal for a Secular Mission: Bringing Gender
to Transitional Justice and Redemption for Feminism' in Z Peterson and S Kuovi (eds), *Feminist Perspectives
on Contemporary International Law: Between Resistance and Compliance* (Oxford, Hart Publishing, 2011)
137.

[11] For instance, in the early years of the International Center for Transitional Justice (ICTJ) it referred to
the field in terms of the four pillars. Even a recent publication on Indonesia refers to 'truth-seeking, judicial
proceedings, reparations, and SSR' as the 'four pillars' of transitional justice. See http://ictj.org/sites/default/
files/ICTJ-Kontras-Indonesia-Derailed-Summary-2011-English.pdf (last accessed on 15 July 2011). However,
this language notwithstanding, over the last decade, as ICTJ has matured it has also developed a more
complex sense of the architecture of the field with increased attention to other initiatives (such as memorials) and other objectives for post-conflict justice (such as developments).

[12] For a discussion of Antigone and the question of reconciliation see V Nesiah, 'Coming to Terms with
Irreconcilable Truths' in E Skaar, S Gloppen and A Suhrke (eds), *Roads to Reconciliation* (Lanham, MD,
Lexington Books, 2004).

[13] These abuses were signature legacies of George W Bush era atrocities and calls to address these violations began to fade from public attention as the Obama period acquired its own horrific record with its
treatment of Bradley Manning, a US soldier held under military detention in conditions described by JE
Méndez, the United Nations Special Rapporteur on torture, as 'cruel, inhuman and degrading', the failure
to close Guantánamo, and the actions of the US in Pakistan and elsewhere.

[14] At first sight, the abuses of the George W Bush administration may seem to be fundamentally different from the historical perspective invoked in more typical transitional justice contexts; however, when
one situates instances such as Guantánamo and Abu Ghraib within a longer time-frame of American
military intervention, the legacies of human rights abuse begin to bear a greater resemblance to the long-
term impact of authoritarian governments. Some groups, including the International Center for Transitional
Justice (ICTJ) and the Center for Constitutional Rights, have initiated US-focused accountability projects
that address US foreign policy in ways that are analogous to other transitional justice projects addressing
systems of entrenched injustice: see the ICTJ's US Accountability Project at http://ictj.org/our-work/regions-
and-countries/usa-accountability (last accessed on 14 July 2011). Moreover, in most transitional justice

Civil Liberties Union (ACLU), Human Rights First and others is that 'We have to look back before we can move forward as a nation'.[15]

From Antigone to the ACLU, I invoke these assertions of the importance of historical accountability because they have resonance with an ethos regarding transitional justice that is frequently advanced by the international human rights community, an ethos captured by the Chilean Truth Commission twenty years ago in its claim that: 'Society cannot simply black out a chapter of its history . . . The unity of a nation depends on a shared identity, which, in turn, depends largely on a shared memory.'[16] Yet, has this invocation of the historical opened the door to grappling with long-enduring injustices or has it channelled the terrain of history to neutralise its most challenging claims? Recognising that the contradictory pressures for accountability and closure can exist simultaneously, this chapter tries to probe these questions by looking at how the historical is defined in specific transitional justice initiatives. I conclude that, too often, the transitional justice field's self-representation as being focused on historical accountability has functioned as a Trojan horse for a project that has, in fact, been directed towards historical closure.

In other work, I have argued that post-conflict human rights intervention is characterised by two important dimensions: the turn to ethics and the turn to expertise.[17] In the field of transitional justice both these broader dimensions garner a very specific articulation in advancing historical closure. The ethical turn is channelled into a focus on the monstrosity of the individual perpetrators and the efforts to hold them accountable for their (abuse of) human rights records. Concomitantly, the expertise turn is channelled into a focus on the minutiae of the technocratic and procedural aspects of institutions such as war crimes courts and truth commissions. I argue in this chapter that, by framing historical space through the dual logics of monstrosity and banality,

---

contexts, the scale of the abuses is quite extensive and is part of the rationale for seeing their impact to be of historic significance. While the American Civil Liberties Union (ACLU) lawsuit against D Rumsfeld, the US Secretary of Defense, dealt with a small number of prisoner-abuse cases, they could provide a window into patterns of atrocity that have accompanied American military interventions historically. In this way, it could be argued that these abuses do raise some of the same issues regarding impunity and accountability that are triggered by the thousands of cases entailed in most transitional justice processes. In fact, as with most transitional justice processes, international actors, norms and laws have played a role in American discussions about dealing with the past. For instance, in discussion of Guantánamo, rendition and related abuses, there has been invocation (be it amongst human rights lawyers or mainstream American media outlets) of international law (particularly the Geneva Conventions) for legal and normative reference in ways that are quite extraordinary in the American context.

[15] This argument is made in the context of the March 2005 lawsuit filed in Illinois's Federal Court by the American Civil Liberties Union and Human Rights First against the then Secretary of Defense, Donald Rumsfeld, accusing him of 'direct responsibility for the torture and abuse of detainees in US military custody'. In addition to violations of the US Constitution, Rumsfeld was charged with violations under international law, including the Convention against Torture and the Geneva Conventions. The suit was eventually dismissed two years later, in March 2007, but the argument regarding criminal accountability for the treatment of prisoners in Guantánamo, Abu Ghraib and elsewhere continues today. As the Justice Department investigates the infamous 'torture memos' and the interrogation techniques used in Guantánamo and elsewhere, many have urged the importance of historical accountability. See ACLU press release, http://www.aclu.org/safefree/torture/39393prs20090416.html (last accessed on 14 July 2011).

[16] Report of the Chilean National Commission (1991). Often referred to as the Rettig Report, after its Chairman, Raul Rettig, the report was the final product of the Chilean Truth Commission. Appointed by President Patricio Aylwin after the end of the Pinochet regime, the Commission was tasked with investigating human rights abuses resulting in death or disappearance during the Pinochet period.

[17] See V Nesiah, 'The Specter of Violence that Haunts the UDHR: The Turn to Ethics and Expertise' (2009) 24 *Maryland Journal of International Law* 135.

the ethics of condemning the monstrous and the expertise in administering the banal, transitional justice initiatives anchor a political horizon that bends towards historical closure and away from historical accountability.

In exploring the distributive and ideological impacts of a closure orientation, this chapter also seeks to situate these technologies of historical closure in the broader arc of the post-conflict human rights interventions that have shaped the delimiting of accountability and the concomitant investment in a redemptive story about the progress of justice. Against the backdrop of the historical rationale for transitional justice, I work through the case studies of Chile and South Africa as windows into how the field defines history in the two countries that are heralded as transitional justice successes and have proved hugely influential in the development of the field.

## II. CHILE, PINOCHET AND THE 'DESPOT CRUSADE': RADICAL EVIL ON TRIAL[18]

Let 100 Pinochets bloom . . . Universal jurisdiction is the law's answer to the spectacle of tyrants and torturers who shield themselves with immunities at home.[19]

Writing in the heady aftermath of Pinochet's arrest in London, Reed Brody, Counsel and Spokesperson for Human Rights Watch (HRW), declared that, 'The Pinochet precedent puts tyrants on notice'.[20] Buoyed by the Pinochet case, and the Habre case that followed, HRW produced a report which explored the doctrine of universal jurisdiction and its potential in prosecuting a range of former heads of states, including Chad's Hissein Habre, Uganda's Idi Amin and Milton Obote, Ethiopia's deposed Mengitsu Haile Mariam, Haiti's Jean-Claude 'Baby Doc' Duvalier and Paraguay's Alfredo Stroessner; HRW described the Pinochet case as a 'wake-up call to tyrants everywhere'.[21]

Historically, the majority of human rights prosecutions were directed at lower ranked trigger-pullers, not at the *Schreibtischtäters*, the higher ranks who issued the orders: to wit, they focused on policeman and ordinary soldiers, ie they used the argument that obeying orders is no defence.[22] The *Pinochet* case was an important

---

[18] My title references two key interventions in the field—the 'Despot Crusade' of Human Rights Watch's Reed Brody (see H Vogt, 'Despot Crusade', available at http://www.hrw.org/en/news/2006/07/02/despot-crusade (last accessed on 14 July 2011) and Carlos Nino's posthumously published book, *Radical Evil on Trial* (New Haven, CT, Yale University Press, 1998).

[19] Human Rights Watch's Reed Brody quoted in T Wilkinson, 'International Justice Faces Crucial Test', *LA Times*, available at http://groups.yahoo.com/group/Nat-International/message/2095 (last accessed on 16 July 2012).

[20] R Brody, 'One year later, The 'Pinochet Precedent' puts Tyrants on Notice', *Boston Globe*, 15 October 1999, available at http://www.hrw.org/news/1999/10/14/one-year-later-pinochet-precedent-puts-tyrants-notice (last accessed on 16 July 2012). Not surprisingly, those targeted call for a different approach to the past. For instance, the Cambodian leader, Hun Sen, urged that 'we should look ahead and dig a hole and bury the past'. See DA Crocker, 'Reckoning with Past Wrongs: A Normative Framework' (1999) 13 *Ethics & International Affairs* 43.

[21] See Human Rights Watch, 'The Pinochet Case—A Wake-up Call to Tyrants and Victims Alike', available at http://www.hrw.org/legacy/campaigns/chile98/precedent.htm (last accessed on 16 July 2012).

[22] Art 8 of the London Charter established that, even if superior orders can mitigate punishment, they do not protect the accused from criminal responsibility. The principle of individual responsibility advanced here was a significant dimension of the Nuremberg justice legacy. Hence the Nuremberg judgment's famous statement that 'Crimes against international law are committed by men, not by abstract entities, and only by

reflection of how contemporary transitional justice initiatives prioritise the prosecution of those giving the orders, rather than those receiving them.[23] International tribunals have established that commanders are responsible for those actions of their subordinates which they could have known and prevented.[24] The subject of a film that dubbed him the 'Dictator Hunter',[25] Mr Brody's HRW office has a 'world map on his wall covered with pictures of dictators he would like to see behind bars'.[26] With echoes of the post-World War II pursuits of Adolf Eichmann and other Nazi officials across continents, propelled by the ideals of historical accountability, the human rights community has pursued Brody's dictators in courtrooms and commission hearings throughout the world. As exemplified in HRW's description of the prosecution of Jean-Claude Duvalier as 'Haiti's rendezvous with history', these cases against past leaders have been seen as efforts to come to terms with a country's past and confront their history head on.[27] This 'despot crusade', which brings together justice and history, represents one of the two central dimensions of transitional justice that I highlight in this chapter, and Chile's transitional justice experience is amongst the best-known exemplars of this effort.

In Chile, the transitional justice story can be traced to 1973, when General Augusto Pinochet took power in a *coup d'état*. Upon taking office, Pinochet made far-reaching changes in a number of areas, including economic policy. Pinochet and Milton Friedman had developed close ties, and Chile emerged as a test case for the free market economic prescriptions identified with the University of Chicago economics department.[28] The wealthy gained much, but the poor suffered: there was a

---

punishing *individuals* who commit such crimes can the provisions of international law be enforced'. Thus, even if you were committing particular acts in a context in which the entire national military enterprise was indifferent to international prohibitions on particular acts, even if superiors required you to commit prohibited acts as a routine aspects of service and even if there were no explicit treaty provision attributing individual responsibility for the violation of those international prohibitions, you were still individually criminally responsible for such violations.

[23] This precedent was explicitly cited in Opinion and Judgment, *Prosecutor v Tadić*, Case No IT-94-1-T, available at http://www.un.org/icty/970507jt.htm (the *Tadić* case) and then in *Prosecutor v Delalić et al*, Case No IT-96-21-T, available at http://www.ess.uwe.ac.uk/documents/part1.htm (the *Čelebići* case) to support the notion that, if certain horrendous acts are prohibited in international law as grave breaches, then it is legitimate to infer that these were the basis for individual criminal responsibility even if there was no explicit treaty provision establishing an enforcement mechanism for individual criminal responsibility in internal armed conflict for those acts; individual criminal responsibility was the logical assumption if the prohibition was to be meaningful. See para 128 of the *Tadić* Jurisdiction Decision and paras 161–62 of the *Čelebići* Appeals Judgment, JL/P.I.S./564-e, available at http://www.icty.org/sid/8021; see also para 153 of the *Čelebići* Appeals Judgment). Moreover, by dint of international customary law, the practice in many domestic legal systems and the evolution of universal jurisdiction over the last half century, there can be no legitimate expectation that grave breaches in the realm of international armed conflict are legal in the realm of internal armed conflict (paras 159–60 of the *Čelebići* Appeals Judgment).

[24] The most important precedent to the *Čelebići* case on command responsibility was the prosecution of the Japanese General Yamashita by a US Military Commission for war crimes committed by his troops in the Philippines; See *in re Yamashita*, 327 US 1 (1946). The most relevant and comprehensive codification of the doctrine (cited by the *Čelebići* court) was in Art 86(2) of the 1977 Additional Protocol 1 to the Geneva Conventions of 1949.

[25] See http://www.thedictatorhunter.com/index.html.

[26] Available at http://www.hrw.org/english/docs/2005/10/05/chad11848.htm.

[27] *Haiti's Rendezvous with History: The Case of Jean-C Duvalier* (Human Rights Watch, 2011) 46; available at http://www.hrw.org/sites/default/files/reports/haiti0411Web.pdf (last accessed on 16 July 2012).

[28] The academic home of Milton Friedman and other influential neoclassical economists, the approach has come to be referred to variously as the 'Chicago school' or the 'Freshwater school'. In Chile, this included the removal of government regulations and subsidies, the shrinking of social spending, and the

rise in 'the national poverty rate from 17 per cent . . . to 45 per cent' in the Pinochet years.[29] Dissent was muted, however, as critics of the regime faced torture, disappearance and death. After almost 20 years, Pinochet was finally ousted from office. His successor, President Aylwin, appointed a truth commission that investigated the disappearances (*los Desaparecidos*),[30] then issued a report outlining its findings and recommended reparations for the families of those who had disappeared.[31] Pinochet, while in office, had granted himself an amnesty, and was thus immune to charges; the military remained a strong force and the government was hesitant to challenge it directly.

But this was not the end of Chile's transitional justice story. In 1998, when Pinochet was visiting London, Spanish courts issued an international warrant for Pinochet's extradition for trial on charges of torture and other abuses of Spanish citizens. After extended debate, the British House of Lords decided that Pinochet's head of state immunity did not trump Britain's own treaty obligations regarding torture; in relation to this, they concluded that the crimes of which he was accused were so heinous that he should be extradited. Despite this decision, citing concerns about his health, the British government chose not to extradite Pinochet, and he returned to Chile in the year 2000. But the political climate had changed in Chile, too, and legal proceedings removed his claim to immunity in key cases; indictments were issued for torture, disappearances and other abuses. Throughout this period, there were calls also to hold Pinochet to account for his economic policy. It was argued that his economic programme had identifiable and quantifiable justiciable impact 'in terms of otherwise avoidable deaths and illnesses'.[32] Ultimately, although he was charged with over 300 crimes, none of these related to the impact of his economic decisions.[33] By the time of Pinochet's death in 2006, another commission had investigated torture during his reign,[34] a reparation policy was developed for torture victims and many court cases against Pinochet were still ongoing; however, the question of economic rights violations never entered any of these proceedings.

The Pinochet case was pivotal for both political inspiration and the legal precedent for the development of the doctrine of command responsibility, and these developments are to be applauded.[35] However, it is striking that the impact of Pinochet's

---

lowering of tariffs and other barriers to a *laissez-faire* market environment. It also included attacks against labour unions and other groups opposed to these economic policies.

[29] C Perez-Bustillo, 'Poverty as a Violation of Human Rights: the Pinochet Case and the Emergence of a New Paradigm' in L Williams, A Kjonstad and P Robson, *Law and Poverty: The Legal System and Poverty Reduction* (London, Zed Books, 2003) 67; among the impoverished, the percentage forced to live in extreme poverty more than doubled.

[30] The term *Desaparecidos* was coined by the de facto President of Argentina, General Jorge Rafael Videla, who said in a press conference: 'They are neither dead nor alive, they are *desaparecidos* (disappeared or missing)'.

[31] See Rettig Report, n 16 above.

[32] Perez-Bustillo, n 29 above.

[33] C Collins, 'Prosecuting Pinochet: Late Accountability in Chile and the Role of the 'Pinochet Case", Project on Human Rights, Global Justice & Democracy Working Paper, No 5 (George Mason University, Spring 2009) 4.

[34] Headed by Bishop Sergio Valech and appointed by President R Lagos, the National Commission on Political Imprisonment and Torture investigated abuses that took place between 1973 and 1990.

[35] Collins, n 33 above.

macroeconomic policies is not part of Chile's transitional justice story.[36] This is especially so as the macroeconomic policies and military policies were intertwined in a
deeply symbiotic relationship.[37] Yet the economic impact has faded from view.

Economic policy is difficult to assimilate into claims about monstrous men or
women—unlike killings, disappearance, torture—acts that more easily embody radical
evil, to use the language of Immanuel Kant that has gained some traction within the
transitional justice literature.[38] Kant referred to the notion of 'radical evil' to describe
the monstrous decisions which we are capable of taking when we allow our baser
instincts to prevail over moral law. These are 'crimes against human rights that are so
grand that no punishment can suffice', yet, for the same reason, there is an imperative
to prosecute these crimes.[39] For Kant, acts of radical evil are acts of will, not natural
inevitability; everyone may have the potential for such evil, and he or she may situate
the conditions of its realisation in social conditions, but individual responsibility
remains a critical preoccupation.[40] Thus, radical evil and individual responsibility are
inextricably intertwined even if accountability mechanisms for the latter are inadequate to capture the monstrosity of the former. Individual responsibility becomes
translated in transitional justice as a call for every country to come to terms with
its past by holding individuals responsible for the monstrosity which they unleashed
and over which they presided. The arrests of Augusto Pinochet, Slobodan Milošević,
Charles Taylor, Hissein Habré/Hissène Habré and Alberto Fujimori are all different
markers of this movement in different parts of the globe. Over the last two decades,
over almost 70 former heads of state have faced criminal charges for abuses conducted
during their reign.[41] In a posthumously published book, *Radical Evil on Trial*, Carlos
Nino, the Argentine philosopher-statesman, situates the post-dictatorship prosecutions (both in his country and in others) of human rights perpetrators as an effort

[36] See D Green, *Silent Revolution: The Rise of Markets and Economics in Latin America*, 2nd edn (New York, Monthly Review Press, 2003); LH Oppenheim, *Politics in Chile: Socialism, Authoritarianism, and Market Democracy* (Boulder, CO, Westview Press, 2007).

[37] There are many dimensions to this symbiosis. Pinochet's *coup d'état* against the Allende government (and what Allende called the 'Chilean Way to Socialism') was backed by the corporate and military
elite. Dissent against Pinochet's regime was catalysed by both his military policies and his macroeconomic
policies, and the left opposition was targeted for heightened repression. Concomitantly, the strengthened
role of the military in the Pinochet years was accompanied by massive increases in the military budget.
The glue holding together the military elite and the economic elite was the marriage between neo-liberal
economics and the policy of terror. For more on the politics of the military in the Pinochet years see KL
Remmer, 'Neopatrimonialism: The Politics of Military Rule in Chile, 1973–1987' (1989) 21 *Comparative
Politics* 149.

[38] I Kant, *Religion within the Boundaries of Mere Reason*, edited by A Wood (Cambridge, Cambridge
University Press, 1999). The invocation of the term by Carlos Nino gave it wider purchase in the transitional
justice field; see Nino, n 18 above.

[39] WA Chaffee, 'Radical Evil on Trial (Review)' (2000) 80 *Hispanic American Historical Review* 217.

[40] See AW Wood, *Kant's Ethical Thought* (Cambridge, Cambridge University Press, 1999), in which he
argues that Kant's anthropological conception of man (rather than his biological conception of man) saw
radical evil as a product of man becoming a competitive social being.

[41] For a brief analysis of these cases see EL Lutz and C Reiger (eds), *Prosecuting Heads of State* (Cambridge, Cambridge University Press, 2009) 12–15. Over half of those indicted were charged with human
rights violations; in many cases, the indictment included other charges, particularly corruption charges.
Moreover, this number reflects only a small subset of those who have faced criminal investigations for
human rights violations; many investigations of former heads of state did not transate into indictments for
political or legal reasons.

to hold radical evil to account.[42] The Deputy Chair of the South African Truth Commission, Alex Boraine, describes the Nuremberg trials as the 'first concerted action by the international community to deal in a systematic manner with what Carlos Nino described as radical evil'.[43] Deaths that do not emerge from the barrel of a gun but from socio-economic policies are rendered invisible on the 'radical evil' audit—and, concomitantly, the transitional justice charge sheet. The field is invested in the monster narrative to fuel its normative rationale and its legal doctrines. Abuses that arise from socio-economic policies, analysis of the interrelationship between abuses that are the results of socio-economic policies and abuses that arise from military policies, systemic responsibilities for these abuses and systemic analysis of the patterns of abuse and their impact are all bracketed off as something outside this arithmetic of justice. Transitional justice knows Pinochet as a monster who tortured and killed, but it does not know the Pinochet who developed budget plans and economic policies that resulted in deaths from typhoid, hepatitis and other preventable illnesses.[44]

Dominant approaches to criminal accountability make two problematical equivalences—monstrous acts are equated with violent acts, and national historical accountability is equated with individual responsibility. Dictators are pursued on the theory that prosecuting these men allows their countries to confront the atrocities of their history.[45] But the complex legacies of macroeconomic policy are not easily channelled into individual decisions. For instance, advancing accountability in Chile may require that we track responsibility for many levels of policy decisions that prioritised the rescue of 'failed banks and large corporations' while deprioritising expenditure on public poverty alleviation.[46] Instead, transitional justice is geared towards the identification and punishment of specific perpetrators. As the star perpetrator absorbs all responsibility, other actors are absolved of responsibility and the stage is depopulated. Chile becomes a story primarily of Pinochet and his victims; his partners in economic leadership, be they internal actors (such as the Chilean bankers and the industrialists

[42] Nino served as human rights advisor to President Alfonsin, and his book grapples with both the legal and normative challenges of criminal accountability.

[43] See www.idrc.ca/uploads/user-S/10829975041revised-boraine-ottawa-2004.pdf. Notably, however, contemporary transitional justice also marks a shift from Nuremburg and its focus on crimes of aggression against other states to trial narratives focused on perpetrators and victims; the Israeli state was interested in having the Eichmann trial enact this shift for the crimes of Nazi Germany and its Jewish victims in particular. See H Arendt, *Eichmann in Jerusalem: A Report on the Banality of Evil* (London, Penguin Books, 1994).

[44] Pinochet's policies had a dramatic impact on basic health care. See, eg AG Frank, *Economic Genocide in Chile: Monetarism versus Humanity* (Nottingham, Spokesman Books, 1976). Noam Chomsky notes that, under Pinochet, 'Per capita health care was more than halved from 1973 to 1985, setting off explosive growth in poverty-related diseases such as typhoid and viral hepatitis. Since 1973, consumption dropped 30 percent for the poorest 20 percent in Santiago and increased 15 percent for the top 20 percent.' See http://psychoanalystsopposewar.org/blog/2006/12/11/chomsky-on-the-pinochet-miracle (last accessed on 15 July 2011). Arguably, there were two phases to the Pinochet regime—while the seventies were characterised by brutal cuts to social welfare, repression of labour rights and such, the eighties saw a gradual thawing of the 'shock therapy' formula. For more detailed historical analysis of economic policy changes over these two decades see S Edwards and A Cox Edwards, 'Economic Reforms and Labor Markets: Policy Issues and Lessons from Chile' National Bureau of Economic Research Working Paper Series No 7646 (2000).

[45] Thus countries are encouraged to come to terms with their past by holding individuals to account rather than 'dig a hole and bury the past'; see Crocker, n 20 above; Chaffee n 39 above, 217–18.

[46] Perez-Bustillo, n 29 above, 65. The Chilean foreign debt was 'the highest per capita foreign debt in Latin America', and the Pinochet government's policy was for 'the government and taxpayers' to finance this 'unprecedented amounts of private debt' to sustain banks and corporations; this budgetary priority was a marked shift away from the pro-poor investments of the Allende administration.

who supported Pinochet) or external actors (such as the Chicago School and the IMF economists), are pre-emptively acquitted. This is problematical on many counts. It means that many of Pinochet's victims are overlooked. It also enables the continued power of both those selfsame actors and institutions that share responsibility for the socio-economic devastation of that period. The doctrinal, normative and institutional architecture of redress can normalise some abuses by focusing exclusively on others. As a result, the effort to settle scores with Pinochet in Chile may have been precisely what diverted attention away from other actors who have also been both the protagonists and the beneficiaries of the abuse.

Hannah Arendt's analysis of Nazi official/officer Adolf Eichmann is instructive here. Eichmann was the logistics czar who oversaw the train system that took millions to their death. In his trial in Israel, he emerged as an ambitious opportunist willing to undertake horrific responsibilities for career success. Arendt argues that it is Eichmann, not Hitler, who exposes the historical truth of the Holocaust; even if Eichmann was not anti-Semitic, as he maintained, even if he did not have the *mens rea* for genocide, he represents the more important, terrible fact that banal, commonplace conformism can enable and implement genocide.[47] Mass atrocity requires many actors; actors driven not by monstrous intent but by ambitions and ideologies which insidiously integrate governance and atrocity. In this way, Arendt pushes us towards complex explanations for the complex regimes that have spawned mass atrocity. In contrast, a focus on monstrous acts shifts our gaze away from how the enabling conditions of abuse become institutionalised.

In the Chilean Truth Commission Report, the commissioners situate their work on Chile's human rights record as an effort to bring historical truth to the surface; they note, however, that 'the truth does not bring the dead back to life, but it brings them out from silence'. The question is, in this focus on individual monstrosity, which silences are broken and which ones rendered quieter still?

## III. SOUTH AFRICA, RACE AND OPERATIONAL PRACTICES: INSTITUTIONALISING JUSTICE

The normative push of transitional justice 'to attend to the past' is accompanied by the development of an array of institutions that are tasked with advancing these goals. The professionalisation of transitional justice as a field has been marked by the identification of a family of institutional pillars of transitional justice—namely, war-crime courts, truth commissions, reparation programmes, memorials and reform initiatives such as human rights vetting processes. These mechanisms are understood and adopted as the path to historical accountability; thus, Neil Kritz recommends that:

---

[47] Reading the transcripts of eight months' of questioning by the Israeli police in the lead-up to the trial, Hannah Arendt notes that one of the most remarkable things that comes across is Eichmann's preoccupation with his rank, and his embarrassment at 'why he had been unable to attain a higher grade in the SS'; Arendt, n 43 above, 49.

With the aid of the international community, each society emerging from genocide, war crimes or sustained mass repression will need to find the specific approach or combination of mechanisms which will best help it achieve the optimal level of justice and reconciliation.[48]

These mechanisms are presented as neutral avenues to clarify the human rights record and to identify the victims and perpetrators, in order to provide reparations to the former and to prosecute the latter. Donor governments have developed budget lines to fund the development of transnationally fungible expertise with regard to these institutions; the field has spawned NGO projects, capacity-building seminars and workshops on best practices in setting up and administering transitional justice mechanisms; there are university courses and diploma programmes focused on transitional justice processes. The field turns to these mechanisms not just as pathways to justice, but as definitions of the parameters of justice. These institutions are justice machines and their output is historical accountability.

The South African Truth and Reconciliation Commission and its global legacy is one of the most important historical markers of this institutional turn. That is, if the Chilean story is about how historical accountability for systemic socio-economic violations are screened out by a focus on the monsters, the South African story is about how historical accountability for systemic racial violations are screened out by a focus on the banal operational preoccupations. By 'banal', I do not mean to imply that these were inconsequential. On the contrary, I want to highlight the enormous reach of institutional practices that are classified as merely technical and operational. The role of the historical context in shaping justice issues fades into the background as the operational is foregrounded. In this way, justice issues become translated into knowledge—arenas of expertise for the provision of technical analysis.[49] In speaking of the role of legal expertise in relation to war, David Kennedy has noted that 'The difficulty is to understand more adequately what these experts do, the nature and limits of their vocabulary, and the possibilities for translating their work into politically contestable terms'.[50]

Within the transitional justice field, we also see that the politically contestable has been translated into the neutral realms of the operational and the mechanical; to understand what is potentially at stake, and expand the possibilities for social change, we need to work at the process of reverse translation.

The broad outlines of the South African story are familiar. Apartheid was born in South Africa when the National Party was voted in on an apartheid platform in 1948. The Group Areas Act was passed in 1950 and the state instituted a regime of far-reaching racial segregation that included the forced relocation of thousands of blacks,

---

[48] N Kritz, 'War Crimes and Truth Commissions: Some Thoughts on Accountability Mechanisms for Mass Violations of Human Rights', paper presented at USAID Conference Promoting Democracy, Human Rights, and Reintegration in Post-conflict Societies, 30–31 October 1997. See http://pdf.usaid.gov/pdf_docs/PNACD090.pdf (last accessed on 15 July 2011).

[49] Janet Halley, Prabha Kotiswaran, Hila Shamir and Chantal Thomas argue that feminism on an international plane also presents as 'expertise' rather than politics; Terming this approach 'Governance Feminism', Halley and her collaborators argue that this new turn has accompanied feminism being infused into statecraft as a mode of legal knowledge. See J Halley et al, 'From the International to the Local in Feminist Legal Responses to Rape, Prostitution/Sex Work and Sex Trafficking' (2006) 29 *Harvard Journal of Law and Gender* 335.

[50] D Kennedy, 'Challenging Expert Rule: The Politics of Global Governance' (2005) 27 *Sydney Law Review* 5.

the denial of civic rights and a whole range of legally sanctioned policies of discrimination. These deprivations had long-term impacts on racial disparities; thus income inequality in South Africa continues to be amongst the worst in the world,[51] and these inequalities remain deeply racialised. During apartheid, public protests against these injustices were met with a policy of brutal repression that included prolonged imprisonment, torture and killings.[52]

As we all know, apartheid came to an end in 1994 following decades of struggle and four years of intense negotiation. Once blacks were allowed to vote, Nelson Mandela and the African National Congress were elected with a mandate not only to build a new South Africa, but also to grapple with the legacies of its racist past.[53] One of the new government's first acts was to establish the South African Truth and Reconciliation Commission to investigate crimes that extended from 1960 to 1994. The Commission was tasked with historical accountability for the crimes of apartheid.[54] Yet what is striking about the Commission's work is that race itself is rendered a footnote in history. This was done through two administrative decisions of the Commission; decisions that informed the everyday tasks of how it read victim statements, processed applications and implemented its protocols. These two decisions were: first, its definition of the victims, and secondly, its definition of the political acts which qualified as eligible for amnesty.

The Commission defined the victims to be those who had suffered deaths, disappearances, torture and other ill-treatment, but not those who had suffered the legalised systemic abuse of *Bantustans* (reservations) and the pass laws.[55] Thus, when victims submitted human rights abuse statements, they qualified for the Commission's purview only if they had suffered a bodily injury, not the systemic abuse of apartheid. The protocol form that needed to be filled out required individuals to report only extraordinary abuses such as disappearances or torture—'statements that dealt with the abuses of "normal" racist practices were excluded'.[56] In fact, Madeleine Fullard, a former

---

[51] The Gini index measures income inequality; South Africa has the most unequal distribution in 2011. As reported by the University of Capetown's Development Policy Research Unit, this reflects long-term patterns: 'For the South African economy as a whole, the Gini coefficient increased from 0.64 in 1995 to 0.72 in 2005'. H Bhorat et al, 'Income and Non-Income Inequality in Post-Apartheid South Africa: What are the Drivers and Possible Policy Interventions?', DPRU Working Paper 09/138 (August 2009), available at http://www.population.gov.za/pop_dev/index2.php?option=com_docman&task=doc_view&gid=51&Itemid=190 (last accessed on 16 July 2012).

[52] The TRC report provides a detailed history of these violations. See http://www.justice.gov.za/trc/report/index.htm (last accessed on 12 July 2011).

[53] See South Africa History Online at http://www.sahistory.org.za/article/trc-grade-12-south-african-history-online (last accessed on 15 July 2011).

[54] Promotion of National Unity and Reconciliation Act 34 of 1995, available at http://www.justice.gov.za/legislation/acts/1995–034.pdf. For more on the commission's interpretation of its mandate see the TRC website at http://www.justice.gov.za/trc.

[55] Forced racial segregation, the creation of a disempowered and primarily migrant labour force, appropriation of land for white farming and mining interests, and a host of other policy objectives of the apartheid state were implemented through a number of mechanisms, including pass laws that defined where you could live and work, and forced relocation to 'Bandustans' or reservations. M Mamdani notes that forced removals and de-urbanisation programmes had ensured that 'by 1990, half of South Africa's black population lived on Bandustans, which together accounted for only 14% of the land in the country'; M Mamdani, *Citizen and Subject: Contemporary Africa and the Legacy of Late Colonialism* (Princeton, NJ, Princeton University Press, 1996) 102.

[56] M Fullard, 'Dis-placing Race: The South African Truth and Reconciliation Commission (TRC) and Interpretations of Violence' (CSVR, 2004) 16 and 17, available at http://www.csvr.org.za/wits/papers/

researcher with the Commission, has noted that 'The TRC appears sharply detached from the concerns with race'; this was partly because the Commission was part of the project of reconciliation, reunification and reconstruction, in which race had to fade into the background 'in order', as Fullard says, 'to "imagine" the new nation'.[57] Thus, by the end of its term, the Commission had, in effect, reduced the victims of apartheid to the 22,000 individuals who qualified through its procedures. As Fullard notes, this has led some to see that 'the TRC was an institutional expression of a "closed master narrative of national reconciliation"'.[58] Ironically, and tragically, the historical legacies of racialised citizenship had become obscured in an institution that was mandated to provide that very call to account. For instance, Fiona Ross analyses the Commission's interpretation of its legal mandate to show how it opted for a strikingly narrow defini-tion that 'considered its subject in terms of injury' and not 'the historical constitution of the subject under apartheid'.[59] The 'subject' generated through the Commission's definitions of victimhood was the universal victim of bodily injury as constituted by dominant traditions of international human rights law.[60] In telescoping its institutional gaze to the global victim of human rights, race becomes just the historical backdrop, and is no longer instrumental to abuse. Ultimately, the focus on the victims of extraor-dinary violence, rather than on the victims of daily racialised humiliations and abuses, produces a narrative of an abusive security force, but not one of apartheid itself.

While, so far, I have considered the Commission's definition of the victims, a second component of the Commission's work that pushed it towards a post-racial reconciliation story was its definition of the perpetrators. The Truth Commission mandate included provisions for a partial and conditional amnesty for the perpetrators who confessed to political crimes. The Truth Commission defined as political those violent actions that were directly associated with supporting or opposing state policy. Thus, if a white man in apartheid South Africa assaulted and maimed a black employee, comfortable in the knowledge that he was protected by a racist system, this act was not classified as political by the Commission—rather, it was personal. If that same black employee came to give testimony about this incident, that is, about the normalised abuses of life under apartheid, he would have been disqualified. For him to be heard by the Commission, be classified as a victim and count as a beneficiary for reparations he needed to report violent acts that were undertaken in supporting or opposing state policy—for instance, if he was assaulted and maimed by a policemen when involved in a street protest. Only then would he qualify as a victim and his assailant as a perpetrator.

The Commission's thematic hearings and final report did address the history of apartheid, but the issue was not central to its public presence and routine operations.[61]

---

paprctp3.htm. My discussion of how race was incorporated into the operations of the South African TRC is deeply indebted to Madeleine Fullard's brilliant paper.

[57] Ibid.

[58] Ibid. Fullard describes this perspective as 'one domestic strand of academic criticism'. Arguably, however, with the passage of time and more critical reflection of the TRC's record, this perspective is more widely shared than is suggested by Fullard's description.

[59] FC Ross, *Bearing Witness: Women and The Truth and Reconciliation Commission in South Africa* (London, Pluto, 2002) 11.

[60] Ibid, 11.

[61] The final report provides a detailed account of its own operations, in addition to a detailed history of apartheid. The report can be read and downloaded from the TRC website. See http://www.justice.gov.za/trc/report/index.htm.

The Commission spoke unequivocally of the moral repugnance of apartheid, but, as Commission researchers have noted, 'questions of race and racism, are strikingly absent from the interrogational framework of the Truth Commission, in both its process and products'.[62] The Commission never explicitly stated that race was not important; rather, through the definitional stipulations of its statement-taking procedures and amnesty-application protocols, the politically contested issue of race was mediated, managed and diffused. These neutral mechanisms ensured that the focus remained on human rights abuse as extraordinary, outside the realm of the routine day-to-day injustices of apartheid. It was an administrative framework that had resonance with the anxiety of some political elites about the need to maintain racial peace after the transition; certainly, in the short term, the commission is lauded by many for having quelled post-transition racial tension and advanced political stability.[63] However, in the quest for what Timothy Garton Ash calls 'usable knowledge' in oiling the wheels of the Truth Commission, historical accountability for apartheid's systemic racial character was sacrificed.[64]

In its eschewing of a broader historical reckoning for a routinised, operational focus, the South African Truth and Reconciliation Commission demonstrates the orientation of the transitional justice field more generally. A recent initiative on 'Strategic Choices in the Design of Truth Commissions' (hereinafter the Strategic Choices initiative) provides an instance of this orientation in a project that seeks to support those setting up of truth commissions. The Strategic Choices initiative distils the strategic choices of 'five key truth commissions' into the details of a truth commission's institutional architecture.[65] It has developed a web portal that identifies the central design factors that commission architects may confront, and also consolidates the lessons learned on these issues in order to help those confronting the 'daunting task' of 'putting a commission together'.[66] Strikingly, the daunting challenge referenced here is not about how the commission grapples with history. In fact, the historical narrative is produced as a self-evident backdrop to the operationalisation of a truth commission's mandate. The authors provide the historical background of each of these commissions as a concise summary at the beginning simply 'to provide some historical context'.[67] In effect, the Strategic Choices initiative presents the real challenge to would-be commission advocates as a long list of neutral tasks and procedural preoccupations that can cement institutional expertise and advance administrative rationality in the setting up of a

---

[62] See Fullard, n 56 above, 8.

[63] It is worth underscoring that the TRC was established under a piece of legislation entitled The Promotion of National Unity and Reconciliation Act.

[64] See the Preface by Timothy Garton Ash, in Hayner, n 3 above, xii. Garton Ash invokes the term 'usable knowledge' to describe the merits of Hayner's analysis of truth commissions as models of the past.

[65] See the website of the Strategic Choices in the Design of Truth Commissions at http://www.truthcommission.org/about.php?Lang=en (last accessed on 15 July 2011). This initiative is a joint initiative of the Program on Negotiation at Harvard Law School (http://www.pon.harvard.edu) and Search for Common Ground, an international conflict resolution and prevention NGO based in Washington, DC, and for the European Centre for Common Ground, in Brussels (http://www.sfcg.org).

[66] The project emerges from the premise that 'Putting a Commission together is a daunting task, one that can benefit greatly from knowing what has been done elsewhere and, where evaluation has been done seeing what impact previous efforts have had'. See the Truth Commission's website at http://www.truthcommission.org/about.php?Lang=en.

[67] Ibid.

commission.[68] For example, the initiative describes the best practices for the organisation of the public hearings in which the victims give testimony; this involves delineating its different elements, such as undertaking advance outreach, the provision for translation services, determining the degree of formality, making provision for psychological support, procedures for legal support, clarifying options for in-camera testimony, and so on. Each of these tasks is described and incorporated into a series of detailed charts and matrixes with reference to the practices adopted by the five commissions that are studied in the portal. Yet, as I have argued in relation to the South African example, the very manner in which these tasks are administered will have enormous consequences for the history that truth commissions narrate. As noted earlier, they will have consequences for whether they legitimate the production and interpretation of South Africa's human rights history as racialised structural violence or as violations of universal human rights. How public hearings are structured may reflect different assumptions regarding the politics of language and silence. For instance, as Fiona Ross notes, with slogans such as 'Revealing is healing', the South African Truth and Reconciliation Commission's discourse on testimonials at public hearings often equated speaking with healing, and individual healing with a therapeutic path to national reconciliation.[69] Moreover, the TRC broadcast these equations nationally through media outreach extolling the healing powers of recounting one's story in a public forum. In fact, Rosalind Shaw notes that the globalised discourse of redemptive memory through speech has become both naturalised and universalised in truth commission processes partly as a result of the South African model.[70] The TRC final report does situate the structures of racial injustice as the background condition of its *raison d'être*, though these structures recede into the background when the Commission channels public testimony into a depoliticised blueprint of truth as institutionally facilitated catharsis. However, rather than foreground the politics at stake in different technologies of truth which are catalysed by public hearings and their attendant institutional ideologies, the Strategic Choices initiative focuses primarily on the mechanics of establishing and administering public hearings, and further naturalises some of the contested ideologies and practices that inform the globalisation of the truth commission model. The

[68] Here, the transitional justice field may have resonance with the international community's broader post-conflict nation-building impetus. As I have explored further in other writing, these initiatives are often informed by the claim that they are fighting the instability and disruption of violence through good governance, ie they take an approach to building justice institutions through analysis of 'best practices, good governance models, and methodologies for implementation. It has indicia of success that establish objective benchmarks and target criteria.' See Nesiah, n 17 above.

[69] Ross cites posters on the walls of the TRC public hearing rooms that carried slogans such as 'Revealing is healing'. She also noted that, in the final report, the TRC presented public testimonials as being not only about 'individual healing processes but also a healing process for the entire nation'. Ross, n 59 above, 78–79.

[70] Shaw's focus is on the Sierra Leone Commission, but she offers a global genealogy of redemptive memory within the transitional justice field that describes the paradigmatic role of the South African TRC in providing an international 'template for healing, redemption and closure'; see R Shaw, 'Memory Frictions: Localizing the Truth and Reconciliation Commission in Sierra Leone' (2007) 1 *The International Journal of Transitional Justice* 183. The Sierra Leone TRC's engagement with the public echoed the engagements of the South African commission noted by Ross: 'Posters, leaflets, radio and television skits and jingles like the one above transated the truth-telling goals of the TRC into Sierra Leone's lingua franca, Krio, urging survivors and perpetrators to "*Come blow your main* [mind]," to vent their thoughts and feelings. "*Blow main*," according to the TRC, not only gives voice to survivors and addresses the impunity of perpetrators, but also transforms subjectivities by generating "*kol at*" ("a cool/settled heart"), making peace "*sidon na Salone*" ("stay in Sierra Leone") and rebuilding the nation. "We and the international community want to give a new face to Sierra Leone . . ." said the Chair of the Commission, Bishop J Humper'; Shaw, ibid, 184.

narrow focus on administrative mechanics obscures how alternative approaches to public hearing processes may entrench or demystify the ideologies that inform alternative accounts of history, and, concomitantly, legitimate particular boundaries for redress and social change over others.

This section has tried to describe the operational turn within the transitional justice field and to illustrate how the field defines its task as ensuring that transitional justice institutions function effectively, ie that they have clear mandates that comply with international law, that they function in accordance with due process norms, that they are grounded in best practices, that they are properly sequenced and co-ordinated, that they are managed professionally and efficiently, and so on. Perhaps one of the best markers of this focus on the banal is that one of the central transitional justice policy initiatives of the Office of the High Commissioner for Human Rights was the production of a series of reports on transitional justice mechanisms which it describes as 'Tools for post-conflict settings'—operational guidelines that identify the technical issues at stake and consolidate the best practices on how such mechanisms should be established, implemented and co-ordinated. Neil Kritz, one of the most prominent spokespersons for the field, has argued that this focus on the fine-tuning and co-ordinating of institutional strategies exemplifies the primary responsibility of the transitional justice field.[71] On this view, the substantive shape of historical work, how transitional justice institutions define their political compass, is not the issue; what needs to be focused on is the mechanics, the neutral, technical questions of institutional pragmatics. Yet, as this chapter has argued, much is at stake in quotidian operational technologies. Particular notions of truth, history and justice can be normalised and legitimated, and others marginalised and excluded, simply through routine operational decisions. Treating these matters as merely technical questions can obscure the ideological and distributive stakes of administrative decisions, deter critical examination, and entrench the most status quo-friendly approaches.

## IV. CONCLUSION: TECHNOLOGIES OF HISTORICAL CLOSURE

I have argued that there are two competing imperatives that have informed how transitional justice institutions approach the historical, namely, accountability and closure. Indeed, in most cases, both of these imperatives operate as simultaneous and warring pressures on the trajectory of transitional justice. I find that, despite the repeated calls to historical accountability, transitional justice processes have often bent towards delimiting accountability to advance closure. Rather than having provided a forum for a national accounting with history, this chapter has highlighted how transitional justice institutions in Chile and South Africa may be better understood as having operated as official gatekeepers—privileging some histories while obscuring others.

---

[71] N Kritz, 'Where We Are and How We Got Here: An Overview of Developments in the Search for Justice and Reconciliation' in A Henkin (ed), *The Legacy of Abuse: Confronting the Past, Facing the Future* (New York, The Aspen Institute/New York University School of Law, 2002), available at http://www.aspen-institute.org/sites/default/files/content/docs/pubs/LEGACY_OF_ABUSE.PDF.

As the Chile and South African case studies have illustrated, two dominant dimensions of the transitional justice field's approach to historical crimes—the focus on monstrous men and the turn to institutional mechanics—have often rendered systemic factors such as economic and racial structures as mere footnotes of history, rather than shining a light on them as enabling conditions of human rights abuse. Focusing on operational banalities, technical design parameters and the norms of legal objectivity as the remedy for historical injustice is not unlike the impact of focusing on monstrous individuals as the cause of that injustice: both moves deter and distract from structural violence. Entering at transitional moments which are pregnant with transformative possibilities, these institutions could play a very different role in catalysing and contributing to critical historical engagement and social change. However, as the field of transitional justice has become ever more significant in the domain of post-conflict policy and international human rights, transitional justice institutions have opted to support the status quo in the name of stability; thus the dynamic described here has become further consolidated.

In addition to this international investment in historical closure and bounded transitions, in many contexts, there may be compelling national arguments for facilitating historical closure in a fragile post-conflict environment. Closure may help consolidate the new regime and enable stable governance. It may also advance moral consensus that can establish social solidarity in a fraught environment.[72] For instance, the telescoping of a nation's justice struggles onto the victims and the perpetrators on a transitional justice stage is designed to ensure a break from endless cycles of collective grievance and retribution. The South African jurist Richard Goldstone lauds transitional justice for enacting this shift from a notion of collective guilt to a focus on individual accountability. This individualisation of responsibility is seen as part of a constructive process of strategic forgetting. Transitional justice institutions are tasked with performing a delicate balancing act of recognising the victims while building barricades against a fraught history.[73]

Undoubtedly, in both Chile and South Africa, transitional justice has achieved much. It has provided a record of abusive security services and the command structure that allowed and encouraged horrific responses to the regime's critics. Even though the harm of those abuses cannot be undone, at least some of the victims of those abuses have received some reparations and some acknowledgement. In some cases, the perpetrators of those abuses have been prosecuted. These are not achievements to be scoffed at—20 years ago none of this was happening.

For this reason, even when the terrain is not fragile, the human rights community has often invested in a closure orientation in order to provide a path to national

---

[72] Mark Osiel explicitly invokes the Durkeimian view of the work that justice can perform in advancing social solidarity, but his focus of civil dissensus as the glue for this solidarity turns Durkheim's interest in moral consensus on its head; M Osiel, 'Ever Again: Legal Remembrance of Administrative Massacre' (1995) 144 *University of Pennsylvania Law Review* 463, 486–88.

[73] Shoshanna Feldman says: 'We needed trials and trial reports to bring a conscious closure to the trauma of the War, to separate ourselves from the atrocities and to restrict, to demarcate, and draw a boundary around a suffering that seemed both unending and unbearable . . . Law distances the Holocaust.' See S Felman, 'Theaters of Justice: Arendt in Jerusalem, the Eichmann Trial, and the Redefinition of Legal Meaning in the Wake of the Holocaust' (2000) 1 *Theoretical Inquiries in Law* 3.

redemption.[74] The case cited in the introduction to this chapter regarding the lawsuit filed by ACLU and Human Rights First against Rumsfeld provides a telling instance of this dynamic as well. In the press statement launching the suit against Rumsfeld, Michael Posner underscored that this was not a case about ordinary Americans, but about Rumsfeld alone; this suit, he said, was 'challenging policy and leadership failures that are the responsibility of Secretary Rumsfeld himself', and was advanced in the name of 'Defending American Values in Court'.[75] In condemning Rumsfeld, the case aims to absolve and redeem the rest of us.[76] In particular, the system itself will mark out prisoner abuse in the context of war as a symptom of exception, rather than symptomatic of patriotism. Rumsfeld was a 'bad apple', but the 'system is bigger and better than him'. Ironically, this was also how Rumsfeld described the abuse at Abu Ghraib in his testimony to the Senate—that these abuses were the un-American exceptions and that the American system was bigger and better.

However, as this chapter has argued, the project of condemning the symptom and saving the system is not without cost.[77] When transitional justice mechanisms have favoured closure over confronting the root causes of conflict, the historical structures that produced and shaped the specific patterns of human rights violations have faded further into the background. In managing and limiting the transformative potential of transitional justice institutions, the goal of securing national redemption has triumphed over critically interrogating cherished national myths.

The parameters within which history is anchored in transitional justice institutions may also reflect the tension between historical time in a national and international framework within the broader arc of governance imperatives in a post-cold war global order. In other words, there may be a tension between the issues that a nation needs to grapple with in dealing with its past and the approach to transitions that is required by the international community's interests in legitimating a global progress narrative. The approach preparing the ground for global governance imperatives over the last two decades entails state-building through the dissemination of human rights ethics and

[74] TS Eliot captures this nexus between history and redemption, urging that, 'A people without history is not redeemed from time, for history is a pattern of timeless moments': TS Eliot, 'Little Gidding' in *Four Quartets*, (London, Faber & Faber, 1983) 48. My thanks to C Engert for this quotation.

[75] See Posner at http://www.humanrightsfirst.org/us_law/etn/lawsuit/statements/lit-posner-030105.aspx; see also http://www.humanrightsfirst.org/us_law/etn/lawsuit/index.aspx. See also P Sands, *Torture Team: Rumsfeld's Memo and the Betrayal of American Values* (New York, Palgrave Macmillan 2008).

[76] Interestingly, Rumsfeld himself was legally absolved on the theory that he was performing his government function and could not be held liable for actions undertaken in that role. District Judge Thomas F Hogan ruled that Rumsfeld could not be held personally responsible in 2007, and this ruling was reinforced in 2011 when ACLU made an unsuccessful attempt to revive the case.

[77] For an alternative route see James Young's discussion of Holocaust memorials and the possibilities of a non-redemptive orientation: JE Young, *At Memory's Edge: After-Images of the Holocaust in Contemporary Art and Architecture* (New Haven, CT, Yale University Press, 2000). For instance, he comments on the process of building the Berlin memorial (an effort that was delayed many years because it catalysed endless debate on the competition entries) to urge that the collective soul-searching that it ignited in Berlin was more valuable than any graveyard that enacted closure on that conversation: 'If the aim is to remember the perpetuity that this great nation once murdered nearly six million human beings solely for having been Jews, then this monument must remain uncompleted and unbuilt, an unfinishable memorial process' (178). Along similar lines, José Alvarez argues that, rather than close the chapter on the past, international criminal trials such as the ICTY trials regarding war crimes in the former Yugoslavia should be aimed at stimulating constructive dialogue on the most divisive issues invoked by the trials. See J Alvarez, 'Rush to Closure: Lessons of the Tadić Judgment' (1998) 96 *Michigan Law Review* 2031. As Alvarez notes, this is closer to the model of 'civil dissensus' that Osiel advocates: see n 72 above.

expertise.[78] This dynamic is not necessarily a repudiation of history, but is a framing of historical time within particular parameters. For instance, Martti Koskenniemi suggests that international tribunals allow the international community to 'contemplate its past and give a moral meaning to disasters such as Rwanda or Srebrenica as a rejected past and a promise of a radiant future'.[79] It is a theory of transitions that has particular traction in an era when many international institutions prioritise state-building as their primary focus.[80] This may be a priority that diverges from that of national activists (as the East German political activist Bärbel Bohley noted, 'we expected justice and we got the rule of law');[81] however, with state-building as the dominant human rights agenda, not only do countries classified as failed states emerge as the primary object of human rights work, but international actors also emerge as its primary agents.[82] Thus, even the achievements of the most celebrated trials (such as the ICTR's finding of Jean-Paul Akayesu to be guilty of genocide) may be best situated within the framework of international jurisprudence, rather than within the framework of political development within Rwanda.[83] Along these lines, Koskenniemi notes, with regard to the ICTY's prosecution of crimes committed in the former Yugoslavia, that:

> It often seems that the memory for which the trial in the Hague is staged is not the memory of Balkan populations but that of an 'international community' recounting its past as a progress narrative from 'Nuremberg to the Hague', impunity to the Rule of Law.[84]

Transitional justice proved a powerful anchor for the agendas at the helm of the post-cold war global order because of a two-pronged achievement that tracked the dual logics of banality and monstrosity and their advancing of closure in different contexts. On the one hand, the transitional justice field's state-building institutional agenda of courts, commissions and the rule of law provided a foundation for international engagement that could be presented as technocratic and politically neutral. On the other, its normative agenda in prosecuting monstrous perpetrators in the name of

---

[78] This is not to say that the push of 'closure' is primarily international; as I have discussed in the Chilean and South African cases, transitional justice institutions were also shaped by powerful national pressures towards political closure, such as the maintenance and reproduction of the socio-economic status quo.

[79] M Koskenniemi, 'Between Impunity and Show Trials' (2002) 6 *Max Planck Yearbook of United Nations Law* 1, 34.

[80] It is a focus that makes a claim to be technocratic, politically neutral and prudent in a context where the quest for 'unbiased' international engagement haunts the world of human rights and humanitarian action. See T Weiss, 'Principles, Politics, and Humanitarian Action' (1999) 13 *Ethics and International Affairs* 1.

[81] Barbel is quoted in AJ McAdams, 'The Honecker Trial: The East German Past and the German Future', Working Paper #216 (Kellogg Institute for International Studies, 1996), available at http://kellogg.nd.edu/publications/workingpapers/WPS/216.pdf (last accessed on 13 July 2011).

[82] The notion of 'failed states' has provided the normative anchor and policy rational for intervention in these contexts. See F Fukuyama, *State-Building: Governance and World Order in the 21st Century* (Ithaca, NY, Cornell University Press, 2004), Often, these approaches have built on and fed into the new imperial logics represented by the George W Bush administration's 'democracy promotion' policies and Huntington's civilisational arguments; see S Huntington, *Clash of Civilizations* (New York, Simon & Schuster, 1996). Countries such as Liberia, Sierra Leone or the Democratic Republic of Congo are classified as 'failed states' that constitute an ideological *terra nulles* to be laid claim to by a universal post-conflict package; Nesiah, n 17 above. See also R Gordon, 'Saving Failed States: Sometimes a Neocolonial Notion' (1997) 12 *American University Journal of International Law and Policy* 903.

[83] *Prosecutor v Akayesu*, Case No ICTR-96-4-T, available at http://www.ictr.org/ENGLISH/cases/Akayesu/judgement/akay001.htm.

[84] Koskenniemi, n 79 above.

justice for victims promised that that engagement would redeem and revitalise the promise of global governance and transnational community. Thus, while the transitional justice field has been shaped by diverse interests and circumstances, both local and global, the field has cohered into a project that has ended up being compatible with, and even complementary to, the dominant structures and dynamics of global governance. Closure on all fronts.

# Part III

# Intersections and Prospects

# 17

# Sociological Jurisprudence 2.0: Updating Law's Inter-disciplinarity in a Global Context*

### PEER ZUMBANSEN

## I. INTRODUCTION

WITH A LOOK at the conference agendas and the tables of contents of edited collections in law, one is tempted to assume that, over the last 20 years or so, there has been a notable shift in the theoretical interests of legal scholars away from domestic law towards a study of law in a global context. A fast growing number of symposia and legal scholarship suggests that legal scholars have been developing a lively interest in obtaining a better grasp and more solid understanding of globalisation and its impact on law, legal research and legal education. Yet, despite ever-increasing efforts among a growing number of lawyers to study the unquestionably complex relationship between domestic and global regulatory developments, the conceptual toolkit used in these undertakings still appears to be incomplete. The same seems true for legal education. While it is true that law schools around the world have been addressing the perceived need to adapt their curricula to the evolving prospects of a legal profession with an increasingly global reach, most such institutional undertakings remain marked by a concern, first and foremost, with how to provide their graduates with the skills to offer optimal legal services in still relatively confined, domestic settings. As a result, law school curricula, while occasionally including introductory courses (such as 'Law and Globalisation', 'Ethical Lawyering in a Global Context' or 'Introduction to International Law'), continue to be primarily structured around core, black letter, bread-and-butter courses, with seminars in comparative or transnational law, legal culture or legal anthropology, and even international business transactions or international business law, taken only by a self-selected group of specialised students in their last year in law school. Law schools, in other words, are still not decided on the profile and prospective professional trajectories of

* An earlier version of this chapter was presented at the 'Regulatory Translations' Conference, hosted by Bogacici University, Istanbul, Rice University, Houston, and the *Indiana Journal of Global Legal Studies*, 16–18 June 2013. I am grateful to Andrea Ballestero, Philip Liste, Anna-Katharina Mangold and Jothie Rajah for excellent feedback.

their future graduates. As a result, curriculum programmes are wavering between the continued commitment of law schools to offer training in core skills, foundations and black letter law, on the one hand, and inducing their future graduates to a fast-paced and complex transactional environment, on the other. The latter, in particular, is seen as a world in which lawyers are expected to navigate complex jurisdictional, cultural and epistemological divides.

How are these debates in legal education connected to legal research? In other words, we need to ask about the reciprocal impact of legal education and research in a context in which it has become obvious that there is much more to the training to think like a lawyer than has traditionally been taught in contract or tort law, constitutional law or civil procedure. The gap between the curriculum-design efforts and legal scholarship of law schools, however, still remains significant. Legal scholars, if the scope of the research disseminated on the Social Science Research Network (www. ssrn.com) is any indication, still appear to be neatly divided into traditionalists and transnationalists.[1] While the latter are divided further into those with a keen interest in either maintaining or breaking down the boundaries between domestic and international law, the so-called traditionalists appear to focus their interests on matters of domestic significance—in the case of SSRN, with an overwhelming focus on US law. The world outside the nation state remains one in which the majority of legal scholars is simply not that interested. In contrast, then, while the apparently transnational scope of some research in the EU appears to be more obviously targeting processes of Europeanisation or, more generally, internationalisation against the background of the undeniably European nature of numerous norms, laws and regulation in force in EU Member States today, there is a distinct blind side, which is noticeable here as well. Pushing the boundaries of the European legal imagination towards a greater appreciation of the significance of studying law from both a comparative and, specifically, from a European and integrationist perspective, this energy-consuming effort almost pushes aside or renders invisible important advances to study law's historical and colonial pasts and to renew legal historical, international and comparative research agendas in order to grasp the inevitably interdisciplinary challenge of studying law in a global, colonial and post-colonial context.[2]

However, in what might appear to be almost a parallel universe to the core of basic legal education and mainstream legal research, an intense debate has been under way about the prospects of, and the forms in which, legal analytical instruments and concepts, categories as well as basic understandings of legal institutions and processes, as they have been developed in the context of the nation state, might or might not be adaptable to the regulatory challenges in a global space. In this vein, scholarship on law and globalisation has arguably become an industry in its own right. Yet, the focal point of this burgeoning scholarship is far from precise. In other words, it does not seem evident what precisely the question is that law and globalisation scholars are trying to answer. What does seem clear, at the same time, is that

---

[1] See KP Berger, *The Creeping Codification of the Lex Mercatoria* (The Hague, Kluwer Law International, 1999).

[2] Indications of such promising initiatives include the recently published *Oxford Handbook of The History of International Law*, by B Fassbender and A Peters (eds) (Oxford, Oxford University Press, 2013), as well as the forthcoming volume entitled *Oxford Handbook of International Legal Theory*, by F Hoffmann and A Orford (eds) (Oxford, Oxford University Press, 2014).

the endeavours of legal scholars in this context have long become part of a multi-disciplinary study of global governance. As such, law and globalisation has become a field of scholarly inquiry belaboured by lawyers, political scientists, sociologists, anthropologists, geographers and political economists alike, which raises important questions regarding how law should situate itself in relation to the approaches and methods of other disciplines.

Admittedly, such a reductionist stance on one the perspective of one's discipline (that of law)—on what has rightly been identified as a multidisciplinary one—bears the risk of closing a door that has hardly been opened. But the intention of choosing law as a starting point and platform for the study of globalisation is to concretise the relation between a still underdefined phenomenon of social and historical processes and a distinct disciplinary framework in an exemplary fashion. In other words, the intention to focus on and to revisit not only law's and legal scholars' but also practitioners' engagement with globalisation phenomena is based upon the assumption that we will be able to identify both specific as well as more generalisable aspects in the way that a social theory has been addressing such developments.

A central contention of this chapter is that the future development of law and globalisation will be significantly shaped by the way in which scholars in law and other social sciences are further able to integrate the respective investigations into the very foundations and methodologies which are already underway in each discipline. The prospect of updating and adapting a primarily nation-state-focused legal discipline to its operation in a global context includes the initiations of concentrated thought exchanges about the different recognisable approaches to make sense, above all, of the very challenges posed by globalisation for law and other social sciences. For a conversation across disciplinary boundaries to develop, it is advisable to give a better picture of law and the current state of legal research (and contemporary developments in legal education). We can today identify a number of thematic clusters which capture the different aspects of contemporary debates around law and globalisation. My contention is that, taken together, these clusters constitute the elements of an emerging legal theory of global governance. Such a theory, to be sure, is no longer a legal theory in its own right, but a social theory of law, and it is in this light that we are now experiencing a strange mixture of both déjà vu and innovation in the engagements between legal theory and social sciences. If we dared to apply a label to these developments, we could venture that of a transition from law and society to law and globalisation, with the term 'transition' marking less of a substitute or replacement than an evolution, a maturing and continuing differentiation. However, having said that, it is clear that the challenges arising from the first phase of law and society are likely to reverberate in the current iteration of law and globalisation. In other words, the pressing questions with regard to the methodology to reveal the relation between law and society cannot be considered to be obsolete. What remains the same is the need to demarcate and motivate the contours of each one and the boundaries between them. This brings us back to the rediscovery of legal sociology in the 1960s and 1970s, the rise of a scientifically driven criminology as one of the launching pads and benchmarks for what was to result in a fast proliferating field of victimology, critical criminal-law theory, implementation and context studies, etc. At the same time, legal pluralism, while echoing the interests of many of the early legal anthropologists and legal sociologists in indigenous legal orders or customary law,[3] became a very ambitious theoretical and practical endeavour in the critical analysis of regulatory regimes in mature welfare states.[4] Today, the resurgence of law and society through the prism of law and globalisation reminds us of these demarcation efforts, while, at the same time, pushing us to recontextualise such concerns in a newly expanded environment—jurisdictionally and geographically,[5] geopolitically[6] and from an epistemological standpoint.[7] What has changed in comparison between the 1960s/1970s constellation and the present time is that the target areas of much of the above-mentioned legal sociological, anthropological and critical work have become decentred, as it were, shifting from a largely state-centred analytical universe to one of hybrid regulatory arenas, described variously as international regimes,[8] transnational spaces,[9] fragmented legal orders[10] and/or collisions.[11] This shift results in what might be called a disembedding of nation-state or jurisdiction-oriented analytical and conceptual approaches. Explanatory frameworks employed to structure and analyse core institutional features of state-based legal regimes such as the 'Rule of Law', the 'Separation of Powers' principle or the ideas of a constitutional order or, simply, normative hierarchy risk missing the unique architectural structure of emerging global governance regimes. It is this disembedding of state-based conceptual toolkits that prompts not so much a full-blown crafting of a new language,[12] but a constant exercise in adaptation, building on reflexive exercises in (discourse–regime–system) translation[13] as well as the continuing engagements with

---

[3] E Ehrlich, *Fundamental Principles of the Sociology of Law* (originally published in German as *Grundlegung der Soziologie des Rechts, 1913*) (New York, Russell & Russell, 1962); E Durkheim, *The Division of Labor in Society*, trans WD Halls (New York, Free Press, 1984); AB Bozeman, *The Future of Law in a Multicultural World* (Princeton, NJ, Princeton University Press, 1971).

[4] SF Moore, 'Law and Social Change: The Semi-autonomous Field as an Appropriate Subject of Study' (1973) 7 *Law & Society Review* 719; G Teubner, 'Substantive and Reflexive Elements in Modern Law' (1983) 17 *Law & Society Review* 239.

[5] R Ford, 'Law's Territory (A History of Jurisdiction)' (1999) 97 *Michigan Law Review* 843; G Handl, J Zekoll and P Zumbansen (eds), *Beyond Territoriality: Transnational Legal Authority in an Age of Globalization* (Leiden, Brill, 2012).

[6] D Held, *Democracy and the Global Order: From the Modern State to Cosmopolitan Governance* (Cambridge, Polity Press, 1995); M Albert and R Schmalz-Bruns, 'Antinomien der Global Governance: Mehr Weltstaatlichkeit, weniger Demokratie?' in H Brunkhorst (ed), *Soziale Welt (Sonderband 18): Demokratie in der Weltgesellschaft* (Baden-Baden, Nomos Verlag, 2009) 57–74.

[7] B de Sousa Santos, 'Beyond Abyssal Thinking. From Global Lines to Ecologies of Knowledge' (2007) *Eurozine*, available at http://www.eurozine.com/articles/2007-06-29-santos-en.html; D Chakrabarty, *Provincializing Europe: Postcolonial Thought and Historical Difference*, 2nd edn (Princeton, NJ, Princeton University Press, 2007); J Comaroff and JL Comaroff, *Theory from the South: Or, How Euro-America is Evolving Toward Africa (The Radical Imagination)* (Boulder, CO, Paradigm Publishers, 2011), especially ch 1, where the authors lay out the different theoretical strands that inform their thesis.

[8] SD Krasner (ed), *International Regimes* (Ithaca, NY, Cornell University Press, 2001).

[9] S Sassen, *Territory, Authority, Rights: From Medieval to Global Assemblages* (Princeton, NJ, Princeton University Press, 2006).

[10] M Koskenniemi and P Leino, 'Fragmentation of International Law? Postmodern Anxieties' (2002) 15 *Leiden Journal of International Law* 553.

[11] A Fischer-Lescano and G Teubner, 'Regime-Collisions: The Vain Search for Legal Unity in the Fragmentation of Global Law' (2004) 25 *Michigan Journal of International Law* 999; G Teubner, *Constitutional Fragments: Societal Constitutionalism and Globalization* (Oxford, Oxford University Press, 2012), especially ch 6, where he analyses the consequences of a constitutional-political challenge arising from regime collisions on a global scale.

[12] In this context see the programme description of 'Language and Globalization' at Tilburg University in the Netherlands: available at http://www.tilburguniversity.edu/research/humanities/language-and-globalization.

[13] See EG Carayannis, A Pirzadeh and D Popiscu, *Institutional Learning and Knowledge Transfer Across Epistemic Communities: Innovation, Technology, and Knowledge Management* (Heidelberg, Springer, 2012),

the tension between government and governance discourses within different social science disciplines.[14]

Such developments can be seen as forming the backdrop for the next stages of globalisation studies, which will, in all likelihood, lead to an ever higher degree of interdisciplinary pollination. For the purposes of the present project, it is necessary to keep this rich background in mind, while continuing our efforts to draw more concrete lessons from this engagement for one's own discipline. This interest in 'one's own' may be justified in light of the consideration that disciplinary frameworks evolve both internally and externally, and, as such, have an inherent quality of instability that needs to be kept in mind when employing its tools and concepts—however critically such employment may occur. What evolutionary theorists have referred to as the tension between routine and innovation,[15] legal scholars have depicted as a state of critical instability, for example, in the case of a normative framework that is rich in its conceptual and, as a result, symbolic aspiration, while being under the constant threat of being unmasked as farcical or worse in light of the unlegitimisable environment that its norms have helped to create.[16] While this instability of theoretical frameworks which results from internal and external challenges[17] might be identified and recognised, the necessary next step is often much harder to formulate. Law's relationship to (global) society is one such constellation in which a crisis of law is widely acknowledged, although nothing that comes close to an idea of consensus is emerging in terms of how to respond to that crisis.[18] Despite this, it is possible to identify a number of thematic clusters which are constantly recurring in related debates about law's status in a global context. These clusters are helpful in that they enable us to distinguish different dimensions of the law-globalisation relationship which this chapter seeks to address. Among these clusters we find:

- the *state-law nexus* and the frequently associated distinction between a (legally structured and operating) state and a (purportedly self-regulatory) society;
- the alleged elusiveness of *transposing nation state-based concepts* such as the 'Rule of Law', 'Separation of Powers' or 'Normative (Constitutional) Hierarchy' into the global sphere (the distinction of domestic and global law);

---

especially ch 2 ('Globalization, Nation-States, and Global Governance'), P Liste, 'The Politics of (Legal) Intertextuality' (2010) 4 *International Political Sociology* 318; idem, *Völkerrecht-Sprechen. Die Konstruktion demokratischer Völkerrechtspolitik in den USA und der Bundesrepublik Deutschland* (Baden-Baden, Nomos Verlag, 2012), especially ch 1, in which the author highlights the different 'international law' discursive spaces that are opening up between state and non-state actors, regimes, movements and individuals.

[14] See, eg JN Rosenau and E-O Czempiel, *Governance without Government: Order and Change in World Government* (Cambridge, Cambridge University Press, 1992); I Ayres and J Braithwaite, *Responsive Regulation: Transcending the Deregulation Debate* (Oxford, Oxford University Press, 1992); C Scott, F Cafaggi and L Senden (eds), *The Challenge of Transnational Private Regulation: Conceptual and Constitutional Debates. Symposium Issue of the Journal of Law and Society, Vol 38, No 1, 1–188* (Chicester, Wiley-Blackwell, 2011).

[15] Eg N Luhmann, 'Evolution und Geschichte' in idem, *Soziologische Aufklärung 2: Aufsätze zur Theorie der Gesellschaft* (Opladen: Westdeutscher Verlag, 1975) 150–69.

[16] S Pahuja, *Decolonising International Law: Development, Economic Growth and the Politics of Universality* (Cambridge, Cambridge University Press, 2011); J Rajah, 'The Gulf between Promise and Claim: Understanding International Law's Failure to Decolonise' (2012) 3 *Transnational Legal Theory* 285.

[17] TS Kuhn, *The Structure of Scientific Revolutions* (Chicago, IL, University of Chicago Press, 1962).

[18] T Murphy, 'Globalization, Legal Pluralism, and the New Constitutionalism' (2007) 25 *Nordic Journal of Human Rights* 1; N McCormick, 'Beyond the Sovereign State' (1993) 56 *Modern Law Review* 73.

- the *relationship between* (formal, institutionalised) *law and* (informal, social) *norms* (the law/non-law distinction);
- the fate of the concept of *legitimacy* in an evolving global legal order (the normative status of global law;
- the *politics* of global law (for example, the tension between progressive and conservative endorsements of concepts such as the Rule of Law);
- the legal-philosophical *foundations of law* as distinct from law seen through the lens of *sociological or regulatory theory* (the interdisciplinary understanding of law).

These identified clusters underscore the previously made observation that the relationship of law and globalisation is, in fact, a label for a multilayered and multitiered theoretical analysis of contemporary social order, as formulated from the unstable epistemological position of law. The purposes of the present project are to investigate the nature of this instability further through a series of applications. Section II of this chapter sets the stage for subsequent analysis by initiating an investigation into the evolution of law and socio-legal studies. Section III builds on this and looks more closely at one of the currently most vibrant discursive playgrounds in globalised socio-legal studies, namely, transnational law (TL). TL is studied here primarily from a methodological perspective, understanding the emergence of this field as an attempt to make sense of law's doctrinal, conceptual and interdisciplinary adaptations to globalisation. The next two sections (IV and V) analyse the role of information and knowledge in the context of this emerging legal-regulatory concept of TL by looking more closely at both facts and norms. The core contention in this part of the chapter is that, while there is an inherently political dimension to the identification and selection of relevant/irrelevant facts, on the one hand, and the recognition versus the dismissal of legal/non-legal norms, on the other, it remains frustratingly difficult to capture or address the nature of this political dimension adequately. It is the ambiguous, illusive nature of both the political status and the framework that I am most interested in here, as I am trying to build further on similar insights from other scholars.[19] Consequently, Section VI introduces two legal fields/arenas/subdisciplines—law and development, on the one hand, and transitional justice, on the other—which may illustrate how law has become an increasingly interdisciplinary and unstable, the merits of which can only be realised in accepting its unstable nature as an unavoidable consequence of law's engagement with its environment. Section VII deepens this analysis by revisiting the earlier findings regarding the role of knowledge in legal governance, but now scrutinising the particular role in these two overarching dynamic areas. Finally, Section VIII reiterates the argument for an understanding of TL not as a field, but as a contemporary methodological engagement. This, in consequence, leads to the emergence of a differentiated analytical framework—under the label of 'transnational legal sociology'—with the help of which it might be possible to think further about the connections and intersections between legal doctrine, legal sociology and social sciences in the present era.

---

[19] Teubner, n 11 above; Liste, *Völkerrecht-Sprechen*, n 13 above.

## II. STRANGE BEDFELLOWS OR A COHABITATION WITH UNCERTAIN EFFECTS: SOCIO-LEGAL STUDIES

Under the constant harassment of the conceptual citadels of legal coherence and unity[20] by social-scientific insights, law eventually morphed into an unbound universe of socio-legal studies. Similar to other hybrid scholarly endeavours,[21] the ambiguity of the politics that are at work in the generation, formation and consolidation of such fields results from both their conceptualisation and impact. The crushing of categories is no longer confined to the internal architecture of a theory, but attains explosive, uncontainable potential in the artificial outside.[22] With this in mind, the chapter is interested in both the trajectories and the politics of the conceptual change in law's efforts to adapt to globalisation. As such, our interest must reach beyond the obvious political categorisation of assertions that globalisation has (rightly[23] or regrettably[24]) put an end to state sovereignty. Instead, the more important task seems to be to understand better the discursive universe in which globalisation is associated either with the death of law (as collateral damage from the decline of the state) or with the resurgence of law as a flexible regulatory asset in globalising markets. Such an understanding cannot be gained from a single vantage point. While the analysis of the contested status and the role of law in global governance is partly an important concern of sociologists and political scientists, the motivations as well as underlying assumptions that guide regulatory scholars—as de facto political philosophers—in their confidence in law in a domestic context, as opposed to the frequently voiced fear of falling into a global void, might be better understood through the lenses of (however crude) behavioural psychology[25] or political philosophy.[26] But only in a combination of these different disciplinary lenses does it seem possible to arrive at halfway appropriate observations of the emerging global regulatory order. Having said that, the contention here is that a legal theory of global governance cannot escape its interdisciplinary reformulation, precisely because its categories have come under such close scrutiny.

Meanwhile, the analysis of law's engagement with globalisation can rest, at least for the time being, on a number of reference points. One of these is the distinction between

---

[20] See, eg M Baldus, *Die Einheit der Rechtsordnung. Bedeutungen einer juristischen Formel in Rechtstheorie, Zivil- und Staatsrechtswissenschaft des 19. und 20. Jahrhunderts* (Berlin, Duncker & Humblot, 1995); D Felix, *Einheit der Rechtsordnung. Zur verfassungsrechtlichen Relevanz einer juristischen Argumentationsfigur* (Tübingen, Mohr Siebeck, 1998); A Hanebeck, 'Die Einheit der Rechtsordnung als Anforderung an den Gesetzgeber? Zu verfassungsrechtlichen Anforderungen wie "Systemgerechtigkeit" und "Widerspruchsfreiheit" der Rechtsetzung als Maßstab verfassungsgerichtlicher Kontrolle' (2002) 41 *Der Staat* 429.

[21] The fitting example often being that of 'cultural studies': see, eg R Terdiman, 'Globalization and Cultural Studies: Conceptualization, Convergence, and Complication' (2001) 21 *Comparative Studies of South Asia, Africa and the Middle East* 82; from the standpoint of legal sociology see D Nelken and J Feest (eds), *Adapting Legal Cultures* (Oxford, Hart Publishing, 2001).

[22] B Latour, 'From Realpolitik to Dingpolitik, or How to Make Things Public' in B Latour and P Weibel (eds), *Making Things Public: Atmospheres of Democracy* (Karlsruhe/Cambridge, MA, ZKM Art and Media Centre/The MIT Press, 2005) 14–41; M Valverde, *Law's Dream of a Common Knowledge* (Princeton, NJ, Princeton University Press, 2003).

[23] M Wolf, *Why Globalization Works* (New Haven, CT, Yale University Press, 2004).

[24] D Grimm, 'The Achievement of Constitutionalism and its Prospects in a Changed World' in P Dobner and M Loughlin (eds), *The Twilight of Constitutionalism* (Oxford, Oxford University Press, 2010) 3–22.

[25] AT Guzman, *How International Law Works: A Rational Choice Theory* (Oxford, Oxford University Press, 2008); EA Posner, *The Perils of Global Legalism* (Chicago, IL, Chicago University Press, 2009).

[26] T Pogge, 'Cosmopolitanism and Sovereignty' (1992) 103 *Ethics* 48.

domestic and international, which—despite its questionable explanatory status in the long run[27]—serves as a productive framework to identify differently bounded regulatory discourses. Against that background, it is possible to get closer to the politics that accompany the emergence of legal fields, which are in themselves neither here nor there, in that they are constantly transgressing the boundaries between the nation-state and the global realm. Two such fields will be at the centre of the forthcoming analysis, namely, the in themselves unruly and seemingly boundaryless fields of law and development and transitional justice. By looking more closely at the continuing conceptualisation of these areas, including their trials and tribulations as law school curriculum entities, it can be shown how the conflict between progressive and conservative politics, well known from nation-state-based disputes regarding the aims of legal governance in different regulatory areas, is repeating itself in the transnational arena.[28] This transnational replay of domestic tensions between progressive versus conservative politics in the global arena can be shown by short-circuiting the related debates within the nation-state context, on the one hand, and within transnational or global governance discourses, on the other. Because the latter is often described as distinctly different from the domestic sphere in light of the absence of a functioning, institutionalised rule of law, a normative-constitutional framework or hierarchy or an adequately designed system of norm-enforcement, the politics of global law are often depicted as being fatally troubled with questions of legitimacy, access to justice or human rights universalism. Meanwhile, it is within the nation-state that the political dimension of legal theory is most frequently associated with crude demarcations of public versus private spheres of regulatory sovereignty, or with claims over contested territory, associated either with state interventionism or societal self-regulation.[29] Law reconceived as socio-legal studies can be seen as a continuing effort to formulate this dependency of law's meaning (its politics) from the context in which it is being evoked. It is this sense of embeddedness that has been crucial to the formation of the legal sociological analysis of law over time. The task at this point in time is how to identify adequately the challenge arising from the globalisation of law, how to build on or reject categories and instruments internal to law as a scholarly discipline, how to relate and, possibly, adapt its conceptual framework to the insights of other disciplines into the nature of global governance, and what lessons to draw from such engagements for law—as a field of doctrine, practice, education and research.[30]

[27] P Zumbansen, 'Administrative Law's Global Dream: Navigating Regulatory Spaces between "National" and "International"' (2013) 11 *International Journal of Constitutional Law* 506.
[28] For a more extensive analysis along those lines see, eg AC Cutler, 'Artifice, Ideology and Paradox: The Public/Private Distinction in International Law' (1997) 4 *Review of International Political Economy* 261; P Zumbansen, 'Sustaining Paradox Boundaries: Perspectives on the Internal Affairs in Domestic and International Law' (2004) 15 *European Journal of International Law* 197; idem, 'Transnational Private Regulatory Governance: Ambiguities of Public Authority and Private Power' (2013) 76 *Law & Contemporary Problems* 117, available at http://ssrn.com/abstract=2252208.
[29] See the pertinent critique by RL Hale, 'Coercion and Distribution in a Supposedly Non-Coercive State' (1923) 38 *Political Science Quarterly* 470.
[30] On this theme see the contributions to the Symposium on W Twining's Montesquieu Lecture, 'Globalization and Legal Scholarship' (2014) 5(2) *Transnational Legal Theory*.

## III. TRANSNATIONAL LAW AS AN ENGAGEMENT WITH GLOBALISATION

In a recent chapter for an essay collection on law and social theory, Ralf Michaels, a prominent participant in the discussions surrounding 'global legal pluralism',[31] surmises that globalisation has become the definitive framing operative of the 'law of our time'.[32] An informed, cursory overview of the challenges arising for law and legal theory from globalisation—above all, law's ties to the concept and the institutions of the Western nation-state—then follows this assumption. At the end of the chapter, Michaels simultaneously appears both to dismiss and to endorse a reading of TL as a theory or a methodological framework in its own right.[33] He suggests that:

> if anything, transnational law is a description of what we find empirically as law beyond the state, and a theoretical conceptualization of law after the breakdown of methodological nationalism. Transnational law describes a starting point, not an endpoint, of thinking about law.[34]

I take the apparent ambiguity of this position as an expression of a dilemma, which we—as legal scholars and de facto social scientists—are facing at almost every turn in our attempt to adapt the conceptual and theoretical instruments of our discipline to the unruly phenomena of globalisation. In turn, globalisation, as Gunther Teubner noted almost 20 years ago, should rightly be seen as the ultimate deconstructor, which, in fact, turns every dearly held assumption and foundation of law as a discipline on its head.[35] As Michaels observes, globalisation 'has remained a remarkably vague concept in general discourse'.[36] While this observation seems to be a valid point when we take into consideration the wide-ranging assessments and appropriations of the term conceptually, politically and theoretically,[37] we still must ask ourselves whether the problem is this lack of definition. After all, if it is true, at the very least, that 'we are all realists now',[38] why further invest our energy in definition games? We know well enough that these only raise further questions as to who does the defining, to

---

[31] See, among his previous contributions to the debate, R Michaels, 'The Re-State-Ment of Non-State Law: The State, Choice of Law, and the Challenge from Global Legal Pluralism' (2005) 51 *Wayne Law Review* 1209; idem, 'The True New Lex Mercatoria: Law Beyond the State' (2007) 14 *Indiana Journal of Global Legal Studies* 447; idem, 'Global Legal Pluralism' (2009) 5 *Annual Review of Law & Social Science* (also Duke Public Law & Legal Theory Research Paper No 259), available at http://papers.ssrn.com/sol3/papers.cfm?abstract_id=1430395.

[32] R Michaels, 'Globalisation and Law: Law Beyond the State' in R Banakar and M Travers (eds), *Law and Social Theory*, 2nd edn (Oxford, Hart Publishing, 2013) 287, available at http://scholarship.law.duke.edu/faculty_scholarship/2862.

[33] P Zumbansen, 'Transnational Comparisons: Theory and Practice of Comparative Law as a Critique of Global Governance' in M Adams and J Bomhoff (eds), *Theory and Practice of Comparative Law* (Cambridge, Cambridge University Press, 2012), available at http://papers.ssrn.com/sol3/papers.cfm?abstract_id=2000803; P Zumbansen, 'Transnational Law, Evolving' in JM Smits (ed), *Elgar Encyclopedia of Comparative Law*, 2nd edn (Cheltenham, Edward Elgar Publishing, 2012) 898–925, available at http://ssrn.com/abstract=1975403.

[34] Michaels, n 32 above, 18.

[35] G Teubner, 'The King's Many Bodies: The Self-Deconstruction of Law's Hierarchy' (1997) 31 *Law & Society Review* 763.

[36] Michaels, n 32 above, 1.

[37] See, eg the tensions between the accounts offered by B de Sousa Santos, 'The Processes of Globalisation' (2002) *Eurozine*, available at http://www.eurozine.com/pdf/2002-08-22-santos-en.pdf, on the one hand, and Wolf, n 23 above, on the other.

[38] JW Singer, 'Legal Realism Now' (1988) 76 *California Law Review* 465.

which purpose and to what effect. In this light, it perhaps appears more productive
to embrace the phenomena which are being associated, for a variety of reasons, with
globalisation as challenges to the foundations of established epistemologies and new
ways of seeing the world. Surely, the ability to see, and then to know, both in and of
itself, is neither an asset nor a self-explanatory competence. That much we ought to
have learned, at least.[39]

From such a starting point, Michaels's assertion of TL merely capturing what we
'find empirically' can be qualified further to hint at the very problem of how we ought
to use frameworks such as a particular theory, an analytical concept or—as in the
case of TL—a field within a discipline to describe (and to construct) reality. Apart
from the question of epistemology and the status of empirical socio-legal studies,[40] the
other part of Michaels's statement deserves equal attention, namely, where he refers
to 'law beyond the state'.[41] If anything, law's engagement with globalisation has been
determined by the category of the state and its significance for our understanding of
law. That is precisely what Michaels depicts as (the need to question and, eventually,
overcome) law's 'methodological nationalism'. So far, so good. But where do we start?

In this chapter, I suggest that, independently of whether or not TL is a theory in
its own right or whether legal pluralism (LP), sharing with TL a keen interest in social
norms and in the tension between law and non-law,[42] should be seen as helpful,[43] we
ought to acknowledge frameworks and approaches such as TL or LP as elements in
what Michaels appropriately, in my view, describes as a reconstruction of 'law as social
science'. As such, the boundaries of law as a discipline tend to be drawn and redrawn
as a result of challenges, the status of which is inevitably going to be as contested and
open for further deconstruction as the nature of law itself. In other words—though it
might be a theoretically obvious and trite point—there is no fixed point from which
it would be possible to treat law as a given, and then to analyse how it changes under
the influence of outside pressures. The problem of law's boundaries and its content,
scope and nature has always been part of the definition of law. Michaels's suggestion
to capture the scope of law as it unfolds under conditions of globalisation through
the study of three determinants or anchor points—territory, population/citizenship
and government—is well suited to explore the inchoate ways in which legal categories
become intertwined with social scientific depictions. Building on these three mini-
excursions, we are able to see how a set of reference points that play an important role
in law are revisited and, in turn, reconfigured and expropriated by an immensely rich
assembly of non-legal analytics that capture their sociological, philosophical, political,

---

[39] See, eg M Foucault, *The Archeology of Knowledge* (Paris, Gallimard, 1973); B Latour, *We Have Never Been Modern*, trans C Porter (Cambridge, MA, Harvard University Press, 1993). See also L Adkins and C Lury, 'What is the Empirical?' (2009) 12 *European Journal of Social Theory* 5 (discussing the different reasons for a perceived 'crisis' of sociology), on the one hand, and the insightful critique of the ways in which the World Bank has been instrumentalising empirical data and human rights research, by GA Sarfaty, *Values in Translation: Human Rights and the Culture of the World Bank* (Stanford CA, Stanford University Press, 2012), on the other.

[40] See, eg G Teubner and J Paterson, 'Changing Maps: Empirical Legal Autopoiesis' (1998) 7 *Social and Legal Studies* 451; for the assessment of legal sociology's contemporary challenges see T Raiser, 'Sociology of Law in Germany' (2010) 11 *German Law Journal* 391; P Zumbansen, 'Law's Effectiveness and Law's Knowledge: Reflections from Legal Sociology and Legal Theory' (2009) 10 *German Law Journal* 417.

[41] Michaels, n 32 above, 1.

[42] Moore, above n 4.

[43] Compare Michaels, n 32 above, 14.

anthropological and/or geographical dimensions. Again, the ensuing question is what the consequences are for law. This question is new only with regard to the context in which it is posed. The fact that this context is labelled as globalisation suggests that it is a different context from that (of the nation state) in which questions regarding the relationship between law and social developments or, more generally, between law and society, have previously been asked.

Globalisation and the various conceptual steps that have been taken by lawyers and socio-legal scholars towards making sense of the impact of globalisation on law appear to place the investigation on an entirely new and distinct foundation. It is against such a background that we might be able to appreciate the anxiety that shines through proclamations such as: 'If everything is transnational law, nothing really is'.[44] Michaels qualifies this statement by referring to the use of TL as encompassing 'all legal (and non-legal!) rules',[45] while underlining that his preferred reading of TL, as alluded to earlier, is one of a description of empirically found instantiations of 'law beyond the state' and as a 'theoretical conceptualization of law after the breakdown of methodological nationalism'.[46]

The problem with these qualifications is that they tend to abbreviate and curtail the necessary inquiries rather than productively draw upon the different already existing investigative strands that have been developing in recent years and that have been benefiting from an increasingly serious engagement across different disciplinary boundaries. The level of complexity that the work carried out under the label of 'socio-legal studies' has reached at this point strongly suggests that we should no longer hope for any 'easy scores' or apodictic truths in this theoretical game. In this vein, it is important to point out and acknowledge that definitions of otherwise unbound experimental frameworks—such as TL—always carry the risk of inadequately reducing complexity. However, they must nevertheless be taken seriously as evolutionary steps in theory-building which is driven by a coalescence of factors. In the area of legal fields, such factors comprise the constant tension between the law on the books and the law in action,[47] the exhaustion of conceptual, analytical and doctrinal categories and instruments in the face of competing interpretations of social facts,[48] and the recognised need to adapt or expand an existing legal framework into a burgeoning set of technological, social and cultural developments.[49] Because law that does not adapt to its times will wither away, we can see these tensions, as well as the attempts to address them, to have been marking any field of law, including contract, tort, property or civil

---

[44] Ibid, 18.

[45] Ibid, emphasis not added. See the expression of a similar anxiety in M Zamboni, '"A Legal Pluralist World" . . . or the Black Hole for Modern Legal Positivism' (2013), available at http://ssrn.com/abstract=2251017, ms 2, referring to the 'black hole represented by legal globalization (and its legal pluralism), a black hole where the distinction between law and non-law (ie the major tenant of legal positivism and, I would dare say, of the modern Western legal culture) seems to vanish, putting the very existence and legitimacy of the legal phenomenon under question'.

[46] Ibid.

[47] See, eg R Pound, 'Law in Books and Law in Action' (1910) 44 *American Law Review* 12; KN Llewellyn, *Bramble Bush (1928/29)* (New York, Oceana Publishing, 1950).

[48] M Galanter, 'In the Winter of our Discontent: Law, Anti-law, and Social Science' (2006) 2 *Annual Review of Law & Social Sciences* 1; O Lobel, 'The Paradox of Extralegal Activism: Critical Legal Consciousness and Transformative Politics' (2007) 120 *Harvard Law Review* 937.

[49] S Jasanoff, *Science at the Bar: Law, Science, and Technology in America* (Cambridge, MA, Harvard University Press, 1997).

procedure: all of these have seen such sieges to their citadels of purported coherence and rationality. As keen observers have pointed out, for example, in the case of private law, the politics of this game of constant change were not first prompted by the emergence of globe-spanning regulatory regimes,[50] but had begun long before. Against this background, who still wants to define what contract (property, constitutional law, etc) law really is, and what it aims for and is designed to demarcate, protect and empower?

Transnational law is just one result of such ongoing attempts to update law and its categorical architecture to fast-moving societal developments. From this viewpoint, the body of TL is driven by the tension as well as by the coexistence of law (legal) and non-law (non-legal rules) as they characterise contemporary regulatory regimes.[51] But this does not define TL; rather, it is but one element of the concept that gives rise to the field. Understood, instead, as a theoretical platform or laboratory, TL allows us to study the ways in which this tension actually unfolds, the forms and instances through which this coexistence occurs and the instances in which legal categories become infiltrated by meanings from other disciplinary discourses. In other words, TL should be seen as doing the exact opposite of equating or levelling legal and non-legal rules. The contention is that TL, instead, problematises the correlation between both normative universes,[52] in that it opens up an increasingly diffuse and complex regulatory landscape to a comprehensive assessment of the status and the function of norms (legal or non-legal) not only inside, but also outside, legal doctrine. For example, rather than contending that the transnational law merchant—the *lex mercatoria*—encompasses the entire universe of legal and non-legal rules in the field of transnational commercial regulation and governance, TL highlights the interaction between legal and non-legal rules in the governance of transnational societal activity.[53]

## IV. THE TRANSNATIONAL LAW PROJECT SCRUTINISES LAW'S 'KNOWLEDGE' PROBLEM 1: FACTS

This leads us to the second contention: if TL is a framework to investigate the correlation between legal and non-legal norms, then it is not just more, but also something different from a mere description of norms that can empirically be found, as alluded to by Michaels. TL problematises the way in which such a finding occurs each time.

---

[50] D Caruso, 'Private Law and State-Making in the Age of Globalization' (2006) 39 *New York University Journal of International Law & Politics* 1.
[51] T Bartley, 'Institutional Emergence in an Era of Globalization: The Rise of Transnational Private Regulation of Labor and Environmental Conditions' (2007) 113 *American Journal of Sociology* 297; idem, 'Transnational Governance as the Layering of Rules: Intersections of Public and Private Standards' (2011) 12 *Theoretical Inquiries in Law* 517; KW Abbott and D Snidal, 'Strengthening International Regulation through Transnational New Governance: Overcoming the Orchestration Deficit' (2009) 42 *Vanderbilt Journal of Transnational Law* 501; P Zumbansen, 'The Ins and Outs of Transnational Private Regulatory Governance: Legitimacy, Accountability, Effectiveness and a New Concept of "Context"' (2012) 13 *German Law Journal* 1269.
[52] For a theoretical account of these universes see RM Cover, 'Nomos and Narrative' (1983) 97 *Harvard Law Review* 4; see also I Augsberg, 'Observing (the) Law: The "Epistemological Turn" in Public Law and the Evolution of Global Administrative Law' in P Jurčys, PF Kjaer and R Yatsunami (eds), *Regulatory Hybridization in the Transnational Sphere* (Leiden, Martinus Nijhoff Publishers, 2013) 11–27.
[53] J Dalhuisen, *Dalhuisen on Transnational, Comparative, Commercial, Financial and Trade Law. Volume 1: Introduction—The New Lex Mercatoria and its Sources* (Oxford, Hart Publishing, 2010); E Gaillard, *Legal Theory of International Arbitration* (Leiden, Martinus Nijhoff Publishers, 2010).

For example, it is from this perspective that we can recognise the factor of agency in identifying and selecting applicable norms in transnational constellations.[54] Meanwhile, from the perspective of TL, it becomes possible to revisit established as well as emerging interpretations of jurisdictional norms: for example, the contested applicability of the US American Alien Tort Statute of 1789,[55] in the context of transnational human rights litigation,[56] is squarely situated in the nexus between legal norms and TL's concerns with the identification and interpretation of norms in accordance with the transnational nature of the underlying issues.[57]

A further contention with regard to the finding of law's instantiation beyond the state can be made with reference to the ways in which the judges in actual cases—be they domestic or involve transnational reach—distinguish between the relevant and irrelevant facts. Judge Posner's opinion in the 2011 *Flomo* decision is a case in point in this regard. Reviewing the applicability of several International Labour Organization (ILO) conventions to the labour practices found at the Firestone Rubber Plantation in Liberia, Judge Posner, at various points, acknowledged the lack of sufficient information or knowledge with regard to the labour practices on the ground, but still did not hesitate to decide on the inapplicability of the conventions.[58] From the perspective of TL, the question of the factual basis upon which decisions regarding the qualification of norms as applicable or non-applicable are made is crucial. The importance here distinctly lies no longer exclusively in the question of whether or not a particular ILO convention is applicable, but how the actual decision of a norm's applicability is shaped by a more comprehensive and adequate understanding of the regulatory regime that, in fact, governs the scenario on the ground that gave rise to the case in the first place. In other words, the application of a legal norm never occurs in a vacuum, but must, instead, be seen as an intervention into an already existing normative system, made up of both official and unofficial norms. The significance of this rudimentary legal pluralist assertion becomes recognisable even from a cursory look behind the obvious facts in a case. In the example of the rubber plantation at the heart of the *Flomo* decision, one quickly begins to wonder about the consequences for the legal assessment of the facts of the case that follow from a consideration of the history

---

[54] For an illustration of such norm selection in the fields of consumer contract law and corporate governance see G-P Calliess and P Zumbansen, *Rough Consensus and Running Code: A Theory of Transnational Private Law* (Oxford, Hart Publishing, 2010) chs 3 and 4.

[55] 28 US C §1350.

[56] For a recent overview see CI Keitner, 'Transnational Litigation: Jurisdiction and Immunities' in D Shelton (ed), *Oxford Handbook of International Human Rights* (Oxford, Oxford University Press, 2013), available at http://ssrn.com/abstract_224000.

[57] Arguably, the US Supreme Court's decision of 17 April 2013, has further decreased the likelihood of consolidating a transnational human rights jurisprudence in the tradition of the decision in *Filártiga v Peña-Irala*, 630 F2d 876 (2d cir 1980): see *Kiobel v Royal Dutch Petroleum Co*, 569 US _(2013). On *Filártiga* see, eg WJ Aceves, *The Anatomy of Torture: A Documentary History of* Filártiga v Peña-Irala (Leiden, Brill, 2007).

[58] *Flomo v Firestone Natural Rubber Co LLC*, 643 F3d 1013 (2011), for example, 1023: 'They can assure fulfillment by hiring other poor Liberians to help them; and because Firestone's Liberian employees are paid well by local standards, they can hire helpers cheaply. But alternatively they can dragoon their wives or children into helping them, at no monetary cost; and this happens, though how frequently we don't know.' See also *ibid*: 'We don't know how many supervisors Firestone has deployed on the plantation, and hence whether there are enough of them to prevent employees from using their children to help them. We don't know the supervisors' routines, or how motivated they are to put a stop to any child labor they observe.'

of the corporate defendant's almost century-long involvement in the country.[59] The facts about which the deciding judge acknowledged that he knew too little were, in fact, available, but only if one began to see the case in hand in a broader context, namely, in a context that was rich in the relevant data and facts. The crucial element of contrasting the case that the judge had before him with a case study of the actually existing context and environment of the case lies in the recognition of the limits of the epistemological categories that informed the construction of the case. The case study, in contrast, does not simply apply established categories first to depict and then to assess legally the interests found to be in obvious conflict (as, for example, between employee and employer, worker and factory owner, or two contracting parties[60]). Instead, its purpose is to highlight the gap between the categories (employee, worker, contractor) and the reality that shapes the case. This gap has been identified as the legitimacy deficit of law from a range of theoretical-political viewpoints, with the interest jurisprudence's attack on legal positivism in late-nineteenth-century Germany[61] and the legal realist attack on legal formalism[62] merely being early instantiations of such efforts. In the attempt to understand this context better, it is necessary to begin to recognise it as being the result of both a detailed field study of work and life conditions on the ground and a comprehensive reconstruction of the historical, socio-economic and political factors that have shaped the conditions of the existing labour practices. While this dimension encompasses what we might call the political economy of the company's actual operation in the region, the community, and the government and stakeholder relations,[63] what also becomes visible is how the labour practices at a plantation such as Firestone's in Liberia are shaped by a multitude of regulatory norms that shape the employees', their dependants' and their peers' relations with regard to the company. Without taking this reality of these complex relationships between the company and its various stakeholders—a label now attached to a group significantly broader than that encompassing the company's official employees—into account, no adequate assessment regarding the labour practices can, in fact, be made on the ground.[64] As ethnographic and political science accounts have shown, the regulatory universe of multinational operations in certain locales is transnational in its reach, and its local effects can only be studied by understanding this complex relation between the local and transnational normative spheres.[65] This is also the reason why there is never a moment in which we can refer to norms that we find empirically as

---

[59] See, eg CM Wilson, *Liberia* (New York, William Sloane, 1947) 80ff.

[60] See the pertinent categorization of the interests at stake in *Lochner v New York*, 45 US 198 (1905).

[61] See R von Ihering, *Der Kampf ums Recht* [1872] (Frankfurt aM, Klostermann, 2003); idem, *Law as a Means to an End* (Boston, MA, Boston Book Company, 1913).

[62] See the comprehensive treatment by N Duxbury, *Patterns of American Jurisprudence* (Oxford, Oxford University Press, 1995).

[63] See, eg C Rodríguez-Garavito, 'Ethnicity.gov: Global Governance, Indigenous Peoples, and the Right to Prior Consultation in Social Minefields' (2011) 18 *Indiana Journal of Global Legal Studies* 263.

[64] For more on this point see Zumbansen, n 51 above, 1269–81; idem, 'Lochner Disembedded: The Anxieties of Law in a Global Context' (2013) 20 *Indiana Journal of Global Legal Studies* 29, available at http://ssrn.com/abstract=2174017.

[65] For a discussion of the public and private rules governing labour relations see Bartley, 'Institutional Emergence in an Era of Globalization', n 51 above, 297–351; see also DM Trubek, J Mosher and JS Rothstein, 'Transnationalism in the Regulation of Labor Relations: International Regimes and Transnational Advocacy Networks' (2000) 25 *Law and Social Inquiry* 1187; DJ Doorey, 'In Defense of Transnational Domestic Labor Regulation' (2010) 49 *Vanderbilt Journal of Transnational Law* 953.

law beyond the state. While we may identify, collect and categorise norms of different status and quality as shaping a particular regulatory area, the selection and ranking of those very norms that we find applicable and determinative in a given context remains a matter of agency and choice.

## V. THE TRANSNATIONAL LAW PROJECT SCRUTINISES LAW'S 'KNOWLEDGE' PROBLEM 2: NORMS

The previous section ended with a reference to the intersecting local and transnational, official and unofficial, hard and soft norms which characterise regulatory arenas such as contemporary labour governance of multinational companies' operations in the Third World. We have referred to this complex interdisciplinary constellation to investigate the ways in which the lawyer in such situations must identify, choose and mobilise norms of different origin and status.[66] A striking feature of this selection process, however, is the effusiveness of the boundaries between the (hard or soft) norms and facts which constitute a social reality. The distinction between the actual facts, allegedly standing for an objective materiality or a state of things, and norms and normativity, by which we refer to the idealistic and symbolic dimensions of the world, is always a constructed one: in pointing to a particular fact, selections and choices have been made, which ultimately rest on value judgements regarding the status being accorded to the facts in question.[67]

In the light of these observations, we now need to further flesh out the proposal made in the previous section, which pertained to the development of a richer concept of context in order to gain a more adequate understanding of the complex qualities and dimensions of the facts that have given rise to cases such as the transnational human rights litigation in the *Firestone* (*Flomo*) case. Taking up the above-cited distinction between a political economy and a normative dimension, we now need to ask about the nature of the relationship between them. The contention made here is that the former takes up the challenge of critically investigating the origin, the nature and the selectivity of the facts being considered in establishing the factual basis of a case, while the latter refers to the idealisation and utopia of fact selection and establishment. Thus, the task becomes one of going beyond a narrow reading of the facts, one that is driven by incomplete testimony and typification, while avoiding being lured down a path that promises to lead to an unbounded history of everything. In other words, we need to identify the moment when and the ways in which lawyers, litigants and judges lose sight of the relevant facts and, instead, consolidate a manageable, ie justiciable, factual basis which, from this point on, will serve as a complete snapshot of the facts of the case. It is precisely here that lawyers will increasingly benefit from the advances made in anthropological and ethnographic methodological research, given that these areas currently display a forceful commitment to revisit and scrutinise long-established

---

[66] Compare Rodriguez-Garavito, n 63 above.

[67] See, eg Latour, n 22 above, 14–41; see also idem, n 39 above; idem, *Science in Action: How to Follow Scientists and Engineers through Society* (Cambridge, MA, Harvard University Press, 1987), in particular chs 2 and 5; meanwhile, Jürgen Habermas has elaborated a comprehensive and ambitious socio-legal theory based upon the critical investigation into the relationship 'between facts and norms'. See J Habermas, *Between Facts and Norms*, trans W Rehg (Boston, MA, The MIT Press, 1996).

research routines and to update methodologies to new circumstances.[68] One particular challenge for lawyers arises from the way in which they are now being pressured into acknowledging and processing numerous research topics that question the epistemological basis of law, but to do so without the proper awareness of the historical traits of this inquiry into the factual basis of legal notions. In other words, lawyers today are thrown into a legal sociological discourse that has greatly advanced from its early beginnings and is no longer concerned merely with the sort of gap critique (between law in books and law in action) that formed the centre of early-twentieth-century legal sociological analysis.[69] While much of early legal sociology aimed at showing how judges were prone to ignore both the (socio-economic and cultural) basis of legal norms and the effects of legal-regulatory intervention,[70] the current iterations of legal sociological analysis are distinctly more interdisciplinary and encompassing in nature. It is in this sense that we can speak of the challenge of legal sociology 2.0 for the majority of lawyers, who were trained in either the Ehrlichian spirit of recognising the undeniable parallels between official and unofficial regulatory regimes or the Dworkinian mindset with an all-else-dismissing focus on legal adjudication, as the key to unlocking the mystery of law.[71] Moving beyond the early analytical interest of legal sociologists in the politics of legal formalism and the rising importance of expert knowledge and scientific governance,[72] intermediate legal sociologists between the 1960s and 1980s pushed decisively for an interdisciplinary reorientation of socio-legal studies.[73] A similar differentiation of a primarily social-justice-focused legal critique into an ever expanding series of critical engagements with developments in race, gender, environment, science or international affairs was witnessed among schools of thought with a significant progressive and legal reformist orientation, such as the Critical Legal Studies movement.[74] In comparison, current legal sociology, if it even still exists in the form of designated law school positions or curricular components,[75] is prone to form alliances with an increasingly far-ranging array of intersections between law and social, media, behavioural, environmental, indigenous, religious or cultural studies. While it is impossible to capture the potential consequences of this

[68] See the contributions to R Hardin and KM Clarke (eds), *Transforming Ethnographic Knowledge* (Madison, WI, Wisconsin University Press, 2012), and the monographic study by LT Smith, *Decolonizing Methodologies: Research and Indigenous Peoples*, 2nd edn (London, Zed Books, 2012), in particular ch 3, 'Colonizing Knowledges'.

[69] See, eg Ehrlich, n 3 above; Durkheim, n 3 above.

[70] See, eg M Rheinstein, 'Review: Two Recent Books on Sociology of Law' [reviewing Timasheff's "Introduction" and Gurvitch's "Elements"] (1941) 51 *Ethics* 220; G Gurvitch, *Sociology of Law* (originally published in French as *Problèmes de la sociologie du droit*) (London, Routledge & Kegan Paul, 1947).

[71] See, eg R Dworkin, *Law's Empire* (Cambridge, MA, Harvard University Press, 1986); in this vein see CR Sunstein, 'Lochner's Legacy' (1987) 87 *Columbia Law Review* 873.

[72] A good illustration is the account given by JM Landis, *The Administrative Process* (New Haven, CT, Yale University Press, 1938).

[73] E Blankenburg, E Klausa, H Rottleuthner and R Rogowski (eds), *Alternative Rechtsformen und Alternativen zum Recht* (Opladen, Westdeutscher Verlag, 1980); P Nonet and P Selznick, *Law and Society in Transition: Toward Responsive Law* (New York, Harper & Row, 1978)

[74] D Kennedy, 'Three Globalizations of Law and Legal Thought: 1850–2000' in DM Trubek and A Santos (eds), *The New Law and Economic Development* (Cambridge, Cambridge University Press, 2006) 19–73.

[75] For an assessment of the relatively sobering institutional state of the discipline see T Raiser, 'Sociology of Law in Germany' (2010) 11 *German Law Journal* 391; M Galanter, 'Farther Along' (1999) 33 *Law & Society Review* 1113.

development in full,[76] it is obvious how the convergence of social science fields that gave rise to hybrid and cross-over academic realms, such as cultural or media studies, can ultimately leave a discipline such as law untouched.

From this perspective, it appears as if a richer account of the relevant facts in a case will, above all, depend on a more contextual identification and reading of the data that can be accounted for as being of an explanatory nature for the case in hand. The bulk of this work still needs to be done in terms of showing how legal sociology 2.0 must now consist not only of the serious engagement on the part of lawyers with the advances in ethnographic research methodology,[77] and with the critique of facts and truth in science and technology studies,[78] but also with critical historiography, as it has become pertinent in selected areas of law.[79]

At the same time, while a more comprehensive approach to an analysis of the facts in a concrete case promises to assist us in obtaining a clearer picture of the actual situation that characterised the conflict between the litigating parties, there will probably always remain a significant gap between a richer factual account of the actual interests and conditions present and the deeper structural frameworks of which a particular conflict scenario is part. It is here where, for example, scholars involved in TWAIL have been able to unveil powerful connections between current governance conflicts and historical pathways, political choices and particular historical, socio-economic and geo-political, circumstances.[80] Another important development that promises to shed more light on the historically grown dimensions of the context in which many of the currently litigated human rights cases involving the operations of multinationals in Third World countries are unfolding is the convergence of law and development (L&D) and transitional justice.

## VI. CONVERGING FIELDS, INTERSECTING EPISTEMOLOGIES

Law and development has always been an area which can neither be neatly or clearly defined nor boxed into clear-cut categories. The field has long been a battlefield for opposing concepts of law, political and economic order, and the role of institutional

---

[76] For a distinctly sceptical assessment from the perspective of law school curricular design see A D'Amato, 'The Interdisciplinary Turn in Legal Education', Bepress Legal Series Working Paper 1901 (2006), available at http://law.bepress.com/expresso/eps/1901.

[77] See Hardin and Clarke, n 68 above. See also DR Holmes and GE Marcus, 'Cultures of Expertise and the Management of Globalization: Toward the Refunctioning of Ethnography' in A Ong and SJ Collier (eds), *Global Assemblages: Technology, Politics, and Ethics as Anthropological Problems* (Oxford, Blackwell Publishing, 2005) 235–252, and AL Tsing, *Friction: An Ethnography of Global Connection* (Princeton, NJ, Princeton University Press, 2005).

[78] See, eg http://sts.cornell.edu.

[79] See the example of the so-called Third World Approaches to International Law (TWAIL). See OC Okafor, 'Critical Third World Approaches to International Law (TWAIL): Theory, Methodology, or Both?' (2008) 10 *International Community Law Review* 371; U Natarajan, 'TWAIL and the Environment: The State of Nature, the Nature of the State, and the Arab Spring' (2012) 14 *Oregon Review of International Law* 177.

[80] See, eg S Pahuja's critique of the Bretton Woods Institutions' embrace of a political sovereignty of post-war nation states without duly recognising the continuing unfulfilment of economic emancipation and sovereignty: Pahuja, n 16 above; for an insightful critique of this analysis see Rajah, n 16 above, 285; see also Natarajan, ibid.

governance,[81] and, as such, has always been a laboratory for audacious experiments with explosive material. Categories such as 'progress', 'development' or 'order' are invariably contentious and, in the context of L&D, are employed as bargaining chips in a high-stakes game over political and economic influence, autonomy and emancipation.[82] While specific local contexts of L&D became the loci of such contestation, often enough, under the magnifying glass of international and national development agendas, market integration and state reform, one of the most striking discoveries to be made here relates to the fact that the contentious items in the L&D context are also those which have long informed a critical analysis of law and governance in the context of the nation state.[83] As such, the boundaries between the developing and the developed world, between the countries receiving and the countries exporting or providing legal (or economic) aid, become porous, and a legal theory of L&D can fruitfully build upon its older domestic sister.

One of the important scholarly projects pursued by L&D scholars has been the discovery and analysis of the legal pluralist nature of the governance orders in the context of development.[84] With a growing awareness of the different existing ordering structures 'on the ground' in the development context came the realisation that any legal order challenges the observer to acknowledge the parallels between, and the coexistence of, formal and informal, hard and soft law, and legal and non-legal norms.[85] This realisation prompted L&D scholars not only to acknowledge but also to build upon the idea that many of the challenges pertaining to a law/non-law distinction that had been identified as specific to the development context were, in fact, detachable from any legal governance framework. Indeed, the inadequacy of existing legal-governance thinking pointed to the need for not only different theoretical, but also different doctrinal, attention.[86]

It is this realisation that grants us a better appreciation of the questionable foundations of a legal order, of the embeddedness of legal governance in a particular institutional setting (for example, the state) and at a particular moment in (geopolitical) time.[87] To the degree that the struggle over law reform in the context of development is seen as not being entirely removed from contestations of legal (political and/or economic) order in the domestic context, L&D emerges as a field which is just as much concerned with the relationship of law to its (in particular, local) social envi-

---

[81] D Kennedy, 'Laws and Development' in J Hatchard and A Perry-Kessaris (eds), *Law and Development: Facing Complexity in the 21st Century—Essays in Honour of P Slinn* (London, Cavendish Publishing Limited, 2003) 17.

[82] For a brilliant deconstruction of the post-war conceptual division between political and economic emancipation of former colonial states see Pahuja, n 16 above.

[83] The masterful analysis is still D Trubek and M Galanter, 'Scholars in Self-Estrangement: Some Reflections on the Crisis in Law and Development Studies in the United States' (1974) *Wisconsin Law Review* 106.

[84] K Pistor and D Berkowitz, 'Of Legal Transplants, Legal Irritants, and Economic Development' in PK Cornelius and B Kogut (eds), *Corporate Governance and Capital Flows in a Global Economy* (Oxford, Oxford University Press, 2003) 347; K Pistor, 'The Standardization of Law and its Effect on Developing Economies' (2002) 50 *American Journal of Comparative Law* 97.

[85] HW Arthurs, *'Without the Law': Administrative Justice and Legal Pluralism in Nineteenth-Century England* (Toronto, University of Toronto Press, 1988); RA Macdonald and J MacLean, 'No Toilets in Park' (2005) 50 *McGill Law Journal* 721; Moore, above n 4.

[86] Macdonald and MacLean, ibid. See also C Scott, 'A Core Curriculum for the Transnational Legal Education of JD and LLB Students: Surveying the Approach of the International, Comparative and Transnational Law Program at Osgoode Hall Law School' (2005) 23 *Penn State International Law Review* 757.

[87] B Aretxaga, 'Maddening States' (2003) 32 *Annual Review of Anthropology* 393.

ronment and to its context as has been the case for all other legal theoretical and legal sociological inquiries.[88] However, accepting this perspective also implies accepting the loss of the standpoint of an outside observer. Precisely by acknowledging the inseparability of critical legal analysis in the domestic and the development context do we lose the comfort of being outside of the sphere which we are purporting both to study and to examine in a disinterested manner.[89] Instead, the demarcation of the L&D context from that of one's home legal system and jurisdiction becomes questionable in itself, because the assertions of the precariousness of law in the development context apply to the domestic home context with equal force. Upon this basis, the distinction between the governance challenges of 'here' and 'there' appears artificial. Indeed, the distinction seems designed to insulate the domestic context from critique while at the same time depicting the development context as deficient and requiring aid and assistance. The identification of a series of legal governance questions as arising from within the context of a developing country inevitably leads to these questions having to be seen as already being pertinent much earlier, that is to say, already present and evident in the context of domestic legal critique.

A striking feature of this contextualisation of L&D as part of a larger exercise in investigating the relationship of law with, and its role in, society is the way in which the field opens itself up to an engagement and exchange with complementary discourses about regulatory places and spaces. Both legal scholars[90] and sociologists[91] have been scrutinising the conceptual and constituted nature of such regulatory spaces—spaces which evade a straightforward depiction from the vantage point of a single discipline. Just as this critique has become pertinent with regard to the analysis of different specialised regulatory arenas, ranging from labour[92] to corporate,[93] from

---

[88] R Cotterrell, 'Why Must Legal Ideas Be Interpreted Sociologically?' (1998) 25 *Journal of Law & Society* 171; R Banakar, 'Law Through Sociology's Looking Glass: Conflict and Competition in Sociological Studies of Law' in A Denis and D Kalekin-Fishman (eds), *The ISA Handbook in Contemporary Sociology* (London, Sage Publications, 2009); Zumbansen, n 40 above.

[89] Trubek and Galanter, n 83 above. See also DM Trubek, 'Toward a Social Theory of Law: An Essay on the Study of Law and Development' (1972) 82 *Yale Law Journal* 1.

[90] R Ford, 'Law's Territory (A History of Jurisdiction)' (1999) 97 *Michigan Law Review* 843.

[91] S Sassen, 'The State and Globalization' in JS Nye and JD Donahue (eds), *Governance in a Globalizing World* (Washington DC, Brookings Institution, 2000) 91; S Sassen, 'The Places and Spaces of the Global: An Expanded Analytic Terrain' in D Held and A McGrew (eds), *Globalization Theory: Approaches and Controversies* (Cambridge, Polity Press, 2007) 79; D Harvey, 'The Sociological and Geographical Imaginations' (2005) 18 *International Journal of Politics, Culture and Society* 211.

[92] Trubek et al, n 65 above; G Mundlak, 'De-territorializing Labor Law' (2009) 3 *Law & Ethics of Human Rights* 188; HW Arthurs, 'Extraterritoriality by Other Means: How Labor Law Sneaks across Borders, Conquers Minds, and Controls Workplaces Abroad' (2010) 21 *Stanford Law & Policy Review* 527.

[93] LC Backer, 'Private Actors and Public Governance Beyond the State: The Multinational Corporation, the Financial Stability Board, and the Global Governance Order' (2011) 18 *Indiana Journal of Global Legal Studies* 751; P Zumbansen, 'Neither "Public" nor "Private", "National" nor "International": Transnational Corporate Governance from a Legal Pluralist Perspective' (2011) 38 *Journal of Law & Society* 50.

environmental[94] to criminal law,[95] which together suggest a methodological shift both away from comparative law and towards transnational law,[96] L&D has become a very active laboratory for a renewed engagement with a critical and contextual analysis of law in a fast-changing and volatile environment.

This aspect has been underlined, perhaps most tellingly, by the recent approximation of L&D with the field of transitional justice (TJ), which testifies to an increasing awareness among interested experts of the close connections between investigations into the legacies of past injustices with programmes of future-directed legal and economic aid.[97] Closely connected to—and often overlapping with—this very vivid scholarly engagement has been an equally vibrant literary[98] and cultural engagement with transition periods. After the seminal (inevitably colonial) portrayals by Joseph Conrad in *An Outpost of Progress* (1897) or *Heart of Darkness* (1899), 'post-colonial' novels such as the late Chinua Achebe's *Things Fall Apart* (1958) or JM Coetzee's *Waiting for the Barbarians* (1980) again poignantly scrutinised the slippery slope between 'us' and 'them' that inescapably pervades any intervention or development context. How, in the context of public international law's attempts to address transnational military and civil conflict, this slope has become painfully obvious again was powerfully illustrated in Anne Orford's critique of the hidden, hegemonic aspirations of recent instances of humanitarian intervention.[99] Excavating the challenges of concepts such as 'change', 'reform' and 'progress', as they have been central to seminal transitional justice debates as those concerning South Africa[100] or Sri Lanka,[101] Achmat Dangor's *Bitter Fruit* (2001) or films such as Prasanna Vithanage's *Purahanda Kaluwara* (*Death on a Full Moon Day*; 1997) have become inseparably intertwined with the scholarly, expert discourse around these instances of transitional justice.

But what can this intersection of scholarly, literary and cultural engagement tell us about the methodological challenges arising in the L&D (and transitional justice) context? To the degree that we can already build on a host of critical work to scru-

---

[94] L Gulbrandsen, S Andresen and JB Skjærseth, 'Non-state Actors and Environmental Governance: Comparing Multinational, Supranational and Transnational Rule Making' in B Reinalda (ed), *The Ashgate Research Companion to Non-state Actors* (Farnham, Ashgate Publishing, 2011) 463; N Craik, 'Deliberation and Legitimacy in Transnational Environmental Governance', IILJ Working Paper 2006/10 (New York University, 2006); C Kamphuis, 'Canadian Mining Companies and Domestic Law Reform: A Critical-Legal Account' (2012) 13 *German Law Journal* 1456; S Seck, 'Home State Regulation of Environmental Human Rights Harms As Transnational Private Regulatory Governance' (2012) 13 *German Law Journal* 1360.

[95] N Boister, 'Transnational Criminal Law?' (2003) 14 *European Journal of International Law* 953; N Boister, *An Introduction to Transnational Criminal Law* (Oxford, Oxford University Press, 2012); RJ Currie, *International and Transnational Criminal Law* (Toronto, Irwin Law, 2010).

[96] CM Scott, '"Transnational Law" as Proto-Concept: Three Conceptions' (2009) 10 *German Law Journal* 859; P Zumbansen, 'Transnational Legal Pluralism' (2010) 1 *Transnational Legal Theory* 141; idem, 'Transnational Law, Evolving', n 33 above.

[97] See, eg R Mani, 'Dilemmas of Expanding Transitional Justice, or Forging the Nexus between Transitional Justice and Development' (2008) 2 *International Journal of Transitional Justice* 253; P de Greiff and R Duthie (eds), *Transitional Justice and Development: Making Connections* (New York, Social Science Research Council, 2009). See also the other chapters in this book.

[98] See the insightful discussion of the prose/poetry debate in India around the work of Rabindranath Tagore, in Chakrabarty, n 7 above.

[99] A Orford, 'Muscular Humanitarianism: Reading the Narratives of the New Interventionism' (2003) 10 *European Journal of International Law* 679.

[100] H Corder, 'Prisoner, Partisan and Patriarch: Transforming the Law in South Africa 1985–2000' (2002) 118 *The South African Law Journal* 772; A Gross, 'Reconciliation in South Africa' (2004) 40 *Stanford Journal of International Law* 40.

[101] J Derges, *Ritual and Recovery in Post-conflict Sri Lanka* (London, Routledge, 2012).

tinise the orientation, method and contentions of L&D and TJ theory, an additional aspect of this enterprise concerns the acknowledgement of and engagement with non-scholarly content. Another question concerns the demarcation of places and spaces in this context. What, we may ask, distinguishes the focus of Achmat Dangor's poignant analysis of family relations in post-apartheid South Africa[102] from the haunting account of Mourid Barghouti's return to Palestine after an involuntary thirty-year exile?[103] Emerging from these accounts is a powerful illustration of what we might call the 'transnational human condition', marked by multilayered and multitiered relations of belonging and citizenship. It is this dimension of the human condition that could arguably be seen as the fourth dimension of Hannah Arendt's depiction of labour-work-action,[104] scrutinising the possibilities of political and social belonging in a post-national environment, which is marked by the fragility of political communities and, again, by an increased precariousness of political voice.[105]

Chinua Achebe recounts, in his 2009 collection of short stories, *The Education of a British-Protected Child*, numerous instances in which he and the audiences he speaks before are confronted with the porosity of the lines that divide 'home' and 'abroad', the 'here' and the 'there'. In Achebe's rendering, these experiences illustrate the tensions in people's lives when trying to make sense of their deeply felt attachments to places of origin, places of meaning, when—at the same time—they find themselves on an inchoate and often swirling trajectory which takes them through different places, communities, spheres of interaction, places of engagement and confrontation—with others who have come to these places through similar patterns of predictable unpredictability. Achebe's stories recount numerous instances of frustration in the face of alienation, cliché and stereotype that seem to repeat themselves over and over again. The author presents them in an uncompromisingly and tirelessly analytical manner, the various accounts underlining the importance of difference in that which seems to be the same, the varying conjectures of people's meetings, confrontations and clashes of viewpoints and observations that cannot be so simply traced back, as emerges from story to story, to one particular stance, one easily demarcated political viewpoint or a comprehensively founded moral choice. Instead, Achebe highlights the numerous cross-roads in people's perceptions and judgements, the complex overlapping of context and intent that shape the moment in which one formulates and utters one's own view. He seems to say 'Look again', 'Think again' and once more 'Look again', and it is this back and forth wandering of our gaze which may help us to grasp better the challenges in contemporary L&D and TJ contexts. These contexts are intricately marked by the simultaneous existence of the new and the old. Yet we are asked to reject this (overly neat) juxtaposition for the ways in which it imposes an evolutionary narrative of progress onto a sphere that needs to be studied through its complex relationship between local and global consciousness.[106] Similarly, both L&D and TJ become mere

---

[102] A Dangor, *Bitter Fruit* (Cape Town, Kwela Books, 2001).

[103] M Barghouti, *I Saw Ramallah* (London, Bloomsbury, 2004).

[104] H Arendt, *The Human Condition* (Chicago, IL, Chicago University Press, 1958).

[105] See R Cotterrell, 'Spectres of Transnationalism: Changing Terrains of Sociology of Law' (2009) 36 *Journal of Law and Society* 481; N Fraser, *Scales of Justice: Reimagining Political Space in a Globalizing World* (New York, Columbia University Press, 2009).

[106] Chakrabarty, n 7 above, ch 5, 'Birth of the Subject'.

instantiations of a renewed effort to reflect critically upon the methodological basis of legal-political governance.

As such, both L&D and TJ can be seen as efforts undertaken from within law as a scholarly discipline and a practical endeavour to illustrate how law is constantly prompted to adapt to its changing environment—both substantively and normatively. This adaptation of law occurs in often unmapped, uncharted and undomesticated spaces. As in Achebe's accounts, these spaces are both geographical and intellectual, both real and constructed. And, as is highlighted by the scholarship in the areas of L&D and TJ, the critical engagement with these allegedly dividing lines between real and constructed, between, say, field work, empirical data, news reports and statistics, on the one hand, and description, critique, deconstruction and argument, on the other, lie at the core of what these two fields are really all about. Both to emphasise and simultaneously to question the very categories by which we draw the lines between 'here' and 'there', 'home' and 'abroad', 'ours' and 'theirs' becomes an existential question for law and for the lawyer employing its label and toolkit. Seen, studied, theorised and practised in this critical way, L&D and TJ become instantiations of a much more comprehensive engagement with the concept of law, with the categories by which lines are drawn in research and curriculum between domestic and foreign laws and legal cultures. Thus, the scholarship of L&D and TJ of such ambitious calibre is likely to be perceived as a threat to the standards and routines of the parochially focused scholarship which still dominates law reviews and conferences and which, in myriad ways, continues to influence and shape law school course design and the programming of legal education. The particular approach here taken to defend L&D and TJ as both critical engagements with and representations of contemporary law threatens the daily routine of law schools that profess to teach their fee-paying clients to think like a lawyer: the approach embraced here critically challenges this entire routine and suggests that it could all, in fact, be very different if only we took the time to reflect more on the connections between 'here' and 'there'. In other words, are the legal conflicts that we are concerned with domestically really so very different from the ones that we identify in foreign places? If this is true, then the question is one of how we can develop an adequate epistemological framework for law in a transnational context. As is clear from Achebe's stories, to think about these connections is a tiresome business, one that must remain cautious, self-critical and never satisfied, one that continues to draw on a wide spectrum of information, data, accounts—in other words, on a complex body of knowledge, on which one draws and to which one already contributes constantly.

## VII. THE CRUCIAL ROLE OF KNOWLEDGE IN DEVELOPMENT AND TRANSITIONAL JUSTICE

The vibrant and increasingly intersecting intellectual discourses around the conceptual and normative foundations of L&D[107] and of TJ[108] are increasingly complemented

---

[107] See the contributions to Trubek and Santos, n 74 above.

[108] N Roht-Arriaza, *The Pinochet Effect: Transnational Justice in the Age of Human Rights* (Philadelphia, PA, University of Pennsylvania Press, 2005); N Roht-Arriazza and J Mariezcurrena (eds), *Transitional Justice*

and contextualised by a critical engagement with the North's[109] legal regulatory and epistemological interventions in the South.[110] Arising from this attention to L&D and TJ is an intensified interest in the nature of knowledge implicated in these different engagements. Knowledge becomes a crucial variable as it applies to a host of divergent conceptual and normative programmes. For example, knowledge is at the heart of the expertise and know-how retained by a governing body or drawn upon by governmental actors when crafting regulatory instruments and interventions.[111] At the same time, knowledge as a variable and an unknown enters both sides of regulatory interventions—pertaining to what the regulator knows and what is known within the sphere acted upon. This double contingency of what law should know, but can never know for certain, has long been a concern of legal regulatory theory, and of legal sociology and criminology in particular.[112] Given the complex interplay of domestic and transnational governance discourses and the centrality of knowledge in both,[113] the intensified interest in scrutinising what we know when unleashing programmes of aid, reform and technical and legal assistance has to be central to any future engagement with L&D and TJ as part of a larger, interdisciplinary theory of global governance.[114] From the vantage point of a critical engagement with knowledge, such an enterprise must develop a methodology able to open up, rather than eclipse, avenues of contestation and mutual learning.[115] We can already see how the parallels and shared interests in contemporary L&D and TJ discourses are echoed by the connections between domestic and transnational governance discourses. Where we find that L&D discourses are inseparably intertwined with TJ-related questions regarding the appropriate and non-universalising,[116] legal/non-legal response to the legacies of suppression, exploitation and domination, we are confronted with the co-evolutionary dynamics of legal/non-legal, hard/soft, formal/informal. In short, attending to knowledge points us to the legal pluralism of modes of governance characteristic in settings

---

in the Twenty-first Century: Beyond Truth versus Justice (Cambridge, Cambridge University Press, 2006); R Nagy, 'Transitional Justice as Global Project: Critical Reflections' (2008) 29 *Third World Quarterly* 275; S Vieille, 'Transitional Justice: A Colonizing Field?' (2012) 4 *Amsterdam Forum* 58.

[109] This depiction is used to mark both economic and ideological characteristics rather than a geographic region.

[110] De Sousa Santos, n 7 above. See also B de Sousa Santos (ed), *Another Knowledge is Possible: Beyond Northern Epistemologies* (London, Verso, 2007); R D'Souza, 'Imperial Agendas, Global Solidarities, and Third World Socio-legal Studies: Methodological Reflections' (2012) 49 *Osgoode Hall Law Journal* 409.

[111] Jasanoff, n 49 above; see also the contributions in G Edmond (ed), *Expertise in Regulation and Law* (Aldershot, Ashgate Publishing, 2004).

[112] KN Llewellyn, 'The Normative, the Legal, and the Law-Jobs: The Problem of Juristic Method' (1940) 49 *Yale Law Journal* 1355; N Luhmann, 'Some Problems with Reflexive Law' in G Teubner and A Febbrajo (eds), *State, Law and Economy as Autopoietic Systems* (Milan, Giuffre, 1992) 389; P Zumbansen, 'Law's Effectiveness and Law's Knowledge: Reflections from Legal Sociology and Legal Theory' (2009) 10 *German Law Journal* 417.

[113] Abbott and Snidal, n 51 above, 501; Zumbansen, n 51 above.

[114] D Held, 'Reframing Global Governance: Apocalypse Soon or Reform!' in Held and McGrew, n 91 above, 240; FE Johns, 'Global Governance: An Heretical History Play' (2004) 4 *Global Jurist Advances* Art 3.

[115] See, eg JN Pieterse, 'Globalization North and South: Representations of Uneven Development and the Interaction of Modernities' (2000) 17 *Theory, Culture & Society* 129; M-R Trouillot, 'The Anthropology of the State in the Age of Globalization: Close Encounters of the Deceptive Kind' (2001) 42 *Current Anthropology* 125; J Ferguson and A Gupta, 'Spatialising States: Toward an Ethnography of Neoliberal Governmentality' (2002) 29 *American Ethnologist* 981.

[116] Vieille, n 108 above.

which we have hitherto tended to study through conventional notions of jurisdiction, that is, through legal spatial lenses.[117] However, these co-evolutionary dynamics between L&D and TJ support the emergence of regulatory regimes which can no longer adequately be captured through categories of state sovereignty or jurisdiction. Instead, the emerging transnational regulatory landscape follows, to a large degree, the fragmenting dynamics of a functionally differentiated world society, prompting, in turn, an intensified investigation as to the legitimacy, that is, the normative and political implications, of the systems theory's world society model.[118]

These debates provide a formidable background to the continuously evolving debate around L&D, in that they complement and expand the highly charged economic and political stakes in this arena. Knowledge occupies a crucial place in L&D scholars' long-standing, persistent engagements with bridging both national and development governance discourses.[119] Taking a closer look at the role of knowledge in the L&D context promises important insights into the future trajectory of this field in the above-sketched context of interdisciplinary global governance studies. What drives and motivates developments such as the World Bank's self-description as a 'knowledge bank'[120] becomes a matter of critical concern, and prompts our reflection on the origins as well as the experiences that have already been made with such data-driven governance approaches in other times and places. In other words, the question regarding the role of knowledge in today's development agendas—in theory and practice—invites us to take a closer look at the connections and the differences between the prominence of knowledge in this context and in domestic contexts in the past. To do so seems especially opportune in light of the crudeness of the assertions, distinctions and categories that continue to characterise global governance discourses, particularly in terms of the descriptions and analysis of constellations that really deserve a more comprehensive and sophisticated conceptual treatment.[121] Indeed, the persistence of inadequate analytical categories in the field of global governance is at considerable odds with contemporary analysis of knowledge-driven governance.[122] Knowledge as an analytical category offers us a way forward.

The overriding challenge arising from a critique of knowledge in the development context, however, consists in the question of frame of reference. Every employed conceptual, analytical and doctrinal toolkit has a history of its own—the way it came to be put together, the order of the instruments that are stored and arranged within it,

---

[117] Ferguson and Gupta, n 115 above; A Mbembe, 'At the Edge of the World: Boundaries, Territoriality, and Sovereignty in Africa' (2000) 12 *Public Culture* 259.

[118] This tension characterises the interchange between, say, Gunther Teubner and Emilios Christodoulidis. See G Teubner, 'Fragmented Foundations: Societal Constitutionalism beyond the Nation State' in Dobner and Loughlin, n 24 above, 327; see also the contributions of E Christodoulidis, G Verschraegen, B Klink and W Martens in (2011) *Netherlands Journal of Legal Philosophy* no 3. For Teubner's most recent, comprehensive attempt to engage with the challenge of normativity see G Teubner, *Constitutional Fragments* (Oxford, Oxford University Press, 2012).

[119] D Trubek, 'Toward a Social Theory of Law: An Essay on the Study of Law and Development' (1972) 82 *Yale Law Journal* 1; D Trubek and Galanter, 'Scholars in Self-estrangement: Some Reflections on the Crisis in Law and Development Studies in the United States' (1974) *Wisconsin Law Review* 1062.

[120] See http://siteresources.worldbank.org/WBI/Resources/KnowledgeBankOct2004.pdf.

[121] RA Posner, 'Creating a Legal Framework for Economic Development' (1998) 13 *The World Bank Research Observer* 1.

[122] K-H Ladeur, 'Constitutionalism and the State of the "Society of Networks": The Design of a New "Control Project" for a Fragmented Legal System' (2011) 2 *Transnational Legal Theory* 463.

and the use that has been made of them over time. The L&D context, in particular, prompts a host of questions regarding the origin, adequacy and transferability of regulatory models. Similar to the seemingly never-ending self-inspection and critique of comparative law,[123] L&D is a field forever belaboured and challenged upon a complex methodological basis, which underscores the relevance of approaching a study of a local regulatory culture from a more comprehensive perspective, eventually allowing for a scrutiny of the actors, norms and processes (A-N-P) which all serve to shape the development context.[124] But how are we to account for the inevitable baggage and background assumptions that accompany and shape the governancem as well as the desired policy ideas transplanted from one context—which in the twentieth-century L&D context has been the post-industrialist and post-welfare constitutional state[125]— into another context with institutional and normative dimensions which we might not be able to map with the cartography that we are used to. This seems to be of particular importance with regard to the implicit assumptions informing an endorsement of regulatory models such as decentralisation, innovation and regulatory competition. In the political and regulatory theory discourses of the last two to three decades, these terms emerged in an intricate intellectual space between economic and political theories, and have by now attained an almost sacrosanct character, both with regard to federal structures in complex polities[126] and in the context of searching for growth models in path-dependent economies.[127] However, as examples of transatlantic transplants already illustrate, the effects of policies that endorse a finely tuned subsidiarity–federalist framework and that place hope in the regulated self-regulatory dynamics of actors at different levels[128] depend greatly on the historically and politically evolved context in which they are implemented. What might be a very promising conceptual approach to the study of multilevel and multipolar regulatory systems—and the EU certainly represents just that[129]—will eventually unfold through highly intricate and unpredictable dynamics in a continuously evolving complex environment.[130]

---

[123] See the contributions to Adams and Bomhoff, n 33 above.

[124] For more background on the A-N-P approach see Zumbansen, n 64 above.

[125] R Cranston, *Legal Foundations of the Welfare State* (London, Weidenfeld & Nicolson, 1985); FG Castles (ed), *The Disappearing State? Retrenchment Politics in an Age of Globalization* (Cheltenham, Edward Elgar Publishing, 2007).

[126] S Rose-Ackerman, 'Risk Taking and Reelection: Does Federalism Promote Innovation?' (1980) 9 *Journal of Legal Studies* 593; GA Bermann, 'Harmonization and Regulatory Federalism' in I Pernice (ed), *Harmonization of Legislation in Federal Systems* (Baden-Baden, Nomos Verlag, 1996); K Nicolaidis and R Howse (eds), *The Federal Vision* (Oxford, Oxford University Press, 2001); B Galle and J Leahy, 'Laboratories of Democracy? Policy Innovation in Decentralized Governments' (2009) 58 *Emory Law Journal* 1333.

[127] W Lazonick, 'Varieties of Capitalism and Innovative Enterprise' (2007) 24 *Comparative Social Research* 21; J P Murmann, *Knowledge and Competitive Advantage: The Coevolution of Firms, Technology and National Institutions* (Cambridge, Cambridge University Press, 2003).

[128] CF Sabel and J Zeitlin, 'Learning from Difference: The New Architecture of Experimentalist Governance in the EU' (2008) 14 *European Law Journal* 271; MC Dorf and CF Sabel, 'A Constitution of Democratic Experimentalism' (1998) 98 *Columbia Law Review* 267.

[129] See, eg G Majone, 'The European Commmunity between Social Policy and Social Regulation' (1993) 31 *Journal of Common Market Studies* 153; KA Armstrong, 'Governance and the Single European Market' in P Craig and G de Búrca (eds), *The Evolution of EU Law* (Oxford, Oxford University Press, 1999).

[130] R Boyer and JR Hollingsworth, 'From National Embeddedness to Spatial and Institutional Nestedness' in J Rogers Hollingsworth and R Boyer (eds), *Contemporary Capitalism: The Embeddedness of Institutions* (Cambridge, Cambridge University Press, 1997); R Dore, W Lazonick and M O'Sullivan, 'Varieties of Capitalism in the Twentieth Century' (1999) 15 *Oxford Review of Economic Policy* 102; G Teubner, 'Legal Irritants: How Unifying Law Ends Up in New Divergences' in PA Hall and D Soskice (eds), *Varieties of Capitalism: The Institutional Foundations of Comparative Advantage* (Oxford, Oxford University Press,

To be sure, it is a trivial insight that these experiences suggest the need to pay close regard to the locally existing rules and regulatory practices—the challenge consists in determining the form and process of context-sensitive regulation. It is with this challenge in mind that we find ourselves torn between opening our toolbox of well-worn and tested tools and concepts, on the one hand, and starting afresh, with open eyes and without prejudice, on the other.[131] What is remarkable in this context is the impossibility of breaking free even from the semantic and symbolic stronghold of certain categories, regardless of the degree to which these have been subjected to critique, deconstruction and demystification. This is as true today[132] as it was in the 1970s:[133] in our search for appropriate regulatory approaches to be taken with regard to development contexts (as well as other, similarly complex, regulatory spaces[134]), we strive to reflect critically upon the usability of the rule of law, and upon lessons learned with regard to democratic accountability, public deliberation and the separation of powers. Meanwhile, we have come to realise how none of these principles can be lifted out of its context without losing some explanatory capacity, leading us back to the motivation of why we intended to draw on a particular regulatory experience in the first place. Again and again, we are confronted with the particularity of an evolutionary process in a specific space that seemingly frustrates all attempts at translation or transplantation.[135] Yet, precisely because of this confrontation, we return again and again to a critical reflection on the categories through which we seek both to explain and to shape spaces of vulnerability and precariousness. There appears to be a crucial difference, however, between an earlier, progressive, critical exercise of such reflection and the more inchoate, interdisciplinary approach that seems to be forming today out of a combination of legal, political, sociological, economic and anthropological theory, on the one hand, and historical and linguistic study, on the other.[136] While this difference is still hard to pinpoint or to make fruitful, it becomes ever more evident that, in close proximity to the continuing stand-offs between conservative and progressive struggles over development policies, the range of theory, vocabulary, categories, frameworks and imaginations is expanding. In this context, the astutely recorded accounts by Chinua Achebe of his interactions with Third World experts,[137] the extermination of interview protocols and legislative materials of law-making processes in Singapore's authoritarian rule of law[138] or the anthropological scrutiny of the World Bank's human rights

---

2001) 417; P Zumbansen, '"New Governance" in European Corporate Governance Regulation as Transnational Legal Pluralism' (2009) 15 *European Law Journal* 246.

[131] See, eg Pistor and Berkowitz, n 84 above.

[132] K Rittich, 'The Future of Law and Development: Second Generation Reforms and the Incorporation of the Social' (2004) 26 *Michigan Journal of International Law* 199.

[133] Trubek and Galanter, n 118 above.

[134] N Krisch, *Beyond Constitutionalism: The Pluralist Structure of Post-national Law* (Oxford, Oxford University Press, 2010) ch 4.

[135] GA Sarfaty, 'Measuring Justice: Internal Conflict over the World Bank's Empirical Approach to Human Rights' in KM Clarke and M Goodale (eds), *Mirrors of Justice: Law and Power in the Post-Cold War Era* (Cambridge, Cambridge University Press, 2009).

[136] J Rajah, *Authoritarian Rule of Law: Legislation, Discourse and Legitimacy in Singapore* (Cambridge, Cambridge University Press, 2012) 37–52, 58–60, 288.

[137] C Achebe, *The Education of a British-Protected Child* (New York, Knopf, 2009).

[138] Rajah, n 136 above, 181–212.

programmes[139] are all crucial elements that help draw a richer and more sophisticated picture of the development context today. In other words, we see a significant analytical expansion and deepening of our knowledge base vis-à-vis the developmental state and the transnational aid and development apparatus that is staring at it. The challenge remains to understand and draw adequate lessons from such an expanding epistemic framework.

## VIII. IN LIEU OF A CONCLUSION: THE SURPRISE THAT IS NOT—ALL LAW IS TRANSNATIONAL

In an effort to connect the preceding sections on the status of knowledge in hybrid legal fields such as L&D and TJ with the opening parts of this chapter on law's general relationship with globalisation, I will briefly address the idea that a project such as TL can function as a 'theoretical conceptualization of law after the breakdown of methodological nationalism'.[140] The contention here would be that such a characterisation bears considerable promise. It is in this spirit that I suggest that the discussion of concepts or proposals such as TL or LP be reopened, rather than dismissing them prematurely, perhaps under the influence that their deliverables' are not yet as clearly defined as one would hope. My contention is that TL and LP are mutually intertwined precisely because both struggle with the how of distinguishing between legal and non-legal rules. The answer cannot be a jurisprudential one alone. Instead, what appears to follow from discussions of TL and LP is, first and foremost, a growing awareness of the epistemological as well as normative fragility of any attempt at boundary-drawing between different norm universes in the sense evoked by Robert Cover.[141] This fragility has become a central concern in the context of debates around the whats and hows of global governance. In the remainder of this chapter, I want to argue that proposals such as TL or LP should be seen as necessary steps in the development of theoretical approaches to a legal theory (or legal theories[142]) of global governance, which appears to operate, in the current debates, as an umbrella term that is employed to capture the still open-ended and non-linear[143] transformation of a nation-state-based model of political rule.[144] One way to address these changes with uncertain outcomes has been through ambitious assessments of the nature and status of law and its tight linkages with Western notions of (different notions, stages and representations of) the state.[145] One reason why TL appears to have gained temporary currency might relatively easily

---

[139] S Engle Merry, 'Transnational Human Rights and Local Activism: Mapping the Middle', Chapter 8 above; Sarfaty, n 39 above.

[140] Michaels, n 32 above, 18.

[141] R Cover, 'Nomos and Narrative' (1983) 97 *Harvard Law Review* 4.

[142] I am grateful to M Goodwin for her insistence on this point.

[143] Compare C Schreuer, 'The Waning of the Sovereign State: Towards a New Paradigm for International Law?' (1993) 4 *European Journal of International Law* 447 with AL Paulus, 'The War against Iraq and the Future of International Law: Hegemony or Pluralism?' (2004) 25 *Michigan Journal of International Law* 691.

[144] See the contributions to JL Dunoff and JP Trachtman (eds), *Ruling the World? Constitutionalism, International Law, and Global Governance* (Cambridge University Press, 2009); see also the contributions to T Hale and D Held (eds), *Handbook of Transnational Governance: Institutions and Innovations* (Cambridge, Polity Press, 2011).

[145] See, eg the interpretation by Grimm, n 24 above, 3–22.

be found in the fact that it both operates as a manageable label to depict, as already suggested by Jessup,[146] the blind spots between categorically distinguished fields (in this case, public and private international law). Another reason can be identified as lying in the interdisciplinary nature of TL, in that it is often referenced from a variety of theoretical and disciplinary backgrounds precisely to capture a multitude of assertions relating to the transformation of jurisdictional (geopolitical, geographical) boundaries,[147] shifts in norm-making competence between nationally based and spatially operating actors,[148] as well as the nature of communities, polities and peoples.[149] A similarly positive assessment seems to be in order with regard to LP, given that legal pluralists' concern with the demarcation and politics of—as well as with the tension between—official and unofficial bodies of norms, rules, recommendations, guidelines and standards arguably does not result in placing everything[150] at the same level, but seeks to expose, again and again, the often questionable and contestable basis upon which the distinction between law and non-law is drawn in the first place.[151]

While the apparent frustration among many legal scholars today with the slippery nature of concepts such as TL or LP is understandable, the task of making sense of this multidisciplinary and multivocal engagement with globalisation will eventually become easier as we all move through such stages of trial and error, exploitation, application and engagements with theory. Revisiting established legal fields, mostly thought of in their domestic, nation-state context but now reflected upon against the background of a globalisation of law, we can see that the above-described dilemma was in fact inherent to every area of law long before we began inventing new names and setting novel boundaries. Examples of labour, corporate or constitutional law illustrate legal fields as epistemological and normative laboratories, through the study of which we can shed more light on the way in which law can only be understood against the background of society. As such, legal theory is inevitably caught up in the multi- and interdisciplinary efforts to depict the contours and nature of today's world society adequately.

---

[146] PC Jessup, *Transnational Law* (New Haven, CT, Yale University Press, 1956).

[147] See, eg Harvey, n 91 above; Sassen, n 9 above.

[148] Scott et al, n 14 above.

[149] PS Berman, *Global Legal Pluralism: A Jurisprudence of Law Beyond Borders* (New York, Cambridge University Press, 2012); see also S Benhabib, *The Rights of Others: Aliens, Residents and Citizens* (Cambridge, Cambridge University Press, 2004); C Dauvergne, *Making People Illegal: What Globalization Means for Migration and Law* (Cambridge, Cambridge University Press, 2008).

[150] But see Michaels, n 32 above, 18: 'If everything is transnational law, nothing really is'.

[151] See, eg Galanter, n 48 above.

# Epilogue: Progressive Law versus the Critique of Law & Development: Strategies of Double Agency Revisited

## BRYANT G GARTH

T HE VERY RICH collection of essays in this volume, which brings together critical literature on human rights, law & development and transnational justice, raises recurring questions about how legal scholars and lawyers situate themselves. The essays, in various ways, address the legal politics of globalisation. There is a strong and refreshing current of criticism of existing legal assumptions and formulations, but it is hard to find a uniform voice or stance.

One of the questions that the editors ask reflects this concern with the stance and/or approach. They ask what 'specifically is the question that law and globalisa- tion scholars are actually trying to answer'.[1] As a way to think about resolving this threshold inquiry, the editors note that the global legal issues today are parallel, in many respects, to issues and theories associated with the US-led Law and Society movement in the 1960s and 1970s, which was—not coincidentally—also the time of the best known critiques of law & development—produced by leading law and society scholars.[2] The relationship of these debates to the present is quite evident and instruc- tive, and it is the main focus in this chapter.

One frame for debates today among the global legal scholars represented in this volume—and, in the 1960s and 1970s, for socio-legal scholars—is the threshold question of how law can be a progressive tool for social change—how to make progress through law. There is no simple answer, and often scholars decide that the better course is not to address this issue directly. Instead, they simply offer their own prescriptions and critiques as such. In fact, as elaborated below, they are typically trying an unreflective version of the double-agent strategy of the 1970s.

Many of the chapters in this book, therefore, simply take a position against dis- courses and practices that appear to undermine the potential of the law to serve causes

---

[1] Introduction, 7.

[2] Peer Zumbansen's chapter thus reads: 'we are now experiencing a strange mixture of both déjà vu and innovation in the engagements between legal theory and social sciences. If we dared to apply a label to these developments, we could venture that of a transition from law and society to law and globalisation, with the term 'transition' marking less of a substitute or replacement than an evolution, a maturing and continuing differentiation. However, having said that, it is clear that the challenges arising from the first phase of law and society are likely to reverberate in the current iteration of law and globalisation. In other words, the pressing questions with regard to the methodology to reveal the relation between law and society cannot be considered to be obsolete. What remains the same is the need to demarcate and motivate the contours of each one and the boundaries between them. This brings us back to the rediscovery of legal sociology in the 1960s and 1970s' (Chapter 18, 333).

such as economic development and social equality. They do so in the hope that the law will do better if it is improved in response to criticisms. Chapters 1, 2, 4, 7, 8 and 11, for example, call for reformulations of law in one way or another to address inequalities in power. Chapter 7 seeks in particular to revive the social struggles embodied in the discourse of labour rights, as opposed to the narrow discourse that treats work only as a general human right; Chapters 1, 2 and 3 call for a breaking away from neo-liberal versions of rights in favour of more social justice; Chapter 10 calls for reparations as a stronger response to past injustices, instead of merely symbolic acts such as apologies; Chapter 16 aspires to unleash the 'transformative potential' of transnational justice; and, through an act of fighting fire with fire, Chapter 6 seeks to unleash the potential progressive role of property rights for developing countries to protect and profit from their cultural heritage. Chapters 5, 8, 9 and 12 also criticise transnational approaches that ignore historical specificity and rely on cookie-cutter measures of the rule of law and effective governance. There is a clear politics of struggle both through and for progressive law in this book. As Peer Zumbansen points out, we see here a '*transnational replay* of domestic tensions between progressive versus conservative politics in the global arena'.[3]

One suggestion to overcome the problem of fostering progressive change, also made by Zumbansen, is to use the knowledge produced by the inter-disciplinary study of the context of legal ambitions and theories to enrich progressive legal arguments and thereby make them more effective. This approach is reminiscent of both the Legal Realists and their descendents in the Law and Society movement. A combination of critical insights and interdisciplinary studies can help to produce more compelling progressive legal theories.

The authors in this book are not naive about the prospects for this change. They recognise not only that the politics is quite contested, but also that the momentum may not be with the progressive side—even if deepened through interdisciplinary research. What is unique about the book, however, is that it raises more basic issues about the search for progressive transnational law. This search does not come from nowhere, however, no matter what the particular stance of the author. The author is embedded in a particular national and imperial context. When domestic struggles for progressive law are exported to, or imported into, other settings, national and transnational complicating issues emerge. One of the strengths of this volume is that it does not shy away from these issues.

The innovative juxtaposition of human rights, transitional justice and law & development complicates, by design, any unreflexive quest for progressive law. One theme of this collection, as noted above, is the politics of progressive law—challenging conservative legal theories in favour of more progressive ones. The other theme is that the politics of progress—or progressivism—is a version of the contested and imperial politics of modernity. The definition of progress, in other words, is inevitably in question. The tension between scholarship on human rights and transitional justice, on the one hand, and scholarship on law & development, on the other, creates real challenges for the progressive legal theorist.

Chapters 1, 5 and 11, on the politics of good intentions, the introduction and 12–16, on narrow readings of history that neglect both the continuing role of empire

---

[3] Chapter 17, 318. Italics added.

and local particularities, and on transnational justice and state-building as imperial or hegemonic projects obscured by technical language and recipes for 'best practices' (Chapter 13 especially), are among the works here that recall the criticisms of law & development from the 1970s. Chapters 8 and 9, on indicators and governance, make clear the hegemonic project embedded in the measures.

Scholars also recognise that these issues, while reminiscent of the 1970s, existed much earlier. There is much in common today with the imperial era of the late nineteenth and early twentieth centuries, when international law both thrived among 'civilised nations' and justified unrestrained violence against the Ottoman Empire and China, for example, which were deemed to be outside the self-defined group of civilised states. Today's language of 'failed states', as Mark Mazower demonstrates, is the modern equivalent of 'uncivilised'—justifying intrusive and unconstrained interventions by imperial and hegemonic powers.[4] Rosa Brooks accordingly notes how humanitarians and national security promoters unite today in finding grounds to overcome the national sovereignty concerns of states targeted for intervention—conveniently legitimating intervention by the strong over the weaker nations.[5] As the editors note, the desire—idealistic or otherwise—to bring a particular version of progress as progressive law is shaped by parochial experiences, specific positions within national contexts, and benign and non-benign imperial ambitions.

Progressive good intentions, we sometimes forget, have much in common with the ambiguous legacy of the missionaries seeking converts to save the souls of the colonial populations. As Jennifer Pitts points out in her discussions of the British Empire in India, to give but one example, the move from legitimating rhetoric based upon the advantages of trade with India to 'arguments that Britain brought (and was alone capable of bringing) good government to India'[6] justified policies in India that were much more intrusive and onerous than those justified merely in the name of trade rather than truth—allowing 'more subtle forms of oppression'.

The tension in the literature between imposing notions of progress, on the one hand, and ideals of progressivism, on the other, is not going to vanish. It is made more complicated by the fact that legal sociology teaches that the reforms brought through good intentions or mercenary activity have a tendency to depend on and thereby to strengthen the position of those who are better endowed socially. Local elites, in fact, are typically in a position to manage even progressive 'reforms' in ways that will not challenge, and may indeed strengthen, their local power. Yves Dezalay and I have noted, for example, how the public interest law movement in India, the 'legal empowerment' movement that began in the Philippines and the NGO explosion in Indonesia all served to strengthen the position of those who had the closest ties to the colonial regimes and the strongest social positions.[7] It was not a matter of a conspiracy, but rather a traceable process built on path-dependency and local and international fields

---

[4] M Mazower, *Governing the World: The History of an Idea, 1815 to the Present* (London, Penguin, 2012).

[5] R Brooks, 'Strange Bedfellows: The Convergence of Sovereignty-Limiting Doctrines in Counter-terrorist and Human Rights Discourse' (2012) 13 *Georgetown Journal of International Affairs* 125.

[6] J Pitts, *A Turn to Empire: The Rise of Imperial Liberalism in Britain and France* (Princeton NJ, Princeton University Press, 2005) 18.

[7] Y Dezalay and BG Garth, *Asian Legal Revivals: Lawyers in the Shadow of Empire* (Chicago IL, University of Chicago Press, 2010).

of power. More generally, in a similar manner, our investigation of famous 'failures' of law & development programmes in Brazil and India showed how they turned out to be very helpful for the careers and positions of those who participated in those programmes.[8] One potential solution to the complexity of progress, progressivism and empire is simply more and more critique, creative legal prescription and hope that ultimately the marketplace of ideas will ensure that progressive ideas get picked up only where appropriate, that they connect with indigenous social movements and that they transform societies in important positive ways. This is a lot to hope for, however, and it masks the actual processes at work.

There is another complicating factor that is not much discussed in the literature—the position of law varies enormously in different places. Because of the influence of the United States and the scholarship produced within the US context, it is often taken for granted that law is central to the fields of political and economic power. It is assumed, for example, that an overstated US claim—that bargaining inevitably takes place 'in the shadow of the law'—is universal. In fact, the critical or prescriptive legal advocacy that comes from a weak position in a local field of power—overpowered by political parties, religious leaders, economists or other governing elites and their legitimating expertises—has little or no impact domestically. It may build international connections and recognition in places where law is important. But we can never take it for granted that the position of law in national or transnational fields of power will be strong. Sociological inquiry into progressive law must take these different positions into account.

There are three matters, then, that might be considered in examining critical international law. One is the position of law, as just mentioned. A second is the effort to find a progressive path—which could be with or without law as a major player.[9] The third is how to relate the progressive ideal to imperial processes that skew what is considered to be legitimate progress and shape the impact of ideas and institutions that move across borders—'texts without contexts', in Pierre Bourdieu's terms.[10] This epilogue will not pretend to help solve this theoretical and practical problem, although I do hope to place it in a more sociological context.

As noted, the editors suggest the value of re-examining the debates in the 1970s, which, in key respects, anticipated the current era and its defining issues, and I also believe this path to be quite promising in order to situate today's debates in the evolving context. The combination of the critique of liberal legalism and the rise of public interest law in the 1970s, in particular, raises instructive issues. We can revisit the contradiction involving legal critique, modernist ideas of progress and progressive law at the time. The work of David Trubek, one of the key figures in the history of both 'law and society' and 'law & development', merits particular attention.

In 1974, David Trubek and Marc Galanter published their famous attack on law &

---

[8] Ibid; Y Dezalay and BG Garth, *The Internationalization of Palace Wars: Lawyers, Economists, and the Contest to Transform Latin American States* (Chicago IL, University of Chicago Press, 2002).

[9] Progressive legal scholars have difficulty with, for example, Venezuela under Hugo Chávez or Bolivia under Evo Morales.

[10] P Bourdieu, 'Les conditions sociales de la circulation internationale des idees' (2002) 145 *Actes de la Recherches en Sciences Sociales* 3.

development—'Scholars in Self-estrangement'.[11] Presented as a self-criticism of their own work in India and Brazil, Trubek and Galanter underlined the fallacy of seeking to export the US ideal of a legal system—which they termed 'liberal legalism', identified as privileging a central role of courts, fostering an anti-formalist legal education, and giving a key role to the legal profession in promoting development and social change. Trubek and Galanter went further in the critique, asking, in fact, whether liberal legalism made sense any longer as a strategy for progressive social change in the United States.[12]

At the same time, however, Trubek (and Galanter[13]) connected to the emerging public interest law movement in the United States, which Trubek described in his well-known response to Isaac Baldus in the *Law and Society Review* in 1977.[14] Offering a 'New Legal Realist' response to Baldus's Marxist questioning of the autonomy of law, Trubek provided both a theoretical critique and a practical inquiry into the relatively new field of public interest law. On the theory side, Trubek argued that:

> *Contra* Baldus, I see the system as partially open and flexible, and therefore as offering support for moral and political 'entrepreneurs' who can take advantage of the pressures of ideals and the legitimation needs of the system to effect changes that can further genuine equality, individuality, and community.[15]

He thus defended the relevance of law and legal strategies to a social change agenda. He then turned to the emerging field of public interest law as a test of this relative autonomy of the law.

Public interest law, he argued, 'reflects the capacity of the legal tradition to generate critical ideas, and the possibility that these ideas can become institutionalized'.[16] But Trubek also did not forget the critique of liberal legalism. Admitting that, 'Public interest law is basically a movement of the legal élite',[17] he stated that it is dangerous to see 'the subsidized law firm as an all-embracing corrective'. Despite the potential for social change, it also 'could fulfill the most pessimistic predictions of scholars like Baldus about the potential of law for mystification'.[18] His conclusion remained tentative in part because of the connection between the general role of lawyers and the public interest law firm: 'the professionalism of the movement may impede its capacity

---

[11] DM Trubek and M Galanter, 'Scholars in Self-estrangement: Some Reflections on the Crisis in Law and Development Studies in the United States' [1974] *Wisconsin Law Review* 1062.

[12] *Ibid*. 'Legal changes ostensibly designed to reform major areas of social life and achieve developmental goals may in fact be a form of symbolic politics, the effect of which is not to cause change but to defeat it by containing demands for protest, thereby strengthening, rather than weakening groups committed to the status quo. And increased instrumental rationality in legal processes together with governmental regulation of economic life may contribute to the economic well being of only a small elite, leaving the mass no better, or even worse, off.'

[13] M Galanter, 'Why the "Haves" Come Out Ahead: Speculations on the Limits of Law and Social Change' (1974) 9 *Law and Society Review* 95, is both a criticism and a call for mechanisms like public interest law to equalize legal advocacy. Galanter was also quite involved in bringing public interest law to India through the Ford Foundation.

[14] DM Trubek, 'Complexity and Contradiction in the Legal Order: Balbus and the Challenge of Critical Social Thought about Law' (1977) 11 *Law & Society Review* 529.

[15] Ibid, 561.

[16] Ibid, 564.

[17] Ibid.

[18] Ibid, 565.

to focus attention on the role of the bar and the symbols of formalism in maintaining existing systems of bias and inequality.'[19]

Trubek did not specifically explore the social context that generated the particular form of public interest law that he examined. Although it went without saying, it is important to remember that the progressive public interest law at the time had the power of the so-called liberal establishment behind it, which also crucially meant the funding of the Ford Foundation, headed by McGeorge Bundy, a pillar of the establishment.[20] This group—up to that point united through the cold war—had split over the Vietnam War and support for authoritarian governments in Chile and elsewhere. But the key institutions of the group—the philanthropic foundations, the elite universities, corporate law firms—remained united in favour of a legal reformist perspective within the United States that made the gap between the 'ideal and the actual' an argument for further reform.[21] No longer controlling the White House because of the division over Vietnam and the conduct of the cold war, this group saw public interest law as a way to continue the reformist agenda even though Richard Nixon was President. Trubek could thus play a double role in the article of both criticising and using the liberal establishment—the classic elite Yale position, as Laura Kalman noted, as the anti-establishment establishment.[22]

Put in more sociological terms, there was considerable social capital behind the legal capital invested in the reformist agenda of public interest law. The Ford Foundation's programme was designed to enhance the credibility of law and to reinforce the position at the top of the legal hierarchy of corporate lawyers representing the biggest businesses. Public interest law was, by design, elitist, moderate and unthreatening to the structure of power.[23] While not writing explicitly about this context, Trubek recognised these limits, and was quite candid about both his hope and his scepticism.

The story of the liberal establishment and the role of the Ford Foundation are also essential to both the critique of law & development and the creation of a kind of public interest project abroad. The liberal establishment (often termed the Foreign Policy Establishment for its dominance of foreign policy during the cold war) had been united during the cold war, had been willing to support state-led development by those who served as allies of the United States, and had sought to make friends and allies through aid policies that especially helped to train economists.[24] Law & development in the 1960s and 1970s promoted legal education reform and corporate law in order to create places for lawyers serving economists and the relatively strong states. The Ford Foundation was one of the key players promoting this kind of legal reform abroad. In addition to the supply side of the Ford Foundation and its conviction that

---

[19] Ibid.

[20] G Kabaservice, *The Guardians: Kingman Brewster, His Circle, and the Rise of the Liberal Establishment* (New York, Henry Holt, 2004).

[21] R Gordon, 'The Ideal and the Actual in the Law: Fantasies and Practices of New York City Lawyers, 1870–1914' in GW Gawalt (ed), *The New High Priests: Lawyers in Post-Civil War America* (Westport CT, Greenwood Press, 1984). Similarly, Trubek, n 14 above, 564, referring to the potential of 'lawyers disturbed by the gap between the promise and the reality of law in America'.

[22] 'Yale had long encouraged students and professors alike to see themselves as both members of, and rebels against, the establishment.' L Kalman, *Yale Law School and the Sixties: Revolt and Reverberations* (Chapel Hill NC, University of North Carolina Press, 2005) 226.

[23] Y Dezalay and BG Garth, 'Preserving Elite Law and Containing Social Change' (draft manuscript).

[24] Dezalay and Garth, nn 7 and 8 above.

lawyers should be important players in the state, the local demand side for law &
development turned typically on a legal professional complaint of a decline in the role
of, and respect for, lawyers—a decline in the position of law. The policies of law &
development hoped to elevate this status and helped lawyers to partner with the state.

The split in the liberal establishment led to a delayed reaction in law & development. Law & development policies had, in many respects, promoted the creation of
lawyers to serve the state, and now the states had become increasingly authoritarian.
The split over the cold war meant that there was no longer a consensus in favour of
authoritarian states as long as they sided with the United States against the USSR. The
Ford Foundation, which increasingly aligned with the 'doves' rather than the 'hawks'
in foreign policy, turned against law & development as it had been practised. The 'kiss
of death' of law & development was John Gardner's aggressively titled *Legal Imperialism*, ultimately published in 1980 (but a draft of which is cited in the Trubek and
Galanter article in 1974).[25] The book, indeed, provides the story of disillusionment
with law & development in Latin America for playing to and serving authoritarian
regimes. The experiences of the military regimes in Brazil and Chile, in particular,
suggested the need for a change in approach.

The critique of law & development, however, was also double-edged and parallel
to Trubek. Gardner had been a top Ford Foundation official, and he wrote his book,
according to interviews with the leading figures of law & development at the time,
precisely in order to pave the way to a full commitment by the Ford Foundation to the
emerging human rights movement embodied in newly created organisations in Brazil,
Chile and elsewhere.[26] The critique of law & development, in short, was made to
facilitate a new progressive law made for export—human rights as a kind of public
interest law abroad directed against authoritarian states.

The success of the human rights movement then came because it had the backing
of key sectors of the still powerful liberal establishment—the corporate bar, the elite
universities, and foundations such as Ford and MacArthur—along with a growing
number of European, Canadian, and other public and private funders that joined in
support. The success also came because it connected these groups to their counterparts in Argentina, Brazil, Chile, Indonesia, South Africa and elsewhere—elites out
of power.[27] There was social capital on both sides. Furthermore, since this was an
establishment movement oriented towards the United States, it evolved mainly in
conjunction with, rather than in opposition to, the basic tenets of neo-liberal economics—with 'civil society' central to the continued attack on relatively strong states.

With regard to the United States, it was constructed precisely not to create too
strong a challenge to structures of power aligned with the United States. From the
point of view of the challenge of progressive law, the elite human-rights movement,
in the same way as elite public interest law in the United States, could draw on substantial social capital, but its progressiveness was closely linked to the legitimacy
(or hegemony) of the US liberal establishment (which, in fact, funded much of the

---

[25] J Gardner, *Legal Imperialism* (Madison WI, University of Wisconsin, 1980).
[26] Dezalay and Garth, n 7 above.
[27] Ibid. See also K Sikkink, *The Justice Cascade: How Human Rights Prosecutions are Changing World
Politics* (New York, WW Norton, 2011).

international human rights movement). The local position of law could, in fact, be strengthened—in part—by drawing on the power of transnational legal capital.

US-style progressive legal globalisation thrived, especially in the 1990s, inviting the double role of embracing and critiquing that Trubek followed for the United States and public interest law. That liberal legal approach, nevertheless, has always been contested both nationally and transnationally. Economics, as noted above, has competed to be the most important language for governance, and international human rights and allied efforts have, from the start, had to take economic orthodoxy into account.[28] The World Bank, in particular, has been dominated by economists since the 1980s, and therefore its development policies have had to be acceptable to evolving economic orthodoxies. Furthermore, the cold war division of the 1970s between the 'hawks' and 'doves' resurfaced in the guise of the war on terror proclaimed by George W Bush. The 'hawks' placed national security over human rights. More generally, there has been the rise of a counter-establishment with its own legal elite in the United States, uniting, to varying degrees, the religious right and conservative businesses.[29]

These groups participate in activities abroad, and both work with, and in opposition to, the more liberal groups. As a result of each of these developments, the situation is much more complicated than in the earlier period. For many reasons, it is more difficult to work out a stance that is both critical and an ally of liberal legalism. The liberal establishment faces many contenders for state power. The effort to muster social capital on behalf of legal capital is no longer just a matter of taking for granted a powerful progressive wing of the establishment that can be both joined and criticised. This is no longer necessarily the case, and the position of the double agent is therefore more complex.

Trubek and Galanter did not need to be explicit about their own position or their relationship to the social capital embedded in the liberal legal establishment. They could take them for granted. I am not sure that the progressives of today can play this game as easily. The argument today is, therefore, even stronger for explicit sociological analyses of the players on all sides, including the producers of critique and reform in this book and elsewhere; the position of law and its competitors; and the links between national and transnational. Lawyers will look to play the double game—or some variation on it—around the issue of progressive law identified with Trubek and many others, but much would be gained by more attention to both the players and the positions.

Many of the issues debated in international law today—the politics of international criminal law,[30] for example, or the rise of international trafficking in women as the highest profile issue internationally,[31] and the other issues mentioned in this volume— can benefit from analyses that look beyond the seemingly progressive rhetoric and a

---

[28] See, eg N Klein, *The Shock Doctrine: The Rise of Disaster Capitalism* (New York, Henry Holt, 2008).
[29] A Southworth, *Lawyers of the Right: Professionalizing the Conservative Coalition* (Chicago IL, University of Chicago Press, 2008); S Teles, *The Rise of the Conservative Legal Movement* (Princeton NJ, Princeton University Press, 2008).
[30] J Wouters, 'Policies, Not Politics, The Pursuit of Justice in Prosecutorial Strategy at the International Criminal Court', available at http://papers.ssrn.com/sol3/papers.cfm?abstract_id=2274766.
[31] See, eg AT Gallagher and R Surtees, 'Measuring the Success of Counter-trafficking Interventions in the Criminal Justice Sector: Who Decides, and How?' (2012) 1 *Anti-Trafficking Review* 10; DF Haynes, 'The Celebritization of Human Trafficking', *Annals of the American Academy of Political and Social Sciences*, forthcoming.

too easy critique. Similarly, the thriving programmes on 'legal empowerment' within the Open Society Institute and within the United Nations, focusing on property rights and access to justice, merit more than simple support or easy critique. They draw on a mixture of sources that are far more complex than the liberal establishment, as is evident in the fact that the Commission on Legal Empowerment of the Poor set up by the United Nations Development Program was co-chaired by Madeleine Albright and Hernando de Soto.[32]

Alliances and potential alliances today—the religious right, neo-liberal economic programmes, progressive US politics, conservative elite politics, national security advocates, humanitarian interventionists—are very complex both nationally and trans-nationally. The double-agency strategy is still there, and we can be sure that lawyers will continue to play both parts—as progressive missionary reformers and as critics of law & development (or aggressive importers of foreign technology and critics of imperialism and hegemony)—but it is no longer as clear-cut as it was in the 1970s. The critics of the legal establishment could comfortably criticise, in part because they could rely implicitly on the power of the legal establishment both within the United States and abroad. The social capital receptive to progressive legal critique and ready to both embrace it and tame it is attenuated and constantly challenged in today's global context. Critique that replays the same approach will not necessarily bring the same consequences or even gain any attention in the current debates.

Legal sociology provides an essential point of entry today as we seek to understand the complex play of alliances and interests evident in legal globalisation—including the double-agent strategies of scholars, activists and critics, as they play out in today's global context. It was too easy in the 1970s to play a double role without examining (or self-reflecting on) the positions of the players, their connections to social capital both domestically and abroad, their own stakes in palace wars between different experts and governing expertise, and even their connections to the different hegemonic powers competing for global dominance. The chapters in this volume, to my mind, merit a complementary interdisciplinary research agenda that takes the positions of critics, scholars and activists within both legal fields and the fields of state power more into account.

---

[32] Commission on Legal Empowerment of the Poor, 'Making the Law Work for Everyone' (New York, Commission on Legal Empowerment of the Poor, UNDP 2008), available at http://www.namati.org.

# Index